Moral Issues
in Global Perspective

Moral Issues
in Global Perspective

second edition

Volume I: Moral and Political Theory

edited by

Christine M. Koggel

broadview press

Library and Archives Canada Cataloguing in Publication

Moral issues in global perspective / edited by Christine M. Koggel. — 2nd ed.

Includes bibliographical references. Contents: v. 1. Moral and political theory
ISBN 1-55111-747-9 (v. 1)

1. Social ethics—Textbooks.   I. Koggel, Christine M.

HM665.M67 2006   170   C2005-907079-X

Broadview Press Ltd. is an independent, international publishing house, incorporated in 1985. Broadview believes in shared ownership, both with its employees and with the general public; since the year 2000 Broadview shares have traded publicly on the Toronto Venture Exchange under the symbol BDP.

We welcome comments and suggestions regarding any aspect of our publications—
please feel free to contact us at the addresses below or at broadview@broadviewpress.com.

North America
Post Office Box 1243, Peterborough, Ontario, Canada K9J 7H5
Post Office Box 1015, 3576 California Road, Orchard Park, NY, USA 14127
Tel: (705) 743-8990; Fax: (705) 743-8353;
email: customerservice@broadviewpress.com

UK, Ireland, and continental Europe
NBN Plymbridge, Estover Road, Plymouth PL6 7PY UK
Tel: 44 (0) 1752 202301   Fax: 44 (0) 1752 202331
Fax Order Line: 44 (0) 1752 202333
Customer Service: cservs@nbnplymbridge.com Orders: orders@nbnplymbridge.com

Australia and New Zealand
UNIREPS, University of New South Wales
Sydney, NSW, 2052 Australia
Tel: 61 2 9664 0999; Fax: 61 2 9664 5420
email: info.press@unsw.edu.au

www.broadviewpress.com

Broadview Press gratefully acknowledges the financial support of the Government of Canada through the Book Publishing Industry Development Program for our publishing activities.

Copy-edited by Betsy Struthers.

Typesetting and assembly: True to Type Inc., Mississauga, Canada.

PRINTED IN CANADA

For Senna and Aiden

Contents

CHAPTER SIX: WAR AND TERRORISM

PREFACE

A central question in ethics is: how should we live our lives and interact with others? Exploring answers to this question in the context of the international community or "global village" in which we live was the prime motivation for putting out the First Edition of this anthology. This motivation persists into the production of this Second Edition, now expanded into three volumes.

The collection works with the idea that we live in an increasingly interdependent world, one in which features and factors of globalization shape the lives and experiences of people no matter who they are or where they live. "Globalization" is a concept used increasingly in a variety of contexts and in ways that are both positive and negative: in discussions of markets, international relations, economic development, human rights, education, health care, the environment, labor, media, and information technology. Globalization can be characterized as increased flows — of people, information, technology, consumer goods, and trade — across ever more permeable borders. Globalization in the form of increased flows of information, for example, has broadened our exposure to beliefs and values very different from our own and allowed us to communicate instantaneously with people from faraway places. The almost limitless access to information through television and the Internet not only makes it possible for us to learn about others, but it also makes it easy to praise or condemn people, policies, practices, values, beliefs, and political structures in other places. Globalization has universalized human rights discourse from its roots in liberal theory and has given a prominent place to international organizations that monitor human rights violations. An important effect of globalization has been to intensify our awareness of the devastating ways in which policies and practices in one area may affect not only the livelihood and choices of people in other areas, but the world as a whole.

Increased globalization not only means that no community is isolated from the world's gaze and influence, but also that virtually no communities remain unaffected by the influx of people from other places. The latter describes the phenomenon of multiculturalism: difference and diversity within a community of people who have various beliefs. Multiculturalism means that we need not look across borders to find instances of discrimination against and unequal treatment of people identified as different. It calls on us to examine the ways in which our embeddedness in particular contexts and practices shapes our perceptions of and interactions with those different from ourselves. Multiculturalism opens the door to examining relationships and to thinking critically about our interactions with others. In making it possible to scrutinize beliefs and practices different from our own, globalization and multiculturalism ask us to critically examine the judgments we render about others both across and within borders.

These facts and effects of globalization and the related phenomenon of multiculturalism raise questions that have become increasingly pressing to moral inquiry. This anthology assumes that these questions are relevant to the central question of how we live our lives and interact with others. Does our situatedness in a Western liberal democratic society generate problematic assumptions about what human beings are like; what we need to flourish; and what rights and responsibilities we hold? Might our commitment to the notion of the primacy of individual liberty rights change if we learned about commitments to rights different from these in contexts, including liberal societies, outside the U.S.? Would our understanding of what constitutes just social and political structures change if we became aware of theories that defend alternative structures, particularly by authors from societies with structures different from our own? Can social relations and policies in other contexts give us insights into ways to approach moral issues of inequality and discrimination in our own context? Does our understanding of the right way to live and of how to determine morally right action reflect the biases of Western liberal beliefs and values? Does the impact of policies in one society on the welfare and well-being of members of another society hinder us from acquiring an adequate understanding of moral, social, and political issues and of how to resolve them? In general, does our view of moral issues change when we turn our attention to the global context?

Most contemporary collections on moral issues make it difficult to raise these questions. They tend to feature the narrow band of agreements and disagreements within Western liberal theory and practice. As with the First Edition, this Second Edition of *Moral Issues in Global Perspective* seeks to challenge our thinking about morality and moral issues as it has been shaped by the Western liberal tradition and to extend the inquiry beyond the context of North America and specifically that of the U.S. It includes analyses of moral issues by both liberal and non-liberal theorists from around the world, many of whom question predominant understandings of human rights, justice, democracy, social welfare, and development. It includes critiques of traditional accounts of moral theory, rights, justice, and democracy, critiques that examine whether these accounts ignore or fail to address the discriminatory treatment of disadvantaged groups inside and outside the borders of countries. It incorporates work by race, class, feminist, and disability theorists that challenges traditional moral and political theory and opens up new perspectives on issues such as reproduction, euthanasia, censorship, animal rights, and environmental ethics.

This collection incorporates these kinds of perspectives into each chapter, more so than is the case with many of the textbooks on practical ethics that are currently available in North America. So, for example, we are asked to confront challenges by non-Western writers that liberal beliefs about the importance of individual rights to free speech and property may reflect a discourse about rights that has little or no application in places with traditions that uphold community values, or with pasts they want to change, or in countries struggling to achieve stability, let alone economic viability. We may need to question our assumptions about gender when we examine the role and activities of women in places like Indonesia. We are asked to think about how issues of reproductive health may be shaped differently in a context like Argentina where a strong tradition of Catholicism pulls against the interests and aspirations of women. This expanded Second Edition gives testimony to the importance of these issues and to the approach to ethics that it adopts.

Even greater efforts were made with this new edition than with the previous to represent the range of theories and the work of theorists from around the world. In its current three volumes, this anthology collects the work of more than 80 authors, thus presenting a broad range of views from all over the world. In doing so, it attempts to show the complexity of moral issues when examined in a global context and the richness and diversity of writing on these issues by authors outside American and Western thought more generally. Of course, one cannot move in new directions without a base in the familiar. Many of the readings are intended to reflect not only the wide spectrum of views among liberal theorists, but also the discussion of moral issues as it takes place in North America. With this background, we can then take up the two challenges of globalization and multiculturalism. A global context of increased awareness of the impact of globalization on the environment, levels of poverty, prospects for human flourishing, and indigenous cultures challenges the notion that answers to complex moral issues can be found by focusing only on Western liberal values in a North American context. *Moral Issues in Global Perspective* stands as an illustration of how the field of moral inquiry is greatly enriched when we turn our attention to disenfranchised voices within particular societies and to contexts outside North America.

This expanded Second Edition is divided into three separate volumes, each of which corresponds roughly with the three parts of the single volume First Edition. Volume I covers kinds of moral and political theory and topics related to these. The first four chapters in Volume I present traditional and contemporary theories of morality and of concepts such as human rights, justice, and democracy. These concepts have been central to Western liberal theory. The fundamental teaching of classical liberal theory that each human being has equal moral value and deserves equal concern and respect has become the foundation for theories about how societies ought to be structured to ensure equal treatment, for accounts of what human beings need in order to flourish, and for attempts to formulate universal human rights. Yet, liberal theory has been criticized for its excessive individualism, an individualism that critics take to be apparent in the policies, structures, and kinds of human rights that liberals tend to defend. This criticism moves to center stage when we turn to a global context and examine theorists who challenge the very framework of individual freedom that dominates accounts of human rights and theories of justice and democracy in Western liberal societies. The final two chapters in Volume I apply insights from these theories to concrete contexts, ones in which awareness of histories and social conditions in specific parts of the world sometimes support and sometimes challenge understandings of justice, human rights, and democracy. Chapter Six applies these insights to the specific and timely issue of war and terrorism.

Volume II continues the exploration of the relevance of globalization and multiculturalism to moral inquiry by zeroing in on accounts of human nature and the moral questions raised by issues of diversity and difference among human beings. Are we all the same? Can we provide a list of essential human functions and capabilities that generates moral imperatives for what it is for human beings to flourish no matter who they are or where they live? Do we operate with a set of assumptions about human beings that result in stereotypes about difference and critical judgments about other people's beliefs and practices? Do facts of discrimination and inequality both across and within borders shape perceptions, self-perceptions, and opportunities in ways that call for international policies to eliminate the resulting injustices? Is it possible to understand the perspectives and life experiences of members of disadvantaged groups from a vantage point of privilege or to speak for them when making judgments about them? Answers to these sorts of questions in the theory chapter that opens Volume II are then followed by several chapters in which discrimination on the grounds of race and ethnicity, gender, sexual orientation, disability, and poverty are examined. These chapters explore moral issues raised by relationships that are shaped by the different histories, identities, and levels of power of people within and across societies. The issues in this volume cut to the heart of the central question of how to interact with others in morally responsible ways.

The relationship of the individual to society tends to be central to most collections about moral issues. Volume III explores the relationship between the individual and society by surveying some of the practical issues that have acquired particular prominence in Western liberal contexts: individual choice and social responsibility at the beginning and end of human life, the value of liberty and its connection to pornography and hate speech, and how we live and interact with animals and the environment. Liberal theory has tended to examine these issues in terms of the conflict between the individual and society: what, if any, restrictions to individual freedom are permissible and what sorts of moral justifications can be provided for using the power of the state to limit individual freedom? The readings in the chapters of Volume III represent both defenses and critiques of this characterization of how practical moral issues need to be resolved, and they open up inquiry into how moral issues are impacted by a global context. Do debates about issues such as reproduction, euthanasia, health care, pornography, hate speech, animals, and the environment change when we learn about concrete practices in non-Western contexts or in places outside North America? Do the policies in place for dealing with these issues in particular contexts have a differential impact on members of traditionally disadvantaged groups?

The three volumes can be used separately or as a whole. Various threads related to globalization and multiculturalism weave their way through all the volumes and allow issues to cross over from one volume to the next. For example, issues of discrimination on the basis of gender and race are covered explicitly in Volume II but can be found in the examination of reproductive issues, pornography, and hate speech in Volume III. Tendencies of ethnocentrism that result in judgments by developed countries about practices and beliefs in developing countries are explored in the conceptions of human rights, justice, and democracy discussed in Volume I and also in the discussions of health care, the environment, and pornography in Volume III. Discussions in Volume I of the significance of historical and cultural contexts in the shaping of beliefs, practices, and values are revisited in Volume II in the examination of discrimination and unequal relations of power between peoples within a country and across the borders of countries. And arguments by theorists in Volume I that defend particular accounts of morally right action or conceptions of justice are applied to specific moral issues in Volume III. While the volumes may have distinctive topics and titles, the issues and themes intersect and are interconnected.

The revision and expansion of the First Edition would not have been possible without the help and support of many people along the way. I want to begin by thanking all the authors who granted permission to reprint their work in the collection, including both the authors who were first time contributors to the First Edition and whose work reappears in this Second Edition and the authors whose work appears for this first time in the Second Edition. Don LePan, the long time President of Broadview Press who stepped down in 2004, was committed to the project from its earliest stages and has provided encouragement and support throughout and into the preparation of this Second Edition. The torch has been passed to Michael Harrison, someone as committed to supporting authors and their work. Broadview people are wonderful to work with and their competence and care are greatly appreciated. The Production Editors, Barbara Conolly, Jennifer Bingham, and Judith Earnshaw handled this large and complex project with professionalism and enthusiasm throughout. Tania Terrien, Jennifer Findlay, Tammy Roberts, and Joelle Dunne dealt with the many details of permissions and my questions of process and procedures along the way. Betsy Struthers edited each of the volumes in a way that made my job easier and the production process smoother. I would like to thank several anonymous reviewers of early versions of the Second Edition for their helpful suggestions concerning the organization, topics, and readings. A special thanks goes to Keith Burgess-Jackson, whose advice and impressive knowledge of the extensive literature in moral theory and practical issues was as important to the Second Edition as it was to the First.

Countless people took an interest in this project and discussions with them sometimes provided valuable advice and sometimes unearthed readings that have turned out to be key pieces in both the First and Second Editions. In this respect, I would like to thank Susan Babbitt, Nathan Brett, Cheshire Calhoun, David Crocker, Jay Drydyk, Marvin Glass, Jennifer Llewellyn, and Janice Newberry. In doing revisions for the Second Edition, I was fortunate to be in the right places at the right times to discover important and innovative work being done at conferences and colloquia. Working with these people on their contributions to the Second Edition has been a pleasure. In particular, I would like to thank Frank Cunningham, Sally Haslanger, Alison Minea, Roland Pierik, Ingrid Robeyns, Asuncion Lera St. Clair, and Kok-Chor Tan.

I could not have completed the painstaking work of preparing the manuscript if it were not for the competence and dedication of two fabulous Bryn Mawr students: Valori Jankowski and Risa Rice. I cannot say enough about how important they were to the completion of this project. Jessica Moss, Erin McCartney, Erin LaFarge, and Lilian Bürgler are just some of the many students who offered valuable advice as I worked my way through the structure of and selections for the Second Edition. Sue Campbell, Lorraine Code, Lorraine Kirschner, Michael Krausz, Ralph Kuncl, Christine Overall, and Susan Sherwin influenced the project and ensured its completion in ways that only they can know. This is not the first project that Andrew Brook has been there to help me through. His help was, as always, matched by his unwavering confidence in my work and his encouragement and support throughout. Finally, I would like to express my gratitude to the many students with inquiring minds and diverse backgrounds who made this exploration possible and to the young people in my life, to whom I dedicate these volumes. It is they who keep me optimistic about the future.

CHAPTER ONE: MORALITY

INTRODUCTION

In the Preface, I described the question "How should we live our lives and interact with others?" as central to ethics and to the approach adopted in this collection of examining ethics in a global context. In moral theory in the Western tradition, the emphasis has tended to be on the first part of the question about how individuals ought to live their lives. In this approach, theorists begin with the individual as the unit of analysis for understanding what human beings are like so that they can determine for themselves morally right action. This approach has been criticized as being too individualist: human beings are conceived as isolated and atomistic entities who best thrive when left on their own to make decisions about their lives. As we proceed through this and the remaining chapters in Volume I, we shall encounter critiques of this approach to moral and political theory. A central purpose of this chapter is to represent the range of approaches, both classical liberal moral theories and contemporary critiques and revisions of them. Another goal is to juxtapose the traditional Western approaches of Kant and Mill, with which we are familiar, with non-Western approaches and theories. This will highlight the contrasts in traditions and allow us to better understand what non-Western traditions can offer by way of insight and criticism. In general, this chapter examines a range of questions about morality when placed in a global context and explores answers to them.

How do we determine what actions we ought to perform and what responsibilities we have to others? Is the whole of morality captured by the notion that there is a formula or set of principles that we can discover and should follow? Is the idea that morality emerges from the rational capacities of individual agents permeated with Western

liberal assumptions about autonomy, agency, and responsibility? What does responsibility mean in a context in which the actions of individuals and the practices and policies of various societies have an increasing impact on other people, societies, and the world as a whole? Is the moral theory that one espouses shaped by factors such as gender, levels of status and power, and historical, social, and political contexts? Can common principles be found in the diverse traditions of Western and non-Western cultures? Is such a project of formulating a universal theory of what it is to live a good life viable or desirable? Volume I explores answers to these kinds of questions in the context of examining a range of moral and political theories.

Immanuel Kant is an important figure in the development of moral theory in the Western tradition. Kant's approach to morality is evident in the kinds of arguments found in the practical issues we shall examine in this and other volumes of the collection. His approach is referred to as deontological, a theory that derives an account of rights and duties independently of the consequences. In such an account, the assumption is that actions determined to be morally right are right no matter who or where the agent is or what the circumstances are. In our reading from Kant, he begins by characterizing morality in terms of distinct capacities possessed by human beings. Human beings are differentiated from non-human entities in having a will: "the will is a faculty of choosing only that which reason, independently of inclinations, recognizes as being practically necessary, i.e., as good." Reason tells us what actions we ought to perform and sets them as imperatives that command categorically. Kant argues that the categorical imperative is distinctive of moral action and that there is only one: "Act only according to that maxim whereby you can at the same time will that it should become a universal law." The categorical imperative can be viewed as a formula for determining one's moral duties. Kant shows how the formula works in practice by applying it to four examples.

The possession of a will gives human beings absolute worth, which is to be contrasted with conditional worth in that the latter is characteristic of non-human entities that have value only insofar as humans give them value. The absolute worth of human beings means that human beings exist as ends in themselves and can never be used merely as a means by another. This leads Kant to the second formulation of the categorical imperative: "Act in such a way that you treat humanity, whether in your own person or in the person of another, always at the same time as an end and never simply as a means." Kant returns to his examples to show the application of this version of the categorical imperative. He argues that the practical necessity of acting according to duty and not feelings, impulses, and inclinations makes each human being a legislating member in a society of self-legislating beings.

Kant provides a formula for determining the moral actions that are one's duty to perform irrespective of inclinations, circumstances, and contexts. Consequentialists argue that inclinations and desires are relevant and that morally right action should be assessed in terms of the consequences of possible actions on oneself and others. Mill's Utilitarianism is an example of consequentialist theory. For Utilitarians, pleasure and pain are the only things desirable as ends, and morally right action is that which results in promoting the good consequences of maximizing pleasure. Mill differentiates his version of Utilitarianism from previous accounts by defending happiness rather than pleasure as such. Some pleasures are more desirable and valuable than others, namely, pleasures associated with human capacities and distinctive to human beings. Pleasures such as those of the intellect, of feelings and imagination, and of moral sentiments are qualitative ones that have a higher value than mere bodily and quantitative pleasures.

According to the greatest happiness principle,

the ultimate end for the sake of which all other things are desirable is an existence as exempt as possible from pain and as rich as possible in pleasure, both quantitative and qualitative. Mill adds the important qualification that the standard for right conduct is not the agent's own happiness but that of all concerned. For Mill, morally right action is that which results in the greatest happiness for the greatest number of people affected by the particular action. Mill responds to Kant's depiction of morality as necessarily motivated by duty by claiming that what is important is not the motive but following the rule that promotes the general interest and performing the action that results in the greatest happiness for the greatest number of people.

Both Kant and Mill emphasize capacities that make individual human beings capable of determining what actions are morally right and performing those actions. In the third reading, V.F. Cordova identifies this Western liberal focus on individuals with self-determining capacities as an "I" approach to morality. She contrasts this with a "we" approach present in the moral theory of the ancient Greek philosophers Socrates and Aristotle in the Western tradition and in Native American beliefs and values. She argues that the "I" conceived of as an essentially isolated, solitary, and self-determining entity reflects a world view or ethical system in sharp contrast with a conception of the human being as foremost and essentially social. The "we" approach begins with behavior toward others and thereby puts one's membership in a group or community as central to what it is to live an ethical life. Defining human beings as social allows recognition of humans as part of a greater whole, where attention to one's behavior toward other individuals, communities, the environment, and the planet itself is foregrounded. This view of the dependency and interdependency of human beings shapes an ethic in which individuals learn to be aware of the needs of others and of what the individual can do for the good of the group. Cordova argues that the "we" ethic of Native American tradition and culture challenges values evident in the contemporary phenomena of consumerism, environmental degradation, and economic development.

In the fourth reading, Margaret Walker pursues the discussion of individualism in moral theory in the Western tradition. She examines Carol Gilligan's work on an ethic of care, an ethic that is contrasted with the ethic of justice taken to be characteristic of Western moral theory. Gilligan's *In a Different Voice* has generated debate and controversy in its apparent endorsement of the claim that care and justice are orientations to morality characteristically adopted by women and men respectively. Gilligan has persistently rejected this interpretation and argues that the different voice of care offers a distinct moral perspective embodying conceptions of self, relationship, and responsibility that challenge the traditional justice approach to morality. Walker explores Gilligan's claim by pursuing questions about whether the ethic of care is a unified perspective, what that perspective is, and whether it offers an important addition or corrective to prevailing philosophical views.

Walker locates two distinct themes in Gilligan's characterization of care as a responsibilities- rather than a rights-based justice approach. The theme of a "care and response orientation" takes sensitivity to the needs of others and concern for relationships, responsibility, attachment, and compassion to be central moral concerns. Caring for others requires minute attention, identification in thought and feeling, precise communication, and sensitivity to rich circumstantial detail and history. The "contextual-deliberative" theme marks the distinction between justice and care in terms of method, approach, and standards for defining and solving moral problems. Whereas justice is moral reasoning that abstracts from interpersonal contexts, prioritizes rules, and arrives at universal formulas, the care perspective rejects this process of decision-making and takes concrete information about the particular case to be relevant to moral decisions. The care orientation rotates the focus so that the particular is always first and the application of generalized standards is derivative. The debate about care as a woman's voice can now be seen in a different light. Because gender roles continue to

have the majority of women involved in initiating new members into the moral community, their perspectives on caring relationships are vantage points contributing to an understanding of what moral concern requires.

In the final reading, Egbeke Aja turns our attention to Africa and to the phenomenon of economic interdependence that is bringing diverse countries and cultures in Africa into closer contact. He argues that for Africans to live together peacefully, a basis for a common understanding of African moral values needs to be developed. Such a common understanding will allow changes to familiar cultural patterns that are needed to address contemporary aspects of colonialism in the form of educational systems and increased scientific and technological innovation. Aja describes the tradition, beliefs, and values of the Igbo, a group in southeastern Nigeria, as a way to explore the possibility of articulating a solid foundation of African moral values, one that is based on universal human needs and social imperatives. Aja finds variation from one society to another in his examination of Igbo values and in his comparison of these values with other African cultural groupings such as the Yoruba and the Akan people of Ghana. Yet, he argues, an analysis of the functions and interrelations of these values allows general principles and a fundamental uniformity to emerge.

Theorists have defended three hypotheses to explain the source and foundation of Igbo values: religion, social necessity and harmony, and common sense. While these reveal different justifications for moral beliefs and values, the commonality of principles is found in the idea that what is moral is what works, what gives happiness, and what enables the group to survive. Aja examines the ways in which Western value systems such as Christianity have influenced Igbo beliefs about issues such as euthanasia, marriage, and family life. He argues that we need to take the best of traditional African (Igbo) values and Western-oriented values to forge a new, hybrid system that can meet challenges in Africa today.

GROUNDWORK FOR THE METAPHYSICS OF MORALS

Immanuel Kant

Immanuel Kant was born in Germany and lived from 1724-1804. His significant contributions to all major areas of philosophy has made him one of the most important philosophers of all time. Some of his most important works include: Critique of Pure Reason, Critique of Practical Reason, Prolegomena to All Future Metaphysics, *and the book from which this reading is taken,* Groundwork for the Metaphysics of Morals.

Kant defines moral action as that which human beings have a duty to perform irrespective of particular motives, desires, and inclinations. Human beings are the kind of rational and self-legislating entities that make it possible for them to determine morally right action in accordance with the dictates of the supreme rule of the categorical imperative. Kant provides several formulations of the categorical imperative, the first and most well-known of which is: act only on that rule that you would be willing to make into a universal law for everyone to follow.

... Everything in nature works according to laws. Rational beings alone have the capacity to act *in accordance with the representation* of laws — that is, according to principles, that is, have a *will*. Since the deduction of actions from principles requires *reason*, the will is nothing but practical reason. If reason infallibly determines the will, then the actions of such a being which are recognized as objectively necessary are subjectively necessary also, that is, the will is a capacity to choose *that only* which reason independent of inclination recognizes as practically necessary, that is, as good. But if reason of itself does not sufficiently determine the will, if the latter is subject also to subjective conditions (particular incentives) which do not always coincide with the objective conditions, in a word, if the will does not *in itself* completely accord with reason (which is actually the case with human beings), then the actions which objectively are recognized as necessary are subjectively contingent, and the determination of such a will according to objective laws is *necessitation*, that is to say, the relation of the objective laws to a will that is not thoroughly good is con-

ceived as the determination of the will of a rational being by principles of reason, but which the will from its nature does not necessarily follow.

The conception of an objective principle, in so far as it is obligatory for a will, is called a command (of reason), and the formula of the command is called an **imperative**.

All imperatives are expressed through an *ought*, and thereby indicate the relation of an objective law of reason to a will which from its subjective constitution is not necessarily determined by it (a necessitation). They say that something would be good to do or to forbear, but they say it to a will which does not always do a thing because it is represented to be good to do it. That is *practically good*, however, which determines the will by means of the representations of reason, and consequently not from subjective causes, but objectively, that is, on principles which are valid for every rational being as such. It is distinguished from the agreeable as that which influences the will only by means of feeling from merely subjective causes, valid only for the senses of this or that one, and not as a principle of reason which holds for everyone.[1]

A perfectly good will would therefore be equally subject to objective laws (viz. laws of good), but could not be conceived as *necessitated* thereby to act lawfully, because of itself from its subjective constitution it can only be determined by the conception of good. Therefore no imperatives hold for the Divine will, or in general for a *holy* will; *ought* is here out of place because the volition is already of itself necessarily in unison with the law. Therefore imperatives are only formulae to express the relation of objective laws of all volition to the subjective imperfection of the will of this or that rational being, for example, a human will.

Now all imperatives command either *hypothetically* or *categorically*. The former represent the practical necessity of a possible action as means to something else that is willed (or at least which one might possibly will). The categorical imperative would be that which represented an action as necessary of itself without reference to another end, that is, as objectively necessary.

Since every practical law represents a possible action as good, and on this account, for a subject who is practically determinable by reason, as necessary, all imperatives are formulae determining an action which is necessary according to the principle of a will good in some respects. If now the action is good only as a means *to something else*, then the imperative is *hypothetical*; if it is conceived as good *in itself* and consequently as being necessarily the principle of a will which of itself conforms to reason, then it is *categorical*.

Thus the imperative declares what action possible by me would be good, and presents the practical rule in relation to a will which does not forthwith perform an action simply because it is good, whether because the subject does not always know that it is good, or because, even if it know this, yet its maxims might be opposed to the objective principles of practical reason.

Accordingly the hypothetical imperative only says that the action is good for some purpose, *possible or actual*. In the first case, it is a **problematic**, in the second an **assertoric**, practical principle. The categorical imperative which declares an action to be objectively necessary in itself without reference to any purpose, without any other end, is valid as an **apodictic** (practical) principle.

Whatever is possible only by the power of some rational being may also be conceived as a possible purpose of some will; and therefore the principles of action as regards the means necessary to attain some possible purpose are in fact infinitely numerous. All sciences have a practical part consisting of problems expressing that some end is possible for us, and of imperatives directing how it may be attained. These may, therefore, be called in general imperatives of **skill**. Here there is no question whether the end is rational and good, but only what one must do in order to attain it. The precepts for the physician to make his patient thoroughly healthy, and for a poisoner to ensure certain death, are of equal value in this respect, that each serves to effect its purpose perfectly. Since in early youth it cannot be known what ends are likely to occur to us in the course of life, parents seek to have their children taught a *great many things*, and provide for their *skill* in the use of means for all sorts of *discretionary* ends, of none of which can they determine whether it may not perhaps hereafter be an object to their pupil, but which it is at all events *possible* that he might aim at; and this anxiety is so great that they commonly neglect to form and correct their children's judgment of the value of the things which may be chosen as ends.

There is *one* end, however, which may be assumed to be actually such to all rational beings (so far as imperatives apply to them, viz. as dependent beings), and therefore, one purpose which they not merely *may* have, but which we may with certainty assume that they all actually *do have* by a natural necessity, and this is *happiness*. The hypothetical imperative which expresses the practical necessity of an action as means to the advancement of happiness is *assertoric*. We are not to present it as necessary for an uncertain and merely possible purpose, but for a purpose which we may presuppose with certainty and *a priori* in every human being, because it belongs to his being. Now skill in the choice of means to his own greatest well-being may be called *prudence*,[2] in the narrowest sense. And thus the imperative which refers to the choice of means to one's own happiness, that is, the precept of prudence, is still always *hypothetical*; the action is not commanded absolutely, but only as means to another purpose.

Finally, there is an imperative which commands a certain conduct immediately, without having as its condition any other purpose to be attained by it. This imperative is **categorical**. It concerns not the matter of the action, or its intended result, but its form and the principle of which it is itself a result; and what is essentially good in it consists in the mental disposition, let the consequence be what it may. This imperative may be called that of **morality**.

There is a marked distinction also between the volitions on these three sorts of principles in the *dissimilarity* of the necessitation of the will. In order to mark this difference more clearly, I think they would be most suitably named in their order if we said they are either *rules* of skill, or *counsels* of prudence, or *commands* (*laws*) of morality. For it is law only that involves the concept of an *unconditional* and objective necessity, which is consequently universally valid; and commands are laws which must be obeyed, that is, must be followed, even in opposition to inclination. *Counsels*, indeed, involve necessity, but one which can only hold under a contingent subjective condition, viz., they depend on whether this or that human being counts this or that as part of his happiness; the categorical imperative, on the contrary, is not limited by any condition, and as being absolutely, although practically, necessary may be quite properly called a command. We might also call the first kind of imperatives *technical* (belonging to art), the second *pragmatic*[3] (belonging to welfare), and the third *moral* (belonging to free conduct as such, that is, to morals). ...

When I conceive a hypothetical imperative, in general I do not know beforehand what it will contain until I am given the condition. But when I conceive a categorical imperative, I know at once what it contains. For as the imperative contains besides the law only the necessity that the maxims[4] shall conform to this law, while the law contains no conditions restricting it, there remains nothing but the general statement that the maxim of the action should conform to universal law, and it is this conformity alone that the imperative properly represents as necessary.

There is therefore but one categorical imperative, namely, this: *Act only on that maxim whereby you can at the same time will that it become a universal law*.[5]

Now if all imperatives of duty can be deduced from this one imperative as their principle, then, although it should remain undecided whether what is called duty is not merely a vain notion, yet at least we shall be able to show what we understand by it and what this notion means.

Since the universality of the law according to which effects are produced constitutes what is properly called *nature* in the most general sense (as to form)—that is, the existence of things so far as it is determined by general laws—the imperative of duty may be expressed thus: *Act as if the maxim of your action were to become by your will a **universal law of nature***.

We will now enumerate a few duties, adopting the usual division of them into duties to ourselves and duties to others, and into perfect and imperfect duties.[6]

1. Someone reduced to despair by a series of misfortunes feels wearied of life, but is still so far in possession of his reason that he can ask himself whether it would not be contrary to his duty to himself take his own life. Now he inquires whether the maxim of his action could become a universal law of nature. His maxim is: From self-love I adopt it as my principle to shorten my life when its longer duration is likely to bring more ill than satisfaction. It is asked then simply whether this principle founded on self-love can become a universal law of nature. Now we can see at once that a system of nature of which it should be a law to destroy life by means of the very feeling whose vocation it is to impel to the improvement of life would contradict itself, and therefore could not exist as a system of nature; hence that maxim cannot possibly exist as a universal law of nature, and consequently would be wholly inconsistent with the supreme principle of all duty.

2. Another finds himself forced by necessity to borrow money. He knows that he will not be able

to repay it, but sees also that nothing will be lent to him unless he promises firmly to repay it within in a determinate time. He wants to make this promise, but he has still so much conscience as to ask himself: Is it not unlawful and inconsistent with duty to get out of a difficulty this way? Suppose, however, that he resolves to do so, then the maxim of his action would be expressed thus: When I think myself in want of money, I will borrow money and promise to repay it, although I know that I never can do so. Now this principle of self-love or of one's own advantage may perhaps be consistent with my whole future welfare; but the question now is, Is it right? I change then the suggestion of self-love into a universal law, and state the question thus: How would it be if my maxim were a universal law? Then I see at once that it could never hold as a universal law of nature, but would necessarily contradict itself. For supposing it to be a universal law that everyone when he thinks himself in a difficulty should be able to promise whatever he pleases, with the purpose of not keeping his promise, the promise itself would become impossible, as well as the end that he might have in view in it, since no one would consider that anything was promised to him, but would ridicule all such statements as vain pretenses.

3. A third finds in himself a talent which with the help of some culture might make him a useful human being in many respects. But he finds himself in comfortable circumstances and prefers to indulge in pleasure rather than to take pain in enlarging and improving his fortunate natural predispositions. He asks, however, whether his maxim of neglect of his natural gifts, besides agreeing with his inclination to indulgence, agrees also with what is called duty. He sees then that a system of nature could indeed subsist with such a universal law, although human beings (like the South Sea islanders) should let their talents rust and resolve to devote their lives merely to idleness, amusement, and propagation of their species — in a word, to enjoyment; but he cannot possibly **will** that this should be a universal law of nature, or be implanted in us as such by a natural instinct. For as a rational being, he necessarily wills that his faculties be developed, since they

serve him, and have been given him, for all sorts of purposes.

4. Yet a fourth, who is in prosperity, while he sees that others have to contend with great wretchedness and that he could help them, thinks: What concern is it of mine? Let everyone be as happy as heaven pleases, or as he can make himself; I will take nothing from him nor even envy him, only I do not wish to contribute anything to his welfare or to his assistance in need! Now no doubt, if such a mode of thinking were a universal law, the human race might very well subsist, and doubtless even better than in a state in which everyone talks of sympathy and good-will, or even takes care occasionally to put it into practice, but, on the other side, also cheats when he can, betrays the rights of human beings, or otherwise violates them. But although it is possible that a universal law of nature might exist in accordance with that maxim, it is impossible to **will** that such a principle should have the universal validity of a law of nature. For a will which resolved this would contradict itself, inasmuch as many cases might occur in which one would have need of the love and sympathy of others, and in which, by such a law of nature, sprung from his own will, he would deprive himself of all hope of the aid he desires.

These are a few of the many actual duties, or at least what we regard as such, which obviously fall into two classes on the one principle that we have laid down. We must *be able to will* that a maxim of our action should be a universal law. This is the canon of the moral judgment of the action generally. Some actions are of such a character that their maxim cannot without contradiction be even *conceived* as a universal law of nature, far from it being possible that we should *will* that it *should* be so. In others, this intrinsic impossibility is not found, but still it is impossible to *will* that their maxim should be raised to the universality of a law of nature, since such a will would contradict itself. It is easily seen that the former violate strict or rigorous (inflexible) duty; the latter only wide (meritorious) duty. Thus it has been completely shown by these examples how all duties depend as regards the nature of the obligation (not the object of the action) on the same principle.

If now we attend to ourselves on occasion of any transgression of duty, we will find that we in fact do not will that our maxim should be a universal law, for that is impossible for us; on the contrary, we will that the opposite should remain a universal law, only we assume the liberty of making an *exception* in our own favor or (just for this time only) in favor of our inclination. Consequently, if we considered all cases from one and the same point of view, namely, that of reason, we should find a contradiction in our own will, namely, that a certain principle should be objectively necessary as a universal law, and yet subjectively should not be universal, but admit of exceptions. As, however, we at one moment regard our action from the point of view of a will wholly conformed to reason, and then again look at the same action from the point of view of a will affected by inclination, there is not really any contradiction, but an opposition (*antagonismus*) of inclination to the precept of reason, whereby the universality (*universalitas*) of the principle is changed into a mere generality (*generalitas*), so that the practical principle of reason shall meet the maxim half way. Now, although this cannot be justified in our own impartial judgment, yet it proves that we do really recognize the validity of the categorical imperative and (with all respect for it) only allow ourselves a few exceptions which we think unimportant and forced upon us.

We have thus established at least this much — that if duty is a conception which is to have any import and real legislative authority for our actions, it can only be expressed in categorical, and not at all in hypothetical, imperatives. We have also, which is of great importance, exhibited clearly and definitely for every practical application the content of the categorical imperative, which must contain the principle of all duty if there is such a thing at all. We have not yet, however, advanced so far as to prove *a priori* that there actually is such an imperative, that there is a practical law which commands absolutely of itself and without any other incentive, and that the following of this law is duty.

With the view of attaining to this it is of extreme importance to remember that we must not allow ourselves to think of deducing the reality of this principle from the *particular attributes of human nature.* For duty is to be a practical, unconditional necessity of action; it must therefore hold for all rational beings (to whom an imperative can apply at all), and *for this reason only* be also a law for all human wills. On the contrary, whatever is deduced from the particular natural characteristics of humanity, from certain feelings and propensities, or even, if possible, from any particular tendency proper to human reason, and which need not necessarily hold for the will of every rational being — this may indeed supply us with a maxim but not with a law; with a subjective principle on which we may have a propensity and inclination to act, but not with an objective principle on which we should be *enjoined* to act, even though all our propensities, inclinations, and natural dispositions were opposed to it. In fact, the sublimity and intrinsic dignity of the command in duty are so much the more evident, the less the subjective impulses favor it and the more they oppose it, without being able in the slightest degree to weaken the obligation of the law or to diminish its validity. ...

The will is conceived as a capacity of determining itself to action in accordance with the *representation of certain laws*. And such a capacity can be found only in rational beings. Now that which serves the will as the objective ground of its self-determination is the *end*, and if this is assigned by reason alone, it must hold for all rational beings. On the other hand, that which merely contains the ground of possibility of the action of which the effect is the end, this is called the *means*. The subjective ground of the desire is the *incentive*, the objective ground of the volition is the *motive*; hence the distinction between subjective ends which rest on incentives, and objective ends which depend on motives valid for every rational being. Practical principles are *formal* when they abstract from all subjective ends; they are *material* when they assume these, and therefore particular incentives. The ends which a rational being proposes to himself at pleasure as *effects* of his actions (material ends) are all only relative, for it is only their relation to the particular desires of the subject that gives them their worth, which therefore cannot furnish principles universal and necessary for all rational beings and for every volition, that is to say, practical laws. Hence all these relative ends can give rise only to hypothetical imperatives.

Supposing, however, that there were something *whose existence* has *in itself* an absolute worth, something which, being *an end in itself*, could be a source of definite laws, then in this and this alone would lie the source of a possible categorical imperative, that is, a practical law.

Now I say: the human being and in general every rational being exists as an end in itself, *not merely as a means* to be arbitrarily used by this or that will, but in all his actions, whether they concern himself or other rational beings, must be always regarded at the same time as an end. All objects of the inclinations have only a conditional worth; for if the inclinations and the needs founded on them did not exist, then their object would be without any value. But the inclinations themselves, being sources of needs, are so far from having an absolute worth for which they should be desired that, on the contrary, it must be the universal wish of every rational being to be wholly free from them. Thus the worth of any object which is *to be acquired* by our action is always conditional. Beings whose existence depends not on our will but on nature's, have nevertheless, if they are non-rational beings, only a relative value as means, and are therefore called *things*; rational beings, on the contrary, are called *persons*, because their very nature restricts all choice (and is an object of respect).[7] These, therefore, are not merely subjective ends whose existence has a worth *for us* as an effect of our action, but *objective ends*, that is, things whose existence is an end in itself — an end, moreover, for which no other can be substituted, to which they should serve *merely* as means, for otherwise nothing whatever would possess *absolute worth*; but if all worth were conditioned and therefore contingent, then there would be no supreme practical principle of reason whatever.

If then there is a supreme practical principle or, with respect to the human will, a categorical imperative, it must be one which, being drawn from the conception of that which is necessarily an end for everyone because it is *an end in itself*, con-

stitutes an *objective* principle of will, and can therefore serve as a universal practical law. The foundation of this principle is: *rational nature exists as an end in itself*. The human being necessarily conceives of his own existence as being so; so far then this is a *subjective* principle of human actions. But every other rational being regards its existence similarly, just on the same rational principle that holds for me;[8] so that it is at the same time an objective principle from which as a supreme practical law all laws of the will must be capable of being deduced. Accordingly the practical imperative will be as follows: *So act as to treat humanity, whether in your own person or in that of any other, in every case at the same time as an end, never as a means only*. We will now inquire whether this can be practically carried out.

To abide by the previous examples:

First, under the head of necessary duty to oneself: Someone who contemplates suicide should ask himself whether his action can be consistent with the idea of humanity *as an end in itself*. If he destroys himself in order to escape from painful circumstances, he uses a person merely as a *means* to maintain a tolerable condition up to the end of life. But a human being is not a thing, that is to say, something which can be used merely as a means, but must in all his actions be always considered as an end in itself. I cannot, therefore, dispose in any way of a human being in my own person by mutilating, damaging, or killing him. (It belongs to morals proper to define this principle more precisely, so as to avoid all misunderstanding, for example, as to the amputation of the limbs in order to preserve myself; as to exposing my life to danger with a view to preserve it, etc. This question is therefore omitted here.)

Second, as regards necessary duties, or those of strict obligation, towards others: He who is thinking of making a lying promise to others will see at once that he would be using another human being *merely as a means*, without the latter at the same time containing in himself the end. For he whom I propose by such a promise to use for my own purposes cannot possibly assent to my mode of acting toward him, and therefore cannot himself contain the end of this action. This violation of the principle of humanity in other human beings is more obvious if we take in examples of attacks on the freedom and property of others. For then it is clear that he who transgresses the rights of human beings intends to use the person of others merely as means, without considering that as rational beings they ought always to be esteemed also as ends, that is, as beings who must be capable of containing in themselves the end of the very same action.[9]

Third, as regards contingent (meritorious) duties to oneself: It is not enough that the action does not violate humanity in our own person as an end in itself, it must also *harmonize with* it. Now there are in humanity capacities of greater perfection which belong to the end that nature has in view with regard to humanity in ourselves as the subject; to neglect these might perhaps be consistent with the *maintenance* of humanity as an end in itself, but not with the *advancement* of this end.

Fourth, as regards meritorious duties toward others: The natural end which all human beings have is their own happiness. Now humanity might indeed subsist although no one should contribute anything to the happiness of others, provided he did not intentionally withdraw anything from it; but after all, this would only harmonize negatively, not positively, with *humanity as an end in itself*, if everyone does not also endeavor, as far as he can, to forward the ends of others. For the ends of any subject which is an end in itself ought as far as possible to be *my* ends also, if that conception is to have its *full* effect in me.

This principle that humanity and generally every rational nature is *an end in itself* (which is the supreme limiting condition of every human being's freedom of action), is not borrowed from experience, *first*, because it is universal, applying as it does to all rational beings whatever, and experience is not capable of determining anything about them; *second*, because it does not present humanity as an end to human beings (subjectively), that is, as an object which human beings do of themselves actually adopt as an end; but as an objective end which must as a law constitute the supreme limiting condition of all our subjective ends, let them be what they will; it must therefore spring from pure reason. In fact the ground of all practical

legislation lies (according to the first principle) *objectively in the rule* and its form of universality which makes it capable of being a law (say, for example, a law of nature); but *subjectively* in the *end*; now by the second principle, the subject of all ends is each rational being inasmuch as it is an end in itself. From this follows the third practical principle of the will, which is the ultimate condition of its harmony with the universal practical reason, viz., the idea of *the will of every rational being as a will giving universal law*.[10]

On this principle all maxims are rejected which are inconsistent with the will being itself universal legislator. Thus the will is not merely subject to the law, but subject to it so that it must be regarded *as itself giving the law*, and on this ground only subject to the law (of which it can regard itself as the author). ...

Looking back now on all previous attempts to discover the principle of morality, we need not wonder why they all failed. It was seen that the human being is bound to laws by duty, but it was not observed that the laws to which he is subject are *only those of his own giving*, though at the same time they are *universal*, and that he is only bound to act in conformity with his own will — a will, however, which is designed by nature to give universal laws. For when one has conceived the human being only as subject to a law (no matter what), then this law required some interest, either by way of attraction or constraint, since it did not originate as a law from *his own* will, but this will was according to a law obliged by *something else* to act in a certain manner. Now by this necessary consequence all the labor spent in finding a supreme principle of *duty* was irrevocably lost. For one never elicited duty, but only a necessity of acting from a certain interest. Whether this interest was private or otherwise, in any case the imperative had to be conditional, and could not by any means be capable of being a moral command. I will therefore call this the principle of **autonomy** of the will, in contrast with every other which I accordingly count under **heteronomy**.

The concept of every rational being as one which must consider itself as giving in all the maxims of its will universal laws, so as to judge itself and its actions from this point of view — this concept leads to another which depends on it and is very fruitful, namely, that of a *kingdom of ends*.

By a *kingdom* I understand the systematic union of different rational beings through common laws. Now since it is by laws that the universal validity of ends are determined, hence, if we abstract from the personal differences of rational beings, and likewise from all the content of their private ends, we shall be able to conceive all ends combined in a systematic whole (including both rational beings as ends in themselves, and also the special ends which each may propose to himself), that is to say, we can conceive a kingdom of ends, which on the preceding principles is possible.

For all rational beings come under the *law* that each of them must treat itself and all others *never merely as means*, but in every case *at the same time as ends in themselves*. From this results a systematic union of rational beings through common objective laws, that is, a kingdom which may be called a kingdom of ends, since what these laws have in view is just the relation of these beings to one another as ends and means. It is certainly only an ideal.

A rational being belongs as a *member* to the kingdom of ends when, although giving universal laws in it, he is also himself subject to these laws. He belongs to it *as sovereign* when, while giving laws, he is not subject to the will of any other.

A rational being must always regard himself as giving laws either as member or as sovereign in a kingdom of ends which is rendered possible by the freedom of will. He cannot, however, maintain the latter position merely by maxims of his will, but only in case he is a completely independent being without needs and with unrestricted power adequate to his will.

Morality consists then in the reference of all action to the legislation which alone can render a kingdom of ends possible. This legislation must be capable of existing in every rational being, and of emanating from his will, so that the principle of this will is never to act on any maxim which could not without contradiction be also a universal law, and accordingly always so to act that *the will could at the same time regard itself as giving through its maxims universal laws*. If now the maxims of rational beings are not by their own nature coincident with this objective principle, then the necessity of acting on it is called practical necessitation, that is, *duty*. Duty does not apply to the sovereign in the kingdom of ends, but it does apply to every member of it and to all in the same degree.

The practical necessity of acting on this principle, that is, duty, does not rest at all on feelings, impulses, or inclinations, but solely on the relation of rational beings to one another, a relation in which the will of a rational being must always be regarded as *legislative*, since otherwise it could not be regarded as *an end in itself*. Reason then refers every maxim of the will, regarding it as legislative universally, to every other will and also to every action towards oneself; and this not on account of any other practical motive or any future advantage, but from the idea of the *dignity* of a rational being, obeying no law but that which he himself also gives. ...

What then is it which justifies virtue or the morally good disposition, in making such lofty claims? It is nothing less than the *privilege* it secures to the rational being of participating *in the giving of universal laws*, by which it qualifies him to be a member of a possible kingdom of ends, a privilege to which he was already destined by his own nature as being an end in itself, and on that account legislating in the kingdom of ends; free as regards all laws of nature, and obeying only those laws which he himself gives, and by which his maxims can belong to a system of universal law to which at the same time he submits himself. For nothing has any worth except what the law assigns it. Now the legislation itself which assigns the worth of everything must for that very reason possess dignity, that is, an unconditional incomparable worth; and the word *respect* alone supplies a becoming expression for the esteem which a rational being must have for it. *Autonomy* then is the basis of the dignity of human nature and of every rational nature.

The three modes of presenting the principle of morality that have been adduced are at bottom only so many formulae of the very same law, and each unites in itself the other two. There is, however, a difference among them, but it is subjectively rather than objectively practical, intended, namely, to bring an idea of reason nearer to intuition (by means of a certain analogy), and thereby nearer to feeling. All maxims, in fact, have —

1. A *form*, consisting in universality; and in this view the formula of the moral imperative is expressed thus, that the maxims must be so chosen as if they were to serve as universal laws of nature.

2. A *matter*, namely, an end, and here the formula says that the rational being, as it is an end by its own nature and therefore an end in itself, must in every maxim serve as the condition limiting all merely relative and arbitrary ends.

3. A *complete determination* of all maxims by means of that formula, namely, that all maxims ought, by their own legislation, to harmonize with a possible kingdom of ends as with a kingdom of nature.[11] There is a progression here in the order of the categories of *unity* of the form of the will (its universality), *plurality* of the matter (the objects, that is, the ends), and *totality* of the system of these. In forming our moral *judgment* of actions it is better to proceed always on the strict method, and start from the universal formula of the categorical imperative: *Act according to a maxim which can at the same time make itself a universal law*. If, however, we wish to gain an *entrance* for the moral law, it is very useful to bring one and the same action under the three specified conceptions, and thereby as far as possible to bring it nearer to intuition.

We can now end where we started at the beginning, namely, with the conception of a will unconditionally good. *That will is absolutely good* which cannot be evil — in other words, whose maxim, if made a universal law, could never contradict itself. This principle, then, is its supreme law: *Act always on such a maxim as you can at the same time will to be a universal law*; this is the sole condition under which a will can never contradict itself; and such an imperative is categorical. Since the validity of the will as a universal law for possible actions is analogous to the universal connection of the existence of things by universal laws, which is the formal notion of nature in general, the categorical imperative can also be expressed thus: *Act on*

maxims which can at the same time have for their object themselves as universal laws of nature. Such then is the formula of an absolutely good will. ...

It follows incontestably that, to whatever laws any rational being may be subject, he (being an end in itself) must be able to regard himself as also legislating universally in respect to these same laws, since it is just this fitness of his maxims for universal legislation that distinguishes him as an end in itself; also it follows that this implies his dignity (prerogative) above all merely natural beings, that he must always take his maxims from the point of view which regards himself, and likewise every other rational being, as a lawgiving being (on which account they are called persons). In this way a world of rational beings (*mundus intelligibilis*) is possible as a kingdom of ends, and this by virtue of the legislation proper to all persons as members. Therefore, every rational being must so act as if he were by his maxims in every case a legislating member in the universal kingdom of ends. The formal principle of these maxims is: So act as if your maxim were to serve also as the universal law (of all rational beings). A kingdom of ends is thus only possible on the analogy of a kingdom of nature, the former, however, only by maxims — that is, self-imposed rules — the latter only by the laws of efficient causes acting under necessitation from without. Nevertheless, although the system of nature is looked upon as a machine, yet so far as it has reference to rational beings as its ends, it is given on this account the name of a kingdom of nature. Now such a kingdom of ends would be actually realized by means of maxims conforming to the canon which the categorical imperative prescribes to all rational beings, *if they were universally followed*. But although a rational being, even if he strictly follows this maxim himself, cannot count on all others being therefore true to the same, nor expect the kingdom of nature and its orderly arrangements to be in harmony with him as a fitting member, so as to form a kingdom of ends to which he himself contributes, that is to say, that it shall favor his expectation of happiness, still that law: Act according to the maxims of a member of a merely possible kingdom of ends legislating in it universally,[12] remains in its full force inasmuch as it commands categorically. And it is just in this that the paradox lies, that the mere dignity of the human being as a rational being, without any other end or advantage to be attained thereby, in other words, respect for a mere idea, should yet serve as an inflexible precept of the will, and that it is precisely in this independence of the maxim on all such incentives that its sublimity consists; and it is this that makes every rational subject worthy to be a legislative member in the kingdom of ends, for otherwise he would have to be conceived only as subject to the natural law of his needs. ...

From what has just been said, it is easy to see how it happens that, although the conception of duty implies subjection to the law, we yet ascribe a certain *dignity* and sublimity to the person who fulfills all his duties. There is not, indeed, any sublimity in him, so far as he is *subject* to the moral law; but inasmuch as in regard to that very law he is likewise a *legislator*, and on that account alone subject to it, he has sublimity. We have also shown above that neither fear nor inclination, but simply respect for the law, is the incentive which can give actions a moral worth. Our own will, so far as we suppose it to act only under the condition that its maxims are potentially universal laws, this ideal will which is possible for us is the proper object of respect; and the dignity of humanity consists just in this capacity of being universally legislative, though with the condition that it is itself subject to this same legislation.

NOTES

1. The dependence of the faculty of desire on sensations is called inclination, and this accordingly always indicates a *need*. The dependence of a contingently determinable will on principles of reason is called an *interest*. This, therefore, is found only in the case of a dependent will which does not always of itself conform to reason; in the Divine will we cannot conceive any interest. But the human will can also *take an interest* in a thing without therefore acting *from interest*. The former signifies the *practical* interest in the action, the latter the *pathological* interest in the object of the action. The former indicates only dependence on

principles of reason for the sake of inclination, reason supplying only the practical rules how the requirement of the inclination may be satisfied. In the first case the action interests me; in the second the object of the action (because it is pleasant to me). We have seen in the first section that in an action done from duty we must look not to the interest in the object, but only to that in the action itself, and in its rational principle (viz., the law). [I.K.]

2. The word *prudence* is taken in two senses: in the one it may bear the name of knowledge of the world, in the other that of private prudence. The former is a human being's ability to influence others so as to use them for his own purposes. The latter is the sagacity to combine all these purposes for his own lasting benefit. This latter is properly that to which the value even of the former is reduced, and when someone is prudent in the former sense but not in the latter, we might better say of him that he is clever and cunning, but, on the whole, imprudent. [I.K.]

3. It seems to me that the proper signification of the word *pragmatic* may be most accurately defined this way. For *sanctions* are called pragmatic which flow properly, not from the law of the states as necessary enactments, but from *precaution* for the general welfare. A history is composed pragmatically when it teaches *prudence*, that is, instructs the world how it can provide for its interests better, or at least as well as the human beings of former time. [I.K.]

4. A *maxim* is a subjective principle of action, and must be distinguished from the *objective principle*, namely, the practical law. The former contains the practical rule set by reason according to the conditions of the subject (often its ignorance or its inclinations), so that it is the principle on which the subject acts; but the law is the objective principle valid for every rational being, and is the principle on which it *ought to act* — that is, an imperative. [I.K.]

5. This formulation of the categorical imperative, the "formula of universal law" (along with its variant, the "formula of the law of nature") has been a primary target for criticism.

6. It must be noted here that I reserve the division of

duties for a future *metaphysics of morals*; so that I give it here only as an arbitrary one (in order to arrange my examples). For the rest, I understand by a perfect duty one that admits no exception in favor of inclination, and then I have not merely external but also internal perfect duties. This is contrary to the use of the word adopted in the schools; but I do not intend to justify it here, as it is all one for my purpose whether it is admitted or not. [I.K.]

7. This passage makes explicit Kant's view that non-rational animals lack the dignity that Kant attributes to persons, and thus cannot be owed respect or consequent duties.

8. This proposition is here stated as a postulate. The ground of it will be found in the concluding section. [I.K.]

9. Let it not be thought that the common: *quod tibi non vis fieri, etc.*, [i.e., what you do not want others to do to you, do not do to them] could serve here as the rule or principle. For it is only a deduction from the former, though with several limita-tions; it cannot be a universal law, for it does not contain the principle of duties to oneself, nor of the duties of benevolence to others (for many a one would gladly consent that others should not benefit him, provided only that he might be excused from showing benevolence to them), nor finally that of duties of strict obligation to one another, for on this principle the criminal might argue against the judge who punishes him, and so on. [I.K.]

10. This is called the "formula of autonomy."

11. Teleology considers nature as a kingdom of ends; ethics regards a possible kingdom of ends as a kingdom of nature. In the first case, the kingdom of ends is a theoretical idea, adopted to explain what actually is. In the latter it is a practical idea, adopted to bring about that which is not yet, but which can be realized by our conduct, namely, if it conforms to this idea. [I.K.]

12. This is called the "formula of the kingdom of ends."

UTILITARIANISM

John Stuart Mill

John Stuart Mill, a British philosopher, lived from 1806-1873. He is most well-known for his works On Liberty *and* Utilitarianism, *both of which have been highly influential in moral and political theory.*

Mill argues that morally right action is that which results in the greatest amount of happiness for the greatest number of people. There are several elements important to his version of utilitarianism. He promotes happiness rather than pleasure and holds, for example, that the quality of intellectual pleasures ranks higher than the quantity of bodily pleasures; the former are distinctive of and important to human happiness. Morally right action is determined by calculating the amount of happiness and unhappiness in terms of quality rather than mere quantity and in the lives of each person affected by the action.

Chapter II / What Utilitarianism is

... The creed which accepts as the foundation of morals "utility" or the "greatest happiness principle" holds that actions are right in proportion as they tend to promote happiness; wrong as they tend to produce the reverse of happiness. By happiness is intended pleasure and the absence of pain: by unhappiness, pain and the privation of pleasure. To give a clear view of the moral standard set up by the theory, much more requires to be said: in particular, what things it includes in the ideas of pain and pleasure, and to what extent this is left an open question. But these supplementary explanations do not affect the theory of life on which this theory of morality is grounded — namely, that pleasure and freedom from pain are the only things desirable as ends; and that all desirable things (which are as numerous in the utilitarian as in any other scheme) are desirable either for pleasure inherent in themselves or as means to the promotion of pleasure and the prevention of pain.

Now such a theory of life excites in many minds, and among them in some of the most estimable in feeling and purpose, inveterate dislike. To suppose that life has (as they express it) no higher end than pleasure — no better and nobler object of desire and pursuit — they designate as utterly mean and groveling, as a doctrine worthy only of swine, to whom the followers of Epicurus were, at a very early period, contemptuously likened; and modern holders of the doctrine are occasionally made the subject of equally polite comparison by its German, French, and English assailants.

When thus attacked, the Epicureans have always answered that it is not they, but their accusers, who represent human nature in a degrading light, since the accusation supposes human beings to be capable of no pleasures except those of which swine are capable. If this supposition were true, the charge could not be gainsaid, but would then be no longer an imputation; for if the sources of pleasure were precisely the same to human beings and to swine, the rule of life which is good enough for the one would be good enough for the other. The comparison of the Epicurean life to that of beasts is felt as degrading, precisely because a beast's pleasures do not satisfy a human being's conceptions of happiness. Human beings have faculties more elevated than the animal appetites and, when once made conscious of them, do not regard anything as happiness which does not include their gratification. I do not indeed, consider the Epicureans to have been by any means faultless in drawing out their scheme of consequences from the utilitarian principle. To do this in any sufficient manner, many Stoic, as well as Christian, elements require to be included. But there is no known Epicurean theory of life which does not assign to the pleasures of the intellect, of the feelings and imagination, and of the moral sentiments a much higher value as pleasures than to those of mere sensation. It must be admitted however, that utilitarian writers in general have placed the superiority of mental over bodily pleasures chiefly in the greater permanency, safety, uncostliness, etc., of the former — that is, in their circumstantial advantages rather than in their intrinsic nature. And on all these points utilitarians have fully proved their case; but they might have taken the other and, as it may be called, higher ground with entire consistency. It is quite compatible with the principle of utility to recognize the fact that some kinds of pleasure are more desirable and more valuable than others. It would be absurd that, while in estimating all other things quality is considered as well as quantity, the estimation of pleasure should be supposed to depend on quantity alone.

If I am asked what I mean by difference of quality in pleasures, or what makes one pleasure more valuable than another, merely as a pleasure, except its being greater in amount, there is but one possible answer. Of two pleasures, if there be one to which all or almost all who have experience of both give a decided preference, irrespective of any feeling of moral obligation to prefer it, that is the more desirable pleasure. If one of the two is, by those who are competently acquainted with both, placed so far above the other that they prefer it, even though knowing it to be attended with a greater amount of discontent, and would not resign it for any quantity of the other pleasure which nature is capable of, we are justified in ascribing to the preferred enjoyment a superiority in quality so far outweighing quantity as to render it, in comparison, of small account.

Now it is an unquestionable fact that those who are equally acquainted with and equally capable of appreciating and enjoying both do give a most marked preference to the manner of existence which employs their higher faculties. Few Human creatures would consent to be changed into any of the lower animals for a promise of the fullest allowance of a beast's pleasures; no intelligent human being would consent to be a fool, no instructed person would be an ignoramus, no person of feeling and conscience would be selfish and base, even though they should be persuaded that the fool, the dunce, or the rascal is better satisfied with his lot than they are with theirs. They would not resign what they possess more than he for the most complete satisfaction of all the desires which they have in common with him. If they ever fancy they would, it is only in cases of unhappiness so extreme that to escape from it they would exchange their lot for almost any other, however undesirable in their own eyes. A being of higher faculties requires more to make him happy, is capable probably of more acute suffering, and certainly accessible to it at more points, than one of an inferior type; but in spite of these liabilities, he can never really wish to sink into what he feels to be a lower grade of existence. We may give what explanation we please of this unwillingness; we may attribute it to pride, a name which is given indiscriminately to some of the most and to some of the least estimable feelings of which mankind are capable; we may refer it to the love of liberty and personal independence, an appeal to which was with the Stoics one of the most effective means for the inculcation of it; to the love of power or to the love of excitement, both of which do really enter into and contribute to it; but its most appropriate appellation is a sense of dignity, which all human beings possess in one form or other, and in some, though by no means in exact, proportion to their higher faculties, and which is so essential a part of the happiness of those in whom it is strong that nothing which conflicts with it could be otherwise than momentarily an object of desire to them. Whoever supposes that this preference takes place at a sacrifice of happiness — that the superior being, in anything like equal circumstances, is not happier than the inferior — confounds the two very different ideas of happiness and content. It is indisputable that the being whose capacities of enjoyment are low has the greatest chance of having them fully satisfied; and a highly endowed being will always feel that any happiness which he can look for, as the world is constituted, is imperfect. But he can learn to bear its imperfections, if they are at all bearable; and they will not make him envy the being who is indeed unconscious of the imperfections, but only because he feels not at all the good which those imperfections qualify. It is better to be a human being dissatisfied than a pig satisfied; better to be Socrates dissatisfied than a fool satisfied. And if the fool, or the pig, are of a different opinion, it is because they only know their own side of the question. The other party to the comparison knows both sides.

It may be objected that many who are capable of the higher pleasures occasionally, under the influence of temptation, postpone them to the lower. But this is quite compatible with a full appreciation of the intrinsic superiority of the higher. Men often, from infirmity of character, make their election for the nearer good, though they know it to be the less valuable; and this no less when the choice is between two bodily pleasures than when it is between bodily and mental. They pursue sensual indulgence to the injury of health, though perfectly aware that health is the greater good. It may be further objected that many who begin with youthful enthusiasm for everything noble, as they advance in years, sink into indolence and selfishness. But I do not believe that those who undergo this very common change voluntarily choose the lower description of pleasures in preference to the higher. I believe that, before they devote themselves exclusively to the one, they have already become incapable of the other. Capacity for the nobler feelings is in most natures a very tender plant, easily killed, not only by hostile influences, but by mere want of sustenance; and in the majority of young persons it speedily dies away if the occupations to which their position in life has devoted them, and the society into which it has thrown them, are not favorable to keeping that higher capacity in exercise. Men lose their high aspirations as they lose their intellectual tastes, because they have not time or opportunity for

indulging them; and they addict themselves to inferior pleasures, not because they deliberately prefer them, but because they are either the only ones to which they have access or the only ones which they are any longer capable of enjoying. It may be questioned whether anyone who has remained equally susceptible to both classes of pleasures ever knowingly and calmly preferred the lower, though many, in all ages, have broken down in an ineffectual attempt to combine both.

From this verdict of the only competent judges, I apprehend there can be no appeal. On a question which is the best worth having of two pleasures, or which of two modes of existence is the most grateful to the feelings, apart from its moral attributes, and from its consequences, the judgment of these who are qualified by knowledge of both, or, if they differ, that of the majority among them, must be admitted as final. And there needs be the less hesitation to accept this judgment respecting the quality of pleasures, since there is no other tribunal to be referred to even on the question of quantity. What means are there of determining which is the acutest of two pains, or the intensest of the two pleasurable sensations, except the general suffrage of those who are familiar with both? Neither pains nor pleasures are homogeneous, and pain is always heterogeneous with pleasure. What is there to decide whether a particular pleasure is worth purchasing at the cost of a particular pain, except the feelings and judgment of the experienced? When, therefore, those feelings and judgment declare the pleasures derived from the higher faculties to be preferable in kind, apart from the question of intensity, to those of which the animal nature, disjoined from the higher faculties, is susceptible, they are entitled on this subject to the same regard.

I have dwelt on this point as being part of a perfectly just conception of utility or happiness considered as the directive rule of human conduct. But it is by no means an indispensable condition to the acceptance of the utilitarian standard; for that standard is not the agent's own greatest happiness, but the greatest amount of happiness altogether, and if it may possibly be doubted whether a noble character is always the happier for its nobleness, there can be no doubt that it makes other people happier, and that the world in general is immensely a gainer by it. Utilitarianism, therefore, could only attain its end by the general cultivation of nobleness of character, even if each individual were only benefited by the nobleness of others, and his own, so far as happiness is concerned, were a sheer deduction from the benefit. But the bare enunciation of such an absurdity as this last renders refutation superfluous.

According to the greatest happiness principle, as above explained, the ultimate end, with reference to and for the sake of which all other things are desirable — whether we are considering our own good or that of other people — is an existence exempt as far as possible from pain, and as rich as possible in enjoyments, both in point of quantity and quality; the test of quality and the rule for measuring it against quantity being the preference felt by those who, in their opportunities of experience, to which must be added their habits of self-consciousness and self-observation, are best furnished with the means of comparison. This, being according to the utilitarian opinion the end of human action, is necessarily also the standard of morality, which may accordingly be defined "the rules and precepts for human conduct," by the observance of which an existence such as has been described might be, to the greatest extent possible, secured to all mankind; and not to them only, but, so far as the nature of things admits, to the whole sentient creation....

I must again repeat what the assailants of utilitarianism seldom have the justice to acknowledge, that the happiness which forms the utilitarian standard of what is right in conduct is not the agent's own happiness but that of all concerned. As between his own happiness and that of others, utilitarianism requires him to be as strictly impartial as a disinterested and benevolent spectator. In the golden rule of Jesus of Nazareth, we read the complete spirit of the ethics of utility. "To do as you would be done by," and "to love your neighbor as yourself," constitute the ideal perfection of utilitarian morality. As the means of making the nearest approach to this ideal, utility would enjoin, first, that laws and social arrangements should place the happiness or (as, speaking practically, it may be called) the interest of every individual as nearly as possible in harmony with the interest of the whole; and, secondly, that education and opinion which have so vast a power over human character, should so use that power as to establish in the mind of every individual an indissoluble association between his own happiness and the good of the whole, especially between his own happiness and practice of such modes of conduct, negative and positive, as regard for the universal happiness prescribes; so that not only he may be unable to conceive the possibility of happiness to himself, consistently with conduct opposed to the general good, but also that a direct impulse to promote the general good may be in every individual one of the habitual motives of action, and the sentiments connected therewith may fill a large and prominent place in every human being's sentient existence. If the impugners of the utilitarian morality represented it to their own minds, in this its true character, I know not what recommendations possessed by any other morality they could possibly affirm to be wanting to it; what more beautiful or more exalted developments of human nature any other ethical system can be supposed to foster, or what springs of action, not accessible to the utilitarian, such systems relay of for giving effect to their mandates.

The objectors to utilitarianism cannot always be charged with representing it in a discreditable light. On the contrary, those among them who entertain anything like a just idea of its disinterested character sometimes find fault with its standard as being too high for humanity. They say it is exacting too much to require that people shall always act from the inducement of promoting the general interest of society. But this is to mistake the very meaning of a standard of morals and confound the rule of action with the motive of it. It is the business of ethics to tell us what are our duties, or by what test we may know them; but no system of ethics requires that the sole motive of all we do shall be a feeling of duty; on the contrary, ninety-nine hundredths of all our actions are done from other motives, and rightly so done if the rule of duty does not condemn them. It is the more unjust to utilitarianism that this particular misapprehension should be made a ground of objection to it, inasmuch as utilitarian moralists have gone beyond almost all others in affirming that the motive has nothing to do with the morality of the action, though much with the worth of the agent. He who saves a fellow creature from drowning does what is morally right, whether his motive be duty or the hope of being paid for his trouble; he who betrays the friend that trusts him is guilty of a crime, even if his object be to serve another friend to whom he is under great obligations. But to speak only of actions done from the motive of duty, and in direct obedience to principle; it is a misapprehension of the utilitarian mode of thought to conceive it as implying that people should fix their minds upon so wide a generality as the world, or society at large. The great majority of good actions are intended not for the benefit of the world, but for that of individuals, of which the good of the world is made up; and the thoughts of the most virtuous man need not on these occasions travel beyond the particular persons concerned, except so far as is necessary to assure himself that in benefiting them he is not violating the rights, that is, the legitimate and authorized expectations, of anyone else. The multiplication of happiness, is, according to the utilitarian ethics, the object of virtue: the occasions on which any person (except one in a thousand) has it in his power to do this on an extended scale — in other words, to be a public benefactor — are but exceptional; and on these occasions alone is he called on to consider public utility; in every other case, private utility, the interest or happiness of some few persons, is all he has to attend to. Those alone the influence of whose actions extends to society in general need concern themselves habitually about so large an object. In the case of abstinences indeed — of things which people forbear to do from moral considerations, though the consequences in that particular case might be beneficial — it would be unworthy of an intelligent agent not to be consciously aware that the action is of a class which, if practiced generally, would be generally injurious, and that this is the ground of the obligation to abstain from it. The amount of regard for the public interest implied in this recognition is no greater than is demanded by every system of

morals, for they all enjoin to abstain from whatever is manifestly pernicious to society.

The same considerations dispose of another reproach against the doctrine of utility, founded on a still grosser misconception of the purpose of a standard of morality and of the very meaning of the words "right" and "wrong." It is often affirmed that utilitarianism renders men cold and unsympathizing; that it chills their moral feelings toward individuals; that it makes them regard only the dry and hard consideration of the consequences of actions, not taking into their moral estimate the qualities from which those actions emanate. If the assertion means that they do not allow their judgment respecting the rightness or wrongness of an action to be influenced by their opinion of the qualities of the person who does it, this is a complaint not against utilitarianism, but against any standard or morality at all; for certainly no known ethical standard decides an action to be good or bad because it is done by a good or bad man, still less because done by an amiable, a brave, or a benevolent man, or the contrary. These considerations are relevant, not to the estimation of actions, but of persons; and there is nothing in the utilitarian theory inconsistent with the fact that there are other things which interest us in persons besides the rightness and wrongness of their actions. The stoics, indeed, with the paradoxical misuse of language which was part of their system, and by which they strove to raise themselves above all concern about anything but virtue, were fond of saying that he who has that has everything; that he, and only he, is rich, is beautiful, is a king. But no claim of this description is made for the virtuous man but the utilitarian doctrine. Utilitarians are quite aware that there are other desirable possessions and qualities besides virtue, and are perfectly willing to allow to all of them their full worth. They are also aware that a right action does not necessarily indicate a virtuous character, and that actions which are blamable often proceed from qualities entitled to praise. When this is apparent in any particular case, it modifies their estimation, not certainly of the act, but of the agent. I grant that they are, notwithstanding, of opinion that in the long run the best proof of a good character is good actions, and resolutely refuse to consider any mental disposition as good of which the predominant tendency is to produce bad conduct. This makes them unpopular with many people, but it is an unpopularity which they must share with everyone who regards the distinction between right and wrong in a serious light; and the reproach is not one which a conscientious utilitarian need be anxious to repel.

If no more be meant by the objection than that many utilitarians look on the morality of actions, as measured by the utilitarian standards, with too exclusive a regard, and do not lay sufficient stress upon the other beauties of character which go toward making a human being lovable or admirable, this may be admitted. Utilitarians who have cultivated their moral feelings, but not their sympathies, nor their artistic perceptions, do fall into this mistake; and so do all other moralists under the same conditions. What can be said in excuse for other moralists is equally available for them, namely, that, if there is to be any error, it is better that it should be on that side. As a matter of fact, we may affirm that among utilitarians, as among adherents of other systems, there is every imaginable degree of rigidity and of laxity in the application of their standard; some are even puritanically rigorous, while others are as indulgent as can possibly be desired by sinner or by sentimentalists. But on the whole, a doctrine which brings prominently forward the interest that mankind have in the repression and prevention of conduct which violates the moral law is likely to be inferior to no other in turning the sanctions of opinion against such violations. It is true, the question "What does violate the moral law?" is one on which those who recognize different standards of morality are likely now and then to differ. But difference of opinion on moral questions was not first introduced into the world by utilitarianism, while that doctrine does supply, if not always an easy, at all events a tangible and intelligible, mode of deciding such differences.

It may not be superfluous to notice a few more of the common misapprehensions of utilitarian ethics....

We not uncommonly hear the doctrine of utility inveighed against a *godless* doctrine. If it be necessary to say anything at all against so mere an assumption, we may say that the question depends upon what idea we have formed of the moral character of the Deity. If it be a true belief that God desires, above all things, the happiness of his creatures, and that this was his purpose in their creation, utility is not only not a godless doctrine, but more profoundly religious than any other. If it be meant that utilitarianism does not recognize the revealed will of God as the supreme law of morals, I answer that a utilitarian who believes in the perfect goodness and wisdom of God necessarily believes that whatever God has thought fit to reveal on the subject of morals must fulfill the requirements of utility in a supreme degree. But others besides utilitarians have been of opinion that the Christian revelation was intended, and is fitted, to inform the hearts and minds of mankind with a spirit which should enable them to find for themselves what is right, and incline them to do it when found, rather than to tell them, except in a very general way, what it is; and that we need a doctrine of ethics, carefully followed out, to interpret to us the will of God. Whether this opinion is correct or not, it is superfluous here to discuss; since whatever aid religion, either natural or revealed, can afford to ethical investigation is as open to the utilitarian moralist as to any other. He can use it as the testimony of God to the usefulness or hurtfulness of any given course of action by as good a right as others can use it for the indication of a transcendental law having no connection with usefulness or with happiness....

Again, defenders of utility often find themselves called upon to reply to such objections as this — that there is not time, previous to actions, for calculating and weighing the effects of any line of conduct on the general happiness. This is exactly as if anyone were to say that it is impossible to guide our conduct by Christianity because there is not time, on every occasion on which anything has to be done, to read through the Old and New Testaments. The answer to the objection is that there has been ample time, namely, the whole past duration of the human species. During all that time mankind have been learning by experience the tendencies of actions; on which experience all the prudence as well as all the morality of life are dependent. People talk as if the commencement of this course of experience had hitherto been put off, and as if, at the moment when some man feels tempted to meddle with the property or life of another, he had to begin considering for the first time whether murder and theft are injurious to human happiness. Even then I do not think that he would find the question very puzzling; but, at all events, the matter is now done to his hand. It is truly a whimsical supposition that, if mankind were agreed in considering utility to be the test of morality, they would remain without any agreement as to what is useful, and would take no measures for having their notions on the subject taught to the young and enforced by law and opinion. There is no difficulty in proving any ethical standard whatever to work ill if we suppose universal idiocy to be conjoined with it, but on any hypothesis short of that, mankind must by this time have acquired positive beliefs as to the effects of some actions on their happiness; and the beliefs which have thus come down are the rules of morality for the multitude, and for the philosopher until he has succeeded in finding better. That philosophers might easily do this, even now, on many subjects; that the received code of ethics is by no means of divine right; and that mankind have still much to learn as to the effects of actions on the general happiness, I admit or rather earnestly maintain. The corollaries from the principle of utility, like the precepts of every practical art, admit of indefinite improvement, and, in a progressive state of the human mind, their improvement is perpetually going on. But to consider the rules of morality as improvable is one thing; to pass over the intermediate generalization entirely and endeavor to test each individual action directly by the first principle is another. It is a strange notion that the acknowledgment of a first principle is inconsistent with the admission of secondary ones. To inform a traveler respecting the place of his ultimate destination is not to forbid the use of landmarks and direction-posts on the way. The proposition that happiness is the end and aim of morality does not mean that no road ought to be laid down to that goal, or that persons going thither should not be advised to take one direction rather than another....

Whatever we adopt as the fundamental principle of morality, we require subordinate principles to apply it by; the impossibility of doing without them, being common to all systems, can afford no argument against any one in particular; but bravely to argue as if no such secondary principles could be had, and as if mankind had remained till now, and always must remain, without drawing any general conclusions from the experience of human life is as high a pitch, I think, as absurdity has ever reached in philosophical controversy.

The remainder of the stock arguments against utilitarianism mostly consist in laying to its charge the common infirmities of human nature, and the general difficulties which embarrass conscientious persons in shaping their course through life. We are told that a utilitarian will be apt to make his own particular case an exception to moral rules, and, when under temptation, will see a utility in the breach of a rule, greater than he will see in its observance. But is utility the only creed which is able to furnish us with excuses for evil-doing and means of cheating our own conscience? They are afforded in abundance by all doctrines which recognize as a fact in morals the existence of conflicting considerations, which all doctrines do that have been believed by sane persons. It is not the fault of any creed, but of the complicated nature of human affairs, that rules of conduct cannot be so framed as to require no exceptions, and that hardly any kind of action can safely be laid down as either always obligatory or always condemnable. There is no ethical creed which does not temper the rigidity of its laws by giving a certain latitude, under the moral responsibility of the agent, for accommodation to peculiarities of circumstances; and under every creed, at the opening thus made, self-deception and dishonest casuistry get in. There exists no moral system under which there do not arise unequivocal cases of conflicting obligation. These are the real difficulties, the knotty points both in the theory of ethics and in the conscientious guidance of personal conduct. They are overcome practically, with greater or with less success, according to the intellect and virtue of the individual; but it can hardly be pretended that anyone will be the less qualified for dealing with them, from possessing an ultimate standard to which conflicting rights and duties can be referred. If utility is the ultimate source of moral obligations, utility may be invoked to decide between them when their demands are incompatible. Though the application of the standard may be difficult, it is better than none at all; while in other systems, the moral laws all claiming independent authority, there is no common umpire entitled to interfere between them; their claims to precedence one over another rest on little better than sophistry, and, unless determined, as they generally are, by the unacknowledged influence of consideration of utility, afford a free scope for the action of personal desires and partialities. We must remember that only in these cases of conflict between secondary principles is it requisite that first principles should be appealed to. There is no case of moral obligation in which some secondary principle is not involved; and if only one, there can seldom be any real doubt which one it is, in the mind of any person by whom the principle itself is recognized.

ETHICS: THE WE AND THE I

V.F. Cordova

V.F. Cordova was one of the first Native Americans to receive a PhD in Philosophy in the U.S. She taught courses in Native American and comparative philosophies at the University of Alaska at Fairbanks, Oregon State University, and Idaho State University. She was founding editor of the American Philosophical Association Newsletter on American Indians in Philosophy. *She died in 2002.*

Cordova describes the Western liberal focus on individuals with self-determining capacities as an "I" approach to morality. She contrasts this with a "we" approach present in the moral theory of the ancient Greek philosophers Socrates and Aristotle and in Native American beliefs and values. The "we" approach begins with behavior toward others and thereby puts one's membership in a group or community as central to what it is to live an ethical life. Attention to one's behavior toward other individuals, communities, the environment, and the planet itself is thereby foregrounded. This view of the dependency and interdependency of human beings shapes an ethic in which individuals learn to be aware of the needs of others and of what the individual can do for the good of the group. Cordova argues that the "we" ethic of Native American tradition and culture challenges values evident in the contemporary phenomena of consumerism, environmental degradation, and economic development.

When we hear the term "ethics" we usually think of that which is moral or that which is legal: religion or law. We also are aware of the fact that various disciplines have a "code of conduct." The code specifies the actions and the goals of the practitioners in a specific discipline, for example, law, medicine, engineering. Ethics, as defined by the discipline of philosophy, is a careful examination of the foundation upon which such codes are based.

Religion and law do engage in the examination of their own bases but usually as a means of clarifying a specific rule for their adherence to the foundations of religion and law. The foundations themselves are seldom called into question. Ethics, as a philosophical discipline, deals primarily with the foundations of such systems. Ethics also has a foundation of its own: it is based on the fact that human beings do not exist as isolated, or solitary, beings. They exist, except in rare and unusual circumstances, as social entities. Ethics is based on the fact that human beings exist in social environments; it deals, primarily, with the sense of the "We" rather than the sense of the "I." A creature that truly leads an isolated and solitary existence has no need to take into consideration the relationship between itself and the other.

In the West, codes of conduct are based on the concept of the individual as the "bargaining unit." That is, there is a fundamental description of the human being as essentially an individual which is potentially autonomous. The term *autonomous* is, in this sense, described as making reference to an individual that exists isolated and solitary. The term implies, also, the notion that this individual can act in such a manner that he can become a law unto himself: the "I" is conceived as containing the capacity to be "self-determining."

A code of conduct, however, can be based on the description of the human being as a social being;

that is, he exists within the confines of the "We." The adjustment of his behavior in the company of others is necessary for the continued existence of the individual. In other words, if there were no others, or if the individual were truly autonomous, there would be no need to adjust one's behavior in order to maintain membership in a group.

Between those who would define the proper behavior of human beings toward others as based on the We or the I lies a tremendous difference. The societies based on the principle of the I as the essential bargaining unit see the individual as being "at war" with each and every other individual. The British philosopher Thomas Hobbes (1588-1679) best outlined this view of the individual; he saw individuals, also, as existing in a state of competition — one against the other — for a limited supply of those goods essential for the survival of the individual. ("If you won't attack me at the watering hole, I won't attack you.") Even in a Christian, or religious, sense this view of the individual is not uncommon in the West. In the religious version, individuals are separated from other individuals through their adherence to a particular set of beliefs; they come to be a group in order to make alliances between believers and against unbelievers. The Christian god sets the stage for this view of humans in groups: the god makes a distinction between those who follow him and those who do not. The believers are "saved"; the unbelievers are condemned. In both the religious and the "natural" (in the Hobbesian manner) Western definitions of the human being, the actual and undeniable existence of humans in groups must be explained or justified.

This view of human beings is very different from that of the Greeks who are seen as the secular forefathers of the West. Aristotle observed that a "man alone was either a god or a beast." A human was, for Aristotle, a social being, first and foremost. The Greeks were not offended when they heard of a comparison between themselves and bees and ants. These creatures shared with humans an inherently social nature. The West, both Christian and secular, is, in general, offended when humans are compared to bees and ants. The vision of a human as a naturally social being calls up

images of "the mindless herd" or "the mass mind" or "the unthinking masses" which can be swayed by a powerful leader. To say to a man of the West that humans are "animals of the herd" is usually seen as an insult. Others would understand this statement to say something "true" or "real" about the species. (To say to a Western person, for example an American, that he is "not like other Americans" is usually taken as a compliment, whereas in other cultures to single someone out as a being "unlike" others of his group can be a cause for unease.)

The heroic figure in the Greek world (despite misinterpretations by the post-Christian West) is that figure who sacrifices his well-being and sometimes his life for the good of the whole. In the West we have an entirely different "hero": the lone figure who stands against the social whole in the name of his own individual perspective. Socrates, so often depicted as a Western hero, in actuality drinks the hemlock and refuses the offer to flee Athens for the good of the society which he has so annoyed. He has a dream in which he converses with the personification of the laws of Athens: he has been duly charged, according to the law, and found guilty, again, through every means provided by the law. He has a right to defend himself against the charges and he even has a right not granted in the West: the right to propose alternative punishment for his act. The personification of the laws reminds Socrates that a society without laws cannot remain a society for long. "The law" reminds Socrates how he has benefited from that very law: his parents have received sanction from the state, thereby granting Socrates legitimacy as a citizen; it has given him an education, and, of his own accord, he has chosen to remain a citizen of Athens. Socrates does not die because he discounts the group, or its laws; he dies because that is the course determined for him by the law. The law and the group have precedence over the whims of an individual, no matter how well-intended.

My "interpretation" of Socrates is rarely encountered, but then who but Westerners are allowed to give interpretations of the Greek works? The Western "hero" tends to be the defiant individual — someone who stands up to and against the group or even the law. We find here a curious situation where both "evil" heroes as well as the "good" exist in the Western context: Jesus Christ and Billy the Kid. Jesus stands against his own people, the Jews, as well as the intruders, the Romans. Billy the Kid, even in Western psychological studies, is a psychopath. Both figures are kept alive through myth and legend in the West. The hero, as well as the anti- hero, appear to those from a different society to bear equal weight in the West.

In a group that defines the individual as a social being, ostracism, exclusion from the group, is a dreaded and extreme form of punishment. In a group that defines the individual as autonomous, ostracism might be a tragedy but never the ultimate punishment. The ostracized is, after all, left with his life. Ostracism, however, in the West, could be as severe as in other societies, if the individual was ousted from all of the Western societies. Socrates sees this clearly when he understands that being ousted from Athens would bring him no honor in other cities/states: one who was deemed threatening to the social order in one city would be so in another as well. He chooses to die for Athens.

Indigenous Americans, just as did the Greeks, found their codes of conduct on the premise that humans are naturally social beings. Humans exist in the state of the "We." Indigenous peoples exist, however, within a colonial structure that adheres, not only to a different definition of what it is to be human, but to the very different social and moral codes that are based on that different definition. From an Indigenous perspective, Westerners are also a conglomeration of the We. The West simply seeks to deny this fact about human existence. Hence the difficulty encountered in the West in explaining or outlining social behavior.

Professional ethicists cannot agree on what constitutes a "right" action because they cannot agree on a foundation from which to derive their pronouncements. Religion is certainly not the answer. Religion, in actuality, has nothing to do with ethics. The religious relationship is between an individual and his god. If the individual commits "good" acts, they are incidental to that relationship. He acts "good" according to his god's standards in order to gain a reward from his god. If his god wishes him to "love his neighbor" he will do so but only until his god commands him to "slay every man, woman, and child." In a supposedly secular society there is no measure of one's actions against the wishes of a god but there still remains the focus on the individual as the source of moral or legal behavior. The West prefers, overall, to believe that all human acts are a *choice*.

The ramifications of those choices, however, are tied to a set of rewards and punishments. Virtue as a reward in itself is not sufficient in the West as it was for the Greeks. Aristotle's *Ethics* are a prescription for the *internalization* of law or of proper social behavior. He offers no rewards and punishments for following or breaking the law. The West, on the other hand, both secular and Christian, bases its moral and legal foundations on the *externalization* of law or social behavior.

The law that is external is an artificial constraint placed on someone's behavior and enforced through the threat of punishment. An internal law is one that has been so assimilated into the individual's character that he is "a law unto himself." An example of internal and externalized laws can be drawn from one's actions at a traffic light. If one approaches a traffic light that requires one to stop one's vehicle at, say, 4 a.m., and one stops even if there is no one around, then one can see an internal law in action. The internal law says: "It is proper, rational, and good that individuals driving cars stop at traffic lights that so signal." Not to do so would probably not bring about immediate retribution from an external source if no one is about. However, the result of breaking one's own internalized law is guilt and shame. The external law, on the other hand, can be broken without any mental anguish: "It is stupid," could be the reaction of someone who adheres only to external laws, "to stop at a traffic light when there is no one about. What difference does it make?" Or, "Who cares?"

Aristotle's *Ethics* offers a recipe for the development of the internal law. He would have us develop this sense through the process of *habituation*. If, for instance, one wants to become an honest person, we become so through practicing honesty. Eventually one need no longer *practice* honesty; one has become *habitually* honest. Honesty becomes part of our character. In the beginning it is presumed that one had a role model for honesty or at least been taught the social definition of honesty.

Ultimately, the foundation for fostering the *internalization* of rules for "proper" social behavior is the assumption that (1) humans are social beings by nature, and (2) humans want to remain in the social group. Internalization of rules is a means of teaching social behavior used by those who subscribe to the sense of the human being as a We. Those who define the individual as an I, separate and apart from the group of which he is a member, use another form of maintaining social harmony: the threat of punishment brought about through the inability, or choice, not to follow the rules. This latter method of bringing about social harmony is also based on two essential assumptions: (1) that the individual is not "naturally" a social being, and (2) that a social identity, as well as social behavior, is artificially imposed upon the individual by others, that is, that such an identity or behavior is "unnatural."

The Native American, like the Greeks, relies on the internalization of rules for proper conduct; but unlike the Greeks, the Native American adds to the We definition of human beings the idea of *equality*. Many outside commentators on Native American lifeways have commented on this notion of equality — that it extends to children; that it promotes an emphasis on consensual decision-making; that it extends even to an individual's actions toward the planet and its many life-forms.

Aside from a recognition of the We-factor in a Native American society, and the accompanying foundational beliefs of humans as wanting to remain as a part of the human society to which they belong, there is one more factor that accounts for the ethical system which the Native American once had as the dominant source of his actions (and in many cases still practices). He recognizes that he is a part of the Earth. He acknowledges that he is a part of a natural process that has led to his existence as well as to the existence of all other things, "animate" and "inanimate." (The terms are not relevant within a Native American context; all that

exists is seen as participating in a life process.) The Native American recognizes his dependence on the Earth and the Universe. He recognizes no hierarchy of "higher" and "lower" or "simple" and "complex," and certainly not of "primitive" and "modern." Instead of hierarchies he sees *differences* which exist among equal "beings" (mountains, as well as water and air and plants and animals would be included here). The equality is based on the notion, often unstated, that everything that is, is of one process. The Native American, in other words, has a more inclusive sense of the We than others who share the sense of humans as *social* beings.

The combination of defining the human as a social being and denying any hierarchical systems, and a recognition of humans as a part of a greater whole, leads to a complete ethical system. This "complete" system includes not only one's behavior toward other individuals and to the society as a whole but toward the planet which has produced one and upon which one is dependent. For those who would raise objections to the validity or the durability of such an ethical system, it must be pointed out that Native American societies existed for tens of thousands of years and have not perished. Despite territorial wars and skirmishes between adjoining groups, when the European arrived on the American continents there was a vast diversity of peoples and languages. Had the Native Americans been as reckless as they are depicted there would have been less diversity. Even among those groups found to be existing in some form of hierarchical system (slave and free, which seemed to be practiced among the Aztecs and the Incas) there were highly ritualized rules for undertaking conquest and conduct in war. The Aztecs went so far as to set the boundaries for gains and losses by each side before going to war. Slavery in such societies was very different from that practiced by Europeans; under the Aztec rules of conduct in war, he who was free today could be a slave tomorrow, and vice versa. The rules of behavior also prescribed a method of dealing with the stranger: no early European colonizer could have survived without the hospitality and lessons in agronomy provided by the Indigenous peoples.

Just what, then, is this ethical system?

Each new human being born into a group represents an unknown factor to that group. The newborn does not come fully equipped to deal with his membership in the group; he must be taught what it is to be a *human* being in a very specific group. "He has never been here before," I have often heard in explanation of why the newborn must be taught. The newborn is at first merely *humanoid* — the group will give him an identity according to their definition of what it is to be human. The primary lesson that is taught is that the individual's actions have consequences for himself, for others, for the world. The newcomer's *humanness* is measured according to how he comes to recognize that his actions have consequences for others, for the world. Usually an infant was accorded "human" status through a naming ceremony around the ages of 8 or 9. (Many anthropologists "explain," mistakenly, the naming ceremonies as a result of a low survival rate; that is, the infant was not given a "real" name until he appeared to have survived infancy.) It was at or around this age when it became obvious to the group that the infant had come to recognize his place as a member of the group. (A naming ceremony without some knowledge of the child's character would be somewhat premature given that names usually depicted character.)

The lessons included an enhanced perception of the needs and emotions of others as well as a keen perception of where the child was in the world (a sense of place). In a society of equals a proper perception of others is necessary. The term *autonomy* takes on a whole different meaning in this environment. In a society of equals no one can order another about. No one can be totally dependent upon another, as that would create an artificial hierarchy (the dependent and the independent) with all of its accompanying ramifications such as authoritarianism and lack of individual initiative. The autonomous person, in this environment, is one who is aware of the needs of others as well as being aware of what the individual can do for the good of the group. "Autonomy," in this case, would be defined as self-initiative combined with a high degree of self-sufficiency. For example, a

simple but unstated rule of behavior is that I cannot ask another to do for me what I can do for myself. Another is that if I am not perceptive enough to discern the needs of another and that other is required to ask something of me, then I have somehow diminished the other's worth. If I tell another what to do or ask the other for something then I have diminished us both.

In a cross-cultural context this training leads to some misconceptions: a native student who is failing a class never asks the white teacher for help because it is obvious to the student that both he and the teacher know that he is failing but the teacher has failed to offer assistance. The teacher, in the student's view, may be seeking to punish the student's failure by forcing him to ask for help. Having to ask for help, on the other hand, diminishes a sense of self-sufficiency on the part of the student; it also puts into question the student's "place" in the group. "She knew I couldn't understand it and she ignored me!" The fact that the teacher is not a product of the same ethical and cultural system as the student does not occur to the student.

A heightened perception of the other as well as an awareness of the consequences of one's own actions is enhanced by offering the child choices. He can choose to bring his mother, who is busy gardening, a glass of water. His father may ask, "Shall we take her a glass of water?" The child must make a choice; he is aware of having made the choice; and he will be aware of the consequences of that choice for his mother and perhaps even his father. His parents (or aunts, uncles, cousins, grandparents) may point out possible consequences of particular actions. An example from my own childhood shows this "pointing out" accompanied by "choice":

When I was a child my sister and I slept in a large old-fashioned bed with a high brass headboard. When my parents left the house we often used the bed as a trampoline (accompanied by my brother with whose welfare my sister and I had been entrusted). One day my father came home unexpectedly and stood in the doorway to watch our antics as gymnasts. During the first lull in our jumping he proceeded to come into the room to show us how the bed was constructed. He showed us sharp metal angles, narrow ledges which held up the metal springs underneath the mattress, and the seemingly small joints that held the bed together. He then proceeded to tell us about the consequences of falling on the floor as the bed collapsed. After pointing out all of the bed's features, he remade the bed and left the room. We three sat on the edge of the mattress thinking about what we'd been taught. My sister and I gave a few sitting jounces to the mattress. My brother took a practice jump. Wordlessly, we decided that we could find another form of entertainment.

My father forced a choice on us. If we continued to jump on the bed and it broke, it could not be replaced. If we fell we might suffer injury. There would be no sympathy accompanying that injury because it would have been "self-inflicted." I would be ashamed in the face of my father because "I knew better." I would, if I were injured in the face of all that information, be the only one responsible for my own condition. Choices and consequences.

By the time my own children reached their early teens I saw that they had absorbed a lesson that I had unconsciously taught them: that they are responsible for their choice of action. Once one of my sons tossed a basketball into a garage window when he was in the process of putting his things away so that we could go out for pizza. He proceeded to get a broom and began to sweep up the broken glass. "Just leave it," one of the younger children said to him. My son's reaction was to say that we were to go on without him. "My share of the pizza will pay for the glass pane," he said. Now his honor was at stake; no one dismissed his comment. I heard, instead, quiet murmurs from the other children. As recognition of my son's honorable action we saved him a piece of pizza and offered to help him replace the glass. "I will earn the money," he said. The situation ended there and he did fix the window.

My son's action was an illustration of what is meant when a Native American uses the term "autonomous." It is also what is meant when we apply the term "responsible." Or, when we are taught to be aware of the consequences of our actions on others. Going out for pizza was an expensive venture in my household at the time. The price of a broken windowpane was another expensive venture. My son's action — a careless toss of a basketball — had consequences that affected his family. No one would have thought of inflicting punishment on him; there was no need to. He was a human being; he knew what he had done, the consequences of what he had done, and he knew what had to be done to negate those consequences. There was no need for recrimination from any other quarter.

One often encounters a description of Native American cultures as being based on "shame" rather than "guilt." Actually both shame and guilt are a part of the internalization of rules of conduct. One experiences shame in the face of those who knew that the course of action would bring about specific consequences. One experiences guilt when one confronts oneself. Shame and guilt, in a Western system of conduct, are emotions that are to be overcome. In a Native American society they are what call us to action.

Another description of the Native American is that "he has no conscience" (usually the judgment of Christian missionaries). The Western notion of conscience appears to be a lingering sense of guilt or shame. If that is the case then there is no conscience: unintended or unforeseen consequences as well as those seen and pursued demand reparation in a Native American ethical system. Once reparation has been made and acknowledged there is no need for lingering shame or guilt. If conscience, however, means something that calls us to action then it is wrong that Native Americans do not have a conscience. I know few Native Americans that would pursue a "successful American lifestyle" without the accompanying guilt that results because they have more than others. Western conscience appears to have more to do with personal matters than with concern over the consequences of their actions for others. A good example of this is the current concern over "environmental ethics."

Americans agonize over the continued destruction of clean air and clean water, over the diminishing forests, over rising suburbanization. They do not agonize over the fact that their own "superior" technology and their own "needs" have created that condition. The rising misery of people in the so-called Third World is largely the result of people displaced from a once self- sufficient lifestyle. They are displaced because their own government has chosen to appropriate the land so that goods might be produced for the "developed" world's needs. The Brazilians do not cut down the rain forest for their own needs; they cut it down for the needs of "modern" societies. One official from a developing country explained to me that if they did not cut down their own trees (or mine their own ores, or create modern enclaves) the developed nation would take over the country and do these things themselves with perhaps greater misery imposed on his country's people.

"Environmental" ethics, in the West, is about "respecting" the rights of trees, and lions, and future generations. It is not ever about a concern that the cheap cup of coffee is purchased with the misery of a coffee plantation worker. Or that the displacement of peoples from rural ("undeveloped") areas into overcrowded urban areas is not "progress" except for a very few. The peoples of the developed nations are quick to see the profit in a global economy but discount the possible dire consequences to the laborers in the plantations and *maquiladoras* that are drawn off their land to produce for the wealthy. They can discount these consequences because they are convinced that it is better for Natives or peasants to have "jobs" than for them to persist in lifestyles that have allowed them to survive for thousands of years without destruction of their lands, water, or air.

In a Native American ethical system, the actions of an individual are like the pebble dropped into a pond. The pebble creates far-reaching ripples throughout the entire pond. The American prefers the analogy of human beings as people aboard a ship in a vast sea. The ship is held together, we can assume, by a single authority — the captain. The "ripples" of the ship proceed, in this analogy, into infinity. There are no consequences, if only people would just take orders. The greatest accomplishment that has resulted from the entire ecological

movement is the development of what is called the "environmental impact statement." The impact statement is an attempt to understand that there are far-reaching consequences to one's actions. Unfortunately, what the impact statement forbids in one place is usually wreaked upon another. But it is a start.

The greatest advance that could be made in ethical systems in the West would be a recognition of the We-factor. If one imagines the We in a circle of its own unity surrounded by circles maintaining their own unity, perhaps the concept of human action as a pebble dropped into a pond would have more meaning. No pebble can be dropped into a pond without its ripples encountering other ripples and those ripples having other consequences through their encounters. Instead, the I-society prefers to picture itself as the captain in the single ship superior to and disconnected from all other things.

The idea that the planet requires a certain degree of "biodiversity" for its well-being has captured the imaginations of scientists and laymen. The fact that the diversity of human lifestyles might also contribute to that necessary biodiversity has not sunk in yet. The planet can afford to have one group maintain a self-absorbed society (the I-society) but only if others are allowed to survive that follow other lifestyles. The I, in other words, can survive and persist only if there is a recognition that it is not isolated from the others.

The I-society imagines the construction of a massive singular, "monocultural," society made up of only Is each pursuing their own individual interests in "healthy" competition with all of the other Is. Carved, as if in stone, on the inside of the foreheads of Western peoples, I imagine the words, "Each man acts so as to enhance his own self-interest." Carved inside my own forehead are two simple letters, W and E. And that WE can be either exclusive (Apache; Native American) or all-inclusive to encompass the many and diverse peoples and their particular homelands. The I-society has no homeland. It sees itself as owner of a lifeless planet, without boundaries, without limitations.

The definitions which humans assign to

unknown processes are not meaningless intellectual acts. The definitions seem to predicate or dictate certain and unavoidable behaviors. If I believe in, for example, and act on, the definition of a human being as "that which acts only in its own self-interest," I will proceed to act on and treat others based on that slogan. Definitions tend to be self-fulfilling. They are so because they serve as the foundational justifications for all subsequent actions. The We and the I produce different lifestyles, different ethical systems, different worlds.

WHAT DOES THE DIFFERENT VOICE SAY?
GILLIGAN'S WOMEN AND MORAL PHILOSOPHY

Margaret Urban Walker

Margaret Urban Walker is Lincoln Professor of Ethics, Justice, and the Public Sphere in the School of Justice and Social Inquiry at Arizona State University. She is the author of Moral Contexts *(2003);* Moral Understandings: A Feminist Study in Ethics *(1998); editor of* Mother Time: Women, Aging, and Ethics *(1999); and co-editor of* Moral Psychology: Feminist Ethics and Social Theory *(2004, with Peggy DesAutels).*

Walker examines Gilligan's account of an ethic of care in order to explore answers to questions about whether the ethic of care presents a unified perspective on morality and, if so, whether it represents an important addition or corrective to prevailing philosophical views on morality. She argues that there are two distinct and mutually independent themes in the care perspective: a substantive one that is a "care and response orientation" and a methodological one that is a "contextual-deliberative picture" of moral thinking. Together these themes make it possible to think of the care perspective as a unified approach distinct from and even challenging traditional accounts of morality evident in a justice approach.

Many want to see psychologist Carol Gilligan as advancing the view that there are "male" and "female" moral voices, a view which she disclaims early on in *In A Different Voice*[1] and in later writings.[2] Gilligan does advance the hypothesis that the different voice — or "care perspective" — is "characteristically a female phenomenon in the advanced populations that have been studied" and holds that this hypothesis receives support from studies other than her own (R, p. 330). But she continues to maintain that what makes this voice different is that it offers "a moral perspective different from that currently embedded in psychological theories and measures" (R, p. 327), one which embodies distinctive conceptions of self, relationship, and responsibility (R, p. 326).

Much discussion of Gilligan's work has centered on whether she has adequate evidence for the claim of significant gender-related differences in moral thinking. I pursue another set of questions here, because the interest of the different voice for moral philosophy lies primarily in *what* it expresses, perhaps some significant part of moral truth.[3] My questions are: whether the differences in moral thinking she outlines amount to a unified perspective on morality; what that perspective is; and whether this (*possibly* more characteristically "feminine") viewpoint represents an important or interesting addition or correction to prevailing philosophical views.[4]

In section I, I distinguish two themes apparently characteristic of the different voice, and in Section II show how plausible versions of each may appear separately in already well-known types of moral views. In Section III I consider two ways in which versions of the themes might be internally related to produce a view which is both unified and distinctive. One of these interpretations is found superior as a rendering of Gilligan's subjects' views; it is also a plausible moral outlook which significantly challenges standard philosophical conceptions about morality. In conclusion (IV) I remark that while the existence and significance of a different moral voice remains in question, women's voices surely matter for moral philosophy in any case.

I

Gilligan holds that the different voice is "characterized not by gender but theme" (p.2). The characterizing theme is referred to by her variously as "care," "responsibility," or "response" (in contrast to the alternative theme of "justice" or "fairness" or "reciprocity"). But in reviewing her presentation of and commentary on those particular quoted voices which are held to exemplify the care perspective, one hears not one theme but two, and these two themes appear not only distinct, but mutually independent.

One focal description of the care and justice perspectives which comes early on in *In A Different Voice* makes the two themes readily apparent:

In this [care] conception, the moral problem arises from conflicting responsibilities rather than from competing rights and requires for its resolution a mode of thinking that is contextual and narrative rather than formal and abstract. This conception of morality as concerned with the activity of care centers moral development around the understanding of responsibility and relationships, just as the conception of morality as fairness ties moral development to the understanding of rights and rules (p.19).

This passage touches on both the *substance* of moral concern in the alternative visions, and on the *method* of definition and construction appropriate to the solutions of moral problems. Both strains recur throughout the book's discussion, sometimes intertwined, sometimes discretely. I will call the substantive one a *care and response orientation*, the methodological one a *contextual-deliberative picture* of moral thinking.[5]

Often Gilligan seems to identify the different voice in terms of a kind of *value* orientation, i.e., what it sees as calling for moral concern. For example:

The moral imperative that emerges repeatedly in interviews with women is an injunction to care, a responsibility to discern and alleviate the "real and recognizable trouble" of this world. For men, the moral imperative appears rather as an injunction to respect the rights of others and thus to protect from interference the rights to life and self-fulfillment (p.100).

The care orientation resides in "sensitivity to the needs of others and the assumption of responsibility for taking care," (p. 16); it is concerned with "equity" in light of persons' very different needs (p. 164). An "overriding concern with relationships and responsibilities" (pp.16-17) makes connection and attachment (pp. 19, 45, 48), compassion (p. 71) and intimacy (p. 17) central moral concerns. As little girls are reported to terminate their games rather than threaten the continuance of their relationships (p.10), so adult women recognize "the continuing importance of attachment in the human life cycle" (p. 23); it "creates and sustains the human community" (p. 156).

Sometimes Gilligan's characterizations are ambiguous between caring as instrumental to the goods of need-fulfillment or non-violence, and caring as itself the object or attainment of moral endeavor. But these are not exclusive alternatives, and often enough Gilligan seems to be saying, and is heard by others as saying, that women care specially *for* relationships or attachments as themselves fundamental goods of our lives. Jean Grimshaw, for example, in a searching consideration of the idea of a "female ethic" concedes: "There is evidence, both from common experience and from the work of Carol Gilligan and others, that women often perceive the maintenance of relationships as very important in their lives, and see it as a moral priority."[6] In a care and response orientation, then, caring relationships and the responsive attitude which sustains them are particularly morally valued, whether as means, ends, or both.

Gilligan, however, understands these women to be describing and exemplifying a different structure of moral understanding as well as a certain set of concerns. Here the difference between care and justice is marked by method, approach, and the standards for defining and solving moral problems. Here thinking that is "contextual and narrative" contrasts with thinking that "abstracts the moral problem from the interpersonal situation" (p. 32) so that a "formal logic" of fairness can take hold (p. 73). The justice perspective drives toward classification of cases at a high level of generality so that antecedently ordered rules and formulas can do their work in deciding the particular case. The different voice, however, strains against schematically depicted situations toward further concrete information about the particular case (pp. 100-101). It is mistrustful about the relevance of prior, abstract moral orderings (p. 101). And it does not necessarily expect moral dilemmas to yield to resolution without remainder on which "all rational men can agree"[7] and no conflicting claims retain authority. This contextual deliberative view rejects a top-down, nomological picture of moral decision as a deductive operation, it views typifications of actions and situations as only, at best, heuristic, and it leaves room for moral remainders. For it a moral problem is not "a math problem with humans." (p. 28) and there is no moral decision procedure, no guarantee of neat closure. Instead, a "narrative of relationships that extends over time" (p. 28) may supply materials for a context-sensitive adjudication of claims.

Here are the two themes, consonant but seemingly addressed to different questions: one to *what* we must think about morally, one to *how* we must do so. This seems not simply an ethic of care nor simply a context-sensitive, particularistic ethic, but instead a *contextualist ethic of care*. Is this *one* thing, or *two* things contingently juxtaposed?

II

It is not difficult to see how a care and response orientation and a contextual deliberative view might be separate commitments. A contextualist, after all, could have many other value orientations than the care and response one. She might believe that what matters morally is self-realization, or eudaimonia, or something else. She might think many things matter — courage, wisdom, integrity, dignity, gratitude — and each in several ways. She might think care matters too, but not see it as a specially dominant or highest-ranked value. But her way of structuring moral deliberation and achiev-

ing resolution will not be a logical deduction or computation defined in advance by a strict formal program, but a minute and concrete exploration of the particulars. She might like "Sharon" in Gilligan's book "try to be as awake as possible, to try to know the range of what you feel, to try to consider all that's involved" (p. 99) and then, to borrow a phrase, let the decision rest with perception.[8] But her perception might be informed by more than considerations of care and response, and perhaps by other kinds of considerations entirely. Aristotelians, ethical individualists, Bradleyan self-realizationists, and Christian agapeists can be (although may not be in every version) contextualists in the relevant sense.

In turning to the reverse case, of an ethic of care that is not particularistic, but is principled and rigorously logical in carrying theory into practice, consider classical utilitarianism (and many contemporary variants) which could lay claim to being the ultimate in care perspectives.[9] The utilitarian sees the world in terms of a single value, happiness, where that is specified in terms of fulfillment, contentment, satisfaction, pleasure, or preference, i.e., the well-being of others in their own terms.[10] But utilitarians are not content to let the concern for well-being play itself out in the commonplace and parochial ways, and so insist on unqualified and impartial commitment to caring — caring for all, counting each for one and no more. When joined to the positive injunction to produce the greatest aggregate amounts of well-being possible, the strenuousness of this caring seems hard to outdo. Further, full-blooded act utilitarians are known for their mitigated commitment to justice: in the face-off between care and justice that is one recurring motif of Western ethical thought,[11] utilitarians know what side they are on.[12]

Utilitarianism thus can see itself as raising on the ground of human interdependence and fellow-feeling a system for responding to human want without compromise and for extending the care of each over the whole human community, and perhaps over the wider community of all feeling, needing beings.[13] Utilitarians also sometimes claim for their view the virtue of sensitivity to context, inasmuch as rights and wrongs are reckoned afresh case by case. But they are reckoned rigorously, by a procedure laid out in advance, one which allows no competitors and which promises decisive resolution where applicable at all. The narrative of relationships could only matter in providing data for prediction of outcomes and payoffs. Utilitarian moral decision making *is* a math problem with humans.

Is the different voice then whole in some way other than being the sum of these two separable parts? Does it matter? Before proceeding to the first question, I touch here briefly on the second.

I think the unity of the different voice does matter. For Gilligan, it must have mattered originally in a special way in her critique of Kohlbergian developmental theory. In laying down the gauntlet on page one of her book, Gilligan claimed that the two ways of speaking about morality, self, and other which she discerned were an ongoing contrapuntal structure of moral life rather than "steps in a developmental progression," i.e., that the ordering of these ways as higher or lower stages *à la* Kohlberg was a mistake. But his challenge itself takes the view that these perspectives on morality are equally *like* Kohlbergian stages — internally differentiated but "logically unified, functionally *holistic* structures"[14] of moral thought — at the *same* level. For the different voice to have been a fragment of a view or worse an unordered set of moral *apercus* would have made a lame case, in Kohlbergian terms.

The interests of moral philosophy are not those of Kohlbergian theory, and moral philosophy is properly eager for any pieces of moral insight with claim to intuitive entrenchment. Still, what seems *exciting* about the different voice for moral philosophy is that it might reveal or suggest a unified and comprehensive view of moral life — one might say a "moral vision" — which is genuinely alternative in important ways to those which are prevalent philosophically. It would not be negligible, although it would not be so exciting, I think, if the news were that women tended to align, say, with Mill on value but with Aristotle on method.

III

The consideration of utilitarianism as a care-ethic provides a useful comparison case in seeking a picture of the different voice whole. Utilitarians are fully committed to caring about welfare, about the "well-being of others in their own terms," about assessing the particular, present situation, and do not traffic in advance ordering of different values (for there is only one) but in reckoning actual consequences. These are all marks of the care perspective Gilligan describes (e.g., pp. 78, 101). But clearly, Gilligan has not meant that women have a bent for utilitarian thinking. This would leave out the emphasis of the different voice on care focused in terms of relationship, intimacy, attachment, and "natural bonds" (pp. 17, 19, 32, 48, 132). Magnification of the "impartial viewpoint" has put both utilitarianism and Kantian ethical views under suspicion of unwisely demoting or neglecting just the special caring bonds on which the different voice dwells.[15] Seeing care in terms of relationship is a clue to understanding how care and contextualism may be more than accidentally conjoined.

I see two different ways of bringing the care-orientation and the contextual-deliberative view into more intimate union. Both turn on an identification of care primarily with the loving attention characteristic of specific personal bonds. This identification joins them in common cause against the utilitarian ideal of uniform generalized benevolence — "administrative care" one might call it, as it undertakes the task of reckoning in common terms the satisfactions of persons close by and familiar alongside those who may be any, distant, and unknown. The emphasis on personal bonds also provides each of these ways with a clear basis for finding universalism and legalism either inappropriate or derivative as views about the structure of moral reasoning and resolution. But these two ways part company decisively over a fundamental issue. On one, the creation and maintenance of caring relations is *itself* the human good; on the other, caring relations are a necessary condition for the practice within which varied human goods might emerge and flourish. The first way is neater, but it is also more reductive about the direction and point of moral life than is the second way. The divergence corresponds to the ambiguity noted earlier in Gilligan's own descriptions of women's valuation of caring.

The first way is represented lucidly and without compromise by Nel Noddings. In *Caring: a Feminine Approach to Ethics and Moral Education*[16] Noddings anchors morality in the human affective response of natural sympathy and its characteristic issue of natural caring, transformed reflectively into a moral ideal of oneself as once-caring. The caring this ideal demands consists in direct relations in which loving attention and minute recognition flow toward the one cared for, who completes the caring by responding in ways which show its nurturant and supportive power (C, pp. 79-84). Such relations can arise only in actual encounters. Since this is so and since the acts constituting care are determined by close perceptions of individuals, the only appropriate methods of moral thought and resolution are those which embody as much concrete detail as possible and which represent as specific a response as can be mustered. Subsuming people's "cases" under generalization and treating them by rule would be not simply inadequate, but a denial of the very nature of the moral demand and a foreclosure of the achievement of the only moral value. Noddings makes this clear. "Rule-bound responses in the name of caring lead us to suspect that the claimant wants most to be credited with caring" (C, p.24). A care-ethic of this kind is necessarily contextualist because of the value it demands be realized morally (a completed instance of a specific caring relation) and the nature of human beings who participate in its realization (psychologically non-interchangeable individuals whose ways of wanting, needing, perceiving, and receiving may be very different). Legalistic reasoning and impartial computations are wholly inapplicable on this view, and the respect or generalized benevolence which are their attitudinal correlates — their "carings" — are found counterfeit, period. On Noddings's view caring is just one thing, and it is, morally speaking, the *only* thing. The presence, ordering, and extent of moral obligation for her

varies with encounters and the possibility of completion, but the object of obligations is invariable; care is both ground and object of the demands morality places upon us.

Noddings's view is one candidate for a consistent systematization of what the different voice is saying. It suggests that women, including Gilligan's subjects, tend to care, ultimately, *about* caring; that is what they seek to initiate or complete in their lives, or at least what they feel (in Noddings's view correctly) obligated to realize. It also suggests that if care as a specific relation is itself what is valued, then caring will be kept close to home, since direct encounters, and primarily those embedded in a prior history of relationship, are the only obligating occasions. Generalized concern — whether benevolence or that yet more astringent attitude, respect — and its concomitant sense of obligation are on this view illusory (C, pp. 18, 29, 90). It is in just these respects that I find Noddings's view less than satisfactory either as rendering of what resides in Gilligan's subjects' voices, or as a moral vision on its own feet.[17]

Are Gilligan's women properly described as caring about care itself? It seems not; different of the different voices invoke, as decisive or central grounds for moral choice, such values as equality (p. 64), honesty (p. 65), authenticity (p. 52), growth (p. 159), safety from danger and hurt (p. 129), self-preservation (p. 111). Further, a striking feature of a number of cited responses is a tendency to extend the scope of concern very widely indeed. One woman feels strongly "responsible to the world" and obligated to better it if only on a small scale (p. 21). Another finds mundane practical decisions open onto agonizing vistas of others' poverty, unknown children in need, and a world full of trouble and headed for "doom"; and it is clear that she does not dismiss the claim this seems to make on her (p. 99). "Claire" articulates the sweeping view positively: other people are "*part of you*" so that link by link is formed a "giant collection of people that you are connected to" (p. 160). A number of Gilligan's women seem *not* at all hesitant to generalize concern and to ponder, troubled, the overwhelming implications. What they seem not to do is to generalize the *other persons*, to view them abstractly as generalizable kinds of cases (p. 11). The distinction is important and is needed to make sense of a certain kind of strain in these voices. A different way of modeling the moral sensibility at work here captures this.[18]

On this second way, an ethic of care might be seen as affirming the *generative* role of caring relations in morality. Caring relations initiate new human beings into the kind of interpersonal acknowledgment that full moral concern requires: of the separate reality of other persons, of the complex and precarious process of communicating and understanding. Ongoing opportunities to care and be cared for continue the education of those dispositions and capacities which allow us to know how it is with another and to make ourselves known as well. Caring relationship provides a *paradigm* of the understanding that determines full and appropriate response to persons: it must be direct, persona, and specific; it requires minute attention, identification in thought and feeling, precise communication. It will be, among other things, "contextual and narrative," that is, defined by reference to rich circumstantial detail, to the history of the episode, and ideally to the history of the person. This understanding carried through to appropriate action, on this view, *is* caring. But to carry through to *appropriate* action requires more. It requires a *conception of human good*, a picture of what's worth aiming at; there is no reason to think that this cannot be a rich and varied conception in which many important goods (intrinsic, internal, contributory) are complexly related. Care itself, this attentive relation of acknowledgment and understanding, will no doubt reappear *within* this conception of value. It is one of those things worth spending the hard-won understanding of care on reproducing. Care plays a very special role in moral life, on this view, but not that of sole or even dominant end. Care appears instead as a condition for the fullest and most direct pursuit of such goods as there may be.[19]

Full, minute, and sensitive attention is a paradigm of how the materials for the exercise of moral concern are had. It is a *paradigm* because it represents the *best* case: it is in this way I know

"fully and directly" to what and to whom I am responding. Yet many cases are not, cannot be, of the best type. Connection may be attenuated, access blocked. If I am not in a position to care in the paradigmatic way I may be reduced to applying incomplete versions of care, or even resorting to surrogates: general benevolence, respect, fair consideration may be the best I can do. It is, I think, important to let this way remain open. The different voice need not be seen as denying any role to generalized concern, but as marking its incompleteness. This truly rotates the usual order of philosophical precedence 180°, saying that the particular is always first, and the application of rules or generalized standards to someone as a kind of "case" is not just a derivative, but in fact a degenerate instance. The conviction that *moral adequacy falls off in the direction of generality* seems to be one of the plaintive notes in this style of moral discourse. The note struck is plaintive because it is understood that this kind of inadequacy is recurrent and inevitable. What is condemnable from this perspective, then, is *not* doing one's inadequate best where that is all one can do, but denying or ignoring how far the principled, universalistic view may be from adequate moral response in many situations, and how much responsibility one has evaded in adopting it. This is our situation when truly personal understanding eludes us. Gilligan's recent work, interestingly, is more concerned with different understandings of the nature of persons, and with questions of adequate knowledge and disclosure than with particular structures of moral judgment.[20]

The combination of indefinite openness to responsibility and of the particularistic paradigm of understanding persons accounts for a certain kind of strain I discern in these voices. The fact of human connectedness that makes for endless vistas of responsibility (both with respect to *any* person and with respect to *all*) runs up against the inescapable arbitrariness and *ad hoc* limitations of actual connections and the moral possibilities they underwrite and exclude. The moral situation appears to these moral agents entangling, compromising, and permanently unwieldy.[21]

IV

These two versions of the different voice rendered unified are, of course, energetic reconstructions and idealizations. One would not expect a view "systematic" in the philosopher's sense to spring full-blown from any survey of opinion. It must be admitted, finally, that perhaps these reconstructions are too energetic. It may be that similar things many women have to say about morality and responsibility are only contingently related by the fact of women's common situation and social training, and not by some deep conceptual structure a moral philosopher might strive (or contrive) to find. It might be that women's preoccupation with care and relationship and their propensity for concrete over abstract are, if a fact, simply each orientations of thought and feeling which serve their traditional social roles of nurturers, helpers, and keepers of the homely but indispensable material conditions of life. It is this possibility that accounts for much of the ambivalent or hostile reaction to Gilligan's work.[22] It can appear as further depressing adumbration of the apparatus which keeps women in their subservient and private places.[23]

Even if the concerns of the different voices are artifacts of an objectionably limiting social assignment, this does not discredit the view (or views) from that particular set of windows on moral reality. This is not only because any human experience yields matter for moral reflection, nor only because the task of enabling the continuance of human life, to which women's traditional roles and the values these embody are so deeply bound, has now on a global scale become precarious and urgent in ways it has not been for human beings before. It is also because women's social assignments, whatever the local variations, involve the majority of them intimately in quite a special endeavor from the viewpoint of morality: initiation of new members into the moral community. A position of social disadvantage may, on the topic of moral education and moral competence, be one of some epistemic privilege.[24] These voices should be heard, whether they have some large thing to say or many smaller ones.

Author's Note

I am grateful for the opportunity to present a shorter version of this paper at the American Philosophical Association Central Division Meeting in April, 1987, in sessions on Carol Gilligan's work sponsored by the American Society for Value Inquiry, organized by Nancy Tuana. In addition to a number of members of that audience, I thank Carol Gilligan, Celeste Schenck, and Arthur Walker for critical comments and encouragement both. I am grateful to Fordham University for a Faculty Fellowship in 1986-87 which provided the time and support that enabled me to write this paper. This author has previously published under the name Margaret Urban Coyne.

NOTES

1. (Cambridge: Harvard University Press, 1982), p. 2. All page references in the text are to this work unless otherwise marked.

2. "Reply," (p. 324) in L. Kerber, C. Greeno and E. Maccoby, Z. Luria, C. Stack and C. Gilligan, "On *In a Different Voice*: An Interdisciplinary Forum," *Signs* 11 (1986):304-333, hereafter cited in the text as R. See also Carol Gilligan and Grant Wiggins, "The Origins of Morality in Early Childhood Relationships," in *The Emergence of Morality in Early Childhood,* ed. Jerome Kagan and Sharon Lamb (Chicago: University of Chicago Press, 1987) for closer discussion of both findings on distribution of moral orientations and their significance.

3. I don't claim that questions about whether certain moral views are significantly gender-related are of no consequence to moral philosophy. They may well be theoretically, methodologically, and sociologically consequential. But one does need to know what those views are before these sorts of consequence may be seriously explored.

4. Since this paper was written a valuable set of papers in response to or occasioned by Gilligan's work has appeared which includes a number of discussions whose aim, like mine, is conceptual exploration of what this work suggests for moral theory. See Eva Feder Kittay and Diana T. Meyers

(eds.), *Women and Moral Theory* (Totowa, NJ: Rowman and Littlefield, 1987).

5. Marilyn Friedman, "Abraham, Socrates, and Heinz: Where Are the Women? (Care and context in Moral Reasoning)," also distinguishes two themes in the different voice. Friedman sees "contextual relativism" as a concern with concrete detail detachable from a relationship orientation, and interprets relationship orientation as special concern with and for relationship as a value or source of norms. For her these features are separable as well as distinct. I find both of these elements more complex and the matter of their connection more puzzling than she does. Neither of the two interpretations I entertain below is identical with her understanding, which she uses to develop a strong criticism of Kohlbergian assumptions and results. In *Moral Dilemmas*, ed. Carol Gibb Harding (Chicago: Precedent Publishing, Inc. 1985), pp. 25-41.

6. *Philosophy and Feminist Thinking* (Minneapolis: University of Minnesota Press, 1986), p. 210. While Grimshaw finds the claim about distinctive values tolerable subject to critical refinement, she rejects any claim that the structure of women's moral thinking is distinctive as confused and dangerous (pp. 204-215).

7. Carol Gilligan, "Woman's Place in Man's Life Cycle," *Harvard Educational Review* 49 (1979):444.

8. Trenchant critiques (from an Aristotelian viewpoint) of legalistic pictures of moral deliberation in favor of context-sensitive ones are: John McDowell, "Virtue and Reason," *The Monist* 62 (1979):331-50, and David Wiggins, "Deliberation and Practical Reason," in *Practical Reasoning*, ed. Joseph Raz (New York: Oxford University Press, 1978), pp. 144-152.

9. One thinks also of a certain kind of rigoristic, impersonal Christian agapeism that takes a dim view of all partiality and special affection. An echo of this resonates in Kant's famous distinction between practical and pathological love. See Gene Outka's *Agape* (New Haven: Yale University Press, 1972), Chapter One, for a discussion of variations of agapeistic care on the issue of love for others.

10. I deliberately use Gilligan's own phrase here for what women are "talking about" from "The Con-

quistador and the Dark Continent: Reflections on the Psychology of Love," *Daedalus* 113 (1984): 78.

11. Gilligan often invokes this duality, e.g., in "Conquistador" (pp. 77-78) and *In A Different Voice* (p. 69). In "Remapping the Moral Domain: New Images of the Self in Relationship" in *Reconstructing Individualism*, ed. Thomas C. Heller et al. (Palo Alto: Stanford University Press, 1986), pp. 241-256, she suggests briefly that this duality reflects universal experiences, in childhood, of inequality and attachment. For a fuller treatment, see Gilligan and Wiggins *"Origins ..."* (note 2, above).

12. See J.S. Mill on expediency over justice in chapter 5 of *Utilitarianism* (New American Library, 1962), pp. 320-321. (Subsequent references to Mill are to this edition.) For a more wistful admission that justice might have to go, see J.J.C. Smart, *Utilitarianism for and against*, with Bernard Williams (Cambridge: Cambridge University Press, 1973). pp. 69-74.

13. It is not cant when Mill says "In the golden rule of Jesus of Nazareth, we read the complete spirit of the ethics of utility. To do as you would be done by, and to love your neighbor as yourself, constitute the ideal perfection of utilitarian morality" (*Utilitarianism*, Chapter 2, 268). Mill's belief in the "powerful natural sentiment" (p. 284) and "contagion" (p. 285) of sympathy are important grounds of his defense of utilitarianism.

14. Bill Puka, "An Interdisciplinary Treatment of Kohlberg," *Ethics* 92 (1982):469. Puka provides a clear statement of the basic commitments of "cognitive-developmentalism" in morality.

15. Mill responded early on to criticisms of the demandingness and coldness of utilitarianism (*Utilitarianism*, chapter 2, pp. 269-272). Contemporary critiques on this score include: Bernard Williams, "Persons, Character, and Morality," in *Moral Luck* (Cambridge: Cambridge University Press, 1981), pp. 1-19; Michael Stocker, "The Schizophrenia of Modern Ethical Theories," *The Journal of Philosophy* 73 (1976):453-466. See also, Linda Nicholson, "Women, Morality, and History," *Social Research* 50 (1983):514-536, especially 524-525, on how both utilitarianism and Kantianism reflect the same historical location and social organization that yield a certain version of the public vs. private split.

16. (Berkeley and Los Angeles: University of California Press, 1984), hereafter cited in the text as C.

17. Noddings does not put her view forward as a representation of Gilligan's different voice, but does identify her view with Gilligan's at points or recruits Gilligan's view in support of hers (e.g., C, pp. 8, 96).

18. See Seyla Benhabib's excellent "The Generalized and The Concrete Other: The Kohlberg-Gilligan Controversy and Moral Theory" in Kittay and Meyers, pp. 154-171.

19. Owen Flanagan, "Virtue, Sex, and Gender: Some Philosophical Reflections on the Moral Psychology Debate," *Ethics* 92 (1982):499-512, claims Gilligan's "contextualism" is really just a general kind of cognitive sophistication, that of making subtle discriminations (p. 511). But this fails to consider that the cognition central to care is understanding *persons*; I do not think intellectual subtlety in, say, mathematics of philosophy indicates cognitive sophistication we should expect to carry over to interpersonal perceptiveness. Nor can Gilligan's claim that the care and justice orientations are "fundamentally incompatible" like two ways of seeing a puzzle picture ("Remapping ... ," pp. 242, 246), be evaluated if the grounding of these two views in different representations of interpersonal relationship and understanding are not fully explored. Yet without considering these different representations at length or in detail, Flanagan and Kathryn Jackson in "Justice, Care and Gender: the Kohlberg-Gilligan Debate Revisited," *Ethics* 97 (1987): 622-637, argue that it is possible to "integrate" perceptions aligned with each into the same episode of moral deliberation (p. 626).

20. See "Remapping the Moral Domain" (note 11, above) and Carol Gilligan and Eve Stern, "The Riddle of Femininity and the Psychology of Love," in *Passionate Attachments*, ed. Willard Gaylin and Ethel Person (New York: Free Press, 1988).

21. Sharon Bishop, "Connections and Guilt," *Hypatia* 2 (1987):7-23, explores the implications of a Gilligan-like ethics of responsibility for the inevitability of moral conflict and the resulting affective binds which require working through over time and may leave intelligible but only partly expungeable remainders of guilt.

22. The *Signs* forum (note 2, above) illustrates this amply; beyond criticism, there is resentment, frustration, and distress. I don't mean to imply, of course, there is no basis for dispassionate criticism.

23. Grimshaw, op. cit., expresses this reservation about "women's viewpoint" theories generally. But even so, exposing "female" morality to view may open a mine of insight into the hidden presuppositions and agendae of "male" (read, public) moralities. See, e.g. Annette Baier, "Poisoning the Wells," in *Postures of the Mind* (Minneapolis: University of Minnesota Press, 1985), pp. 263-291, especially pp. 273-276.

24. Sara Ruddick's excellent studies, "Maternal Thinking," and "Preservative Love and Military Destruction" are exemplars for examining the intelligent structure of "women's work." In Joyce Trebilcot (ed.), *Mothering* (Totowa, NJ: Rowman and Allanheld, 1984), pp. 213-230, 231-262. In a related vein, see Virginia Held, "Feminism and Moral Theory," in Kittay and Meyers, pp. 111-128, on the understanding of human relationship that grows out of the mothering experience.

CHANGING MORAL VALUES IN AFRICA: AN ESSAY IN ETHICAL RELATIVISM

Egbeke Aja

Egbeke Aja teaches philosophy at the University of Nigeria in Nsukka, Nigeria. He is the author of numerous articles on African moral traditions and Igbo moral values in journals such as Metaphysics, Philosophy and the Contemporary World, *and* Ethics.

   Aja argues that for Africans to live together peacefully in a time of economic interdependence that is bringing diverse countries and cultures into closer contact, a basis for a common understanding of African moral values needs to be developed. A common understanding will permit changes to familiar cultural patterns and help African countries address contemporary aspects of colonialism. Aja describes the tradition, beliefs, and values of the Igbo in Nigeria to explore the possibility of articulating a foundation for African moral values, one that is based on universal human needs and social imperatives. He finds variation within Igbo societies and between Igbo values and those in other African cultural groupings such as the Yoruba and the Akan people of Ghana. Yet, Aja argues, an analysis of the functions and interrelations of these values allows general principles and a fundamental uniformity to emerge.

1. Introduction

Rapid transportation and the increased economic interdependence of parts of Africa are bringing into close contact groups of diverse cultures. If Africans are to live together peacefully, they must develop a basis for common understanding and for the creation of new patterns controlling the interaction of individuals of different cultural groups. Such common understandings, in the field of ethical systems, are the only lasting foundation upon which a modern Africa can be built. If the various African societies cannot agree to adhere to basic moral values in their dealings with each other, their strength will be spent in wars and preparations for wars, and civilization as we know it will elude the countries.

   Another condition which adds urgency to the quest for the understanding of African moral values is the necessity for revising many of our familiar cultural patterns to meet the new conditions imposed by colonialism, especially its edu-

cational system and consequent mechanical civilization. The rapid scientific and technological progress of the current era bids fair to alter our daily lives and even our ways of thinking so profoundly that new African moral values will have to be based on the universal human needs and social imperatives. We will have to get down to bedrock to create new understandings of social interaction which our new situation requires. Such an exercise will be better done by studying definite cultural groups in Africa. Hence, the Igbo, a linguistic group in the Southeastern part of Nigeria, with a population of about ten million, is the focus of this essay. For purposes of comparative study, the Yoruba, the Akan people of Ghana, and other African cultural groupings shall be examined.

   It is incumbent on both the social scientist and the philosopher to seek for the solid foundation of African (Igbo) moral values, a process which involves, first of all, ascertaining whether such a foundation really exists.

2. The Foundation of Traditional Igbo Moral Values

The first impression which you receive from the study of a series of unrelated African societies is of almost unlimited variety of cultures. Since all the varied patterns function successfully as parts of one society or another, the stage is set for the development of the concept of cultural relativity and then ethical relativity. Values seem to vary from one society to another in Igboland. However, when these African values are analyzed, in terms of their functions and inter-relations, some general principles emerge. Behind the seemingly endless diversity of traditional Igbo moral values, there is fundamental uniformity.

What is the basis of traditional Igbo morality? According to Victor C. Uchendu, "To know how a people view the world around them is to understand how they evaluate life; and a people's evaluation of life both temporal and non-temporal, provides them with a 'charter' of action, a guide to behavior."[1] Attempts to examine the traditional Igbo evaluation of life which provides the Igbo with a charter of action, a guide to behavior, have resulted in three hypotheses on the basis of Igbo moral values.

First, is the religious view. Exponents of this view are mainly theologians: John S. Mbiti, Bolaji Idowu, and Edmund Ilogu. However, a non-theologian, Moses Makinde, has also been identified as defending the idea of a religious foundation for morality in Africa. According to Idowu,

> Morality is basically the fruit of religion and that to begin, it was dependent upon it. Man's concept of the Deity has everything to do with what is taken to be the norm of morality. God made man, and it is He who implants in him the sense of right and wrong. This is a fact the validity of which does not depend upon whether man realizes and acknowledges it or not.[2]

Idowu is using "man" to stand for human beings. Similarly, Ilogu has this to say about the Igbo: "In Igbo traditional society, religion is the basis or morality both through the beliefs of the people as well as through the sanctions imposed by customs and prohibitions."[3]

For the Igbo, the world is created by God, *Chineke*, who makes animal and plant life grow. *Chineke*, as the source of life and sustenance, which to the Igbo is the chief good, becomes, therefore, the source of goodness and benevolence. God gives to each person, at the time of birth that person's portion of divine essence known as his or her *Chi*. Hence the Igbo, according to Ilogu, name God *Chi-ukwu*, meaning the Great *Chi* in whom all human life and the sum total of individual *Chis* are gathered up.

Adding to the above arguments, Mbiti maintains that Africans live in a religious universe. Religion, he observes, plays a great role in the lives of African peoples. Therefore, an African system of morality, based on African cultural beliefs, must have a religious foundation.[4]

Against the religious foundations of traditional African moral values, I note that the arguments though cleverly thought out, are a long way from the conclusion that traditional African morality must have a religious foundation. At best, we may conclude that religions may have influence on traditional African morality. For the Igbo, for example,

> traditional religion and morality are closely interwoven. In fact they are not only complementary, but also inseparable. In spite of this marriage of morality and religion, there is nevertheless a well defined code of morality in Igbo society.[5]

It does not follow that religion is the foundation; to say it must be the foundation is to suggest that without religion a given human society cannot have any conception of what is good or bad. It is one thing to claim that religion influences a people's approach to moral behavior, but it is another thing to argue that religion must be the foundation of their morality. That would mean that without religions the Igbo or the Yoruba could not behave in a morally responsible manner. One might be tempted to think so with regard to some

African societies, for example, the Yoruba. The Yoruba trace nearly every aspect of their lives to one deity or the other. But, in respect of the Igbo, G.T. Basden testifies:

> In the majority of Ibo towns, very clearly defined codes of morals exist theoretically. Infringements on these laws may lead to severe penalties being inflicted.[6]

The religious view begs the question: Which comes first, religion or morality? Any answer is bound to be conjectural.

A second school of thought traces traditional African moral values to society, as essentially social phenomena. "Society must keep itself alive and its machinery smooth-running, and to this end, it evolves a system of self preservation."[7] Conscience, according to this school of thought, is nothing more than a complex of residual habits, which society implants in man as it brings him up. This seems to be the main plank on which the traditional Igbo found their moral values. "For the Igbo, the classical sinner is the thief. This is because theft is seen as an aggression and an infringement on other people's right which, in turn, is a violation of social justice."[8] Igbo moral values, in this view, revolve around justice.[9]

The third school of thought holds that traditional Igbo morality is a product of common sense. "In order to live, human beings must adapt themselves to their environment. Experience soon taught them what could be done and what must be avoided. A steady accumulation of this experience over a long period has resulted in a very strong sense of what has come to be popularly known as 'right' and 'wrong'."[10] That is, depending upon the people's experience and needs, by generalization and projection, the Igbo built their conception of "good" and "bad." Being continuous with their direct perception of reality, this conception is confirmed by what they see, and when it takes into account what they expect of life, it answers their psychological requirements. Thus, the Igbo society, in which all adult members must spend the greater part of their energy wresting enough food for their needs from their environment, will have a different view of morality from that of a group in which a few of the members can produce plenty of food for all.

Kwasi Wiredu is in the forefront of those who hold the common-sense view. He opines that at least for the Akan of Ghana, the moral outlook is "logically independent of religion."[11] And Kwame Gyekye holds the same view.[12]

The common-sense school of thought and the school that traces morality to society are vehemently attacked by the exponents of the religious foundation of morality in traditional Africa. Idowu rejects both hypotheses on the ground that they are partial explanations. For him, they "have conveniently overlooked two vital questions: The social school still has to make it explicit why this 'mass' which is called society should be so keen on its own preservation."[13] His point may be that if the society were a soulless machine, it would not bother about its breakdown. For Idowu, that it does bother indicates that it has a soul; so someone — God — is needed as a basis for society's concern for morality.

If one says that society creates morality to avoid its own self-destruction, this is enough reason. We need not assume, as Idowu would like us to do, that there is some other being responsible for putting the soul in the traditional African to think of his or her survival.

Idowu demands that the common-sense view of the foundation of morality tell us what puts so much common sense in human beings. Why, like the candle-drawn moth, do not human beings fly into the flame and be burnt?[14] On the denial of the sufficiency of common sense as a basis for traditional African morality, are we being asked to agree that if a child puts its finger in the fire a first time, he or she cannot on the basis of that experience refrain from fire next time? The life experiences of the Africans are different. However, they have this in common: obtaining the necessities of life is not easy and requires constant effort; survival is always unsure, for the margin is narrow, and every year there is a critical period of scarcity. In this narrow but fundamental aspect, the African's existential experience is everywhere the same. Experience, need, and societal demands make the African know what to do and what to avoid. If we follow through Idowu's claim that God is the source of the traditional African's conscience and, therefore, of notions of right and wrong, everything will be traceable to God. But, if in fact, human beings can discern on their own what is good, even to please God, then the identification of morality with religion is not as tight as first assumed. In other words, since the people are credited with discerning what is good or bad as in the Yoruba concept, *eewo*, they should be credited with independently arriving at the notions of right and wrong by using their reasoning ability which is granted to be God-given.[15]

Theologians are not the only defenders of the idea of a religious foundation of morality in traditional Africa. Moses Makinde, a philosopher, has presented arguments drawn from authorities like Kant, Mill, and Mbiti in defense of the religious hypothesis.[16]

Evidence exists for the view that some African moral values have religious influence, but that does not mean that morality is founded on religion or that a further ultimate source cannot be found for our moral ideas. A common belief among the Igbo and even the Yoruba is that a person who is morally good, who is generous in giving, or respectful to elders, or chaste in words and deeds, would find favor with the gods, and barring the evil machinations of the people of the world, he or she would prosper. African moral values are also justifiable by reference to their consequences for the individual and the society. The answer to the question, "Why respect your elders?" among the Igbo is not only the prudential one: "It will pay you." It is also teleological and by deduction, utilitarian. According to the Igbo, *Ife ojo na agba ugwo* (Evil deed demands reparation). The Igbo also have it that *Isi meturu ebu, ka ebu n'agba* (The head that touches the wasp's nest, is the head that will be stung by the wasp). Or, stated differently, *Isi ebughi ibu, ibu anaghi anyi ya* (A head carrying no load, feels no weight on it). The prudential, teleological, and utilitarian considerations appear to be the ultimate appeals for Igbo moral values.

Igbo moral values can be described as theistic in that what is of moral value relates to the creative source of humanity, and the higher moral values of the society could be known from their pre-existing order. The values can be described as teleological. Social actions and relationships are guided by the consideration of the purpose of the universe. Taboos, for example, are observed, because to contravene their proscriptions disturbs the harmonious relationship between human beings and the cosmos. A third kind of classical ethical system can be distilled from traditional Igbo morality: utilitarianism. Bentham's famous formula of utilitarianism that the good is "the greatest happiness of the greatest number" is interpreted by the Igbo to mean the greatest happiness of the greatest number of the Igbo race instead of humankind as a whole. Whatever the twist, Igbo traditional moral values emphasize what is prescribed as what works, what gives happiness, and what had enabled the group to survive. To that extent, Igbo ethical system can be characterized as pragmatic. For the Igbo, the *summum bonum* to which persons must aspire is the performance of those acts which will enhance the ontological well-being of their community. This is the basis of all ethical considerations in traditional Igbo culture.

3. Moral Values in Contemporary African (Igbo) Societies

Pioneer works on African religions stressed a close connection between ethics and religion in traditional African cultures. Right and wrong continued to be defined by reference to God's will and human life came to be regarded as meaningful only because of its place in God's plan. Traditional African religions were the guardians of the moral community and its main authority.

By the eighteenth and nineteenth centuries, these ideas had begun to lose their grip on the traditional African minds, largely because of changes that had taken place in the continent. With European colonization of the African continent, Western systems of education, religion, science, and technology were introduced among the Igbo. Material and cultural conditions of self-aggrandizing and metaphysical delusion were institutionalized and incarnated in the consciousness of the

Igbo. Simultaneously, this same delusionary meta-physical belief, that is, to be was to be like the other, and to be like the other was to act, dress, and talk like the other, also provided the evidence — in the material instantations and inculcation in the consciousness of the colonized — for its own veracity. The very fact of conquest was taken as metaphysical proof of the unhistoricality — the lack of humanness — of the colonized.

In the traditional African world, power was God's. Human beings did all they could to avoid incurring divine displeasure which manifested itself in pestilence, famine, and defeats in wars. Since such phenomena were frequent, it appeared as if it was easy to incur divine pleasure in tradi-tional Igbo society. Judging by the analogy of earthly monarchs, the Igbo concluded that the thing most displeasing to the Deity is a lack of humility. If you wished to slip through life without disaster, you must be meek; you must be aware of your defenselessness and constantly ready to confess your wrong-doings and atone for them. But the God before whom you humbled yourself was conceived in the likeness of human beings; so the Igbo universe seemed human and warm and cozy, like home if you are the youngest of a large family, painful at times, but never alien and incom-prehensible.

All this is different in the views of the contem-porary Africans. Western education has trans-formed and is still transforming modern African societies into scientific worlds. In African tradi-tional thought, humankind was seen and treated as the center of the created universe. All other beings in the universe were on hand for the services of human beings. The earth was thought to be all that makes up the universe. The physical sciences have challenged the ancient African beliefs. Instead, they have recognized that the earth, compared to other bodies in the created universe, is an insignif-icant speck. This has led to a de-emphasis on the human species in the scheme of things in the uni-verse *vis-à-vis* other created beings. Armed with ingenious arguments by Western thinkers like David Hume, educated Africans now defend the permissibility of such hitherto abominable crimes as suicide and abortion.[17]

It is no longer by prayer, sacrifice, and humility that you cause things to go as you wish in contem-porary Africa, but by acquiring a knowledge of natural laws. The power you acquire in this way is much greater and much more reliable to the modern Igbo than that formerly supposed to be acquired by prayer. This is because you never could tell whether your prayer would be favorably heard in heaven. The power of prayer had recog-nized limits; it would have been impious to ask too much from the gods. But no limits to the power of science exist. The traditional Igbo were told by the missionaries that faith could remove mountains, but no one believed it; we are now told that the hydrogen bomb can remove the mountains, and everyone believes it. These changes have telling effects on moral relationship on contemporary Igbo culture. For example, people no longer fear the displeasure of the gods and the resultant effects on themselves should they infringe upon the rights and property of other people. The contemporary Igbo society is rife with crimes of various dimen-sions.

Apart from defending the permissibility of suicide, Hume was eager to separate religious from moral notions and to dispel the idea that human life is a gift from God. The thought that we are the products of an evolutionary history much like that of all other animals has further eroded the modern Igbo confidence about any special place of human-ity in the scheme of things as posited by the tradi-tional African concept of humanity.

In contemporary Igbo culture, the social sci-ences have presented the greatest challenge to tra-ditional ideas about human beings. Sociologists have impressed upon us that moral standards differ from culture to culture: what the "natural light of reason" reveals to one people may be radically dif-ferent from what is obvious to another. This has been known for a long time.

Herodotus made the point clearly in the fifth century B.C. when he narrated thus:

Darius, after he had got the kingdom called into his presence certain Greeks who were at hand, and asked — "what he should pay them to eat the bodies of their fathers when they died?" To which they answered, that there is no sum that would tempt them to do such a thing. He then sent for certain Indians, of the race called Callatians, men who eat their fathers, and asked them, while the Greeks stood by and know by the help of an interpreter at what was said — "What he should give them to burn the bodies of their fathers at their decease?" The Indians exclaimed aloud and bade him forbear such language. Such is man's wont herein and Pindar was right, in my judgment, when he said, "custom is the King of all."[18]

Today, in African society many an educated person can list similar examples among various cultural groups in the continent. Muslims practice polygamy, while to the Christians it has to be avoided and rejected. Many African societies do not eat snails, while to others it is a delicacy. Among the Igbo, the practice of a man marrying the wife of his deceased relation is encouraged, yet in some sections of Igboland such an act is seen as an abomination.

With the communication media providing constant contact with other parts of Igboland and the world at large, traditional Igbo moral values are not what they used to be. They are more than one cultural product. In many people's minds, Igbo moral values can no longer exist as a subject having as its aim the discovery of what is right and what is wrong in any given Igbo society. This is due to several factors, some of which follows.

3.1. The quest for rationality

Hitherto, according to Igbo customary morality, acts were accounted moral and by deduction juridical because they accorded with the people's customs and tradition. That was enough reason. But now, most skeptical thinkers among the Igbo agree that reason has a role to play in moral judgments: reason establishes the facts of any particular moral value. Unfortunately, attaining a rational view of the facts is not always a simple matter. We often need to know what the consequences of a course of action will be, and this may be impossible to determine with precision or certainty. Take

the issue of mercy-killing or euthanasia. Suppose it is legalized. What will be the consequences, say, among the Igbo? Opponents of euthanasia — a practice which was in vogue in traditional African set-ups — sometimes claim that if mercy-killing were legalized, it would lead to diminished respect for human life throughout the society. Some Christian denominations are of the same view with regard to abortion. Concerning euthanasia, the opponents contend that we would end up caring less about the elderly, the mentally retarded, and so forth. The defenders of euthanasia, on the other hand, heatedly deny this. What separates the two camps is a disagreement about the facts, but we cannot settle the issue in the same way we could settle an argument about what would happen if Coca-Cola were boiled. We are stuck with different estimates of what would happen if most of the taboos in Igbo societies were legalized, which may be more or less reasonable, but which we cannot definitely adjudicate. Moreover, consistency is the prime requirement of rationality. If we accept some of the consequences of our actions, but not others, then we are inconsistent. This point, which has fundamental consequences will be missed if we are blinded by overly simple doctrine like, "Reason establishes the facts; sentiment makes the choice," especially in relation to most African moral values.

The requirement of consistency forces a change in contemporary Igbo moral traditions. For most Westerners and contemporary Africans with a Western frame of mind, a moral value, if it is to be acceptable, must be backed by reasons. This does not hold in traditional Igbo set-ups. Consistency requires that if exactly the same reasons support one course of conduct as there are supporting another, those actions are equally right or equally wrong. We cannot say that action X is right but that action Y is wrong, unless there is a relevant difference between X and Y. This is a familiar principle in many contexts. It cannot be right for a teacher to give students different grades unless a relevant difference exists in the work that they have done; it cannot be right to pay workers different wages unless some relevant differences between the jobs they do can be established. This principle underscores the social ideal of equality. But in African morality, actions can only be tolerated in respect of people affected.

Recently, this principle has acquired more radical implications that egalitarians have realized. For, if applied consistently, it would require that we rethink our treatment of fellow citizens *vis-à-vis* employment opportunities and political appointments. A reflection on traditional and contemporary Igbo moral values reveals that the difference between moral values and other values is in the involvement of the emotions in the moral ones. In order for anything to count as a value, we must care about that thing in some way. In the absence of any emotional involvement we have no reasons for action. For example, the fact that children are starving is a reason for their parent to do something only if he or she cares about their plight. People might care about different things and so accept different ultimate principles between which reason can not adjudicate: this possibility continues to undermine the credibility of some traditional moral values in contemporary Africa.

3.2. The Christian ethics versus traditional Igbo morality

No acceptable body of knowledge that can be called Christian ethics exists. But some doctrines are basic to Christianity. They express the main Christian motif. Christians, all over the world, believe and proclaim that:

1. God is the Creator and Jesus Christ is the redeemer of the world.
2. God is the final arbiter and ruler in the affairs of the world.
3. The measure of the importance of believers' worth is determined by the fact that Jesus Christ died for humanity.
4. Sin is a reality in human experience.[19]

From these four teachings are distilled four basic tenets of what can be referred to as Christian ethics: a theological corpus understood in terms of self-emptying or self-sacrifice that enriches the life of others. It demands a life of love which is essentially social and required of the individual clear understanding of the Christian's relation to others. It educates the Christians to accept that each person, by faithfulness to her or his special function in society, promotes the welfare and advances the happiness of others. In this social concern, love, the main motive force of Christian ethics, provides the bond of sympathy and the motive of service. The exercise of love does not ask what is easiest or most pleasant, but what is best. Hence, the Christian can say "No" and bear the misunderstanding and reproach which refusal might entail. Individual merit is not sought after nor general principles indiscriminately applied as a quick and ready way out.

Christian ethics has some problems to contend with *vis-à-vis* Igbo converts. The behavior patterns and social practices of the traditional Igbo contradict the meaning of the love ethics of Christianity. Four areas of moral conflict readily come to mind.

1. Nepotism. This has been described as enlightened self-interest. Nepotism is the practice of filling all existing vacancies in public services with members of one's relations. Though this may be said to be practiced in other societies, including Christian Europe, in Africa it is culture-bound. In traditional Africa, relationship goes back to twenty or more generations of both mother and father and all relations by marriage within the long line of extended family system. Someone who happens to occupy a public office of high standing is persuaded by pressure from the hundreds or thousands of relations to employ, first and foremost, members of her or his family. Public opinion, based on traditional Igbo ethics, justifies her or him. And where one person goes out of her or his way to employ anyone who is not related by traditional definition, she or he is considered as showing special favor for which the newly employed should express thanks or give a bribe. The family of the person offering such bribes does not see anything wrong in doing so because the person expressing the favor is not a member of their extended family.

Despite the official provision that jobs are open to every qualified candidate, the cultural and moral background of the Igbo still holds people tight to their old and traditional concept of family. By that conception, bribery, for example, is not seriously condemned, while nepotism, as a social evil, is not frowned at. The contemporary Igbo is in a state of moral dilemma imposed on them by their new religious and social order.

2. *Group solidarity and Christian ethics.* Another important culture-bound moral value that stands in opposition to the modern Igbo morality is the emphasis on the group. For the African, the group is crucial. Obedience to the laws and the prescriptions of the tradition maintains the harmony between the group and the cosmos. As a result, a customary ethics develops among the Igbo. The desire to do as others do creates the "shame-oriented ethics" characteristic of Igbo morality rather than the "guilt-oriented ethics" of the Christian faith. So all moral acts are in response to avoiding detection rather than avoiding the wrong actions. The desire to do as others do perpetuates the *status quo* and destroys the chances of rearing people with prophetic voice and insight by which society is enabled to start afresh along a more deserving moral route. This accounts for the bandwagon effect of moral decadence among contemporary Africans.

3. *Marriage and family life.* In Western societies, monogamy has been maintained through state and church laws. In Igboland, only some churches maintain sanctions against polygamy. Both traditional law and public opinion approve polygamy in Igboland. Polygamy is a factor in the economic life of the Igbo, and it adds to a man's, but not a woman's, social prestige. The shift in emphasis in contemporary African society to Western education, commerce, politics, public office held, and wealth accumulated in landed properties, the economic and prestigious attraction for polygamy is fast disappearing among the Igbo. But the desire for male heirs and the social preference for boys in traditional Igbo families have induced Christians apparently happily married as monogamists to turn polygamists. Contrary to expectations, the church, for practical purposes, does not condemn the acts nor does public opinion. A man's sex relation with all the wives does not qualify as adultery in tradi-

tional Igbo moral law. So the lapse into polygamy from Christian monogamy does not qualify for ridicule in the shame-oriented morality of the Igbo, nor does it apparently earn from the offender pricks of conscience in the guilt-oriented morality of Christian ethics. There is no pressure from the women either, since a large number, including educated women, accept that it is better to have a husband shared with other women than die a spinster.

How does the contemporary Igbo solve the dilemma posed by Christianity's insistence on monogamy and the traditional encouragement for polygamy? The situation is complicated by the various groups of African churches which do not insist on monogamy. The moral issue is, then, can both monogamy and polygamy grow together till the "harvest"? as the Christian theologian would put it. If that is granted, then the exotic religions among the Igbo need a new theological approach to the problem. Rather than approving of, say, monogamy and disapproving of polygamy, we would better give African Christians a chance to make a choice of the type of marriage they prefer. The situation requires a marriage of both traditional and Christian, or other religious moral values. Although everyone who becomes a Christian must become a new creature, yet the person need not be a stranger in her or his environment. The environment is the social and cultural milieu which is the only reality in which individuals can love their neighbor as themselves.

4. *Sanctions.* One of the characteristics of African morality is the use of sanction as means of ensuring compliance. Oath-taking at the shrine of a chosen divinity is one of the methods employed by the Igbo in obtaining sanctions against destroyers of traditional moral values. Some exotic religions, for instance, Christianity, brand as superstitious this practice of oath-taking. In contemporary Igboland, the conflict is of traditional oath-taking with the Western legal system practiced in Igboland and with the teachings of Christianity. The issue is: What then will take the place of oath taking or any other sanctions against deviance from moral prescription? In the past, a young

woman, newly married, could be sent back to her parents by the relatives of the husband if she was found to have broken her virginity before marriage. The sanction here is loss of face, and in itself it was a good means of protecting young girls from sexual indulgence. Among the Cross-river Igbo, though the woman is no longer sent back to her parents, the inquiries made by the Age Grade of the newly married man on the first morning after wedding, indicate the demand for virginity placed on the wife. For instance, the Age Grade would like to know whether the bed was stained with blood, or whether the wife exhibited signs of being inflicted with pain during intercourse.

The Western legal system and Christian conscience would revolt against this type of differential morality because the husband is never subjected to such loss of face if he had indulged in a good deal of sexual license before marrying his young bride.

4. Conclusion

As societies change, so their moral values change. African values are grounded on common sense and societal needs: whence the multiplicity of values among the various societies in Africa. Contemporary Africans are at the cross-roads; they are sitting on two moral stools. They are not comfortably seated on any of the value systems — Western and African — with which they are confronted. Contemporary Africans no longer appreciate their environment through the erstwhile value systems of their traditional society; neither are they of a piece with the Western values that Western education with which has acquainted them. The theistic and teleological considerations that accounted for what passed as value among the Igbo have been replaced with utilitarian and materialistic considerations. This trend is not peculiar to the Igbo or Africa; it is a common feature of the contemporary world. It is therefore imperative that we sieve out the best from the traditional African (Igbo) values and the Western-oriented values so as to forge a

new value system — a hybrid — that will meet the challenges of our time.

NOTES

1. Victor C. Uchendu, *The Igbo of Southeast Nigeria* (New York: Holt, Rinehart and Winston, 1965), p. 12.
2. Bolaji Idowu, *Olódùmaré: God in Yoruba Belief* (Lagos: Longmans, 1962), p. 145.
3. Edmund Ilogu, *Igbo Life and Thought* (Onitsha: University Publishing Company, 1985), p. 24.
4. John S. Mbiti, *African Religions and Philosophy* (London: Heinemann, 1977), pp. 48-57.
5. F.U. Okafor, *Igbo Philosophy of Law* (Enugu: Fourth Dimension Publishers, 1992), p. 32.
6. G.T. Basden, *Niger Ibos* (London: Frank Cass and Co. Ltd.), p. 34.
7. Idowu, *Olódùmaré*, p. 144.
8. Okafor, *Igbo Philosophy of Law*, p. 33.
9. Francis Arinze, *Sacrifice in Igbo Religion* (Ibadan: University Press, 1970), pp. 29-30.
10. Idowu, *Olódùmaré*, p. 144.
11. Kwasi Wiredu, "Morality and Religion in Akan Thought," H. Odera Omka and D.A. Masolo, (eds). *Philosophy and Culture* (Nairobi: Bookwise, 1983), p. 13.
12. Kwame Gyeke, *An Essay on African Philosophical Thought: Akan Conceptual Scheme* (New York: Cambridge University Press, 1987), p. 155.
13. Idowu, *Olódùmaré*, p. 145.
14. Ibid.
15. Segun Gbadegesin, *African Philosophy: Traditional Yoruba Philosophy and Contemporary African Realities* (New York: Peter Lang, 1991), p. 70.
16. H. Gene Blocker, *Ethics: An Introduction* (New York: Haven Publishing Corporation, 1988), p. 97.
17. Mbiti, *African Religions and Philosophy*, p. 33.
18. See Edward LeRoy Long, Jr., *A Survey of Christian Ethics* (New York: Oxford University Press, 1967), p. 27.
19. Ilogu, *Igbo Life and Thought*, p. 30.

STUDY QUESTIONS

1 According to Immanuel Kant, what is the difference between a hypothetical and a categorical imperative and why is the latter distinctive of morality?

2 What is the distinction between perfect and imperfect duties meant to capture? Describe the relevance of the distinction by discussing the four examples that Kant provides.

3 Kant gives several formulations of the categorical imperative. What are they? Explain how these formulations are taken to be equivalent by applying the different formulations to at least one of Kant's examples of moral dilemmas.

4 What is the principle of utility? Why does John Stuart Mill distinguish between quantity and quality of pleasures? Does the distinction capture an account of human nature that is, in the end, similar to Kant's account of the dignity of human beings? Why or why not?

5 How does Mill answer the kind of objection that Kant would make that morality has to do with determining one's duty and not with maximizing happiness either for the individual or for the greatest number of individuals?

6 When deciding what is morally right, is the best way to calculate consequences and maximize happiness or to determine one's duty in accordance with universal moral laws? Formulate your answer to this question by exploring cases that present problems for one or the other kind of moral theory.

7 Would V.F. Cordova characterize both Kant's and Mill's moral theories as an "I" approach to morality? What features of these theories would characterize them as such?

8 What distinguishes a "we" approach to morality from an "I" approach? Would the "we" approach give us answers different to those provided by Kant and Mill as to how we determine morally right actions? If so, what are the differences?

9 In what ways does Kant's moral theory fit the description of an ethic of justice as described in Margaret Walker's account of Gilligan's work on justice and care? In what ways is a care perspective similar to and different from Utilitarianism?

10 Are there similarities between the "we" approach described by Cordova and the ethic of care described by Walker? Are there differences? Defend your answers.

11 Do you think that women tend to adopt an ethic of care? Is this question relevant to an evaluation of care as a way of thinking about morality and resolving moral issues? How does Walker answer these questions? How would you?

12 Outline the two themes that Walker identifies in a care orientation. Does Walker's strategy of bringing the care-orientation and contextual-deliberative view together work to capture the differences between an ethic of care and an ethic of justice? Does it succeed in showing how an ethic of care challenges traditional accounts of morality and enriches moral theory? Provide reasons for your answers.

13 Is Egbeke Aja also critical of traditional Western-oriented accounts of morality? Why does he want to find values that are common to African tradition and beliefs?

14 Aja surveys three hypotheses that explain the source and foundation for Igbo values. What are these hypotheses? What commonalities among different African systems does Aja identify?

15 Do you agree with Aja that the best of Western-oriented values can be combined with African ones to shape a system that can meet contemporary challenges in Africa today? Provide reasons for your answer.

SUGGESTED READINGS

Annas, Julia. "Virtue and Eudaimonism." *Social Philosophy & Policy*, v. 15, no. 1 (Winter 1998): 37-55.

Baier, Annette C. "The Need For More Than Justice." *Canadian Journal of Philosophy*, Supplementary vol. 13 (1987): 41-56.

Bok, Sissela. "What Basis for Morality? A Minimalist Approach." *The Monist*, v. 76 (1993): 349-59.

Brennan, Samantha (editor). *Canadian Journal of Philosophy. Supplementary Volume: Feminism and Moral Philosophy*, v. 33, no. 2 (2003).

Calhoun, Cheshire. "Responsibility and Reproach." *Ethics*, v. 99 (January 1989): 389-406.

Card, Claudia (editor). *On Feminist Ethics and Politics*. Lawrence, KS: University Press of Kansas, 1999.

Debold, Elizabeth. "Shifting Moral Ground: The Dilemmas of Ethics in an Out-of-Control World." *What is Enlightenment?* (February-April 2004): 51-59.

Etzioni, Amitai. "Cross-Cultural Judgments: The Next Steps." *Journal of Social Philosophy*, v. 28, no. 3 (Winter 1997): 5-15.

Friedman, Marilyn. "Feminism and Modern Friendship: Dislocating the Community." *Ethics*, v. 99 (1989): 275-90.

Gilligan, Carol. *In a Different Voice: Psychological Theory and Women's Development*. Cambridge, MA: Harvard University Press, 1982.

Hekman, Susan. "Moral Voices, Moral Selves: About Getting it Right in Moral Theory." *Human Studies*, v. 16 (1993): 143-62.

Isaacs, Tracy. "Cultural Context and Moral Responsibility." *Ethics*, v. 107 (July 1997): 670-84.

Jackson, W.M. "Rules Versus Responsibility in Morality." *Public Affairs Quarterly*, v. 3, no. 2 (April 1989): 27-40.

LeMoncheck, Linda. "Academic Feminism and Applied Ethics: Closing the Gap Between Private Scholarship and Public Policy." *International Studies in Philosophy*, v. 29, no. 1 (1997): 69-77.

Louden, Robert. "Some Vices of Virtue Ethics." *American Philosophical Quarterly*, v. 21 (1984): 227-36.

Manning, Rita C. *Speaking From the Heart: A Feminist Perspective on Ethics*. Lanham, MD: Rowman & Littlefield, 1992.

Matilal, Bimal Krishna. "Ethical Relativism and Confrontation of Cultures." In *Relativism: Interpretation and Confrontation*, edited by Michael Krausz. Notre Dame, IN: University of Notre Dame Press, 1989.

Moody-Adams, Michele. "Culture, Responsibility, and Affected Ignorance." *Ethics*, 104 (January 1994): 291-309.

Nedelsky, Jennifer. "Reconceiving Autonomy: Sources, Thoughts, and Possibilities." *Yale Journal of Law and Feminism*, v. 1, no. 7 (Spring 1989): 7-36

Nussbaum, Martha, and Amartya Sen. "Internal Criticism and Indian Rationalist Traditions." In *Relativism: Interpretation and Confrontation*, edited by Michael Krausz. Notre Dame, IN: University of Notre Dame Press, 1989.

Pazenok, Victor S. "The Values and Ethics of a Changing Society." *Journal of Value Inquiry*, v. 30 (June 1996): 135-44.

Razin, Alexander V. "Value Orientation and the Well-Being of Humanity." *Journal of Value Inquiry*, v. 30 (June 1996): 113-24.

Rorty, Richard. "Solidarity or Objectivity?" In *Anti-Theory in Ethics and Moral Conservatism*, edited by Stanley G. Clarke and Evan Simpson. Albany, NY: SUNY Press, 1989.

Sher, George. "Ethics, Character, and Action." *Social Philosophy & Policy*, v. 15, no. 1 (Winter 1998): 1-17.

Sherman, Nancy. "Concrete Kantian Respect." *Social Philosophy & Policy*, v. 15, no. 1 (Winter 1998): 119-48.

Slote, Michael. "The Justice of Caring." *Social Philosophy & Policy*, v. 15, no. 1 (Winter 1998): 171-95.

Walker, Margaret Urban. *Moral Understandings: A Feminist Study of Ethics*. New York, NY: Routledge, 1998.

Wolf, Susan. "Moral Saints." *Journal of Philosophy*, v. 79 (1982): 419-39.

Wong, David B. *Moral Relativity*. Berkeley, CA: University of California Press, 1984.

CHAPTER TWO: HUMAN RIGHTS

INTRODUCTION

This chapter opens with the United Nations Universal Declaration of Human Rights, signed by 48 countries on December 10, 1948. The idea underlying the Declaration is that all human beings are equal by virtue of the fact that they share basic human capacities that make them deserving of respect. The moral principle of equal treatment flows from this account of the equality of shared capacities. This idea has been enormously influential in creating a global community, one in which virtually all countries express, if not always honor, a commitment to human rights and reject discrimination based on morally irrelevant differences such as race, ethnicity, and gender. The idea of human rights has its most obvious source and development in the Western tradition beginning with classic liberal theorists such as Locke, Kant, and Mill. Yet it is well known that some of these theorists propounded equality for all people at the same time as they justified inequality and unequal treatment for some, including women and people of different ethnicity and race. It is also well known that liberal theory has tended to emphasize the primacy of individual rights to free speech, property, and assembly, for example. How human rights are conceived is important because rights articulate what human beings need to flourish and are, therefore, intricately connected with accounts of what is needed by way of political structures and institutions for meeting the demands of equality and justice.

One of the central questions to be explored in this chapter is whether the Universal Declaration of Human Rights reflects a Western notion of human rights rather than one that speaks for and meets the needs of people in countries with diverse people, beliefs, and values. A corollary to this question is whether the charge that current conceptions of human rights are predominantly Western undermines the validity or desirability of trying to

formulate a list of human rights that are genuinely universal. The project of producing a list assumes that there is a set of rights and corresponding institutions that are valid everywhere. This assumption is taken to generate several tendencies discussed in Volume I and examined in various chapters in all three volumes. The first is *ethnocentrism*, the disposition to judge foreign peoples or groups by the standards and practices of one's own culture or ethnic group. The term *Eurocentrism* is reserved for the particular bias in favor of the culture and values of Western liberal thinking. *Universalism* is the tendency to view human rights or justice ahistorically and in isolation from their social, political, and economic habitat. Often this tendency emerges from generalizing from one's own social context with specific values and political structures to all contexts and all people. Lastly, there is *essentialism*, the tendency to characterize all human beings as having the same features, capacities, and needs irrespective of social conditions, political contexts, and the particular circumstances of people's lives.

The Universal Declaration of Human Rights that opens this chapter lists liberty rights familiar in Western liberal contexts such as freedom to own property; freedom of thought, conscience, and religion; freedom of opinion and expression; and freedom of peaceful assembly and association. These civil and political rights are often referred to as negative rights because they flow from the notion that the state should refrain from interfering in the lives of its citizens. Those who defend negative rights and non-interference by the state argue that this context allows individuals to develop their capacities, pursue their aspirations and goals, meet their needs, and thereby flourish as human beings. Sections of the Declaration also propound positive rights such as the right to work, the right to equal pay for equal work, the right to education, and the right to a standard of living adequate for health and well-being. These positive rights are economic and social rights, and those who defend them justify and endorse state interference through minimum wage laws, for example, or through positive measures to ensure that basic human needs such as food and shelter are provided.

In the second reading, Adamantia Pollis and Peter Schwab examine this distinction between negative, or civil and political rights, and positive, or economic and social rights, and point out that the former tends to be closely aligned with Western liberal values. They argue that cultural, developmental, and ideological differences have shaped beliefs and values in non-Western countries that stand in sharp contrast with those in the West. On their account, the emphasis in the West on individuals and individual rights has little or no meaning in non-Western contexts in which the individual is conceived as an integral part of a greater whole, a whole that has primacy over the individual. Moreover, they argue that many non-Western countries emerging from colonialism may need to suspend certain rights so that they can gain economic viability and meet the needs of their citizens. They argue that because human rights originated in Western political thought and because the United Nations was dominated by the West, the Universal Declaration of Human Rights is actually the expression of legal and political thought in the West and has limited applicability in non-Western contexts. However, Pollis and Schwab do not reject the notion of human rights as such. Instead, they take the realization of differing historical conditions and of a multiplicity of philosophies and ideologies to be the occasion for uncovering and discovering any universals that may exist.

In the third reading, Jay Drydyk takes the current trend of increased globalization with respect to economic development and labor as an important reason for reexamining the criticism that human rights are Eurocentric constructs. Drydyk rejects Eurocentrism but not the project of formulating a universal set of rights. He does the latter by uncovering a common ground for human rights discourse in what motivates discussions of rights and responsibilities at all. According to Drydyk, a human right to something is "calling for social protection against standard threats that exemplify a particular type of danger for humans." Such a general understanding, he argues, allows us to derive a concept of human rights from the beliefs, values, and laws of both Western and non-Western countries. More importantly, it also allows us to take account of different cultural contexts and to provide a critical analysis of the accounts of danger and social protection assumed by some cultures. According to Drydyk, the emergence of a global public sphere of moral deliberation makes it possible to come up with a full set of human rights applicable on a global scale. At the center of such moral deliberation is knowledge of care, neglect, and abuse — knowledge that is specific to cultures with different conditions and circumstances that may require specific kinds of response. Drydyk thinks there is convergence on these matters and that this should form the bedrock for ridding moral discourse of its Eurocentrism, correcting for defective and incomplete conceptions of human rights, and making human rights useful for eliminating the damage caused by globalization in the areas of development and labor.

In the fourth reading, Kenneth Inada develops the critique of human rights from a non-Western perspective and lends support to Pollis and Schwab's argument that many non-Western ideologies are holistic rather than individualistic by examining the philosophical underpinnings of the Buddhist "holistic cosmological framework." Inada argues that the tension between the tradition of Buddhism and the Western notion of rights elucidates a difference in perspective with respect to how human relationships are conceived. The Western view of human rights is based on "hard relationships" in that people are treated as separate and independent entities each having his or her own identity and self-concepts. Inada takes hard relationships to be exemplified in the work of modern liberal thinkers who theorize about the need to make contracts that set limits to their freedom so that liberty, security, and peaceful coexistence can be enhanced for themselves and all individuals like them. Inada argues that a Buddhist view of human rights emerges from recognition and knowledge of the soft side of human interaction. The soft side is characterized by openness, depth, flexibility, and creativity and by the features of mutuality, holism, and emptiness. Together these characteristics shape relationships that emphasize virtues such as patience, trust, humility, tolerance, deference, concern, honesty, responsibility, respectfulness, and compassion. According to Inada, these virtues supersede the need for rights that define boundaries and emphasize liberty. Inada's argument is not that human rights are meaningless in Buddhism, but rather that soft relationships are inclusive in a way that can accommodate hard relationships and allow for interaction and complementarity between these two sets of beliefs and values.

So far, the discussion of rights in this chapter shows the focus to be on issues of the diversity and possible irreconcilability of beliefs across cultures that make it difficult to formulate a set of human rights applicable to all people and all places. The last reading moves the focus from rights as freedoms owed to individuals to an account of rights as expressive of and emerging from relationships in particular social contexts. Jennifer Nedelsky follows feminists and communitarians in their criticism of the individualism at the base of liberalism and traditional Western moral theory. She takes Canada's commitment to rights discourse, evident in the 1982 adoption of its *Charter of Rights and Freedoms*, as the occasion for examining a conception of rights as relational. Nedelsky contrasts the structure of Canada's Charter with the American conception of constitutional rights to equality and property to argue that conventional understandings of rights as non-interference with the autonomous decisions of individuals are inadequate. For autonomy to serve as a measure of democratic outcomes, we need a conception of autonomy not as independence, protection, and separation from others, but as a capacity that develops and is enhanced in relationships with significant people, such as parents, teachers, and friends who nurture this capacity. The constitutional protection of autonomy should be less about carving out a separate sphere into which the collective cannot intrude than a means of structuring relationships between individuals so that autonomy is fostered rather than undermined.

Nedelsky puts her conception of rights as relational to work on the right to property so central to liberal theory. Property should be viewed as less about things and erecting boundaries to protect those things than about people's relationships to each other as they affect and are affected by those things. In liberal societies with market economies, property is a great source of inequality. Nedelsky argues that because the fundamental premise of constitutional rights is equality, the tension created between the inequalities generated by property and the claims of equal rights need to be debated so as to determine the meaning, kinds of power, and limits on power that property has and can have in market economies.

UNIVERSAL DECLARATION OF HUMAN RIGHTS

United Nations

The Universal Declaration of Human Rights was approved by the General Assembly of the United Nations on December 10, 1948, by 48 nations with eight abstentions. The Declaration is formulated as a universal standard of human rights for all nations and peoples and enumerates the rights and freedoms of individuals irrespective of "race, color, sex, language, religion, political or other opinion, national or social origin, property, birth or other status."

Whereas Member States have pledged themselves to achieve, in co-operation with the United Nations, the promotion of universal respect for and observance of human rights and fundamental freedoms.

Whereas a common understanding of these rights and freedoms is of the greatest importance for the full realisation of this pledge,

Now, therefore, the General Assembly, Proclaim this Universal Declaration of Human rights as a common standard of achievement for all peoples and all nations, to the end that every individual and every organ of society, keeping this Declaration constantly in mind, shall strive by teaching and education to promote respect for these rights and freedoms and by progressive measure, national and international, to secure their universal and effective recognition and observance, both among the peoples of Member States themselves and among the peoples of territories under their jurisdiction.

Article 1

All human beings are born free and equal in dignity and rights. They are endowed with reason and conscience and should act towards one another in a spirit of brotherhood.

Article 2

1. Everyone is entitled to all the rights and freedoms set forth in this Declaration, without distinction of any kind, such as race, colour, sex, language, religion, political or other opinion, national or social origin, property, birth or other status.

2. Furthermore, no distinction shall be made on the basis of the political, jurisdictional or international status of the country or territory to which a person belongs, whether it be independent, trust, non-self-governing or under any other limitation of sovereignty.

Article 3

Everyone has the right to life, liberty and security of person.

Article 4

No one shall be held in slavery or servitude; slavery and the slave trade shall be prohibited in all their forms.

Article 5

No one shall be subjected to torture or to cruel, inhuman or degrading treatment or punishment.

Article 6

Everyone has the right to recognition everywhere as a person before the law.

Article 7

All are equal before the law and are entitled without any discrimination to equal protection of the law. All are entitled to equal protection against any discrimination in violation of this Declaration and against any incitement to such discrimination.

Article 8
Everyone has the right to an effective remedy by the competent national tribunals for acts violating the fundamental rights granted him by the constitution or by law.

Article 9
No one shall be subjected to arbitrary arrest, detention or exile.

Article 10
Everyone is entitled in full equality to a fair and public hearing by an independent and impartial tribunal, in the determination of his rights and obligations and of any criminal charge against him.

Article 11
1. Everyone charged with a penal offence has the right to be presumed innocent until proved guilty according to law in a public trial at which he has had all the guarantees necessary to his defence.
2. No one shall be held guilty of any penal offence on account of any act or omission which did not constitute a penal offence, under national or international law, at the time when it was committed. Nor shall a heavier penalty be imposed than the one that was applicable at the time the penal offence was committed.

Article 12
No one shall be subjected to arbitrary interference with his privacy, family, home or correspondence, nor to attacks upon his honour and reputation. Everyone has the right to the protection of the law against such interference or attacks.

Article 13
1. Everyone has the right to freedom of movement and residence within the borders of each State.
2. Everyone has the right to leave any country, including his own, and to return to his country.

Article 14
1. Everyone has the right to seek and to enjoy in other countries asylum from persecution.

2. This right may not be invoked in the case of prosecutions genuinely arising from non-political crimes or from acts contrary to the purposes and principles of the United Nations.

Article 15
1. Everyone has the right to a nationality.
2. No one shall be arbitrarily deprived of his nationality nor denied the right to change his nationality.

Article 16
1. Men and women of full age, without any limitation due to race, nationality or religion, have the right to marry and to found a family. They are entitled to equal rights as to marriage, during marriage and at its dissolution.
2. Marriage shall be entered into only with the free and full consent of the intending spouses.
3. The family is the natural and fundamental group unit of society and is entitled to protection by society and the State.

Article 17
1. Everyone has the right to own property alone as well as in association with others.
2. No one shall be arbitrarily deprived of his property.

Article 18
Everyone has the right to freedom of thought, conscience and religion; this right includes freedom to change his religion or belief, and freedom, either alone or in community with others and in public or private, to manifest his religion or belief in teaching, practice, worship and observance.

Article 19
Everyone has the right to freedom of opinion and expression; this right includes freedom to hold opinions without interference and to seek, receive and impart information and ideas through any media and regardless of frontiers.

Article 20
1. Everyone has the right to freedom of peaceful assembly and association.
2. No one may be compelled to belong to an association.

Article 21
1. Everyone has the right to take part in the government of his country, directly or through freely chosen representatives.
2. Everyone has the right of equal access to public service in his country.
3. The will of the people shall be the basis of the authority of government; this will shall be expressed in periodic and genuine elections which shall be by universal and equal suffrage and shall be held by secret vote or by equivalent free voting procedures.

Article 22
Everyone, as a member of society, has the right to social security and is entitled to realisation, through national effort and international co-operation and in accordance with the organization and resources of each State, of the economic, social and cultural rights indispensable for his dignity and the free development of his personality.

Article 23
1. Everyone has the right to work, to free choice of employment, to just and favorable conditions of work and to protection against unemployment.
2. Everyone, without any discrimination, has the right to equal pay for equal work.
3. Everyone who works has the right to just and favourable remuneration ensuring for himself and his family an existence worthy of human dignity, and supplemented, if necessary, by other means of social protection.
4. Everyone has the right to form and to join trade unions for the protection of his interest.

Article 24
Everyone has the right to rest and leisure, including reasonable limitation of working hours and periodic holidays with pay.

Article 25
1. Everyone has the right to a standard of living adequate for the health and well-being of himself and of his family including food, clothing, housing and medical care and necessary social services, and the right to security in the event of unemploy-

ment, sickness, disability, widowhood, old age or other lack of livelihood in circumstances beyond his control.
2. Motherhood and childhood are entitled to special care and assistance. All children, whether born in or out of wedlock, shall enjoy the same social protection.

Article 26
1. Everyone has the right to education. Education shall be free, at least in the elementary and fundamental stages. Elementary education shall be compulsory. Technical and professional education shall be made generally available and higher education shall be equally accessible to all on the basis of merit.
2. Education shall be directed to the full development of the human personality and to the strengthening of respect for human rights and fundamental freedoms. It shall promote understanding, tolerance and friendship among all nations, racial or religious groups, and shall further the activities of the United Nations for the maintenance of peace.
3. Parents have a prior right to choose the kind of education that shall be given to their children.

Article 27
1. Everyone has the right freely to participate in the cultural life of the community, to enjoy the arts and to share in scientific advancement and its benefits.
2. Everyone has the right to the protection of the moral and material interests resulting from any scientific, literary or artistic production of which he is the author.

Article 28
Everyone is entitled to a social and international order in which the rights and freedoms set forth in this Declaration can be fully realised.

Article 29
1. Everyone has duties to the community in which alone the free and full development of his personality is possible.
2. In the exercise of his rights and freedoms, everyone shall be subject only to such limitations as are determined by law solely for the purpose of secur-

ing due recognition and respect for the rights and freedoms of others and of meeting the just requirements of morality, public order and the general welfare in a democratic society.

3. These rights and freedoms may in no case be exercised contrary to the purposes and principles of the United Nations.

Article 30

Nothing in this Declaration may be interpreted as implying for any State, group or person any right to engage in any activity or to perform any act aimed at the destruction of any of the rights and freedoms set forth herein.

HUMAN RIGHTS: A WESTERN CONSTRUCT WITH LIMITED APPLICABILITY

Adamantia Pollis and Peter Schwab

Adamantia Pollis is Professor Emerita and Senior Lecturer in Political Science at the New School for Social Research, New York. She has published numerous articles on topics related to Greece, Cyprus, and the Southern Mediterranean region and on rights more generally. She is co-editor with Peter Schwab of Human Rights: Cultural and Ideological Perspectives *(1979),* Toward a Human Rights Framework *(1982), and* Human Rights: New Perspectives, New Realities *(2000).*

Peter Schwab is Professor of Political Science at the State University of New York at Purchase. In addition to the co-edited books listed above, he is the author of Cuba: Confronting the US Embargo *(1999) and* Africa: A Continent Self-Destructs *(2001).*

Pollis and Schwab claim that international documents such as the Universal Declaration of Human Rights contain strong biases that reflect Western conceptions of human rights. As evidence for this cultural and ideological ethnocentrism, they cite the emphasis given in Western political thinking both to individual civil and political rights over economic rights and to individual freedom over social relations and community values. They question the assumption that doctrines originating in the West and concerned with human rights are applicable in non-Western contexts, and they call for greater efforts to formulate human rights that are truly universal and capture values common to a multiplicity of philosophies and divergent beliefs in the world.

Recently there has been increasing concern that notwithstanding the Charter of the United Nations and the Universal Declaration of Human Rights, universal consensus on the concept of human rights and the content of fundamental freedoms does not exist. It is becoming increasingly evident that the Western political philosophy upon which the Charter and the Declaration are based provides only one particular interpretation of human rights, and that this Western notion may not be successfully applicable to non-Western areas for several reasons: ideological differences whereby economic rights are given priority over individual civil and political rights and cultural differences whereby the philosophic underpinnings defining human nature and the relationship of individuals to others and to society are markedly at variance with Western individualism. Consequently, application in non-Western countries of Western-originated doctrines such as the Universal Declaration of Human Rights has frequently meant that legal norms whose implementation is contingent upon the state lack the substantive meaning such rights have in the West.

If it is valid that there is no universal concurrence as to the meaning of human rights, human dignity, and freedom — and in fact there is marked diversity of opinion — then efforts to enforce the provisions of the Universal Declaration of Human Rights in states that do not accept its underlying values are bound to fail. What is needed is a rethinking of the conception of human rights; an effort must be made to distill from the multiplicity of philosophies and ideologies and their divergent values any universals that may exist. The analysis that follows is a beginning effort to deal with the problem of cultural and ideological ethnocentrism in the area of human rights and human dignity.

Human Rights and the West

From the seventeenth to the twentieth centuries in England, France, and the United States, the legal and political roots of human rights were formulated. Through the philosophic and legal writings of Grotius, Locke, Montesquieu, and Jefferson a new conception of popular sovereignty and individual rights was conceived. This in turn was grounded in a new view of the nature of man, and the relationship of each individual to others and to society.[1] From these revolutionary ideas stemmed the basic premises of the Declaration of Independence and the Declaration of the Rights of Man and Citizen: "all men are created equal ... endowed ... with certain inalienable rights ... among these ... life, liberty, and the pursuit of happiness"; "Men are born and remain free and equal in rights, the aim of every political association is the preservation of the natural and imprescriptible rights of man. These rights are liberty, the ownership of property, security and the right to resist oppression." These radical concepts understood man as an autonomous being possessed of rights in nature, rights that were not dependent upon a sovereign grant or legislative statute. Liberty and democracy, therefore, were not consequences of a particular set of political institutions, but were based on natural rights that were prior to and supreme over the sovereignty of the state. The late eighteenth century revolutions in the United States and France legitimized within the context of the state the philosophical and legal justifications of natural rights. That man had certain inherent natural rights "found practical expression and legal reality in the historical documents that embodied the constitutional principles of the new American state and of revolutionary France."[2]

The seventeenth and eighteenth centuries witnessed such landmarks as the English Petition of Rights (1627), the Habeas Corpus Act (1679), the American Declaration of Independence (1776), the United States Constitution (1787), the American Bill of Rights (1791), and the French Declaration of the Rights of Man and Citizen (1789), all of which constitutionalized and institutionalized a Western standard of human rights and liberties. That standard still exists today. As Myres McDougal, Harold Lasswell, and Lung-Chu Chen wrote in 1969:

> Let it be said immediately that a certain minimum of values indispensable to a dignified human existence must be described as immune from all claims of derogation at all times. Notably among these are the right to life, freedom from torture and inhuman treatment, freedom from involuntary human experimentations, freedom from slavery, the slave trade and servitude, freedom from imprisonment for debt, freedom from retroactive application of criminal punishment, the right to recognition as a human being, and freedom of thought conscience and religion. These rights and freedoms are indispensable to a dignified human existence and remain wholly intact from derogation upon grounds of crisis. In terms of our basic postulation, it can never be necessary to encroach upon these rights and freedoms, even in times of emergency.[3]

The seventeenth- and eighteenth-century postulate that there are rights and freedoms that are not amenable to state legislation, control, or abrogation, has been carried through in the twentieth century in the conception of "minimum of values."

It is important to note that the philosophic and ideological revolution of the seventeenth and eighteenth centuries regarding the nature of man and his inalienable rights was accompanied by radical socioeconomic transformations and changing societal values. In Western Europe the communal bonds of feudalism had collapsed and extended family ties were disrupted by the Industrial Revolution — by urbanization and the factory. A capitalist system came into existence and a new industrial class rebelled against the constraints of government, demanding political participation and political freedoms and arguing the ethics of social contract. In the United States a new land was being settled where individual initiative and competition frequently were requisites for survival. Hence the new philosophic doctrines of the autonomous individual and his inherent rights were assimilated both as an explanation of and a justification for the new social order. In time such doctrines became part of the prevailing shared values of Western societies.

Whereas the seventeenth to the nineteenth centuries were eras during which the concept of natural rights was institutionalized within the context of the nation-state in the West, the twentieth century witnessed the extension of this concept and its institutionalization in regional and international organizations, particularly in the Council of Europe and the United Nations. The Universal Declaration of Human Rights, adopted by the United Nations General Assembly in 1948, for example, is based on the Jeffersonian credo, and states in its preamble that "recognition of the *inherent dignity and of the equal and inalienable rights* of all members of the human family is the foundation of freedom, justice and peace in the world ..." (our emphasis). Egon Schwelb, in his study of human rights, categorically states that the roots of the Universal Declaration of Human Rights "are in the legal and political thought of the seventeenth to twentieth centuries" in France, England, and the United States.[4]

Hence it is clear that human rights as a twentieth-century concept and as embedded in the United Nations can be traced to the particular experiences of England, France, and the United States. In turn the experiences of these states through the centuries have led directly to the concern with human rights as expressed in the Universal Declaration. It should not be forgotten that the San Francisco Conference which established the United Nations in 1945 was dominated by the West, and that the Universal Declaration of Human Rights was adopted at a time when most Third World countries were still under colonial rule. Thus to argue that human rights has a standing which is universal in character is to contradict historical reality. What ought to be admitted by those who argue universality is that human rights as a Western concept

based on natural right *should* become the standard upon which all nations ought to agree, recognizing however, that this is only one particular value system. And in fact, as McDougal makes evident, this is what is really being said.[5] The critical question, however, is whether there is a universal consensus regarding the Western definition of human rights based on natural right or whether there are alternative conceptions of human rights and human dignity that merit consideration. Before discussing the extent to which individual and human rights based on Western philosophy are accepted or rejected by non-Western nations and the extent to which alternative concepts may contain significant values, it will be instructive to investigate the extent to which the rights embodied in the Universal Declaration of Human Rights are obligatory or enforceable on the states of the world.

Obligation and Enforcement of the Universal Declaration of Human Rights

On December 20, 1948 the General Assembly of the United Nations, by a vote of 48 for, none against, and eight abstentions (including the Soviet Union, South Africa, and Saudi Arabia), adopted and proclaimed the Universal Declaration of Human Rights. Although not spelled out in detail, the Declaration indicated that human rights and freedoms were related to "race, colour, sex, language, religion, political or other opinion, national or social origin, property, birth or other status" (in Article 2). A perusal of the provisions regarding rights makes it abundantly clear that the overriding philosophy underlying them is the Western concept of political liberty and democracy, inclusive of property rights in contradistinction to economic rights or egalitarianism. The rights and freedoms enumerated in the articles are life, liberty, the illegality of torture, equality before the law, prohibition against arbitrary arrest, fair trial by impartial tribunal, the right to be presumed innocent until proven guilty, freedom of travel, the right to marry freely, the right to own property, freedom of assembly, and so on. The primacy of political rights in the Declaration is clear: of the thirty articles only three, one of them dealing with property rights, can be considered as dealing with economic rights.[6] In prefacing his discussion of human rights, Moses Moskowitz articulates the extent to which the political philosophy of liberalism has dominated the conceptualization of the Universal Declaration of Human Rights over and above any other system of values or any other ideology such as socialism:

> Two hundred years ago Immanuel Kant argued that it was illusory to expect an international association to enforce peace among nations without a common morality of democratic values. ... He asserted the rights and liberties of the individual as a condition for all true morality.[7]

The Declaration itself reads like a political "bill of rights," and according to Schwelb that is precisely how it was viewed during the drafting stage.[8]

Many authorities on human rights contend that the Declaration is not merely a recommendation to states, but a set of standards that must be applied. According to Leland Goodrich, it seems evident that at the time of adoption, although the Declaration was passed by the General Assembly without a dissenting vote, "it was not a treaty and was not intended to impose legal obligations."[9] In the words of Eleanor Roosevelt, who chaired the Commission of Human Rights, the Declaration is "not a treaty; it is not an international agreement, it is not and does not purport to be a statement of law or of legal obligation."[10] Nevertheless it is argued that subsequent international conventions have reaffirmed the Declaration's principles and consequently, regardless of the original intent of the drafters of the Universal Declaration of Human Rights, it has now become mandatory for at least the signatory states. One example cited is the convention on the Elimination of all Forms of Racial Discrimination, adopted by the General Assembly and put into force in 1969, which states in Article 6 that "parties shall assure to everyone within their jurisdiction effective protection and remedies ... against any acts of racial discrimination which violate his human rights and fundamental freedoms. ..." Similarly the International Covenant on

Economic, Social, and Cultural Rights (1966) which, in the words of its Preamble, was written in "accordance with the Universal Declaration of Human Rights," is considered a legitimizing action making the Declaration binding on member states.

Others argue that since the Declaration has been in existence for nearly 30 years it has become binding under customary law. But as J. L. Brierly explains, this is dubious.

> Custom ... is a usage felt by those who follow it to be an obligatory one. There must be present a feeling that, if the usage is departed from some form of sanction will probably or at any rate ought to, fall on the transgressor.[11]

The Statute of the International Court of Justice specified in Article 38 that customary law can be considered binding when the alleged custom shows "evidence of a general practice accepted as law." Hence although what is customary law cannot be precisely defined, the principles of human rights do not fall within the domain of customary law and states are not bound by them. If one surveys the states that compose the international community, no general practice regarding human rights is evident and there is no feeling or expectation of sanctions if the Declaration of Human Rights or the subsequent covenants are violated.

By contrast, among states in the West, for example in the Council of Europe, some human rights are perceived as inviolate by the state under any conditions whereas others can be infringed only under extraordinary political circumstances such as a clear national emergency.[12] The European Convention on Human Rights, unlike the Universal Declaration, has a standing in law and is obligatory on the signatories. Evidence of this perception has been the relative willingness of the European states to abide by findings charging violation of rights by the European Commission of Human Rights and the European court of Human Rights. Most striking was the action of the Council of Europe in the expulsion of Greece in 1969 for gross violations of human rights, a decision that was not implemented due to

Greece's withdrawal the day prior to the vote for expulsion.[13]

To the extent that the Western European states and the United States adhere to the principles of human rights and are responsive to criticisms for their violation, it is not a consequence of the European Convention of Human Rights or the Universal Declaration of Human Rights. On the contrary, the historical experiences of both these areas had defined the issue well before 1948. Both in Western Europe and in the United States conceptions of individual human rights were assimilated over the centuries into the political cultures of these societies. The holocaust of World War II precipitated the drafting of the Universal Declaration of Human Rights which, however, was an articulation and a reinforcement of political values that had a prior existence.

It is frequently argued that many non-Western states have incorporated the values and rights of the Universal Declaration into their own constitutions and into the charters of regional organizations such as the Organization of American States (OAS) and the Organization of African Unity (OAU), hence giving these rights a universal legal standing. But such a claim ignores several factors that vitiate these rights and make them substantively meaningless. The dominance of the United States over Latin America, particularly in 1948 when the OAS was formed, is well known. Furthermore, at the time of independence countries under colonial rule wrote constitutions in accord with and often along with former colonial administrators. For British colonies the Westminster model, including its provisions for individual rights, became practically the *sine qua non* for independence. The failure of the Westminster model is now generally accepted in light of the prevalence of military regimes that in many cases threw out colonial-inspired constitutions along with civilian regimes. Even in cases where provisions guaranteeing human rights remain in the books such as in Senegal, or where constitutions are not a direct colonial legacy, as in Greece, human rights are perceived as a grant by the state and as something that the state can give or withhold. In turn the charters of regional organizations,

also written under external pressure and influence, do not necessarily bind member states to adhere to human rights. As the Organization of African Unity charter states in its preamble, it adheres "to the principles of the Charter of the United Nations and of the Universal Declaration of Human Rights as a solid foundation for peaceful and positive cooperation among states."[14] No member state is bound in any way to enforce the provisions of the Universal Declaration.

Summarizing then, in essence the Universal Declaration of Human Rights is a document whose underlying values are democratic and libertarian, based on the notion of atomized individuals possessed of certain inalienable rights in nature. These political values, as distinct from economic rights or communal rights, can be traced directly to the experiences of France, England, and the United States. The Declaration is predicated on the assumption that Western values are paramount and ought to be extended to the non-Western world. It is clear that at present the Universal Declaration of Human Rights is not binding upon states; many adhere to the International Court of Justice's interpretation of customary law implying that the Declaration is unenforceable since its functional acceptance and usage is limited. States do violate the Declaration, they do not feel bound by it, and there is little evidence that the practice of states regarding human rights follows any established norm. The discussion that follows will analyze some of the factors that account for the neglect and violation of human rights in regions other than the West.

Human Rights and the Non-Western World: Cultural, Developmental, and Ideological Differences

An interrelated and interdependent set of factors account for the limited viability and applicability of the Western concepts of human rights and human dignity in the non-Western world. Broadly speaking these factors can be divided into two categories: the cultural patterns and the developmental goals of new states including the ideological framework within which they were formulated. Traditional cultures did not view the individual as autonomous and possessed of rights above and prior to society. Whatever the specific social relations, the individual was conceived of as an integral part of a greater whole, of a "group" within which one had a defined role and status. The basic unit of traditional society has varied — the kinship system, the clan, the tribe, the local community — but not the individual. (This notion of the group defining the self, it should be mentioned, was equally valid in the West prior to the advent of individualism.) The colonial experience in the Third World did little to alter traditional conceptualizations of the social order. Regardless of specific colonial policies and political structures, all colonized peoples were subject to ultimate authority in the form of the colonial ruler, and doctrines of inalienable rights — clearly a threat to the interests of the colonial powers — were not disseminated.

With independence a multiplicity of new "sovereign" nation-states were established and at least in theory these new entities defined group membership. The notion of the primacy of the group and the submission of the individual to the group persisted, although the confines and boundaries of the group had changed to become coterminous with the state. As a consequence whatever rights an individual possesses are given to him by the state, and this state retains the right and the ability to curtail individual rights and freedoms for the greater good of the group. Inevitably constitutional government has come to be identified with a particular set of democratic political institutions but not with the doctrines of individualism or inalienable rights which constitute the philosophic underpinnings of democracy in the West.

The pervasiveness of the notion of the "group" rather than the "individual" in many cultures is evident even in concepts of property ownership. The Universal Declaration maintains in Article 17 that "everyone has the right to own property. ..." Yet in many cultures, among them the Gojami-Amhara of Ethiopia, land is owned communally and there is no "right" to individual ownership of holdings. This conception of social ownership predates by centuries any Marxist or socialist doctrines, but it is evident how such traditional conceptions can be incorporated into the different ideological frameworks of Third World countries. Furthermore, Article 16 states that the "family is the fundamental group unit of society." For many societies the nuclear family (as implied in this article) clearly is not the fundamental unit; in hunting and gathering societies the kinship group, and in China the clan, have been more "natural."[15]

The irrelevance of the Western conception of human rights founded on natural rights doctrines is not rooted solely in traditional cultural patterns, but is also a consequence of the articulated modernization goals of Third World countries. The ideology of modernization and development that has attained universal status has come to be understood primarily in terms of economic development. The colonial experience of economic exploitation gave credence to the notion of human dignity as consisting of economic rights rather than civil or political rights. Freedom from starvation, the right for all to enjoy the material benefits of a developed economy, and freedom from exploitation by colonial powers became the articulated goals of many Third World countries. The strategies that evolved for the attainment of these goals incorporated an admixture of old concepts and values frequently reinterpreted and redefined in light of contemporary realities and goals. Thus the state was to replace traditional group identities but was to retain the same supremacy as traditional groups. By the same token the state's responsibility is to free its people from colonial exploitation and to attain economic betterment. Essentially this is the conceptual framework that has structured the world view of many Third World countries and within which human rights and human dignity are understood. Democratic government is perceived as an institutional framework through which the goals of the state are to be achieved, and if it fails or becomes an impediment it can be dispensed with impunity. Individual political rights, so revered in the West, at most take second place to the necessity of establishing the legitimacy of the new group — the state — and to the priority of economic rights that necessitate economic modernization.

It is within this context that the doctrines and policies of many African states can be understood. As early as the 1960s such leaders as Nkrumah, Toure, and Nyerere rejected democratic political institutions as undesirable for their societies. They argued forcefully that a one party state, by contrast to a multiparty state, was necessary because Ghana, Guinea, and Tanzania needed to prevent political dissension among their populations. The multiparty state was perceived as counterproductive both to the development of a nation-state and to the development of the economy; parties represented classes or ethnic or tribal groups and would foster political dissension at a time when those states had to concentrate on national unity and on social and economic change. As Nkrumah said, "the Convention People's Party (CPP) is Ghana and Ghana is the CPP."[16] Thus the CPP could do no wrong because it spoke for the entire population. With the establishment of priorities and of one-party ideologies in the new states, politically restrictive statutes were adopted.

The conjunction of a traditional culture that defined the individual in terms of group membership, the need to transpose this group identity to the nation-state level, a definition of modernization in terms of economic development, and the evolution of the notion of a one-party state as the embodiment of the people facilitated the adoption of decrees limiting freedom of speech, the adoption of preventive detention laws, the outlawing of rival political parties, the placing of the judiciary under party control, and the incorporation of all voluntary associations under the rubric of the one party. These actions were not viewed as antidemocratic but as requisites whereby ethnically diverse, extremely poor states could create the unified political framework essential for economic development. As Nkrumah and Nyerere often said, if political differences were permitted to rule the state the economy would be stymied as the unity necessary for development would be absent.[17] Social change, a process fraught with political problems, was the major priority, and its perceived importance is evident in the national leaderships' argument that "the maintenance of order becomes necessary if national goals are to be concentrated

upon and achieved."[18] Democratic political institutions were to be sacrificed to some future time, while economic development was to be concentrated upon. The fact that many of these states (Ghana as a case in point) have failed to attain their articulated goals does not invalidate the conceptual framework in terms of which Third World leaders perceive their goals and the strategy of their attainment.[19]

It is perhaps instructive to keep in mind the experience of Turkey which more than 50 years ago was one of the first states to consciously and explicitly embark on a program of "westernization" (as Kemal Ataturk labeled it). Ataturk attempted to transform the Ottoman Empire into a modern Turkish nation-state. His concept of modernization did not include an ideology of individual political rights or even democratic government. In reaction to the defeat and dismemberment of the Ottoman Empire at the hands of advanced industrial states, just as African states reacted to colonial exploitation and domination, Ataturk was concerned with secularizing society, introducing a modern educational system, adopting Western technology and industry, creating new political structures, and defining Turkish nationalism.[20] On the question of even a formally democratic polity he argued that the above-mentioned goals had priority over such institutions as a multiparty system; only after Turkey had attained the goals of modernization and the unity of the state could it afford and risk a democratic political system. Ataturk, who led his revolution in the aftermath of defeat in World War I, predated the post-World War II universalization of the goal of economic growth through economic planning. Even so, he did not consider individual human rights or a multiparty system as ingredients in the modernization efforts.

The role of the state in the contemporary non-Western world cannot be overemphasized. Regardless of articulated ideology the underlying conceptual framework views the state — sometimes but not always equated with the party — as the communal group through which the goals of economic development and modernization (which will provide for human dignity) will be attained. The state or party is the dispenser of all political and economic goods and economic goods have the highest priority. In fact, in the Nkrumah school of thought, democracy itself was seen as having an economic meaning: it enabled masses of poverty-stricken people to secure minimal economic liberties. The dominant role of the state and restrictions on political liberties were not consequences only of the corporation of traditional values into a new framework and of the ideological rhetoric of socialism, but also of the empirical realities facing many new countries. The new African states were inadequate in infrastructure, had little capital for development, had extraordinarily high rates of unemployment and underemployment, were basically one-crop economies at the mercy of Western capital, and had a history of oppression through the slave trade. Colonialism left them bereft of viable political and economic structures, concurrently disrupting and distorting traditional institutions. Toure and Nkrumah saw little choice but to make the state or party the instrument of change, and economic development the primary goal. Freedom from want, from hunger, and from economic deprivation necessitated limiting political liberties that could destroy the party or state in its initial stages. Developmental success was seen as dependent on preventing opposition by those who propagated alternative political and economic models. In this context human rights were of limited importance or were directly related to the attainment of self-sufficiency, which in turn was a function of the state. In some cases this led to state capitalism, in some to state socialism. The impact of the Nkrumah ideology was widespread; even pro-Western states such as Senegal adopted a similar political framework premised on a similar conceptualization. By the 1970s African leaders generally perceived this ideology of economic statism not as pro-Western or pro-Eastern but as a specifically African solution to their monumental problems.[21]

In state constitutions and in the OAU charter, African states have given lip service to the Universal Declaration of Human Rights, and they have affixed their signatures to United Nations documents that reinforce the Declaration. It is evident from the above analysis, however, that human rights are not perceived along Western lines by African leaders. The world is seen in economic terms that are more akin to those of Karl Marx than to the classical economists and liberal political thinkers. Human rights as formulated in the West, at least in their political and legal aspects, can come into existence only after a stable economic life with a minimum of economic prosperity is assured to the African population. Furthermore, it is critical to realize that the Western-based notions of human rights, to the extent that they are articulated by Third World political elites, reflect these elites' "westernization." It cannot be assumed that the mass of people hold these concepts.

The Western conception of human rights is not only inapplicable to third World countries or to socialist states, but also to some states that profess to adhere to democratic precepts and to states that are considered part of the West. The cultural heritages of Spain, Portugal, and Greece do not include a Western conception of inalienable human rights, any more than do the African. All three countries have recently emerged from periods of dictatorial rule. Democracy is understood as a particular set of political institutions, including a multiparty system, but the philosophic underpinnings differ from those of the West. Rights are political and legal, and not attributes of individuals *qua* individuals. The state retains a preeminent position and has an existence other than and prior to the individuals that compose it.[22]

In fact the absence of a concept of inalienable human rights indirectly facilitated the military takeover of Greece in 1967 and the subsequent dictatorial rule. The justification that the military officers used — the threat of chaos stemming from demonstrations, strikes, and protest marches — seemed valid ground to many Greeks for the abrogation of political freedoms. Democracy is seen by the Greeks and other peoples as a set of formal institutions and individual rights that emanate from and are granted by the state, rather than being inalienable and natural. No rights exist except those specified by law, and if there is no law protecting a particular right, that right does not exist — and hence there is no question of its violation or infringement. Illustrative were the trials of torturers held after the collapse of the Greek military dictatorship in 1974. The torturers were not charged with gross violations of human rights, but with "misuse of authority"; there was and is no law specifically making torture illegal.[23] Furthermore, the absence of a notion of the autonomous individual and of individual rights, and the communal basis of traditional Greek society has led in Greece to an exalted view of the state — which is perceived as the embodiment of the Greek people.

In summary then, it is evident that in most states in the world, human rights as defined by the West are rejected or, more accurately, are meaningless. Most states do not have a cultural heritage of individualism, and the doctrines of inalienable human rights have been neither disseminated nor assimilated. More significantly the state — as a substitute for the traditional communal group — has become the embodiment of the people, and the individual has no rights or freedoms that are natural and outside the purview of the state. It is a Platonic world in that Plato "justified the ultimate right of the state to suppress dissidents since the individual owes his existence to and was a product of, the state."[24] As Indira Gandhi said, "it is not individuals who have rights but states."[25] Further limiting the significance of Third World countries of Western conceptions of human rights are the societal goals and priorities set by their leaderships. Economic development is the primary objective, for it is only through this that economic rights can be attained, and these provide for human dignity by freeing individuals from exploitation and dependence. Perhaps the best that can be expected in the political realm is what may be happening in India — the establishment of political institutions that define the rights of individuals not under the rubric of natural law but under the structure of political law.

Toward a Reevaluation of Human Rights

The cultural patterns, ideological underpinnings, and developmental goals of non-Western and socialist states are markedly at variance with the prescriptions of the Universal Declaration of Human Rights. Efforts to impose the Declaration as it currently stands not only reflect a moral chauvinism and ethnocentric bias but are also bound to fail. In fact, the evidence of the last few decades shows increasing violations of the Declaration rather than increasing compliance.

The conceptualization of human rights is in need of rethinking. It should be recognized that the Western notion of human rights evolved historically, under a particular set of circumstances, in the most highly industrialized and developed areas of the world — areas that subsequently have dominated the remainder of the world. While espousing and to a great extent implementing human rights doctrines domestically, the Western industrial states nonetheless denied them to peoples they controlled for generations. In large measure both the nationalist movement efforts to create new nations and socialist revolutionary movements are reactions and responses to this domination and control. Hence, rather than focusing on additional legal mechanisms for imposing the West's philosophic doctrines of the individual and inalienable human rights on the non-Western world, discussion of the issue of human rights should begin with the differing historical and contemporary circumstances of non-Western societies. Given differences in historical experience and contemporary conditions, what was a "natural" evolution in the West may not appear so "natural" in the Third World.

Realization that differing historical experiences and cultural patterns have led to differing notions of human nature and to marked differences in the articulated goals of political elites should facilitate investigation and analysis of those fundamental aspects of society from which may be derived a new conceptualization of universal human rights. All societies cross-culturally and historically manifest conceptions of human dignity and human rights. If the notion of human rights is to be a viable universal concept it will be necessary to analyze the differing cultural and ideological conceptions of human rights and the impact of one on the other. There are many societies in which human dignity is culturally defined in terms of excelling in the fulfillment of one's obligation to the group, a concept that has been incorporated in a radically altered form in socialist ideology. In many states human rights are ideologically defined in terms of one's being a functionally useful member of society — through guaranteed employment and provision of the basic needs of life: food, shelter, and clothing. From this perspective, clearly, Western countries can be accused of gross violations of human rights.

In the international arena and among many human rights advocates the argument is couched in terms of political versus economic rights; which of the two has, or should have, priority. Such a simplistic categorization is reductionist and overlooks the philosophies and cultural premises underlying such a division. The Western notion of inalienable rights, whose substance is predominantly political and civil, nevertheless includes the right to private property, a right that is central to an understanding of the development of Western pluralist and capitalist societies. Similarly, despite their apparent emphasis on economic rights, socialist societies incorporate notions of political participation. Thus although the ontology and ideology of societies differ, they incorporate the totality of what is and what should be.

Despite divergences in conceptions of what constitutes the substance of human dignity there seem to be certain shared commonalities that warrant further investigation. All societies impose restraints on the use of force and violence by their members and all apply sanctions on those who, within their particular cultural or ideological context, violate their norms and values. Hence it is important to analyze both issues further. What are the societal and political limits on the use of force or violence, and to what extent and in terms of what criteria is individual or group behavior restrained? No cultural or ideological system, for example, condones arbitrary and indiscriminate destruction of life or incarceration. Thus the killings in Uganda and Ethiopia, genocide in Paraguay, and torture in Iran and Chile are not justifiable in terms of any philosophical system. Such actions, in addition to raising the basic moral question of the right to life, are arbitrary and without any specification as to the violations that lead to such extreme sanctions. If a differentiation were made in terms of the ideological or cultural context

in which violations of human rights took place, then it would be easier, for example, to obtain broad African support for sanctions against Idi Amin. He would be hard pressed to justify his mass killings and torture in terms of any ideology.

Clearly there are marked differences in the specification of the areas where conformity is demanded by a polity. In the West violations of property rights are considered crimes justifying sanctions and punishment for the transgressor; in socialist societies dissent from the official ideology is considered a crime and elicits sanctions; and in many traditional societies ostracism is the consequence when norms are violated.

If a meaningful conception of human rights is to be formulated, the interrelationship between human rights and socioeconomic developments must be scrutinized. Historically Western Europe underwent an era of absolute monarchy and state building before any notion of individual human rights was extant. Given the fact that many non-Western countries are currently undergoing the process of state building — in fact attempting to form a state and a nation simultaneously — and therefore lack consensus regarding the state and the rules of the game, is a Western conception of human rights feasible? To what extent have social, political, and economic ferment eroded traditional conceptions of rights and human dignity without the formulation and implementation of alternative or reinterpreted concepts of human rights? Historical analysis of the dissemination of human rights doctrines in the West, and the question of requisites for their existence, may shed some light on the conditions prevailing in non-Western societies today.

In the contemporary world, where the legitimate order is one of sovereign nation-states, all societies regardless of ideological commitments violate their particular conceptions of human rights and human dignity under certain conditions. A more extensive investigation of the situational and empirical factors both internal and external to the state that may constrain the implementation of human rights would seem critical. In the United States for example, the perceived threat of communism was used as the justification for the infringement and violation of the civil and political rights of many individuals, particularly during the McCarthy era. Hence an investigation of the restraints, "perceived" or "real," under which Western and non-Western countries operate in implementing human rights may lead to a clarification of what societies believe constitute "emergencies" justifying restrictions of human rights however defined.

Several developments not only in third World countries but in the West itself raise fundamental issues regarding the boundaries within which doctrines of human rights are applicable. Human rights, whatever their ideological or cultural content, are largely viewed as extant within the confines of the state. The Western emphasis on individual rights vis-à-vis the state has resulted by and large in ignoring the entire question of communal rights. Yet in the West itself — in Great Britain with the resurgence of Scottish and Welsh nationalism, in France with the movement for autonomy in Brittany, in the United States with the American Indian Movement, and in Canada with the demand for independence by the French Canadians — charges of violations of human rights are heard with increasing frequency. This challenge in the West to individual rights operative within the state to the neglect of communal rights acquires heightened importance in the Third World. A significant philosophic and empirical question is the extent to which granting legitimacy to the state has enabled central governments to diffuse and destroy the authority of traditionalism and the rights incorporated within traditional societies without providing adequate alternatives. Concomitantly the universal legitimacy accorded to the state and the demands it places on all citizens — primarily but not limited to loyalty to the state and all the attendant requisite behavior — by definition limits and restricts individual political freedoms.

The many fundamental questions that have been raised in the previous pages should be more thoroughly analyzed if the prospects for a world community geared toward enhancing human dignity are to improve. Unfortunately not only do human rights as set forth in the Universal Declaration reveal a strong Western bias, but there has been a tendency to view human rights ahistorically and in isolation from their social, political, and economic milieu. What is being advocated here is a rethinking of the conception of human rights that both takes into account the diversity in substance that exists and recognizes the need for extensive analysis of the relationship of human rights to the broader societal context. Through this process it may become feasible to formulate human rights doctrines that are more validly universal than those currently propagated.

NOTES

1. It is interesting that the modern political philosophers with the exception of John Stuart Mill in *The Subjection of Women* (1869) did not concern themselves with women. Inalienable human rights were viewed as qualities of men, not of women.

2. Alessandra Luini del Russo, *International Protection of Human Rights* (Washington, DC: Lerner Law Book Co., 1971), p. 11.

3. Myres McDougal, H.D. Lasswell, and Lung-Chu Chen, "Human Rights and World Public Order: A framework for Policy Oriented Inquiry," *American Journal of International Law* (1969): 237.

4. Egon Schwelb, *Human Rights and the International Community* (Chicago: Quadrangle Books, 1964), p. 12.

5. See McDougal et al., "Human Rights," pp. 237-69.

6. Articles 17, 23, and 24. Article 17 deals with private property rights; Article 23 with the right to work, equal pay for equal work, and just remuneration; and Article 24 with the right to leisure.

7. Moses Moskowitz, *The Politics and Dynamics of Human Rights* (Dobbs Ferry: Oceana Publications, 1968), p. 75.

8. Schwelb, *Human Rights*, p. 32.

9. Leland M. Goodrich, *The United Nations* (New York: Thomas Y. Crowell, 1959), p. 249.

10. United Nations General Assembly, Official Records: Third Session, First Part, Plenary, 180th Meeting (New York), p. 860.

11. J. L. Brierly, *The Law of Nations* (New York: Oxford University Press, 1963), p. 59.

12. See *Convention on the Council of Europe and Sup-*

porting Protocols. Collected Texts, European Convention on Human Rights (Strasbourg, 1977).

13. *New York Times*, December 13, 1969.

14. For the full charter see Colin Legum, *Pan-Africanism* (New York: Praeger, 1965).

15. For an interesting and significant study on the utilization of traditional notions of small group relatedness and its reinterpretation and restructuring within a socialist ideology see Martin King Whyte, *Small Groups and Political Ritual in China* (Los Angeles: University of California Press, 1974).

16. Kwame Nkrumah, *I Speak of Freedom* (New York: Praeger, 1961). See Chapter 6, "The Party and its Progress."

17. Julius K. Nyerere, *Freedom and Socialism* (London: Oxford University Press, 1968), see Chapter 26, "The Arusha Declaration and Ujamaa"; Nyerere, *Essays on Socialism* (London: Oxford University Press, 1968), pp. 1-12. Kwame Nkrumah, *Consciencism* (New York: Monthly Review Press, 1964), see Chapter 3.

18. Peter Schwab, "Human Rights in Ethiopia," *Journal of Modern African Studies* 14 (1976): 159.

19. An analysis of the failure of African and Asian countries to achieve their economic development goals and the growing disparity between the haves and the have-nots (both within countries such as Ghana and between the industrialized countries and the Third World) is beyond the scope of this essay.

20. Lord Kinross, *Ataturk: A Biography of Mustafa Kemal, Father of Modern Turkey* (New York: Morrow, 1965), p. 518. Ataturk's famous six principles were republicanism, nationalism, populism, elitism, secularism, and revolution.

21. Nyerere, "Socialism and Rural Development," in *Essays on Socialism.*

22. Adamantia Pollis, "The Impact of Traditional Cultural Patterns on Greek Politics," *The Greek Review of Social Research* 29 (1977).

23. For a criticism of Greece's failure, with the reestablishment of a parliamentary regime, to enact a law for torture see *Torture in Greece: The First Torturers' Trial 1975* (Amnesty International Publications, 1977).

24. Adamantia Pollis, "Traditional Cultural Patterns," p. 2.

25. *New York Times*, July 3, 1975.

GLOBALIZATION AND HUMAN RIGHTS

Jay Drydyk

Jay Drydyk teaches philosophy and is currently Chair of the Philosophy Department at Carleton University in Ottawa. He is co-editor of Global Justice, Global Democracy *(1997, with G. Peter Penz) and the author of articles on ethics, human rights, and international development.*

   Drydyk critically evaluates a wide range of views on the question of whether human rights are ethnocentric and biased in favor of Western values. He argues that we can formulate human rights that avoid the Eurocentrism evident in the dominant discourse on human rights and that are sensitive to cultural contexts. He discusses two areas affected by globalization as a way of defending the need for human rights and for an expansion of them. First, the damaging effects of globalization with respect to the subcontracting and the informalization of labor calls for the development of international labor rights. Second, an ever-growing context of a "global public sphere of moral deliberation" makes cross-cultural communication and agreement about the language of rights possible.

In the face of economic globalization, what are we to think of human rights? Globalization is a complex trend, including globalization of production processes, global capital mobility, neoliberal development agendas, and finally globalization of subcontracting and informalization of labour, as a source of competitive advantage. In much of the debate about globalization, the labour dimension — subcontracting and informalization of labour — tends to be overshadowed by the first three. My view is the opposite, that the labour dimension of globalization is the most important. In an orgy of subcontracting, employers all over the world have been eliminating jobs and shifting their work through labour contractors, nominal self-employment, and other schemes into the "informal sector," so that ever more of the work is performed by jobless workers, at low cost and with no security or regulation. As a result the movement of production to the South has not always brought jobs, much less prosperity.[1] The subcontracting trend, by itself, is clearly damaging to labour rights — for example, safety, equal pay for equal work, protec-

tion against unemployment, and the right to organize. Subcontracting and informalization of work also conspire with globalized production and finance to vitiate the taxation bases that nation-states need to finance their protection of social rights — for example, to subsistence, housing, health, education, social services, and welfare security.

Arguably these pressures undermine not only labour rights and social welfare rights but also civil and political rights. This argument exactly is made by Pierre Sané, the secretary-general of Amnesty International:

> The globalization of the world economy continues apace. The debt burden and the world recession exact their toll. Massive international speculation and large foreign investments chase the best returns. Millions of people move across borders in search of a better life, or any life at all. ...
>
> Everywhere, people feel powerless in the face of these global trends. And in reaction, they turn

to their group for identity. Religion, race, tribe, nation — the ties of blood — all take on a new importance. ...

The nation state cannot control the global trends. It cannot easily accommodate the demands of different groups living in the same country.

And so the institution itself loses legitimacy.

The question for us, therefore, is how to develop a global countermovement to protect all the rights of all the people from the global trends that threaten to destroy the very fabric of society in many countries. [I believe that] we need a new paradigm in which "substantive participation" — at local, national and international levels — is the primary goal, not an afterthought. It should integrate the values emerging from the human rights and other social movements that are developing worldwide. It should put back the human being as the subject of history.[2]

I. Eurocentrism

This raises a further question for philosophers. How well can such a movement be served by current conceptions of human rights? After all, aren't the received notions of human rights Eurocentric? If so, how could they serve the self-understanding of a movement that is to be global, culturally pluralistic, and counter-hegemonic to Northern capital? My answer is: it is not human rights that are Eurocentric, but only certain conceptions of human rights. Properly understood, human rights are justifiable from within all cultures. Moreover, current conceptions of human rights are not as narrow as they were in 1948, when the Universal Declaration was drafted. Nearly five decades of international dialogue have transformed human rights discourse in ways that are profoundly anti-Eurocentric, and further transformations are already under way.

A wide range of views are held on the Eurocentricity of human rights:

- The *triumphalist* view is that human rights are superior, and only Western cultures can support

them. Thus Jack Donnelly has argued that the concept of human rights is foreign to all but Western cultures.[3]

- The *rejectionist* view agrees that only Western cultures can support human rights, but it denies that human rights have any value. The Ayatollah Khomeini was a rejectionist, as he made perfectly clear when he said, "The Universal Declaration of Human Rights is a 'collection of mumbo-jumbo by disciples of Satan'" and "What they call human rights is nothing but a collection of corrupt rules worked out by Zionists to destroy all true religion."[4]

These two views agree that human rights concepts and beliefs are exclusively Western; they disagree as to whether human rights have any value. Alternatively, there are a number of views that both value human rights and argue for their justifiability within all existing cultures.

- *Assimilationists* argue that because we know, on independent grounds, that current international human right standards are more or less correct, further grounds can and ought to be found within all cultures for accepting them. Once this is done, according to Abdullahi Ahmed An-Na'im, human rights will have "cultural legitimacy," and they will not be so easily portrayed as foreign impositions.[5]
- *Revisionists* argue that human rights have been understood and justified within non-Western cultures all along, and they have been understood there perfectly well. This view has been espoused by the authors of the Universal Islamic Declaration of Human Rights of 1981, who claim that "Islam gave to mankind an ideal code of human rights fourteen centuries ago."[6]
- *Transformationists* argue for the most complex position:

  (i) In all cultural traditions, some people at some time or other have employed concepts of human rights that are "defective" in the sense that they limit human rights protection to in-groups, while out-groups are excluded.

  (ii) Still, there are features of cross-cultural

dialogue that forbid these sorts of defects —
if the dialogue is not abused.

(iii) Now let us say that an "incomplete" list
of human rights is one that overlooks certain
protections that people are due. These can
also be found in all cultural traditions.

(iv) On the other hand, there are resources of
moral and political experience, within all cultures, which argue strongly against this sort of
incompleteness. Therefore, a consistent and
complete knowledge of human rights can
emerge cross-culturally, if the dialogue is not
abused and if the relevant moral and political
experience is let into the dialogue, from all
quarters.

I will defend these four claims of the transfor-
mationist position in this and the next section.
First, though, it will be constructive to consider
what is mistaken about two of the other views: tri-
umphalism and rejectionism.

The Western triumphalist position on human
rights is represented prominently by Jack Donnelly. Typically Donnelly argues that the concept
of human rights is foreign to non-Western political
cultures. Depending on which culture is in question, he relies on one or another of the following
arguments. (1) Some basic protections that are
provided and justified in non-Western societies
and cultures are not universal; only some people
are protected, not all. (2) Some of these protections
are conceived as grants that the community gives
to people conditionally, because they accept
responsibilities to and within the community. In
other words, these protections are not thought of as
being owed to persons just because they are
persons. (3) In some non-Western contexts, basic
protections are not justified as entitlements inherently belonging to individuals; rather, they are justified as other people's duties.

The latter line of argument I find particularly
scandalous. It is quite right that in many cultures
the political discourse of duty is far more convincing than rights talk, because it has a deeper cultural
resonance. This difference is reflected in many of
the regional human rights documents. For
example, the document drafted in 1948 by the

Ninth International Conference of American States
was called the "American Declaration of the
Rights *and* Duties of Man." Chapter 1 lists the
Rights, and chapter 2 lists the duties. A similar
format is followed in the Banjul Declaration of the
Organization of African Unity: the twenty-six articles specifying rights in chapter 1 are followed by
a list of duties in articles 27, 28, and 29, chapter 2.
A comparable declaration for the member countries of ASEAN (Association of Southeast Asian
Countries) has been proposed not by the governments but by the ASEAN Regional Council, a non-
governmental organization composed of jurists
and others interested in human rights. As the document title—"Declaration of the Basic Duties of
ASEAN Peoples and Governments" — would
suggest, each article specifies a duty. In those articles in which rights are declared, they are presented as grounded in a specific duty.

For the moment, let us pass over the fact that the
ASEAN Declaration calls for more extensive protections than any Western government has ever
accepted. Imagine that a Western government and
an Asian government each provided its people with
exactly the same basic protections against the standard threats to life and development that you wish
to consider basic. Imagine, further, that these protections were justified, in the Western country, as
rights. In the Asian country, imagine that the very
same protections were conceived and justified as
duties. Donnelly would be committed to the absurd
position that the Asian country had no conception
of human rights. Yet, *ex hypothesi*, they provided
human rights protections identical to those provided in the West. What is scandalous about Donnelly's position is that it betrays a greater concern
for how people think about human rights than for
how well they protect them.

This is not only scandalous, but ironic. Donnelly
takes pains to distinguish the concept of human
rights from its various conceptions. Yet what he
has done is to replace the core working concept of
human rights with his own pet conceptions. If we
want to know what the core concept of "human
rights" is, then what we must want to know is what
this phrase is used to refer to. The workaday world
of human rights is focused on saving people's

lives, their wellness, and their basic opportunities. While there are some cultural barriers to recognizing the greatest dangers to life, wellness, and opportunity, there are not many, and they are not insurmountable. Cross-cultural understanding is not terribly difficult when we are dealing with what Henry Shue has called "the morality of the depths," where the dangers fall under commonly recognizable types, starting with threats to personal safety and threats to subsistence. Every type of danger is understood by certain standard threats that exemplify it. Standard threats vary from region to region, yet what may be a threat in one place (such as the risk of being struck by falling ice in Ottawa) can be understood as a threat elsewhere (for example, in Honduras) even though *there* it is no threat at all.

Following Shue, and indeed John Stuart Mill, I believe that calling for a human right to something is calling for social protection against standard threats that exemplify a particular type of danger for humans. The point of saying that the human right to free speech is honoured or implemented in, say, South Africa, is to say that social protection of free speech against standard threats of censorship and harassment is adequate there. The point of saying that there is a breakdown of the human right to shelter in, say, New York or London, is to say that social protection against homelessness is inadequate there. The point of saying that the human right to security was violated in East Timor is to say not only that social protection against violence failed, but also that the standard threat, here violence, against which people were to be protected, was willfully inflicted upon them. However human rights language may be used, it must refer to the presence, absence, or violation of social protection against standard threats exemplifying some type of danger to humans.

These dangers will be recognized differently, with different language and under different descriptions, in different cultural contexts. Protections against them will also be justified differently. But as long as this kind of protection can be described within a culture, no matter how it is conceived or described, then we cannot say, as Donnelly does, that the concept of this human right is foreign to this culture. The concept of universal health care seems foreign to the minds of many Americans; shall we infer that the concept of a human right to health protection is "foreign" to them?

Another one of Donnelly's usual lines of argument targets cultures that justify extensive protection for their members, but only as the result of duties that are owed to group members in recognition of their membership. This was indeed the case in many traditional African cultures. As Kwasi Wiredu points out with reference to the Akan peoples of West Africa,

> On the face of it, the normative layer in the Akan concept of person brings only obligations to the individual. In fact, however, these obligations are matched by a whole series of rights that accrue to the individual simply because he lives in a society in which everyone has those obligations.[7]

The notion that people are entitled to these protections is not absent from Akan thought; it is simply justified in other terms, in which recognition that humans are frail, vulnerable, and dependent on one another is central. Wiredu argues:

> A number of Akan sayings testify to this conception, which is at the root of Akan communalism. One ... points out that to be human is to be in need of help. Literally it says simply "a human being needs help" (*onipa hyia mmoa*). The Akan verb *hyia* means "is in need of." In this context it also has the connotation of merits, "is entitled to," so that the maxim may also be interpreted as asserting that a human being, simply because he is a human being, is entitled to help from others.[8]

Nor are the rights to which a person is entitled limited in this culture to the matters of subsistence and material need. As Wiredu goes on to say,

> One finds a veritable harvest of human rights. Akan thought recognized the right of a newborn to be nursed and educated, the right of an adult

to a plot of land from the ancestral holdings, the right of any well-defined unit of political organization to self-government, the right of all to have a say in the enstoolment or destoolment of their chiefs or their elders and to participate in the shaping of governmental policies, the right of all to freedom of thought and expression in all matters, political, religious, and metaphysical, the right of everybody to trial before punishment, the right of a person to remain at any locality or to leave, and so on.[9]

In response it could be argued that, in similar cultures, only members of this society who accept the culture, its responsibilities, and their place within it are recognized as persons. Thus Francis Deng, who finds similar support for human rights among the Dinka people, who live mainly in the Sudan, also observes that these commitments, like other "Dinka cultural values tend to weaken as the community widens, and they become minimal in relations with foreigners." This, however, is a different problem. The problem here is not that Dinka culture accords too little respect to individuals. The problem is that it respects too few individuals; what is missing is not individualism, but universality.

On the other hand, this lack of universality is hardly a minor problem if we are discussing a culture's supportiveness for human rights — which, after all, are meant to protect all humans. Indeed, the particularism of non-Western cultures is the feature which Donnelly seizes most firmly in arguing for their incapacity to support human rights.

Clearly one does not support human rights unless one supports their protection for everyone. Otherwise we should have to allow that General Mladic supports human rights — for Serbs only. Yet Donnelly wants to say something stronger: if a group fails to recognize that outsiders deserve basic protections no less than members, then that group has no concept of human rights. I find this claim too strong. Any group can recognize the similarities between dangers to them and dangers to outsiders. They are also capable of recognizing some cases in which general social protection

against these dangers is deserved — namely, within their own group. If they had no concept of human rights, then they would be unable to pick out any communities in which such social protection is warranted. But they can pick out at least one such community, namely their own. What they cannot do so easily is to pick out others. Their knowledge of how to use the language of human rights is not absent; it is more accurate to call it "defective."

Take the case of John Locke. As we all know, Locke believed that anyone who would but consult their own Reason would conclude that behaviour threatening life, liberty or property was a danger against which social protection was warranted. Men were warranted in providing and enforcing this protection spontaneously, as required, or they could contract the work out. However, there was notoriously more male liberty and property to be protected within this view, and Locke was also the second-largest shareholder in the Royal Africa Company, "explicitly a slave trading enterprise."[10] In Locke's own thought, then, was the concept of human rights wholly lacking, or was it just horribly defective? If Donnelly wants to hold that Locke did, after all, have something to say about human rights, not just white men's rights, then he should choose the latter. To be consistent, however, he should in that case say that in certain traditional cultures — as well as in Christianity and Islam — the concept of human rights, though it may have been applied defectively, is not altogether absent.

Rejectionists hold that human rights beliefs are inconsistent with non-Western moral and political cultures — and so much the worse for human rights. The Ayatollah Khomeini was a rejectionist, as he indicated in his statements about the Universal Declaration of Human Rights being a "collection of mumbo-jumbo by disciples of Satan" and human rights being "nothing but a collection of corrupt rules worked out by Zionists to destroy all true religion."[11] There are also Western rejectionists, for example Adamantia Pollis and Peter Schwab, who claim, "It is evident that in most states in the world, human rights as defined by the West are rejected, or more accurately, are meaningless."[12] Yet on closer inspection their arguments, like Donnelly's, have more to do with favoured Western conceptions than with human rights themselves. They object to biased construals of human rights that favour individualism over communalism, private property over group property, and nuclear over extended families, and they object to the crude and clumsy sorts of moral realism and universalism that abandon historical understanding of the variable social formations in which human rights can be implemented in favour of a simple and uniform conception of each right. On the other hand, as they themselves point out, some of the social protections to which human rights language refers can be justified in "all societies ... within their particular cultural or ideological context ... norms and values."[13]

Rejectionism, then, is better exemplified by Khomeini than by Pollis and Schwab. We can see what is wrong with Khomeini's view by examining some of the human rights debates that have occurred amongst Muslims themselves. Some Muslims have argued that a full set of human rights, comparable to those listed by the Universal Declaration, have always been prescribed by Islam. An example is the Universal Declaration of Human Rights of 1981 — which, we should note, is a declaration not of any governments but rather of the Islamic Council, a private group based in London. The authors preface their Declaration with the claim that "Islam gave to mankind an ideal code of human rights fourteen centuries ago."[14] Critics of this Declaration argue that, at best, the conception of human rights it expresses is defective, because it is limited by provisions of Islamic law that deny equal rights not only to women but to all persons who are not "people of the book" — that is, Muslim, Christian, or Jewish. Nevertheless, it seems to me that the fact that this debate has occurred at all supports the following arguments.

"Believing in" a human right means believing that wide social protection against standard threats exemplifying some fundamental type of danger to humans is justified. Now, we want to be able to discuss whether each other's beliefs in human rights are defective. I want to distinguish between human rights beliefs that are "defective" and

others that are "incomplete." By "defective," I mean this: while someone understands why social protection against a given type of danger is justified, that person fails to understand why this protection is justified for everyone. By "incomplete" I mean something else: while a person understands why protection against one danger is justified, she or he cannot justify protection against other dangers that are comparably serious threats to the person's life-prospects.

The debate surrounding the Islamic Declarations shows that some social protections against some basic human dangers are justifiable on the basis of Islamic beliefs. But believing that such protection is justified is a belief in human rights. That belief may be defective, but a defective belief in human rights is still some belief in human rights. No matter which side in this debate is right — whether it is the authors of the Islamic Declaration or their critics — it is clear that some belief in human rights is part of Islam.

In other words, the very occurrence of a revisionist position — such as that of the Islamic Council — refutes rejectionism. If human rights can be debated on Islamic grounds, then this is a debate that can occur within Islam, not between Islam and the disciples of Satan.

On the other hand, what revisionists assert — that their tradition holds a complete set of human rights — is extremely unlikely to be true. There are two general reasons for this: one is the universality of ethnocentrism, combined with the absence, until recently, of any global context for moral discourse, and the other is the historical tendency to expand the list of dangers against which social protection is deserved.

While there is indeed some concept of human rights to be found in Islam and traditional African thought as well as Lockean liberalism, these conceptions of human rights are also defective, since their arguments privilege protection of one's own group over protection of others — if, indeed, the others are recognized as persons at all. While Eurocentrism is arguably more than — and more vicious than — ethnocentrism generally, cultural history leaves little room to doubt that all cultures have ethnocentric tendencies, and therefore they have been generally unlikely to put the other on the same footing, morally, as "their own." Historically, a necessary condition for overcoming these otherwise pervasive ethnocentric tendencies is the emergence of a worldwide context for moral discussion, a global public sphere of moral deliberation, open to the participation of all. In saying this, I have in mind a specific — yet, I hope, not question-begging — conception of moral discussion. What I mean by "moral" discussion is not technical discussion about the most effective way to make something happen, nor is it negotiation, mediation or any other way of "getting your way" with others by using words. What I have in mind as "moral discussion" is typified by a mutual commitment to reach an understanding of what is the right thing to do, bringing to bear the best available resources for reaching this understanding, and seeking to reduce manipulation in the discussion as far as possible. Prior to the emergence of the United Nations and parallel international institutions, what global discussions took place were either strategic or sectarian. One might argue that previously the Christian moral discourse was global; however, it was far from all-inclusive, and it was always sectarian. One might argue that the international workers' movements were international, and had they lived up to their promise as "universal class," they might have come to create a context for global moral discourse; however, they too remained sectarian.

Admittedly, international institutions have always been arenas for strategic interactions between states and power blocs. Nevertheless, they have also created a public context in which moral discourse sporadically emerges and carries some weight, at least enough to cause minor embarrassments to governments that subordinate it to strategic manipulation, and enough to give opposition movements moral high ground from which to question the legitimacy of government policies. While global communications have made it easier to know what happens in distant parts of the world, global communications have done little to make voices from distant parts of the world audible to each other. The notion that when normative claims are put forward they can be challenged from any-

where on Earth has little currency unless there are contexts in which everyone is to some degree represented and where either one achieves mutual understanding or one courts the risk of embarrassment for defecting from a consensus that is understood by others to be plausibly justified.

We should not fool ourselves by thinking that the world public sphere, morally, has any great strength at this present time. Commitments to reaching global understandings are weak and sporadic, and their power to embarrass governments that defy or ignore them is minimal. Nevertheless, shaky though it is, a global public sphere does exist, and so we do have at least this necessary condition for moral knowledge on a global scale. This is something that all of our traditions were lacking. And therefore, I submit, it is no wonder that the understanding of human rights contained in our traditions was defective.

II. How a Fuller Set of Human Rights Can Be Known

I shall proceed now to the claims of transformationism, which, I think, support the sort of political goals that Sané has proposed. The first two claims are: (i) in all cultural traditions, some people at some time or other have employed concepts of human rights that are "defective" in the sense that they limit human rights protection to in-groups while excluding out-groups; (ii) still, there are features of cross-cultural dialogue that forbid these sorts of defects — if the dialogue is not abused.

Clearly the sort of understanding we want, when we want *moral understanding*, is not an agreement based on cajoling or tricking each other. In other words, a group that is committed to reaching such an understanding is thereby committed to reducing the degree of manipulation in the discussion. To such a group, *not* giving each other equal standing and equal consideration would be irrational: any implication that someone ought to be demoted in standing or considerability will find the force of analogical reasoning (to treat like cases alike) weighing against it; meanwhile, reasons adduced in favour of the demotion will be suspected as manipulative, self-serving ideologies. Consequently, if social protection against a basic danger to humans is warranted for some, the rationality of excluding others from this protection will always be questionable.

The next claim that transformationists make is that (iii) the lists of human rights that can be generated from received cultural norms are generally *incomplete*, by which I mean that they overlook certain protections that people are due. Three "generations" of human rights have been claimed, declared or enacted since the founding of the United Nations. In this process the United States, backed occasionally but not reliably by some of its allies, has fought a prolonged losing battle to delete or demote all but the civil and political rights from the list. Initially it succeeded in separating implementation of these "first-generation" rights from social, cultural and economic rights, which, as a result of being separated and deferred, came to be known as the "second generation" of human rights.[15] Later, once more against U.S. resistance, it was argued that both lists were formulated too abstractly, in ways that permitted equivalent protection for some groups to be ignored. On these grounds a "third generation" of rights was called for, including women's rights, rights of peoples (as distinct from states), the right to development, and others.[16] Transformationists see this trend as essentially progressive. What they claim is not only that these new rights are justified, but that (iv) the justification rests on resources for moral knowledge that exists in all cultures.

To examine this, let's begin with some second-generation rights. According to Article 25 of the Universal Declaration:

Everyone has the right to a standard of living adequate for the health and well-being of himself and of his family, including food, clothing, housing and medical care and necessary social services, and the right to security in the event of unemployment, sickness, disability, widowhood, old age or other lack of livelihood in circumstances beyond his control.

How do we know that these things ought to be socially protected? What are the cognitive resources, available in our culture, for knowing this? They are located at two levels: moral principles that are plausible within the culture, and the knowledge of care, neglect, and abuse that informs people's treatment of each other — especially their treatment of those for whom they feel some responsibility.

First consider cultural norms. Protection of people in relation to their needs is hardly a new idea. In some traditional cultures it is justified in terms of dignity — a good example of which can be found in Francis Deng's discussion of virtue and dignity for the Dinka people of Sudan. In others, protection against need is to be rooted in the prevailing concept of personhood, as Kwasi Wiredu has shown with regard to the Akan peoples of West Africa. These cultural beliefs, then, can support recognition of human rights relating to need.

However, there are other cultural beliefs that may, in particular cases, argue for other priorities. The question, then, is whether there is any deeper resource that enables us to know that needs protection is not to be overridden by other norms or considerations. My claim is that all cultures do have such a resource, which I am calling "knowledge of care, neglect, and abuse." What this knowledge does within moral discussion is to block the use of cultural norms to justify or condone neglect or abuse. If people's common knowledge of care, neglect and abuse is allowed to prevail in a discussion, the result will be to shape the discussion. Where knowledge of care and neglect prevails, those cultural norms justifying protection against need will also prevail. One can see this influence at work particularly in the interpretation of religious traditions, such as in social Buddhism, in Christian liberation theology and among the Islamic left.

In different cultures, knowledge of care, neglect and abuse is expressed differently, and under different conditions the requirements of care will vary, as for example adequate shelter is exemplified differently in different climates. Nevertheless, when it comes to identifying the most important types of protection, and probably even to ranking the worst cases of neglect and abuse, there is remarkable convergence.[17] As a resource for moral understanding, this convergence is bedrock. Were this convergence not possible, neither would it be possible for us to know anything about human rights.

Some of the third-generation rights are supported by this same resource, social knowledge of care, neglect and abuse. This is clearly the case for the emergence of women's rights as human rights. The protections that women seek, as Charlotte Bunch and others have pointed out, include protection from domestic, sexual, and other violence that targets them as women, protection from torture and sexual abuse while in custody, subordination and sexual exploitation of women refugees, feminization of poverty, and sex discrimination. All of these could be seen as violations of already-listed first-generation and second-generation rights. Why, then, add more rights? The reason is to ensure that these will be seen as instances of human rights violations, no less serious than comparable violations that are more typically encountered by men. Moreover, our understanding of a human right is not complete without a full understanding of the *standard threats* against which this right is meant to protect people.

Consider the right to security as an example. Some male interpreters have in fact denied that the right to security includes the right of women not to be beaten by their husbands. Clearly their understanding of the broad right — of security against violence — needs to be completed by specifying that domestic violence against women by husbands is a standard threat. How do we know about these as standard threats? There is some academic study, of course, but there is also an informal basis in experience: we come to know these are standard threats through women's experiences of having to care for and protect themselves, and each other, from violence that targets them specifically as women. With this addition, our understanding of human rights is, as Bunch argues, transformed. Without it, without understanding human rights as women's rights, our understanding of human rights is incomplete.[18]

Other emerging third-generation rights rely for their justification on *political experience* of barriers to the implementation of first-generation and second-generation rights. From various histories of Southern countries we can see that not all ways of enacting civil and political rights enable nations to enact, with equal effectiveness, their social and economic rights. The last half of the twentieth century has revealed specific social and political dangers that have become standard threats to the institutionalization of social and economic rights. One such threat has been the emergence of elites, which, though they may once have wished to lead their people to prosperity and development, have been unable to do so, partly because of their subordinate positioning within international economic systems. The result has been the well-known tendency towards internal repression by domestic elites. As one African writer sums it up,

> Political independence coupled with the failure of the new elites to carry out an appreciable level of socioeconomic and political transformation generated apathy, opposition, and revolutionary pressures. These pressures in turn compelled African leaders to resort to repression; the manipulation of religion and ethnicity; alliances with powerful foreign interests, particularly for support; ideological containment; and defensive radicalism.[19]

By endangering democratic development, this syndrome makes the rights of the first and second generations insecure. The solution is seen as twofold. First, international barriers to resources for development must be removed. Second, so must barriers to widespread public participation — both democratic participation and private participation — be removed, while organizations and institutions empowering people to participate in and share in control over the development process must be promoted. These are the two main elements of the third generation of human rights, which are sometimes called, "the right to development," or "people's rights," or, more prosaically, "peoples' rights to development." Why should this third generation of rights be recognized? One argument is that the failure to secure people's rights to development yields political structures (the repressive subaltern elite, powerless to lead development) that predictably fail to protect not only socio-economic rights but also first-generation rights. It is argued on the basis of this political experience that enacting third-generation rights is the only process that can effectively enact first-generation and second-generation rights in Third World contexts.

In principle, then, a full list of human rights can be known. A full understanding and a complete set of human rights can be justified by moral discourse, so long as that discourse is not abused, and so long as it is open to two sorts of cognitive resources. One of these is the varied yet convergent knowledge of care, neglect and abuse that informs personal and social life in all cultures. The other is not moral but political experience of barriers to achieving social protections, including those recognized as human rights.

What we will accomplish, in struggling for the inclusion of this knowledge and experience in the moral discourse of human rights, is to rid the discourse of its former Eurocentrism and in this way render it more capable and appropriate for articulating at least some goals of the kind of world movement that Sané has called for in response to the human damage being caused by globalization. It is part of the process that South Asian feminist Corinne Kumar D'Souza has called "the Wind from the South," which fills our sails "to move outside the universal, Eurocentric, patriarchal patterns ... [and] develop a new universalism."[20]

Defending Human Rights in the Context of Globalization

Recall what labour force dualization is, and how it undermines human rights. Corporations buy the loyalty of some workers whom they employ in formal, regulated jobs, paid according to a market influenced by labour productivity and collective bargaining. On the other hand, much of the labour that the corporation requires is procured now by other means, indirectly, through subcontracting into labour pools where market conditions are far less favourable for the workers. If the labour market were unified, labour of a given type would obtain a single equilibrium price, but here, in the

dual labour market, this is not the case. As long as this rift endures, "equal pay for equal work" and "just and favourable remuneration ensuring [oneself and one's] family an existence worthy of human dignity" are protected, if at all, only for workers who continue to possess jobs in the formal sector; on the other side of the rift, these protections are only dreams — or, as well, they are seen as other workers' privileges.

One would think that once this phenomenon becomes at all widespread within a country it could also have a damaging effect on state finances. We are all familiar with the pressure on countries to strip away state spending and social protections in order to reduce budget deficits and become more "competitive" in relation to other countries. Subcontracting must be one factor contributing to this "race for the bottom." The competitive advantage that capital achieves by these means seems to be reflected in reduced earning power by workers, which must ultimately be reflected in reduced taxation power for their governments. Thus the capacity of governments to finance social rights is curtailed. It is not just labour rights that are undermined but social rights as well.

Those who are seriously committed to preserving the substance of human rights on our planet must address the problem of healing this rift in the world's workforce. The solutions, if there are any, will be complex.

To begin looking at solutions, we need to ask why it is that subcontracting gives a corporation competitive advantage. Three sources of advantage need to be distinguished. In part, there may be efficiencies of allocation: just as the "parts-on-time" system achieves economies, by analogy so too does subcontracting, as a "labour-on-time" system. For this there may be no solution; yet, at the same time, it is not clear that this aspect of subcontracting causes harm. In part — arguably the greater part — the competitive advantage comes from the kind of labour pools that capital seeks out through subcontracting. For the labour that capital was, in a previous century, able to create, infamously, through such measures as enclosures, it must now scour the earth, as the world's workforce becomes more highly educated, and more expensive. In the long term, the only solution is to increase the value of Southern labour. On the one hand, this requires social investment in education and other forms of human development. As Mahbub ul Haq has observed,

> Investing in human development has been a key strategy of economic growth in East Asia. In the Republic of Korea, labour productivity grew by 11 % a year between 1963 and 1979 — with only half that growth due to increased capital investment.[21]

Consequently, one part of the solution is (a) to raise the value of labour — especially at capital's new and last frontiers — by investment in human development. However, the ability of labour to realize this value, to capture the proceeds of productivity increases, depends on its bargaining power. What subcontracting allows corporations to do is reduce the cost of labour by reducing the bargaining power of labour. This is accomplished by evading labour regulation: in export processing zones, and in the informal sector (where workers are nominally entrepreneurs) there is no collective bargaining. In these two different cases — export processing zones and the informal sector — different responses are required.

(b) Export processing zones would seem to require re-regulation. This would seem easy enough to justify on human rights grounds, inasmuch as labour rights are human rights. However, the issue has been clouded by demands by France and the United States to enforce labour standards by means of trade sanctions and "social clauses" attached to trade agreements.[22]

Labour regulation is also absent from the informal sector. The informal sector is a cash economy from which regulation and taxation are largely absent. People who work it are nominally self-employed; the earnings of many are at subsistence level, and for them this is the sector of last resort. Others manage modest accumulation, and some are able to "graduate" into formal businesses with more or less stable assets and employees. In some of the recently successful Asian economies, the graduation process has all but eliminated the informal sector.[23] Consensus among development analysts is that the best approach to the informal sector is to facilitate the graduation process, which benefits not only the entrepreneurs but workers as well — since graduation transforms jobless work into formal employment. Three requirements are generally recognized for greater chances of success by these micro-enterprises: marketing networks, credit, and business skills.[24]

(c) The task, then, is to "graduate" the informal sector. Credit and empowerment (including marketing and business skills) seem essential. All three can be called for under a new human right, a "third-generation" right: people's right to development.

In the "Declaration on the Right to Development," adopted by resolution of the General Assembly in 1986, we find a sophisticated view of the development process, of obstacles that may thwart it, and of agents that must co-ordinate their work in order to lead development through the obstacles. The conception of development that informs it is one in which welfare, autonomy, and justice are interdependent. Perhaps in order to confront exclusively welfarist conceptions of development, the document stresses from the start that individuals are to be active participants and peoples are to be self-determining in development, which is then implicitly defined as the "constant improvement of the well-being of the entire population and of all individuals, on the basis of their active, free and meaningful participation in development and in the fair distribution of the benefits resulting therefrom."[25] Major obstacles to development are identified as: lack of international co-operation; colonialism, racism, and other violations of the self-determination of peoples; violation of other human rights; threats to peace and security; and unequal access to resources — for example, by women. What the right calls for is co-ordination at all levels — local, national, and international — which promotes participatory development and surmounts these obstacles.

This is, of course, an extremely rich and powerful claim. I will discuss its justification later. For now, I want to note its consequences for the informal sector. "Graduating" the informal sector requires credit and empowerment (especially in the areas of marketing and business management). These necessities are being provided increasingly by community organizations, self-help groups, co-operatives, and similar organizations of civil society — some of them initially formed by NGOs. These popular grassroots organizations also contribute politically to participatory development by focusing demands to pry resources from a self-serving state apparatus.[26] For this and other reasons, these very organizations, which have a central role to play in the process of graduating micro-enterprises from the informal sector, have come to be interpreted as important means of realizing the right to development. The UN secretary general's report *Realizing the Right to Development*, resulting from the 1991 Global Consultation on the Right to Development as a Human Right, included these organizations within the interpretation of "participation." Thus the right to development, including participation, was seen to include the growth of these organizations.[27]

It also addresses the need for credit. Article 8 of the Declaration calls upon states to "ensure ... equality of opportunity for all in their access to basic resources," and this has been interpreted to include access to productive resources. The Global Consultation included availability of credit among its list of "criteria which might be used to measure progress" in implementing the right to development.[28]

Let us see where we stand. I began by observing that labour force dualization is a pervasive threat not only to labour rights but also to social rights generally. I have identified three types of action that will need to be taken to mend the rift in the world's workforce: (a) raising the value of Southern labour through human development investment, (b) re-regulating the EPZs, preferably through international agencies, and (c) graduating the informal sector through credit and empowerment. I have shown that the first two are justifiable under currently recognized social and economic rights, and the third can be justified on the basis of the newer human right of peoples to development. Therefore, if a global movement of the kind Sané

calls for is to address this issue, its goals can be articulated and justified in terms of human rights.

NOTES

1. In a recent interview, Sandra Ramos, National Co-ordinator of the Movement of Working and Unemployed Women, gave the following description of conditions in Nicaragua:

   > Some 70 percent of the labour force is unemployed. So jobs and the right to healthcare and education are the basic demands for women. Neo-liberalism is working towards the privatization of healthcare and education, and also to reduce the number of jobs required to produce goods.
   >
   > The Government's only alternative in terms of jobs is to go work in the *maquilas* (export-only factories). This strategy is based on the poorly paid labour of women workers. There are 20 international companies investing here — mostly Korean and Taiwanese — all producing for the North American market. The women who work here have no benefits and are entirely outside the normal labour-law requirements. Women earn an average of $70 a month — less than a third of what they need to survive. They work 10 to 15 hours a day.

   Sandra Ramos, interviewed by Richard Swift, "The NI Interview," *The New Internationalist* 279 (May 1996): 31. See also Henk Thomas, ed., *Globalization and Third World Trade Unions: The Challenge of Rapid Economic Change* (London: Zed Books, 1995).

2. Pierre Sané, "Human Rights: An Agenda for Action," *West Africa* 3978 (Dec. 20, 1993): 2294.

3. Jack Donnelly, "Human Rights and Human Dignity: An Analytic Critique of Non-Western Conceptions of Human Rights," *American Political Science Review* 76 (1982): 303-16.

4. Bassam Tibi, "The European Tradition of Human Rights and the Culture of Islam," in *Human Rights in Africa: Cross-Cultural Perspectives*, ed. Abdullahi Ahmed An-Na'im and Francis M. Deng (Washington, D.C.: The Brookings Institution, 1990): 118.

5. Abdullahi Ahmed An-Na'im, "Islam, Islamic Law and the Dilemma of Cultural Legitimacy for Universal Human Rights," In *Asian Perspectives on Human Rights*, ed. Claude E. Welch Jr. and Virginia A. Leary (Boulder, Col.: Westview Press, 1990); Abdullahi Ahmed An-Na'im and Francis M. Deng, eds., *Human Rights in Africa: Cross-Cultural Perspectives* (Washington, D.C.: The Brookings Institution, 1990); Abdullahi Ahmed An-Na'im, "Problems of Universal Cultural Legitimacy for Human Rights," in *Human Rights in Africa*; Abdullahi Ahmed An-Na'im, *Human Rights in Cross-Cultural Perspectives: A Quest for Consensus* (Philadelphia: University of Pennsylvania Press, 1992).

6. Quoted by Ann Elizabeth Mayer, "Current Muslim Thinking on Human Rights," in *Human Rights in Africa*, 138.

7. Kwasi Wiredu, "An Akan Perspective on Human Rights," in *Human Rights in Africa*, p. 247.

8. *Ibid.*: p. 247.

9. *Ibid.*: p. 257.

10. Wayne Glausser, "Three Approaches to Locke and the Slave Trade," *Journal of the History of Ideas* 51 (1990): 199-216.

11. Bassam Tibi, "The European Tradition of Human Rights and the Culture of Islam," in *Human Rights in Africa*, 118.

12. Adamantia Pollis and Peter Schwab, "Human Rights: A Western Construct with Limited Applicability," in *Human Rights: Cultural and Ideological Perspectives*, ed. Adamantia Pollis and Peter Schwab (New York: Praeger, 1980): 13.

13. Pollis and Schwab, "Human Rights," 15.

14. Quoted by Mayer, "Current Muslim Thinking on Human Rights," 138. This list is extensive, including rights to life, freedom, procedural justice, political participation, free speech, religion, and association, protection of property, dignity of workers, social security, marital rights and rights of women, and rights to education, privacy, and free movement. "Universal Islamic Declaration of Human Rights," in *Human Rights Sourcebook*, ed. Albert P. Blaustein, Roger S. Clark, and Jay A. Sigler (New York: Paragon House, 1987): 917-23. However, as Tibi notes ("European Tradition," n. 4 above), the declaration stipulated that all of these rights are to be interpreted consistently with Sha'riah.

15. Virginia A. Leary, "The Effect of Western Perspectives on International Human Rights," in *Human Rights in Africa*.

16. Philip Alston, "Making Space for the New Human Rights: The Case of the Right to Development," *Harvard Human Rights Yearbook* 1 (1988): 3-40.

17. I want to stress that the underlying beliefs about care, neglect, and abuse are in principle a form of *knowledge*. It is fallible and corrigible knowledge, but knowledge nonetheless. It is a form of knowledge that no culture can afford not to have. Every culture — if it is going to sustain itself — must include practices of direct personal care and support. In some cases we take direct responsibility for the well-being of others — for example, our children. We also take on similar responsibilities towards adult friends and loved ones, although these responsibilities are limited by respect for their autonomy. To carry out these practices and responsibilities, people need a great deal of knowledge. Modernity has rendered some of this knowledge formal and testable, but a great deal more of the knowledge we need in order to provide each other with humane care and support is informal, a cultural reservoir of knowledge based on current and received experience. It is against this vast informal knowledge of how people are to be cared for and supported that we can also recognize neglect. Care and support are eventually concerned with providing conditions for growth and socialization, but they begin with providing protection. Consequently, those who can recognize good care can also recognize abuse.

18. Charlotte Bunch, "Women's Rights as Human Rights: Toward a Re-Vision of Human Rights," in *Applied Ethics: A Multicultural Approach*, ed. Larry May and Shari Collins Sharratt (Englewood Cliffs, N.J.: Prentice-Hall, 1994): 41-9.

19. Julius O. Ihonvbere, "Underdevelopment and Human Rights Violations in Africa," In *Emerging Human Rights: The African Political Economy Context*, ed. George W. Shepherd Jr. and Mark Anikpo (New York: Greenwood, 1990): 58.

20. Corinne Kumar D'Souza, "A New Movement, a New Hope: East Wind, West Wind, and the Wind

from the South," in *Healing the Wounds: the Promise of Ecofeminism*, ed. Judith Plant (Toronto: Between the Lines, 1989): 38.

21. Mahbub ul Haq, *Reflections on Human Development* (New York: Oxford University Press, 1995).

22. See Paul Waer, "Social Clauses in International Trade," *Journal of World Trade* 30 (1989): 25-42. One of the arguments made by Southern governments has some merit: the intent and effect of trade sanctions would not be to transform unregulated EPZs into regulated EPZs; the intent and effect would be, on the contrary, protectionist, to keep production out of EPZs altogether. On the other hand, there is another argument against trade sanctions that goes — fallaciously, in my view — against regulation altogether. Social development, it is argued, requires economic development. Economic development must be encouraged first through unregulated EPZs; only subsequently can social development, in the form of labour regulation, be introduced. If the premise were true, then corporate users of EPZs would simply move away later, rather than accept the costs of regulation. This sort of economic development will be of little lasting benefit to the host country. It is even less beneficial than exporting workers to foreign jobs, from which at least a portion of the higher earnings will be sent home in the form of remittances. In some EPZs, women are offered sub-subsistence wages, which they accept as long as these earnings are enough to "top up" family earnings to subsistence level. There is a vast difference, then, between exporting labour to an unregulated EPZ, and exporting labour to a regulated labour market abroad: from the EPZs there are likely to be no remittances.

23. Thomas, *Globalization and Third World Trade Unions*, 50.

24. Sadig Rasheed and David Fasholé Luke, *Development Management in Africa: Toward Dynamism, Empowerment, and Entrepreneurship* (Boulder, Col.: Westview Press, 1995): 165-6, 256-7.

25. *The Realization of the Right To Development: Global Consultation of the Right To Development as a Human Right*, Centre for Human Rights, Geneva (New York: United Nations, 1991).

26. James C.N. Paul, "Participatory Approaches to Human Rights in Sub-Saharan Africa," in *Human Rights in Africa*, 213-39; George W. Shepherd Jr., "African People's Rights: The Third Generation in a Global Perspective," in *Emerging Human Rights*, 39-54.

27. *Realization of the Right to Development*, 37, 53.

28. *Ibid.*, 67, 49.

A BUDDHIST RESPONSE TO THE NATURE OF HUMAN RIGHTS

Kenneth K. Inada

Kenneth K. Inada is an Emeritus faculty member in the Philosophy Department at the State University of New York at Buffalo. He is the author of Guide to Buddhist Philosophy *(1985), co-editor of* Buddhism and American Thinkers *(1984, with Nolan P. Jacobson), and editor of the* Journal of Buddhist Philosophy.

Inada describes fundamental elements of Buddhism in order to identify areas of contrast and commonality between Buddhist values and Western human rights discourse. He argues that the Western notion of rights is premised on what he calls hard relationships, which are based on notions of the separateness and independence of individuals. He contrasts this with the Buddhist emphasis on soft relationships and argues that because soft relationships are more flexible, compassionate, and holistically oriented than hard relationships, Buddhist values can form the base for a conception of human rights that places less emphasis on legal remedies for settling conflicts amongst individuals than does the Western conception.

It is incorrect to assume that the concept of human rights is readily identifiable in all societies of the world. The concept may perhaps be clear and distinct in legal quarters, but in actual practice it suffers greatly from lack of clarity and gray areas due to impositions by different cultures. This is especially true in Asia, where the two great civilizations of India and China have spawned such outstanding systems as Hinduism, Buddhism, Jainism, Yoga, Confucianism, Taoism and Chinese Buddhism. These systems, together with other indigenous folk beliefs, attest to the cultural diversity at play that characterizes Asia proper. In focusing on the concept of human rights, however, we shall concentrate on Buddhism to bring out the common grounds of discourse.

Alone among the great systems of Asia, Buddhism has successfully crossed geographical and ideological borders and spread in time throughout the whole length and breadth of known Asia. Its doctrines are so universal and profound that they captured the imagination of all the peoples they touched and thereby established a subtle bond with all. What then is this bond? It must be something common to all systems of thought which opens up and allows spiritual discourse among them.

In examining the metaphysical ground of all systems, one finds that there is a basic feeling for a larger reality in one's own experience, a kind of reaching out for a greater cosmic dimension of being, as it were. It is a deep sense for the total nature of things. All this may seem so simple and hardly merits elaborating, but it is a genuine feeling common among Asians in their quest for ultimate knowledge based on the proper relationship of one's self in the world. It is an affirmation of a reality that includes but at once goes beyond the confines of sense faculties.

A good illustration of this metaphysical grounding is seen in the Brahmanic world of Hinduism. In it, the occluded nature of the self (*atman*) constantly works to cleanse itself of defilements by yogic discipline in the hope of ultimately identifying with the larger reality which is Brahman. In the process, the grounding in the larger reality is always kept intact, regardless of whether the self is impure or not. In other words, in the quest for the purity of things a larger framework of experience is involved from the beginning such that the ordinary self (*atman*) transforms into the larger Self (*Atman*) and finally merges into the ultimate ontological Brahman.

A similar metaphysical grounding is found in Chinese thought. Confucianism, for example, with its great doctrine of humanity (*jen*), involves the ever-widening and ever-deepening human relationship that issues forth in the famous statement, "All men are brothers." In this sense, humanity is not a mere abstract concept but one that extends concretely throughout the whole of sentient existence. Confucius once said that when he searched for *jen*, it is always close at hand.[1] It means that humanity is not something external to a person but that it is constitutive of the person's experience, regardless of whether there is consciousness of it or not. It means moreover that in the relational nature of society, individual existence is always more than that which one assumes it to be. In this vein, all experiences must fit into the larger cosmological scheme normally spoken of in terms of heaven, earth and mankind. This triadic relationship is ever-present and ever-in-force, despite one's ignorance, negligence or outright intention to deny it. The concept that permeates and enlivens the triadic relationship is the *Tao*. The *Tao* is a seemingly catchall term, perhaps best translated as the natural way of life and the world. In its naturalness, it manifests all of existence; indeed, it is here, there and everywhere since it remains aloof from human contrivance and manipulation. In a paradoxical sense, it depicts action based on non-action (*wu-wei*), the deepest state of being achievable. The following story illustrates this point.

A cook named Ting is alleged to have used the same carving knife for some 19 years without sharpening it at all. When asked how that is possible, he simply replied:

What I care about is the way (*Tao*), which goes beyond skill. When I first began cutting up oxen, all I could see was the ox itself. After three years I no longer saw the whole ox. And now — now I go at it by spirit and don't look with my eyes.

Perception and understanding have come to a stop and spirit moves where it wants. I go along with the natural makeup, strike in the big hollows, guide the knife through the big openings, and follow things as they are. So I never touch the smallest ligament or tendon, much less a main joint. ... I've had this knife of mine for nineteen years and I've cut up thousands of oxen with it, and yet the blade is as good as though it had just come from the grindstone.[2]

Such then is the master craftsman at work, a master in harmonious triadic relationship based on the capture of the spirit of *Tao* where the function is not limited to a person and his or her use of a tool. And it is clear that such a spirit of *Tao* in craftsmanship is germane to all disciplined experiences we are capable of achieving in our daily activities.

Buddhism, too, has always directed our attention to the larger reality of existence. The original enlightenment of the historical Buddha told of a pure unencumbered experience which opened up all experiential doors in such a way that they touched everything sentient as well as insentient. A Zen story graphically illustrates this point.

Once a master and a disciple were walking through a dense forest. Suddenly, they heard the clean chopping strokes of the woodcutter's axe. The disciple was elated and remarked, "What beautiful sounds in the quiet of the forest!" To which the master immediately responded, "You have got it all upside down. The sounds only makes obvious the deep silence of the forest!" The response by the Zen master sets in bold relief the Buddhist perception of reality. Although existential reality refers to the perception of the world as a singular unified whole, we ordinarily perceive it in fragmented ways because of our heavy reliance on the perceptual apparatus and its consequent understanding. That is to say, we perceive by a divisive and selective method which however glosses over much of reality and indeed misses its holistic nature. Certainly, the hewing sounds of the woodcutter's axe are clearly audible and delightful to the ears, but they are so at the expense of the basic silence of the forest (i.e., total reality). Or, the forest in its silence constitutes the necessary back-ground, indeed the basic source, from which all sounds (and all activities for that matter) originate. Put another way, sounds arising from the silence of the forest should in no way deprive nor intrude upon the very source of their own being. Only human beings make such intrusions by their crude discriminate habits of perception and, conse-quently, suffer a truncated form of existence, unknowingly for the most part.

Now that we have seen Asian lives in general grounded in a holistic cosmological framework, we would have to raise the following question: How does this framework appear in the presence of human rights? Or, contrarily, how does human rights function within this framework?

Admittedly, the concept of human rights is rela-tively new to Asians. From the very beginning, it did not sit well with their basic cosmological outlook. Indeed, the existence of such an outlook has prevented in profound ways a ready accept-ance of foreign elements and has created tension and struggle between tradition and modernity. Yet, the key concept in the tension is that of human relationship. This is especially true in Buddhism, where the emphasis is not so much on the perfor-mative acts and individual rights as it is on the matter of manifestation of human nature itself. The Buddhist always takes human nature as the basic context in which all ancillary concepts, such as human rights, are understood and take on any value. Moreover, the context itself is in harmony with the extended experiential nature of things. And thus, where the Westerner is much more at home in treating legal matters detached from human nature as such and quite confident in forging ahead to establish human rights with a dis-tinct emphasis on certain "rights," the Buddhist is much more reserved but open and seeks to under-stand the implications of human behavior, based on the fundamental nature of human beings, before turning his or her attention to the so-called "rights" of individuals.

An apparent sharp rift seems to exist between the Western and Buddhist views, but this is not really so. Actually, it is a matter of perspectives and calls for a more comprehensive understanding of what takes place in ordinary human relation-ships. For the basic premise is still one that is focused on human beings intimately living together in the selfsame world. A difference in per-spectives does not mean non-communication or a simple rejection of another's view, as there is still much more substance in the nature of conciliation, accommodation and absorption than what is ini-tially thought of. Here we propose two contrasting but interlocking and complementary terms, namely, "hard relationship" and "soft relation-ship."

The Western view on human rights is generally based on a hard relationship. Persons are treated as separate and independent entities or even bodies, each having its own assumed identity or self-identity. It is a sheer "elemental" way of per-ceiving things due mainly to the strong influence by science and its methodology. As scientific methodology thrives on the dissective and analytic incursion into reality as such, this in turn has resulted in our perceiving and understanding things in terms of disparate realities. Although it makes way for easy understanding, the question still remains: Do we really understand what these realities are in their own respective fullness of existence? Apparently not. And to make matters worse, the methodology unfortunately has been uncritically extended over to the human realm, into human nature and human relations. Witness its ready acceptance by the various descriptive and behavioral sciences, such as sociology, psychol-ogy and anthropology, On this matter, Cartesian dualism of mind and body has undoubtedly influ-enced our ordinary ways of thinking is such a manner that in our casual perception of things we habitually subscribe to the clearcut subject-object dichotomy. This dualistic perspective has natu-rally filtered down into human relationships and has eventually crystallized into what we refer to as the nature of a hard relationship. Thus, a hard rela-tionship is a mechanistic treatment of human beings where the emphasis is on beings as such regardless of their inner nature and function in the fullest sense; it is an atomistic analysis of beings where the premium is placed on what is relatable and manipulable without regard for their true potentials for becoming. In a way it is externalization in the extreme, since the emphasis is heavily weighted on seizing the external character of beings themselves. Very little attention, if any, is given to the total ambience, inclusive of inner contents and values, in which the beings are at full play. In this regard, it can be said that postmodern thought is now attempting to correct this seemingly lopsided dichotomous view created by our inattention to the total experiential nature of things. We believe this is a great step in the right direction. Meanwhile, we trudge along with a heavy burden on our backs, though unaware of it for the most part, by associating with people on the basis of hard relationships.

To amplify on the nature of hard relationships, let us turn to a few modern examples. First, Thomas Hobbes, in his great work, *Leviathan*,[3] showed remarkable grasp of human psychology when he asserted that people are constantly at war with each other. Left in this "state of nature," people will never be able to live in peace and security. The only way out of this conundrum is for all to establish a reciprocal relationship or mutual trust that would work, i.e., to strike up a covenant by selfish beings that guarantees mutual benefits and gains, one in which each relinquishes certain rights in order to gain or realize a personal as well as an overall state of peace and security. This was undoubtedly a brilliant scheme. But the scheme is weak in that it treats human beings by and large mechanically, albeit psychologically too, as entities in a give-and-take affair, and thus perpetuates the condition of hard relationships.

Another example can be offered by way of the British utilitarian movement which later was consummated in American pragmatism. Jeremy Bentham's hedonic calculus[4] (e.g., intensity of pleasure or pain ... etc.) is a classic example of quantification of human experience. Although this is a most expedient or utilitarian way to treat and legislate behavior, we must remind ourselves that we are by no means mere quantifiable entities. John Stuart Mill introduced the element of quality in order to curb and tone down the excesses of the quantification process,[5] but, in the final analysis, human nature and relationships are still set in hard

relation. American pragmatism fares no better since actions by and large take place in a pluralistic world of realities and are framed within the scientific mode and therefore it is unable to relinquish the nature of hard relationships.

In contemporary times, the great work of John Rawls, *A Theory of Justice*,[6] has given us yet another twist in pragmatic and social contract theories. His basic concept of justice as fairness is an example of the reciprocal principle in action, i.e., in terms of realizing mutual advantage and benefit for the strongest to the weakest or the most favored to the least favored in a society. Each person exercises basic liberty with offices for its implementation always open and excess available. It is moreover a highly intellectual or rational theory. It thus works extremely well on the theoretical level but, in actual situations, it is not as practical and applicable as it seems since it still retains hard relationships on mutual bases. Such being the case, feelings and consciousness relative to injustice and inequality are not so readily spotted and corrected. That is to say, lacunae exist as a result of hard relationships and they keep on appearing until they are detected and finally remedied, but then the corrective process is painfully slow. Thus the theory's strongest point is its perpetually self-corrective nature which is so vital to the democratic process. Despite its shortcomings, however, Rawls' theory of justice is a singular contribution to contemporary legal and ethical thought.

By contrast, the Buddhist view of human rights is based on the assumption that human beings are primarily oriented in soft relationships; this relationship governs the understanding of the nature of human rights. Problems arise, on the other hand, when a hard relationship becomes the basis for treating human nature because it cannot delve deeply into that nature itself and functions purely on the peripheral aspects of things. It is another way of saying that a hard relationship causes rigid and stifling empirical conditions to arise and to which we become invariably attached.

A soft relationship has many facets. It is the Buddhist way to disclose a new dimension to human nature and behavior. It actually amounts to a novel perception or vision of reality. Though contrasted with a hard relationship, it is not in contention with it. If anything, it has an inclusive nature that "softens," if you will, all contacts and allows for the blending of any element that comes along, even incorporating the entities of hard relationships. This is not to say, however, that soft and hard relationships are equal or ultimately identical. For although the former could easily accommodate and absorb the latter, the reverse is not the case. Still, it must be noted that both belong to the same realm of experiential reality and in consequence ought to be conversive with each other. The non-conversive aspect arises on the part of the "hard" side and is attributable to the locked-in character of empirical elements which are considered to be hard stubborn facts worth perpetuating. But at some point, there must be a break in the lock, as it were, and this is made possible by knowledge of and intimacy with the "soft" side of human endeavors. For the "soft" side has a passive nature characterized by openness, extensiveness, depth, flexibility, absorptiveness, freshness and creativity simply because it remains unencumbered by "hardened" empirical conditions.

What has been discussed so far can be seen in modern Thailand where tradition and change are in dynamic tension. Due to the onslaught of elements of modernity, Buddhism is being questioned and challenged. Buddhist Thailand, however, has taken up the challenge in the person of a leading monk named Buddhadasa who has led the country to keep a steady course on traditional values.[7]

The heart of Buddhadasa's teaching is that the Dhamma (Sanskrit, Dharma) or the truth of Buddhism is a universal truth. Dhamma is equated by Buddhadasa to the true nature of things. It is everything and everywhere. The most appropriate term to denote the nature of Dhamma is *sunnata* (Sanskrit, *sunyata*) or the void. The ordinary man considers the void to mean nothing when, in reality, it means everything — everything, that is, without reference to the self.

We will return to the discussion of the nature of the void or *sunnata* later, but suffice it to say here

that what constitutes the heart of Buddhist truth of existence is based on soft relationships where all forms and symbols are accommodated and allows for their universal usage.

Robert N. Bellah has defined religion as a set of normative symbols institutionalized in a society or internalized in a personality.[8] It is a rather good definition but does not go far enough when it comes to describing Buddhism, or Asian religions in general for that matter. To speak of symbols being institutionalized or internalized without the proper existential or ontological context seems to be a bit artificial and has strains of meanings oriented toward hard relationships. Bellah, being a social scientist, probably could not go beyond the strains of a hard relationship, for, otherwise, he would have ended in a nondescriptive realm. The only way out is to give more substance to the nature of religious doctrines themselves, as is the case in Buddhism. The Buddhist Dharma is one such doctrine which, if symbolized, must take on a wider and deeper meaning that strikes at the very heart of existence of the individual. In this respect, Donald Swearer is on the right track when he says:

the adaptation of symbols of Theravada Buddhism presupposes an underlying ontological structure. The symbol system of Buddhism, then, is not to be seen only in relationship to its wider empirical context, but also in relationship to its ontological structure. This structure is denoted by such terms as Dhamma or absolute Truth, emptiness and non-attachment. These terms are denotative of what Dhiravamsa calls "dynamic being." They are symbolic, but in a universalistic rather than a particularistic sense.[9]

Swearer's reference to an underlying ontological structure is in complete harmony with our use of the term soft relationship. And only when this ontological structure of soft relationship is brought into the dynamic tension between tradition and modernity can we give full accounting to the nature of human experience and the attendant creativity and change within a society.

Let us return to a fuller treatment of soft relationships. In human experience, they manifest themselves in terms of the intangible human traits that we live by, such as patience, humility, tolerance, deference, non-action, humaneness, concern, pity, sympathy, altruism, sincerity, honesty, faith, responsibility, trust, respectfulness, reverence, love and compassion. Though potentially and pervasively present in any human relationship, they remain for the most part as silent but vibrant components in all experiences. Without them, human intercourse would be sapped of the human element and reduced to perfunctory activities. Indeed, this fact seems to constitute much of the order of the day where our passions are mainly directed to physical and materialistic matter.

The actualization and sustenance of these intangible human traits are basic to the Buddhist quest for an understanding of human nature and, by extension, the so-called rights of human beings. In order to derive a closer look at the nature of soft relationships, we shall focus on three characteristics, namely, mutuality, holism, and emptiness or void.

Mutuality

Our understanding of mutuality is generally limited to its abstract or theoretical nature. For example, it is defined in terms of a two-way action between two parties and where the action is invariably described with reference to elements of hard relationships. Except secondarily or deviously, nothing positive is mentioned about the substance of mutuality, such as the feelings of humility, trust and tolerance that transpire between the parties concerned. Although these feelings are present, unfortunately, they hardly ever surface in the relationship and almost always are overwhelmed by the physical aspect of things.

What is to be done? One must simply break away from the merely conceptual or theoretical understanding and fully engage oneself in the discipline that will bring the feelings of both parties to become vital components in the relationship. That is, both parties must equally sense the presence and value of these feelings and thus give substance and teeth to their actions.

Pursuing the notion of mutuality further, the Buddhist understands human experience as a totally open phenomenon, that persons should always be wide open in the living process. The phrase, "an open ontology," is used to describe the unclouded state of existence. An illustration of this is the newborn child. The child is completely an open organism at birth. The senses are wide open and will absorb practically anything without prejudice. At this stage, also, the child will begin to imitate because its absorptive power is at the highest level. This open textured nature should continue on and on. In other words, if we are free and open, there should be no persistence in attaching ourselves to hard elements within the underlying context of a dynamic world of experience. The unfortunate thing, however, is that the open texture of our existence begins to blemish and fade away in time, being obstructed and overwhelmed by self-imposed fragmentation, narrowness and restriction, which gradually develop into a closed nature of existence. In this way, the hard relationship rules. But the nature of an open ontology leads us on to the next characteristic.

Holism

Holism of course refers to the whole, the total nature of individual existence and thus describes the unrestrictive nature of one's experience. Yet, the dualistic relationship we maintain by our crude habits of perception remains a stumbling block. This stunted form of perception is not conducive to holistic understanding and instead fosters nothing but fractured types of ontological knowledge taking. Unconscious for the most part, an individual narrows his or her vision by indulging in dualism of all kinds, both mental and physical, and in so doing isolates the objects of perception from the total process to which they belong. In consequence, the singular unified reality of each perceptual moment is fragmented and, what is more, fragmentation once settled breeds further fragmentation.

The Buddhist will appeal to the fact that one's experience must always be open to the total ambience of any momentary situation. But here we must be exposed to a unique, if not paradoxical, insight of the Buddhist. It is that the nature of totality is not a clearly defined phenomenon. In a cryptic sense, however, it means that the totality of experience has no borders to speak of. It is an open border totality, which is the very nature of the earlier mentioned "open ontology." It is a non-circumscribable totality, like a circle sensed which does not have a rounded line, a seamless circle, if you will. A strange phenomenon, indeed, but that is how the Buddhist sees the nature of individual existence as such. For the mystery of existence that haunts us is really the nature of one's own fullest momentary existence. Nothing else compares in profundity to this nature, so the Buddhist believes.

Now, the open framework in which experience takes place reveals that there is depth and substance in experience. But so long as one is caught up with the peripheral elements, so-called, of hard relationships one will be ensnared by them and will generate limitations on one's understanding accordingly. On the other hand, if openness is acknowledged as a fact of existence, the way out of one's own limitations will present itself. All sufferings (*duhkha*), from the Buddhist standpoint, are cases of limited ontological vision (*avidya*, ignorance) hindered by the attachment to all sorts of elements that obsess a person.

Holism is conversant with openness since an open experience means that all elements are fully and extensively involved. In many respects, holistic existence exhibits the fact that mutuality thrives only in unhindered openness. But there is still another vital characteristic to round out or complete momentary experience. For this we turn to the last characteristic.

Emptiness

Emptiness in Sanskrit is *sunyata*.[10] Strictly speaking, the Sanskrit term, depicting zero or nothing, had been around prior to Buddhism, but it took the historical Buddha's supreme enlightenment (nirvana) to reveal an incomparable qualitative nature inherent to experience. Thus emptiness is not sheer voidness or nothingness in the nihilistic sense.

We ordinarily find it difficult to comprehend emptiness, much less to live a life grounded in it.

Why? Again, we return to the nature of our crude habits of perception, which is laden with unwarranted forms. That is, our whole perceptual process is caught up in attachment to certain forms or elements which foster and turn into so-called empirical and cognitive biases. All of this is taking place in such minute and unknowing ways that we hardly, if ever, take notice of it until a crisis situation arises, such as the presence of certain obviously damaging prejudice or discrimination. Then and only then do we seriously wonder and search for the forms or elements that initially gave rise to those prejudicial or discriminatory forces.

Emptiness has two aspects. The first aspect alerts our perceptions to be always open and fluid, and to desist from attaching to any form or element. In this respect, emptiness technically functions as a force of "epistemic nullity,"[11] in the sense that it nullifies any reference to a form or element as preexisting perception or even postexisting for that matter. Second and more importantly, emptiness points at a positive content of our experience. It underscores the possibility of total experience in any given moment because there is now nothing attached to or persisted in. This latter point brings us right back to the other characteristics of holism and mutuality. Now, we must note that emptiness is that dimension of experience which makes it possible for the function of mutuality and holism in each experience, since there is absolutely nothing that binds, hinders or wants in our experience. Everything is as it is (*tathata*), under the aegis of emptiness; emptiness enables one to spread out one's experience at will in all directions, so to speak, in terms of "vertical" and "horizontal" dimensions of being. As it is the key principle of enlightened existence, it makes everything both possible and impossible. Possible in the sense that all experiences function within the total empty nature, just as all writings are possible on a clean slate or, back to the Zen story, where the sounds are possible in the silence (emptiness) of the forest. At the same time, impossible in the sense that all attachments to forms and elements are categorically denied in the ultimate fullness of experience. In this way, emptiness completes our experience of reality and, at the same time, provides the grounds for the function of all human traits to become manifest in soft relationships.

It can now be seen that three characteristics involve each other in the selfsame momentary existence. Granted this, it should not be too difficult to accept the fact that the leading moral concept in Buddhism is compassion (*karuna*). Compassion literally means "passion for all" in an ontologically extensive sense. It covers the realm of all sentient beings, inclusive of non-sentients, for the doors of perception to total reality are always open. From the Buddhist viewpoint, then, all human beings are open entities with open feelings expressive of the highest form of humanity. This is well expressed in the famous concept of *bodhisattva* (enlightened being) in Mahayan Buddhism who has deepest concern for all beings and sympathetically delays his entrance to nirvana as long as there is suffering (ignorant existence) among sentient creatures. It depicts the coterminous nature of all creatures and may be taken as a philosophic myth in that it underscores the ideality of existence which promotes the greatest unified form of humankind based on compassion. This ideal form of existence, needless to say, is the aim and goal of all Buddhists.

As human beings we need to keep the channels of existential dialogue open at all times. When an act of violence is in progress, for example, we need to constantly nourish the silent and passive nature of nonviolence inherent in all human relations. Though nonviolence cannot counter violence on the latter's terms, still, its nourished presence serves as a reminder of the brighter side of existence and may even open the violator's mind to common or normal human traits such as tolerance, kindness and non-injury (*ahimsa*). Paradoxically and most unfortunately, acts of violence only emphasize the fact that peace and tranquility are the normal course of human existence.

It can now be seen that the Buddhist view on human rights is dedicated to the understanding of persons in a parameter-free ambience, so to speak, where feelings that are extremely soft and tender, but nevertheless present and translated into human traits or virtues that we uphold, make up the very fiber of human relations. These relations, though

their contents are largely intangible, precede any legal rights or justification accorded to human beings. In brief, human rights for the Buddhists are not only matters for legal deliberation and understanding, but they must be complemented by and based on something deeper and written in the very feelings of all sentients. The unique coexistent nature of rights and feelings constitutes the saving truth of humanistic existence.

NOTES

1. *Lu Yu* (The Analects of Confucius) VII, 29.
2. *The Complete Works of Chuang Tzu*, translated by Burton Watson (New York: Columbia University Press, 1960), pp. 50-1.
3. Thomas Hobbes, *Leviathan* (New York: Hafner, 1926).
4. Jeremy Bentham, *An Introduction to the Principles of Morals and Legislation* (New York: Hafner, 1948).
5. John Stuart Mill observed, "It is better to be a human being dissatisfied than a pig satisfied; better to be a Socrates dissatisfied than a fool satisfied." *Utilitarianism*, cited in Louis P. Pojman, *Philosophy: The Quest for Truth* (Belmont CA: Wadsworth, 1989), p. 357.
6. John Rawls, *A Theory of Justice* (Cambridge: Harvard University Press, 1971). Rawls also has a chapter on civil disobedience but it too is treated under the same concept of justice as fairness and suffers accordingly from the elements of hard relationships.
7. Donald K. Swearer, "Thai Buddhism: Two Responses to Modernity," in Bardwell L. Smith, ed., *Contributions to Asian Studies, Volume 4: Tradition and Change in Theravada Buddhism* (Leiden: E.J. Brill, 1973), p. 80. "Without reference to the self" means to uphold the Buddhist doctrine of non-self (Sanskrit, *anatman*) which underlies all momentary existence and avoids any dependence of a dichotomous self-oriented subject-object relationship. For an updated and comprehensive view of Buddhadasa's reformist's philosophy, see Donald K. Swearer, ed., *Me and Mine: Selected Essays on Bhikkhu Buddhadasa* (Albany: State University of New York Press, 1989).

8. Robert N. Bellah, "Epilogue," in Bellah, ed., *Religion and Progress in Modern Asia* (New York: Free Press, 1965), p. 173.

9. Swearer, "Thai Buddhism," p. 92.

10. Etymologically *sunyata* (in Pali, *sunnata*) means the state of being swollen, as in pregnancy, or the state of fullness of being. Thus, from the outset the term depicted the pure, open and full textured nature of experiential reality.

11. Kenneth Inada, "Nagarjuna and Beyond," *Journal of Buddhist Philosophy* 2 (1984), pp. 65-76, for development of this concept.

RECONCEIVING RIGHTS AS RELATIONSHIP

Jennifer Nedelsky

Jennifer Nedelsky is in the Faculty of Law at the University of Toronto. In addition to her book Private Property and the Limits of American Constitutionalism *(1990), she is co-editor with Ronald Beiner of* Judgment, Imagination and Politics: Themes from Kant and Arendt *(2001). She is currently working on two books:* Law, Autonomy and the Relational Self: A Feminist Revisioning of the Foundations of Law *and* Human Rights and Judgment: A Relational Approach.

Nedelsky uses Canada's 1982 adoption of its own Charter of Rights and Freedoms as the occasion for reconceiving rights as relational. She is critical of the traditional liberal understanding of rights and argues that the protection of autonomy is less about carving out a separate sphere into which the collective cannot intrude than about structuring relationships between individuals so that autonomy is fostered rather than undermined. Nedelsky applies her conception of rights as relational to the right to property so central to liberal theory. She argues that because the fundamental premise of constitutional rights is equality, the tension created between the inequalities generated by property and the claims of equal rights need to be debated so as to determine the meaning, kinds of power, and limits on power that property has and can have in market economies.

I. Introduction

In adopting the *Charter of Right and Freedoms*, Canada chose to make "rights" a central and permanent part of its political discourse just when the meaning and legitimacy of judicial review and, more generally, of "rights talk," was increasingly contested among legal scholars. Of course, one might see these contests as an arcane scholarly preoccupation, since the invocation of rights can be heard in North America in every sphere from self-help groups to environmentalists and is a growing practice world wide. But I think there are problems with rights that we ought to take seriously. In this essay, I identify a set of problems with how we are to understand the meaning of "rights" and to institutionalize those understandings. The problems fall into two broad categories: justifying the constitutionalization of rights and the critiques of "rights talk" in general. In response to each problem, I will suggest how a central tenet of feminist theory, its

focus on relationship, directs us toward solutions. My primary focus is on the constitutional sphere, for which I propose a conception of constitutionalism as a "dialogue of democratic accountability" that provides a better model than rights as "trumps."[1] I will not enter the debate about whether it was a good idea to adopt a charter at all, but I will suggest that the structure of the Canadian *Charter* lends itself to a constructive approach to rights as relationship. In closing, I will try to show how this framework helps us to better understand a set of specific constitutional problems.

II. Justifying Constitutional Rights

A. Rights as Collective Choices

Let us begin with the powerful American conception of constitutional rights so that we can see the need for an alternative paradigm. The notion that there are certain basic rights that no government, no matter how democratic, should be able to violate is a basic idea behind the U.S. Constitution and its institution of judicial review.[2] But the simple, compelling clarity of this idea is difficult to sustain in modern times. The Framers of the U.S. Constitution did not worry much about whether there were such basic rights and what they were. The Framers were even sure that although there was no consensus on what constituted the violation of rights such as property, *they* knew what property rights really were and what kind of legislation would violate them. Their confidence was the foundation for their vision of constitutionalism. Today, however, we have before us 200 years of the vicissitudes of rights jurisprudence in the U.S.: for example, neither property nor equality look today like they did in 1787. It is hard to believe in timeless values with immutable content. We have disputes about rights at every level: whether natural rights are the source of our legal rights, what would count as basic among a list of rights, and whether there is any value in using the term "rights" at all. My own view is that it is useful to use the term, and in any case we are institutionally committed to doing so. But if we are to invoke rights to constrain democratic outcomes, we must do so in a way that is true to the essentially contested and shifting meaning of rights.

We need to confront the history of rights and acknowledge the depth of the changes that have taken place in both popular and legal understandings of rights. Consider, for example, our understanding of equality. It was not so long ago that great restrictions on both the legal rights and the actual opportunities for women were widely (though I am sure not unanimously) believed to be consistent with a basic commitment to equality for all. And the changes do not exist only at the level of big general terms like equality. Consider the changes in common law conceptions of contract between the mid-nineteenth century and today. At the popular level, we have come to expect constraints on individual contracts such as minimum wage legislation, and in the courts we continue to work out concepts of unjustifiable enrichment and unconscionability in ways that would have been hard to imagine at the turn of the century. These

shifts are not just a matter of past history of conflicts, now long since settled. A workable conception of rights needs to take account of the depth of the ongoing disagreement in Canadian society about, for example, the meaning of equality and how it is to fit with our contemporary — and contested — understanding of the market economy and its legal foundations, property and contract.

Once we acknowledge the mutability of basic values, the problem of protecting them from democratic abuse is transformed. We do not have to abandon the basic insight that democracy can threaten individual rights, but we need to reconsider all of those terms: democracy, individual rights, and the nature of the tension between them. First we must see that the problem of defending individual rights is inseparable from the problem of defining them. Even if there are deep, immutable truths underlying the shifting perceptions of the terms that capture those truths, the ongoing problem of defining the terms remains. And then the relation to democracy becomes more complex, for the definition of rights, as well as the potentially threatening legislation, is the product of shifting collective choice.[3]

We find that the neat characterization of constitutionalism as balancing a tension between democracy and individual rights is not adequate for the actual problem. As a society that gives voice and effect to its collective choices and values through government institutions, both the courts and the legislatures[4] must be seen as expressing those choices and values. Courts have traditionally expressed those shifting collective choices in terms of rights, but we must recognize rights to be just that: terms for capturing and giving effect to what judges perceive to be the values and choices that "society" has embedded in the "law." (Here I am being deliberately vague as to how values come to be seen to be basic to the legal system, and which components of "society" end up affecting the choice of values.) Consider, for example, the choices between the right to use one's property as one wishes and the competing values of the right to quiet enjoyment. Judges make those choices, whether they think of the choice as dictated by the basic values of the common law, or as reflecting the choices already made by "society at large" as expressed through custom and common acceptance, or as choices guided by the best interest of all. Other examples are judicial decisions about the conflicts that arise over the importance of environmental health, or the "rights" of tenants to heat and safety.

My first point, then, in seeing the hidden complexity of "rights vs. democracy" is that rights are as much collective choices as laws passed by the legislature. And if rights no longer look so distinct from democratic outcomes, democracy also blurs into rights, for, of course, democracy is not merely a matter of collective choice, but the expression of "rights" to an equal voice in the determination of those collective choices.

The problem of constitutionalism thus can no longer simply be protecting rights from democracy. The more complex problem can be posed in various ways, with either rights or collective choice on both sides of the "balance": why should some rights (such as freedom of conscience) limit other rights, namely the rights to have collective choices made democratically? Or, why do we think that some collective choices, that is those we constitutionalize as rights, should limit other collective choices, that is the outcomes of ordinary democratic processes?[5] Since the idea of a "limit" is itself problematic, I think a more helpful way to put it is this: we need a new way of understanding the source and content of the values against which we measure democratic outcomes. Later, I will offer an example of how a conception of rights as relationship helps in this process, by looking at the question of why property should *not* be constitutionalized. First, however, I want to look more closely at some of the prevalent objections to constitutional rights as violations of democratic principles.

B. Beyond the "Pure Democracy" Critique

The pure democracy critique is primarily aimed at rights as judicially enforced limits on democratic outcomes (rather than "rights talk" more generally, which might include common law rights or statutory rights). The argument comes in two forms.

One rejects any judicial oversight of democratic bodies. The underlying claim can be that, in principle, there are no rights claims that can legitimately stand against democratic outcomes, or that there is no justifiable way of *enforcing* such claims, or that, in practice, the best way of ensuring rights in the long run is through democratic procedures, not through efforts to circumvent them. The more common form of the argument acknowledges that even if democracy is accepted as the sole or supreme value of a political system, there may be times when the courts can play a useful role in making sure the procedural conditions of democracy are met. John Hart Ely[6] in the U.S. and to some extent Patrick Monahan in Canada defend judicial review in these terms, and each claims that the Constitution in his country[7] authorizes judicial review primarily or exclusively for democracy enhancing purposes.

My view is that democracy has never been the sole or even primary value of either the U.S. or Canada, and it *could* never be the sole basis for a good society. There have been and always will be other values that are not derivative from democracy. Autonomy is one. The development of our spiritual nature is another, captured by notions of freedom of conscience and religion.[8] And of course these values can be threatened by democratic majorities wielding the power of the state. If one accepts that there are values we cherish for reasons other than their relevance to the functioning of democracy and that these values may need protection from democratic outcomes, then neither form of the pure democracy critique of rights is persuasive.[9] However, as I have already suggested, the conventional formulations of rights as limits to democracy are not adequate. Fortunately, I think it is possible to do a better job of capturing the multiple values we care about. If we look more deeply at a value like autonomy, we can begin to see that the value itself is best understood in terms of relationship, and once we see that, we can begin to rethink what it means conceptually and institutionally for autonomy to serve as a measure of democratic outcomes.

First let me contrast my conception of autonomy[10] with the kind of vision that I think underlies the American conception of rights as limits. (I also think that this conception has deep roots in Anglo-American liberalism, more broadly.) There the idea is that rights are barriers that protect the individual from intrusion by other individuals or by the state. Rights define boundaries others cannot cross and it is those boundaries, enforced by the law, that ensure individual freedom and autonomy. This image of rights fits well with the idea that the essence of autonomy is independence, which thus requires protection and separation from others. My argument is that this is a deeply misguided view of autonomy. What makes autonomy possible is not separation, but relationship.

This approach shifts the focus from protection against others to structuring relationships so that they foster autonomy. Some of the most basic pre-suppositions about autonomy shift: dependence is no longer the antithesis of autonomy but a precondition in the relationships — between parent and child, student and teacher, state and citizen — which provide the security, education, nurturing, and support that make the development of autonomy possible. Further, autonomy is not a static quality that is simply achieved one day. It is a capacity that requires ongoing relationships that help it flourish; it can wither or thrive throughout one's adult life. Interdependence becomes the central fact of political life, not an issue to be shunted to the periphery in the basic question of how to ensure individual autonomy in the inevitable face of collective power. The human interactions to be governed are not seen primarily in terms of the clashing of rights and interests, but in terms of the way patterns of relationship can develop and sustain both an enriching collective life and the scope for genuine individual autonomy. The whole conception of the relation between the individual and the collective shifts: we recognize that the collective is a source of autonomy as well as a threat to it.

The constitutional protection of autonomy is then no longer an effort to carve out a sphere into which the collective cannot intrude, but a means of structuring the relations between individuals and the sources of collective power so that autonomy is fostered rather than undermined.[11] The first thing

to note in this reformulation is that it becomes clear that the relation between autonomy and democracy is not simply one of threat and tension — just as the relation between autonomy and the collective is not simply a matter of threat. Autonomy means literally self-governance and thus requires the capacity to participate in collective as well as individual governance. In addition, the long-standing argument in favour of democracy is that it is the best way of organizing collective power so that it will foster the well-being, which must include the autonomy, of all. So autonomy demands democracy, as both a component and a means — even though democracy can threaten autonomy. (And, of course, the ideals of democracy require autonomous citizens so that each expresses her own rather than another's judgments, values and interests.)

With this relationship-focused starting point, how do we move beyond "rights as limits to democratic outcomes"? We shift our focus from limits, barriers and boundaries to a dialogue of democratic accountability — which does not make the mistake of treating democracy as the sole value. We require two things for this dialogue. We need a mechanism, an institutionalized process, of articulating basic values — particularly those that are not derivative from democracy – which is itself consistent with democracy, and we need ways of continually asking whether our institutions of democratic decision-making are generating outcomes consistent with those values, or, to stick with the autonomy example, of asking whether those outcomes foster the structures of social relations that make the development of autonomy possible. This mechanism for holding governments accountable to basic values should take the form of institutional dialogue that reflects and respects the democratic source and shifting content of those values. (Of course, judicial review has for a long time in the U.S. and recently in Canada been the primary vehicle for the articulation of values against which democratic outcomes can be measured. I will return at the end to a proposal for such a mechanism that is significantly different from judicial review.)

The example of autonomy as relation already

helps solve one of the puzzles of justifying rights as limits: how to justify their supremacy over democracy when rights themselves are shifting values. First we no longer have, and thus need no longer justify, simple supremacy, but a more complex structure of democratic accountability to basic values. Second, the shifting quality of those basic values makes more sense when our focus is on the structure of relations that fosters those values. It is not at all surprising that what it takes to foster autonomy, or what is likely to undermine it, in an industrialized corporate economy with an active regulatory-welfare state is quite different from the relationships that would have had those effects in mid-nineteenth century Canada. These may be different still in Eastern Europe or South Africa. A focus on relationship automatically turns our attention to context, and makes sense of the commonly held beliefs that there are some basic human values *and* that how we articulate and foster those values varies tremendously over time and place.

In this vision, rights do not "trump" democratic outcomes, and so they and the institutions that protect them do not have to bear a weight of justification that is impossible to muster. Rather when we begin with a focus on the relationships that constitute and make possible the basic values, which we use rights language to capture, then we have a better understanding not only of rights, but of how they relate to another set of values, for which we use the short hand "democracy." The mechanisms for institutionalizing both sets of values must aim at maintaining an ongoing dialogue that recognizes the ways democracy and autonomy are both linked together as values requiring each other *and* potentially in conflict with one another.

It will probably have already become apparent to many of you that the Canadian *Charter* is much better suited to implementing such a dialogue than the American system of judicial review, for which, at least formally, "rights as trumps" is an accurate metaphor. The *Charter*'s "override" provision in s. 33 may be seen as an effort to create a dialogue about the meaning of rights that would take place in public debate, the legislature, and the courts.[12] Section 1 invites a dialogue internal to the courts,

or to any body considering the constitutionality of a law, by opening the *Charter* with an assertion that rights are not to be seen as absolute.[13] Legislatures are to be held accountable to the basic rights outlined in the *Charter*, but that accountability must be determined in light of the (implicitly shifting) needs of a free and democratic society.

Perhaps some readers have had occasion to try to explain s. 1 and s. 33 to incredulous Americans — who usually conclude that Canadians simply still do not *really* have constitutional rights. The American vision of rights as trump-like limits is so central to their understanding of constitutionalism that they have a hard time imagining that "rights" could mean anything else. This it true despite the fact that the increasingly obvious problems with this notion drive American scholars to produce thousands of pages each year in efforts to explain and defend it. Rights as trumps is a catchy phrase and an apparently graspable, even appealing, concept, but it cannot capture the complex relations between the multiple values we actually care about. I think "dialogue of democratic accountability," though not quite as pithy, is truer both to the best aspirations of constitutionalism and to the structure of the *Charter*.

III. Critiques of "Rights Talk"

Let me turn now to some of the critiques of "rights talk" in general: 1) "rights" are undesirably individualistic; 2) rights obfuscate the real political issues; 3) rights serve to alienate and distance people from one another. I will not be trying to present these critiques in detail, but merely to sketch them to show how a focus on relationship helps construct a response.

I will begin with the claim that rights talk is hopelessly individualistic, which my argument above has already begun to address. Of course, I am not going to try here to summarize the ongoing communitarian versus liberal individualism debate — which, in any case, is only one form of the critique of individualism.[14] Let me simply note the core of the critique that I find persuasive (and have participated in myself) and then suggest how rights as relationship helps to meet it. The charge that

Charter rights express individualistic values will be familiar to many — for example in arguments about why they should not apply to the collective decisions of First Nations. There are good reasons to believe that the *Charter* draws on a powerful legacy of liberal political thought in which rights are associated with a highly individualistic conception of humanity ("mankind" historically, and there are persuasive arguments that link this gender specificity with individualism[15] — but I cannot go into that here). Indeed, the "rights bearing individual" may be said to be the basic subject of liberal political thought. Now, to compress many long, complicated, and different arguments into a sentence or two, what is wrong with this individualism is that it fails to account for the ways in which our essential humanity is neither possible nor comprehensible without the network of relationships of which it is a part. It is not just that people live in groups and have to interact with each other — after all liberal rights theory is all about specifying the entitlements of people when they come in conflict with one another. The anti-individualism theorists claim that we are literally constituted by the relationships of which we are a part.[16] Virtually all these theories also recognize some significant degree of choice and control over how these relationships shape us. But even our capacity to exercise this choice can and should be understood as shaped by our relationships — hence my argument about the centrality of relationship for autonomy. Most conventional liberal rights theories, by contrast, do not make relationship central to their understanding of the human subject. Mediating conflict is the focus, not mutual self-creation and sustenance. The selves to be protected by rights are seen as essentially separate and not creatures whose interests, needs, and capacities routinely intertwine. Thus one of the reasons women have always fit so poorly into the framework of liberal theory is that it becomes obviously awkward to think of women's relation to their children as *essentially* one of competing interests to be mediated by rights. So, it is not that I think the concerns about the individualism associated with rights are unjustified. Rather, it is my hope that the notion of rights can be rescued from its historical association with individualistic theory and practice. Human beings are *both* essentially individual and essentially social creatures. The liberal tradition has been not so much wrong as seriously and dangerously one-sided in its emphasis.

What I have tried to do elsewhere and just alluded to here, is to take the concept of autonomy and identify its core elements — which of course are connected to our sense of ourselves as distinct individuals — and to see how these elements themselves are best understood as developing in the context of relationship. Here I have used autonomy as an example of a value that is not derivative from democracy and to which democratic decision-making should be held accountable. Now I want to suggest that all rights, the very concept of rights, is best understood in terms of relationship. Again, I will be quickly condensing a much longer argument so that we can move on to see how this conception of rights meets the critiques and helps us with concrete problems.

In brief, what rights in fact do and have always done is construct relationships — of power, of responsibility, of trust, of obligation. This is as true of the law of property and contract as it is of areas like family law in which the law obviously structures relationships. For example, as lawyers know, property rights are not primarily about things, but about people's relation to each other as they affect and are affected by things.[17] The rights that the law enforces stipulate limits on what we can do with things depending on how our action affects others (for example, nuisance), when we can withhold access to things from others and how we can use that power to withhold to get them to do what we want (we are now into the realm of contract), and what responsibilities we have with respect to others' well-being (for example, tort law and landlord-tenant law). The law also defines fiduciary relationships. It defines particular relationships of trust and the responsibilities they entail. In the realm of contract, the law takes account of relationships of unequal bargaining power, and it defines certain parameters of employment and of landlord-tenant relationships. In deciding on the importance to give instances of reliance, judges must make choices about the patterns of responsibility and trust the law will foster.

I run through this list only to make it easier to think about my claim that in defining and enforcing rights, the law routinely structures and sometimes self-consciously takes account of relationship. What I propose is that this reality of relationship in rights becomes the central focus of the concept itself, and thus of all discussion of what should be treated as rights, how they should be enforced, and how they should be interpreted. It is really a matter of bringing to the foreground of our attention what has always been the background reality. My claim is that we will do a better job of making all these difficult decisions involving rights if we focus on the kind of relationships that we actually want to foster and how different concepts and institutions will best contribute to that fostering. I hope my closing examples will give a better sense of this.

My point here is that once rights are conceptualized in terms of the relationships they structure, the problem of individualism is at least radically transformed. There will almost certainly still be people who *want* the kind of relationships of power and limited responsibility that the individualistic liberal rights tradition promotes and justifies. But at least the debate will take place in terms of why we think some patterns of human relationships are better than others and what sort of "rights" will foster them.

Suppose we have some initial agreement about what we think optimal human autonomy would look like. We could then proceed beyond conclusory claims that autonomy requires individual rights to a close look at what really fosters the human capacity for autonomy and in what ways the relationships involved can be promoted and protected by legally enforced "rights." For example, I have looked at how administrative law can be understood as protecting rights in this sense and how we can structure our provision of public services so that they foster autonomy-enhancing relationships.[18] I think all of the traditionally cherished individual rights such as freedom of conscience, of speech, of "life, liberty and security of the person" can most constructively be understood

in these terms. It is extremely unlikely that any of them would, under this form of analysis, appear unnecessary. They would thus not disappear. They would not be swamped or overturned by the claims of community. Indeed in constitutional terms their function would still be to stand as an independent measure of the legitimacy of collective decisions (though the determination of that legitimacy would be a process of dialogue, not a one shot, trump-like decision). However, the specific meaning of each right would probably be transformed as people deliberated on the patterns of relationship that they wanted to characterize their society.

Rights debated in terms of relationship seem to me to overcome most of the problems of individualism without destroying what is valuable in that tradition. Of course, when dealing with such an old and powerful tradition, one has to be ever on guard against the conventional meanings of long standing terms insinuating themselves back into the conversation. But since I think we do not have the option to simply drop the term "rights," and because I think it can be used constructively, that vigilance is the price we will have to pay.

Finally, I will just offer brief suggestions about how this approach can meet the diverse body of criticism (often associated with critical legal studies) that I have lumped into my second category of objection to "rights talk" as obfuscating. One of the most important parts of this set of critiques is the objection that when "rights" are central to political debate, they misdirect political energies because they obscure rather than clarify what is at issue, what people are really after. As with the objection of individualism, this critique points to serious problems, but those problems are transformed when we understand rights as structuring relationship.

I think it is in fact the case that many rights claims, such as "it's *my* property" have a conclusory quality. They are meant to end, not to open up debate. As is probably clear by now, I am sympathetic to the idea that whether the issue is a plant-closing, or an environmentally hazardous development project, or a person who wants to rent a room in her home only to people with whom she feels comfortable, simply invoking property rights does not help, and in some circumstances can hurt — by treating as settled what should be debated. That is only the case, however, if the meaning of property rights is taken as self-evident, or if the right questions are not asked in determining their meaning.

If we approach property rights as one of the most important vehicles for structuring relations of power in our society and as a means of expressing the relations of responsibility we want to encourage, we will start off the debate in a useful way. For example, if we ask whether ownership of a factory should entail some responsibility to those it employs and how to balance that responsibility with the freedom to use one's property as one wishes (a balance analogous to that in traditional nuisance law), then we can intelligently pursue the inevitable process of defining and redefining property. We can ask what relationships of power, responsibility, trust, and commitment we want the terms of ownership of productive property to foster, and we can also ask whether those relationships will foster the autonomy, creativity, or initiative that we value. By contrast, to say that owners can shut down a plant whenever and however they want because it is their property, is either to assert a tautology (property *means* the owner has this power) or an historical claim (property has in the past had this meaning). The historical claim does, of course, have special relevance in law, but it can only be the beginning not the end of the inquiry into what property should mean. The focus on relationship will help to give proper weight and context to the historical claims and to expose the tautological ones.

One common form of the allegation of obfuscation is the objection that rights are "reified." They appear as fixed entities, whose meaning is simply taken as a given. This thing-like quality of rights prevents the recognition of the ways in which rights are collective choices which require evaluation. Descriptively, I think this is a valid concern about the dominant traditions of rights. But, as is no doubt already clear, I do not think it is inevitable. I think that if we always remember that what rights do is structure relationships, and that we interpret them in that light, and make decisions about what ought to be called rights in that light,

then we will not only loosen up the existing reification, but our new conceptions of rights as relationship are not as likely to once again harden into reified images that dispel rather than invite inquiry.

Finally, there is the important critique that rights are alienating and distancing, that they express and create barriers between people.[19] Rights have this distancing effect in part because, as they function in our current discourse, they help us avoid seeing some of the relationships of which we are in fact a part. For example, when we see homeless people on the street, we do not think about the fact that it is in part our regime of property rights that renders them homeless. We do not bring to consciousness what we in fact take for granted: our sense of our property rights in our homes permits us to exclude the homeless persons. Indeed, our sense that we have not done anything wrong, that we have not violated the homeless persons' rights, helps us to distance ourselves from their plight. The dominant conception of rights helps us to feel that we are not responsible.

If we come to focus on the relationships that our rights structure, we will see the connection between our power to exclude and the homeless persons' plight. We might still decide to maintain that right of exclusion, but the decision would be made in full consciousness of the pattern of relationships it helps to shape. And I think we are likely to experience our responsibilities differently as we recognize that our "private rights" always have social consequences.[20]

Thus my response to the critique of distancing is that rights conceived as relationship will not foster the same distancing that our current conception does. Rights *could*, however, still serve the protective function that thoughtful advocates of rights-based distance, like Patricia Williams,[21] are concerned about. Not only does my vision of rights as relationship have equal respect at its core, but optimal structures of human relations will always provide both choice about entering relationships and space for the choice to withdraw.[22]

These, then, are the outlines of my responses to the critiques of "rights-talk" as individualistic, obfuscating, and alienating. Before going on to my constitutional examples, let me reiterate what is novel and what is not about my approach. It is important to my argument to claim that thinking about rights as relationship offers a new and better way of resolving a set of problems about rights. But part of what I think makes the argument compelling is that it is not in fact a radical departure from what is currently entailed in legal decision making, including judicial decision-making. As my earlier examples were intended to show, the novelty lies only in bringing into focus what has always been in the background.

It is important to recognize the *existing* role of relationship in rights in order to see that what I am proposing can happen immediately, without the radical restructuring of our legal system. It is also important to meet the objection that what I am calling for dangerously expands — or creates — a policy-making role for judges. My argument is that recognizing rights as relationship only brings to consciousness, and thus open to considered reflection and debate, what already exists. Here I join a growing chorus of voices that urge that judges will do a better job if they are self-conscious about what they are doing, even if that new self-consciousness seems very demanding.[23]

IV. Applying "Rights as Relationship"

I turn now finally to my sketches of how my approach helps with some specific problems. I begin with the question of whether property belongs in the *Charter*. This question has the virtue of making more concrete the abstract question I began with of how we are to understand the idea of constitutionalizing rights. Once we acknowledge that constitutional rights are collective choices, we not only make the simple "democracy vs. rights" formulation untenable, we make it a great deal more difficult (or we make it more obvious why it is difficult) to explain why some things we call rights (like freedom of speech or conscience) should be constitutionalized in my dialogue of democratic accountability and others, like property, should not.

My idea of constitutionalism is to make democracy accountable to basic values, to have mechanisms of ongoing dialogue about whether the col-

lective choices people make through their democratic assemblies are consistent with their deepest values. Now there is a certain irony to this idea of "deepest values" as what constitutionalism protects. When we choose to constitutionalize a value, to treat it as a constitutional right, we are in effect saying both that there is a deeply shared consensus about the importance of that value *and* that we think that value is at risk, that the same people who value it are likely to violate it through their ordinary political processes. Now, in fact, I think this ironic duality makes sense. There are lots of values like that. Once we recognize the duality, we know that it is not a sufficient argument *against* constitutionalizing a right either to say that it is contested so it does not belong in a Charter of Rights and Freedoms or to say that it is so well accepted that it does not need to be in the *Charter*. Of course, those are both arguments one might make about property.

I think that in Canada, and probably more generally in constitutional democracies, the fundamental premise of constitutional rights is equality. Constitutional rights define the entitlements that *all* members of society must have, the basic shared terms that will make it possible not just to flourish as individuals, but to relate to each other on equal terms. (Which is not to say that the values we protect constitutionally — autonomy, privacy, liberty, security — are themselves identical to or derivative from equality.) Now this sounds at first perilously close to the basic notion of liberal theory: that people are to be conceived of as rights-bearing individuals, who are equal precisely in their role as rights-bearers, abstracted from any of the concrete particulars, such as gender, age, class, abilities, which render them unequal. This conception has been devastatingly criticized by feminist scholars such as Iris Young.[24] My notion is subtly, but I think crucially, different. The question of equality (to be captured in constitutional rights) is the meaning of equal moral worth *given* the reality that in almost every conceivable concrete way we are not equal, but vastly different, and vastly unequal in our needs and abilities. The object is not to make these differences disappear when we talk about equal rights, but to ask how we can structure relations of equality among people with many different concrete inequalities.

The law will in large part determine (or give effect to choices about) which differences matter and in what ways: which will be the source of advantage, power, privilege and which the source of disadvantage, powerlessness, and subordination. One might say that whatever the patterns of privilege and disadvantage the ordinary political and legal processes may generate, the purpose of equal constitutional rights is to structure relations so that people treat each other with a basic respect, acknowledge and foster each other's dignity, even as they acknowledge and respect differences. Constitutional rights define indicia of respect and requirements for dignity — including rights of participation. Constitutional rights define basic ways we must treat each other as equals as we make our collective choices.

Property fits very awkwardly here. It is, at least in the sorts of market economies we are familiar with, the primary source of *inequality*. Of course, formally, everyone who has property *has* the same rights with respect to it. Nevertheless, property is the primary vehicle for the allocation of power from state to citizen, and in market economies, the presumption has been that that power must and should be distributed unequally — for purposes of efficiency and prosperity and, on some arguments, merit as well. The result, of course, is an ongoing tension between the inequality of power generated by property through the market and the claims of equal rights. ...

All of this suggests to me that debates over the meaning of property, of the kinds of power that should be allocated to individuals and the limits on that power (as in my earlier examples of landlord-tenant law, environmental regulation, and minimum wage law) should be part of the ongoing vigorous debate of the most popularly accessible bodies, the legislative assemblies. ...

V. Conclusion

When we understand the constitutionalization of rights as a means of setting up a dialogue of democratic accountability, we redefine the kinds of justification necessary for constitutional constraints on democratic decision-making. Perhaps even more importantly for the world outside of academia, we provide a conceptual framework that will help us to design and assess workable mechanisms for constitutionalizing rights in modern democracies. This conception of constitutionalism both requires and fosters a new understanding of rights — rights as structuring relationships. This approach to rights, in turn, helps to overcome the most serious problems with the dominant conceptions of our liberal tradition. When we understand rights as relationships and constitutionalism as a dialogue of democratic accountability, we can not only move beyond long-standing problems, but we can create a conceptual and institutional structure that will facilitate inquiry into the new problems that will inevitably emerge.

Author's Note

The author would like to thank the audience of the 1992 McDonald Lecture and the participants at the legal theory workshops at New York University Law School and Columbia University Law School for their helpful questions and comments.

NOTES

1. Ronald Dworkin coined this now widely used phrase in R. Dworkin, *Taking Rights Seriously* (Cambridge: Harvard University Press, 1978).
2. As I have argued elsewhere, the Constitution of 1787 did not focus primarily on rights as limits in the sense we now understand as the purpose and legitimacy of judicial review. The Constitution of 1787 was designed to structure the institutions so as to ensure that the sort of men who knew how to govern, including how to respect rights, would be the ones in office. See J. Nedelsky, *Private Property and the Limits of American Constitutionalism: The Madisonian Framework and its Legacy* (Chicago: University of Chicago Press, 1990).
3. This paragraph is drawn from *ibid*. c. 6.
4. To leave aside the complexities of cabinet and administrative bodies.
5. One workshop participant suggested that this for-

mulation rested on a mistake: confusing the question of limits on democracy with the process of determining or enforcing those limits. To the participant, the content of the rights that should serve as limits is given by a theory of rights, derived, I assume, from human nature or the nature of agency or freedom. My point, however, is that we cannot rely on such theoretically derived conceptions to justify limits on democracy. At the least, as I noted in the text above, the legal meaning of such rights must be determined, and the legitimacy of the process of that determination is inseparable from the legitimacy of treating rights as limits. And, in my terms, that process will inevitably be a collective determination and thus choice. More broadly, the historical shifts in meaning and the diversity of constitutionalized rights in different democracies make it difficult to believe that we can rely on a transcendent, universal, immutable source for the content of rights.

In B.A. Ackerman, *We, the People: Foundations* (Cambridge: Harvard University Press, 1991), Bruce Ackerman also has a compelling argument that the American Constitution is structured in a way that treats "the people" as the source of the meaning of rights rather than transcendent meaning. Here he contrasts the American Constitution with the German Constitution. In this regard, the Canadian Constitution is like the American.

6. J.H. Ely, *Democracy and Distrust: A Theory of Judicial Review* (Cambridge: Harvard University Press, 1980).

7. Monahan draws on Ely, but thinks Ely is wrong descriptively about the U.S. P. Monahan, *Politics and the Constitution: The Charter, Federalism and the Supreme Court of Canada* (Toronto: Carswell/Methuen, 1987).

8. Of course it is possible to work back from democracy, asking what all the preconditions are for democratic participation, and from that process generate a very wide range of values, including autonomy. But I think such a process distorts our understanding of the genuine diversity of values that in fact are necessary for an optimal society or for the possibility of pursuing a full and good life. It has always struck me as particularly implausible to believe that the value of freedom of religion

could be derived from even the most all encompassing conception of the conditions for democracy. Here I think the distortion involved in such derivation is obvious.

9. Unless one wants to make the strong claim that even though in principle it would be legitimate to protect those values, there is no institutional mechanism of doing so that could be legitimate.

10. I have developed this conception in more detail in J. Nedelsky, "Reconceiving Autonomy: Sources, Thoughts, and Possibilities" (1989) 1 *Yale Journal of Law and Feminism* 7.

11. Note that the sources of collective power might include large scale corporations, but here I will just focus on the government.

12. Section 33, the so-called override provision or notwithstanding clause, allows legislatures to expressly state that a piece of legislation shall operate notwithstanding provisions in s. 2 (fundamental freedoms of conscience, expression, assembly and association) or ss. 7-15 ("legal rights" and "equality rights"). Such legislation has effect for 5 years and may then be reenacted.

13. Section 1 reads: "The *Canadian Charter of Rights and Freedoms* guarantees the rights and freedoms set out in it subject only to such reasonable limits prescribed by law as can be demonstrably justified in a free and democratic society."

14. An excellent critique and historical account not widely known among legal and political science academics is C. Keller, *From a Broken Web: Separation, Sexism and Self* (Boston: Beacon Press, 1986).

15. *Ibid.*

16. For example, C. Taylor, *Philosophy and the Human Sciences* (Cambridge: Cambridge University Press, 1985), particularly c. 7, "Atomism"; C. Keller, *ibid.*; M.J. Sandel, *Liberalism and the Limits of Justice* (Cambridge: Cambridge University Press, 1982); I.M. Young, "Impartiality and the Civic Public" and S. Benhabib, "The Generalized and the Concrete Other" in S. Benhabib and D. Cornell, eds. *Feminism as Critique* (Minneapolis: University of Minnesota Press, 1987).

17. For a discussion of property rights from a relational perspective see J. Singer, "The Reliance Interest in Property" (1987-88) 40 *Stanford Law Review* 577.

My conversations with Joe Singer were also helpful in the early stages of working on this essay.

18. *Supra* note 11.

19. Peter Gabel offers an excellent, thoughtful statement of this perspective in P. Gabel, "The Phenomenology of Right-Consciousness and the Pact of the Withdrawn Selves" (1984) 62 *Texas Law Review* 1563.

20. This seems an appropriate place for a note of response to the allegation that my theory of "rights as relationship" is consequentialist, and that I must therefore enter into the debate over deontological vs. consequentialist theories of rights. A series of questions and the Legal Theory workshop at Columbia helped me to see why this debate is peripheral to my concerns here. The division between consequentialist and deontological theories is premised on the possibility of a useful conception of human beings whose nature can be understood in abstraction from any of the relations of which they are a part. Once one rejects this premise, the sharp distinction between rights defined on the basis of human nature vs. rights defined in terms of the desirability of the relationships they foster simply dissolves. Since there is no free-standing human nature comprehensible in abstraction from all relationship from which one could derive a theory of rights, the focus on relationship does not constitute a failure to respect the essential claims of humanness. The focus on relationship is a focus on the nature of humanness, not a willingness to sacrifice it to the collective.

21. P.J. Williams, *The Alchemy of Race and Rights* (Cambridge: Harvard University Press, 1991).

22. There are still some unresolved problems here. We need to figure out both the scope for withdrawal that is optimal and the ways of structuring choice about entering relationships. These are complicated problems once one starts from a framework that treats relationships as primary and in some ways given rather than chosen.

23. See, for example, M. Minow, *Making All the Difference: Inclusion, Exclusion and American Law* (Ithaca: Cornell University Press, 1990).

The strongest argument that I have heard against this position has come from some of my students, in particular black students. The argument is that even if judges are always engaged in what they would call policy-making, if they were conscious of it, they should remain unconscious because that constrains them more. Contrary to my claim that we can move forward in the direction I advocate in the absence of radical reform, they say given the current composition of the judiciary, they want the judges to feel as constrained as possible about innovation. They seem to suggest that we should wait until we have a vastly more representative judiciary before we advocate a shift in their understanding of their job.

24. See I.M. Young, "Impartiality and the Civic Public" in S. Benhabib and D. Cornell, eds., *supra* note 16 at 56.

STUDY QUESTIONS

1 What is the starting point for the Universal Declaration of Human Rights? Are some rights in the UN Declaration more familiar to you than others? If so, which ones? Are there some rights that do not strike you as universal? If so, which ones?

2 What evidence do Adamantia Pollis and Peter Schwab provide to substantiate their claims that "the political philosophy of liberalism has dominated the conceptualization" of human rights?

3 What arguments do Pollis and Schwab make to substantiate their claim that human rights as defined by the West are meaningless in most states in the world?

4 Do you think Pollis and Schwab are right to suggest that we can reformulate human rights so that they truly reflect universal values underlying the multiplicity of philosophies and divergent beliefs in the world? What do they identify as universal? Would your answer be different from theirs? Defend your answers.

5 What arguments does Jay Drydyk use to answer the claim by Pollis and Schwab that human rights are meaningless in most places in the world?

6 Drydyk takes up the challenge posed by Pollis and Schwab to reformulate human rights by making use of the notion of a "global public sphere of moral deliberation." What does he mean by this? Can it be used to avoid Eurocentrism? Why or why not?

7 Explain what Drydyk means when he says that a human right to something is "calling for social protection against standard threats that exemplify a particular type of danger for humans." Do the third generation rights that Drydyk describes fit this definition? What about first and second generation rights? Defend your answers.

8 Drydyk uses the phenomena of the "globalization of subcontracting and informalization of labour" not only as a call for an international movement to address the violation of labor rights, but as a way of formulating a full set of human rights that are sensitive to conditions in various social and political contexts. Is the case he presents convincing? Why or why not?

9 Like Pollis and Schwab, Kenneth Inada thinks non-Western cultures tend to value the community and relationships in it over the individual rights to freedom and property emphasized in the West. According to Inada, how do soft relationships as described in Buddhist beliefs exemplify these values?

10 Explain what Inada means by hard relationships by outlining how the values underlying these kinds of relationships are evident in Western philosophical thinkers such as Hobbes and Rawls. Evaluate Inada's attempt to use the Buddhist understanding of soft relationships as a way of reconceiving the Western notion of human rights.

11 Why, according to Jennifer Nedelsky, is an individualist conception of autonomy problematic for a conception of rights?

12 Nedelsky retains the goal of enhancing autonomy, but argues that the liberal ideal of rights as setting limits to state interference needs to be reconceived. How does she reconceive rights? Is this relevant to a discussion of the differences between the *Canadian Charter of Rights and Freedoms* and the American conception of constitutional rights?

13 How does Nedelsky apply insights from her relational conception of rights to the right to property so central to liberal societies? Does this make you think differently about the right to property? Why or why not?

SUGGESTED READINGS

Ake, Claude. "The African Context of Human Rights." *Africa Today*, v. 34, no. 142 (1987): 5-13.

An-Na'im, Abdullahi Ahmed. "Islam, Islamic Law and the Dilemma of Cultural Legitimacy for Universal Human Rights." In *Asian Perspectives on Human Rights*, edited by Claude E. Welch and Virginia Leary. Boulder, CO: Westview Press, 1990.

An-Na'im, Abdullahi Ahmed, and Francis M. Deng (editors). *Human Rights in Africa: Cross-Cultural Perspectives*. Washington, DC: The Brookings Institution, 1990.

Bahar, Saba. "Human Rights are Women's Right: Amnesty International and the Family." *Hypatia*, v. 11, no. 1 (Winter 1996): 105-34.

Bauer, Joanne, and Daniel A. Bell (editors). *The East Asian Challenge for Human Rights*. Cambridge: Cambridge University Press, 1999.

Bell, Daniel A. "The East Asian Challenge to Human Rights: Reflections on an East-West Dialogue." *Human Rights Quarterly*, v. 18, no. 3 (1996): 641-67.

Berlin, Isaiah. *Four Essays on Liberty*. Oxford: Oxford University Press, 1969.

Bunch, Charlotte. "Women's Rights as Human Rights: Toward a Re-Vision of Human Rights." *Human Rights Quarterly*, v. 12, no. 4 (1990): 486-98.

Cook, Rebecca (editor). *Human Rights of Women: National and International Perspectives*. Philadelphia, PA: University of Pennsylvania Press, 1994.

Donnelly, Jack. "Human Rights and Human Dignity: An Analytical Critique of Non-Western Conceptions of Human Rights." *The American Political Science Review*, v. 76 (1982): 303-16.

Dworkin, Ronald. "Taking Rights Seriously." In *Taking Rights Seriously*. Cambridge, MA: Harvard University Press, 1978: 184-205.

Howard, Judith A., and Carolyn Allen (editors). "Reflections on the Fourth World Conference on Women and NGO Forum '95." *Signs: Journal of Women in Culture and Society*, v. 22, no. 1 (1996): 181-226.

Hunt, Krista. "The Strategic Co-optation of Women's Rights." *International Feminist Journal of Politics*, v. 4, no. 1 (April 2002): 116-21.

Ignatieff, Michael. *The Rights Revolution*. Toronto, ON: House of Anansi Press, 2000.

Ignatieff, Michael, *et al*. *Human Rights as Politics and Idolatry*. Edited and introduced by Amy Gutmann. Princeton, NJ: Princeton University Press, 2001.

Kahn, Paul. "American Hegemony and International Law: Speaking Law to Power: Popular Sovereignty, Human Rights, and the New International Order." *Chicago Journal of International Law*, v. 1, no. 1 (Spring 2000): 1-18.

Li, Xiaorong. "'Asian Values' and the Universality of Human Rights." *Report from the Institute of Philosophy & Public Policy*, v. 16, no. 2 (Spring 1996): 18-23.

Meyer, Lucas, Stanley Paulson, and Thomas Pogge (editors). *Rights, Culture and the Law: Themes from the Legal and Political Philosophy of Joseph Raz*. Oxford: Oxford University Press, 2003.

Monshipouri, M., *et al*. (editors). *Constructing Human Rights in the Age of Globalization*. Armonk, NY: M.E. Sharpe, 2003.

Nussbaum, Martha. "Capabilities and Human Rights." *Fordham Law Review*, v. 66 (1997): 273-300.

Peter, Julie, and Andrea Wolper (editors). *Women's Rights, Human Rights: International Feminist Perspectives*. New York, NY: Routledge, 1994.

Pogge, Thomas. "How Should Human Rights be Conceived?" in *Jahrbuch für Recht und Ethik* 3, (1995): 103-20.

Pollis, Adamantia. "Liberal, Socialist, and Third World Perspectives on Human Rights." In *Toward a Human Rights Framework*. New York, NY: Praeger, 1982.

Sen, Amartya. "Human Rights and Asian Values." *The New Republic* (July 14 and 21 1997).

Shapiro, Ian (editor). *Ethnicity and Group Rights*. NOMOS v. 39 (1997).

Waldron, Jeremy (editor). *Theories of Rights*. Oxford: Oxford University Press, 1984.

Walters, Lynn (editor). *Women's Rights: A Global View*. Westport, CT: Greenwood Press, 2001.

Williams, Patricia. *The Alchemy of Race and Rights*. Cambridge, MA: Harvard University Press, 1991.

CHAPTER THREE: JUSTICE

INTRODUCTION

Theories of what justice is and demands have had a longer history in moral and political theory than those of rights. Plato and Aristotle understood justice to be a virtue of individuals in their interactions with others as well as the principal virtue of social institutions. As a social virtue, justice has been closely associated with ideas of equality and what people are owed — as is reflected in Aristotle's tenet that justice demands that equals be treated equally. This tenet of treating equals equally divides justice into two kinds of theories: those that provide accounts of compensation and punishment for the infliction of harm or damage and those that provide accounts of the proper distribution of benefits or goods. These theories vary from those that hold that what people are owed is determined by the particular laws, customs, and shared values of the community in which a person lives to those that hold that justice is the maximization of a particular good for a community (such as Mill's Utilitarian account of happiness in Chapter One) to those that hold that justice is the set of rules or principles that emerge in conditions under which people reach an agreement or social contract about how to cooperate with others for mutual advantage (such as John Rawls's theory in this chapter).

The first reading presents some of the basic ideas from Rawls's highly influential theory of justice. Recall from the previous chapter that Inada takes Rawls to be an example of a modern liberal thinker who uses the notion of a social contract to generate a set of principles that members of a community agree to abide by. In *A Theory of Justice* (1971), Rawls asks us to imagine ourselves in an original position behind a veil of ignorance, a veil that conceals from us knowledge about the specific details of our lives: who we are, where we live, whether we are rich or poor, black or white. We do know that we have goals and interests that we will want to pursue, and we have general knowledge that social and political structures can determine our fate with respect to the distribution of social goods. For Rawls, these conditions enable us to reach agreement about principles of justice for shaping political structures so that people are treated equally and for determining the fair distribution of social goods.

Rawls argues that the two principles that would be reached through an agreement in an original position of fairness and equality are 1) each person is to have an equal right to the most extensive basic liberty compatible with a similar liberty for others; and 2) social and economic inequalities are to be arranged so that they are both a) reasonably expected to be to everyone's advantage and b) attached to positions and offices open to all. The first principle takes priority and guarantees equal liberty to all. The second justifies inequalities in the distribution of goods, but only if it is to the benefit of the worst off. The first principle defends negative or civil and political rights and the second, referred to as the difference principle, defends positive or social and economic rights. The difference principle allows a redistribution of goods such as wealth through measures such as taxation so that those who are disadvantaged through no fault of their own are treated fairly.

Rawls's theory of justice has generated numerous critiques, some of which are examined in the readings that follow his. Rawls's defense of positive rights has him described as a liberal egalitarian or a substantive equality theorist. This is contrasted with libertarians or formal equality theorists who make liberty rights (in the first principle) both necessary and sufficient for equal treatment. The libertarian argument is presented by Richard Garner. Other criticisms come from feminists who argue that Rawls makes assumptions about what sort of person is behind the veil of ignorance. That person, they argue, reflects the norm of male citizen in the workplace and in positions of power and status. Virginia Held's defense of an ethic of care reflects this sort of criticism. Rawls has also been charged with assuming that the person behind the veil of ignorance is already a citizen of liberal democratic societies with beliefs and values about what equality and liberty entail. The final reading by Nira Yuval-Davis explores this kind of criticism by providing a gendered account of citizenship.

The libertarian account of justice, which rejects Rawls's theory of justice, is defended by Garner in the second reading. Like Rawls, Garner works within the tradition of social contract theory. But he disagrees with Rawls that the second principle that justifies state welfare policies would be chosen in a hypothetical contract that establishes the rules of justice. Garner argues that the only guiding principle for political and social arrangements is that of individual liberty. Like other libertarians, Garner defends the negative right to liberty, one that produces a duty in others and in the state to refrain from interfering with one's freedom. On this view, positive rights cannot be justified because they ask individuals to give up some of what they have acquired through their own means and actions. On this view as well, liberty and private property are integrally connected — my freedom to pursue desires, projects, and goals leads to the moral imperative that I have the freedom to acquire the things I want and to control what I use and have without interference from others or the state.

To answer possible objections that non-interference by the state deprives some people of basic goods such as education, minimum guaranteed income, old age security, and health care, Garner argues that having these measures as compulsory violates freedom in a way that cannot be justified. What can be justified and help those in need are voluntary mechanisms such as charity and philanthropy. Garner speculates, in fact, that individuals would be more inclined to voluntarily support those in need if the welfare state that taxes people and redistributes wealth were abolished.

In the third reading, Virginia Held presents a critique of justice that applies to both Rawls's and Garner's theories of justice. Justice, argues Held, in its alignment with conceptions of individual rights, equality, and universal law, is to be contrasted with an ethic of care that views persons as relational and interdependent and in which the interests of the self and others are intertwined. An ethic of care, therefore, is concerned with responsibilities for meeting the needs of others and with maintaining and sustaining caring relations. Mutual concern, trustworthiness, attentiveness, and responsiveness are thereby promoted by a care approach to morality. Though an ethic of care has tended to be associated with moral theory and, more specifically, with moral relations in the private sphere, Held argues that it has potential as a political theory that can inform and transform contemporary problems in international relations and global politics. As caring values became more influential within a society, for example, resolutions of conflict through threat, force, and violence could decrease at national and international levels of relations within and between states.

While Held credits feminist theory for developing an ethic of care, she also notes that there are similarities between the ethic of care and Confucianism or "Asian values" more generally. In the fourth reading, A.T. Nuyen turns our attention back to correspondences between Confucianism and Western theories of justice. He argues that globalization has resulted in a move to universalism that should be embraced rather than resisted and that a universal account of global justice is desirable and attainable. He examines the question of whether Confucianism can contribute to the project of articulating a universal account of global justice that can help resolve conflicts, including those of cultural identities. He argues that Confucianism need not be conceived as blocking the progress of universal justice or being a helpless victim of that progress and has the potential to contribute to the development of a notion of universal justice that respects and promotes cultural difference.

Yuval-Davis provides a gendered reading of citizenship in a world where the borders of nations are becoming more permeable and globalization affects everyone. She argues that women's citizenship needs to be discussed as different from men's. Moreover, citizenship is also impacted by factors such as ethnicity, origin, and urban or rural residence — all of which are in turn affected by trans- and cross-border as well as global understandings of what constitutes citizenship. In the liberal tradition, citizens are presumed to be basically the same; their differences of class, ethnicity, gender, and so on are considered irrelevant to their status as citizens. Yuval-Davis uses the binaries of individual/group, public/private, and active/passive pervasive in Western liberal thinking to show that citizens have not been and are not actually treated the same. She argues that in an era of increased multiculturalism within states and increased globalization across states citizenship should be conceived as a "multi-tiered construct," one that conceives of persons as members of groups of various kinds within and across national collectivities as well as in states. Such a strategy of expanding the notion of citizenship, she argues, can help to integrate the struggles of women in places across the world with respect to issues such as reproductive rights, political participation, poverty, and the oppression and exploitation that exists in the name of culture and tradition.

A THEORY OF JUSTICE

John Rawls

John Rawls was the James Bryant Conant University Professor Emeritus at Harvard University. He is the author of the path-breaking A Theory of Justice *(1971) as well as* Political Liberalism *(1996),* The Law of Peoples *(1999),* Collected Papers *(1999),* Lectures on the History of Moral Philosophy *(2000), and* Justice as Fairness: A Restatement *(2001). Rawls is considered by many to be the most important political philosopher of the twentieth century and a powerful advocate of the liberal perspective. He died in 2002.*

The reading provides excerpts from A Theory of Justice. *It gives a skeletal account of Rawls's project of using social contract theory to generate principles of justice for assigning basic rights and duties and determining the division of social benefits in a society. Rawls argues that the two principles that would be reached through an agreement in an original position of fairness and equality are 1) each person is to have an equal right to the most extensive basic liberty compatible with a similar liberty for others; and 2) social and economic inequalities are to be arranged so that they are both a) reasonably expected to be to everyone's advantage, and b) attached to positions and offices open to all.*

---

1. The Role of Justice

Justice is the first virtue of social institutions, as truth is of systems of thought. A theory however elegant and economical must be rejected or revised if it is untrue; likewise laws and institutions no matter how efficient and well-arranged must be reformed or abolished if they are unjust. Each person possesses an inviolability founded on justice that even the welfare of society as a whole cannot override. For this reason justice denies that the loss of freedom for some is made right by a greater good shared by others. It does not allow that the sacrifices imposed on a few are outweighed by the larger sum of advantages enjoyed by many. Therefore in a just society the liberties of equal citizenship are taken as settled; the rights secured by justice are not subject to political bargaining or to the calculus of social interests. The only thing that permits us to acquiesce in an erroneous theory is the lack of a better one; analo-

gously, an injustice is tolerable only when it is necessary to avoid an even greater injustice. Being first virtues of human activities, truth and justice are uncompromising.

These propositions seem to express our intuitive conviction of the primacy of justice. No doubt they are expressed too strongly. In any event I wish to inquire whether these contentions or others similar to them are sound, and if so how they can be accounted for. To this end it is necessary to work out a theory of justice in the light of which these assertions can be interpreted and assessed....

2. The Subject of Justice

Many different kinds of things are said to be just and unjust: not only laws, institutions, and social systems, but also particular actions of many kinds, including decisions, judgments, and imputations. We also call the attitudes and dispositions of persons, and persons themselves, just and unjust.

Our topic, however, is that of social justice. For us the primary subject of justice is the basic structure of society, or more exactly, the way in which the major social institutions distribute fundamental rights and duties and determine the division of advantages from social cooperation. By major institutions I understand the political constitution and the principal economic and social arrangement. Thus the legal protection of freedom of thought and liberty of conscience, competitive markets, private property in the means of production, and the monogamous family are examples of major social institutions. Taken together as one scheme, the major institutions define men's rights and duties and influence their life-prospects, what they can expect to be and how well they can hope to do. The basic structure is the primary subject of justice because its effects are so profound and present from the start. The intuitive notion here is that this structure contains various social positions and that men born into different positions have different expectations of life determined, in part, by the political system as well as by economic and social circumstances. In this way the institutions of society favor certain starting places over others. These are especially deep inequalities. Not only are they pervasive, but they affect men's initial chances in life; yet they cannot possibly be justified by an appeal to the notions of merit or desert. It is these inequalities, presumably inevitable in the basic structure of any society to which the principles of social justice must in the first instance apply. These principles, then, regulate the choice of a political constitution and the main elements of the economic and social system. The justice of a social scheme depends essentially on how fundamental rights and duties are assigned and on the economic opportunities and social conditions in the various sectors of society....

3. The Main Idea of the Theory of Justice.

My aim is to present a conception of justice which generalizes and carries to a higher level of abstraction the familiar theory of the social contract as found, say, in Locke, Rousseau, and Kant.[1] In order to do this we are not to think of the original

contract as one to enter a particular society or to set up a particular form of government. Rather, the guiding idea is that the principles of justice for the basic structure of society are the object of the original agreement. They are the principles that free and rational persons concerned to further their own interests would accept in an initial position of equality as defining the fundamental terms of their association. These principles are to regulate all further agreements; they specify the kinds of social cooperation that can be entered into and the forms of government that can be established. This way of regarding the principles of justice I shall call justice as fairness.

Thus we are to imagine that those who engage in social cooperation choose together, in one joint act, the principles which are to assign basic rights and duties and to determine the division of social benefits. Men are to decide in advance how they are to regulate their claims against one another and what is to be the foundation charter of their society. Just as each person must decide by rational reflection what constitutes his good, that is, the system of ends which it is rational for him to pursue, so a group of persons must decide once and for all what is to count among them as just and unjust. The choice which rational men would make in this hypothetical situation of equal liberty, assuming for the present that this choice problem has a solution, determines the principles of justice.

In justice as fairness the original position of equality corresponds to the state of nature in the traditional theory of the social contract. This original position is not, of course, thought of as an actual historical state of affairs, much less as a primitive condition of culture. It is understood as a purely hypothetical situation characterized so as to lead to a certain conception of justice.[2] Among the essential features of this situation is that no one knows his place in society, his class position or social status, nor does anyone know his fortune in the distribution of natural assets and abilities, his intelligence, strength, and the like. I shall even assume that the parties do not know their conceptions of the good or their special psychological propensities. The principles of justice are chosen behind a veil of ignorance. This ensures that no one is advantaged or disadvantaged in the choice of principles by the outcome of natural chance or the contingency of social circumstances. Since all are similarly situated and no one is able to design principles to favor his particular condition, the principles of justice are the result of a fair agreement or bargain. For given the circumstances of the original position, the symmetry of everyone's relation to each other, this initial situation is fair between individuals as moral persons, that is, as rational beings with their own ends and capable, I shall assume, of a sense of justice. The original position is, one might say, the appropriate initial status quo, and the fundamental agreements reached in it are fair. This explains the propriety of the name "justice as fairness": it conveys the idea that the principles of justice are agreed to in an initial situation that is fair. The name does not mean the concepts of justice and fairness are the same, any more that the phrase "poetry as metaphor" means that the concepts of poetry and metaphor are the same.

Justice as fairness begins, as I have said, with one of the most general of all choices which persons might make together, namely, with the choice of the first principles of a conception of justice which is to regulate all subsequent criticism and reform of institutions. Then, having chosen a conception of justice, we can suppose that they are to choose a constitution and a legislature to enact laws, and so on, all in accordance with the principles of justice initially agreed upon. Our social situation is just if it is such that by this sequence of hypothetical agreements we would have contracted into the general system of rules which defines it. Moreover, assuming that the original position does determine a set of principles (that is, that a particular conception of justice would be chosen), it will then be true that whenever social institutions satisfy these principles those engaged in them can say to one another that they are cooperating on terms to which they would agree if they were free and equal persons whose relations with respect to one another were fair. They could all view their arrangements as meeting the stipulations which they would acknowledge in an initial situation that embodies widely accepted and reasonable constraints on the choice of principles. The general recognition of this fact would provide the basis for a public acceptance of the corresponding principles of justice. No society can, of course, be a scheme of cooperation which men enter voluntarily in a literal sense; each person finds himself placed at birth in some particular position in some particular society, and the nature of this position materially affects his life prospects. Yet a society satisfying the principles of justice as fairness comes as close as a society can to being a voluntary scheme, for it meets the principles which free and equal persons would assent to under circumstances that are fair. In this sense its members are autonomous and the obligations they recognize self-imposed.

One feature of justice as fairness is to think of the parties in the initial situation as rational and mutually disinterested. This does not mean that the parties are egoists, that is, individuals with only certain kinds of interests, say in wealth, prestige, and domination. But they are conceived as not taking an interest in one another's interests. They are to presume that even their spiritual aims may be opposed, in the way that the aims of those of different religions may be opposed. Moreover, the concept of rationality must be interpreted as far as possible into the narrow sense, standard in economic theory, of taking the most effective means to given ends. I shall modify this concept to some extent, as explained later (§25), but one must try to avoid introducing into it any controversial ethical elements. The initial situation must be characterized by stipulations that are widely accepted.

In working out the conception of justice as fairness one main task clearly is to determine which principles of justice would be chosen in the original position. To do this we must describe this situation in some detail and formulate with care the problem of choice which it presents. These matters I shall take up in the immediately succeeding chapters. It may be observed, however, that once the principles of justice are thought of as arising from an original agreement in a situation of equality, it is an open question whether the principle of utility would be acknowledged. Offhand it hardly seems likely that persons who view themselves as equals, entitled to press their claims upon one another, would agree to a principle which may require lesser life prospects for some simply for the sake of a greater sum of advantages enjoyed by others. Since each desires to protect his interests, his capacity to advance his conception of the good, no one has a reason to acquiesce in an enduring loss for himself in order to bring about a greater net balance of satisfaction. In the absence of strong and lasting benevolent impulses, a rational man would not accept a basic structure merely because it maximized the algebraic sum of advantages irrespective of its permanent effects on his own basic rights and interests. Thus it seems that the principle of utility is incompatible with the conception of social cooperation among equals for mutual advantage. It appears to be inconsistent with the idea or reciprocity implicit in the notion of a well-ordered society. Or, at any rate, so I shall argue.

I shall maintain instead that the persons in the initial situation would choose two rather different principles: the first requires equality in the assignment of basic rights and duties, while the second holds that social and economic inequalities, for example inequalities of wealth and authority, are just only if they result in compensating benefits for everyone, and in particular for the least advantaged members of society. These principles rule out justifying institutions on the grounds that the hardships of some are offset by a greater good in the aggregate. It may be expedient but it is not just that some should have less in order that others may prosper. But there is no injustice in the greater benefits earned by a few provided that the situation of persons not so fortunate is thereby improved. The intuitive idea is that since everyone's well-being depends upon a scheme of cooperation without which no one could have a satisfactory life, the division of advantages should be such as to draw forth the willing cooperation of everyone taking part in it, including those less well situated. Yet this can be expected only if reasonable terms are proposed. The two principles mentioned seem to be a fair agreement on the basis of which those better endowed, or more fortunate in their social position, neither of which we can be said to deserve, could expect the willing cooperation of others when

some workable scheme is a necessary condition of the welfare of all.[3] Once we decide to look for a conception of justice that nullifies the accidents of natural endowment and the contingencies of social circumstance as counters in a quest for political and economic advantage, we are led to these principles. They express the result of leaving aside those aspects of the social world that seem arbitrary from a moral point of view....

4. The Original Position and Justification

I have said that the original position is the appropriate initial status quo which insures that the fundamental agreements reached in it are fair. This fact yields the name "justice as fairness." It is clear, then, that I want to say that one conception of justice is more reasonable than another, or justifiable with respect to it, if rational persons in the initial situation would choose its principles over those of the other for the role of justice. Conceptions of justice are to be ranked by their acceptability to persons so circumstanced. Understood in this way the question of justification is settled by working out a problem of deliberation: we have to ascertain which principles it would be rational to adopt given the contractual situation. This connects the theory of justice with the theory of rational choice.

If this view of the problem of justification is to succeed, we must, of course, describe in some detail the nature of this choice problem. A problem of rational decision has a definite answer only if we know the beliefs and interests of the parties, their relations with respect to one another, the alternatives between which they are to choose, the procedure whereby they make up their minds, and so on. As the circumstances are presented in different ways, correspondingly different principles are accepted. The concept of the original position, as I shall refer to it, is that of the most philosophically favored interpretation of this initial choice situation for the purposes of a theory of justice.

But how are we to decide what is the most favored interpretation? I assume, for one thing, that there is a broad measure of agreement that principles of justice should be chosen under certain conditions. To justify a particular description of the initial situation one shows that it incorporates these commonly shared presumptions. One argues from widely accepted but weak premises to more specific conclusions. Each of the presumptions should by itself be natural and plausible; some of them may seem innocuous or even trivial. The aim of the contract approach is to establish that taken together they impose significant bounds on acceptable principles of justice. The ideal outcome would be that these conditions determine a unique set of principles; but I shall be satisfied if they suffice to rank the main traditional conceptions of social justice.

One should not be misled, then, by the somewhat unusual conditions which characterize the original position. The idea here is simply to make vividly to ourselves the restrictions that it seems reasonable to impose on arguments for principles of justice, and therefore on these principles themselves. Thus it seems reasonable and generally acceptable that no one should be advantaged or disadvantaged by natural fortune or social circumstances in the choice of principles. It also seems widely agreed that it should be impossible to tailor principles to the circumstances of one's own case. We should insure further that particular inclinations and aspirations, and a person's conceptions of their good do not affect the principles adopted. The aim is to rule out those principles that it would be rational to propose for acceptance, however little the chance of success, only if one knew certain things that are irrelevant from the standpoint of justice. For example, if a man knew that he was wealthy, he might find it rational to advance the principle that various taxes for welfare measures be counted unjust; if he knew that he was poor, he would most likely propose the contrary principle. To represent the desired restrictions one imagines a situation in which everyone is deprived of this sort of information. One excludes the knowledge of those contingencies which sets men at odds and allows them to be guided by their prejudices. In this manner the veil of ignorance is arrived at in a natural way. This concept should cause no difficulty if we keep in mind the constraints on arguments that it is meant to express. At any time we can enter the original position, so to speak, simply by following a certain procedure, namely, by arguing for principles of justice in accordance with these restrictions.

It seems reasonable to suppose that the parties in the original position are equal. That is, all have the same rights in the procedure for choosing principles; each can make proposals, submit reasons for their acceptance, and so on. Obviously the purpose of these conditions is to represent equality between human beings as moral persons, as creatures having a conception of their good and capable of a sense of justice. The basis of equality is taken to be similarity in these two respects. Systems of ends are not ranked in value; and each man is presumed to have the requisite ability to understand and to act upon whatever principles are adopted. Together with the veil of ignorance, these conditions define the principles of justice as those which rational persons concerned to advance their interests would consent to as equals when none are known to be advantaged or disadvantaged by social and natural contingencies.

There is, however, another side to justifying a particular description of the original position. This is to see if the principles which would be chosen match our considered convictions of justice or extend them in an acceptable way. We can note whether applying these principles would lead us to make the same judgments about the basic structure of society which we now make intuitively and in which we have the greatest confidence; or whether, in cases where our present judgments are in doubt and given with hesitation, these principles offer a resolution which we can affirm on reflection. There are questions which we feel sure must be answered in a certain way. For example, we are confident that religious intolerance and racial discrimination are unjust. We think that we have examined these things with care and have reached what we believe is an impartial judgment not likely to be distorted by an excessive attention to our own interests. These convictions are provisional fixed points which we presume any conception of justice must fit. But we have much less assurance as to what is the correct distribution of wealth and authority. Here we may be looking for a way to remove our doubts. We can check an interpretation of the initial situation, then, by the capacity of its principles to accommodate our firmest convictions and to provide guidance where guidance is needed.

In searching for the most favored description of this situation we work from both ends. We begin by describing it so that it represents generally shared and preferably weak conditions. We then see if these conditions are strong enough to yield a significant set of principles. If not, we look for further premises equally reasonable. But if so, and these principles match our considered convictions of justice, then so far well and good. But presumably there will be discrepancies. In this case we have a choice. We can either modify the account of the initial situation or we can revise our existing judgments, for even the judgments we take provisionally as fixed points are liable to revision. By going back and forth, sometimes altering the conditions of the contractual circumstances, at others withdrawing our judgments and conforming them to principle, I assume that eventually we shall find a description of the initial situation that both expresses reasonable conditions and yields principles which match our considered judgments duly pruned and adjusted. This state of affairs I refer to as reflective equilibrium.[4] It is an equilibrium because at last our principles and judgments coincide; and it is reflective since we know to what principles our judgments conform and the premises of their derivation. At the moment everything is in order. But this equilibrium is not necessarily stable. It is liable to be upset by further examination of the conditions which should be imposed on the contractual situation and by particular cases which may lead us to revise our judgments. Yet for the time being we have done what we can to render coherent and to justify our convictions of social justice. We have reached a conception of the original position.

I shall not, of course, actually work through this process. Still, we may think of the interpretation of the original position that I shall present as the result of such a hypothetical course of reflection. It represents the attempt to accommodate within one scheme both reasonable philosophical conditions on principles as well as our considered judgments of justice. In arriving at the favored interpretation

of the initial situation there is no point at which an appeal is made to self-evidence in the traditional sense either of general conceptions or particular convictions. I do not claim for the principles of justice proposed that they are necessary truths or derivable from such truths. A conception of justice cannot be deduced from self-evident premises or conditions on principles; instead, its justification is a matter of the mutual support of many considerations, of everything fitting together into one coherent view.

A final comment. We shall want to say that certain principles of justice are justified because they would be agreed to in an initial situation of equality. I have emphasized that this original position is purely hypothetical. It is natural to ask why, if this agreement is never actually entered into, we should take any interest in these principles, moral or otherwise. The answer is that the conditions embodied in the description of the original position are ones that we do in fact accept. Or if we do not, then perhaps we can be persuaded to do so by philosophical reflection. Each aspect of the contractual situation can be given supporting grounds. Thus what we shall do is to collect together into one conception a number of conditions on principles that we are ready upon due consideration to recognize as reasonable. These constraints express what we are prepared to regard as limits on fair terms of social cooperation. One way to look at the idea of the original position, therefore, is to see it as an expository device which sums up the meaning of these conditions and helps us to extract their consequences. On the other hand, this conception is also an intuitive notion that suggests its own elaboration, so that led on by it we are drawn to define more clearly the standpoint from which we can best interpret moral relationships. We need a conception that enables us to envision our objective from afar: the intuitive notion of the original position is to do this for us....

11. Two Principles of Justice.

I shall now state in a provisional form the two principles of justice that I believe would be chosen in the original position. In this section I wish to make only the most general comments, and therefore the first formulation of these principles is tentative. As we go on I shall run through several formulations and approximate step by step the final statement to be given much later. I believe that doing this allows the exposition to proceed in a natural way.

The first statement of the two principles reads as follows.

First: each person is to have an equal right to the most extensive basic liberty compatible with similar liberty for others.

Second: social and economic inequalities are to be arranged so that they are both (a) reasonably expected to be to everyone's advantage, and (b) attached to positions and offices open to all....

By way of general comment, these principles primarily apply, as I have said, to the basic structure of society. They are to govern the assignment of rights and duties and to regulate the distribution of social and economic advantages. As their formulation suggests, these principles presuppose that the social structure can be divided into two more or less distinct parts, the first principle applying to the one, the second to the other. They distinguish between those aspects of the social system that define and secure the equal liberties of citizenship and those that specify and establish social and economic inequalities. The basic liberties of citizens are, roughly speaking, political liberty (the right to vote and to be eligible for public office) together with freedom of speech and assembly; liberty of conscience and freedom of thought; freedom of the person along with the right to hold (personal) property; and freedom from arbitrary arrest and seizure as defined by the concept of the rule of law. These liberties are all required to be equal by the first principle, since citizens of a just society are to have the same basic rights.

The second principle applies, in the first approximation, to the distribution of income and wealth and to the design of organizations that make use of differences in authority and responsibility, or chains of command. While the distribution of wealth and income need not be equal, it must be to everyone's advantage, and at the same time, posi-

tions of authority and offices of command must be accessible to all. One applies the second principle by holding positions open, and then, subject to this constraint, arranges social and economic inequalities so that everyone benefits.

These principles are to be arranged in a serial order with the first principle prior to the second. This ordering means that a departure from the institutions of equal liberty required by the first principle cannot be justified by, or compensated for, by greater social and economic advantages. The distribution of wealth and income, and the hierarchies of authority, must be consistent with both the liberties of equal citizenship and equality of opportunity.

It is clear that these principles are rather specific in their content, and their acceptance rests on certain assumptions that I must eventually try to explain and justify. A theory of justice depends upon a theory of society in ways that will become evident as we proceed. For the present, it should be observed that the two principles (and this holds for all formulations) are a special case of a more general conception of justice that can be expressed as follows.

All social values — liberty and opportunity, income and wealth, and the bases of self-respect — are to be distributed equally unless an unequal distribution of any, or all, of these values is to everyone's advantage.

Injustice, then, is simply inequalities that are not to the benefit of all. Of course, this conception is extremely vague and requires interpretation.

As a first step, suppose that the basic structure of society distributes certain primary goods, that is, things that every rational man is presumed to want. These goods normally have a use whatever a person's rational plan of life. For simplicity, assume that the chief primary goods at the disposition of society are rights and liberties, powers and opportunities, income and wealth. (Later on in Part Three the primary good of self-respect has a central place.) These are the social primary goods. Other primary goods such as health and vigor, intelligence and imagination, are natural goods;

although their possession is influenced by the basic structure, they are not so directly under its control. Imagine, then, a hypothetical initial arrangement in which all the social primary goods are equally distributed: everyone has similar rights and duties, and income and wealth are evenly shared. This state of affairs provides a benchmark for judging improvements. If certain inequalities of wealth and organizational powers would make everyone better off than in this hypothetical starting situation, then they accord with the general conception.

Now it is possible, at least theoretically, that by giving up some of their fundamental liberties men are sufficiently compensated by the resulting social and economic gains. The general conception of justice imposes no restrictions on what sort of inequalities are permissible; it only requires that everyone's position be improved. We need not suppose anything so drastic as consenting to a condition of slavery. Imagine instead that men forego certain political rights when the economic returns are significant and their capacity to influence the course of policy by the exercise of these rights would be marginal in any case. It is this kind of exchange which the two principles as stated rule out; being arranged in serial order they do not permit exchanges between basic liberties and economic and social gains. The serial ordering of principles expresses an underlying preference among primary social goods. When this preference is rational so likewise is the choice of these principles in this order.

In developing justice as fairness I shall, for the most part, leave aside the general conception of justice and examine instead the special case of the two principles in serial order. The advantage of this procedure is that from the first the matter of priorities is recognized and an effort made to find principles to deal with it. One is led to attend throughout to the conditions under which the acknowledgement of the absolute weight of liberty with respect to social and economic advantages, as defined by the lexical order of the two principles, would be reasonable. Offhand, this ranking appears extreme and too special a case to be of much interest; but there is more justification for it than would appear at first sight. Or at any rate, so

I shall maintain ('82). Furthermore, the distinction between fundamental rights and liberties and economic and social benefits marks a difference among primary social goods that one should try to exploit. It suggests an important division in the social system. Of course, the distinctions drawn and the ordering proposed are bound to be at best only approximations. There are surely circumstances in which they fail. But it is essential to depict clearly the main lines of a reasonable conception of justice; and under many conditions anyway, the two principles in serial order may serve well enough. When necessary we can fall back on the more general conception.

The fact that the two principles apply to institutions has certain consequences. Several points illustrate this. First of all, the rights and liberties referred to by these principles are those which are defined by the public rules of the basic structure. Whether men are free is determined by the rights and duties established by the major institutions of society. Liberty is a certain pattern of social forms. The first principle simply requires that certain sorts of rules, those defining basic liberties, apply to everyone equally and that they allow the most extensive liberty compatible with a like liberty for all. The only reason for circumscribing the rights defining liberty and making men's freedom less extensive than it might otherwise be is that these equal rights as institutionally defined would interfere with one another.

Another thing to bear in mind is that when principles mention persons, or require that everyone gain from an inequality, the reference is to representative persons holding the various social positions, or offices, or whatever, established by the basic structure. Thus in applying the second principle I assume that it is possible to assign an expectation of well-being to representative individuals holding these positions. This expectation indicates their life prospects as viewed from their social station. In general, the expectations of representative persons depend upon the distribution of rights and duties throughout the basic structure. When this changes, expectations change. I assume, then, that expectations are connected: by raising the prospects of the representative man in one position we presumably increase or decrease the prospects of representative men in other positions. Since it applies to institutional forms, the second principle (or rather the first part of it) refers to the expectations of representative individuals. As I shall discuss below, neither principle applies to distributions of particular goods to particular individuals who may be identified by their proper names. The situation where someone is considering how to allocate certain commodities to needy persons who are known to him is not within the scope of the principles. They are meant to regulate basic institutional arrangement. We must not assume that there is much similarity from the standpoint of justice between an administrative allotment of goods to specific persons and the appropriate design of society. Our common sense intuitions for the former may be a poor guide to the latter.

Now the second principle insists that each person benefit from permissible inequalities in the basic structure. This means that it must be reasonable for each relevant representative man defined by this structure, when he views it as a going concern, to prefer his prospects with the inequality to his prospects without it. One is not allowed to justify differences in income or organizational powers on the ground that the disadvantages of those in one position are outweighed by the greater advantages of those instead, the two principles require that everyone benefit from economic and social inequalities....

17. The Tendency to Equality

I wish to conclude this discussion of the two principles by explaining the sense in which they express an egalitarian conception of justice. Also I should like to forestall the objection to the principle of fair opportunity that it leads to a callous meritocratic society. In order to prepare the way for doing this, I note several aspects of the conception of justice that I have set out.

First we may observe that the difference principle gives some weight to the considerations singled out by the principle of redress. This is the principle that undeserved inequalities call for redress; and since inequalities of birth and natural endowment are undeserved, these inequalities are to be somehow compensated for.[5] Thus the principle holds that in order to treat all persons equally, to provide genuine equality of opportunity, society must give more attention to those with fewer native assets and to those born into the less favorable social positions. The idea is to redress the bias of contingencies in the direction of equality, in pursuit of this principle greater resources might be spent on the education of the less rather than the more intelligent, at least over a certain time of life, say the earlier years of school.

Now the principle of redress has not to my knowledge been proposed as the sole criterion of justice, as the single aim of the social order. It is plausible as most such principles are only as a prima facie principle, one that is to be weighed in the balance with others. For example, we are to weigh it against the principle to improve the average standard of life, or to advance the common good.[6] But whatever other principles we hold, the claims of redress are to be taken into account. It is thought to represent one of the elements in our conception of justice. Now the difference principle is not of course the principle of redress. It does not require society to try to even out handicaps as if all were expected to compete on a fair basis in the same race. But the difference principle would allocate resources in education, say, so as to improve the long-term expectation of the least favored. If this end is attained by giving more attention to the better endowed, it is permissible; otherwise not. And in making this decision, the value of education should not be assessed solely in terms of economic efficiency and social welfare. Equally if not more important is the role of education in enabling a person to enjoy the culture of his society and to take part in its affairs, and in this way to provide for each individual a secure sense of his own worth.

Thus although the difference principle is not the same as that of redress, it does achieve some of the intent of the latter principle. It transforms the aims of the basic structure so that the total scheme of institutions no longer emphasizes social efficiency and technocratic values. We see then that the difference principle represents, in effect, an agreement to regard the distribution of natural talents as a common asset and to share in the benefits of this distribution whatever it turns out to be. Those who have been favored by nature, whoever they are, may gain from their good fortune only on terms that improve the situation of those who have lost out. The naturally advantaged are not to gain merely because they are more gifted, but only to cover the costs of training and education and for using their endowments in ways that help the less fortunate as well. No one deserves his greater natural capacity nor merits a more favorable starting place in society. But it does not follow that one should eliminate these distinctions. There is another way to deal with them. The basic structure can be arranged so that these contingencies work for the good of the least fortunate. Thus we are led to the difference principle if we wish to set up the social system so that no one gains or loses from his arbitrary place in the distribution of natural assets or his initial position in society without giving or receiving compensating advantages in return.

In view of these remarks we may reject the contention that the ordering of institutions is always defective because the distribution of natural talents and the contingencies of social circumstance are unjust, and this injustice must inevitably carry over to human arrangements. Occasionally this reflection is offered as an excuse for ignoring injustice, as if the refusal to acquiesce in injustice is on a par with being unable to accept death. The natural distribution is neither just nor unjust; nor is it unjust that persons are born into society at some particular position. These are simply natural facts. What is just and unjust is the way that institutions deal with these facts. Aristocratic and caste societies are unjust because they make these contingencies the ascriptive basis for belonging to more or less enclosed and privileged social classes. The basic structure of these societies incorporates the arbitrariness found in nature. But there is no necessity for men to resign themselves to these contingencies. The social system is not an unchangeable order beyond human control but a pattern of human action. In justice as fairness men agree to share one another's fate. In designing institutions they undertake to avail themselves of the accidents

of nature and social circumstance only when doing so is for the common benefit. The two principles are a fair way of meeting the arbitrariness of fortune; and while no doubt imperfect in other ways, the institutions which satisfy these principles are just.

A further point is that the difference principle expresses a conception of reciprocity. It is a principle of mutual benefit. We have seen that, at least when chain connection holds, each representative man can accept the basic structure as designed to advance his interests. The social order can be justified to everyone, and in particular to those who are least favored; and in this sense it is egalitarian. But it seems necessary to consider in an intuitive way how the condition of mutual benefit is satisfied. Consider any two representative men A and B, and let B be the one who is less favored. Actually, since we are most interested in the comparison with the least favored man, let us assume that B is this individual. Now B can accept A's being better off since A's advantages have been gained in ways that improve B's prospects. If A were not allowed his better position, B would be even worse off than he is. The difficulty is to show that A has no grounds for complaint. Perhaps he is required to have less than he might since his having more would result in some loss to B. Now what can be said to the more favored man? To begin with, it is clear that the well-being of each depends on a scheme of social cooperation without which no one could have a satisfactory life. Secondly, we can ask for the willing cooperation of everyone only if the terms of the scheme are reasonable. The difference principle, then, seems to be a fair basis on which those better endowed, or more fortunate in their social circumstances could expect others to collaborate with them when some workable arrangement is a necessary condition of the good of all.

There is a natural inclination to object that those better situated deserved their greater advantages whether or not they are to the benefit of others. At this point it is necessary to be clear about the notion of desert. It is perfectly true that given a just system of cooperation as a scheme of public rules and the expectations set up by it, those who, with the prospect of improving their condition, have done what the system announces that it will reward are entitled to their advantages. In this sense the more fortunate have a claim to their better situation; their claims are legitimate expectations established by social institutions, and the community is obligated to meet them. But this sense of desert presupposes the existence of the cooperative scheme; it is irrelevant to the question whether in the first place the scheme is to be designed in accordance with the difference principle or some other criterion.

Perhaps some will think that the person with greater natural endowments deserves those assets and the superior character that made their development possible. Because he is more worthy in this sense, he deserves the greater advantages that he could achieve with them. This view, however, is surely incorrect. It seems to be one of the fixed points of our considered judgments that no one deserves his place in the distribution of native endowments, any more than one deserves one's initial starting place in society. The assertion that a man deserves the superior character that enables him to make the effort to cultivate his abilities is equally problematic; for his character depends in large part upon fortunate family and social circumstances for which he can claim no credit. The notion of desert seems not to apply to these cases. Thus the more advantaged representative man cannot say that he deserves and therefore has a right to a scheme of cooperation in which he is permitted to acquire benefits in ways that do not contribute to the welfare of others. There is no basis for his making this claim. From the standpoint of common sense, then, the difference principle appears to be acceptable both to the more advantaged and to the less advantaged individual. Of course, none of this is strictly speaking an argument for the principle, since in a contract theory arguments are made from the point of view of the original position. But these intuitive considerations help to clarify the nature of the principle and the sense in which it is egalitarian....

77. The Basis of Equality

I now turn to the basis of equality, the features of human beings in virtue of which they are to be treated in accordance with the principles of justice. Our conduct toward animals is not regulated by these principles, or so it is generally believed. On what grounds then do we distinguish between mankind and other living things and regard the constraints of justice as holding only in our relations to human persons? We must examine what determines the range of application of conceptions of justice.

To clarify our question, we may distinguish three levels where the concept of equality applies. The first is to the administration of institutions as public systems of rules. In this case equality is essentially justice as regularity. It implies the impartial application and consistent interpretation of rules according to such precepts as to treat similar cases similarly (as defined by statutes and precedents)[7] and the like. Equality at this level is the least controversial element in the common sense idea of justice.[8] The second and much more difficult application of equality is to the substantive structure of institutions. Here the meaning of equality is specified by the principles of justice which require that equal basic rights be assigned to all persons. Presumably this excludes animals; they have some protection certainly but their status is not that of human beings. But this outcome is still unexplained. We have yet to consider what sorts of beings are owed the guarantees of justice. This brings us to the third level at which the question of equality arises.

The natural answer seems to be that it is precisely the moral persons who are entitled to equal justice. Moral persons are distinguished by two features: first they are capable of having (and are assumed to have) a conception of their good (as expressed by a rational plan of life); and second they are capable of having (and are assumed to acquire) a sense of justice, a normally effective desire to apply and to act upon the principles of justice, at least to a certain minimum degree. We use the characterization of the persons in the original position to single out the kind of beings to whom the principles chosen apply. After all, the parties are thought of as adopting these criteria to regulate their common institutions and their conduct toward one another; and the description of their nature enters into the reasoning by which these principles are selected. Thus equal justice is owed to those who have the capacity to take part in and to act in accordance with the public understanding of the initial situation. One should observe that moral personality is here defined as a potentiality that is ordinarily realized in due course. It is this potentiality which brings the claims of justice into play. I shall return to this point below.

We see, then, that the capacity for moral personality is a sufficient condition for being entitled to equal justice.[9] Nothing beyond the essential minimum is required. Whether moral personality is also a necessary condition I shall leave aside. I assume that the capacity for a sense of justice is possessed by the overwhelming majority of mankind, and therefore this question does not raise a serious practical problem. That moral personality suffices to make one a subject of claims is the essential thing. We cannot go far wrong in supposing that the sufficient condition is always satisfied. Even if the capacity were necessary, it would be unwise in practice to withhold justice on this ground. The risk to just institutions would be too great.

It should be stressed that the sufficient conditions for equal justice, the capacity for moral personality, is not at all stringent. When someone lacks the requisite potentially either from birth or accident, this is regarded as a defect or deprivation. There is no race or recognized group of human beings that lacks this attribute. Only scattered individuals are without this capacity, or its realization to the minimum degree, and the failure to realize it is the consequence of unjust and impoverished social circumstances, or fortuitous contingencies. Furthermore, while individuals presumably have varying capacities for a sense of justice, this fact is not a reason for depriving those with a lesser capacity of the full protection of justice. Once a certain minimum is met, a person is entitled to equal liberty on a par with everyone else. A greater capacity for a sense of justice, as shown say in a greater skill and facility in applying the principles of justice and in marshaling arguments in particular cases, is a natural asset like any other ability.

The special advantages a person receives for its exercise are to be governed by the difference principle. Thus if some have to a preeminent degree the judicial virtues of impartiality and integrity which are needed in certain positions, they may properly have whatever benefits should be attached to these offices. Yet the application of the principle of equal liberty is not affected by these differences. It is sometimes thought that basic rights and liberties should vary with capacity, but justice as fairness denies this: provided the minimum for moral personality is satisfied, a person is owed all the guarantees of justice.

NOTES

1. As the text suggests, I shall regard Locke's *Second Treatise of Government*, Rousseau's *The Social Contract*, and Kant's ethical works beginning with the *Foundation of the Metaphysics of Morals* as definitive of the contract tradition. For all of its greatness, Hobbes's *Leviathan* raises special problems. A general historical survey is provided by J.W. Gough, *The Social Contract*, 2nd ed. (Oxford, The Clarendon Press, 1957), and Otto Gierke, *Natural Law and the Theory of Society*, trans. with an introduction by Ernest Barker (Cambridge, The University Press, 1934). A presentation of the contract view as primarily an ethical theory is to be found in G. R. Grice, *The Grounds of Moral Judgment* (Cambridge, The University Press, 1967).

2. Kant is clear that the original agreement is hypothetical. See *The Metaphysics of Morals*, pt. I (Rechtslehre), especially '' 47, 52; and pt. II of the essay "Concerning the Common Saying: This May Be True in Theory but It Does Not Apply in Practice," in Kant's *Political Writings*, ed. Hans Reiss and trans. by H.B. Nisbet (Cambridge, The University Press, 1970), pp. 73-87. See Georges Vlachos, *La Pensée Politique de Kant* (Paris, Presses Universitaires de France, 1962) pp. 326; and J.G. Murphy, *Kant: The Philosophy of Right* (London, Macmillan, 1970), pp. 109-112, 133-136 for a further discussion.

3. For the formulation of this intuitive idea, I am indebted to Allan Gibbard.

4. The process of mutual adjustment of principles and

considered judgments is not peculiar to moral philosophy. See Nelson Goodman, *Fact, Fiction, and Forecast* (Cambridge, Mass., Harvard University Press, 1955), pp. 65-68, for parallel remarks concerning the justification of the principles of deductive and inductive inference.

5. See Herbert Spiegelberg, "A Defense of Human Equality." *Philosophical Review*, vol. 53 (1944), pp. 101, 13-123; and D.D. Raphael, "Justice and Liberty," *Proceedings of the Aristotelian Society*, vol. 51 (1950-1951), pp. 187f.

6. See for example, Spiegelberg. pp.120f.

7. On this last point, see Travers, *ibid.*, pp. 47-54.

8. See Sidgwick, *Methods of Ethics*, p. 496.

9. This fact can be used to interpret the concept of natural rights. For one thing, it explains why it is appropriate to call by this name the rights that justice protects. These claims depend solely on certain natural attributes the presence of which can be ascertained by natural reason pursuing common sense methods of inquiry. The existence of these attributes and the claims based upon them is established independently from social conventions and legal norms. The propriety of the term "natural" is that it suggests the contrast between the rights identified by the theory of justice and the rights defined by law and custom. But more than this, the concept of natural rights includes the idea that these rights are assigned in the first instance to persons, and that they are given a special weight. Claims easily overridden for other values are not natural rights. Now the rights protected by the first principle have both of these features in view of the priority rules. Thus justice as fairness has the characteristic marks of a natural rights theory. Not only does it ground fundamental rights on natural attributes and distinguish their bases from social norms, but it assigns rights to persons by principles of equal justice, these principles having a special force against which other values cannot normally prevail. Although specific rights are not absolute, the system of equal liberties is absolute practically speaking under favorable conditions.

LIBERTARIANISM, INSURANCE ARGUMENTS, AND GENERAL STATE WELFARE

Richard A. Garner

Richard A. Garner, a PhD student at Nottingham University in England, researches political legitimacy from the libertarian standpoint. He first got interested in politics as an anarchist communist before becoming a free market anarchist who now advocates such policies as the abolition of taxation. The reading in this chapter is one of several articles that he has written for the Libertarian Alliance in London, England.

Garner argues that measures such as state welfare policies would not be chosen in a hypothetical contract that establishes the rules of justice. Like other libertarians, Garner defends negative rights as both necessary and sufficient. Negative rights produce a duty in others and in the state to refrain from interfering with an individual's freedom. On this view, liberty and private property are integrally connected — my freedom to pursue desires, projects, and goals requires that I have the freedom to acquire the things I want and to control what I have without interference from others or the state. To answer objections that non-interference by the state deprives people of basic goods such as minimum guaranteed income, old age security, and health care, Garner argues that having these as compulsory measures violates freedom in a way that cannot be justified. Only voluntary mechanisms such as charity and philanthropy can be justified.

A Defence of Contractarianism

For those of us that reject traditional "natural law" or intuitive arguments for libertarianism, but instead draw upon contractarian justifications for our moral principles, we may face problems. Many modern defences of general state welfare are likewise grounded in contractarian philosophical defences. The contractarian libertarian has to argue why the principles underlying welfare statism would not be chosen as the principles of a hypothetical contract establishing the rules of justice.

Libertarianism and Contractarian Moral Philosophy

Liberty as a Right

Libertarianism is the political philosophy that says that the guiding principle for our political and social arrangements should be that of individual liberty. It is a political philosophy concerned with individual rights, or, more properly, with the idea that we have only one fundamental right: that of liberty. Hence the name "libertarianism."

In examining the question of what is meant by the word "liberty," two questions arise. Firstly, what is the subject of liberty, the thing whose liberty we are meant to be concerned with? And secondly, what is it for this entity to be free or unfree? The answer to the first is that what is free is the practical agent, anything with a rational will to act. The answer to the second question, and perhaps the more controversial answer, is that to be free means that one is able to act without impediment, imposition, or restriction. Since we are concerned with moral philosophy, which is about how humans should act towards one another, and political philosophy, which is about the structuring of our human societies, it follows that the impediments and restrictions we are concerned with are human ones.

The right to liberty is a right to be free, and to be free means to be free to do what one wants. The question that often arises in libertarian discourse, however, is whether this right to liberty is, or should be, a negative or a positive right. You see, the study of rights has revealed the interesting connection between rights and duties. Rights, in effect, are claims on others — they constitute demands we make on other people. This claim can either be that these others do something, or that they refrain from doing something. The former is a positive duty, and the latter is a negative one, and so a positive right is one that produces a positive duty, and a negative right is one that produces a negative duty.

Applied to the context of liberty, a negative right to liberty produces a duty in others that they refrain from interfering with our freedom, or, better, with our actions. Hence we can be said to be free in the sense of enjoying our negative right to liberty if nobody is purposefully curtailing our ability to act.

On the other hand, a positive right to liberty would imply not simply that people refrain from curtailing our ability to act, but that they also provide for it. Libertarians believe that a proper understanding of the right to liberty reveals that the negative view is the only acceptable one for the simple reason that positive rights infringe on both negative and positive rights, and are incompatible with the notion of equality of rights.

For instance a libertarian will assert that Sam has a right to liberty which implies that he has a right to play football. When libertarians say this, they simply mean that people have an obligation to refrain from preventing Sam from playing football, or interfering with his doing so. This is the negative view. If we were to accept the positive view then we would have to say that people are obliged to enable Sam to play football. The dilemma comes in if we embellish the story further by saying that Sam has arthritis so severe that his ability to play football is nigh-on non-existent. Suppose that Harry is a doctor with the ability to cure Sam, and so enable him to play football. The only trouble is that he doesn't want to.

In the negative view, Sam's rights remain intact. Nobody is stopping him from playing football. Nobody is curtailing his ability to do so. They simply aren't contributing to it. If his right to liberty is enforceable then there is no need to do so at this stage. However, in the positive view his rights are violated and other people's moral obligations go unfulfilled. For Sam's right to play football, his right to be free to play football, and so his liberty, if the positive view is correct, imply that the doctor is morally obliged to treat Sam's arthritis. Whether he wants to or not. What then becomes of all the doctor's projects? What becomes of his wants and aims, his goals in life and his ability to pursue his conception of the good? Firstly the enforcement of Sam's right would interfere with whatever it was that the doctor was doing rather than treat Sam. This would violate his right to liberty in the negative sense. Secondly, the enforcement of Sam's right would reduce the doctor's ability to do something other than treat Sam, hence meaning that making Sam able to play football means making the doctor less able to do something else, thus violating any positive right to liberty.

So liberty should properly be understood as a negative right. And so we may further develop our definition of libertarianism: a libertarian is somebody who believes that all our rights are negative. Liberty is the right to do what you want, in the sense that people don't purposefully interfere with, restrict, or otherwise inhibit your ability to go about your affairs as you see fit. In this way, liberty provides a framework within which each of us is able to pursue his or her own conception of the good, provided none of us interferes with liberty. Since the right to liberty is an obligation on others to refrain from interfering with our liberty, it follows that nobody has a right to interfere with other people's liberty. Therefore liberty must be an equal right.

Property Rights Derived From a Negative Right to Liberty

Libertarians, it is known, are strong believers in the right of private property for the basic reason that the libertarian believes that liberty and property are connected. How? Well, first, what do we mean by the word "property"? When libertarians use the word they mean, basically, the right to control a resource; the right to decide over it, or to determine its disposition. Hence Murray Rothbard argued that there is no public sector, that "public property" is really simply government property, since the government controls it.

We have a negative right to do what we want. However, in order to do what we want we necessarily must be doing what we want with something, even if that something is only a part of ourselves. My right to wave my arm in the air implies that I have right to do something with my arm, namely to wave it in the air. Hence:

> …it is plausible to construe *all* rights as property rights. Whenever anybody has a right, Rx, to engage in any sort of actions x, we can find some thing or things y, such that that person must be understood to have, given that he has a right to engage in those actions, the right Ry, to use that thing or those things: Rx entails Ry. At a minimum, y is some part of that person's body or mind; the agent in question must employ his body and/or mind to do anything, and the liberty to do it will follow automatically from the liberty to use those pieces of human equipment as the person will.[1]

So liberty, the (negative) right to do as we want, implies the (negative) right to decide over the various things we do as we want with. After all, how could John Stuart Mill have had the right to write *On Liberty*, part of his freedom of discourse or expression, and so his basic liberties, if he didn't have a right to decide over the stylus he used to do it? And remember, this is a negative right, so his right to decide over it implies the question "how could he have had the right to write *On Liberty* if other people weren't morally obliged to refrain from interfering with or curtailing his ability to decide over the stylus he was using to do so?" His right to write his essay was part and parcel of his right to decide over that stylus. And a right to decide over, to control, to determine the disposition of something is what libertarians mean when they use the term "property." Hence Jan Narveson says:

Out there in the world people do things, and move about. They start using things, in various ways. By and by, established patterns of use will be confirmed with recognitions of rights. If I'm doing something with something, and was the first person to do so, and intend to keep doing it, then other people who propose to use it would be interfering with me if they didn't clear it with me. The general right to do what we wish enables us to claim items in the world as our property: property rights are nothing but non-interference rights over identifiable, establishable patterns of action. Often, of course, we will cross paths with others, and in the course of interaction we will come to make some agreements about who gets to do what, and with what. These agreements emerge from a background of freedom plus path-crossing. To enable each of us to have a rightful area of freedom, we swap our powers of action in such a way that this person is recognised as having this, that person as having that, and so on. Also we may find it helpful to establish common areas, such as parklands and sidewalks, which may be used by any peaceable person…[2]

So then, the general right to liberty is really only a right to self-ownership,[3] property in ourselves, plus extension to that initial area that we form by our plans and actions in relation to other people. The general principle of initial acquisition is that you get whatever you are the first to use, since, if you are the first to use it your use cannot be interfering with the usage of anybody else, whilst anybody else coming along after you start using it and themselves proposing to use it will be interfering with your usage, and so violating your right to liberty.

From this, people's liberty rights are fairly easy to identify, since you simply do whatever you wish on your property so long as you don't interfere with the rights of anybody else over their property. Property, then, makes interpersonal liberty possible and coherent. The right to do as you want with your own property clearly involves the right to give it to somebody else. This you might do because you care about them very deeply. Alternatively, and more likely, it is something you might do in order to get that somebody else to give you something else you value more than the original item. On the whole, then, our lives would mainly consist of series of voluntary exchanges between people who would otherwise keep interfering with each other with no clear view of who gets right of way.

Why Accept Libertarianism? The Contractarian Argument

This goes on to answer the further question: Why believe that we have rights, especially the libertarian view of them?

The answer to this question, I believe, lies in *contractarian* moral philosophy. Contractarianism is good for when other moral philosophies don't work. For instance, if you are debating a theist on the existence of God then you may well come across the objection, "but if God doesn't exist, why be moral?" Or when pointing out that there are no natural moral laws, a natural law theorist will often say, "well, why be moral then?"

These people are scared. That's simply it: They recognise that morality is of value, and they want a means to secure it. But that is the answer to their own question: Why be moral? Because morality is valuable.

Contractarianism is not the belief that we have, at sometime, entered into a contract to agree to abide by certain moral precepts. This would be an indefensible position for two reasons: Firstly, no such contract exists. Secondly, question of keeping your contracts or even keeping promises and not lying is itself a moral question. Instead Contractarians ask what the contents of such a contract might well be, against the background that the moral rules that we ought to abide by are those that it is reasonable to expect rational people to adopt.

However, it is necessary to expand this point by examining just what is meant by the term "morality."

Firstly, I can start by rejecting a particular view of Natural Moral Laws. There are those who believe that, since man is, then man is *something*, i.e. man (meaning mankind here) has a specific

nature. Natural law theorists then go on to say that moral precepts are discernible from the nature of man just as any other existing thing. One argument is that all morality centres around the idea of values, but that all values are secondary to life, since no other value can be pursued if we are dead. However, in order to survive and live an enriching life, we have to produce, and in order to do this we have to use our minds. This means we must be free to plot our courses of actions and to carry out these plans. Hence our natures seem to dictate that we need liberty.

The trouble is that this provides good reason as to why I want liberty, but absolutely no reason why you should grant it to me and absolutely no reason why I should grant it to you. This is the flaw: It fails as a moral theory because it fails to provide a body of *generalisable* rules, a body of rules that binds everybody.

This is because moral laws are prescriptive, not descriptive. So, when looking for moral rules, so far we know that we want moral rules that are binding on everyone, which is reflected in the fact that moral rules are prescriptive.

So, the contractarian position is actually that the moral rules we should follow are those that it would be reasonable to expect all rational people to adopt. It says that since there are no natural moral laws, no God-given moral guides, and that we cannot rely on moral intuitions since intuitions often contradict each other, the only moral rules that should constrain our actions are those that rational individuals would choose for themselves. However, whilst it is true that people need to choose, it must be understood what it is they are choosing. This is because of our insights as to what a morality is for. For example, you may decide your morals — for instance, the view that theft is morally justifiable if the need is great enough — but only for yourself. The trouble is you are not the only pebble on the beach. We live in social surroundings, under which circumstances we are likely to come into contact with each other. Couple this with the fact that we all have different values and desires, often very different, and we basically get the question of how this helps us at all? How has choosing a morality only for ourselves made any difference to not choosing one at all? Morality is necessary in order to regulate the behaviour of everybody, because there are things we don't want others doing, things we want to be able to do, and vice versa.

This is the point: The morality I choose can't only be the one that is the best choice for me, or the one you choose should only be the one that is the best, most rational choice for you. It has to be the best for all of us. This is because morality is necessary only because we are social, and come into contact with others. If you think we should choose only for ourselves, then consider this: What point would there be in choosing a morality if you were the only person in the world? None. Why would you care if you led a moral life then?

Hence Jan Narveson writes:

What we are arguing for is *general* principles of action for regulating our mutual behaviour. We would like to have the best such principles... We interact with lots and lots of people, most of them total strangers. Which principles, limiting our own and everyone else's conduct, would the rational person go for? Well, this question surely segues into another: what is it reasonable to expect of them, and what is it reasonable for them to expect of us? Obviously we need a principle that people with different values would all find it rational to accept. Precisely because they are so different, if they were to act exclusively on the variable values they have, we'd soon get into trouble.[4]

We can, therefore, talk about which is the correct moral theory by attacking the groundwork of others as not being satisfactory to the social contract — not being a set of principles that would be accepted by everybody. This is one answer to many who reject the contractarian thesis. They observe what is basically true: That in choosing the moral principle I think I should live under, I would choose the one that does best for me, you would choose the one that does best for you, etc. and we would wind up with the kind of mess we think morality is necessary to prevent, the kind of mess that we are trying to contract out of. The key,

though, is that the principle to be chosen can't be just a personal principle, precisely because that leads to a situation no different from one in which no principle was chosen at all. Instead, the contractarian is saying that the principle of morality or justice will be that which is best for me, provided that it is also best for you, him, her, and everybody.

So which principle of justice is that likely to be? The answer is that we should prohibit just those actions that would worsen the situation of others. Worsen in relation to the way things would be were the offending agent not around — in short, by comparing what I actually do with what would have occurred in my absence. As Narveson goes on:

Borrowing a famous analogy from Nozick, suppose that people lived on separate islands, with no knowledge of each other's existence. Then it can hardly be reasonable to impute injustice into any of their activities: no one can worsen the situation of others relative to one's absence, because everyone is absent. Once interaction sets in, however, injustice can arise. If the As take from the Bs what the latter have produced by their own efforts, without recompense, they better their own situation *by* worsening the situation of the Bs, as to how it would be for the Bs if the As didn't exist. In short, they take advantage of the Bs.[5]

You can do what you like, so long as you do not make others worse off than were you not around. This view smacks very heavily of libertarianism. David Gauthier expands on this:

Each person, in the absence of his fellows, may expect to use his own powers but not theirs... Thus the proviso, in prohibiting each from bettering his own position by worsening that of others, but otherwise leaving each free to do as he pleases, not only confirms each in the use of their powers, but in denying to others the use of those powers, affords to each exclusive use of his own. The proviso thus converts the unlimited liberties of Hobbesian nature [the moral-less situation we were trying to escape by establishing the contract] into exclusive rights and duties. Each person has a right to the exercise of his own powers without hindrance from others, and a duty to refrain from the use of others' powers in so far as this would hinder their exercise by those with direct access to them.[6]

As Narveson notes, this amounts to a prohibition on force or fraud. It definitely amounts to a prohibition against interference with the actions of other people, and, perhaps less stringently, with their plans and goals. Thus it amounts to the liberty principle. It is rational because violations of this principle are Pareto inefficient. That is to say, one person could be made better off without making anybody else worse off. If agents are rational, then we cannot expect voluntary agreement to anything less. The principle of justice does prohibit violations of the Pareto condition measured against the baseline of zero social interaction. We can expect this principle of justice to be the outcome of the social contract, in short, because we have no good reason to believe that anybody would voluntarily enter a contract that established as a principle that it would be just if they made be worse off than if they did not interact with anybody.

This last point can be emphasised by examining competing political philosophies. Take strict egalitarianism, which says that everybody should be equally well off (in a simplistic view of egalitarianism). The implication of this is that we should prohibit anybody from being made better off unless everybody is made equally better off at the same time, even if nobody is made worse off.

A problem with this theory, though, is that it would justify actually making everybody worse off than they would otherwise be, just so long as they are all equally badly off! It is clear that this principle would not be chosen as a principle of justice or morality, then. To see why, imagine two countries, A and B. In country A strict equality pertains and nobody is better off than anybody else is. In country B, however there are great inequalities. However, even the worst off in country B will be better off than anybody in country A. Which country would the rational person choose to live in? Surely B.

This argument is that egalitarianism restricts Pareto improvements. A situation is efficient in a Paretian sense when it cannot be improved upon, meaning that nobody can be made better off without making anybody worse off. If there were a change under which the situation of one person could be improved without harming that of others, the strict egalitarian principle would forbid it. This is unlikely to be the choice of rational agents forming an agreement on principles to mutually bind their behaviour.

Suppose we soften the egalitarianism by introducing a theory popular among some liberal philosophers: That we permit some inequalities, but only if the inequalities make people in general better off, or at least make the worst of members of society better off, than they would otherwise be. There has been some argument to suggest that this would be a rational principle for reasonable people to adopt in the social contract. After all, if everybody in country B were actually worse off than those in country A, then the egalitarian country would be the rational choice… But not for the sake of its equality, only because it made everybody, including the worst off sections of society, better off than they would otherwise have been.

However, I suggest that this principle will not be adopted in the social contract. Note that its implication is that inequalities are justified *if and only if* they benefit either the rest of society, or/and the worst off members of society. However, it is logically possible for an inequality to *neither benefit nor worsen* anybody in society, including members of the worst off. The softer egalitarian position would still prohibit such an inequality. Hence the soft egalitarian principle is still likely to be rejected by rational people forming an agreement on principles that would mutually constrain their actions. Harry is likely to reject a principle that would allow Mary to better herself at Harry's expense, and so Mary would reject it too, since mutually agreed principles are what we are looking for. But why would Mary adopt a principle that would forbid her from bettering herself in relation to Harry, but without harming Harry? Especially since Harry has no reason to object to Mary making herself better off if he himself isn't being made worse off by her actions.

The egalitarian may claim to be able to water his argument down further: The principle we shall adopt is that inequalities will be justified if and only if they make nobody worse off than they would otherwise have been. This clearly seems to be more rational for reasons given above.

But what difference is there between this and the liberty principle? This is a general principle that says that you can do what you want so long as you don't worsen the situation of others. It amounts to not interfering in the actions that people are performing and not taking away the things they are using or feature in their plans. This is identical to the principle libertarianism suggests. It does not suffer the same Paretian deficiencies that egalitarianism suffers, for, though it doesn't guarantee that anybody's situation will be improved by its adoption, it does guarantee that nobody will be made worse off. And it also guarantees that nobody will be prohibited from attempting to make himself or herself better off so long as they don't harm the situations of others.

We have thus grounded the right to liberty by showing why it would be the principle of justice that it would be reasonable to expect everybody to adopt. The liberty principle gives us all a basic right to do what we want, constrained only by a similar right belonging to others. This is barely different from the principle we said would be established by the moral social contract, that people be free to do as they want so long as they don't worsen the situation of others compared to how those others would be were the offender not around. This gives us liberty in the negative sense of being free to utilise our powers without them being utilised by others without compensation, and so free to do as we want without interference. Being free to do as we want without interference or impediment means being free to control what we are using to do what we want without impediment. This establishes a negative right to property.

Summary of Libertarianism, and its Implications

Hence people should not interfere with what we do with our own person or property. Since governments are people, this means that governments should not interfere with what we do with our person or property either. Nozick tells us why this frightens the non-libertarian horses:

> Two noteworthy implications are that the state may not use its coercive apparatus for the purpose of getting some citizens to aid others, or in order to prohibit activities to people for their own good or protection.

> Despite the fact that it is only coercive routes toward these goals that are excluded, while voluntary ones remain, many persons will reject our conclusions instantly, knowing they don't *want* to believe anything so apparently callous toward the needs and sufferings of others.[7]

The only just social arrangement, then, is that which arises spontaneously from the free interactions of each agent in full possession of his powers, i.e. that which is consented to rather than that to which he is forced to contribute. Some opponents of libertarianism, such as Alan Howarth or G.A. Cohen object that the market economy cannot satisfy this, since, whilst each person can be said to consent to his part of the market process, he knows nothing about the multitude of other interactions nor about their likely consequences, and so does not consent to the arrived at arrangements of the entire market system. However, when we use the word consent here, we are saying that each person is able to act unmolested, not that each person knowingly chooses a particular outcome. In other words, that they are not coerced into choosing an outcome, not that they know the outcome they are choosing.

Only if the state can be shown to come about by these spontaneous arrangements can its existence be justified.

Insurance Arguments for Compulsory Social Insurance

As libertarians, we know our views are unpopular. They imply extreme laissez faire, in the literal sense — *leave it alone; hands off.*

People tend to disagree with us, because they assume that the possibility of a libertarian society would threaten their attainment of various ends. Often they argue against us in terms of justice, asserting that attainment of these ends can be viewed as part of our rights. They argue that ends such as a universal attainment of a certain level of education, a universal minimum income regardless of desert, the extension of this basic income into old age to cover against insecurity, and high levels of medical attention are requirements of justice, and hence the welfare state is justified in providing them for us. However, it is difficult to see how these could be requirements of justice if justice is only concerned with fundamental rights, and more so if these rights are generated in a contractarian manner. They cannot simply snatch their moral views from the air!

However, many modern theorists do not argue for the welfare state in this manner. Instead they frame the issue as an insurance argument. These arguments avoid any claims to rights. Instead, their premise is simply that the things in question, such as a minimum guaranteed income, especially in old age, are sufficiently important from the point of view of any person that he or she would do well to take out insurance against them. For example, we have the position of the modern egalitarian philosopher, Ronald Dworkin.[8] Dworkin, on one hand, argues that markets are just. He holds that to show respect and concern for people who have different, but peaceful, views of the good life, different preferences and ambitions, etc., justice mandates that individuals have the right to act in accordance with those views and have the freedom to pursue, revise, and realise their ambitions and goals. Further to this, such respect requires that one be held responsible for one's own choices, since it would be grossly unfair to expect those who are morally obliged to respect people's rights and not interfere with the choices they make to then also have to subsidise the costs of the right holder's choices. Hence, Dworkin argues, a system which allows people to make choices, gives people information about the costs of their choices so that these choices can be informed ones, and holds people responsible for their choices, would be just. Markets do all three things. So, if we lived in a world in which we all began in roughly equal cir-

cumstances, then any inequality in wealth and income that resulted would be just, for it would simply reflect people's choices about how to live their lives, as revealed by their trade-offs of work and leisure, their trade-offs between savings and investment for consumption, the extent to which they discount the future, their occupational choices, etc.

However, Dworkin goes on, we obviously do not live in such a world. Here in the real world people find themselves in unchosen circumstances with varying degrees of advantage or disadvantage. Dworkin holds that when markets reflect or compound unchosen disadvantages that may result from one's natural endowments, or one's race, or family or social background, etc., then markets do not embody justice, but injustice. Hence, for Dworkin, welfare state policies that interfere with the workings of the market are justified insofar that they correct for the unchosen disadvantages whilst still leaving people free to act on their peaceful ambitions and conceptions of the good.

Insurance arguments, and positions like Dworkin's, ask, basically, do we want to throw ourselves entirely on the tender mercies of the free market for these essential goods in life, without protection against the exigencies in life. These might, in particular, include unexpectedly high health care costs, job loss not due to culpable incompetence (because, for people like Dworkin, culpable incompetence is something that you are responsible for — it is a choice you make), inability to make a living due to the death or desertion of a spouse or family member (or anybody else) upon whom you were dependent, being suddenly left with the family in one's sole care, or just plain unemployability due to the present situation of the job market.

The argument thus goes that if the typical rational adult would take out insurance against these things then a further move towards the state leans on premises about efficiency and certainty. If the state guarantees the benefits we don't need to worry about our insurance company going broke or making a bad choice in our case. If everybody is covered, then economics of scale are realised. The resulting insurance will be cheaper and better, then, if it is universal. But if the benefits are worth it to everybody, then those accepting them without paying would be free-riders of the culpable kind, i.e. those who free ride even though it is perfectly possible for them to avoid the benefits. Thus, then, insurance may be financed out of general taxation.

How, then, does the libertarian answer this argument for compulsory social insurance?

The Libertarian Response

Good libertarians have an answer to all objections, and the libertarian answer to this one is, at least abstractly, very compelling. In fact, I would agree with Jan Narveson that the argument I am about to present is utterly decisive.

Insurance and the Tender Mercies of the Market

The answer comes in two parts. Firstly, the alternatives of "throwing oneself on the tender mercies of the market" and having sufficient insurance against these unchosen disadvantages are not exclusive alternatives and never have been: It is perfectly possible to throw one's self on the tender mercies of the free market and cover one's self against the exigencies in question by simply taking out free-market-generated insurance against whatever unchosen and risky thing you are inclined to feel the need for protection against. In that classic work of libertarian Science Fiction, *The Moon Is a Harsh Mistress*, Robert Heinlein describes a world without social insurance. When asked how society manages without all the things that Earth's governments provide, the chief protagonist responds:

> Free Hospitals — aren't any on Luna. Medical insurance — we have that but apparently not what you mean by it. If a person wants insurance he goes to a bookie and works out a bet. You can hedge anything, for a price. I don't hedge my health, I'm healthy. Or was 'til I came here.[9]

In one sense, this is all insurance is. If you are worried that something bad will happen to you, you find someone willing to take your bet, bet them that this bad thing will happen to you during some period of time, whilst they bet you that it won't. If it does, they pay you. …

But What if the Market Doesn't Provide Enough Coverage?

The second part of this argument concentrates on the important question of whether the free market will supply "enough" protection, especially to those who cannot afford it. The reply to these challenges is in three parts:

(1) Compulsory protection may well not be able to supply "enough" either. As Jan Narveson notes, "certainly we will be able to find, for any level you care to name, some individual who wants more; and it is difficult to see how any premises that allow scope for freedom could claim to identify a 'correct' amount for all and sundry."

In fact we may go further than this with two other points. Firstly, the effects of providing a good at lower than its market price are that the good will be over consumed. When the state provides us with something for free, or at a lower than normal price, it effectively creates a form of market failure called a negative externality. You see, when a person gets both the costs and the benefits of his actions, if he is rational he will only perform those actions he thinks are worth doing; i.e., the actions he thinks deliver benefits that are worth enduring the costs. If somebody else is paying the costs, on the other hand, perhaps because they have been forced on somebody else via state action, he won't have to consider whether his actions are worth their costs. We know that the cheaper something is, the more of it people are likely to consume, so the end result is that in effect the state is likely to supply not "enough" insurance, but too much — more than its recipient would actually think is worth providing. This will lead to perpetual complaints of shortages, whilst the taxes used to subsidise the lower prices will lead to a fall in productivity throughout the economy.

On top of this, production necessarily precedes charity. You cannot feed the poor if there is no food. The philanthropist cannot give the needy his money if he has no money or if there is nothing to spend it on. Therefore you cannot help the poor by using policies that would be deleterious of production. And all taxes and regulations reduce productivity.

(2) The second response cuts back to the ethical and philosophical issue at hand: The cost of protection in the compulsory scheme is thrown on all whether they want to pay that much or not; however, surely no contractarian moral philosophy could provide a principle that could be foreseen to require people to pay for things they don't want whether they like it or not and independently of any benefit to them. This is clear for the same reason that contractarianism yields the liberty principle: Nobody would agree to an arrangement that would leave them worse off than they would otherwise be.

But if contractarianism cannot yield this principle, what moral philosophy could. Where do these moral imperatives come from? We would have to go back to flawed moral theories such as utilitarianism, natural law, or divine will.

(3) Now, though, we reach what I consider to be the most damning argument the libertarian can present against at least most advocates of compulsory social insurance. This argument is that nobody advocates such measures independently of democratic procedures. Proponents of compulsory social insurance generally insist that their scheme would be popular with voters and that it would not be legitimate to impose it were this not the case. So let us imagine that it is indeed highly popular, then. But then, if the value of having this insurance is so great and the scheme is as popular as the argument demands, it would also be possible to form a private insurance scheme with essentially the same schedule of costs and benefits, but which extended its benefits and costs only to those who were interested in sharing in those benefits at those costs. So why would we need to go all the way to a compulsory scheme?

Narveson sums this point up:

> The point about this last argument is that some necessary conditions of the acceptability and workability of the compulsory scheme under

consideration are such that a noncompulsory scheme must be possible offering the same advantages but without the disadvantage of being compulsory. And so it merely remains to point out that one who was contracting for general social arrangements could not be understood to consent to arrangements requiring us to pay costs for unnecessary benefits.

This last argument is, then, a dominance argument. It says that from the contractarian point of view, libertarian systems dominate their alternatives. The fulcrum of such arguments is that rational persons cannot be in favour of outcomes that, by definition, they are not in favour of. It's pretty difficult to knock that principle, I should think. And so it seems that, at least abstractly, the argument goes through pretty smoothly.

In other words, if this insurance scheme is popular enough with voters that they would vote for their money to be used in such a fashion, it is plainly going to be popular enough for them to voluntarily spend their money on it. And if it was not popular enough for them to choose to use their money to support it, it then cannot be presumed that they would vote for it. As Narveson wrote elsewhere:

> It's a bit crazy to try to justify an involuntary exchange with an argument that it is such a keen deal that we would take it even if we had the choice. For if that were true, then it of course would not need to be involuntary, now, would it? For then we'd do it anyway! Freedom is all we need to get the benefits of freely made deals. And it is very much what we need to avoid the downsides of unfreely made ones.[10]

Extending the Argument to Apply to Charity

The Economics of Charity

Many people don't object to libertarianism as a threat to things they already enjoy. They accept that they could just as easily get them through the free market: "Sure, I can afford health insurance, so I certainly don't need taxation to provide me with health care... but what about the poor?" "What about the Poor?" can just as readily apply to "What about the Handicapped?" especially the paraplegic? The position is basically, "sure, I can help myself so I don't need someone to do it for me, and on those grounds, sure I object to being forced to pay the guy supposedly helping. But what about those that can't help themselves?"

Libertarians are often strong in their principles and unyielding in the face of this objection: They might sometimes turn around and say, sure, worst comes to the worst, those born disabled can starve in the gutters, and that would be a more just outcome than if people were forced to provide for them. On philosophical grounds I might agree with this. Forcing people to provide for others certainly violates rights that I think are the likely outcome of the only reasonable basis for a moral philosophy I know of: Either it is wrong to force people to provide for others, or morality doesn't exist. That's my basic position.

However, this ends up being unpersuasive, and definitely very unattractive. An alternative is to say that simply because libertarianism is opposed to forcing people to provide, through labour or through commitment of resources, for the good of others, there is nothing in libertarianism that prohibits people voluntarily helping others. Indeed, it follows from the assumption at the core of libertarianism, that each of us should be at liberty to dispose of ourselves and whatever resources we justly acquire, however we choose, that any prohibition of charity would be an injustice. If you want to help others, especially those who can't help themselves, you could donate to charity. Even a philosopher as sceptical of the libertarian position as Jonathon Wolff notes that "The distinction between the morally right and the rightfully enforceable is one we commonly make in other cases."[11] So whilst it may be absolutely wrong and utterly unforgivable for me not to cross the road and go to the aid of someone collapsed on the pavement, we might still be unhappy with the prospect of this immoral choice being made illegal. Wolff notes that "libertarians point out that taxation for redistributive purposes does in fact make it illegal not to contribute to alleviating the plight of

the badly off. But it is quite consistent to believe that morally one should aid the poor and sick, and yet that one should not be forced to do this." ...

But How Can We Know That Enough People Will Give to Charity?

How much aid would be forthcoming if all aid were voluntary? This is a speculative question, of course. However, there have been those who have said that philanthropy and charity are actually curtailed by the welfare state and its taxes. Abolish state welfare and drastically reduce or abolish taxes, it is said, and the well springs of philanthropy will flow once more. ...

So, in answer to the question, *"But how do you know if there will be plenty of people willing to support those in need through private charity?"* the answer is that we don't. However, if I am too selfish to give voluntarily to charity, then it follows that I would be too selfish to vote for someone to take my money and give it instead. And so, if we can't expect that most people will be generous enough to give voluntarily to help the poor, then we also can't expect enough people to vote for a scheme of compulsory charity instead. People cannot rationally be expected to consent to that which they would not rationally consent to. Therefore the libertarian argument wins. The libertarian position dominates the alternatives since, if enough people care about the poor enough to vote for a welfare scheme to take their money and give it to the poor, there would be enough to help the poor through charity. But if there are not enough to help the poor through charity, then how could there be the political will to arrange the welfare policy?

NOTES

1. Jan Narveson, *The Libertarian Idea*, Temple University Press, 1988, p. 66.
2. Jan Narveson "Foundations of Liberty: Contract Law Vs. Government Coercion," http://www.libertyconferences.com/sp_narveson.htm. Lecture given to the International Society for Individual Liberty, 2000.
3. Many people have a curious objection to the notion

of self-ownership. They regard it as incoherent because they are of the opinion that the statement "I own myself" is somehow circular or that it raises the Cartesian paradigm of mind-body dualism — that some part of me must be separate from another part of me if I can own myself — the "I" and the "myself" are separate. (In fact, it is worse than the Cartesian paradigm in that it involves an infinite regress: If I own myself, then not only must "I" be separate from "myself," but also this thing called "I" must also be something I control, etc, etc.) However, these people are perfectly happy to use logically identical phrases in everyday language. If they really think that "I control myself" is incoherent due to some suspected circularity, ask them if they have ever hurt themselves? Ask them if they have ever been proud of themselves? But don't get too close, they clearly never wash themselves! In fact, stay away from them completely ... they are dangerous ... after all, they can't control themselves!

4. Jan Narveson, "Foundations of Liberty: Contract Law Vs. Government Coercion," http://www.libertyconferences.com/sp_narveson.htm. Lecture given to the International Society for Individual Liberty 2000.

5. Jan Narveson, *The Libertarian Idea*, Temple University Press, 1988, p. 176.

6. David Gauthier, *Morals by Agreement*, Oxford University Press, 1986, pp. 209-10.

7. Robert Nozick, *Anarchy, State and Utopia*, Routledge, 1974, p. ix.

8. See Ronald Dworkin "What is Equality? Part 1: Equality of Welfare," *Philosophy and Public Affairs*, Vol. 10, No. 3 1981; "What is Equality? Part 2: Equality of Resources," *Philosophy and Public Affairs*, Vol. 10, No. 4 1981; "What is Equality? Part 3: The Place of Liberty," *Iowa Law Review*, Vol. 73, No. 1 1987.

9. Robert Heinlein, *The Moon is a Harsh Mistress*, New English Library, 1967, p. 184.

10. Jan Narveson, "Foundations of Liberty: Contract Law Vs. Government Coercion," www.libertyconferences.com/sp_narveson.htm. Lecture given to the International Society for Individual Liberty, 2000.

11. Jonathon Wolff, *Robert Nozick: Property, Justice, and the Minimal State*, Polity Press, 1991, p. 12.

CARE AND JUSTICE IN THE GLOBAL CONTEXT

Virginia Held

Virginia Held is Distinguished Professor Emerita in Philosophy and Women's Studies at the Graduate Center of the City University of New York. She is the author of numerous articles on feminist ethics; has authored Rights and Goods: Justifying Social Action *(1989), and* Feminist Morality: Transforming Culture, Society, and Politics *(1993); and edited* Justice and Care: Essential Readings in Feminist Ethics *(1995).*

Virginia Held contrasts justice in its alignment with moral and political conceptions of individual rights, equality, and universal law with care in its alignment with relationships, equity, and responsibility to others. While care has tended to be associated with moral theory and, more specifically, with moral relations in the private sphere, Held argues that it has potential as a political theory for informing and transforming contemporary problems in international relations and global politics. Mutual concern, trustworthiness, attentiveness, and responsiveness are promoted by a care approach to morality. As caring values become more influential within a society, argues Held, resolutions of conflict through threat, force, and violence could decrease at national and international levels of relations within and between states.

The field of study known as international relations tries to guide our thinking about the world and about relations between states. On the one hand it has had a normative component from the beginning, concerning itself with avoiding the mistakes that led, for instance, to the First World War (Grant and Newland 1991, 3). On the other hand, it has tried to be an empirical social science, and what is called "realism" has been dominant in international relations for a long time, at least since the Second World War.

It has sometimes been acknowledged that what people *think* about the morality of a state's behavior can influence that state's standing, and thus power. But the world has largely been seen as a global near-anarchy of rival states each pursuing its national interest. This national interest can sometimes be thought to include entering into agreements with other states. But trying to assess what really would be the moral course of action for states to pursue has usually been dismissed as pointless.

Of course, it has not been pointless to everyone, and a number of philosophers and others have concerned themselves with ethics and international affairs.[1] And, in the last decade or so, there seem to have been within the field of international relations, more serious discussions than before of what morality — if it were taken seriously — would require of states. Also, international law, with its inherent or arguably normative aspects, has, despite serious challenges, continued to grow (Henkin 1989). In short, much work has been done to develop the morality of *justice*, with its associated moral conceptions of individual rights, equality, and universal law, for the arena of international relations and politics. Global justice has come to be a familiar topic, along with just war.

This is sometimes seen as part of the "third debate" in international relations theory — after the idealism of the first debate, which was replaced by the realism of the second. Also in this third debate within international relations are the very different approaches of critical theory, postmodernism, and feminist theory (Steans 1998). From many such perspectives it is apparent how ideological the "realism" that passed for factual and scientific has been. And receptivity towards new ways of understanding international reality and what to do within it has grown (Keohane 1998).

International relations has been among the last of the social sciences to be affected by the awareness of gender issues that made such strides in the last quarter of the 20th century (Halliday 1991). As J. Ann Tickner (1992, 4) writes, "with its focus on the 'high' politics of war and Realpolitik, the traditional Western academic discipline of international relations privileges issues that grow out of men's experiences; we are socialized into believing that war and power politics are spheres of activity with which men have a special affinity [...]" and to which women are irrelevant. Gradually, however, as the equation of what is human with what is masculine is being questioned, the implications of attending to gender are becoming apparent for this field as for others. It is being shown how "the values and assumptions that drive our international system are intrinsically related to concepts of masculinity [...]" (Tickner 1992, 17).

Meanwhile, within feminist theorizing and in the area of moral theory, an alternative to the ethics of justice has been developed. This alternative moral approach is the ethics of care. It is beginning to influence how philosophers and scholars in international relations and global politics see the world, and our responsibilities.

1. The Ethics of Care

In the last few decades, a very short time in the history of moral theorizing, the ethics of care has given rise to an extensive literature, and has affected many moral inquiries in many areas.[2] It is changing the ways moral problems are often interpreted, and changing what many think the recommended approaches to moral problems ought to be. It offers promising possibilities for improving morality, and quite possibly for understanding what we ought to be doing at the global level.

The ethics of care offers a distinctive challenge to the dominant moral theories — Kantian moral theory, utilitarianism, and virtue ethics. Kantian moral theory can most easily be seen as a morality of justice. Its expression in works such as John Rawls' *A Theory of Justice* is emblematic. And many recent discussions of global justice illustrate the application of this sort of theory to international affairs. It can be seen, for instance, in the work of Charles Beitz, Onora O'Neill, and Thomas Pogge. Such theory requires abstract, universal principles to which all, taken as free, equal, and autonomous individual persons choosing impartially, can agree. It sees justice as the most important basis on which to judge the acceptability of political and social arrangements. It insists on respecting persons through recognition of their rights, and provides moral constraints within which individuals may pursue their interests. It seeks fair distributions of positions of differential power and of the benefits of economic activity.

Utilitarianism is less obviously a morality of justice. It recommends maximizing the utility of all taken as individuals pursuing their own interests. But in its requirement that the utility of each individual is to be seen as of equal importance to that of any other, it tries to build justice into its foundations. And it justifies the political recognition of individual rights as highly conducive to general utility. Like Kantian moral theory's Categorical Imperative, utilitarianism has one very general universal principle, the Principle of Utility on which it relies.

The ethics of care differs from these theories in its assumptions, goals, and methods. It is closer to virtue ethics, which has enjoyed a recent revival, and it is sometimes thought to be a kind of virtue ethics (Tessman 2001, McLaren 2001). But the ethics of care is sufficiently different from virtue ethics as well as other theories to be counted, in my view, as a new and distinct kind of moral theory (Held, forthcoming). Of course it has precursors, but it is built on different foundations and has developed in distinctive ways.

Among the characteristics of the ethics of care is

its view of persons as relational and as interdependent. Kantian and consequentialist moral theories focus primarily on the rational decisions of agents taken as independent and autonomous individuals. Even virtue theory focuses on individuals and their dispositions. In contrast, the ethics of care sees persons as partly constituted by their relations with others. It pays attention primarily to relations between persons, valuing especially caring relations. Rather than assuming, as do the dominant moral theories, that moral relations are to be seen as entered into voluntarily by free and equal individuals, the ethics of care is developed for the realities, as well, of unequal power and unchosen relations; salient examples are relations between parents and children, but the ethics of care is not limited to such "private" contexts. It understands how our ties to various social groups and our historical embeddedness are also part of what make us who we are.

For the dominant moral theories, there is attention to individual aims and interests on the one hand, and to universal moral norms on the other. Conflicts between the egoistic desires of the self, and the moral claims of everyone seen from an impartial perspective, are recognized. But anything between these extremes of individual self and all others is virtually invisible. To the ethics of care, in contrast, moral life is populated by caring relations in which the interests of self and other are mingled, and trust is crucial. In caring for her child, for instance, a mother may often be pursuing not her own individual interest, or altruistically her child's as if it were in conflict with her own, but the mutual interest of both together. And she will characteristically value her child and her relation to the child for their own sakes, not to satisfy her own preferences. Her moral concern may well be not that of all persons universally, but that of the particular others with whom she shares such caring relations. And such caring relations are not limited to the personal contexts of family and friends. They can extend to fellow members of groups of various kinds, to fellow-citizens, and beyond. We can, for instance, develop caring relations for persons who are suffering deprivation in distant parts of the globe. Moral theories that assume only

individuals pursuing their own interests within the constraints supplied by universal rules are ill-suited to deal with the realities and values of caring relations and of relational persons.

In sum, then, an ethic of justice focuses on issues of fairness, equality, and individual rights, seeking impartial and abstract principles that can be applied consistently to particular cases. Individual persons are seen as instances of the general and timeless conception of person. In contrast, the ethics of care focuses on attentiveness to context, trust, responding to needs, and offers narrative nuance; it cultivates caring relations. Persons are seen as enmeshed in relations and unique. An ethic of justice seeks fair decisions between competing individual rights and interests. The ethics of care sees the interests of carers and cared-for as importantly shared. While justice protects equality and freedom from interference, care values positive involvement with others and fosters social bonds and cooperation.

In trying to ascertain what we morally ought to do, Kantian moral theory and utilitarianism rely entirely on reason. The ethics of care, instead, appreciates the contribution of the emotions in helping us to understand what morality recommends. For instance, empathy, sensitivity, and responsiveness to particular others may often be better guides to what we ought to do than are highly abstract rules and principles about "all men." In place of what has traditionally been thought of as "moral knowledge," Margaret Walker (1989), for instance, advocates "attention, contextual and narrative appreciation, and communication in the event of moral deliberation," holding that "the adequacy of moral understanding decreases as its form approaches generality through abstraction."

From the perspective of law, emotion is seen as a threat to the impartiality law requires; emotion is then to be discounted and dismissed. But from the perspective of care, the social relations that must exist before law can get off the ground are, importantly, a form of caring relations between, say, fellow citizens, or, potentially, fellow members of regions or of the globe.

Dominant moral theories seem to have general

ized to what they take to be the whole of morality the outlooks thought to be appropriate for the impartial decisions of judges and legislators, or the pursuits of rational self-interest in the marketplace. The concerns of women in the family have been thought to lie "outside" morality, governed by "natural" inclinations. However, with the rise of women's reliance on their own experiences and feminist insights, the relevance to morality of the concerns and responsibilities of caring, in the family and far beyond, have been appreciated. And it is becoming apparent that this requires profound changes in the way morality is understood.

In my view, the ethics of care should not be thought of as a naturalized ethic, as some of its advocates propose. To provide the full normativity of this approach, persons engaged in caring activities and relations, as I see them, must be taken to be moral subjects not reducible to the objects of scientific description (Held 2002b, 7-24). But caring persons will draw greatly on the understanding of care that can be developed from actual experiences of caring and being cared for.

2. Care as Practice and Value

There is not yet agreement on the precise meaning of "care" as it figures in the ethics of care, but taking care of a child, providing care for the ill, and caring strongly about how those without adequate food are to be fed are examples. Care is concerned with meeting the needs of those dependent on us, and the ethics of care values caring relations and their associated concerns of trust and mutual responsiveness.

Care is a practice involving the work of caregiving and the standards by which the practices of care can be evaluated. Care must concern itself with the effectiveness of its efforts to meet needs, but also with the motives with which care is provided. Recipients of care sustain caring relations through their responsiveness — the look of satisfaction in the child, the smile of the patient. Relations between persons can be criticized when they become dominating, exploitative, mistrustful, or hostile. Relations of care can be encouraged and maintained.

Care is also a value (Held 2003). We value caring relations and caring persons. We can understand many aspects of how persons are interrelated through a constellation of moral considerations associated with care: mutual concern, trustworthiness, attentiveness, responsiveness. To advocates of the ethics of care, care involves moral considerations at least as important as those of justice. And, when adequately understood, it is an ethics as appropriate for men as for women. Both men and women should acknowledge the enormous value of the caring activities on which society relies, and should share these activities fairly. They should recognize the values of care, as of justice.

One should not equate the ethics of care with feminist ethics. Some feminists are critical of the emphasis on care, seeing it as reinforcing traditional stereotypes of women as selfless nurturers, "naturally" suited to staying home and leaving the "public" sphere to men. Onora O'Neill, for instance, writes that "a stress on caring and relationships [...] may endorse relegation to the nursery and the kitchen, to purdah and to poverty. In rejecting 'abstract liberalism,' such feminists converge with traditions that have excluded women from economic and public life" (O'Neill 1992, 55; Okin 1989; Nussbaum 1999). But Fiona Robinson, arguing for the relevance of the ethics of care to international relations, writes that "it is only a narrow, 'orthodox' ethics of care — the view of care as essentially a morality for women, belonging in the private sphere [...] to which these criticisms apply" (Robinson 1999, 20). And I agree. The ethics of care has gone *far* beyond its earliest formulations. Although there are similarities between ethics of care and communitarianism, and between the ethics of care and Confucianism and what are sometimes thought of as "Asian values," many now argue that any *satisfactory* ethics of care, or perhaps even any ethic that deserves the name "ethics of care," will be a feminist ethics that includes an insistence on the equality of women, not one accepting a traditional gender hierarchy.

3. Justice and Caring Relations

Some writers defending the dominant moral theories acknowledge that care is important and has been neglected. They think a concern for care can be added to theories that focus on justice without requiring significant changes in those theories (Darwall 1998, chap. 19). They see moral terms as requiring universalizability, but think duties to care can be universalized. They continue to hold that impartial principles of justice have priority, but suggest that such principles can permit us to be partial towards our families and friends in appropriate ways, as when we prefer to spend time with one friend rather than another.

Advocates of the ethics of care believe this misunderstands the issues (Held 2001). To the ethics of care, the moral claims of partial caring relations may indeed challenge the priority of universal rules and the perspective of impartiality. The question "why should I give priority to justice over my relations with those I most care about?" can be a meaningful question not answerable by an appeal to the meaning of the terms in the languages of the dominant moralities. As Annette Baier has expressed this thought, in noting the resistance of many women to Kantian morality, "[w]here Kant concludes 'so much the worse for women,' we can conclude 'so much the worse for the male fixation on the special skill of drafting legislation, for the bureaucratic mentality of rule worship, and for the male exaggeration of the importance of independence over mutual interdependence'" (Baier 1994, 26).

This is not to say that care excludes justice. Justice should be incorporated into morally acceptable practices of care. Parents of two or more children, for instance, ought to treat each fairly; the care given to a frail old person should respect her autonomy when possible. Within caring relations of a personal kind, competition may sometimes arise as when siblings engage in a competitive game, and fairness should prevail. At the social level, institutions that provide care ought to assure that the rights of recipients are respected and paternalism avoided. But in contexts of care, care should have priority, and justice be developed within caring relations.

At the level of society, justice now has overwhelming priority, as care is marginalized to private provision or grudging and stingy public support. From the perspective of the ethics of care, this is highly unsatisfactory. Care should at least be on a par with justice, and should perhaps have priority even in the social order, as it certainly has priority in the contexts of family and friends. Consider the case for the priority of care. Care is probably the most fundamental value of all. There can be care without justice: There has been little justice in traditional families but care has been provided. There can be no justice without care, for neither persons nor societies could exist without the enormous amount of care, with its associated values, involved in raising and educating children.

It is plausible to see caring relations as the wider and deeper context within which we seek justice and, in certain domains, give it priority.[3] In the domain of law, for instance, the language and principles of justice ought to have priority even though any "justice system" can and ought to be more caring than it almost surely is at present. At the same time, we should not lose sight of how the domain of law, with justice its priority, should be a limited domain and *not* imagined to be the model for the whole of moral life.

The values of care are already roughly incorporated into existing practices of care; they need to be better reflected and the practices improved and expanded. With better and more extensive practices of care, the needs for law and the enforcement mechanisms of the state could shrink. With better care in childhood and adolescence, fewer persons would turn to crime. But also, a care perspective would recommend a liberation of culture from the domination of commercial interests, and greatly enlarged opportunities for social decisions to be arrived at through dialogue and discourse rather than through imposed governmental determination (Held 1993, chap. 5). Environmental concerns would be accorded the importance they deserve. As the culture disapproved of those failing to take responsibility for the effects of their activities and for their failures to sustain caring relations, less enforcement would be required.

From the perspective of care, markets should be limited rather than ever more pervasive, as they undermine the caring, relations in which persons and the relations between them are valued for their own sakes (Held 2002a, 19-33). To the market, everything is a fungible commodity, and economic gain is the highest priority (Radin 1996). In the United States, more and more activities that were previously not in the market, such as child care and health care, and varieties of public services that are being "privatized," are being pushed into the market. Even persons and their labor are increasingly seen as commodities, as, for instance, labor markets become more often spot markets, and replace relations between employers and employees that once had at least some elements of caring (Kuttner 1998).

We can see how rights presuppose care. Respecting rights within a society requires that persons care enough about each other to be willing to think of each other as fellow members of whatever group or political entity is asserting or recognizing such rights (Held 2000). In recent years, more and more attention has been paid to the practices of civil society on which satisfactory political institutions depend. Such practices build connections between persons and ties that hold people together into a group capable of democratic self-government. They often foster caring relations. Various advocates of the ethics of care explicitly include citizenship among the practices of care. Peta Bowden, for instance, examines four types of caring practice: mothering, friendship, nursing, and citizenship. Those who do not yet think of citizenship in terms of care can come to see why they should. Bowden resists undue generalizations and abstract theorizing about care, but notes resemblances among its various forms. These include their emphases on the interdependence of persons and the quality of their relationships. All caring practices have been devalued; all should be accorded recognition of their enormous ethical significance.

4. Global Implications of the Ethics of Care

There is wide agreement among advocates of the ethics of care that it is not to be limited to the "private" spheres of family and friendship, and that it is a political as well as personal ethic. It clearly implies that society must recognize its responsibilities to its children and others who are dependent, enabling the best possible bringing up and educating of its future generations, appropriate responses to its members in need of health care, and assistance with the care of dependents. Relying largely or entirely, as societies have traditionally done, on the unpaid labor of women in the household for the provision of care is inconsistent with the values of care as well as of justice. The ethics of care calls for increased state support of various forms of caring, and for meeting people's needs in caring ways. It recommends the equal participation of men in caring activities and of women in the political and economic structures that affect the circumstances in which caring takes place. It guides the practices that encourage cooperation between persons and groups, and the caring that is needed to uphold the values of citizenship.

The ethics of care calls for the transformation of the different segments of society, with caring values and cooperation replacing the hierarchies and dominations of gender, class, race, and ethnicity. It recommends families characterized by mutual care; child care, education, and health care institutions well supported and developed; economies focused on actually meeting needs rather than enriching the powerful; military-industrial power under social constraints and decided about by women as well as men in the military services, defense industries, and diplomatic and political institutions; legal and political systems more expressive of the values of care as well as justice; and cultures free to present imaginative alternatives and to inspire cooperative and creative solutions to contested issues. But in addition to transforming each of such given domains, the ethics of care would transform the relations between domains (Held 1993). Instead of domination by military and economic and political power and the marginalization of caring activities, the latter would move to the center of attention, effort, and support. Bringing up new persons in caring relations that would be as admirable as possible would be seen as society's most important goal.

We can also begin to see how the ethics of care should transform international politics, and relations between states as well as within them. Building on its feminist roots, the ethics of care notices rather than ignores the role of the cultural construct of masculinity in the behavior of states. There are many men whom this image of masculinity does not actually characterize, and it can be aspired to by women as well as by men. But it does shape what those in positions of power, including the voters who support them, aim to do. Among its influences are the overemphasis on the part of states on military security and economic pre-emi nence, and the neglect of other aspects of security such as environmental and ecological concerns, the moral acceptability of policies to those affected, and the cultivating and maintaining of cooperative relations with others. The behavior of the United States in its near unilateral war against Iraq, its bullying of potential allies, its rejection of UN restraints and of the Kyoto and other treaties, illustrates the kind of foreign policies that almost certainly bear the influence of an exaggerated image of masculinity. The fear of being less than "tough," the prejudice that cooperation is for sissies, infects the possibilities for improving relations between states.

Feminists have demonstrated the gender bias in Hobbes' view of the political world (Di Stefano 1991). Realists and neorealists in international relations have transferred this Hobbesian view to the international arena, advocating preparation for war and the avoidance of dependence on others as the road to security. For Hans Morgenthau and Kenneth Waltz, for instance, maximizing military power and maintaining effective autonomy lead to states' success (Tickner 1992, 32). The ethics of care, in contrast, understands the importance of cultivating relations of trust, listening to the concerns of others, fostering international cooperation, and valuing interdependence.

In the usual construal of the global context, states are thought of as regions of security and order while the world beyond is seen as dangerous, anarchic, and frequently violent — Hobbes' war of all against all. This picture is analogous to that of the household as "haven in a heartless world." And military might is seen as analogous to the male "protector" of hearth and home. Feminists have cracked this picture of the household, making

visible the enormous amount of family violence that occurs within it. They have noted the special ways in which women throughout the world are threatened: Women are subject to rape, forced marriage, female infanticide, and the denial of health care and nutrition, merely because they are female (Charlesworth 1994). And feminists are cracking the picture of military strength, and the willingness to use it, as offering protection. They note, for instance, that "civilians now account for about 90 percent of war casualties, the majority of whom are women and children" (Tickner 2001, 6). From the perspective of the ethic of care, the militarized state may be more threat than protector. When in possession of overwhelming force, the temptation may be overwhelming to use it; the result may be arms races among all who feel threatened, and ever less attention to the real sources of security.

Feminists have also examined the image of the "citizen-warrior" at the heart of so much political theory and international relations thinking (Tickner 1992, chap. 2). They make explicit its devaluation of women and women's activities, and call for the revision of this constructed social ideal and of the way it has been transferred to the international arena of imagined personified states.

When the needs for law and restraint are acknowledged in relations between states, the model is then usually contractual, as within states, with the gender bias of law within states magnified on the international stage. However, as relations between states are re-examined, it is apparent how far they are from the assumptions of those who imagine their liberal democracies to be based on freely chosen contracts between equal individuals,[4] and see this as the model for the world. In fact, states have been created and their boundaries determined largely by force, and fraud has usually played a large role. Disparities between the global North and the global South are fraught with involuntary aspects and unequal power. Net capital flows during the 1980's and 1990's have been from South to North, and the gaps between poor and rich are growing alarmingly, with women increasingly the most vulnerable (Tickner 2001).

Alongside a gendered international law, the recommendations and requirements of economic development have also not been gender neutral. The effects of "restructuring" for the global market, for instance, have often been especially harmful to women as well as to other marginalized groups. During the 1990's, feminist scholars began to show how "women have been, not the beneficiaries, but significant victims" of globalization "not only in the South but also in the North [...]" (Sisson Runyon 1999, 215-6). A paper from this period was called, appropriately, "Wealth of Nations-Poverty of Women" (WIDE 1995).

For women in Central and Eastern Europe, for instance, globalization brought unprecedented unemployment rates and the loss of state-funded maternity healthcare, maternity leave, and childcare. Women became "unattractive employees" to privatized industries that wanted to avoid providing benefits (Sisson Runyon 1999, 216). Restructuring has led to an intensification of pro-patriarchal family policies generally, pushing women out of the jobs they previously held and often into the sex trade (Uçarer 1999). The globalization so aggressively promoted by those with a neoliberal agenda has often been deleterious to many, but it has had an especially unfortunate impact on many women (Halliday 1991, 161).

Mainstream international relations theory, meanwhile, has paid inadequate attention to such global economic realities, or to the gross inadequacy of the way mainstream economics views social reality.

5. The Future of Care

Fiona Robinson argues that both mainstream international relations theory and mainstream normative theory about international relations have "resulted in the creation of a global 'culture of neglect' through a systematic devaluing of notions of interdependence, relatedness, and positive involvement in the lives of distant others" (Robinson 1999, 7). A morality suited to unchosen relations between agents of unequal vulnerability, as is the ethics of care, might often have more relevance to global realities than have versions of social contract theory.

In addition, the ethics of care, with its attention to actual differences between persons and groups and its resistance to universalizing all into an abstraction of the ahistorical rational-individual-as-such, may be more suited to the realities of global differences of culture, felt identity, resources, and group exclusion, the sources of much recent conflict.

Within the ethics of justice, respect for human rights has played a central role, and this concern has been increasingly apparent at the global level. But as feminist scholars have shown, the human rights of women have been woefully neglected. Until recently, violence against women was not part of the international human rights agenda. The public/private distinction was reproduced at the international level, with the many forms of violence against women — from rape to patterned malnutrition to bride-burning — considered "unfortunate cultural practices outside of the state's or international system's responsibilities" (Meyer 1999, 60).

In this and other ways it can be seen how international law has been deeply gendered. Issues traditionally of concern to men have been seen as general human concerns, while "women's concerns" have been relegated to a special category, and marginalized. Strong efforts are now being made to recognize and to protect the human rights of women. But in addition, feminist moral theorists have been showing how the ethics of justice, itself, is gendered, and they have been developing the ethics of care.

As the ethics of care requires not only transformations of given domains — the legal, the economic, the political, the cultural, etc. — within a society, but also a transformation of the relations between such domains, so would it in the global context. Taking responsibility for global environmental well-being would become among the central concerns of a caring global policy. Fostering the kinds of economic development that actually would meet human needs and enable the care needed by all to be provided would also be seen as of primary importance. Ecofeminists, for instance, offer an ethic of care for nature and call for a radically different kind of economic progress. They ask that development be sustainable, ecologically sound, non-patriarchal, non-exploitative, and community oriented (Mies and Shiva 1993).

As caring values would became more influential within a society, resolutions of conflict through the threat and use of force would decrease; so would they on the international level as relations between states would be influenced by the ethics of care. This would not mean that at this stage of development there should be less rather than more support for whatever restraints can be provided by international law. Where the unrestrained use of force and violence is the norm, accepting legal restraints is more expressive of care than disregarding them. Some enforcement of law may always be needed between states as within them, though international police actions should be carried out by international bodies, not unilaterally by superpowers. But where caring relations have been adequately developed within a society, the need for legal enforcement can be reduced. The same could be looked forward to in the global context.

At the current stage of development, efforts to achieve progress in respect for human rights are also certainly to be supported rather than neglected. But in a world in which the multiple ties of care would have expanded to encompass the whole human family, and poverty and exclusion really would be on the wane rather than, as at present, increasing, caring relations might make appeals to human rights less important.

A vast number of efforts, through non-governmental organizations, and state and international agencies, could do much to establish the ties of care between actual persons within and across state boundaries that can enable the decrease of violence and exploitation. Ties among poor women within a state, for instance, have potential for transforming economic and gender hierarchies. Ties between persons from different states can contribute to decreasing international hostility and resort to violence. They should be far more adequately supported. Those from the global North need to listen and understand, as in friendship, rather than bestow limited benevolence. And those in the global South need to overcome humiliation and participate in the discourses that will determine their circumstances, enabling caring economic

development rather than unfettered capitalism.

It is caring relations rather than what persons do as individuals that exemplify the values of caring. The small societies of family and friendship are formed by caring relations. More attenuated but still evident caring relations between more distant people enable them to trust each other enough to form political entities and to accept each other as fellow citizens of states. A globalization of caring relations would help to enable people of different states and cultures to live in peace, to respect each other's rights, to care together for their environments, and to improve their lives so that all their children might have hopeful futures.

NOTES

1. A few titles are: Falk 1968, Wasserstrom 1970, Held, Morgenbesser, and Nagel 1974, Aiken and LaFollette 1977, Walzer 1977, Beitz 1979, Hoffman 1981, Holmes 1989, Luper-Foy 1988, Valls 2000.

2. Some major titles are: Gilligan 1982, Noddings 1986, Kittay and Meyers 1987, Ruddick 1989, Sherwin 1992, Friedman 1993, Held 1993, Tronto 1993, Bubeck 1995, Held 1995, Clement 1996, Bowden 1997, Sevenhuijsen 1998, Walker 1998, Kittay 1999; MacKenzie and Stoljar 2000.

3. For a pluralistic view in which different values are seen as appropriately having priority in different domains, see Held 1989.

4. The equality imagined has been not only moral but empirical — Hobbes' equal vulnerability to the sword of one's neighbor, for instance. When, on the world stage, states are imagined to be individuals, the removal from reality increases.

REFERENCES

Aiken, William, and Hugh LaFollette, eds. 1977. *World Hunger and Moral Obligation.* Englewood Cliffs, N.J.: Prentice-Hall.

Baier, Annette C. 1994. *Moral Prejudices: Essays on Ethics.* Cambridge, Mass.: Harvard University Press.

Beitz, Charles R. 1979. *Political Theory and International Relations.* Princeton, N.J.: Princeton University Press.

Bowden, Peta. 1997. *Caring: Gender Sensitive Ethics.* London: Routledge.

Bubeck, Diemut. 1995. *Care, Gender and Justice.* Oxford: Oxford University Press.

Charlesworth, Hilary. 1994. What Are "Women's International Human Rights"? In *Human Rights of Women: National and International Perspectives.* Ed. R.J. Cooke. Philadelphia, Penn.: University of Pennsylvania Press.

Clement, Grace. 1996. *Care, Autonomy, and Justice.* Boulder, Co.: Westview.

Darwall, Stephen. 1998. *Philosophical Ethics.* Boulder, Co.: Westview.

Di Stefano, Christine. 1991. *Configurations of Masculinity: A Feminist Perspective on Modern Political Theory.* Ithaca, N.Y.: Cornell University Press.

Falk, Richard. 1968. *Legal Order in a Violent World.* Princeton, N.J.: Princeton University Press.

Friedman, Marilyn. 1993. *What Are Friends For? Feminist Perspectives on Personal Relationships.* Ithaca, N.Y.: Cornell University Press.

Gilligan, Carol. 1982. *In a Different Voice: Psychological Theory and Women's Development.* Cambridge, Mass.: Harvard University Press.

Grant, Rebecca, and Kathleen Newland, eds. 1991. *Gender and International Relations.* Bloomington, Ind.: Indiana University Press.

Halliday, Fred. 1991. Hidden From International Relations: Women and the International Arena. In *Gender and International Relations.* Ed. R. Grant and K. Newland. Bloomington, Ind.: Indiana University Press.

Held, Virginia. 1989. *Rights and Goods: Justifying Social Action.* Chicago, Ill.: University of Chicago Press.

—. 1993. *Feminist Morality: Transforming Culture, Society, and Politics.* Chicago, Ill.: University of Chicago Press.

—, ed. 1995. *Justice and Care: Essential Readings in Feminist Ethics.* Boulder, Co.: Westview.

—. 2000. Rights and the Presumption of Care. In *Rights and Reason: Essays in Honor of Carl Weilman.* Ed. M. Friedman et al. Dordrecht: Kluwer.

—. 2001. Caring Relations and Principles of Justice. In *Controversies in Feminism.* Ed. J. P. Sterba. Lanham, Md.: Rowman and Littlefield.

—. 2002a. Care and the Extension of Markets. *Hypatia* 17: 19-33.

—. 2002b. Moral Subjects: The Natural and the Normative. Presidential Address-Eastern Division. *Proceedings and Addresses of the American Philosophical Association* 76: 7-24.

—. 2003. Taking Care: Care as Practice and Value. In *Setting the Moral Compass.* Ed. C. Calhoun. New York, N.Y.: Oxford University Press.

—. Forthcoming. The Ethics of Care. In *Oxford Handbook of Moral Theory.* Ed. D. Copp. New York, N.Y.: Oxford University Press.

Held, Virginia, Sidney Morgenbesser, and Thomas Nagel, eds. 1974. *Philosophy, Morality, and International Affairs.* New York, N.Y.: Oxford University Press.

Henkin, Louis. 1989. The Use of Force: Law and U.S. Policy. In *Right v. Might: International Law and the Use of Force.* Ed. L. Henkin. New York, N.Y.: Council on Foreign Relations.

Hoffman, Stanley. 1981. *Duties Beyond Borders: On the Limits and Possibilities of Ethical International Politics.* Syracuse, N.Y.: Syracuse University Press.

Holmes, Robert L. 1989. *On War and Morality.* Princeton, N.J.: Princeton University Press.

Keohane, Robert O. 1998. International Relations Theory: Contributions of a Feminist Standpoint. In *Gender and International Relations.* Ed. R. Grant and K. Newland. Bloomington, Ind.: Indiana University Press.

Kittay, Eva, Feder. 1999. *Love's Labor: Essays on Women, Equality, and Dependency.* New York, N.Y.: Routledge.

Kittay, Eva, Feder, and Diana T. Meyers, eds. 1987. *Women and Moral Theory.* Lanham, Md.: Rowman and Littlefield.

Kuttner, Robert. 1998. *Everything for Sale: The Virtues and Limits of Markets.* New York, N.Y.: Knopf.

Luper-Foy, Steven, ed. 1988. *Problems of International Justice.* Boulder, Co.: Westview.

MacKenzie, Catriona, and Natalie Stoljar, eds. 2000. *Relational Autonomy: Feminist Perspectives on Autonomy, Agency, and the Social Self.* New York, N.Y.: Oxford University Press.

McLaren, Margaret. 2001. Feminist Ethics: Care as a Virtue. In *Feminists Doing Ethics.* Ed. P. DesAutels and J. Waugh. Lanham, Md.: Rowman and Littlefield.

Meyer, Mary K. 1999. Negotiating International

Norms: The Inter-American Commission of Women and the Convention on Violence against Women. In *Gender Politics in Global Governance.* Ed. M. Meyer and E. Prülg. Lanham, Md.: Rowman & Littlefield.

Mies, Maria, and Vandana Shiva, eds. 1993. *Ecofeminism.* London: Zed.

Noddings, Nel. 1986. *Caring: A Feminine Approach to Ethics and Moral Education.* Berkeley, Cal.: University of California Press.

Nussbaum, Martha C. 1999. *Sex and Social Justice.* New York, N.Y.: Oxford University Press.

Okin, Susan Moller. 1989. *Justice, Gender, and the Family.* New York, N.Y.: Basic.

O'Neill, Onora. 1992. Justice, Gender, and International Boundaries. In *International Justice and the Third World.* Ed. R. Attfield and B. Wilkins. London: Routledge.

Radin, Margaret Jane. 1996. *Contested Commodities: The Trouble with Trade in Sex, Children, Body Parts and Other Things.* Cambridge, Mass.: Harvard University Press.

Robinson, Fiona. 1999. *Globalizing Care: Ethics, Feminist Theory, and International Relations.* Boulder, Co.: Westview.

Ruddick, Sara. 1989. *Maternal Thinking: Toward a Politics of Peace.* Boston, Mass.: Beacon.

Runyan, Anne Sisson. 1999. Women in the Neoliberal "Frame." In *Gender Politics in Global Governance.* Ed. M.K. Meyer and E. Prülg. Lanham, Md.: Rowman & Littlefield.

Sevenhuijsen, Selma. 1998. *Citizenship and the Ethics of Care.* London: Routledge.

Sherwin, Susan. 1992. *No Longer Patient: Feminist Ethics and Health Care.* Philadelphia, Penn.: Temple University Press.

Steans, Jill. 1998. *Gender and International Relations: An Introduction.* New Brunswick, NJ.: Rutgers University Press.

Tessman, Lisa. 2001. Critical Virtue Ethics: Understanding Oppression as Morally Damaging. In *Feminists Doing Ethics.* Ed. P. DesAutels and J. Waugh. Lanham, Md.: Rowman and Littlefield.

Tickner, J. Ann. 1992. *Gender In International Relations: Feminist Perspectives on Achieving Global Security.* New York, N.Y.: Columbia University Press.

—. 2001. *Gendering World Politics.* New York, N.Y.: Columbia University Press.

Tronto, Joan C. 1993. *Moral Boundaries: A Political Argument for an Ethic of Care.* New York, N.Y.: Routledge.

Uçarer, Emek M. 1999. Trafficking in Women: Alternate Migration or Modern Slave Trade? In *Gender Politics in Global Governance.* Ed. M.K. Meyer and F. Prülg. Lanham, Md.: Rowman & Littlefield.

Valls, Andrew, ed. 2000. *Ethics in International Affairs.* Lanham, Md.: Rowman & Littlefield.

Walker, Margaret. 1989. Moral Understandings: Alternative "Epistemology" for a Feminist Ethics. *Hypatia* 4: 19-20.

—. 1998. Moral Understandings: A Feminist Study in Ethics. New York, N.Y.: Routledge.

Walzer, Michael. 1977. *Just and Unjust Wars.* New York, N.Y.: Basic.

Wasserstrom, Richard, ed. 1970. *War and Morality.* Belmont, Cal.: Wadsworth.

WIDE, NAC Canada, ALT-WID, CRIAW. 1995. *Wealth of Nations-Poverty of Women: Framework Paper for the "Globalization of the Economy and Economic Justice for Women."* Workshop. ECE Regional Preparatory Meeting for the Fourth World Conference on Women, Vienna, October 1994.

CONFUCIANISM, GLOBALISATION AND THE IDEA OF UNIVERSALISM

A.T. Nuyen

A.T. Nuyen teaches Philosophy at the National University of Singapore. He has published in international journals in the areas of the philosophy of Hume and Kant, ethics and applied ethics, Continental Philosophy, and comparative (Chinese/Western) philosophy.

   Nuyen points out that increased globalization has yielded benefits but also conflicts. One source of conflict is the desire to maintain cultural identity in the face of increased pressure from globalizing factors to erase difference. Yet, argues Nuyen, globalization has resulted in a move to universalism that should be embraced rather than resisted. He investigates whether Confucianism can contribute to the project of articulating a universal account of global justice that can help resolve conflicts, including those of cultural identities. He argues that Confucianism can be part of the globalization process without sacrificing its cultural identity and that it has the potential to contribute to the development of a notion of universal justice that respects and promotes cultural difference.

The pace of globalisation has quickened considerably in the last 10-15 years, owing in part to changing economic and political forces, and in part to recent advances in computer and information technologies. The process of globalisation has certainly yielded considerable benefits, but it has also resulted in conflicts, some of which take the form of violent protests at international meetings. Protesters, naturally, draw attention to what they take to be the high costs of globalisation. Observers generally agree that the forces and technologies that have brought about the globalisation process are such that a slow down, let alone reversal, is ruled out. If this is true, it makes no sense trying to slow down the process, and worse sense to stop it. Whether or not this is true, the more sensible thing to do is to ensure that the benefits can be enhanced and enjoyed by as many people as possible, and the costs minimised.

   One distinct feature of globalisation is the move towards universalism: the world is increasingly moving towards universal technical formats and languages, universal procedures, universal rules and regulations. For supporters of globalisation, the ultimate prize to be had is universal global justice, administered in the context of a universal culture. Yet, while the benefits of adopting universal formats, procedures and the like are clear enough, and the costs are few, there are problems with the notion of a global, universal justice and the related idea of a universal culture. Supporters of universal, or global, justice point out that it offers the best hope of solving conflicts arising from cultural differences. Critics argue that universalism is problematic precisely because it leaves no room for cultural differences. It will be good if the supporters' hope can be realised and the critics' fear can be avoided. Thus, the question is how to steer a safe path between the Charybdis of cultural strife — the clash of civilisations as Huntington has famously called it — and the Scylla of a universalism that devours cultural particularities. Can Confucianism help steer this safe path?[1] Both supporters and critics of universalism have tended to ignore this question, the former taking Confucianism to be a protagonist in the cultural clash that universalism will avoid, and the latter having it in mind as a victim of universalism. I will argue that Confucianism is neither a villain blocking the progress of universal justice, nor a helpless victim of that very progress. On the contrary, Confucianism has the potential to contribute to the development of a notion of universal justice that respects cultural differences, a kind of universalism that can actually promote cultural diversity.

Universalism and Confucianism

Many supporters of globalisation focus on the ultimate prize, namely universal justice. The case for universal justice is largely a Kantian one. As is well known, Kant argues for a variety of globalisation that he calls "cosmopolitanism" as a means to bring about "perpetual peace" through the instrument of a cosmopolitan, or universal, justice. To avoid the "clash of civilisations," there has to be a means of resolving conflicts arising from cultural differences, and they can be resolved only if there is a standard of justice to which different cultures are willing to submit, a universal standard that adjudicates competing cultural claims. Since willingness to submit depends on the perception that the rules of justice are impartial, what is necessary for "perpetual peace" is a universal justice that operates impartially at the global level. For many thinkers, both the need for and the justification of universal justice are self evident, although some have chosen to argue further that, morally, the claim for a universal justice rests on a deeper claim that there is a common humanity that obligates us to regard all others as having a moral status equal to our own. That common humanity dictates that disputes be settled not by appealing to what is judged good or right or valuable by the standard of one's own culture, but by applying standards that transcend cultural values. Practically, the hope for a universal justice rests on a belief in the universal process of practical reason, something that Kant clearly takes for granted. Indeed, if Kant is right in his optimistic belief in the inevitable progress of reason, the human world must be moving ever

closer to universal justice, and the present trend in globalisation may be proof of this.

Not everyone is as optimistic as Kant. There are skeptics who do not see that universalism is either inevitable or desirable. Given the moral and practical basis of universal justice, it is understandable that skeptics of the idea have sought to undermine that very basis. It might be said that thinkers such as Herder have denied that there is such a thing as a common humanity, at least the kind that motivates against privileging one culture, our own, over others.[2] Such denial, it might be said also, gains support from the views of many anthropologists who have found what they take to be evidence for cultural relativism. More recently, post-modernists have been interpreted as standing against the idea of universalism. For instance, it may be said that Lyotard would regard the idea of a universal justice as a "meta-narrative" that has no legitimacy in the post-modern condition. It is not within the scope of this paper to judge these skeptical claims. Suffice it to say that while Herder and anthropologists such as Franz Boas and Ruth Benedict may support relativism as a *factual* claim, there is enough evidence to suggest that they advocate universalism as a claim of *value*. Thus, Isaiah Berlin believes that Herder (and Vico) "insist on our need and ability to transcend the values of our own culture or nation or class, or those of whatever other windowless boxes some cultural relativists wish to confine us to."[3] Such "need and ability" are endorsed by both Boas and Benedict.[4] As for Lyotard, I have argued elsewhere that there is enough universalism in his idea of "just gaming."[5] For my purpose, what is relevant is not so much how to deal with the arguments against the possibility of a universal justice, but the claim that such an idea sounds the death knell of cultural identity. The other side of this claim is the view that the demand for cultural identity sounds the death knell of universalism, or universal justice in particular.

Depending on which side of the claim we apply to Confucianism, we have either the charge that Confucianism will stand in the way of the progress towards universalism, or the fear that Confucianism will be the victim of the latter. In either case, Confucianism is perceived as a unique cultural phenomenon, incompatible with any universal ideal or principle. Perceiving Confucianism in this way, we seem to be confronted with the choice between on the one hand defending universalism but accepting that Confucianism must be sacrificed in the process, and on the other defending Confucianism against universalism but at the risk of contributing to the "clash of civilisations." The fact that the same thing can be said about many other particular "isms" only deepens the problem. The threat of the Scylla and the Charybdis seems to loom very large. Many theorists have taken this threat seriously. However, they contend that the way to deal with the threat is from the outside of any particular cultural framework, arguing for political arrangements that ensure both the key universal values and the protection of cultural identities. It is often taken for granted that we have to approach the problem from the outside in order to avoid cultural bias, which lies at the root of the problem. I will argue instead that we can deal with the problem from the inside of Confucianism. Before doing so, it will be useful to examine some of the attempts that are claimed to be made from the outside.

Many attempts have been made by people who consider themselves liberal thinkers. It may be thought that because liberals are committed to universalism, they are willing to sacrifice particular cultural demands to universal values, thus succumbing to the Scylla that devours cultural identities. However, Bhikhu Parekh claims that liberals are in fact bound to protecting cultural identities, arguing as follows: "The liberal is committed to equal respect for persons. Since human beings are culturally embedded, respect for them entails respect for their cultures and ways of life."[6] Along similar lines, James Tully argues that self-respect is a Rawlsian primary good, and since a person's culture is a part of that self-respect, it cannot be sacrificed for other goods.[7] Will Kymlicka, too, accepts this liberal vision: "The individuals who are an unquestionable part of the liberal moral ontology are viewed as individual members of a particular cultural community, for whom cultural membership is an important good."[8] For thinkers such as these, the question is how to render consis-

tent universal liberal values and the respect for cultural identities. Kymlicka argues that this can be achieved in what he calls "multicultural citizenship."[9] The key universal values are embedded in the idea of citizenship, while the protection of cultural identities can be effected through multiculturalism. Similar suggestions have been made. For instance, Iris Young urges that we construct universal values on the. basis of a "politics of difference" so as to protect the interests of minorities.[10] More recently, Aihwa Ong argues for a "flexible citizenship" that allows expatriates in a state to participate in the citizenship of that state while retaining their cultural identities in being citizens of their home states.[11]

It has to be said that what to do with minorities within a state is an important issue in the theory of citizenship, but it is one that is present whether or not there is any movement towards globalisation. In comparison, the issue I want to focus on is much larger than this, an issue that has to do with different cultures in the global community, and arises specifically in the context of globalisation. Of course, if we extend the notion of citizenship and speak of "global citizenship," as some have done,[12] then we will have the right focus, but it is no longer clear whether suggestions made by Kymlicka and others are still applicable, and even if they are applicable, they may still be ineffective. For one thing, certain state-wide interests that may be said to override minority interests, such as territorial integrity, will disappear as we shift the focus from states to the global community. More importantly, something else is at stake when we try to generalise suggestions made by liberals such as Kymlicka. One fundamental assumption that needs to be questioned is the assumption that liberal values are universal and provide the neutral basis on which we can erect a framework hospitable to all different cultures. As we have seen, liberals such as Parekh are confident that we can start with the liberal values and end up with a global community in which all cultures can flourish, given the liberal commitment to respecting all cultures.[13] The standard to be used in adjudicating competing cultural claims will be the liberal standard, incorporating liberal values, among which is the toleration of different cultures. To be more specific, the assumption we need to question is that liberalism itself is not culture-specific, that it is not on the same level as, say, Confucianism. If this assumption is false then the liberal approach is no longer an approach from without as many liberals think, but rather an approach from within a particular culture, the liberal culture.

While many liberals would like to think that liberal values are universal, Martin Hollis has reminded us that "liberalism is for the liberals" no less than "cannibalism is for the cannibals."[14] Indeed, Hollis suspects that all claims of universalism are ethnocentric. However, as pointed out above, I do not wish to enter the debate concerning the possibility of true universalism. I simply assume that it is both necessary and possible to arrive at impartial rules of justice, at what might be called global justice. The only question is whether this global justice is inherently liberal, as many liberals would have us believe. Deep down, liberalism is a philosophy, a *Western* philosophy. More specifically, it is a doctrine borne out of a specific philosophical tradition stretching from Plato to Descartes and beyond. As such, it is part of the general culture of the West. To see how it is culture-specific, we need only look at the liberal metaphysics of personhood. In the liberal metaphysics, the individual person is a rational, autonomous and self-sufficient being, who chooses to associate with others, acknowledged to be his or her equals, to further his or her interests. This is reflected in, among other things, the liberal idea of citizenship, according to which citizenship consists of a set of rights protecting the individual from the state and from other individuals. Compare this with the Confucian understanding of the individual person, according to which a person is a socially embedded being, not an individual standing apart from, or over and against the community, or the society. As Julia Ching has reminded us, "the Chinese view of the human being tends to see the person in the context of a social network rather than as an individual."[15] Based on a *Western* metaphysics of personhood, liberalism is thoroughly *Western*. We have good reasons, then, to question its claim to be universal. A liberal notion of global

justice will be a notion arrived at from the inside, not from the outside.

Arguably, the point above concerning the liberal conception of universalism is what lies behind recent criticisms of the idea of universalism, particularly those coming from the East. As one critic has put it, "universality is actually the western approach in disguise."[16] However, to throw universalism out with the liberal, western, conception of it is surely to throw the baby out with the bath water. From whatever perspective, western or eastern, justice requires impartiality, and impartiality can only be guaranteed by an appeal to standards acceptable to all, or universal standards. What we need is a universalism that is not "the western approach in disguise," or anything else in disguise. The question is whether a notion of global justice arrived at from the inside of any particular cultural framework is really that culture's viewpoint in disguise, hence not truly universal, or not workable as a means of justly adjudicating competing cultural claims. In this respect, Hollis's suggestion that any claim to universalism will prove to be ethnocentric, that is, some particular culture's viewpoint in disguise, is too pessimistic. At best, it can be taken to mean only that we have no choice but to work out a conception of a global justice from within a particular culture. It does not mean that the result cannot be truly universal. I will argue for this indirectly in the next section. Naturally, if I am right then liberals are perfectly entitled to arrive at the notion of global justice from within the liberal tradition and to claim universality for it, provided that they are honest about its origin and are prepared to subject the outcome to the test of universality. Part of that test is to see how the liberal conception compares with other conceptions. What liberals should not do is to assume that theirs is the only possible conception, that we cannot work out a notion of global justice from the inside of any other cultural tradition, such as Confucianism. Equally, what the critics of the liberal conception of universalism should not do is to reject the idea of universal justice altogether. Instead, efforts should be made to arrive at an idea of global justice from the inside of something other than liberalism, such as Confucianism. In what follows, I try to show that Confucianism at least has the resources that enable us to do so. Assuming that the Confucian conception passes the test of universality, something that is beyond the scope of this paper to demonstrate, we can say that it is possible for a culture to embrace global justice without losing its identity. That it is necessary for a culture to do so in the age of globalisation is, I take it, beyond argument.

Confucianism and the Idea of Global Justice

As argued above, we need something like a global justice, a set of rules that can be applied impartially, to adjudicate competing cultural claims. This global justice and the institutional framework that supports it will need to stand over and above all cultures, to be seen as universal. Can a culture submit itself to this kind of universalism without losing its cultural identity? My contention is that we can answer this question in the positive if the global justice that the culture submits itself to is something that is worked out from the inside of that culture and thus bears the very hallmark of that culture. In support of this contention, two analogous cases can be cited. First, consider Kant's Moral Law. If anything is truly universal, Kant's Moral Law is. Yet, Kant would not accept that one loses one's individuality in submitting oneself to the Moral Law. This is because the Moral Law is arrived at from the inside of one's own practical reason. Indeed, were it to come from the outside, the Law would be heteronomous, not autonomous. Of course, things are easy for Kant because he presumes, perhaps rightly, that we all share the same faculty of practical reason. However, and second, things are somewhat tougher for Rawls' principles of justice. They too are meant to be universal but neither do they rob the individual of his or her individuality. Again, this is so because they too are arrived at from the inside of an individual's practical reasoning, which has to do not with the Kantian goodwill, but with the desire to fare well in the society, a desire that determines the individual to accept the Rawlsian principles of justice. While we may assume that we all share the same desire, things are tougher for Rawls because different

people may have different ideas concerning how that same desire can be met. Thus, it may be more difficult for Rawls to convince us of the universality of his principles. However, the case of Rawls' principles of justice and that of Kant's Moral Law indicate that we can have a universalism that does not obliterate particularity if it is something arrived at from within the particularity. We can have a global justice that does not devour a cultural identity if it is something arrived at from within that identity. Naturally, the cultural identity in question must have sufficient internal resources to enable it to transcend its cultural boundaries, and it is not clear that all cultures have the necessary resources. I shall make a general comment about cultures in general later, but my immediate task is to show that Confucianism does have the resources not only to contribute to the idea of global justice but also to maintain its identity in a universal framework of global justice.

The first thing that has to be done is to counter the charge that Confucianism is so ethnocentric that it has no chance of contributing to any universal idea. Critics are apt to claim that Confucianism has resulted in, among other things, a rigid hierarchical social system that is unpalatable to more liberal cultures, in an emphasis on the group over the individual that is incompatible with the democratic values held in high regard in some cultures, and in an elitism that is objectionable to cultures that value equality. In support of such claim, critics often rely on the fact that these characteristics were found in the Confucian society of the past, and to a lesser extent, in the many present societies that claim to be Confucian. At least two points can be made in reply. First, the sociologist Peter Berger has drawn our attention to Max Weber's distinction between "the vulgar and the 'high' versions" of any set of ideas, and to Weber's observation that it is the vulgar version that would "have the most historical efficacy."[17] The historical and social evidence that critics have cited to support the claim that Confucianism is ethnocentric is almost certainly evidence of the efficacy of the vulgar version of Confucianism. It is in no way an indictment of the "high" version of Confucianism. Citing Tu Wei-ming, Francis Fukuyama has drawn a similar distinction between "political Confucianism" and philosophical Confucianism, and attributes much of the hierarchical rigidity to the former.[18] We may support this claim by pointing out that the notorious "Three-Bond Doctrine" is discussed only in *The Hanfeizi,* a legalist text, and not mentioned anywhere in the Confucian classics. Arguably, the Han "Confucians" found it politically convenient to advocate that the wife, the son and the subject should show absolute obedience to, respectively, the husband, the father and the sovereign. Thus, Tu Wei-ming contends that "the Han ideologists, like the Legalists, were mainly concerned about the functional utility of the Three Bonds as mechanism of symbolic control for the primary purpose of social control."[19] Looking into the Confucian classics, the only thing close enough to the "Three-Bond Doctrine" we can find is the discussion of the "five relationships" in *The Mencius,* which stresses, not the hierarchical structure, but the reciprocal nature of the relationship between friends, the young and the old, husband and wife, the children and their parents, and the subjects and their sovereign (*Mencius* III.i.4.8).

Second and much more importantly, the charges that Confucianism promotes inequality, blind obedience, and the subordination of the individual to the group, can be directly challenged. Three kinds of confusion are involved in these charges. The first is the confusion of meritocracy with inequality.[20] It is true that Confucianism advocates meritocracy, but elsewhere I have argued that the Confucian notion of meritocracy should not be confused with inequality. Indeed, Confucius himself advocated equality of the most basic kinds, namely equality of human worth and equality of educational opportunity. What Confucianism acknowledges is that, given the same circumstances, free choice will result in different achievements: "By nature close together, through practice set apart" (*Analects* 17:2).[21] Just as meritocracy should not be confused with inequality, loyalty and respect should not be confused with blind obedience. What we do find in Confucianism is the stress on loyalty and respect. However, there is enough evidence in *The Mencius* to show that Mencius was in favour of the idea of the people

opposing, even rebelling against, a tyrant who abused his power at the expense of the people (*Mencius* I.i. 7; VII.ii.14). Kung-chuan Hsiao interprets these passages as saying that the people do not have "any absolute duty of obedience to the government."[22] Daniel Bell goes further and claims that, in Imperial China, Confucianism was frequently "criticized ... for encouraging disobedience and fostering a critical perspective *vis-á-vis* the state."[23] Finally, the Confucian stress on the community should not be confused with the Maoist doctrine that each individual is merely a "cog in the machine" and that ultimately it is the machine that matters. In all the Confucian classics, the stress is always on the development of the individual, on the process of individual learning, and on becoming a gentleman (*junxi*). The teachings in the Confucian classics make use of exemplary individuals with distinct and unique characteristics, individuals who are the driving force of the moral society, not anonymous and dispensable cogs of a social machine. It is true that, as pointed out above, individuality is not seen as something formed in isolation from the community, or the society, but this only means that an individual's interests are more likely to be shaped by his or her social relationships, not that they are discouraged nor must they be ultimately sacrificed for the sake of community interests.

We can now turn to the positive task of exploring the possibility of working toward an idea of global justice from within the Confucian perspective. It is certainly beyond the scope of this paper actually to build the structure of such an idea. All that can be done here is to show that Confucianism has the necessary resources for such a task, keeping in mind the twin requirements that the end result must be universal so as to serve as an anchor for impartial judgments -although, as pointed out above, showing that it passes the test of true universality is beyond the scope of this paper - and at the same time, must be something that the Confucian culture can subscribe to without losing its identity.

The first thing to notice is that Confucianism is committed to a movement towards universalism. More importantly, the movement starts from the individual. The Confucian vision is a vision of a peaceful and harmonious world that extends beyond the individual and beyond a particular community, or a local culture. However, the understanding of that world does not come to the Confucians from any outside source, but grows out of the Confucian understanding of ourselves as members of the Confucian culture, much as the Kantian vision of the universal Moral Law growing out of the moral agent's own practical reason, not from an outside source, such as God. As stated in *The Great Learning (Dai-xue),* the idea of learning is initially to "rectify the mind" in order to "cultivate the person," but in learning, the individual person must aim, beyond the person, at "regulating the family," then beyond the family, at promoting harmony in the community, and then beyond one's community, at contributing to peace and prosperity of one's country, and then finally beyond one's country, at making the whole world virtuous.[24] In *The Great Learning* and elsewhere, there is a clear commitment to an outward expansion of the individual self to a universal framework that encompasses the whole world. A gentleman (*junxi*) is committed to bringing about a virtuous world. Insofar as a virtuous world is first and foremost a just world, it may be said that the Confucian vision envisages the very idea of global justice. It is certainly not a narrow, ethnocentric vision. On the other hand, it is not a vision that is focused so exclusively on the universal as to blur the image of the individual and his or her community, his or her culture.

What then is the gentleman to learn, if he is to attain the Confucian vision? Above all, it is to learn to cultivate virtues such as humanity *(ren),* propriety (*li*) and righteousness *(yi).* The first two virtues combined dictate that we love and respect our fellow human beings. With *ren,* we can develop a sense of love and benevolence that will bring us closer to each other. With *li,* we can develop a sense of propriety that creates a respectful distance between oneself and one's fellow human beings.[25] Loving our fellow human beings, we will want all to live in peace and harmony, and respecting our fellow human beings, we will want to move toward the setting up of rituals *(li)* whereby disputes are

amicably and justly settled. Thus, it can be argued that by emphasizing *ren* and *li,* Confucianism practically commits itself to some form of global justice. In support of this claim, it can be pointed out that in the Confucian classics, it is clear that the basis for both love and respect is our common humanity, not membership of any particular culture, arguably the same common humanity that, as pointed out earlier, provides the moral ground for the idea of global justice. Thus, while *ren* and *li* are personal virtues (which, presumably, develop and manifest differently in different individuals), they propel us toward a universal standpoint. Interestingly, Kant himself declares that the *"love* and *respect"* that we experience personally and individually are the "feelings that accompany the practice of ... duties [to others]."[26] Duties, in turn, are universal. Clearly then, there are resources within the personal ethics of Confucianism for a move toward the adoption of a universal idea. We can perhaps even say that the virtues of *ren* and *li* find their ultimate manifestation in a universal ethics.

In particular, there is some scope for interpreting *li* as an idea perfectly compatible with, if not one that entails, the idea of a global justice. This scope can be more clearly seen once we have cleared up two misunderstandings about *li.* According to the first misunderstanding, *li* has to do with rigid social rituals, and the Confucian emphasis on *li* serves to highlight the ethnocentricity of Confucianism, which has to be sacrificed if we are to attain the universalism necessary for global justice. However, contrary to this not uncommon perception of *li,* the virtue of *li* is not the virtue of adhering to inflexible rituals — Confucius himself declares that he "detest(s) inflexibility" (*Analects* 14.32). It is rather the virtue of following the rules of orderly conduct. In practice, of course, the observance of *li* amounts to the observance of rites, or ceremonies, and it is this practical aspect that is at the heart of the misunderstanding. But to focus on the actual rites, or ceremonies, is to focus on the wrong aspect of *li.* Impatiently, Confucius told his followers: "Surely when one says 'The rites, the rites,' it is not enough merely to mean presents of jade and silk" (*Analects* 17.11). Beyond the presents of jade and silk is the orderly conduct that *li* ultimately aims at, and beyond it, humanity, and righteousness. It is this aspect of *li*, among other things, that makes it a virtue that leads to global justice. Thus, the question of orderly conduct arises typically in situations involving competing claims. In observing *li*, we aim to avoid conflicts arising from competing claims. Unless conflicts can be amicably settled by observing *li*, we risk treating without humanity and righteousness, hence without justice, those with whom we are in conflict. Hence, Confucius says: "If a man is not humane *(ren)*, what has he to do with *li*?" *(Analects* 3.3), and "The gentleman is on the side of *yi"* *(Analects* 4.10). Clearly, while *li* is embodied in rites and rituals, the latter are not rigid, and not to be followed for their own sake, but for the sake of humanity and righteousness.

Orderly conduct, in turn, will bring about harmony *(ho)*. The idea of harmony lies at the very heart of *li*. As stated in *Analects* 1.12, the main effect of ritual propriety is the harmonization of competing forces ("Of the things brought about by rites, harmony is the most valuable"). The idea of harmony is subject to a misunderstanding (the second one in addition to the misunderstanding above) that also serves to make Confucianism stand opposed to universalism, and risk losing its identity if it has to submit to any universal standard. Accordingly, harmony is taken to mean the same thing as conformity. Understood, or misunderstood, as such, critics might say that any universalism that Confucianism subscribes to can only be a uniformalism, precisely that which obliterates cultural identities. However, the Confucian idea of harmony is anything but conformity and uniformity. We have seen above that Confucian teachings rely heavily on the idea of exemplary individuals, the *junxi*. There cannot be such individuals if all have to conform to a uniformity. Furthermore, it is precisely in a Confucian harmony that differences are maintained. The Confucian harmony is like orchestral harmony, which requires the blending of different sounds in producing music that stands over and above all the instruments, but in such a way that each instrument can still be heard and identified in the music. It is like the harmony of the various ingredients that a good cook produces in a dish, in which the distinctness of each particular ingredient is preserved.

Once the above two misunderstandings about *li* are cleared up, and once we focus correctly on what is important in *li*, namely the virtue of orderly conduct aiming at harmony, to be cultivated by a person with *ren* and *yi* who acts towards others with humanity and righteousness, the global significance of *li*, and of Confucianism, becomes clear. A person with *li* must strive to arrive at and abide by rites and rituals that aim at establishing social order. This is surely a necessary virtue if we are to avoid the "clash of civilisations" in the context of globalisation. It is no wonder that Lin Yutang renders *li* as the "principles of social order."[27] If Lin Yutang had had in mind the global context, he most probably would have rendered *li* as the "principles of world order." We can argue, then, that accepting and abiding by the principles of a global justice can be made into a Confucian virtue. To say the same thing differently, we can move out toward a notion of global justice from within Confucianism, or from the *li* of Confucianism understood in combination with the key virtues of *ren* and *yi*. Far from Confucianism standing in the way of the development of global justice, and far from the universalism of global justice obliterating the culture of Confucianism, it can be said that the idea of global justice is the natural extension of the *li* of Confucianism. Indeed, as I have argued elsewhere,[28] Confucianism may be said to be aiming at a justice that harmonises with the cosmic forces of the *dao*, a justice that is not just global but also cosmic.

It may be objected at this point that, even if I am right, what we have is an idea of global justice worked out from the inside of Confucianism, and that may still come into conflict with a global justice worked out from the inside of some other cultural perspective, including the liberal perspective. If this is so then the threat of a "clash of civilisations" remains, although the clash would now take place at a different location. To avoid the clash, so the objection goes, we need some universal standard to adjudicate the different conceptions of global justice worked out from the inside of different cultures, and that standard will have to be worked out from the outside of any culture. But the application of any such standard will threaten cultural identities. We are then back to the proverbial square one.

The obvious reply to the above objection is that the notion of global justice worked out from the inside of any cultural perspective is only the first step towards true universalism. It can only be an offer put on the table, subject to further negotiations. My concern has been to argue against both the critics and sympathisers of Confucianism who believe that since Confucianism has nothing to put on the table, it is either an impediment to global justice (for the critics) or victim of it (for the sympathisers). If I am right in my claims above concerning the nature of Confucianism, then not only is it capable of coming up with a conception of global justice, it is also committed to further negotiations once its conception has been put on the table. If I am right, the Confucian gentlemen (*junxi*) will not rest until there is a world order, a virtuous and harmonious world. As Confucius said (*Analects* 4.10), "[I]n his dealings with the world, the gentleman is not invariably for or against anything. He is on the side of what is moral." It is un-Confucian, then, to be invariably for one's own position and invariably against what others might put forward. It is Confucian to negotiate with others in the world to bring about what is moral, namely a global justice. At *Analects* 5.11, Confucius declares: "I have never met anyone who is truly unbending" and goes on to ask that if one is full of desires, "how can he be unbending?" If we are full of desires for our and others' flourishing, how can we be unbending when it comes to competing cultural claims?

Indeed, in any further negotiations with other cultural representatives, the Confucian gentlemen have the advantage of not just practical flexibility and the willingness to bend, but also of cultural generality and flexibility in theoretical beliefs. The fact that the Confucian emphasis on the flourishing of the individual and his or her family is found in almost all other cultures should provide a broad agreement from the start. Then there is the fact that Confucian values such as humanity, propriety and righteousness are general and basic enough to be adapted, if not adopted, by most other cultures. Indeed, Chinese history shows that even "barbarian" invaders could easily absorb the Confucian culture. But the biggest advantage that the Confucians have in negotiating for a global justice is that they are not bound by any rigid understanding of Confucianism. As cited above, Confucius himself said that he hated inflexibility. Again, history has demonstrated that the Confucian culture has managed to adapt to historical circumstances. While it is true that the Confucian culture can be said to be enjoying a continuous existence for more than two thousand years, it has not remained unchanged in that period, and it would not have enjoyed a continuous existence for such a long time without considerable flexibility. Intellectually, Confucianism underwent a great transformation at the hands of the Neo-Confucians a few centuries after Confucius. Tu Wei-ming claims that right now it is undergoing another transformation in response to modern challenges such as globalisation. Tu refers to this transformation as a move "toward a third epoch of Confucian humanism,"[29] and argues that the "core values" of Confucianism are general and basic enough for it to contribute to and to be a part of a "fiduciary global community."[30] Insofar as a fiduciary global community is not possible without global justice, Tu's view supports my contention that Confucians have what it takes to negotiate with others for a truly universal notion of global justice, but one that does not obliterate the Confucian cultural identity, precisely because the outcome will be what has been worked out from within the Confucian cultural tradition. More importantly, there are resources within Confucianism to negotiate a global justice that respects other cultural identities. As *Analects* 6.30 makes clear, Confucianism is committed to helping others establishing themselves as well as enlarging themselves: "Wishing to establish oneself, one establishes others; wishing to enlarge oneself, one enlarges others." Given the global conditions, this is a commitment to the enlargement of oneself and others into a global community as well as to the establishment of oneself and others as distinct identities in it.

In many ways, the world is already a global

village. Many problems we are facing have globalised themselves, such as pollution, climate
change, terrorism and so on, even if we have not
globalised enough of our values and practices to
match. Yet, concerns voiced by critics of globalisation are real enough. One such concern is the
loss of cultural identity. In the global context, cultural commitments are seen as either impediments
to a universal global justice necessary to adjudicate competing claims, or as victims of it. I have
argued that for Confucianism at least, there is no
cause for concern for both critics and sympathizers. I leave the fate of other cultures to others, but
with the assurance that the universalism that Confucianism takes to the negotiating table will
neither threaten other cultural values, nor regard
them as barriers to the idea of global justice. As
pointed out above, Confucianism is committed to
enlarging oneself and others into a global and just
community as well as to establishing oneself and
others as distinct and flourishing identities in it.
Fortunately for Confucians (as well as others from
other cultures), the chances of a successful negotiation is more than average in view of the fact, as
pointed out by many keen observers of cultures,
that cultures are not rigid entities with clear and
impermeable defining boundaries. We have seen
Isaiah Berlin's denial that cultures are "windowless boxes." Typically, a culture has an identifying
core but also open borders, allowing for
exchanges with other cultures and for transformation as a result of such exchanges. As Mary
Midgley puts it, cultures are "more like climactic
regions or ecosystems than ... like the frontiers
drawn between nation states."[31] If I am right, the
inevitable coming together of the Confucian "climactic region" with others in the globalisation
process need not result in the dissipation of the
Confucian "climate" or any particular cultural
"climate," nor in a massive storm that engulfs us
all.

NOTES

1. In what follows, I shall use the term "Confucianism" to refer to both the Confucian philosophy and
the Confucian culture. I take it that to belong to the

Confucian culture is at least to live by the moral
code based on Confucian philosophy.
2. See for instance Berlin, Isaiah (1976), *Vico and
Herder* (London, Hogarth Press).
3. Berlin, Isaiah (1990), *The Crooked Timbre of
Humanity,* H. Hardy (Ed.) (London, John Murray),
p. 85.
4. On Boas, see Cook, J.W. (1999), *Morality and Cultural Differences* (Oxford, Oxford University
Press). See also Benedict, R. (1957), *Patterns of
Cultures* (New York, New American Library).
5. See Nuyen, A.T. (1996), Lyotard's postmodern
ethics, *International Studies in Philosophy,* 28, pp.
75-86.
6. Parekh, Bhikhu (1994), Superior people: the narrowness of liberalism from Mill to Rawls, *Times
Literary Supplement,* 25 February, p. 13.
7. See Tully, James (1995), *Strange Multiplicity: Constitutionalism in the Age of Diversity* (Cambridge,
Cambridge University Press).
8. Kymlicka, Will (1989), *Liberalism, Community
and Culture* (Oxford, Clarendon Press), p. 162.
9. Kymlicka, Will (1995), *Multicultural Citizenship:
A Liberal Theory of Minority Rights* (Oxford,
Clarendon Press).
10. Young, Iris (1990), *Justice and the Politics of Difference* (Princeton, NJ, Princeton University Press).
11. Ong, Aihwa (1999), *Flexible Citizenship: The Cultural Logics of Transnationality* (Durham, NC,
Duke University Press).
12. See for instance Falk, R., (1995) *On Human Governance* (Cambridge, Polity).
13. See for instance Parekh, Bhikhu (1998), Cultural
diversity and liberal democracy, in: Gurpreet
Mahajan (Ed.) *Democracy, Difference and Social
Justice* (Delhi, Oxford University Press).
14. Hollis, Martin (1999), Is universalism ethnocentric?,
in: C. Joppke and S. Lukes (Eds) *Multicultural
Questions* (Oxford, Oxford University Press), p. 36.
15. Ching, Julia (1998), Human rights: a valid Chinese
concept? in: W.T. De Bary and Tu Wei-ming (Eds)
Confucianism and Human Rights (New York,
Columbia University Press), pp. 67-82 at p. 72.
16. Bauer, Joanne (1995), International human rights
and Asian commitment, in: *Human Rights Dialogue 3* (New York, Carnegie Council of Ethics and
International Affairs), pp. 1-4 at p. 2.

17. Berger, Peter L. (1986), *The Capitalist Revolution* (New York, Basic Books), p. 101.

18. Fukuyama, Francis (1995), Confucianism and democracy, *Journal of Democracy,* 6, pp. 20-33.

19. Tu Wei-ming, Probing the "Three Bonds" and "Five Relationships" in Confucian humanism, in: W.H. Slote and G.A. De Vos (Eds), *Confucianism and the Family* (Albany, NY, State University of New York Press), pp. 121-136 at p. 122.

20. Nuyen, A.T. (2001), Confucianism and the idea of equality, *Asian Philosophy,* 11, pp. 61-71.

21. Translations of *The Analects* and *The Mencius* have been adapted from various sources.

22. Kung-chuan Hsiao (1979), *A History of Chinese Political Thought.* Vol. 1. *From the Beginnings to the Sixth Century A.D.,* trans. F.W. Mote (Princeton, NJ, Princeton University Press), p. 159.

23. Bell, Daniel A. (1999), Democracy with Chinese characteristics: a political proposal for the post-communist era, *Philosophy East and West,* 49, pp. 451-491 at p. 463.

24. See Wing Tsit Chan (1963), *A Source Book of Chinese Philosophy* (Princeton, NJ, Princeton University Press), p. 87.

25. For a full discussion, see Nuyen, A.T. (2003), Love and respect in the Confucian family, in: K.C. Chong, S.H. Tan and C.L. Ten (Eds) *The Moral Circle and the Self* (Chicago, IL, Open Court), pp. 93-105.

26. Kant, Immanuel (1964), *The Doctrine of Virtue,* trans. Mary J. Gregor (New York, Evanston), p. 115. Interestingly, Kant himself has compared the feelings of love and respect that regulate human relationships with the attractive and repulsive forces in the cosmos that keep the heavenly bodies in a cosmological balance: "... *attraction* [due to love] and *repulsion* [due to respect] bind together rational beings ..."

27. In Lin Yutang (Ed.) (1938), *The Wisdom of Confucius* (New York, The Modern Library).

28. Nuyen, A.T. (1999), *Chung Yung* and the Greek conception of justice, *Journal of Chinese Philosophy,* pp. 187-202.

29. See Tu Wei-ming, (1986), Toward a third epoch of Confucian humanism: a background understanding, in: Irene Eber (Ed.) *Confucianism: The Dynamics of Tradition* (New York, Macmillan), pp. 3-21.

30. See Tu Wei-ming (1992), Core values and the possibility of a fiduciary global community, K. Tehranian and M. Tehranian (Eds) *Restructuring for World Peace* (Cresskill, Hampton Press), pp. 333-345.

31. Midgley, Mary (1991), *Can't We Make Moral Judgements?* (Bristol, Bristol Press), p. 84.

WOMEN, CITIZENSHIP AND DIFFERENCE

Nira Yuval-Davis

Nira Yuval-Davis is a Professor and Graduate Course Director in Gender, Sexualities and Ethnic Studies at the University of East London. She has written extensively on theoretical and empirical aspects of nationalism, racism, fundamentalism, citizenship, and gender relations. Among her written and edited books are Gender and Nation *(1997);* The Gulf War and the New World Order *(1992);* Women, Citizenship & Difference *(1999); and* Warning Signs of Fundamentalisms *(2004).*

Yuval-Davis argues for a gendered reading of citizenship in a world where the borders of nations are becoming more permeable and globalization affects everyone. She argues that women's citizenship is not like that of men and is further impacted by factors such as ethnicity, origin, and urban or rural residence — all of which are in turn affected by trans- and cross-border as well as global understandings of what constitutes citizenship. She defends an understanding of citizenship as a "multi-tiered construct," one in which persons are members in groups of various kinds within and across national collectivities as well as in states. Expanding the notion of citizenship, she argues, can help to integrate the struggles of women in places across the world and with respect to issues such as reproductive rights, political participation, poverty, and the oppression and exploitation that exists in the name of culture and tradition.

"Citizenship" has become a very popular subject of debate in the last few years, appropriated nationally and internationally, by both Left and Right, as well as by feminists. The interest in citizenship is not just in the narrow formalistic meaning of having the right to carry a specific passport. It addresses an overall concept encapsulating the relationship between the individual, state and society.

This article discusses some of the major issues which need to be examined in a gendered reading of citizenship. Its basic claim is that a comparative study of citizenship should consider the issue of women's citizenship not only by contrast to that of men, but also in relation to women's affiliation to dominant or subordinate groups, their ethnicity, origin and urban or rural residence. It should also take into consideration global and transnational positionings of these citizenships.

T.H. Marshall (1950, 1975, 1981), the most

influential theorist of citizenship in Britain, has defined citizenship as "a status bestowed on those who are full members of a community" (1950: 14), which includes civil, political and social rights and obligations. By formally linking citizenship to membership in a community rather than to the state, as liberal definitions of citizenship do, Marshall's definition enables us analytically to discuss citizenship as a multi-tier construct, which applies to people's membership in a variety of collectivities — local, ethnic, national and trans-national. Such a multi-tier construction of citizenship is particularly important these days when neo-liberal states redefine and reprivatize their tasks and obligations. It also enables us to raise the question of the relationship between "the community" and the state and how this affects people's citizenship. The debates in the literature between the "liberals" and the "communitarians" (see, for example, Avineri and Shalit, 1992; Daly, 1993; Nimni, 1996;

Phillips, 1993) and the "republicans" (Peled, 1992; Roche, 1987; Sandel, 1982; Oldfield, 1990) relate to these issues. The article examines some of the implications of this debate for notions of social rights and social difference.

Bryan Turner (1990) has constructed an influential typology of citizenship based on two dimensions — the public/private and the active/passive. Turner's typology, sadly, is completely Euro- or, rather, Westocentric (Yuval-Davis, 1991a), his "universal" typology being based on the development of citizenship in four Western countries — France, the USA, England and Germany. Even more astonishing perhaps, is the fact that Turner's typology is gender blind (Yuval-Davis, 1991a; Walby, 1994), although the two dimensions he considers are ones which have often been used in order to describe gender differences in general and difference in relation to women's citizenship in particular (Pateman, 1988; Grant and Newland, 1991). The article, therefore, explores these two dimensions and how they should be theorized when seeking to construct a comparative non-Westocentric framework of analysis of gendered citizenship which incorporates notions of difference.

A word of warning, however, is necessary before the exploration of the various issues considered in the paper can start. When dealing with the notion of citizenship it is also important to remember that, as Floya Anthias and myself have commented before (Yuval-Davis and Anthias, 1989: 6), on its own, the notion of citizenship cannot encapsulate adequately all the dimensions of control and negotiations which take place in different areas of social life, nor can it adequately address the ways the state itself forms its political project. Studying citizenship, however, can throw light on some of the major issues which are involved in the complex relationships between individuals, collectivities and the state, and the ways gender relations (as well as other social divisions) affect and are affected by them.

Citizenship, Nationalism and "the Community"

As Roche (1987) describes it, in the liberal tradition individual citizens are presumed to have equal status, equal rights and duties, etc., so that princi-

ples of inequality deriving from gender, ethnic, class or other contexts are *not* supposed to be of relevance to the status of citizenship as such. The citizens are therefore constructed not as "members of the community" but as *strangers* to each other, although they are sharing a complex set of assumptions about and expectations of each other which, when not fulfilled, can be enforceable by the state.

This liberal abstraction of self has been criticized, however, by the "communitarians" who claim that notions of rights and duties, as well as those of equality and privacy, have no meaning outside the context of particular communities (Ackelsberg, 1995). On different grounds, the proponents of republicanism such as Sandel (1982), also find the individualistic construction of citizenship highly unsatisfactory. They argue that such a construction of citizenship denies the possibility of citizenship as constituting a membership in a moral community in which the notion of the common good is antecedent to the individual citizenship choice. Liberal construction of citizenship, according to Sandel, assumes the priority of right over good. Republicanism, on the other hand, constructs citizenship not only as a status but also as a means of active involvement and participation in the determination, practice and promotion of the common good.

However, as Peled comments (Peled, 1992: 433), "This raises the question of how the republican [moral] community is constituted and what qualities are required for active participation in it." According to him, two distinct notions of community can be discerned in the current revival of republicanism: a weak community, in which membership is essentially voluntary, and a strong, historical community that is *discovered*, not formed by its members. In a strong community its "ongoing existence is an important value in and of itself" and becomes one of the, if not the most, important imperatives of the "moral community" (ibid.).

Membership in such a community involves "enduring attachment," often a myth of common origin, and is clearly bonded by a myth of common destiny. In other words, this "strong community" is the national "imagined community" (Anderson,

1983). There is no difference between republican constructions of the "moral community" and the *gemeinschaft*-like constructions of the "national community."

The question arises, then, what should happen to those members of the civil society who cannot or will not become full members of that "strong community." In virtually all contemporary states there are migrants and refugees, "old" and "new" minorities and in settler societies there are also indigenous people who are not part of the hegemonic national community (Stasiulis and Yuval-Davis, 1995). In addition, there are many other members of the civil society who, although they might share the myth of common origin of "the community," do not share important hegemonic value systems with the majority of the population in sexual, religious and other matters.

Peled's solution (following Oldfield, 1990) is a two-tier construction of citizenship: a full membership in the "strong community" for those who can be included, and for people who cannot:

> a residual, truncated status, similar to the liberal notion of citizenship as a bundle of rights. Bearers of this citizenship do not share in attending to the common good but are secure in their possession of what we consider essential human and civil rights. (Peled, 1992)

In other words, Peled is suggesting the institutionalization of an exclusionary two-tier system of citizenship as a way of solving the discrepancy between the boundaries of the civil society and the boundaries of the national collectivity. This solution is far from being satisfactory. Politically it openly condones discrimination and racialization of citizens on national grounds (Peled brings Israel and its treatment of the Palestinians who have been citizens of the state since 1948 as the ideal case of a state which successfully managed to do so). Theoretically, this model dichotomizes the population into two homogenous collectivities — those who are in and those who are out of the national collectivity, without paying attention to other dimensions of social divisions and social positionings, such as gender, intra-national ethnicity, class, sexuality,

ability, stage in the life cycle, etc., which are crucial to constructions of citizenship.

Yet, with all these reservations, the above position at least recognizes the potential inherently contradictory nature of citizenship as individual and communal, inclusionary and exclusionary. In Marshall's works, these issues were not problematized at all and there has been an automatic assumption of an overlap between the boundaries of civil society and those of the national community. Not incidentally, as Theodor Shanin (1986) has commented, in English, unlike other languages (such as Russian or Hebrew), there is a missing term which expresses the notion of ethnic nationality, to differentiate it from nationality which is equivalent to formal citizenship in the state. In different states and societies the relationship between the two differs hugely and can be structured formally or informally, in ways which prioritize one hegemonic ethnic/national collectivity or several; in which such a membership would be primarily important for one's identity or not; which could provide members easier or more difficult access to a whole range of social, economic and political facilities; and which may or may not actually ground legally that members in different collectivities would be entitled to a differential range of civil, political and social citizenship rights. A common status in Europe, for instance, is that of the "denizen": someone who is entitled to most social and civil rights but is deprived of the political rights of national voting.

Paradoxically, although Marshall's theory of citizenship does not relate to any of these issues, his conceptual definition of citizenship as a membership of the community rather than of the state can provide us with the framework to study specific cases of the differential multi-tier citizenship. A word of caution is necessary here, however. As elaborated elsewhere (Cain and Yuval-Davis, 1990; Yuval-Davis, 1991a) it is important not to view "the community" as a given natural unit. Collectivities and "communities" are ideological and material constructions, whose boundaries, structures and norms are a result of constant processes of struggles and negotiations, or more general social developments (Anthias and Yuval-Davis,

1992). The moral imperative which interprets the "good of the community" as a support for its continuous existence as a separate collectivity can become an extremely conservative ideology which would see any internal or external change in the community as a threat.

Social Rights and Social Difference

The liberal definition of citizenship constructs all citizens as basically the same and considers the differences of class, ethnicity, gender, etc., as irrelevant to their status as citizens.[1] On the other hand, the welfare state assumes a notion of difference, as determined by *social needs*. In the words of Edwards "Those with similar needs ought to get similar resources and those with different needs, different resources, or — more succinctly — treatment as equals rather than equal treatment" (1988: 135). These differences were initially conceived exclusively as class differences. As originally envisaged by Beveridge (1942), social welfare rights were aimed at improving the quality of life of the working classes (as well as the smooth working of capitalism). As Harris (1987) put it, welfare was conceived as the institutionalized recognition of social solidarity within the political community of the citizens.

This social solidarity is being threatened by a variety of groupings, ethnic, racial, religious and sexual sub-collectivities which exist within the marginal matrix of society and "which experience informal and formal discrimination consonant with their credited lower social worth" (Evans, 1993: 6). A primary concern of many relevant struggles and debates (Gordon, 1989; Hall and Held, 1989) has been around the right to enter or to remain in a specific country. The "freedom of movement within the European community," the Israeli Law of Return and the Patriality clause in British immigration legislation are all instances of ideological, often racist, constructions of boundaries which allow unrestricted immigration to some and block it completely to others.

Even when questions of entry and settlement have been resolved, the concerns of groupings constituted as ethnic minorities might be different from those of other members of the society. For example, their right to formal citizenship might depend upon the rules and regulations of their country of origin in addition to those of the country where they live, as well as the relationship between the two. Thus, people from some Caribbean Islands who have been settled in Britain for years were told that they could not have a British passport because their country does not recognize dual citizenship and because they had not declared on time their intent to renounce the citizenship of their country of origin after it received independence. Concern over relatives and fear of not being allowed to visit their country of origin prevent others (such as Iranians and Turks) from giving up their original citizenship. Women workers who have children in other countries are often ineligible to receive child benefits like other mothers. Countries like Israel and Britain confer citizenship on those whose parents are citizens rather than on those born in the country. Further, the right of entry to a country is often conditional on a commitment by the immigrant that neither s/he or any other member of their family will claim any welfare benefits. Citizenship needs to be examined, therefore, not just in terms of state, but often in relation to multiple formal and informal citizenships in more than one country, and most importantly, to view them from a perspective which would include the different positioning of different states as well as the different positionings of individuals and groupings within states (Bakan and Stasiulis, 1994).

A whole different set of citizenship issues relates to indigenous minorities in settler societies (Stasiulis and Yuval-Davis, 1995; Dickanson, 1992). It is not just that in many societies indigenous populations have been very late, if at all, entrants to the formal citizenship body of the state. It is that if their claim on the country — in the form of land rights — were to be taken seriously and in full, this would totally conflict with the claim of the settler national collectivity for legitimacy. Attempts to solve the problem by transforming the indigenous population into another "ethnic minority" have usually met with a strong and understandable resistance (de Lepervanche, 1980). Formal treaties, which would institutionalize and anchor in law the relations between what Australian Aboriginals have been calling "the imposing society" and the indigenous people, often create a complex situation in which there exist two national sovereign entities over the same territory — one which owns the state and one which attempts to establish a sovereign stateless society within it. Somewhat similar, if less racialized, struggles are present in the many regionalist secessionist movements which claim the right of national self-determination *vis-à-vis* their states which themselves have been constructed as nations.

The most problematic aspects of citizenship rights for racial and ethnic minorities relate to their social rights and to the notion of multi-culturalism (Parekh, 1990; Jayasuriya, 1990; Yuval-Davis, 1992, 1997). For some (e.g. Harris, 1987; Lister, 1990), the problem remains within the realm of individual, though different, citizens. The homogenous community of Marshall is being transformed into a pluralist one by the reinterpretation of his emphasis on equality of status into mutual respect (Lister, 1990: 48). However, such a model does not take into account potential conflicts of interest among the different groupings of citizens, nor does it consider the collective, rather than the individual, character of the special provisions given to members of groupings defined as ethnic minorities (Jayasuriya, 1990: 23).

The question of a collective provision to meet the needs of "ethnic minorities" relates to policies of positive action aimed at group rather than individual rights. Multiculturalist policies construct these populations, or rather, effectively, the poor and working classes within them, in terms of ethnic and racial collectivities. These collectivities are attributed with collective needs, based on their different cultures as well as on their structural disadvantages. Resistance to these policies has been expressed by claims that constructing employment and welfare policies in terms of group rights can conflict with individual rights and are therefore discriminatory. However, at least in countries which officially adopted multiculturalist policies, such as Canada, Britain and the USA, it has been widely accepted, at least until recently, that in order to overcome the practical effects of racism

rather than just its ideology, collective provisions and positive action, based on group membership, are the only effective measures to be taken (see Burney, 1988; Young, 1989; Cain and Yuval-Davis, 1990). Similar policies have been constructed in other pluralist states, such as India and South Africa.

The question becomes more problematic when positive provisions relate to the different "cultural needs" of different ethnicities. These can vary from the provision of interpreters to the provision of funds to religious organizations. In the most extreme cases, as in the debates around Aboriginals, on the one hand, and Muslim minorities around the Rushdie affair, on the other hand, there have been calls to enable the minorities to operate according to their own customary and religious legal systems. While the counter-arguments have ranged from the fact that this would imply a *de facto* apartheid system to arguments about social unity and political hegemony, those who support these claims have seen it as a natural extrapolation of the minorities' social and political rights.

This raises the question of how one defines the boundaries of citizens' rights. Kymlicka (1995) suggests a differentiation between "two kinds of group rights": one which involves the claim of a group against its own members and one which involves the group's claim against the larger society (or the state). Kymlicka opposes the use of state powers in the support of claims of the first kind, because he suspects that very often individuals within the group would be oppressed in the name of culture and tradition. In the second case, however, the issue often involves protection of a disadvantaged group by others and so, in this case, state intervention should be welcome. While the general line of argument of Kymlicka can be supported, he reifies and naturalizes the groups' boundaries and does not differentiate between people with specific power positionings within the groups (which are not homogenous and can be with differing and conflicting interests) and "the group."

Jayasuriya (1990), in a somewhat different terminology when grappling with the same question, suggests a distinction between needs, which are essential and which therefore require satisfaction by the state, and wants, which fall outside the public sector and are to be satisfied within the private domain in a voluntary way. This conceptualization of "wants" and "needs" as objective differences between essential and non-essential cultural demands of specific sub-collectivities within the civil society is, of course, highly suspect. Cultural needs are not fixed a-historical essentialist characteristics of collectivities. Cultures are highly heterogeneous resources which are used selectively, and often in contradictory ways, in different ethnic projects which are promoted by members of specific collectivities, often in a way which disadvantages women. Women often suffer from the acceptance by the state of the definition of what constitutes "the cultural needs of the community" in matters of education, marriage and divorce and other provisions such as women's refuges (Sahgal and Yuval-Davis, 1992; for testimonies on these issues from women activists from various post-colonial countries in a South African mobilization conference on this issue, see Amy Biehl, 1994).

The Private and the Public

Jayasuriya establishes the boundary line of provision by the state in between the public and private domains, as if this boundary is natural and static. This boundary is, however, highly problematic and is both gender and culture specific. ...

If we accept the meaning of "private" as that in which the individual is autonomous, then this can be exercised to a lesser or greater extent in all social spheres, where people — and not just women — can act both as part of social structures and collectivities with all the constraints these provide, and as autonomous individual agents, whether it is in the family, in the civil or in the political domain. Similarly, depending on people's preferences and hobbies, leisure and self-enhancement activities can be spent with the family or other personal friends, with the trade union, church or ethnic sports associations, or as a councillor in the local government in the political domain. At the same time, political power relations with their own dynamics exist in each social sphere. The

most important contribution of feminism to social theory has been the recognition that power relations operate within primary social relations as well as within the more impersonal secondary social relations of the civil and political domains.

The recognition that power lines operate horizontally as well as vertically has given rise to the Foucauldian perspective that there is no need to theorize the state as a separate unitary sphere. However, as elaborated elsewhere (Anthias and Yuval-Davis, 1989: 6), while the state is not unitary in its practices, its intentions or its effects, there is a need to retain the state as a separate sphere, "a body of institutions which are centrally organized around the intentionality of control with a given apparatus of enforcement at its command or basis." While ideological production, like education and the media, can lie both inside and outside the state, the exercise of individual and collective rights continues to be tied to the state (Soysal, 1994). Thus control over the state continues to be the primary political target. Especially in the modern welfare state, there is no social sphere which is protected from state intervention. Even in cases where there is no direct intervention, it is the state which has usually established, actively or passively, its own boundaries of non-intervention. In other words, the construction of the boundary between the public and the private is a political act in itself.

Given all these inconsistencies and confusions in the determination of the "private" domain, I suggest that we abandon the public/private distinction. Rather, we should differentiate between three distinct spheres of the state, civil society and the domain of the family, kinship and other primary relationships. Feminists, such as Ann Orloff (1993) and Julia O'Connor (1993), have already pointed out that there is a need to add the family domain to that of the state and the market when examining the ways societies organize the provision of welfare. However the family domain has also to be added when we discuss different locations for political organization and power....

Welfare states are considered to be those where the influence of civil society is the greatest in terms of the location of political, as well as economic power. Marshall (1981) described the capitalist society as the hyphenated society in which there are inevitable tensions between a capitalist economy and the welfare state. Esping-Andersen (1990) described the variations between different welfare state regimes as dependent on the extent to which the market forces or the state have the upper hand in the struggle for domination. It is important to remember, however, that the civil domain is not just the market. It is not only economic, but political and social relations which operate there, in collusion and/or resistance to the market forces. Political parties, social movements and trade unions are not part of the state even if they are often organized and focus their activities on the state. Education and media can be owned or not by the state and can have ideological projects which are autonomous to a larger or lesser extent from the state. Of particular importance to our concern here are formal and informal organizations, associations and institutions in civil society which are organized by/for members of a particular ethnic/racial/national collectivity. Such collectivities play a larger or smaller role in the construction of state policies and social and political relations. The formal ethnicization of the different regions in Yugoslavia in the revised constitution approved by Tito during the last years in his life has been a major stepping stone in its history and a partial explanation of later developments.

In general terms the above examples demonstrate the differential relative importance of the familial, the civil and state agencies domains in the determination of the social, political and civil rights of citizens. Any comparative theory of citizenship, therefore, must include an examination of the individual autonomy allowed to citizens (of different gender, ethnicity, region, class, stage in the life cycle, etc.) *vis-à-vis* their families, civil society organizations and state agencies.

Active/Passive Citizenship

The other axis of Bryan Turner's comparative typology of citizenship is that of active-passive which he defines as "whether the citizen is conceptualized as merely a subject of an absolute authority or as an active political agent" (1990: 209). The conventional differentiation, then, between "citizen" and "subject" is removed in Turner's definition, and instead becomes a continuum of passivity and activity.

The history of citizenship is different in different countries. In some countries, like in France and the USA, it has been the result of a popular revolutionary struggle, while in others, like Britain and Germany, it has been more of a "top to bottom" process. Similarly, in some post-colonial countries, like in India or Kenya, national independence was achieved after a long period of popular struggle, while in others, like in certain islands of the Caribbean, that transition was much more peaceful and political rule was passed smoothly from the colonial elite to the local one. Today, virtually all the world's population live in countries in which some form of citizenship exists, at least in the Marshallian sense of being a member of a community.

As to participating in some form in ruling as well as being ruled, the Aristotelian definition of citizenship (Allen and Macey, 1990), the picture is, of course, very different. Only a minority of people, in probably the minority of world states, can be said to have this kind of active citizenship status. This is not just a question of formal rights. Even in the most democratically active societies there are strata of the population which are passive, too disempowered and/or alienated to participate even in the formal act of voting. Among them can be not only children, migrants, ethnic minorities and indigenous people in settler societies, but also what has come to be labelled as the "underclass," which in the USA is to a large extent black, but which in Britain and other countries can also be largely white, and in which lone mothers loom large (Lister, 1990; Morris, 1994). Gender, sexuality, age and ability as well as ethnicity and class are important factors in determining the relationship of people to their communities and states.

The notion of the "active citizen" has been a focus of debates and policies in recent years within both the "Left" and the "Right," especially in Britain. The recent growth in interest in citizenship among the Left has coincided with signs that many of the social rights which have come to be taken for granted in the welfare state have come under threat, in the areas of health care, education, retirement, child benefits, etc. Rather than concentrating on social rights, however, the Left (and Centre) has used citizenship as a call for political mobilization and participation and in Britain it also became part of a campaign for a written constitution (Charter 88) in which social citizenship entitlement would be enshrined so that a radical Rightist government would not again be able to transform the relationship between people and state so easily.

The language of citizenship has also been a major discourse of the Right. In Britain "the active citizen" has been put forward as an alternative to the welfare state, in which "the citizen," constructed as an economically successful middle-class male head of a family, would fulfill his citizenship duties by giving his spare money and time "to the community" (Lister, 1990; Evans, 1993). In this discourse, therefore, citizenship stops being a political discourse and becomes a voluntary involvement within civil society, in which the social rights of the poor are transferred, at least partly, from entitlements into charities. Lister (1990:14) quotes the Conservative Minister Douglas Hurd defining active citizenship: "Public service may once have been the duty of an elite, but today it is the responsibility of all who have time or money to spare." Obligations are shifted from the public sphere of tax-financed benefits and services to the private sphere of charity and voluntary service. Rights become gifts and active citizenship assumes a top-down notion of citizenship. Typically, quangos, which are appointed rather than elected, have come to be the means by which various public services, like health and welfare, are being managed.

This depoliticization of the notion of citizenship has been enhanced with the publication of the government's Citizen's Charter in 1992 which constructs citizens as consumers whose prime rights are to have the freedom to make well-informed choices of high-quality commodities and services in public and private sectors and to be treated with due regard for their "privacy, dignity, religious and cultural beliefs" (Evans, 1993: 10). The balance of citizenship rights has shifted away from social

rights of welfare towards civil rights of an economic kind. Its aim is to promote individual persona and autonomy rather than the relationship between the individual and community and would clearly fall within the liberal mode of citizenship described above.

The Thatcherite notion of citizenship as consumerism is not based on a completely free market model, in spite of its universalist rhetoric. There are legal and moral constraints which prevent a variety of marginal or minority groups from pursuing their religious and cultural beliefs or economic needs in equal measure (Evans, 1993: 6). The state's management of these "moral aliens," who are to be found in the marginal matrix of citizenship, is exercised in social, political and economic arenas. This is the twilight zone between the liberal and republican constructions of citizenship, where religious, ethnic and sexual minorities are located outside the national "moral community" but inside the civic nation.

To those who can afford it, this is not a completely closed-off system. Evans describes how sexual minority groups have developed socio-economic "community" infrastructures around their identities, organized to obtain further housing, insurance, medical, parenting, marital rights, etc., and spend a significant proportion of their income on distinguishable lifestyles in segregated or specifically gay social and sexual territories (1993: 8). Multiculturalism which is aimed at ethnic minorities can be described in similar terms. Multiculturalist policies are aimed at simultaneously including and excluding the minorities, locating them in marginal spaces and secondary markets, while reifying their boundaries.

The question of citizenship rights and social difference has been a difficult one in feminist political theory. Iris Young (1989) has suggested that representative democracy should treat people not as individuals but as members of groups. She argues that a discourse of universal citizenship which would ignore these differences would just enhance the domination of groups which are already dominant, and would silence the marginal and oppressed groups. She suggests, therefore, that special mechanisms have to be established to represent these groups as groups. Such an approach, however, can easily fall into politics, in which the groups are constructed as homogenous and with fixed boundaries, the interests of specific individuals within groups constructed as representing the interests of the whole group and the advancement of the specific group becomes primary....

Suggestions of other feminists and activists who attempted to deal with the question of citizenship rights and social difference focus differentially on the social and on the political. Correa and Petchesky (1994) argue that, rather than abandoning rights discourse, we should reconstruct it so that it both specifies differences, such as gender, class, cultural and other differences and recognizes social needs. Sexual and reproductive (or any other) rights, understood as private "liberties" or "choices," are meaningless, especially for the poorest and most disenfranchised, without enabling conditions through which they can be realized. In the post-GLC era in London with the massive backlash against the identity politics which was practised there, some black and other radical activists came to the conclusion that the alternative to group politics should be a politics of confronting these disabling conditions. The argument has been that, if black people suffer disproportionally from unemployment, for instance, political discourse which focuses on unemployment will particularly benefit black people. However, this approach would not exclude, nor create a construction of otherness for other unemployed (Wilson, 1987)....

Instead of a given unitary standard, there has to be a process of constructing a standard norm for each specific political project. Black feminists like Patricia Hill Collins (1990) and Italian feminists like Raphaela Lambertini and Elizabetta Dominini (see Yuval-Davis, 1994, 1997) have focused on the transversal politics of coalition building, in which the specific positioning of political actors is recognized and considered. This approach is based on the epistemological recognition that each positioning produces specific situated knowledge which cannot be but an unfinished knowledge, and therefore dialogue among those differentially positioned should take place in order to reach a common perspective. Transversal dialogue should be based on the principle of remaining centred in one's own experiences while being empathetic to the differential positionings of the partners in the dialogue, thus enabling the participants to arrive at a different perspective from that of hegemonic tunnel vision. The boundaries of the dialogue would be determined, as Hill Collins has argued (1990), by the message rather than its messengers. The result of the dialogue might still be differential projects for people and groupings positioned differently, but their solidarity would be based on a common knowledge sustained by a compatible value system. The dialogue, therefore, is never boundless.

Of course, in "real politics," unlike in grassroots social movements, there is often no time for extensive continuous dialogue. When the Women's Unit in the GLC in the early 1980s tried to work in this manner, it ended up being largely ignored by the daily hierarchical structures of decision making which were working at a much faster pace. Transversal politics should not be seen as necessarily opposing the principle of delegation, so long as the political delegates are seen as advocates, rather than representatives, of specific social categories and groupings and so long as their message is a result of transversal dialogues....

Concluding Remark

The article discusses some of the issues which are relevant to the development of a theory of citizenship which will not only be non-sexist, non-racist and non-Westocentric, but would also be flexible enough to deal with the far-reaching changes in the global (dis)order and reconstructions of state and society. Such a theory needs to dismantle the identification of the private with the family domain and the political with the public domain; it needs to construct citizenship as a multi-tier concept and to sever it from an exclusive relation to the state. The various sub-, cross- and supra-national and state collectivities of which people are formally and informally citizens can exist in a variety of co-operative and conflicting relationships which would differentially determine the positionings and the access to resources of different people at different times.

Considering these complexities and separating the notion of citizenship from the notion of the "nation-state" is probably more prevalent than ever in these days of "glocalization" (as Zygmund Bauman entitled his closing plenary address at the 1997 BSA annual conference). Similarly, such an analytical separation is necessary given the growing number of states which privatize a growing number of their institutions. Many feminists — most notably the Latin American ones (Vargas, 1996) — have found the notion of "citizenship" to be the most appropriate political mobilization tool in the post-Beijing era. It could be used to integrate separate feminist struggles, such as those about reproductive rights, political participation, poverty, etc. Moreover, once the notion of citizenship is understood as a concept wider than just a relationship between the individual and the state, it could also integrate the struggles of women against oppression and exploitation in the name of culture and tradition within their own ethnic and local communities and transcend the politically dangerous but intellectually sterile debate which took place in the UN conference on human rights in Vienna in 1993 about whether the struggle for human rights should be on an individual or a "group" level. Power relations and conflict of interests apply within "groups" as well as between them. At the same time, individuals cannot be considered as abstracted from their specific social positionings.

As I discuss elsewhere (Yuval-Davis, 1997: ch.6), there is no "end of history," nor is there an "end goal" for political struggles. Transversal politics might offer us a way for mutual support and probably greater effectiveness in the continuous struggle towards a less sexist, less racist and more democratic society, a way of agency within the political, economic and environmental continuously changing contexts in which we live and act. The struggle for citizenship should engage us in our homes, our local, ethnic and national collectivities as well as in our struggles with states and international agencies. It is quite an agenda!

Author's Note

A version of this paper was circulated as a background paper among the participants of the conference *Women, Citizenship and Difference* organized by Nira Yuval-Davis and Pnina Werbner at the University of Greenwich, July 1996. The conference was funded by the Equal Opportunity Unit of the EU and by the Wenner-Gren Foundation for Anthropological Research.

NOTES

1. This view, incidentally, was also shared by Marx, as has been developed in his article "On the Jewish Question" (1975)

REFERENCES

Ackelsberg, Martha (1995) "Liberalism" and "Community Polities," unpublished papers written as draft entries for the *Encyclopedia of Women's Studies* London: Simon and Schuster.

Allen, Sheila and Macey, Marie (1990) "At the cutting edge of citizenship: race and ethnicity in Europe 1992," a paper presented at the conference on New Issues in Black Politics, University of Warwick, May.

Anderson, Ben (1983) *Imagined Communities* London: Verso.

Anthias, Floya and Yuval-Davis, Nira (1989) "Introduction" in Yuval-Davis and Anthias (1989).

—- (1992) *Racialized Boundaries: Race, Nation, Gender, Colour and Class and the Anti-Racist Struggle* London: Routledge.

Arendt, Hannah (1951) *The Origins of Totalitarianism* New York: Harcourt, Brace.

Avineri, S. and Shalit, A. (1992) editors *Communitarianism and Individualism* Oxford: Oxford University Press.

Bakan, Abigail B. and Stasiulis, Daiva (1994) "Foreign domestic worker policy in Canada and the social boundaries of modern citizenship," *Science and Society* Vol.58, No. 1: 7-33.

Barbalet, J.M. (1988) *Citizenship*, Milton Keynes: Open University Press.

Beveridge, William (1942) *Report on Social Insurance and Allied Services* London: HMSO.

Bhabha, Jacqueline and Shutter, Sue (1994) *Women's Movement: Women under Immigration, Nationality and Refugee Law* Stoke-on-Trent: Trentham Books.

Biehl, Amy (1994) "Custom and religion in a non-racial, non-sexist South Africa," *Women Against Fundamentalism Journal*, No. 5: 51-4.

Burney, Elizabeth (1988) *Steps to Social Equality: Positive Action in a Negative Climate* London: Runnymede Trust.

Cain, Harriet and Yuval-Davis, Nira (1990) "'The Equal Opportunities Community' and the anti-racist struggle," *Critical Social Policy* No. 29: 5-26.

Chhachhi, Amrita (1991) "Forced Identities: the State, Communalism, Fundamentalism and Women in India" in D. Kandiyoti editor, *Women, Islam and the State* London: Macmillan, pp. 144-75.

Correa, Sonia and Petchesky, Rosalind (1994) "Reproductive and social rights: a feminist perspective" in G. Sen, A. Germain and L.C. Cohen editors, *Population Policies Considered*, HCPD and IWHC, pp. 107-26.

Daly, M. (1993) editor, *Communitarianism: Belonging and Commitment in a Pluralist Democracy* New York: Wadsworth Publishing Company.

Dean, Mitchel (1992) "Review essay: Pateman's dilemma: women and citizenship," *Theory and Society* No. 21: 121-30.

de Lepervanche, Marie (1980) "From race to ethnicity," *Australian and New Zealand Journal of Sociology* Vol. 16, No. 1.

Dickanson, Olive P. (1992) *Canada's First Nations* Toronto: McClelland and Stewart.

Dietz, Mary G. (1987) "Context is all: feminism and theories of citizenship," *Daedalus* 116: 4.

Edwards, J. (1988) "Justice and the bounds of welfare," *Journal of Social Policy* No. 18.

Eisenstein, Zillah R. (1989) *The Female Body and the Law* Berkeley: University of California Press.

—- (1993) *The Color of Gender - Reimaging Democracy* Berkeley: University of California Press.

Esping-Anderson, Gosta (1990) *The Three Worlds of Welfare Capitalism* Cambridge: Polity Press.

Evans, David T. (1993) *Sexual Citizenship: The Material Construction of Sexualities* London: Routledge.

Evans, Mary (1994) editor, *The Woman Question* London: Sage.

Gordon, Paul (1989) *Citizenship for Some? Race and Government Policy 1979-1989* London: Runnymede Trust.

Grant, Rebecca and Newland, Kathleen (1991) editors, *Gender and International Relations* Bloomington: Indiana University Press.

Hall, Catherine (1994) "Rethinking imperial histories: the Reform Act of 1867" *New Left Review* No. 208: 3-29.

Hall, Stuart and Held, David (1989) "Citizens and citizenship," in Stuart Hall and Martin Jacques editors, *New Times* London: Lawrence and Wishart.

Harris, D. (1987) *Justifying State Welfare: The New Right v The Old Left* Oxford: Blackwell.

Hernes, Helga Maria (1987) "Women and the welfare state: the transition from private to public dependence" in Anne Showstack Sassoon (1987).

Hill Collins, Patricia (1990) *Black Feminist Thought* Boston: Unwin Hyman.

Ignatieff, Michael (1993) *Blood and Belonging: Journeys into the New Nationalisms* London: BBC and Chatto and Windus.

Jayasuriya, Laksiri (1990) "Multiculturalism, citizenship and welfare: new directions for the 1990s," a paper presented at the 50th Anniversary Lecture Series, Dept. of Social Work and Social Policy, University of Sydney.

Jones, Kathleen B. (1990) "Citizenship in a woman-friendly polity," *Signs* Vol. 15, No. 4.

Joseph, Suad (1993) "Gender and civil society," *Middle East Report* No. 183: 22-6.

Kandiyoti, Deniz (1991) "Identity and its discontents: women and the nation," *Millennium*, Vol. 20, No. 3: 429-44.

Kosmarskaya, Natalya (1995) "Women and ethnicity in former day Russia — thoughts on a given theme" in H. Lutz, A. Phoenix and N. Yuval-Davis editors, *Crossfires: Nationalism, Racism and Gender in Europe* London: Pluto Press.

Kymlicka, Will (1995) *Multicultural Citizenship: A Liberal Theory of Minority Rights* Oxford: Clarendon Press.

Lechte, John (1994) "Freedom, community and cultural frontiers," paper presented to the Citizenship and Cultural Frontiers conference at Staffordshire University, Stoke-on-Trent, 16 September.

Lister, Ruth (1990) *The Exclusive Society: Citizenship and the Poor* London: Child Poverty Action Group.

Mann, Michael (1987) "Ruling class strategies and Citizenship," *Sociology* No. 21: 339-54.

Marshall, T.H. (1950) *Citizenship and Social Class* Cambridge: Cambridge University Press.

—- (1975) (original edition 1965) *Social Policy in the Twentieth Century* London: Hutchinson.

—- (1981) *The Right To Welfare and Other Essays* London: Heinemann Educational.

Marx, Karl (1975) "On the Jewish question," *Early Writings* Harmondsworth: Penguin, pp. 211-42.

Molyneux, Maxine (1994) "Women's rights and international context: some reflections on the post communist states," *Millennium: Journal of International Studies* Vol. 23, No. 2.

Morris, Lydia (1994) *Dangerous Classes: The Underclass and Social Citizenship* London: Routledge.

Mouffe, Chantal (1993) "Liberal socialism and pluralism: which citizenship" in J. Squires editor *Principled Positions* London: Lawrence and Wishart.

Nimni, Ephraim (1996) "The limits of Liberal Democracy," unpublished paper given at the departmental seminar for the Sociology Subject Groups at the University of Greenwich, London.

O'Connor, Julia S. (1993) "Gender, class and citizenship in the comparative analysis of welfare state regimes: theoretical and methodological issues," *British Journal of Sociology* Vol. 44, No. 3: 501-18.

Oldfield, Adrian (1990) *Citizenship and Community: Civic Republicanism and the Modern World* London: Routledge.

Oliver, Michael (1995) *Understanding Disability: From Theory to Practice* Basingstoke: Macmillan.

Orloff, Ann Shola (1993) "Gender and the social rights of citizenship: the comparative analysis of gender relations and welfare states," *American Sociological Review* Vol. 58: pp. 303-28.

Parekh, Bhiku (1990) "The Rushdie affair and the British press: some salutary lessons," in *Free Speech*, a report of a seminar by the CRE, London.

Pateman, Carole (1988) *The Sexual Contract* Cambridge: Polity Press.

—- (1989) *The Disorder of Women* Cambridge: Polity Press.

Peled, Yoav (1992) "Ethnic democracy and the legal construction of citizenship: Arab citizens of the Jewish state" *American Political Science Review*, Vol. 86, No. 2: 432-42.

Pettman, Jan (1992) *Living in the Margins: Racism, Sexism and Feminism in Australia* Sydney: Allen and Unwin.

Phillips, Anne (1993) *Democracy and Difference* Cambridge: Polity Press.

Phillips, Melanie (1990) "Citizenship sham in our secret society," *Guardian*, 14 September.

Roche, Maurice (1987) "Citizenship, social theory and social change," *Theory and Society* No. 16: 363-99.

Sahgal, Gita and Yuval-Davis, Nira (1992) editors, *Refusing Holy Orders: Women and Fundamentalism in Britain* London: Virago.

Sandel, Michael J. (1982) *Liberalism and the Limits of Justice* Cambridge: Cambridge University Press.

Shanin, Theodore (1986) "Soviet concepts of ethnicity: the case of a missing term," *New Left Review* No. 158: 113-22.

Showstack Sassoon, Anne (1987) editor, *Women and the State: The Shifting Boundaries of Public and Private* London: Hutchinson.

Smith, Anthony D. (1986) *The Ethnic Origins of Nations* Oxford: Blackwell.

Soysal, Yasemin (1994) *Limits of Citizenship: Migrants and Postnational Membership in Europe* Chicago: University of Chicago Press.

Stasiulis, Daiva and Yuval-Davis, Nira (1995) editors, *Unsettling Settler Societies: Articulations of Gender, Ethnicity, Race and Class* London: Sage.

Turner, Bryan (1990) "Outline of a theory on citizenship," *Sociology* Vol. 24, No. 2: 189-218.

Vargas, Virginia (1996) presentation in panel 3: "Unity, equality and difference: women's citizenship in contemporary Europe and beyond" at the Greenwich conference on Women, Citizenship and Difference, London.

Vogel, Ursula (1989) "Is citizenship gender specific?," paper presented at PSA Annual Conference, April.

Voronina, Olga A. (1994) "Soviet women and politics: on the brink of change" in B.J. Nelson and N. Chowdhury editors, *Women and Politics Worldwide* New Haven, Conn.: Yale University Press pp., 722-36.

Walby, Sylvia (1994) "Is citizenship gendered?," *Sociology* Vol. 28, No. 2: 379-95.

Wilson, William J. (1987) *The Truly Disadvantaged* Chicago: University of Chicago Press.

WING (Women, Immigration and Nationality Group)

(1985) *Worlds Apart: Women under Immigration and Nationality Laws* London: Pluto Press.

Young, Iris Marion (1989) "Polity and group difference: a critique of the ideal of universal citizenship," *Ethics* No. 99.

Yuval-Davis, Nira (1985) "Front and rear: sexual divisions of labour in the Israeli military," *Feminist Studies* Vol. 11, No. 3.

—- (1991a) "The citizenship debate: women, ethnic processes and the state," *Feminist Review* No. 39: 58-68.

—- (1991b) "The gendered Gulf War: women's citizenship and modern warfare," in Haim Breshceth and Nira Yuval-Davis, *The Gulf War and the New World Order*. London: Zed Books.

—- (1992). "Multi-culturalism, fundamentalism and women" in J. Donald and A. Rattansi editors, *Race, Culture and Difference*. London: Sage.

—- (1993) "Gender and nation," *Ethnic and Racial Studies* Vol. 16, No. 4: 621-32.

—- (1994) "Women, ethnicity and empowerment," *Feminism and Psychology* Vol. 4, No. 1: 179-97.

—- (1997) "Colour, culture and anti-racism" in C. Lloyds, F. Anthias and N. Yuval-Davis editors, *Rethinking Racism and Anti-Racism in Europe*. London: Macmillan.

Yuval-Davis, Nira and Anthias, Floya (1989) *Woman-Nation-State*. London: Macmillan.

STUDY QUESTIONS

1 How does John Rawls defend the idea of the primacy of justice? What is the original position? What purpose is served by the veil of ignorance? What principles of justice emerge from the original position?

2 The first principle of justice takes priority over the second and outlines the fundamental liberty rights of individuals. What are these liberty rights? What is the purpose of the second principle? What kinds of positive rights might be defended through it? Does Rawls provide a defense of strong welfare rights? Defend your answers.

3 Is the problem of Western biases as outlined by some of the other authors in Chapters 1 and 2 evident in Rawls's principles of justice? If so, does it undermine the possibility of giving Rawls's principles of justice universal application? Defend your answers.

4 Richard Garner argues that people in the hypothetical original position would not choose the second principle of justice. How does he argue for this? According to Garner, what would they choose and why?

5 How does Garner connect liberty rights to property rights? Does this support his conclusion that taxation is not justified? How does Garner answer the charge that without taxation allowing a redistribution of wealth, some people would be deprived of basic goods such as education, old age security, and health care?

6 Do you agree with Garner that abolishing taxation and the welfare state would probably make people more inclined than they are now to be charitable and philanthropic? Why or why not?

7 In what ways does Virginia Held's critique of justice apply to each of the accounts given by Rawls and Garner?

8 What are some of the features characterizing an ethic of care that distinguish it from an ethic of justice?

9 Do you agree with Held that an ethic of care has the potential to inform and transform our contemporary context of international relations and global politics? Why or why not?

10 Why does A.T. Nuyen defend the idea of formulating a universal account of justice? In what ways can Confucianism contribute to this project?

11 From what you have learned about Confucianism, do you agree with Nuyen's assessment that it can help resolve conflicts and at the same time promote cultural difference? Defend your answer.

12 Nira Yuval-Davis can be said to cast doubt on the project of providing a universal account of justice that relies on an account of the sameness of human beings. How and why does she undermine the notion of sameness at the bottom of liberal accounts of justice?

13 What does Yuval-Davis mean by a conception of citizenship as a "multi-tiered construct"? How does she defend this conception? What does this account of citizenship mean for the project of articulating an account of what justice demands?

14 Take a position on the question of whether Rawls's principles of justice can be applied to non-Western settings by outlining and evaluating how the different authors in this chapter would answer that question.

SUGGESTED READINGS

Baier, Annette C. "The Need for More than Justice." *Canadian Journal of Philosophy*. Supplementary Volume 13 (1987): 41-56.

Barry, Brian. "Humanity and Justice in Global Perspective." In *Ethics, Economics, and the Law* edited by J. Roland Pennock and John W. Chapman. New York, NY: New York University Press, 1982.

—. *Justice as Impartiality*. Oxford: Oxford University Press, 1995.

Benhabib, Seyla. *Situating the Self: Gender, Community, and Postmodernism in Contemporary Ethics*. New York, NY: Routledge, 1992.

Carens, Joseph H. *Culture, Citizenship, and Community: A Contextual Exploration of Justice as Evenhandedness*. Oxford: Oxford University Press, 2000.

Fraser, Nancy. *Justice Interruptus: Critical Reflections on the "Postsocialist" Condition*. New York, NY: Routledge, 1997.

Freeman, Samuel (editor). *The Cambridge Companion to Rawls*. Cambridge: Cambridge University Press, 2003.

Friedman, Marilyn. *What are Friends For? Feminist Perspectives on Personal Relationships and Moral Theory*. Ithaca, NY: Cornell University Press, 1993.

Held, Virginia. *Justice and Care: Essential Readings in Feminist Ethics*. Boulder, CO: Westview Press, 1995.

Jones, Charles. *Global Justice: Defending Cosmopolitanism*. Oxford: Oxford University Press, 1999.

Kymlicka, Will (editor). *Justice in Political Philosophy*. Aldershot, UK: E. Elgar, 1992.

Li, Xiaorong. "A Critique of Rawls's 'Freestanding' Justice." *Journal of Applied Philosophy*, v. 12, no. 3 (1995): 263-71.

Narveson, Jan. *The Libertarian Idea*. Philadelphia, PA: Temple University Press, 1988.

Nielsen, Kai. *Globalization and Justice*. New York, NY: Humanity Books, 2003.

—. "Relativism and Wide Reflective Equilibrium." *The Monist*, v. 76 (1993): 316-32.

Nozick, Robert. *Anarchy, State, and Utopia*. New York, NY: Basic Books, 1974.

Okin, Susan Moller. *Justice, Gender, and the Family*. New York, NY: Basic Books, 1989.

O'Neill, Onora. *Bounds of Justice*. Cambridge: Cambridge University Press, 2000.

Pettit, Philip. *Judging Justice: An Introduction to Contemporary Political Philosophy*. London: Routledge and Kegan Paul, 1980.

Pogge, Thomas. *Realizing Rawls*. Ithaca, NY: Cornell University Press, 1989.

Pogge, Thomas (editor). *Global Justice*. Oxford: Blackwell Publisher, 2001.

Rawls, John. *Justice as Fairness: a Restatement*. Cambridge, MA: Harvard University Press, 2001.

—. *The Law of Peoples: with, The Idea of Public Reason Revisited*. Cambridge, MA: Harvard University Press, 1999.

—. *Political Liberalism*. New York, NY: Columbia University Press, 1996.

Sandel, Michael. *Liberalism and the Limits of Justice*. 2nd edition. Cambridge: Cambridge University Press, 1998.

Solomon, Robert C., and Mark C. Murphy (editors). *What is Justice?: Classic and Contemporary Readings*. New York, NY: Oxford University Press, 1990.

Tan, Kok-Chor. *Toleration, Diversity and Global Justice*. University Park, PA: Pennsylvania State University Press, 2000.

Tronto, Joan. *Moral Boundaries: A Political Argument for an Ethic of Care*. New York, NY: Routledge, 1993.

Walzer, Michael. *Spheres of Justice: A Defense of Pluralism and Equality*. New York, NY: Basic Books, 1983.

Young, Iris Marion. *Justice and the Politics of Difference*. Princeton, NJ: Princeton University Press, 1990.

CHAPTER FOUR: DEMOCRACY

INTRODUCTION

In the final reading in Chapter Two, Jennifer Nedelsky introduced the idea of a tension between democratic processes of majority rule and the rights enshrined in constitutions that "trump" these democratic processes. Democracy is rule by the people, but constitutional rights are viewed as fixed and not revisable by the people. Democracy is a system of decision-making in which everyone is treated as equal with respect to having a say in the structures and policies of their group or state. The right to vote, for example, is itself a liberty right enshrined in many constitutions. We will find out, however, that who gets to participate and decide has been and continues to be shaped by the histories, traditions, and beliefs of peoples, countries, and states.

As with justice, there are competing theories of democracy. One theory holds that democracy means allowing everyone to vote for proposals or for representatives who are then entrusted with making the decisions. On this voting conception, the proposal or representative with the most votes wins. While some take it to be obvious that democracy in the sense of one person-one vote promotes liberty and equality, some argue that this may not be so in practice. On the voting conception, the majority who wins has their say and the minority lack liberty in the sense that they are controlled by the majority. Others object that it is problematic that the only say that citizens have may be at election time, where factors such as advertising, the media, and election manipulation or fraud may influence who wins and gets to make the decisions for all. Some theorists attempt to alleviate the difficulties with the pure voting model of democracy by arguing that features such as mutual discussion, deliberation, participation, and decision-making are central to what constitutes democracy. The idea here is that everyone should participate in making decisions that emerge from a full discussion. On

these models, voting by itself is not sufficient for achieving equality and liberty. Rather, equality and liberty are needed *first* for democracy as deliberation, participation, and public discussion to work properly. The authors in this chapter survey some of these theories and models of democracy, examine the well-known criticism that democracy is a Western construct and concept, and explore issues and problems with the workings of democracy in the contemporary context of globalization.

Recall Rawls's theory of justice from the previous chapter. In his early work, at least, Rawls tends to assume that his principles of justice are those that would be chosen in the hypothetical thought experiment of the original position — no matter who the people are or where they live. As was noted in the previous chapter, one criticism of Rawls's theory of justice emerges from communitarians and feminists who argue that Rawls makes assumptions about what sort of person is behind the veil of ignorance. Does Rawls already assume that people in the original position hold the beliefs and values of a liberal democratic society? If so, does his theory of justice lack proper grounding and have limited applicability in non-liberal or non-Western contexts? These criticisms continue even in the face of revisions that Rawls has made to his theory since 1971.

In his recent work, Rawls admits that his theory of justice applies to a democratic political culture, one in which citizens are already committed to a view of themselves as free and equal and have divergent and conflicting religious, philosophical, and moral beliefs. He takes his principles of justice to be free-standing in that they are not grounded in any religious, philosophical, or moral doctrine. They are chosen in and apply to liberal democratic societies and have their legitimacy and foundation there and not elsewhere. Some have objected that Rawls's admission that his principles of justice emerge from liberal democratic societies weakens his theory because it lacks the foundational arguments that would make it applicable to other cultures. Without a commitment to any comprehensive moral doctrine, Rawls has little to say about why liberty and equality are superior to slavery or subjugation, for example. These critics argue that Rawls's theory of justice needs foundational arguments to provide a firm defense of liberal democratic institutions against totalitarian or authoritarian repression.

The question of foundations for liberal democratic values is taken up by Amy Gutmann in the first reading. Gutmann argues that democracy does not need foundations in the strong sense that it must rest on self-evident truths about human nature, human rights, rationality, or politics. Instead, justifications can be given for why democracies as they currently exist in various non-ideal forms can provide the conditions for human flourishing. She characterizes non-ideal democracies by features such as guarantees of free speech, press, and association; the right to run for political office; the rule of law; and frequent and procedurally fair elections. She argues that because these features enhance human dignity and maximize social welfare, they provide justifications for non-ideal democracies as at least better than non-ideal non-democracies. However, Gutmann acknowledges that this justification does not satisfy the political philosopher's goal of articulating a democratic ideal that can tell us what *kind* of democracy is most justified. She then provides a brief outline of this ideal in her account and defense of deliberative democracy.

In the second reading, Chenyang Li takes China to be a good context for exploring the clash and conflict between democratic and non-democratic values. Li answers the question of whether liberal democratic values of liberty, equality, and pluralism are compatible with values in a strong tradition of Confucianism in China by examining and rejecting attempts by theorists to find compatibilities between democracy and Confucianism. He argues that Confucianism has no place for the concept of rights because there is no need for them in the society Confucius envisioned, where an

emphasis on duty, loyalty, and responsibility places value on paternalism over individual liberty and autonomy. Li argues that defenses of Confucianism without democracy or democracy without Confucianism as well as attempts to integrate the two are all misguided and threaten the integrity of each. Li maintains that both sets of values are worthwhile and desirable and proposes that they co-exist in China in the same way that the different value systems of Confucianism, Taoism, and Buddhism have co-existed in harmony in the lives of many individuals in China.

The third reading by Nadirsyah Hosen examines the perceived conflict between Islamic values and the idea of constitutionalism at the heart of Western democracies. Hosen examines the question of whether the Shari'ah is compatible with Western constitutionalism by surveying the arguments of those who oppose the very idea of Islamic constitutional law. Constitutionalism has been characterized as having features such as government according to the constitution, sovereignty of the people and democratic government, constitutional review, independent judiciary, limited government subject to a bill of individual rights, civilian control of the military, and no or very limited state power to suspend a constitution itself. As thus defined, opponents to the idea of Islamic constitutional law argue that constitutionalism is a Western notion and product. Moreover, they argue that the Shari'ah meets Muslim needs and provides a unique system of government that makes constitutionalism unnecessary.

Hosen reviews and rejects both the fundamentalist and secularist interpretations of the Shari'ah as in tension with constitutionalism. He argues that the Shari'ah is not final and static and can be reformed and amended in line with democracy and constitutionalism. He argues that the Shari'ah's underlying principles of consensus (*ijmā*), elections (*bay'ah*), and broad deliberation (*shūrā*) can and should be a source and inspiration to a constitution that respects democratic principles of rule by the people.

Amartya Sen continues the exploration of whether democracy is a Western construct with limited or no applicability in non-Western contexts. He examines two kinds of objections to the advocacy of democracy worldwide: 1) democracy deflects attention from state control in developing countries where economic and social programs of providing food and jobs are needed, and 2) democracy involves an imposition of Western values and practices on non-Western societies. Sen argues that those defending these objections view democracy too narrowly — as constituted merely by freedom of elections and ballots. Viewing democracy more broadly in terms of being able to participate in public discussions and influence public choice allows us to understand that the roots of democracy go beyond the basic institutions of elections and voting emphasized in Western democracies. Sen retrieves aspects of a broad conception of democracy as involving public reasoning in intellectual heritages in the West as well as in those of China, Japan, East and Southeast Asia, Iran, the Middle East, and Africa. He argues that neglecting the roots and value of public reasoning in non-Western thinking is not only a loss in itself, but it undermines the positive role that democracy could play in the contemporary world if the West did not claim democracy as its own and was not viewed as imposing it on the non-Western world.

In the final reading, Thomas Pogge sheds light on limits to deliberation and participation in a world impacted by factors of economic globalization. Pogge is critical of judgments by Western countries that responsibility for poverty in developing countries rests with the countries themselves and their histories and cultures of spawning incompetent, oppressive, and corrupt governments. While it is true that the eradication of poverty in developing countries depends on changing these features of third world governments and political institutions, Pogge argues that several aspects of the global order and our global economic system actively contribute to the perpetuation of corruption, lack of democracy, and poverty.

First, rules of the global order are shaped through negotiations among governments with large differences in bargaining power and expertise. The affluent states, in other words, use their power to shape the rules of the global economic order in their own favor in a cycle that further strengthens their bargaining power. Second, developing countries suffer the effects of pollution, global warming, and the depletion of natural resources, much of which is caused by developed countries and could be alleviated if developed countries reduced their high consumption patterns. Third, the global order plays an important part in sustaining corruption and oppression in poorer countries by giving international borrowing privileges to any person or group in power, no matter how they got or exercise that power, and providing international resource privileges that allow this person or group to freely dispose of their country's resources. Pogge uses these descriptions of global systemic factors to undermine the belief that the causes of severe poverty are indigenous to developing countries. He ends by suggesting policies for enhancing democratic procedures that can modify and eliminate the detrimental effects of the global economic order and help establish democratic structures that serve the needs of a developing country's present and future people rather than the interests of authoritarian rulers and corrupt elites.

DEMOCRACY, PHILOSOPHY, AND JUSTIFICATION

Amy Gutmann

Amy Gutmann is President of the University of Pennsylvania. She was formerly the Laurance S. Rocke-feller University Professor of Politics, Director of the University Center for Human Values, and Provost at Princeton University. She is the author of Identity in Democracy *(2003) and* Democratic Education *(revised edition, 1999); co-author with Dennis Thompson of* Why Deliberative Democracy? *(2004) and* Democracy and Disagreement *(1996); and co-author with Anthony Appiah of* Color Conscious: The Political Morality of Race *(1996).*

Gutmann answers the question "does democracy need foundations?" by clarifying what is meant by both democracy and foundations. She argues that if we think of democracy in non-ideal terms as those political institutions characterized by features such as free speech, the right to vote, competitive elections, and the rule of law, there is no need for foundations in the strong sense of reliance on self-evident truths about human nature, human rights, or rationality. Gutmann defends a version of ideal democracy that she refers to as deliberative democracy, one that is based on moral and political argument and justification and is neither foundationalist nor anti-foundationalist.

Does democracy need foundations? We cannot adequately answer the foundationalist question without first asking how democracy is best defended. When we answer this question, however, the foundational question becomes moot. Democracy needs justifications, not foundations — at least, not foundations in the strict sense suggested by Richard Rorty and other antifoundationalists. If we cannot justify democracy, then neither can we know what kind of democracy is worth defending. If we can justify democracy, then we should not worry about whether our justification is, in the strict sense, foundationalist. Justifications need not be foundationalist or antifoundationalist. I will first suggest some reasons why this is so, and then briefly sketch a justification of deliberative democracy that is neither foundationalist nor antifoundationalist.

Foundationalism in political philosophy, if it is not to be trivially identified with any reason-giving defense of a conception of politics, is the claim that justification must rest upon truths about human nature, human rights, rationality, or politics that are self-evident, rationally incontestable, or axiomatic. Does an adequate theoretical defense of democracy need foundations in this nontrivial sense? Before answering this question, we should be clear not to confuse it with the more practical question of whether actual democracies need to rely upon philosophy in addition to, or instead of, education, elections, legislation, constitutions, and force, if necessary, in order to defend themselves against threats to their well-being that variously come from intolerance, apathy, corruption, and violent aggression. We are rather asking the theoretical question of what it takes to sustain the claim that democracy is a justified (or the most justified) form of government

First, let us consider democracy as it is often understood today to describe an increasingly common set of political institutions the world over, for which Robert Dahl coined the term "polyarchy." Polyarchies, or what we might call non-ideal democracies, are characterized, at minimum, by guarantees of free political speech, press, association, and equal suffrage for all adults, the right of all adults above a certain age to run for political office, the rule of law, and frequent, competitive elections that are procedurally fair. How can non-ideal democracy best justify itself against undemocratic forms of government?

Democracy, Winston Churchill noted, is the worst form of government except all the others. He was referring to actual, nonideal democracies and comparing them to nonideal nondemocracies. Many people today, many of whom were raised in nondemocratic societies, defend nonideal democracy on Churchillian grounds even though their nascent democratic governments are falling far short of satisfying many of their basic needs. Why are nonideal democracies better than their nonideal alternatives? Political philosophers have offered several practically compatible (yet theoretically distinct) reasons, the first having to do with the centrality of democratic liberties to human dignity, the second with the instrumental value of democratic liberties in resisting political tyranny, and the third connecting democratic liberties with the maximization of social welfare. The moral and intellectual force of these (contestable) reasons notwithstanding, the Churchillian defense of democracy is largely negative and therefore uninspiring to many citizens of nonideal democracies who take for granted the basic accomplishments of democratic government and are aspiring for something more. The Churchillian defense of nonideal democracy is also doubly inadequate to the aspirations of political philosophy. Because it stops short of articulating a full-fledged democratic ideal, it does not expect enough of democracy and also fails to tell us what kind of democracy is most justified. It therefore provides only a partial defense of even nonideal democracy.

Nonetheless, to say that nonideal democracy is better than the available nonideal alternatives is to say something practically and theoretically important. The Churchillian defense offers some insight into why, despite the failures of every existing democratic government to secure for all its citizens some basic goods such as an adequate income, employment, health care, and education, most citizens of nonideal democracies, including many who are deprived of these basic goods, support them over their undemocratic alternatives.

Notice that the Churchillian defense of democracy is neither foundational nor antifoundational. It is agnostic on the question of whether democracy rests on certain rationally undeniable facts about human nature and politics. (We could say the defense is foundational in the loose sense of offering reasons for defending nonideal democracies against their undemocratic alternatives but this is to confuse foundationalism with reasonableness. Antifoundationalists do not deny the need to give reasons in defense of democracy against undemocratic — or less democratic — alternatives.) Despite its lack of what we might call Cartesian foundations, the Churchillian defense of democracy is as salient in today's world as it was in Churchill's and its force is not limited to any particular culture, or a few idiosyncratic ones.

Why should anyone think that the Churchillian position constitutes even a partial justification of nonideal democracy, as opposed to an indication of what "we democrats" just happen (without any reason) to believe in by virtue of our socialization? Ordinary people, not only political philosophers, think about whether and why they should support nonideal democratic governments rather than undemocratic ones. The theoretical question of whether nonideal democracy is justified is typically connected to a practical question: is this nonideal democracy deserving of support? Now, what else could justify the precarious support for democracy among former subjects of Soviet-style communism but the comparative advantage of nonideal democratic governments over nonideal autocratic governments? And what else but the value of civil and political liberties could account for the moral strength of nonideal democracy? The short-run economic benefits of democracy have been conspicuous by their absence. The claim that the long-run benefits of democracy outweigh its short-term costs is doubly dubious, first for sacrificing the well-being of present people for future ones, and second for its unwarranted confidence in such long-term social forecasting and calculating. Democracy needs to be justified to the people who are bound by its practices and policies. Long-term benefits may be there; yet without the basic liberties that democracy brings, those benefits would be insufficient to justify nonideal democracies to people here and now.

Consider this typical story about the extraordinary economic problems facing the new Baltic republics, featured on the front page of the *New York Times*, April 10, 1993. This story happened to be about Lithuania, whose citizens had experienced over the past year one of the worst economic situations of their lifetimes. Inflation in consumer goods was over 600 percent, and inflation in agricultural products over 700 percent. Industrial output had declined over 50 percent, and new housing had declined by over 20 percent. Unemployment was estimated at 200,000 (out of 3.7 million), an enormous shock to a citizenry completely unaccustomed to worrying about job security. Not surprisingly, Lithuanian citizens have voted out of office the more liberal president (Landsbergis) and voted in a former communist, newly turned social democratic president (Brazauskas). What is surprising is that they did not vote for a return to authoritarian rule.

The story featured an ordinary citizen, Rimantas Pirmaitis, who had, along with many of his compatriots, joined the protests of 1989-90 that led to Lithuania's democratization and independence from Soviet rule. Pirmaitis was employed under the communist regime as a construction engineer, where he made a decent living. But under the new democracy he has been reduced to selling flowers from a street stand in central Vilnius to support his family. He nonetheless remains a democrat, notwithstanding runaway inflation. "But we are past the time for marches and anthems," he says. "What we need now is something real, something we can eat and touch."

Were it not the case that the civil and political liberties of a democratic society are as real as economic benefits, the belief in a *democratic* Lithuania would be considerably less defensible. Although liberties are inedible and untouchable, they are not always overlooked by people who are

struggling to survive. An appreciation of basic freedoms and their centrality to human dignity, self-respect, and well-being often makes nonideal democracy both apparently and really better than its alternatives. An understanding of the degrading experience of people living under the undemocratic alternatives to nonideal democracies may be sufficient for a nonfoundationalist defense of nonideal democracy. This defense is distinct from that of an ideal conception of democracy, but the favorable comparison with available nonideal alternatives is a strong defense nonetheless. The comparison provides reasons to people who doubt that democracy is better than the alternatives, as well as to people who are drawn to democracy but wonder why. Although much more may be said in defense of nonideal democracy, this much should suffice to show that justification, at least at the nonideal level, need not be either foundationalist or antifoundationalist to be reasonable, and useful as well.

But political philosophers aspire to something more than the defense of nonideal democracy as we now know it. We try to construct out of our inheritance, and imagine beyond it, a more fully justifiable set of social and political institutions, which we can call democracy without qualification, or at least without neologism. Political philosophers who defend a democratic *ideal* may therefore seem committed to some form of foundationalism. What else but some self-evident or rationally incontrovertible truth could support our claims for an ideal conception of democracy, which would (if democratically instituted) realize the political ideal of collective self-government? How else are we to interpret and defend such an ideal?

Suppose that a fully justified democracy authorizes all adult members of society to share, either directly or through their accountable representative, in deliberatively shaping their collective life in a way that is consistent with respecting the basic liberties and opportunities of all individuals. Suppose also that deliberation is the give-and-take of argument in a public form (not necessarily a legislature) that aims at, and results in, provisionally justified decision-making, decisions that are respectful of the basic liberties and opportunities of all members of society. Deliberation also helps shape our understanding of basic opportunities and liberties. But if the results of democratic deliberation are to be provisionally justified, they must respect the basic liberties and opportunities of all citizens on some reasonable understanding. The arguments offered in a public forum also should be reasonable by some public standard. Deliberation at various levels of government and in different political arenas is, as far as I can discern, the most legitimate means of settling principled conflicts over social justice, conflicts that are inescapable in any free society.

This is an abbreviated outline of one interpretation of deliberative democracy. An interpretation of deliberative democracy as a political ideal, suitably expanded and more fully defended, is bound not only to be incomplete and controversial but also to be reasonably contested. Prominent among its democratic contesters are what might be called populist democracy, participatory democracy, perfectionist liberal democracy, and ultra constitutionalist democracy. Deliberative democracy has two important advantages over these and other democratic alternatives that bear on the foundationalist question.

The first advantage of deliberative democracy is its recognition of the provisional nature of justification in politics. The empirical and moral understandings of citizens change not only over time and social space but also by virtue of deliberative interchange, the give-and-take of sometimes complementary, often conflicting, political insights and arguments (including conflicts over what counts as the political realm). Deliberative democracy therefore leaves a lot of room for "difference." Differences in practices and policies that result from deliberating among an inclusive citizenry are democratically legitimate, even if no one knows whether they are just in the strict foundational sense. Whether or not foundational claims are metaphysically possible is a moot point as far as the ideal of deliberative democratic politics is concerned. The alternative is not antifoundationalism, but fairly conducted collective deliberations that yield provisionally justified practices and policies.

A second significant advantage of deliberative democracy is its compatibility with some other conceptions of democracy, insofar as these conceptions result from democratic deliberations. Upon deliberation, citizens may decide to institute some form of perfectionist democracy. But if they decide to reject perfectionist policies, then what can philosophy divorced from democratic deliberation say in their favor? Perfectionist critics can say that the standpoint of deliberative democracy is not neutral among democratic (or undemocratic) alternatives. Of course it is not, and it need not claim to be. Critics can also say that deliberative democracy lacks incontestable foundations. Of course it does. There is neither a neutral substitute for foundationalism, as some liberal philosophers have claimed, nor a foundationalist substitute for democracy, as some perfectionist philosophers have suggested.

Defenders of deliberative democracy can offer only a moral and political argument (with the hope that it catches on). The argument, in brief, might be that the legitimate exercise of political authority requires justification to those people who are bound by it, and decision-making by deliberation among free and equal citizens is the most defensible justification anyone has to offer for provisionally settling controversial issues. This justification, once elaborated, would be compatible with respecting many moral and cultural differences within and across societies. If citizens deliberatively decide to constitute themselves as a participatory or perfectionist liberal democracy, then those forms of democracy are also provisionally justified, provided they respect the basic liberties and opportunities of all individuals and leave citizens free to deliberate in the future. (The freedom to deliberate in the future is necessary to ensure that provisional justifications are not treated as foundationalist truths.)

This defense of deliberative democracy is not an example of either foundationalism or antifoundationalism. Foundationalism tells us that we must defend democracy on the basis of human nature, natural rights, or self-evident reason; antifoundationalism tells us that reason has nothing to do with defending democracy.

Both perspectives presuppose a metaphysical truth without warrant.

The foundationalist defense, sometimes attributed to Aristotle, bases deliberative democracy on an alleged truth about human nature, that human beings are rational, deliberative animals. According to this defense, only a deliberative democracy expresses the true, rational nature of individuals and offers all people the opportunity to perfect their natures through public deliberation. Every other form of government falls short of this foundational standard, because other forms of government encourage only one or a few people to deliberate on political questions, whereas all human beings are by nature deliberative beings in political as well as personal realms. Is this true? Are all people natural deliberators in politics? Maybe so, maybe not. We really do not know. The claim that people are by their very nature deliberative beings in the strong sense claimed by some Aristotelians is not self-evidently true (or false). It is subject to reasonable doubt (and defense). Far from being axiomatic, such substantive claims about human nature are reasonably contestable, and contested. This foundationalist defense of deliberative democracy does not satisfy foundationalist standards; its claims about human nature are not self-evident, rationally incontestable, or axiomatic. The claim that human beings are natural deliberators is as subject to reasonable doubt as nonfoundationalist claims about democracy. Saying that democracy is grounded in human nature cannot therefore substitute for showing that democracy gives actual people something that is valuable to them, where what is valuable includes a wide range of liberties and opportunities as well as economic well-being.

Saying that democracy needs no foundations does not leave us with anything more than a critical stance toward foundationalists, who claim or expect too much from philosophical argument. To show that democracy does not need foundations does not tell us what we need to say in its defense. We need to say something more than what is suggested by the strong antifoundationalist view, which runs roughly as follows: if we, the members of a democratic cultural community, believe in democracy happens not to satisfy the best philosophical conception of human nature or basic human needs, then so much the worse for philosophical justifications of democracy. I do not see how our widely shared belief in democracy can suffice to justify imposing a democratic government on disbelieving minorities. We need to say something to them about the political virtues of democracy. Besides, most of us believe in democracy, and in a particular kind of democracy, because we think there are good reasons to defend it against the alternatives. Our reasons will of course come from within some social understandings, but this is not to say that our reasons are therefore unnecessary, or merely a reflection of our upbringing about which we cannot critically reflect. "Our" believing in democracy is not a substitute for our offering arguments in favor of some conception of democracy. Nor is our offering good arguments a substitute for our believing in democracy. The truth in antifoundationalism is that much of what we say is going to be contestable, subject to reasonable doubt. If we take such doubt to be devastating of the philosophical case for democracy then we capitulate to critics of democracy without good cause.

All anyone can do is try to address the doubt. Few political philosophers actually argue that democracy can be defensibly dissociated from a form of deliberative self-government that secures the basic liberties and opportunities of all members of society. Most neglect the importance of deliberation. The neglect of deliberation is untenable because the defense of democracy against traditional hierarchy, enlightened autocracy, liberal perfectionism, ultraconstitutionalism, and other credible political alternatives is weakened to the extent that we imagine a democracy that does not collectively deliberate over controversial matters of political importance. Briefly and roughly, one might say that populist democracy reduces citizenship to formal political rights and majoritarian procedures; participatory democracy not only takes too many meetings but also disrespects those people who would, quite reasonably, rather be represented than represent themselves; ultraconstitutionalism identifies justice with a comprehensive set of substantive principles, as if someone could design a government that institutes the comprehensive set of just policies, known prior to deliberative decision-making among citizens or their accountable representatives.

Suppose that, with regard to the many politically controversial matters that divide democratic societies, some philosophers think that they know what is just and do not need to deliberate with other citizens who see things differently in order to figure out what is just. It is quite another question, however, as to whether, in the absence of collective deliberation, their supposedly just policies, which are meant to be socially binding, can be justified to all those other people who are to be bound by them. And it is yet another question as to how a society, without deliberating, can distinguish the philosopher who really knows what is just from all those who are no less convinced that they know, but do not.

If all foundationalists claim is that democracy can be defended by publicly accessible reasons, then we are (almost) all foundationalist. If all antifoundationalists claim is that democracy cannot be deduced from self-evident truths, then we are (almost) all antifoundationalists. But if some kind of deliberative democracy is defensible, then democracy does not need either foundationalism or antifoundationalism. It needs to be liberated from this dead-end debate. Political philosophers can contribute more to both political philosophy and democracy when we stop metatheorizing and start arguing about the substantive problems that animate contemporary politics, including the continually contested question of what *kind* of democracy is most defensible.

CONFUCIAN VALUE AND DEMOCRATIC VALUE

Chenyang Li

Chenyang Li teaches in and is currently Chair of the Department of Philosophy at Central Washington University. He has published articles in the areas of metaphysics, philosophy of language, and comparative philosophy. He is the author of The Tao Encounters the West: Explorations in Comparative Philosophy *(1999) and editor of* The Sage and the Second Sex: Confucianism, Ethics, and Gender *(2000).*

Li uses the perceived clash between democracy and Confucianism in China as an opportunity to examine the values underlying each and to explore the possibility of their mutual co-existence. He rejects various theoretical attempts to find compatibilities between democracy and Confucianism and argues that the values associated with each make them inherently incompatible. He further rejects calls for replacing Confucian beliefs and values with democratic ones. Instead, Li argues that China needs both democratic and Confucian values and that Confucianism and democracy can and should co-exist independently in China.

Introduction

Samuel P. Huntington asserts that the world is now entering an age of "the clash of civilizations."[1] Specifically, the clash is between democratic Western civilizations and undemocratic civilizations in the rest of the world, Confucian and Islamic civilizations in particular. Huntington also suggests that in order for democracy to take roots in a Confucian society, undemocratic elements in Confucianism must be superseded by democratic elements.[2] The purpose of this essay is to examine the future relationship between democracy and Confucianism in the part of the world where they are most likely to clash, namely China.

1. What Democracy Is and What China Needs

The word "democracy" has been used in so many ways that people today often disagree about exactly what it means. Many controversies about democracy concern whether it is merely a procedural method for political decisions or something

more substantive that has value content.[3] Joseph Schumpeter, for example, has proposed as a minimal definition of democracy:

> the democratic method is that institutional arrangement for arriving at political decisions in which individuals acquire the power to decide by means of a competitive struggle for the people's vote.[4]

His use of "democratic method," instead of "democracy," indicates that he takes democracy primarily as a procedural form.

Francis Fukuyama has recently argued that the consolidation of democracy must occur on four levels: ideology, institutions, civil society, and finally, culture. He regards culture as the "deepest level" of democracy.[5] Many people would agree with Fukuyama in as much as democracy penetrates culture and is therefore value-loaded. Jürgen Domes, for instance, also defines democracy primarily as a value-loaded political system. In addition to its formal dimension, Domes characterizes democracy specifically by three principles: liberty, equality, and pluralism.[6] This is sometimes said to characterize liberal democracy.

Without a context, it makes little sense to ask whose definition is right. The question we should ask here is, what kind of democracy does China need? I believe the answer is the kind of democracy with the values of individual liberty, equality, and pluralism. These values, as I will show, make the clash between democracy and Confucianism possible. Confucianism is no longer an institutional arrangement, and such a clash cannot take place anywhere but on the dimension of value.

Without the values of individual liberty, equality, and pluralism, democracy as a mere procedure is merely a technique of formality. This technique has been and continues to be misused in China. Unless we make explicit the values found in democracy, the misuse is likely to continue. For example, within the Chinese Communist Party (CCP), democracy as a voting procedure has been practiced. Missing, however, is the value of individual liberty. Within the CCP, members can vote, but the party leadership demands absolute loyalty. The value of loyalty takes the place of individual liberty in the current mainland Chinese version of democracy. Even when the voting procedure is carried through, the outcome has almost always been a unanimous decision. In *Democracy in America* Alexis de Tocqueville wrote:

> if a democratic republic, similar to that of the United States, were ever founded in a country where the power of a single individual had previously subsisted, and the effects of a centralized administration had sunk deep into the habits and the laws of the people, I do not hesitate to assert, that in that country a more insufferable despotism would prevail than any which now exists in the monarchical states of Europe; or indeed than any which could be found on this side of the confines of Asia.[7]

When democracy is taken to be merely a voting procedure, it can be counterproductive in countries like China where people have formed the habits of following a centralized administration which they

may have mistakenly identified as representing their own interest and to which they habitually render unconditional loyalty. Unless individual liberty is valued, voters will not realize that they ought to feel free in choosing their representatives; and unless voters can freely choose to vote for their candidates, there cannot be true democracy. Here "free choice" does not merely mean choice without external coercion. It also means choosing candidates on the basis of individual liberty. Imagine a people in whom loyalty to their leader is such an overwhelming value that no matter what happens they will always cast their votes for their own leader. Such a so-called democracy would be no better than a tyranny. This form of government is not worth fighting for, except perhaps as a mere preliminary step from totalitarianism to real democracy. What China needs is democracy with the value of individual liberty, equality, and pluralism.[8]

While acknowledging that democracy has institutional forms, I will focus on democracy on a cultural level and consider democracy mainly as a value system which is centered on the rights of individual liberty and equality. In that value system, pluralism is also an important element. If we recognize that democracy is value-loaded, then no matter how we think about democracy and Confucianism, we have to think about how values from both sides interact.[9]

2. Is Confucianism Democratic?

Among influential Confucian thinkers Mencius had a thought which is probably closest to one that might be considered democratic and is most often cited by those looking for democratic elements in traditional Chinese thought.[10] Mencius said: "(In a state) the people are the most important; the spirits of the land and grain (guardians of territory) are the next; the ruler is of slight importance."[11] This thought is often called the thought if *min-ben*, or people-rootedness. Some people think this is the model for Chinese democracy. For example, Sun Yat-sen said that Confucius and Mencius more than two thousand years ago already advocated democracy because they advocated the common good and emphasized the importance of the people.[12]

However, Mencius' thought is not democracy as defined by individual liberty and equality. First of all, Mencius' thought does not exclude having a king as the sole decision-maker for social affairs. As Shu-hsien Liu properly pointed out, Mencius' idea of people-rootedness and the idea of having a good king mutually depend on each other.[13] When a king makes a decision, he should consider the well-being of the people first.[14] It would be unreasonable if we were to look for a form of government without a king in Mencius. The point here is that Mencius' form of government is what Lin Yutang has called "parental government."[15] It requires a king to treat people as he treats his children *ai min ru zi*. But even though a king considers the well-being of the people first, the form of government is not democratic. For even if a parent has the children's well-being in mind, the parent is the sole decision-maker. As the decision-making power of a parent does not come from children, a king's power comes from Heaven, not from popular free choice. In this picture there is no room for individual liberty and equality, both of which are essential for democracy. This kind of government is at most, in the phrasing of Lincoln, "for the people." It is highly questionable whether it is "of the people." It is clearly not "by the people."

Secondly, the question of whose well-being should be put first has little to do with democracy. A dictator might put the people's well-being first. The Confucian concept of government is government by gentlemen and governance by moral force. But gentlemen may be mistaken in believing that they make decisions on behalf of the people and in their best interests; or they may really represent the best interests of the people, without the people, due to lack of knowledge or wisdom, wanting them to do so. In each case the Confucian form of government would not be democratic.

Among prominent classic Confucian philosophers, Mencius' thought is considered the closest to the idea of democracy.[16] If his idea is not that of real democracy, we can conclude that democracy is not an influential value in traditional Confucianism.

While there may be practical reasons for Confucians today to make Confucianism look democratic, the claim that Confucianism is democratic is seriously flawed and, as I will show later, the move to make Confucianism democratic is misguided.

3. Are Confucianism and Democracy Compatible?

If democracy has not been at the heart of traditional Chinese culture, are democracy and Confucianism compatible? Liang Shu-ming for example, thought that there is no room in Chinese culture for democracy. He wrote that, "it is not that China has not entered democracy, it is rather that China cannot enter democracy."[17] He believed that traditional Chinese value systems alone provide a solid foundation for a good civil society. Mou Tsung-san, a prominent contemporary New-Confucian, sees the inadequacy of traditional Confucianism and believes that through a transformation of the Confucian moral subjectivity into a cognitive subjectivity, Confucianism will provide an adequate foundation for democracy. But it is not clear how such a transformation can actually take place.[18] Mou includes liberty, equality, and human rights in democracy.[19] It is doubtful that these values can be integrated into Confucianism. Shu-hsien Liu, in contrast, sees many difficulties in grafting democracy onto Confucianism and maintains that unless politics is separated from morals, democracy will not find a home in China.[20] Liu is certainly right in thinking that democracy must take the political realm as a social institution. But what about the value content of democracy? If democratic values are to enter the culture, then we cannot ignore the relationship between democratic values and Confucian values.

There are fundamentally conflicting values between democracy and Confucianism. Democracy, as we have seen, presupposes the concept of right. A democratic society is one in which individual rights are recognized and respected. This requires the recognition that some basic rights of individuals are inalienable. Confucianism, at least in the traditional form, has no place for the concept of rights.[21] It is, however, a serious mistake to think that Confucius left out the concept of rights by negligence. In the ideal society that Confucius envisioned, there is just supposed to be no need for rights. On the issue of whether human nature is good or bad, rights-based theories typically lean toward the view that human nature is bad or flawed. Rights are viewed as the basis for individuals to stand up for themselves. When others impose on someone, the person can stand on a right. The Confucian social ideal is one of *jen*, which signifies humanity, compassion, and benevolence. Unlike rights-based social theories, which tend to regulate society by giving weapons to the weak to protect themselves, Confucian theory promotes the view that *jen* regulates society and protects the weak by placing moral restraints on the strong and powerful. If all people are to embody *jen* as Confucius wished, no one would inflict pain on others unjustly and everyone would be taken care of.

In Confucianism the primary concern for individuals has to do with duty, not liberty. The Confucian motto is "to return to the observance of the rites through overcoming the self constitutes benevolence (*jen*)."[22] Overcoming ourselves implies suppressing our desires of self-interest, including the desire for individual liberty. For Confucians the first order of a person's social life concerns family life, where liberty is typically not a primary concern.[23] In a family model of society, people are defined by their social roles that come with responsibilities. In Confucianism responsibilities override liberty.

Closely connected to duty is the Confucian notion of loyalty (*zhong*). Loyalty is not only a virtue of the subject to the ruler, but also a virtue among people in general. Replying to Fan Chi's question on the meaning of *jen*, Confucius said: "Be respectful in private life, be serious (*ching*) in handling affairs, and be loyal in dealing with others."[24] In a broad sense, a child's filial piety to parents and trust between friends are also forms of loyalty. Loyalty implies being bound to other people. As long as people have to be loyal to others, they are not really free in the liberal sense. Thus, there is an essential tension between loyalty and liberty as two values. Of course someone can

freely *choose* to be loyal. But that does not mean that liberty and loyalty, as primary virtues, point in the same direction. Someone can freely choose to be a slave too.

Confucian loyalty becomes even more binding when it is coupled with another cardinal Confucian value, *yi*. Usually translated in English as "righteousness," *yi* has more than one meaning. In a primary sense, *yi* requires that we do not abandon friends when they are in trouble or in need of our help and that we do not let friends down even under extreme circumstances. Heavy emphasis on loyalty and *yi* as central Confucian virtues can be seen throughout history. For instance, in 1948 after Chiang Kai-shek was forced to resign from the presidency of the Republic of China, he still had almost full control of the government. The acting president, Li Tsung-jen, formally in the post, was simply unable to perform his duties without having his own people in the government. A main reason for this was that people in the government had an overwhelmingly strong sense of duty of loyalty to Chiang. The kind of loyalty he felt is almost incomprehensible to many Westerners. In contrast a democratic society such as the United States characteristically lacks for loyalty. Voters are willing to readily withdraw their support from a leader and turn to someone else at almost any time. Elected officials simply cannot count on loyalty from their voters.

As we have seen, a fundamental value for democracy is equality, whereas in Confucianism equality receives only minimal recognition. In Confucianism, while people may have equal opportunities for laboring through the role of an obedient young person to become a respected old person, there is little hope for submissive ministers to rule. Confucians believe that we are what we make ourselves to be. While everyone has the potential to make themselves a sage or superior person (*jun zi*), in practice because people are inevitably at different stages of this process, they are not on the same footing. Therefore they are not equal. To add the value of equality to Confucianism would inevitably undermine the Confucian ideal of superior person which is at its core.

Confucianism is characteristically paternalistic.

Paternalism may be seen as a necessary consequence of the lack of equality within the tradition,
a natural extension from the concept of *jen*, and a
corollary of the Confucian ideal of meritocracy.
Confucius said: "the character of a ruler (*jun zi*) is
like wind and that of the people is like grass. In
whatever direction the wind blows, the grass
always bends."[25] Mencius advocated that those
who use their minds should rule those who use
their muscles.[26] A cardinal Confucian virtue for
the able and wise is to direct and take care of the
less able and wise. For example, it is the
inescapable duty of Confucian intellectuals to
speak on behalf of the masses. In contrast, in
democracy, the concepts of liberty and individual
rights assure that individuals are entitled to make
choices for themselves even if they are wrong or
unwise.[27] For that, Confucianism leaves little
room. In Confucianism, under the name of
common good, paternalism prevails over individual liberty and individual autonomy.

Confucians place a strong value on unity (*da yi
tong*), not plurality. "Unity" here means not only
political and territorial unity, but also unity in
thought and ideology.[28] Confucians place paramount importance on following the way of the
Chou dynasty and thereby excluded other
options.[29] While Mencius believed that the only
way to settle the empire was through unity, Xun Zi
advocated the idea of using a unitary principle in
deciding world-affairs. The Confucian classic *Li Ji*
states: "Today throughout the empire carts all have
wheels with the same gauge; all writing is with the
same character; and for conduct there exist the
same rules."[30] This is stated with enthusiastic
approval. The Kung-Yang School of Confucianism
almost took unity to be the only manifestation of
Tao or the Way. In this tradition pluralism has no
place.

The problem between Confucian and democratic values is that both sets of values are worthwhile. On the one hand, such democratic values as
liberty, equality, and pluralism are desirable; and
on the other, so are Confucian values like the
family, duty loyalty, and unity. Confucian values
are as cherishable as democratic values. Traditional Confucian virtues such as loyalty, filial

piety, paternalism, and unity are good values and
ought to be retained. Just because Confucian
virtues are in conflict with some democratic
values, that does not mean they are less good or
less valuable. The real strength of Confucianism is
not in being or becoming democratic, but in the
traditional virtues that are not democratic. It is a
simple-minded fallacious inference that, since
democracy is good, anything that is undemocratic
must be bad. An argument can be made that in the
United States and throughout the democratic West,
healthy society has been threatened precisely by
the diminishing of traditional values similar to
these undemocratic Confucian values. Scholars
like Samuel Huntington have made much the same
mistake in thinking that because democratic values
are good, undemocratic or non-democratic Confucian values must be abandoned or superseded.

At this historically critical and conceptually per-
plexing point, where ought China to go? Or, as the
Confucian would ask, what ought Chinese intellectuals to advocate?

4. Democracy as an Independent Value System in China

Since Confucianism is the predominant value
system in China and is not compatible with democracy in one integrated value system, will the two
value systems clash with one another as democracy enters China? There are at least four possible
answers to this question.

Let us call the first answer "Confucianism but
not democracy." Among its proponents, besides
those outrightly rejecting democracy, I include
people who would want China to have minimal
democracy, or democracy without pluralism or
rights to individual liberty and equality. Lian Shu-
ming outrightly rejected democracy. Recently
Western scholars such as Henry Rosemont, Jr. also
have appeared to favor the alternative of minimal
democracy in China.[31] Yet since the May Fourth
Movement of 1919 some people have chosen the
opposing view of complete Westernization in
China. Westernization may include democratization. Therefore this view may be called "democracy but not Confucianism."

Samuel Huntington provides a third answer. Pointing out the impending clash between democracy and some traditional culture in some parts of the world, Huntington writes:

> Great historic cultural traditions, such as Islam and Confucianism, are highly complex bodies of ideas, beliefs, doctrines, assumptions, writings, and behavior patterns. Any major culture, including even Confucianism, has some elements that are compatible with democracy, just as Protestantism and Catholicism have elements that are clearly undemocratic. Confucian democracy may be a contradiction in terms, but democracy in a Confucian society need not be. The question is: What elements in Islam and Confucianism are favorable to democracy, and how and under what circumstances can these supersede the undemocratic elements in those cultural traditions?[32]

Huntington is evidently applying a Western hierarchical model of thinking here. For him, Confucianism can survive democratization by superseding or abandoning its undemocratic values. Admittedly, this option is not entirely impossible, just as a China with only residual Confucian values is not entirely impossible. But is that too great a price for Confucianism to pay? Can Confucianism do better than that?

I propose a fourth answer: that Confucianism and democracy independently co-exist in China. I believe that China needs both democratic and Confucian values. Because of essential tensions between democratic values and some undemocratic Confucian values, the two value systems cannot be integrated into a single system without undermining their integrity. Therefore the only way out has to be for democracy to exist in China independently of Confucianism. Chinese should not pursue a single integrated system of values, whether it is called "democratic Confucianism" or "Confucian democracy."

Because of the tensions between democratic values and some undemocratic Confucian values, the two sets of values cannot be integrated into one coherent value system without substantially sacri-

ficing either democratic or Confucian values. Unfortunately some New-Confucians try to do just that. Any attempt to make Confucianism democratic will only make it nondescript. As a value system, Confucianism is not unchangeable. It has changed in many ways since Confucius' time, and it needs to change further. To some extent the vitality of Confucianism lies in its potentialities for change. But it does have some elements which are so central to Confucianism that it cannot survive substantially without them. Features like its emphasis on the family, filial piety, and self-cultivation and self-constraint are an indispensable part of Confucianism. Since Confucian emphases lead away from individual liberty and equality, if the emphases were to shift, how Confucian would a democratic Confucianism be? Any attempt to democratize Confucianism by superseding its traditional values would jeopardize the integrity of Confucianism. This kind of integration, if applied to all the non-Western world, would indeed lead to "the end of history."[33]

China should become democratic and retain its Confucian heritage. The co-existence of two value systems cannot be that of institutional Confucianism with democracy as a social institution. Confucianism as a social institution no longer exists. As value systems, democracy and Confucianism may influence each other, even as they remain independent. Confucianism and democracy may co-exist in two ways. Some people are more Confucian than democratic, and value Confucian values more than democratic values, while others are more democratic than Confucian, and value democratic values more than Confucian values. Perhaps more important, the values of Confucianism and democracy may co-exist in the same individual. Various values that are not consistent with each other may be worth pursuing. Where that is the case, we need to achieve a delicate balance among them.

History hints at how to balance the values. The three major existing value systems in China, Confucianism, Taoism, and Buddhism, have co-existed for a long time. As Wing-Tsit Chan observed: "most Chinese follow the three systems of Confucianism, Taoism, and Buddhism, and usually take

a multiple approach to things."[34] Tao Yuanming
was a Taoist and a Confucian at the same time; the
so-called last Confucian, Liang Shu-ming,
remained a Buddhist throughout his life.

Thinking is not a linear process that always
follows a consistent pattern. In the West, people
tend to overlook this by overemphasizing a unitary
rationality. People have different values, desires,
and needs which can be alternately pursued. A
Confucian scholar once said that Buddhism is like
floating on the water, drifting wherever the current
takes you, and Confucianism is like having a
rudder in the boat to guide it in a certain direction.
This analogy was meant to show the advantage of
Confucianism over Buddhism. But if we read it
from a different perspective, we can find new
meanings. Is it always so bad to drift along the
current? Perhaps it is better to drift for a while
before using the rudder again. Sometimes it may
be better to follow both ways at different times.
Reading the analogy this way may help us understand how someone can adopt Confucianism along
with Buddhism.[35]

Democracy may enter China similarly. The Confucian, the Taoist, and the Buddhist, who have
been engaged in a dialogue for an extended period
of time, may invite another participant, the democrat, to join them. Then we will see the four different value systems side by side. The primary characteristic of the dialogue should be one of
harmony. When one party is too loud, it is time to
shift attention to another party. For instance, the
concept of rights should be voiced when there is
too much emphasis on paternalism and the paternalistic practice has become oppressive; but Confucianism, Taoism, and perhaps Buddhism should
be voiced when right-based talk has aroused too
much individualism. Thus, despite tensions
between Confucianism and democracy, the four
systems can nevertheless keep themselves in
balance and harmony in the same land.

Author's Note

An earlier version of this paper was presented at
the Seventh East-West Philosophers' conference at
the East-West Center and the University of Hawaii.

I would like to thank Joel Kupperman, Charles
Hayford, Craig Ihara, Ira Smolensky, Walter
Benesch, Ruiping Fan, and Qingjie Wang for
reading previous drafts of the paper, and the
Midwest Faculty Seminar, the Center for East
Asian Studies of the University of Chicago, the
Center of Chinese studies of the University of
Michigan, and Monmouth College for their gener-
ous support.

NOTES

1. Samuel P. Huntington, "The clash of civilizations,"
   Foreign Affairs, 72:3 (Summer 1993), pp. 22-49.

2. *Ibid.*

3. For different versions of democracy, see C. B.
   Macpherson, *The Real World of Democracy* (New
   York: Oxford University Press, 1972).

4. Joseph A. Schumpeter, *Capitalism, Socialism, and
   Democracy*, 2nd ed. (New York: Harper, 1947), p.
   269.

5. Francis Fukuyama, "The primacy of culture,"
   Journal of Democracy, 6:1 (January 1995), pp. 7-
   14.

6. Jürgen Domes, "China's Modernization and the
   Doctrine of Democracy," in *Sun Yat-Sen's Doctrine
   in the Modern World,* ed. Chu-yuan Cheng
   (Boulder, Colo.: Westview Press, 1989), pp. 202-
   224.

7. Alexis de Tocqueville, *Democracy in America,* Vol.
   1 (New York: Schocken Books, 1974), p. 320.

8. For some liberal views on what kind of democracy
   China needs, see Hua Shiping, "All roads lead to
   democracy: A critical analysis of the writings of
   three Chinese reformist intellectuals," *Bulletin of
   Concerned Asian Scholars* (January-March 1992),
   pp. 43-58; and Yu-sheng Lin, "Reluctance to mod-
   ernize: The influence of Confucianism on China's
   search for political modernity," in *Confucianism
   and Modernization: A Symposium*, ed. Joseph P. L.
   Jiang (Taipei, Freedom Council, 1987), pp. 21-33.

9. The relation between democracy on the one hand
   and Taoism and Buddhism on the other is complex
   and cannot be adequately dealt with in this essay.
   Confucianism, the predominant value system in
   Chinese culture, is my main concern here.

10. For the view that Confucianism is democratic, see

Leonard Shihlien Hsü, *The Political Philosophy of Confucianism* (New York: Harper and Row, 1975), particularly Chapter IX: Democracy and Representation, pp. 174-197; Huang Chun-chieh and Wu Kuang-ming, "Taiwan and the Confucian aspiration: Toward the twenty-first century," in *Cultural Change in Postwar Taiwan*, ed. Stevan Harrell and Huang Chun-chieh (Boulder, Colo.: Westview Press, 1994), pp. 69-87; and more recently, Lee Teng-hui, "Chinese culture and political renewal," *The Journal of Democracy*, 6:4 (October 1995), pp. 3-8.

11. Wing-Tsit Chan, *A Source Book in Chinese Philosophy* (Princeton, N. J.: Princeton University Press, 1963), p. 81.

12. Sun Yat-sen, "First lecture on democracy," in *The teachings of the Nation-Founding Father [Guo Fu Yi Jiao]* (Taiwan: Cultural Book Inc., 1984), Section 3. p. 70.

13. Shu-hsien Liu, *Confucianism and Modernization [Ru Jia Si Xiang Yu Xian Dai Hua]*, ed. Jing Hai-feng (Beijing: Chinese Broadcasting and TV Publishing House, 1992), p. 19.

14. Female monarchs were evidently not a possibility at Mencius's time.

15. Lin Yutang, *My Country and My People* (New York: The John Day Company Books, 1939), p. 206.

16. Other liberal Confucian philosophers like Huang Zongxi (1610-1695) were much less influential in the society. For some marginal liberal elements in Confucian tradition, see Wm. Theodore de Barry, *The Liberal Tradition in China* (Hong Kong: The Chinese University Press and New York: Columbia University Press, 1983), and his "Neo-Confucianism and human rights," in *Human Rights and the World's Religions*, ed. Leroy S. Rouner (Notre Dame, Ind.: University of Notre Dame Press, 1988), pp. 183-198.

17. Liang Shu-ming, "Elements of Chinese culture [Zhong Guo Wen Hua Yao Yi]," Chapter 2, Section 5; in *Collected Works of Liang Shu-ming*, vol. 3 (Jinan, China: Shandoing People's Publishing House, 1990), p. 48.

18. Mou Tsung-san, "Preface to *Philosophy of History*," in *Reconstruction of Moral Idealism*, ed.

Zheng Jiadong (Beijing: China Broadcasting TV Publishing House, 1992), pp. 128-132.

19. *Ibid.*, p. 15.

20. Shu-hsien Liu, *op. cit.*, pp. 17-40.

21. See Henry Rosemont Jr., "Why take rights seriously? A Confucian critique," in *Human Rights and the World Religions*, ed. Leroy Rouner (Notre Dame Ind.: University of Notre Dame Press, 1988), pp. 167-182.

22. Confucius, *Analects*, 12:1, trans. D.C. Lau (New York: Penguin Books, 1979), p. 112.

23. See Fung Yu-lan, "China's road to freedom [*Xin Shi Lun*]," Chapter 4: On the Family and State, in *Collected Work of Fung Yu-lan*, ed. Huang Kejian and Wu Xiaolong (Beijing: Qun-Yan Publishers, 1993), pp. 270-280. Also Liang Shu-ming, op. cit., pp.19-24.

24. Wing-Tsit Chan, *op. cit.*, p. 41.

25. *Ibid.*, p. 40.

26. *Ibid.*, p. 69.

27. See Michael Walzer, "Philosophy and Democracy," *Political Theory*, 9:3 (August 1981) pp. 379-399.

28. See Yu Rubo, "On the Confucian thought of Great Unity [*Rujia Da Yitong Sixiang Jianyi*]," *The Academic Journal of Qilu [Qilu Zuekan],* No. 1 (1995), pp. 51-54.

29. Confucius, *Analects* 3:14, *op. cit.* p. 69.

30. Quoted from Fung Yu-lan's *A History of Chinese Philosophy* Vol. 1 (Princeton: Princeton University Press, 1952), p. 370.

31. Henry Rosemont, Jr., *A Chinese Mirror: Moral Reflections on Political Economy and Society* (La Salle, Ill.: Open Court, 1991).

32. Samuel P. Huntington, *The Third Wave: Democratization in the Late Twentieth Century* (Norman, Okla.: University of Oklahoma Press, 1991), p. 310.

33. Francis Fukuyama, "The end of history?" *The National Interest*, 16 (Summer 1989), pp. 3-18.

34. Wing-Tsit Chan, *op. cit.*, pp. 184-185.

35. For a detailed account of how a person can incorporate different values, see my "How can one be a Taoist-Buddhist-Confucian?," *International Review of Chinese Religion and Philosophy* 1 (March 1996), pp. 29-66.

IN SEARCH OF ISLAMIC CONSTITUTIONALISM

Nadirsyah Hosen

Nadirsyah Hosen is Lecturer at the State University of Islamic Studies (UIN) Syarif Hidayatullah Jakarta. He was awarded a graduate diploma in Islamic studies and an MA from the School of Classics, History, and Religion (University of New England). He obtained his Master of Laws in comparative law from the Northern Territory University, Australia.

Hosen examines the perceived conflict between Islamic values and those of democracy and constitutionalism. Constitutionalism comprises features such as government according to the constitution, sovereignty of the people and democratic government, independent judiciary, limited government subject to a bill of individual rights, and no or very limited state power to suspend a constitution. As thus defined, opponents to the very idea of Islamic constitutional law argue that constitutionalism is a Western notion and that the Shari'ah provides a unique system of government that makes constitutionalism unnecessary. Hosen argues that the Shari'ah's underlying principles of consensus (ijmā), elections (bay'ah), and broad deliberation (shūrā) can and should be sources for a constitution that respects democratic principles of rule by the people

Introduction

While constitutionalism in the West is mostly identified with secular thought,[1] Islamic constitutionalism, which incorporates some religious elements, has attracted growing interest in recent years. For instance, the Bush administration's response to the events of 9/11 radically transformed the situation in Iraq and Afghanistan, and both countries are now rewriting their constitutions. As Ann Elizabeth Mayer points out, Islamic constitutionalism is constitutionalism that is, in some form, based on Islamic principles, as opposed to the constitutionalism developed in countries that happen to be Muslim but which has not been informed by distinctively Islamic principles.[2]

Several Muslim scholars, among them Muhammad Asad[3] and Abul A' la al-Maududi,[4] have written on such aspects of constitutional issues as human rights and the separation of powers.

However, in general their works fall into apologetics, as Chibli Mallat points out:

> Whether for the classical age or for the contemporary Muslim world, scholarly research on public law must respect a set of axiomatic requirements. First, the perusal of the tradition cannot be construed as a mere retrospective reading. By simply projecting present-day concepts backwards, it is all too easy to force the present into the past either in an apologetically contrived or haughtily dismissive manner. The approach is apologetic and contrived when Bills of Rights are read into, say, the Caliphate of 'Umar, with the presupposition that the "just" qualities of 'Umar included the complex and articulate precepts of constitutional balance one finds in modern texts.[5]

The fall of the Ottoman Empire also contributed to the lack of Islamic constitutional thought, since it was the last caliphal state. Even books on political law (fiqhsiyasāh) written in the twentieth century by 'Abdurrahman Taj[6] and Ahmad Shalabi,[7] for instance, refer to the ideas and practices of an Islamic state that existed more than a thousand years ago.[8] This means that they are simply repeating opinions from fiqh books written several centuries ago without making any modifications through Ijtihād (reinterpretation) and without trying to link the Qur'anic revelation and modern problems in a modern nation-state. In other words, what Islamic constitutionalism entails remains contested among Muslims, as well as among western scholars who study the topic.[9]

Constitutional law can be defined as the law that regulates a state's government. It is concerned with the struggle between rival contenders for power and the question of what limits should be imposed on the government. In a minimalist sense of the term, a constitution consists of a set of rules or norms that create, structure, and define the limits of governmental power or authority. In this way, all states have constitutions and all states are constitutional states. However, it should be noted that having a constitution — written or unwritten — does not necessarily mean that a state follows constitutionalism. In other words, constitutionalism does not reside only in the powers of the state.

When scholars talk of constitutionalism, they normally mean not only that rules create legislative, executive, and judicial powers, but that these rules impose limits on those powers. As a concept, constitutionalism is wider and broader than the text of a constitution. For instance, a state can have a written constitution that is against the spirit of constitutionalism.

Louis Henkin defines constitutionalism as constituting the following elements: (1) government according to the constitution, (2) separation of power, (3) sovereignty of the people and democratic government, (4) constitutional review, (5) independent judiciary, (6) limited government subject to a bill of individual rights, (7) controlling the police, (8) civilian control of the military, and (9) no state power, or very limited and strictly circumscribed state power, to suspend the operation of some parts of, or the entire, constitution.[10] The

philosophy behind the doctrine is that the people become the best judges about what is and what is not in their own interest.[11]

The main question is: What is the relationship between the Shari'ah and constitutionalism? This article will answer this question by looking at the arguments put forward by opponents of Islamic constitutional law and their counter-arguments. One group takes the view that not only is the Shari'ah sufficient to meet the Muslims' needs, and that, therefore, they do not need constitutionalism, but also that the Shari'ah, as God's law, is above the constitution. The Shari'ah has already provided a unique system of government or politics. Another group believes that Islam (including the Shari'ah) has no relationship with state affairs. According to this group, a constitution should not be used to enforce the Shari'ah.

Although both groups have different arguments, they share the same conclusion: The nature and characteristics of the Shari'ah do not permit them to acknowledge the relationship between the Shari'ah and constitutionalism. This article argues that the Shari'ah is neither above nor outside the constitution. Instead, the principles of the Shari'ah and constitutionalism can walk together. However, reform of the Shari'ah is needed to articulate the procedural and institutional mechanisms of Islamic constitutional law, particularly to draw a clear line of authority and accountability.

Authoritarianism and Secularism

In this section, I discuss the arguments opposing the compatibility of the Shari'ah and constitutionalism. The first four arguments are offered by fundamentalist groups, while the rest are provided by secularist groups. As pointed out above, although each authoritarian and secularist group has its own reasons, they share a similar view that the Shari'ah is not compatible with constitutionalism.

The Fundamentalists' Arguments.

Argument 1: Islamic law is immutable because the authoritarian, divine, and absolute concept of law in Islam does not allow change in legal concepts and institutions. The Shari'ah is immutable, regardless of history, time, culture, and location, as it did not develop an adequate methodology of legal change. Muslims may change, but Islam will not. This means that the rulings pronounced by the Shari'ah are static, final, eternal, absolute, and unalterable. In other words, its idealistic nature, its religious nature, its rigidity, and its casuistic nature lead to the Shari'ah's immutability.[12] This position is not compatible with the nature of a constitution which can be amended, modified, reformed, or even replaced.

Argument 2: The Shari'ah is based on God's revelation. Thus, the source of Islamic law is God's will, which is absolute and unchangeable. There has always been a close connection between Islamic law and theology. This means that the existing laws must operate within the boundaries set by the Shari'ah. In other words, real power lies with God.[13] This condition contradicts the nature of constitutionalism, which is based on the people's will. Following the point above, the Shari'ah states that sovereignty belongs to God, not to the people.[14] This means that the government must act according to the Shari'ah. This group also argues that the fact that a legislative measure is supported by a majority does not necessarily imply that it is a "right" measure. The underlying assumption here is that the majority, however large and even well-intentioned, might sometimes make a mistake, while the minority, despite its small numbers, may be right. What is right and what is wrong should be based on the Shari'ah, not on the popular vote.[15]

Argument 3: Constitutionalism is not drawn originally from Islam; rather, it is a western product and part of western hegemony. The tension between church and state in the western tradition is evident in all European constitutional traditions, as well as in the constitutions of such former colonies as the United States and Australia.[16] This group argues that adopting constitutionalism, which is outside of the Islamic discourse, will lead Muslims to abandon Islam by separating it from politics. Moreover, democracy and the rule of law are con-

cepts alien to Islam and were introduced by western tradition. Unlike the law in a secular state, the Shari'ah makes no distinction and separation between religion and state. Islam is a religion and a state (dīn wa dawlah).[17] State politics is part of Islamic teachings, in that Islam is a religion as much as it is a legal system.

Secularization, the separation of religion and politics, is seen as the product of western colonialism and a conspiracy directed against Islam. During the colonial era, accordingly, the concept of secularization was introduced into Muslim society in order to maintain western power. With the separation of religion and politics, jihad would be meaningless. The word and the idea of secularization have become very pejorative terms. Any Muslim scholar who supports this concept would allegedly be seen as a supporter of western hegemony. Accordingly, constitutionalism is the product of this western idea.[18]

Argument 4: The Shari'ah is perfect, for it is based on the Qur'an (5:3)[19] and therefore covers broad topics (e.g., ritual, social interaction, criminal law, and political law) and can answer every single problem. In other words, it was designed for all times and places, for a universal application to all people. It is comprehensive and so encompasses all aspects of law, be they personal, societal, governmental, constitutional, criminal, mercantile, war and peace, and international treaties. Hence, Islam is an ideology that address all of life's affairs.[20] Meanwhile, constitutionalism will not (and cannot) provide answers for all of humanity's problems.

As mentioned earlier, these arguments are supported by authoritarian groups. Authoritarians view the Shari'ah as incompatible with constitutionalism in the modern, legal, and secular sense. Instead, the Qur'an and the Hadith literature should be seen as the Islamic constitution. Meanwhile, the secular groups reject the Shari'ah's constitutionalization on the grounds that it was never the constitution of the traditional Islamic caliphate, which was, in fact, an "absolute monarchy." Therefore, the Shari'ah cannot be enforced through a constitution, because they contradict each other.

The Secularists' Arguments.

According to the secular groups, the Shari'ah is a matter for individual compliance and therefore is incompatible with constitutionalism. States do not have the right to intervene nor to enforce the Shari'ah on the public. One may observe that Islamic law began with the activities of jurists owing to religious motives, rather than being created by state legislation. This results in the jurists' conviction of the independence of Islamic law from state control. States can encourage their citizens' compliance with the Shari'ah (e.g., paying zakat, fasting, making the pilgrimage to Makkah), but cannot force them to comply. Unlike the authoritarians' view, this group believes in the secular state, and therefore say that the Shari'ah cannot (and should not) take the place of the constitution. They introduce the idea of de-politicizing Islam and determining it solely as a religious faith, as once articulated by the Islamic scholar 'Ali 'Abd al-Raziq.[21]

The Shari'ah, developed many centuries ago, is fit only for the conditional, political, and institutional conditions of that time. In other words, it can function only in a traditional state (or city-state) that is based on the leader's personal charisma rather than on the constitutional system. Fifteen centuries ago, there was no Parliament, system of checks-and-balances, judicial review, good governance, separation of powers, and so on.

Implementing the Shari'ah, therefore, is in contradiction with modern institutions and concepts. Moreover, constitutions cannot be viable documents in the absence of the ideological, cultural, and political prerequisites for constitutional life. How can constitutionalism emerge in societies in which liberalism and secularism are so far from hegemonic?

If constitutionalism is defined as a set of ideologies and institutions predicated on the idea of enabling the law to limit and regulate government authority, the Shari'ah does not limit the power of governments. In the Islamic tradition, the caliph could do anything he wanted without the fear of facing an opposition party or even impeachment procedures. Implementing the Shari'ah would lead to an undemocratic state, for the caliph's power would be unlimited. In the words of Bassam Tibi, "none of them was a legal ruler in the modern constitutional sense."[22] One of the reasons for this situation was that no institutional authority was able to enforce the caliph's compliance with the Shari'ah.

This leads us to discuss the rule of law. The modern conception of the rule of law derives from the late-nineteenth and early-twentieth-century movements in Anglo-American legal scholarship. This movement sought to convey the operation of the law, law-making, and functioning of the legal system as scientific processes governed by ascertainable and predictable rules.[23] The rule of law, as the embodiment of governance by fixed principles rather than the discretion of political expediency, fits into this mode by serving, in the view of Albert Venn Dicey, its best known exponent of that period, three functions: the supremacy of the law and the absence of arbitrariness, equality before the law, and constitutional law as part of the ordinary law of the land.[24]

Since then, the exposition of this concept has largely revolved around subjecting the government and, in particular, the lawmakers to the same laws as ordinary people. That is, the law effectively restrains and, where necessary, punishes the abuse of political power. Considering the historical context in which the concept was propounded, it is not surprising that its focus was political.[25] Though some effort has been made since the 1960s to direct the concept to economic issues, it has largely remained a political imperative.[26] In addition, Lon Fuller claimed that the rule of law is part of the "internal" morality of law.[27] M. J. Radin interprets this to mean that the complex of ideas associated with the term rule of law is essential for the efficacy of any system of legal rules.[28]

Meanwhile, the topic of the rule of law in Islam remains controversial. The image is that Islamic law allows the ruler (e.g., the king, prime minister, or president) to govern as a dictator: Whatever his decision, it is always right. This follows with other images that the Shari'ah does not provide procedural regulations to control the government, does not have a clear rule on how to elect the government and how to limit its powers, and enjoys no judicial independence in the countries where it is applied.

Historically, it is the ruler's discretion — not the rule of law — that plays a greater part in Islamic constitutional law. Islamic jurisprudence came to accept the idea of siyasāh shar'īyah, which accords the terrestrial ruler a reservoir of discretionary power of command in the public interest. If "deviations from the strict Shari'ah doctrine"[29] were required to protect the maslahah al-'āmmah[30] (public interest) in implementing its guiding principles, then such deviations were allowed. This expansive doctrine of government discretion was justified in terms that reflected the caliph's privileged position as the Islamic nation's head of state. Since caliphs were presumed to possess keen piety and the ability to engage in ijtihād, they were also presumed to be ideally qualified for their office and were to be allowed the discretion to take such steps as they, in their wisdom, saw fit.[31]

However, if taken too far or granted carte blanche, such discretion can be inimical to efficiency, stability, and transparency. Discretion, which is prone to ad hoc decision-making, does not lend itself to long-term planning and certainty and, in such circumstances, runs counter to the doctrine of the rule of law. Moreover, it can confer too much power that could corrupt and be abused. Factors other than transparent scientific considerations also could infect the decision-making process. Historically, the caliph's decision would be based heavily on his personal discretion or interpretation of the Shari'ah, not on the rule of law.

Historically, Muslim scholars have divided the world into two divisions: the territory of Islam (dar al-Islām), comprising Islamic and non-Islamic communities that had accepted Islamic sovereignty, and the rest of the world (dār al-hārb) or the territory of war.[32] Muslims enjoyed the rights of full citizenship, while non-Muslims enjoyed only partial civil rights. For instance, a non-Muslim could not be appointed as a caliph or any other type of ruler. The non-Muslims' concern over their status under the Shari'ah can be understood by looking at the concept of dhimmī, which does not give them the governing rights and, while guaranteeing them security of life and property, does not permit them to become an integral part of the ruling class.[33] Such treatment violates the understanding of religious freedom enshrined in international human rights instruments.

This means that there would be no equality before the law, should the Shari'ah be implemented. In other words, the Shari'ah does not guarantee and protect the rights of minority groups. The problem of equality in Islamic society is centered around, as pointed out by John Esposito and James Piscatori, the "unequal status between Muslims and non-Muslims as well as between men and women."[34] For instance, Muslim women's testimony is accepted in civil matters, but it takes two of them to make a single witness. A Muslim man is always a fully competent witness under the Shari'ah.[35] Another example of gender discrimination is found in the law of inheritance: A woman is entitled to half the share of a man who has the same degree of relationship to the deceased.[36] Some Muslim politicians go further by stating that women cannot become president, citing the Prophet's saying: "Those who entrust their affairs to a woman will never know prosperity."[37] They interpreted this as implying that a woman cannot lead a Muslim state. This restriction should be seen as violating the spirit of constitutionalism. Once again, accordingly, these examples provide evidence that the Shari'ah should not be put into a constitution.

The Shari'ah and Constitutionalism

As seen from the discussion above, both authoritarian and secularist groups believe that the Shari'ah is not compatible with constitutionalism. Although both have similar views, they have different arguments in support of these views. While authoritarians believe that the Shari'ah is better than constitutionalism, secularists take the position that the Shari'ah is part of a religious faith and not a system of government. It seems that both groups put different interpretations on the word and the meaning of Shari'ah. Therefore, the idea of the Shari'ah and its relationship with the idea of constitutionalism will be examined critically.

Kurzman opines that within the Islamic discourse, there are three main tropes of the Shari'ah. The first one is the liberal Shari'ah, which argues that the Qur'anic revelation and the Prophet's practices command Muslims to follow liberal positions. The second trope, the silent Shari'ah, holds that coexistence is not required but is allowed, and that the Shari'ah is silent on certain topics not because divine revelation was incomplete or faulty, but because the revelation intentionally left certain issues for humans to choose. The first trope holds that the Shari'ah requires democracy, while the second trope holds that the Shari'ah allows democracy.

However, the third trope, that of interpreted Islam, takes issue with each of the first two. According to this view, revelation is divine, but interpretation is human, fallible, and inevitably plural. This third trope suggests that religious diversity is inevitable, not just among religious communities but within Islam itself.[38] Despite their different opinions, those tropes can simply be classified as the substantive Shari'ah, meaning that the Shari'ah should be reinterpreted along the lines of democracy and constitutionalism. Using this substantive Shari'ah approach, I take the position that no inherent contradiction exists between the principles of the Shari'ah and constitutionalism.

Contrary to the (religious) authoritarians' views, such other Muslim scholars as Abdullahi Ahmed An-Na'im[39] and Muhammad Sa 'id Al-Ashmawy[40] advocate an emancipated understanding of the Shari'ah, stressing its original meaning as a "path" or guide rather than a detailed legal code. The Shari'ah must involve human interpretation. Islamic law is, in fact, the product of a very slow and gradual process of interpreting the Qur'an and collecting, verifying, and interpreting the Sunnah during the first three centuries of Islam (the seventh to the ninth centuries C.E.). This process was undertaken by scholars and jurists who developed their own methodology for classifying sources, deriving specific rules from general principles, and so forth.

This led the scholars to distinguish between the Shari'ah and fiqh. While the Shari'ah can be seen as the totality of divine categorizations of human acts, fiqh might be described as the articulation of the divine categorizations by human scholars. These articulations represent or express the scholars' understanding of the Shari'ah. In other words, these jurists or scholars, however highly respected they may be, can present only their own personal views or understanding of what the Shari'ah rules on any given matter. Moreover, the Qur'an and the Sunnah cannot be understood or have any influence on human behavior except through the efforts of (fallible) human beings.

Bernard Weiss has correctly pointed out that:

> Although the law is of divine provenance, the actual construction of the law is a human activity, and its results represent the law of God as humanly understood. Since the law does not descend from heaven ready-made, it is the human understanding of the law — the human fiqh (literally meaning understanding) — that must be normative for society.[41]

Therefore, even though the Shari'ah is based on God's revelations, it cannot be drawn up except through human understanding, which means both the inevitability of different opinions and the possibility of error, whether among scholars or the community in general. Khaled Abou El Fadl explains further:

> All laws articulated and applied in a state are thoroughly human, and should be treated as such. Consequently, any codification of Shari'ah law produces a set of laws that are thoroughly and fundamentally human. These laws are a part of Shari'ah law only to the extent that any set of human legal opinions is arguably a part of Shari'ah. A code, even if inspired by Shari'ah, is not Shari'ah — a code is simply a set of positive commandments that were informed by an ideal but do not represent the ideal. In my view, human legislation or codifications, regardless of their basis or quality, can never represent the Divine ideal.[42]

Since the Shari'ah involves human understanding, its social norms follow the nature of human beings, because they are derived from specific historical circumstances. For instance, the caliphate was the product of history, an institution of human (rather than divine) origin, a temporary convenience, and therefore a purely political office. This means that most Islamic legal regulations, including the status of non-Muslims and women, may be amended, changed, altered, and adapted to social change.[43] While the Qur'an contains a variety of elements (e.g., stories, moral injunctions, and general, as well as specific, legal principles), it prescribes only those details that are essential. It thus leaves considerable room for development and safeguards against restrictive rigidity. The universality of Islam lies not in its political structure, but in its faith and religious guidance.

Another source of Islamic jurisprudence, secondary only to the Qur'an, consists of the examples and words of Prophet Muhammad (the Sunnah). The Qur'an and the Sunnah quite often use words that have speculative, interpretable, and debatable meanings. This leads to the third source, Ijtihād, which can be defined simply as "interpretation." The main difference between Ijtihād and both the Qur'an and the Sunnah is that Ijtihād is a continuous process of development, whereas the Qur'an and the Sunnah are fixed sources of authority and were not altered or added to after the Prophet's death.[44]

Ijtihād literally means "striving, or self-exertion in any activity which entails a measure of hardship."[45] According to al-Amidi,[46] Ijtihād is defined as "the total expenditure of effort made by a jurist to infer, with a degree of probability, the rules of Islamic law."[47] In this sense, al-Gazali defined Ijtihād as "the expending, on the part of a mujtahid, of all that he is capable of in order to seek knowledge of the injunctions of Islamic law."[48]

Ijtihād can be conducted in one of at least three ways: Ijtihādbayānī, Ijtihādqiyāsī, and Ijtihādistislahī.[49] Ijtihādbayānī may be applied to cases that are mentioned explicitly in the Qur'an or Hadith literature but need further explanation. Ijtihādqiyāsī may be applied to cases that are not mentioned in these two sources, but that are similar to cases mentioned in either of them. Ijtihādistislahī may be applied to those cases that are not regulated by either source and cannot be solved through analogical reasoning. In this case, maslahah (utilities) is considered to be the basis for legal decisions.

From the short discussion above, it can be stated that Ijtihād is a tool for Muslims to understand and practice the Shari'ah in line with human nature and characteristics. Having performed ijtihād, Muslim scholars can build a fresh theoretical construct, as well as a contextual approach, to legal language and legal interpretation in order to follow the dynamic character of human beings. Thus the secularist views discussed above, that the Shari'ah fits only with the conditional, political, and the institutional occasions of 15 centuries ago, can be rejected.

The rule of Ijtihād might also be seen to indicate "the imperfectness of the Shari'ah." This means that the Shari'ah alone does not cover all issues, as claimed by authoritarian groups. Their interpretation of Qur'an 5:3, as mentioned above, could be criticized. The verse only deals with the complete and perfect teachings of Islamic rituals, from prayers to pilgrimage. After Allah revealed this verse, there were other verses, such as the verse on kalalah (4:176). This means that "This day I have perfected your religion for you" should be read in the context only of this verse. Qur'an 5:3 actually discusses such prohibitions as eating some foods, using arrows to seek luck or decisions, and fearing unbelievers. Accordingly, the word perfect should be understood as referring only to Islam's mandates and prohibitions, not as regulating the caliphate's establishment.

In other words, based on this verse, one could not argue that the Shari'ah deals with any specific form of government. In fact, no verse directly regulates a state's power. If the Qur'an is a comprehensive compendium of knowledge on every issue, then why does it not clarify this issue? As will be explained below, the Qur'an provides only some basic principles on this matter.

Scholars who believe that Islam was meant to be a political order have performed their Ijtihād according to their understanding and interpretation of the Shari'ah's rule. While their interpretations should be respected as intellectual exercises, their

Ijtihād is neither legally binding on all Muslims nor can it be regarded as the Shari'ah itself. This means that scholars who have different opinions have performed their Ijtihād and that the outcome of their intellectual activities cannot be seen as being against the Shari'ah. The issue of whether or not the Shari'ah is compatible with constitutionalism is the issue of ijtihād.

Following on the point made above, one may argue that our understanding of the Shari'ah is not perfect, in the sense that it is changeable through the Ijtihād of Muslim scholars according to the requirements of different places and times. For instance, al-Shafi'i changed several of his views in Iraq (qawl qadīm) when he moved to Cairo (qawl jadīd). Much earlier, 'Umar ibn al-Khattab was known as a caliph who practiced Ijtihād on several occasions when there was no guidance in the Qur'an and the Hadith literature, and when he thought that the law mentioned in both sources was no longer suitable for dealing with the circumstances of his era. The two texts below provide examples of how 'Umar's Ijtihād differs from the Prophet's decision:

> Narrated 'Imran: "We performed Hajj al-Tamattu' in the lifetime of Allah's Apostle and then the Qur'an was revealed (regarding Hajj al-Tamattu') and somebody ['Umar] said what he wished (regarding Hajj al-Tamattu') according to his own opinion (ra'y)."[50]

Yahya related to me from Malik, from Ibn Shihab, that Muhammad ibn ' Abdillah ibn al-Haris ibn Nawfal ibn 'Abd al-Muttalib told him that he had heard Sa'd ibn Abi Waqqas and al-Dahhak ibn Qays discussing tamattu' (performing 'umrah first, then Hajj) in between 'umrah and Hajj. Al-Dahhak ibn Qays said, "Only someone who is ignorant of what Allah, the Exalted and Glorified, says would do that." Whereupon Sa'd said, "How wrong is what you have just said, son of my brother!" al-Dahhak said, "'Umar ibn al-Khattab forbade that," and Sa'd said, "The Messenger of Allah, may Allah bless him and grant him peace, did it, and we did it with him."[51]

'Umar believed that the situation had changed, and this forced him to apply ijtihād. Hence, in several cases, his decision differed from the position adopted by the Prophet. 'Umar's decision not to distribute the lands of Iraq and Syria among the Companions is another example. Muslims insisted on following the Prophet's practice. 'Umar replied that if he kept on distributing the lands, where would he maintain the army to protect the borders and the newly conquered towns? The Companions, therefore, finally agreed with him and remarked: "Al-ra'y ra'yuka" (Yours is the correct opinion). He later justified this decision by citing 59:6-10.[52] 'Umar actually preferred actions that benefited Muslims in general, rather than individuals. During his time, social justice demanded that conquered lands should not be distributed among the army. Another interesting example occurred when a thief was captured but 'Umar did not amputate his hand, citing an ongoing famine.[53] In deciding this, it seems that 'Umar contravened the formal Qur'anic injunction.[54] However, since he was still regarded and respected as one of the four rightly-guided caliphs, these cases suggest that the Shari'ah is not unchangeable.

The Shari'ah is also considered not to be "perfect" on the grounds that there is a great deal of disagreement and disputation among scholars concerning the meaning and significance of different aspects of the sources with which they are working. For example, one school considers analogy as a source of Islamic law, while others reject it. Furthermore, as the case of al-Shafi'i shows, the scholars' work cannot be done in isolation from the prevailing conditions of their communities in local as well as broader regional contexts. The interpretations of scholars, 'ulama, and mujathidiū would reflect the state of their human and political consciousness, and usually that of their people, at that particular time and place. Disagreements among schools, not to mention among scholars of the same school, provide other evidence that understanding the Shari'ah, in human terms, is not static, final, eternal, absolute, and unalterable.

The Qur'an encourages ethnic and other types of diversity as blessings from God. Consequently, classical Muslim jurists recognized the fact that what may suit one culture may not be quite so suitable for another. For this reason, they encouraged each country to introduce its own customs into its laws, provided that these customs did not contradict basic Islamic principles. As a result, even today the Islamic laws of Muslim countries differ significantly on various matters.

While rejecting the Qur'an and the Hadith literature as the Islamic constitution (authoritarian view), at the same time I also reject the secularist view that Islam is a religion, in the western sense, that regulates only the relationship between humanity and the Supreme Creator. The Qur'an and the Hadith literature cannot be seen as the Islamic constitution, but perhaps as its code of high constitutional principles. They comprise guidance on legislation, morality, and meaningful stories, all of which, unlike other constitutions and laws, were not recorded systematically. Although both the Qur'an and the Hadith literature do not prefer a definite political system, both primary sources have laid down a set of principles, or ethical values and political morals, to be followed by Muslims in developing life within a state.

For instance, Muhammad Husayn Haykal takes the view that Islam does not provide direct and detailed guidance on how the Islamic community should manage state affairs. According to him, Islam lays down the basic principles for human civilization, not the basic provisions that regulate human behavior in life and in association with fellow humans, and which, in turn, will characterize the pattern of politics. In short, according to Haykal, there is no standard system of government in Islam. The Islamic community is free to follow any governing system that ensures equality among its citizens (both in rights and responsibilities) and in the sight of the law, and manages affairs of state based on shūrā (consultation) by adhering to Islam's moral and ethical values.

Haykal believes that a governmental system based on Islamic provisions ensures freedom and is based on the principle of appointing a head of state with the people's approval, and that the people have the right to control how the government operates and to call it to account. Islam appeals to all people, especially Muslims, to make an effort to carry out those above-mentioned principles as far as possible. This position is located right in the middle, between authoritarian and secularist views. In this context, one may see that Haykal's views clearly oppose the strict authoritarian groups' opinions that sovereignty belongs to Allah and not to the people. However, at the same time, he also opposes the view that Islam does not teach how to live within a community and a state.[55]

Principles of Islamic Constitutional Law

The counter-arguments above specifically reject some ideas of the incompatibility of the nature and the characteristics of the Shari'ah and constitutionalism. The following arguments will focus on examining the Shari'ah's principles in relation to constitutionalism. By doing so simultaneously, the arguments are presented to counter secular views on this matter.

Secularist groups hold that the caliph's power was historically unlimited, and that therefore the Shari'ah is incompatible with constitutionalism. This view could be rejected on the grounds that Islam has provided a wilāyahal-mazālim (the redress of wrongs), the embryo of administrative tribunal or constitutional court in the modern sense. Al-Mawardi outlines ten areas that can be reported to this tribunal, including government officials' oppression and maltreatment of the public and not implementing sentences when judges cannot enforce them due to the sentenced person's power or social standing.[56]

Abd al-Wahhab Khallaf goes even further by stating that the Islamic government is a constitutional, as opposed to a tyrannical, government."[57] In other words, based on his understanding of the Shari'ah, government in Islam is not based on the charisma of the person. He also opines that Islam guarantees individual rights (huqūq al-afrād) and separates power into al-sultah al-tashri 'iyah, al-sultah al-qada 'iyah, and al-sultah al-tanfizīyah'[58]— which could easily be classified as the legislative, judiciary, and executive powers, respectively. Khallaf's views can be justified on the grounds that the Qur'an provided the basic principles for a constitutional democracy without providing the details of a specific system. Muslims were to interpret these basic principles in light of their customs and the demands of their historical consciousness. Once again, this partly explains why Muslims currently need a new ijtihād.

In addition, advocates of Islamic constitutional law have sought to broaden the classic understanding of ijmā (consensus). In the past, only Muslim scholars had a role in reaching consensus; the general public had little significance.[59] Fazlur Rahman argues that the classical doctrine of consultation was in error because it was presented as the process of one person, the ruler, asking subordinates for advice. In fact, the Qur'an calls for "mutual advice through mutual discussions on an equal footing."[60] In this context, ijmā is closely related to shūrā (consultation) and, therefore, can be implemented as a legislative power in the modern sense. Louay M. Safi also notes that the "legitimacy of the state ... depends upon the extent to which state organization and power reflect the will of the ummah [the Muslim community], for as classical jurists have insisted, the legitimacy of state institutions is not derived from textual sources but is based primarily on the principle of ijmā'."[61] According to this understanding, an Islamic constitution is a human product of legislation based on the practices of consultation and consensus, and thus, virtually, no longer the result of a divine act. It is set and approved by the people. In other words, consensus and consultation offer a justification of Islamic constitutional law.

Nathan J. Brown points out that the Shari'ah does provide such a basis for constitutionalism and that Islamic political thought is increasingly inclined toward constitutionalist ideas. While it is true that attempts to implement these ideas have not been successful, the problem could be seen to lie in the lack of attention given to the structures of political accountability, rather than to any flaws in the concept of Islamic constitutionalism.[62]

Azizah Y. al-Hibri explains some key concepts of Islamic law in order to support the view that the Shari'ah is compatible with constitutionalism. A state must satisfy two basic conditions to meet Islamic standards: the political process must be based on "elections" (bay'ah), and the elective and governing process must be based on "broad deliberation" (shūrā). These two principles are part of the criteria employed to determine or to judge Islamic constitutional law. According to al-Hibri, these two principles, together with other factors (e.g., a Muslim ruler has no divine attributes and Islam has no ecclesiastical structure), indicate that there is, in fact, little difference between an Islamic constitutional setting and a secular one.[63]

Given the alleged parallels she discovers between the Constitution of Madinah and the American Constitution, al-Hibri considers the possibility that the Founding Fathers were either directly or indirectly influenced by the Islamic precedent. She notes that Thomas Jefferson was aware of Islam, since he had in his library a copy of George Sale's translation of the Qur'an. Al-Hibri suggests that Sale presented Islam in as fair a light as possible, under the circumstances of the eighteenth century, thereby making the Prophet's precedent amenable to Jefferson. Furthermore, she argues that if the Founding Fathers were, in fact, influenced by the Islamic model of constitutionalism, then this would "support the argument that American constitutional principles have a lot in common with Islamic principles. Such a conclusion would be helpful in evaluating the possibility of exporting American democracy to Muslim countries."[64]

Although her argument could be considered apologetic,[65] it seems that she has attempted to show some similarities between the two traditions by using the American standard as the standard of evaluation. The comparison between two legal traditions is, to borrow Patrick Glenn's term, a multivalent thinking. Glenn takes the view that all traditions contain elements of others. Thus, western legal traditions may contain some elements of eastern legal traditions. In other words, "there are always common elements and common subjects of discussion."[66] Glenn rejects the proposition that "you can't have your cake and eat it too."[67] He offers the multivalent view that everything is a matter of degree. It is possible to compare apples and oranges. In other words, you can have your cake and eat it too, if you eat only half of it.[68] Therefore, he rejects the claim that a religious legal tradition is incompatible or incommensurable with a secular legal tradition.

In addition, Muslim scholars could readily conclude that a Muslim country may choose to be a republic and still be in compliance with the Shari'ah, as long as the presidential election is genuinely free and the consultation among all branches of government is broad. Furthermore, the existence of a House of Representatives would ensure that the people's voice is heard in legislative matters, even if indirectly. Other scholars, however, may make similar arguments for a constitutional monarchy based on the British example. One can see that Muslim countries may or may not satisfy the two criteria above in their constitutions.

In relation to protecting the citizens' rights, despite some rights that are established in the Qur'an and the Sunnah,[69] the maqāsid al-Sharī'ah (the objectives of Islamic law) should become another principle or criterion of Islamic constitutional law, a view supported by El Fadl.[70] According to Muhammad Husein Kamali, the maqāsid al-Sharī'ah is an important but neglected aspect in the Shari'ah's discourse. He claims that even today many reputable textbooks on usūl al-fiqh do not include the maqāsid al-Sharī'ah in their usual coverage of familiar topics. Generally those textbooks are more concerned with conforming to the letter of the divine text. This, directly or not, has contributed to the literalist orientation of juristic thought.

The maqāsid al-Sharī'ah consists of five juristic core values of protection (al-darūrīyah al-khams): religion, life, intellect, honor or lineage, and property. Basically, the Shari'ah, on the whole, primarily seeks to protect and promote these essential values and validates all measures necessary for their preservation and advancement. El Fadl argues that protecting religion would have to mean protecting the freedom of religious belief; protecting life would mean that the taking of life must be for a just reason and the result of a just process; protecting the intellect would have to mean the right to freedom of thought, expression, and belief; protecting honor or lineage would have to mean protecting each person's dignity; and protecting property would ensure the right to compensation for the taking of property.

As he also points out, these five core values are human — not divine — values, since they were developed by Muslim jurists based on their interpretations of the Qur'an and the Sunnah. This could mean that the maqāsid al-Sharī'ah are not limited to the five core values. Ibn Taymiyah departs from the notion of confining the maqāsid al-Sharī'ah to a specific number of values.[71] Yusuf al-Qardawi takes a similar approach, for he extends the list of the maqāsid al-Sharī'ah to include human dignity, freedom, social welfare, and human fraternity among the higher maqāsid al-Sharī'ah.[72] The existence of additional objectives is upheld by the weight of both the general and detailed evidence found in the Qur'an and the Sunnah.

A new ijtihād could be performed by considering the theory of the maqāsid al-Sharī'ah and examining the Shari'ah as a unity in which detailed rules are to be read in light of their broader premises and objectives. This means that by looking at the maqāsid al-Sharī'ah, the Shari'ah could be analyzed beyond the particularities of the text. In Kamali's words, "the focus is not so much on the words and sentences of the text, as on the purposes and goals that are being upheld and advocated."[73] It is worth noting that the principles and the procedural form of Islamic constitutional law could be found through the theory of the maqāsid al-Sharī'ah.

In relation to the position of religion vis-à-vis the state, another principle or criterion could be drawn from the Charter of Madinah.[74] One of the challenges for Islamic constitutional law is the position of Islam (or the Shari'ah) in the constitution. This could be examined on three levels: the position of Islam within the Muslim community itself, in relation to other religions, and its relationship with the state. The Charter of Madinah is a document reportedly drawn up by Prophet Muhammad upon his migration from Makkah to Madinah. The document establishes the rights and obligations of the Ansar of Madinah, the Muhajir who left Makkah with the Prophet, and Madinah's Jewish tribes as they embarked upon a new journey of coexistence and cooperation in the nascent Muslim polity. The text itself consists of a preamble and 47 clauses outlining various aspects of community organization, procedures for common defense, and the relationship between the Muslim and Jewish inhabitants of Madinah.

This declared that all of Madinah's Muslim and Jewish tribes (apparently, there were no Christians) to be one community. It also stipulated that non-Muslim minorities (Jews) had the same right to life as Muslims; guaranteed peace and security for all Muslims based on equality and justice; guaranteed freedom of religion for both Muslims and Jews; and ensured equality between the rights of the Jewish tribes of Banu Najjar and Banu 'Awf.

Instead of strictly using the text, the spirit of this document could be used as a principle or criterion of modern Islamic constitutional law. Although this constitution does not mention an Islamic state, the text states that "where a contention arises between two parties on a matter, the issue is to be referred to God and to Muhammad for a decision." Using both an historical and a legal approach, one may examine the significance of textual ambiguity in a modern pluralistic society. This would help to clarify the debate between authoritarians and secularists on Islam being both a religion and a state (dīn wa dawlah).

Conclusion

As may be seen from the foregoing discussion, the substantive Shari'ah approach has been taken. This holds that the Shari'ah, in this context, should be reinterpreted in line with democracy and constitutionalism. This substantive approach is based on the belief that any understanding of the Shari'ah cannot be static and final. As argued earlier, it can be amended, reformed, modified, or even altered — as long as its fundamental basis is not neglected. The Shari'ah is changeable and adaptable to social change, and thus follows the dynamics and the characteristics of human beings. Revelation is divine, whereas interpretation is human, fallible and inevitably plural. It is also suggested that religious diversity is inevitable, not just among religious communities, but within Islam itself.

This approach leads to the following position: The Shari'ah is compatible with constitutionalism.

This position rejects both the authoritarian and the secularist views. The Shari'ah's principles could be a formal source for, or be used only as an inspiration for, a constitution. The phrase al-maqāsid al-Sharī'ah should be distinguished from the divine ideal or the Shari'ah itself. With this approach, Islamic constitutional law does not stop at the point reached by the secularists — that the Shari'ah can borrow from western constitutionalism. Rather, it goes further by asking: Can the Shari'ah develop a new theory, type, idea, of form of constitutionalism? It is possible to produce some criticisms on the current discourse of constitutionalism by using the substantive Shari'ah approach. This is a real challenge for Islamic constitutionalists.

NOTES

1. Graham Hassal and Cheryl Saunders, *Asia-Pacific Constitutional Systems* (Cambridge: Cambridge University Press, 2002), 42.

2. See Ann Elizabeth Mayer, "Conundrums in Constitutionalism: Islamic Monarchies in an Era of Transition," *UCLA J. Islamic and Near E.L.*, no. 1 (2002): 183.

3. Muhammad Asad, *The Principles of State and Government in Islam* (Kuala Lumpur: Islamic Book Trust, 1980).

4. For example, Abul A'la al-Maududi, *Political Theory of Islam* (Lahore: Islamic Publications, 1985).

5. Chibli Mallat (ed.), *Islam and Public Law: Classical and Contemporary Studies* (London: Graham and Trotman, 1993), 1-2.

6. 'Abdurrahman Taj, Al-Siyāsah al-Shar'iyah wa al-Fiqh al-Islāmī (al-Qahirah: Dar al-Ta'rif, 1953).

7. Ahmad Shalabi, Al-Siyāsah fī al-Fikr al-Islāmī (al-Qahirah: Nahdah al-Misriyah, 1983).

8. The common sources are al-Mawardi, Al-Ahkām al-Sultāniiyah (Cairo: Mustafa Babi al-Halabi wa Auladuh, 1996); Ibn Khaldun, Muqaddimah (Beirut: Dar al-Fikr, n.d.).

9. In April 2000, a major international conference on Islam and constitutionalism, held by the Islamic Legal Studies Program, Faculty of Law, Harvard University. The papers will be edited by

Sohail Hashmi and Houchang Chehabi and published by Harvard University Press (forthcoming).

10. Louis Henkin, "Elements of Constitutionalism," Occasional Paper Series (Center for the Study of Human Rights: 1994). See also Dario Castiglione, "The Political Theory of the Constitution," in *Constitutionalism in Transformation*, ed. Richard Bellamy and Dario Castiglione (London: Blackwell Publishers, 1996), 5; Francis D. Wormuth, *The Origins of Modern Constitutionalism* (New York: Harper and Brothers, 1949).

11. Alan S. Rosenbaum (ed.), *Constitutionalism: The Philosophical Dimension* (Connecticut: Greenwood Press, 1988), 8 (introduction); see also J. Lane, *Constitutions and Political Theory* (Manchester: Manchester University Press, 1996), 25.

12. See the discussion in Muhammad Khalid Masud, *Shatibi's Philosophy of Islamic Law* (Pakistan: Islamic Research Institute, 1995), 17.

13. Ahmad Shalabi, Al-Hukūmah wa al-Dawlah fī al-Islām (Cairo: Maktabah al-Nahdah al-Misriyah, 1958), 23.

14. See M. 'Abd al-Qadir Abu Faris, Al-Nizāam al-Siyāsī fī al-Islām (Beirut: Dar al-Qur'an al-Karim, 1984), 15-40.

15. Asad, *The Principles of State and Government*.

16. See Said Amir Arjomand, "Religion and Constitutionalism in Western History and in Modern Iran and Pakistan," in *The Political Dimensions of Religion*, ed, Said Amir Arjomand (Albany: State University of New York Press, 1993), 69-99.

17. See Muhammad Salim al-'Awwa, Fī al-Nizām al-Siyāsī li al-Dawlah al-Islāmī yah (Cairo: al-Maktab al-Misri al-Hadith, 1983).

18. Husain Ya'qub, Al-Nizām al-Siyāsī fī al-Islām (Iran: Mu'assasah Ansariyan, 1312 A.H.), 250.

19. "...This day, I have perfected your religion for you, completed My Favor upon you, and have chosen for you Islam as your religion ..." (Qur'an 5:3).

20. Taqiyuddin al-Nabhani, Nizām al-Islām. Online at www.hizb-ut-tahrir.org/arabic/kotobmtb/htm/Olndam.htm.

21. 'Ali'Abd al-Raziq (1888-1966) was the most controversial Islamic political thinker of the twentieth century. His book, Al-Islam wa Usūl al-Hukm, written in 1925, aroused great criticism within the Muslim world. He was then condemned and isolated by al-Azhar's 'ulama council, dismissed from his position as a judge, and prohibited from assuming a position in the government. Raziq disagreed with many 'ulama, who considered the establishment of the khilāfah as obligatory and therefore it would be sinful if it were not carried out. Raziq could not find a strong foundation to support this belief.

22. Bassam Tibi, *The Challenge of Fundamentalism: Political Islam and the New World Disorder* (Berkeley: University of California Press, 1998), 160.

23. Information on the origins of the rule of law can be obtained from F. A. Hayek, *The Rule of Law* (California: Institute for Humane Studies, 1975); see also Robert S. Summers, "A Formal Theory of the Rule of Law," *Ratio Juris* 6, no. 2 (July 1993): 127-42.

24. See A. V. Dicey, *Introduction to the Study of the Law of the Constitution* (London: Macmillan, 1959).

25. For more information see Judith N. Shklar, "Political Theory and the Rule of Law," in *The Rule of Law: Ideal or Ideology*, ed. Allan C. Hutchinson and Patrick Monahan (Vancouver: Carswell, 1987), 2-16.

26. Maxwell O. Chibundu, "Law in Development: on Taping, Gourding and Serving Palm-wine," *Case Western Reserve Journal of International Law*, no. 29 (spring 1997): 178.

27. Lon Fuller, *The Morality of Law* (New Haven: Yale Univ. Press, 1969), 157.

28. M. J. Radin, "Reconsidering the Rule of Law," *Boston University Law Review*, no. 69 (1989): 785.

29. Taj, Al-Siyāsah al-Shar'īyah,10-11.

30. More information on the concept of public interest in Islam can be found in Husain Hamid Hasan, Nazarīyah al-Maslahah fī al-Fiqh al-Islāmī (Cairo: Dar al-Nahdah al-'Arabiyah, 1971).

31. Nabhani, Nizām al-Islām.

32. For a full account, see Patricia Crone, *Medieval Islamic Political Thought* (Edinburgh: Edinburgh University Press, 2004), 358-92.

33. Ann K. S. Lambton, *State and Government in Medieval Islam* (New York: Oxford University Press, 1991), 203-08.

34. John L. Esposito and James P. Piscatori, "Democratization and Islam," *Middle East Journal* 45, no. 3 (1991): 428.

35. The Qur'an 2:282 says: "... if the two be not men, then one man and two women, such witnesses as you approve of, that if one of the two women errs the other will remind her ..."

36. For a full account, see Zainab Chaudhry, "Myth of Misogyny: A Reanalysis of Women's Inheritance in Islamic Law," no. 61, *Alb. L. Rev.* (1997): 511.

37. For full discussion, see Nadirsyah Hosen, "Can a Woman Become the President of the World's Largest Muslim Country? Megawati — An Indonesian Political Victim" (paper presented at Women in Asia Conference, Australian National University, Canberra, 23-26 September 2001).

38. Charles Kurzman, "Liberal Islam: Prospects and Challenges," *Journal Middle East Review of International Affairs* 3, no. 3 (September 1999).

39. See Abdullahi Ahmed An-Na'im, *Toward an Islamic Reformation: Civil Liberties, Human Rights, and International Law* (Syracuse, NY: Syracuse University Press, 1996).

40. See Carolyn Fluehr-Lobban (ed.), *Against Islamic Extremism: The Writings of Muhammad Sa'id al-Ashmawy* (Gainesville: University Press of Florida, 1998).

41. Bernard Weiss, *The Spirit of Islamic Law* (Athens: University of Georgia Press, 1998), 116.

42. Khaled Abou El Fadl, "Constitutionalism and the Islamic Sunni Legacy," *UCLA J. Islamic and Near E.L.*, no. 1 (2002): 67.

43. For instance, Amina Wadud al-Muhsin, a professor at Virginia Commonwealth University, offers a hermeneutical approach to understand the Qur'an on women. See her article, "Qur'an and Woman," in *Liberal Islam: A Source Book*, ed. Charles Kurzman (Oxford: Oxford University Press, 1998), 127-38. For the interpretation and historical context of the Prophet's statement "Those who entrust their affairs to a woman will never know prosperity," see Fatima Mernissi, "A Feminist Interpretation of Women's Rights in Islam," in ibid, 112-26.

44. Mohammad Hashim Kamali, *Principles of Islamic Jurisprudence* (Cambridge: The Islamic Text Society, 1991), 366.

45. Ibid., 367; Hans Wehr, *A Dictionary of Modern Written Arabic* (London: Macdonald and Evans LTD, 1974), 142-43.

46. Sayf al-Din al-Amidi was a noted scholar who wrote Al-Ihkām fī Usūl al-Ahkām. After the first edition of this work appeared, Bernard Weiss of the University of Utah published an exhaustive study of al-Amidi's work in a volume entitled *The Search for God's Will: Islamic Jurisprudence in the Writings of Sayf al-Din al-Amidi* (Utah: University of Utah Press, 1992).

47. Sayf al-Din al-Amidi, Al-Ihkām fī Usūl al-Ahkām (Cairo: Dar al-Kutub al-Khidiwiya, 1914), 4:218. See also Kamali, *Principles*; Muhammad Taqi al-Hakim, Usūl al-'Āmmahli al-Fiqh Muqārin (Beirut: Dar al-Andalas, 1963), 561-62.

48. Abu Hamid Muhammad al-Gazali, Al-Mustaqsfā 'Ilm al-Usūl (Madinah: Al-Jami'ah al-Islamiyah, n.d.), 4:4. See also Taha Jabir al-Alwani, "The Crisis of Thought and Ijtihad," *The American Journal of Islamic Social Sciences* 10, no. 2 (1993): 237.

49. Muhammad Ma'ruf al-Dawalibi uses these classifications in his book Al-Madkhal Ilā 'Ilm al-Usūl al-Fiqh (Damascus: Matba'ah Jami'ah Dimashq, 1959), 389. Muhammad Salam Madkur mentioned Dawalibi's book when discussing this issue (see Manāhij al-Ijtihād fī al-Islām [Matba'ah al-'Asriyah al-Kuwayt, 1974], 396) and, shortly afterwards, Wahbah al-Zuhaili also referred to this book in 1977 (see Al-Wasīt fī Usūl al-Fiqh al-Islāmi [Matba'ah Dar al-Kitāb, 1977], 484). However, Muhammad Taqi al-Hakim criticizes these categorizations and, therefore, proposes only two classifications, namely, al-Ijtihādal-'aqli and al-Ijtihad al-shar'i. (See Al-Hakim, Usūl al-'Āmmah).

50. Al-Bukhari, "Kitāb al-Hajj," Sahīh Bukhārī (Beirut: Dar al-Qalam, 1987), no. 1469.

51. Abu 'Abd Allah Malik, "Kitāb al-Hajj," Al-Muwattā", (al-Sharikah al-'Alamiyah, 1993), no. 671. See also al-Darimi, "Kitāb al-Manāsik," no. 1745.

52. Fazlur Rahman, *Islamic Methodology in History* (Lahore: 1965), 180-81.

53. Ahmad Hasan, *The Early Development of Islamic Jurisprudence* (Islamabad: Islamic Research Institute, 1970), 120.

54. The decision of 'Umar ibn al-Khattab to suspend the hadd penalty (a penalty prescribed by the Qur'an and the Sunnah) of amputating a thief s hand during a time of famine is an example of istihsān (juristic preference). Here the law was suspended as an exceptional measure in an exceptional situation. Istihsān is considered a method of seeking facility and ease in legal injunctions and is in accord with Qur'an 2:185. This suggests that the Companions were not merely literalists. On the contrary, their rulings were often based on their understanding of the spirit and purpose of the Shari'ah.

55. More information can be found in Musdah Mulia, *Negara Islam: Pemikiran Politik Husain Haikal* (Jakarta: Paramadina, 2001).

56. Al-Mawardi, Al-Ahkām al-Sultānīyah 80-92.

57. Abd al-Wahhab Khalaf, Al-Siyāsah al-Shar'īyah (Cairo:Salafīyah1350 A.H.), 25.

58. Ibid., 41-51.

59. The doctrine of ijmā (consensus) was introduced in the second century A.H./ eighth century C. E. in order to standardize legal theory and practice and to overcome individual and regional differences of opinion. Though conceived as a "consensus of scholars," in actual practice ijmā' was a more fundamental operative factor. From the third century A.H., ijmā' has amounted to a principle of rigidity in thinking; points on which consensus was reached in practice were considered closed, and further substantial questioning was prohibited. Accepted interpretations of the Qur'an and the actual content of the Sunnah all rest finally on ijmā', which, according to one definition, should be attended by all mujathidūn only. The problem is, if one refers to all books of Islamic legal theory, no definition of ijmā' is accepted by all mujathidūn. There is no consensus (mujma' 'alayhi) in defining ijmā' itself. See 'Ali 'Abd al-Raziq, Al-ijmā' f al-Shari'ah al-Islamiyah (Dar al-Fikr al-'Arabi, 1948), 6.

60. Fazlur Rahman, "The Principle of Shura and the Role of the Ummah in Islam," in *State, Politics, and Islam*, ed. Mumtaz Ahmad (Indianapolis: American Trust Publications, 1986), 90-91 and 95.

61. Louay M. Safi, "The Islamic State: A Conceptual Framework," *The American Journal of Islamic Social Sciences* (September 199): 233.

62. See Nathan J. Brown, *Constitutions in a Non-Constitutional World: Arab Basic Laws and the Prospects for Accountable Government* (Albany, NY: State University of New York Press, 2002), 162.

63. Azizah Y. al-Hibri, "Islamic Constitutionalism and the Concept of Democracy," in *Border Crossings: Toward a Comparative Political Theory*, ed. Fred Dallmayr (Maryland: Lexington Books, 1999), 63-87.

64. Azizah Y. al-Hibri, "Islamic and American Constitutional Law: Borrowing Possibilities or a History of Borrowing?" *U. Pa. J. Const. L.*, no. 1 (1999): 492 and 497.

65. El Fadl, "Constitutionalism." See also Anver Emon, "Reflections on the 'Constitution of Madinah: An Essay on Methodology and Ideology in Islamic Legal History," no. 1, *UCLA J. Islamic and Near E.L.* (2002): 103.

66. H. Patrick Glenn, *Legal Traditions of the World* (New York: Oxford University Press, 2000), 35.

67. Ibid., 325.

68. See also Glenn, "The Capture, Reconstruction and Marginalization of 'Custom,'" *Am. J. Comp. L.*, no. 45 (summer 1997): 613.

69. Many Muslim scholars are firm in their belief that the Shari'ah addresses the fundamentals of human rights. For instance, they identify the most important human rights principles in Islam to be dignity and brotherhood; equality among members of the community, without distinction on the basis of race, color, or class; respect for the honor, reputation, and family of each individual; the right of each individual to be presumed innocent until proven guilty; and individual freedom. See Tahir Mahmood (ed), *Human Rights in Islamic Law* (New Delhi: Genuine Publications, 1993). This book compiles articles from such leading Muslim scholars as Abul A 'la Maududi, M. I. Patwari, Majid Ali Khan, Sheikh Showkat Husain, and Parveen Shaukat Ali.

70. El Fadl, "Constitutionalism."

71. Taqi al-Din ibn Taimiyah, Majmu' al-Fatāwā (Beirut: Mu'assasat al-Risalah, 1398 A.H.), 32:134.

72. Yusuf al-Qardawi, Madkhal U Dirāsah al-Sharī'ah, 75.

73. Kamali, *Principles*, 408.

74. The Charter of Madinah's full text can be found online at http://islamicworld.net/islamic-state/macharter.htm.

DEMOCRACY AND ITS GLOBAL ROOTS:
WHY DEMOCRATIZATION IS NOT THE SAME
AS WESTERNIZATION

Amartya Sen

Amartya Sen is Lament University Professor and Professor of Economics at Harvard University. Until recently, he was Master of Trinity College, Cambridge. Sen received the Nobel Prize for Economics in 1998. He is the author and editor of numerous books, some of the most recent of which include Development as Freedom *(1999),* Hunger and Public Action *(1989, with Jean Dreze),* The Political Economy of Hunger in 3 volumes *(1990 and 1991, co-edited with Jean Dreze), and* The Quality of Life *(1993, co-edited with Martha Nussbaum).*

Sen examines two kinds of objections to the idea that democracy is applicable in non-Western contexts: 1) democracy deflects attention from the need for state control in developing countries, and 2) democracy involves an imposition of Western values and practices on non-Western societies. Sen argues that these objections rely on a too narrow view of democracy as constituted merely by the free elections and ballots emphasized in Western democracies. By broadening an account of democracy as being able to participate in public discussions and as involving public reasoning, Sen retrieves the roots of democracy in intellectual heritages in China, Japan, East and Southeast Asia, Iran, the Middle East, and Africa. Sen argues that neglecting the value of public reasoning in non-Western traditions undermines the positive role that democracy could play in the contemporary world if the West did not claim democracy as its own and the non-Western world did not view the West as imposing it on them.

I

There is no mystery in the fact that the immediate prospects of democracy in Iraq, to be ushered in by the American-led alliance, are being viewed with increasing skepticism. The evident ambiguities in the goals of the occupation and the lack of clarity about the process of democratization make these doubts inescapable. But it would be a serious mistake to translate these uncertainties about the immediate prospects of a democratic Iraq into a larger case for skepticism about the general possibility of — and indeed the need for — having democracy in Iraq, or in any other country that is deprived of it. Nor is there a general ground here for uneasiness about providing global support for the struggle for democracy around the world, which is the most profound challenge of our times. Democracy movements across the globe (in South Africa and Argentina and Indonesia yesterday, in Burma and Zimbabwe and elsewhere today) reflect people's determination to fight for political participation and an effective voice. Apprehensions about current events in Iraq have to be seen in their specific context; there is a big world beyond.

It is important to consider, in the broader arena, two general objections to the advocacy of democracy that have recently gained much ground in international debates and which tend to color discussions of foreign affairs, particularly in America and Europe. There are, first, doubts about what democracy can achieve in poorer countries. Is democracy not a barrier that obstructs the process of development and deflects attention from the priorities of economic and social change, such as providing adequate food, raising income per head, and carrying out institutional reform? It is also argued that democratic governance can be deeply illiberal and can inflict suffering on those who do not belong to the ruling majority in a democracy. Are vulnerable groups not better served by the protection that authoritarian governance can provide?

The second line of attack concentrates on historical and cultural doubts about advocating democracy for people who do not, allegedly, "know" it. The endorsement of democracy as a general rule for all people, whether by national or international bodies or by human rights activists, is frequently castigated on the ground that it involves an attempted imposition of Western values and Western practices on non-Western societies. The argument goes much beyond acknowledging that democracy is a predominantly Western practice in the contemporary world, as it certainly is. It takes the form of presuming that democracy is an idea of which the roots can be found exclusively in some distinctively Western thought that has flourished uniquely in Europe — and nowhere else — for a very long time.

These are legitimate and cogent questions, and they are, understandably, being asked with some persistence. But are these misgivings really well-founded? In arguing that they are not, it is important to note that these lines of criticism are not altogether unlinked. Indeed, the flaws in both lie primarily in the attempt to see democracy in an unduly narrow and restricted way — in particular, exclusively in terms of public balloting and not much more broadly, in terms of what John Rawls called "the exercise of public reason." This more capacious concept includes the opportunity for citizens to participate in political discussions and so to be in a position to influence public choice. In understanding where the two lines of attack on democratization respectively go wrong, it is crucial to appreciate that democracy has demands that transcend the ballot box.

Indeed, voting is only one way — though certainly a very important way — of making public

discussions effective, when the opportunity to vote is combined with the opportunity to speak, and to listen, without fear. The force and the reach of elections depend critically on the opportunity for open public discussion. Balloting alone can be woefully inadequate, as is abundantly illustrated by the astounding electoral victories of ruling tyrannies in authoritarian regimes, from Stalin's Soviet Union to Saddam Hussein's Iraq. The problem in these cases lies not just in the pressure that is brought to bear on voters in the act of balloting itself, but in the way public discussion of failures and transgressions is thwarted by censorship, suppression of political opposition, and violations of basic civil rights and political freedoms.

The need to take a broader view of democracy — going well beyond the freedom of elections and ballots — has been extensively discussed not only in contemporary political philosophy, but also in the new disciplines of social choice theory and public choice theory, influenced by economic reasoning as well as by political ideas. The process of decision-making through discussion can enhance information about a society and about individual priorities, and those priorities may respond to public deliberation. As James Buchanan, the leading public choice theorist, argues, "The definition of democracy as 'government by discussion' implies that individual values can and do change in the process of decision-making."

All this raises deep questions about the dominant focus on balloting and elections in the literature on world affairs, and about the adequacy of the view, well articulated by Samuel P. Huntington in *The Third Wave*, that "elections, open, free and fair, are the essence of democracy, the inescapable sine qua non." In the broader perspective of public reasoning, democracy has to give a central place to guaranteeing free public discussion and deliberative interactions in political thought and practice — not just through elections nor just for elections. What is required, as Rawls observed, is the safeguarding of "diversity of doctrines — the fact of pluralism," which is central to "the public culture of modern democracies," and which must be secured in a democracy by "basic rights and liberties."

The broader view of democracy in terms of public reasoning also allows us to understand that the roots of democracy go much beyond the narrowly confined chronicles of some designated practices that are now seen as specifically "democratic institutions." This basic recognition was clear enough to Tocqueville. In 1835, in *Democracy in America*, he noted that the "great democratic revolution" then taking place could be seen, from one point of view, as "a new thing," but it could also be seen, from a broader perspective, as part of "the most continuous, ancient, and permanent tendency known to history." Although he confined his historical examples to Europe's past (pointing to the powerful contribution toward democratization made by the admission of common people to the ranks of clergy in "the state of France seven hundred years ago"), Tocqueville's general argument has immensely broader relevance.

The championing of pluralism, diversity, and basic liberties can be found in the history of many societies. The long traditions of encouraging and protecting public debates on political, social, and cultural matters in, say, India, China, Japan, Korea, Iran, Turkey, the Arab world, and many parts of Africa, demand much fuller recognition in the history of democratic ideas. This global heritage is ground enough to question the frequently reiterated view that democracy is just a Western idea, and that democracy is therefore just a form of Westernization. The recognition of this history has direct relevance in contemporary politics in pointing to the global legacy of protecting and promoting social deliberation and pluralist interactions, which cannot be any less important today than they were in the past when they were championed.

In his autobiography, *Long Walk to Freedom*, Nelson Mandela describes how impressed he was, as a young boy, by the democratic nature of the proceedings of the local meetings that were held in the regent's house in Mqhekezweni:

Everyone who wanted to speak did so. It was democracy in its purest form. There may have been a hierarchy of importance among the speakers, but everyone was heard, chief and subject, warrior and medicine man, shopkeeper and farmer, landowner and laborer....The foundation of self-government was that all men were free to voice their opinions and equal in their value as citizens.

Meyer Fortes and Edward E. Evans-Pritchard, the great anthropologists of Africa, argued in their classic book *African Political Systems*, published more than sixty years ago, that "the structure of an African state implies that kings and chiefs rule by consent." There might have been some over-generalization in this, as critics argued later; but there can be little doubt about the traditional role and the continuing relevance of accountability and participation in African political heritage. To overlook all this, and to regard the fight for democracy in Africa only as an attempt to import from abroad the "Western idea" of democracy, would be a profound misunderstanding. Mandela's "long walk to freedom" began distinctly at home.

Nowhere in the contemporary world is the need for more democratic engagement stronger than in Africa. The continent has suffered greatly from the domination of authoritarianism and military rule in the late twentieth century, following the formal closure of the British, French, Portuguese, and Belgian empires. Africa also had the misfortune of being caught right in the middle of the Cold War, in which each of the superpowers cultivated military rulers friendly to itself and hostile to the enemy. No military usurper of civilian authority ever lacked a superpower friend, linked with it in a military alliance. A continent that seemed in the 1950s to be poised to develop democratic politics in newly independent countries was soon being run by an assortment of strongmen who were linked to one side or the other in the militancy of the Cold War. They competed in despotism with apartheid-based South Africa.

That picture is slowly changing now, with post-apartheid South Africa playing a leading part. But, as Anthony Appiah has argued, "ideological decolonization is bound to fail if it neglects either endogenous 'tradition' or exogenous 'Western' ideas." Even as specific democratic institutions developed in the West are welcomed and put into practice, the task requires an adequate understanding of the deep roots of democratic thought in Africa itself. Similar issues arise, with varying intensity, in other parts of the non-Western world as they struggle to introduce or consolidate democratic governance.

II

The idea that democracy is an essentially Western notion is sometimes linked to the practice of voting and elections in ancient Greece, specifically in Athens from the fifth century B.C.E. In the evolution of democratic ideas and practices it is certainly important to note the remarkable role of Athenian direct democracy, starting from Cleisthenes's pioneering move toward public balloting around 506 B.C.E. The term "democracy" derives from the Greek words for "people" (*demos*) and "authority" (*kratia*). Although many people in Athens — women and slaves in particular — were not citizens and did not have the right to vote, the vast importance of the Athenian practice of the sharing of political authority deserves unequivocal acknowledgment.

But to what extent does this make democracy a basically Western concept? There are two major difficulties in taking this view. The first problem concerns the importance of public reasoning, which takes us beyond the narrow perspective of public balloting. Athens itself was extremely distinguished in encouraging public discussion, as was ancient Greece in general. But the Greeks were not unique in this respect, even among ancient civilizations, and there is an extensive history of the cultivation of tolerance, pluralism, and public deliberation in other societies as well.

The second difficulty concerns the partitioning of the world into discrete civilizations with geographical correlates, in which ancient Greece is seen as part and parcel of an identifiable "Western" tradition. Not only is this a difficult thing to do given the diverse history of different parts of Europe, but it is also hard to miss an implicit element of racist thinking in such wholesale reduction of Western civilization to Greek antiquity. In this perspective, no great difficulty is perceived in

seeing the descendants of, say, Goths and Visigoths and other Europeans as the inheritors of the Greek tradition ("they are all Europeans"), while there is great reluctance to take note of the Greek intellectual links with ancient Egyptians, Iranians, and Indians, despite the greater interest that the ancient Greeks themselves showed — as recorded in contemporary accounts — in talking to them (rather than in chatting with the ancient Goths).

Such discussions often concerned issues that are directly or indirectly relevant to democratic ideas. When Alexander asked a group of Jain philosophers in India why they were paying so little attention to the great conqueror, he got the following reply, which directly questioned the legitimacy of inequality: "King Alexander, every man can possess only so much of the earth's surface as this we are standing on. You are but human like the rest of us, save that you are always busy and up to no good, traveling so many miles from your home, a nuisance to yourself and to others! ... You will soon be dead, and then you will own just as much of the earth as will suffice to bury you." Arrian reports that Alexander responded to this egalitarian reproach with the same kind of admiration as he had shown in his encounter with Diogenes, even though his actual conduct remained unchanged ("the exact opposite of what he then professed to admire"). Classifying the world of ideas in terms of shared racial characteristics of proximate populations is hardly a wonderful basis for categorizing the history of thought.

Nor does it take into account how intellectual influences travel or how parallel developments take place in a world linked by ideas rather than by race. There is nothing to indicate that the Greek experience in democratic governance had much immediate impact in the countries to the west of Greece and Rome — in, say, France or Germany or Britain. By contrast, some of the contemporary cities in Asia — in Iran, Bactria, and India incorporated elements of democracy in municipal governance, largely under Greek influence. For several centuries after the time of Alexander, for example, the city of Susa in southwest Iran had an elected council, a popular assembly, and magistrates who were proposed by the council and elected by the assembly. There is also considerable evidence of elements of democratic governance at the local level in India and Bactria over that period.

It must be noted, of course, that such overtures were almost entirely confined to local governance, but it would nevertheless be a mistake to dismiss these early experiences of participatory governance as insignificant for the global history of democracy. The seriousness of this neglect has to be assessed in light of the particular importance of local politics in the history of democracy, including the city-republics that would emerge more than a millennium later in Italy, from the eleventh century onward. As Benjamin I. Schwartz pointed out in his great book *The World of Thought in Ancient China*, "Even in the history of the West, with its memories of Athenian 'democracy,' the notion that democracy cannot be implemented in large territorial states requiring highly centralized power remained accepted wisdom as late as Montesquieu and Rousseau."

Indeed, these histories often play inspirational roles and prevent a sense of distance from democratic ideas. When India became independent in 1947, the political discussions that led to a fully democratic constitution, making India the largest democracy in the twentieth century, not only included references to Western experiences in democracy but also recalled India's own traditions. Jawaharlal Nehru put particular emphasis on the tolerance of heterodoxy and pluralism in the political rules of Indian emperors such as Ashoka and Akbar. The encouragement of public discussion by those tolerant political orders was recollected and evocatively linked to India's modern multi-party constitution.

There was also, as it happens, considerable discussion in the early years of Indian independence of whether the organization of "the ancient polity of India" could serve as the model for India's constitution in the twentieth century, though that idea was actually even less plausible than would have been any attempt to construct the constitution of the United States in 1776 in line with Athenian practices of the fifth century B.C.E. The chair of the committee that drafted the Indian constitution, B.R. Ambedkar, went in some detail into the history of local democratic governance in India to assess whether it could fruitfully serve as a model for modern Indian democracy. Ambedkar's conclusion was that it should definitely not be given that role, particularly because localism generated "narrow-mindedness and communalism" (speaking personally, Ambedkar even asserted that "these village republics have been the ruination of India"). Yet even as he firmly rejected the possibility that democratic institutions from India's past could serve as appropriate contemporary models, Ambedkar did not fail to note the general relevance of the history of Indian public reasoning, and he particularly emphasized the expression of heterodox views and the historical criticism of the prevalence of inequality in India. There is a direct parallel here with Nelson Mandela's powerful invocation of Africa's own heritage of public reasoning in arguing for pluralist democracies in contemporary Africa.

III

The established literature on the history of democracy is full of well-known contrasts between Plato and Aristotle, Marsilius of Padua and Machiavelli, Hobbes and Locke, and so on. This is as it should be; but the large intellectual heritages of China, Japan, East and Southeast Asia, the Indian subcontinent, Iran, the Middle East, and Africa have been almost entirely neglected in analyzing the reach of the ideal of public reasoning. This has not favored an adequately inclusive understanding of the nature and the power of democratic ideas as they are linked to constructive public deliberation.

The ideal of public reasoning is closely linked with two particular social practices that deserve specific attention: the tolerance of different points of view (along with the acceptability of agreeing to disagree) and the encouragement of public discussion (along with endorsing the value of learning from others). Both tolerance and openness of public discussion are often seen as specific — and perhaps unique — features of Western tradition. How correct is this notion? Certainly, tolerance has by and large been a significant feature of modern Western politics (leaving out extreme aberrations like Nazi Germany and the intolerant administration of British or French or Portuguese empires in Asia and Africa). Still, there is hardly a great historical divide here of the kind that could separate out Western toleration from non-Western despotism. When the Jewish philosopher Maimonides was forced to emigrate from an intolerant Europe in the twelfth century, for example, he found a tolerant refuge in the Arab world and was given an honored and influential position in the court of Emperor Saladin in Cairo — the same Saladin who fought hard for Islam in the Crusades.

Maimonides's experience was not exceptional. Even though the contemporary world is full of examples of conflicts between Muslims and Jews, Muslim rulers in the Arab world and in medieval Spain had a long history of integrating Jews as secure members of the social community whose liberties — and sometimes leadership roles — were respected. As María Rosa Menocal notes in her recent book *The Ornament of the World*, the fact that Cordoba in Muslim-ruled Spain in the tenth century was "as serious a contender as Baghdad, perhaps more so, for the title of most civilized place on earth" was due to the joint influence of Caliph Abd al-Rahman III and his Jewish vizier Hasdai ibn Shaprut. Indeed, there is considerable evidence, as Menocal argues, that the position of Jews after the Muslim conquest "was in every respect an improvement, as they went from persecuted to protected minority."

Similarly, when in the 1590s the great Mughal emperor Akbar, with his belief in pluralism and in the constructive role of public discussions, was making his pronouncements in India on the need for tolerance and was busy arranging dialogues between people of different faiths (including Hindus, Muslims, Christians, Parsees, Jains, Jews, and even atheists), the inquisitions were still taking place in Europe with considerable vehemence. Giordano Bruno was burned at the stake for heresy in the Campo dei Fiori in Rome in 1600 even as Akbar was speaking on tolerance in Agra.

We must not fall into the trap of arguing that there was in general more tolerance in non-Western societies than in the West. For no such generalization can be made. There were great examples of tolerance as well as of intolerance on both sides of this allegedly profound division of the world. What needs to be corrected is the under-researched assertion of Western exceptionalism in the matter of tolerance; but there is no need to replace it with an equally arbitrary generalization of the opposite sort.

A similar point can be made about the tradition of public discussion. Again, the Greek and Roman heritage on this is particularly important for the history of public reasoning, but it was not unique in this respect in the ancient world. The importance attached to public deliberation by Buddhist intellectuals not only led to extensive communications on religious and secular subjects in India and in East and Southeast Asia, but also produced some of the earliest open general meetings aimed specifically at settling disputes regarding different points of view. These Buddhist "councils," the first of which was held shortly after Gautama Buddha's death, were primarily concerned with resolving differences in religious principles and practices, but they dealt also with demands of social and civic duties, and they helped to establish the practice of open discussion on contentious issues.

The largest of these councils — the third — occurred, under the patronage of Emperor Ashoka in the third century B.C.E., in Pataliputra, then the capital of India, now called Patna (perhaps best known today as a source of a fine long-grain rice). Public discussion, without violence or even animosity, was particularly important for Ashoka's general belief in social deliberation, as is well reflected in the inscriptions that he placed on specially mounted stone pillars across India — and some outside it. The edict at Erragudi put the issue forcefully:

... the growth of essentials of Dharma [proper conduct] is possible in many ways. But its root lies in restraint in regard to speech, so that there should be no extolment of one's own sect or disparagement of other sects on inappropriate occasions, and it should be moderate even on appropriate occasions. On the contrary, other sects should be duly honoured in every way on all occasions.... If a person acts otherwise, he not only injures his own sect but also harms other sects. Truly, if a person extols his own sect and disparages other sects with a view to glorifying his own sect owing merely to his attachment to it, he injures his own sect very severely by acting in that way.

On the subject of public discussion and communication, it is also important to note that nearly every attempt at early printing in China, Korea, and Japan was undertaken by Buddhist technologists, with an interest in expanding communication. The first printed book in the world was a Chinese translation of an Indian Sanskrit treatise, later known as the "Diamond Sutra," done by a half-Indian and half-Turkish scholar called Kumarajeeva in the fifth century, which was printed in China four and half centuries later, in 868 C.E. The development of printing, largely driven by a commitment to propagate Buddhist perspectives (including compassion and benevolence), transformed the possibilities of public communication in general. Initially sought as a medium for spreading the Buddhist message, the innovation of printing was a momentous development in public communication that greatly expanded the opportunity of social deliberation.

The commitment of Buddhist scholars to expand communication in secular as well as religious subjects has considerable relevance for the global roots of democracy. Sometimes the communication took the form of a rebellious disagreement. Indeed, in the seventh century Fu-yi, a Confucian leader of an anti-Buddhist campaign, submitted the following complaint about Buddhists to the Tang emperor (almost paralleling the current official ire about the "indiscipline" of the Falun Gong): "Buddhism infiltrated into China from Central Asia, under a strange and barbarous form, and as such, it was then less dangerous. But since the Han period the Indian texts began to be translated into Chinese. Their publicity began to adversely affect the faith of the Princes and filial piety began to degenerate. The people began to shave their heads and refused to bow their heads to the Princes and their ancestors." In other cases, the dialectics took the form of learning from each other. In fact, in the

extensive scientific, mathematical, and literary exchanges between China and India during the first millennium C.E., Buddhist scholars played a major part.

In Japan in the early seventh century, the Buddhist Prince Shotoku, who was regent to his mother Empress Suiko, not only sent missions to China to bring back knowledge of art, architecture, astronomy, literature, and religion (including Taoist and Confucian texts in addition to Buddhist ones), but also introduced a relatively liberal constitution or *kempo*, known as "the constitution of seventeen articles," in 604 C.E. It insisted, much in the spirit of the Magna Carta (signed in England six centuries later), that "decisions on important matters should not be made by one person alone. They should be discussed with many." It also advised: "Nor let us be resentful when others differ from us. For all men have hearts, and each heart has its own leanings. Their right is our wrong, and our right is their wrong." Not surprisingly, many commentators have seen in this seventh-century constitution what Nakamura Hajime has called Japan's "first step of gradual development toward democracy."

There are, in fact, many manifestations of a firm commitment to public communication and associative reasoning that can be found in different places and times across the world. To take another illustration, which is of particular importance to science and culture, the great success of Arab civilization in the millennium following the emergence of Islam provides a remarkable example of indigenous creativity combined with openness to intellectual influences from elsewhere — often from people with very different religious beliefs and political systems. The Greek classics had a profound influence on Arab thinking, and, over a more specialized area, so did Indian mathematics. Even though no formal system of democratic governance was involved in these achievements, the excellence of what was achieved — the remarkable flourishing of Arab philosophy, literature, mathematics, and science — is a tribute not only to indigenous creativity but also to the glory of open public reasoning, which influences knowledge and technology as well as politics.

The idea behind such openness was well articulated by Imam Ali bin abi Taleb in the early seventh century, in his pronouncement that "no wealth can profit you more than the mind" and "no isolation can be more desolate than conceit." These and other such proclamations are quoted for their relevance to the contemporary world by the excellent "Arab Human Development Report 2002" of the United Nations. The thesis of European exceptionalism, by contrast, invites the Arabs, like the rest of the non-Western world, to forget their own heritage of public reasoning.

IV

To ignore the centrality of public reasoning in the idea of democracy not only distorts and diminishes the history of democratic ideas, it also detracts attention from the interactive processes through which a democracy functions and on which its success depends. The neglect of the global roots of public reasoning, which is a big loss in itself, goes with the undermining of an adequate understanding of the place and the role of democracy in the contemporary world. Even with the expansion of adult franchise and fair elections, free and uncensored deliberation is important for people to be able to determine what they must demand, what they should criticize, and how they ought to vote.

Consider the much-discussed proposition that famines do not occur in democracies, but only in imperial colonies (as used to happen in British India), or in military dictatorships (as in Ethiopia, Sudan, or Somalia, in recent decades), or in one-party states (as in the Soviet Union in the 1930s, or China from 1958 to 1961, or Cambodia in the 1970s, or North Korea in the immediate past). It is hard for a government to withstand public criticism when a famine occurs. This is due not merely to the fear of losing elections, but also to the prospective consequences of public censure when newspapers and other media are independent and uncensored and opposition parties are allowed to pester those in office. The proportion of people affected by famines is always rather small (hardly ever more than 10 percent of the total population), so for a famine to become a political nightmare for the government it is necessary to generate public sympathy through the sharing of information and open public discussion.

Even though India was experiencing famines until its independence in 1947 — the last one, the Bengal famine of 1943, killed between two and three million people — these catastrophes stopped abruptly when a multi-party democracy was established. China, by contrast, had the largest famine in recorded history between 1958 and 1961, in which it is estimated that between twenty-three and thirty million people died, following the debacle of collectivization in the so-called "Great Leap Forward." Still, the working of democracy, which is almost effortlessly effective in preventing conspicuous disasters such as famines, is often far less successful in politicizing the nastiness of regular but non-extreme undernourishment and ill health. India has had no problem in avoiding famines with timely intervention, but it has been much harder to generate adequate public interest in less immediate and less dramatic deprivations, such as the quiet presence of endemic but non-extreme hunger across the country and the low standard of basic health care.

While democracy is not without success in India, its achievements are still far short of what public reasoning can do in a democratic society if it addresses less conspicuous deprivations such as endemic hunger. A similar criticism can also be made about the protection of minority rights, which majority rule does not guarantee until and unless public discussion gives these rights enough political visibility and status to produce general public support. This certainly did not happen in the state of Gujarat last year, when politically engineered anti-Muslim riots led to unprecedented Hindu sectarian militancy and an electoral victory for the Hindu-chauvinist state government. How scrupulously secularism and minority rights will be guarded in India will depend on the reach and the vigor of public discussion on this subject. If democracy is construed not merely in terms of public balloting, but also in the more general form of public reasoning, then what is required is a strengthening of democracy, not a weakening of it.

To point to the need for more probing and more

vigorous public reasoning even in countries that formally have democratic institutions must not be seen as a counsel of despair. People can and do respond to generally aired concerns and appeals to tolerance and humanity, and this is part of the role of public reasoning. Indeed, it is not easy to dismiss the possibility that to a limited extent just such a response may be occurring in India in the wake of the Gujarat riots and the victory of Hindu sectarianism in the Gujarat elections in December 2002. The engineered success in Gujarat did not help the Bharatiya Janata Party, or BJP, in the state elections in the rest of India that followed the Gujarat elections. The BJP lost in all four state elections held in early 2003, but the defeat that was particularly significant occurred in the state of Himachal Pradesh, where the party had actually been in office but was routed this time, winning only sixteen seats against the Congress Party's forty. Moreover, a Muslim woman from the Congress Party won the mayoral election in Ahmadabad, where some of the worst anti-Muslim riots in Gujarat had occurred only a few months earlier. Much will depend on the breadth and the energy of public reasoning in the future — an issue that takes us back to the arguments presented by exponents of public reasoning in India's past, including Ashoka and Akbar, whose analyses remain thoroughly relevant today.

The complex role of public reasoning can also be seen in the comparisons between China's and India's achievements in the field of health care and longevity over recent decades. This happens to be a subject that has interested Chinese and Indian public commentators over millennia. While Faxian (Fa-Hien), a fifth-century Chinese visitor who spent ten years in India, wrote admiringly in effusive detail about the arrangements for public health care in Pataliputra, a later visitor who came to India in the seventh century, Yi Jing (I-Ching), argued in a more competitive vein that "in the healing arts of acupuncture and cautery and the skill of feeling the pulse, China has never been surpassed [by India]; the medicament for prolonging life is only found in China." There was also considerable discussion in India on *chinachar* — Chinese practice — in different fields when the two countries were linked by Buddhism.

By the middle of the twentieth century, China and India had about the same life expectancy at birth, around forty-five years or so. But post-revolution China, with its public commitment to improve health care and education (a commitment that was carried over from its days of revolutionary struggle), brought a level of dedication in radically enhancing health care that the more moderate Indian administration could not at all match. By the time the economic reforms were introduced in China in 1979, China had a lead of thirteen years or more over India in longevity, with the Chinese life expectancy at sixty-seven years, while India's was less than fifty-four years. Still, even though the radical economic reforms introduced in China in 1979 ushered in a period of extraordinary economic growth, the government slackened on the public commitment to health care, and in particular replaced automatic and free health insurance by the need to buy private insurance at one's own cost (except when provided by one's employer, which happens only in a small minority of cases). This largely retrograde movement in the coverage of health care met with little public resistance (as it undoubtedly would have in a multi-party democracy), even though it almost certainly had a role in slowing down the progress of Chinese longevity. In India, by contrast, unsatisfactory health services have come more and more under public scrutiny and general condemnation, with some favorable changes being forced on the services offered.

Despite China's much faster rate of growth since the economic reforms, the rate of expansion of life expectancy in India has been about three times as fast, on the average, as that in China. China's life expectancy, which is now just about seventy years, compares with India's figure of sixty-three years, so that the life expectancy gap in favor of China has been nearly halved, to seven years, over the last two decades. But note must be taken of the fact that it gets increasingly harder to expand life expectancy further as the absolute level rises, and it could be argued that perhaps China has now reached a level at which further expansion would be exceptionally difficult. Yet this explanation does not work, since China's life expectancy of seventy years is still very far below the figures for many countries in the world — indeed, even parts of India.

At the time of the economic reforms, when China had a life expectancy of about sixty-seven years, the Indian state of Kerala had a similar figure. By now, however, Kerala's life expectancy of seventy-four years is considerably above China's seventy years. Going further, if we look at specific points of vulnerability, the infant-mortality rate in China has fallen very slowly since the economic reforms, whereas it has continued to fall extremely sharply in Kerala. While Kerala had roughly the same infant mortality rate as China — thirty-seven per thousand — in 1979, Kerala's present rate, between thirteen and fourteen per thousand, is considerably less than half of China's thirty per thousand (where it has stagnated over the last decade). It appears that Kerala, with its background of egalitarian politics, has been able to benefit further from continued public reasoning protected by a democratic system. The latter on its own would seem to have helped India to narrow the gap with China quite sharply, despite the failings of the Indian health services that are widely discussed in the press. Indeed, the fact that so much is known — and in such detail — about the inadequacies of Indian health care from criticisms in the press is itself a contribution to improving the existing state of affairs.

The informational role of democracy, working mainly through open public discussion, can be pivotally important. It is the limitation of this informational feature that has come most sharply to attention in the context of the recent SARS epidemic. Although cases of SARS first appeared in southern China in November 2002 and caused many fatalities, information about the deadly new disease was kept under wraps until this April. Indeed, it was only when that highly infectious disease started spreading to Hong Kong and Beijing that the news had to be released, and by then the epidemic had already gone beyond the possibility of isolation and local elimination. The lack of open public discussion evidently played a critical part in the spread of the SARS epidemic in particular, but the general issue has a much wider relevance.

V

The value of public reasoning applies to reasoning about democracy itself. It is good that the practices of democracy have been sharply scrutinized in the literature on world affairs, for there are identifiable deficiencies in the performance of many countries that have the standard democratic institutions. Not only is public discussion of these deficiencies an effective means of trying to remedy them, but this is exactly how democracy in the form of public reasoning is meant to function. In this sense, the defects of democracy demand more democracy, not less.

The alternative — trying to cure the defects of democratic practice through authoritarianism and the suppression of public reasoning — increases the vulnerability of a country to sporadic disasters (including, in many cases, famine), and also to the whittling away of previously secured gains through a lack of public vigilance (as seems to have happened, to some extent, in Chinese health care). There is also a genuine loss of political freedom and restrictions of civil rights in even the best-performing authoritarian regimes, such as Singapore or pre-democratic South Korea; and, furthermore, there is no guarantee that the suppression of democracy would make, say, India more like Singapore than like Sudan or Afghanistan, or more like South Korea than like North Korea.

Seeing democracy in terms of public reasoning, as "government by discussion," also helps us to identify the far-reaching historical roots of democratic ideas across the world. The apparent Western modesty that takes the form of a humble reluctance to promote "Western ideas of democracy" in the non-Western world includes an imperious appropriation of a global heritage as exclusively the West's own. The self-doubt with regard to "pushing" Western ideas on non-Western societies is combined with the absence of doubt in viewing democracy as a quintessentially Western idea, an immaculate Western conception.

This misappropriation results from gross neglect of the intellectual history of non-Western societies, but also from the conceptual defect in seeing democracy primarily in terms of balloting, rather than in the broader perspective of public reasoning. A fuller understanding of the demands of democracy and of the global history of democratic ideas may contribute substantially to better political practice today. It may also help to remove some of the artificial cultural fog that obscures the appraisal of current affairs.

THE INFLUENCE OF THE GLOBAL ORDER ON THE PROSPECTS FOR GENUINE DEMOCRACY IN THE DEVELOPING COUNTRIES

Thomas W. Pogge

Thomas Pogge is in the Department of Philosophy at Columbia University. He has published numerous articles on the topics of global justice, poverty, and democracy. His books include Realizing Rawls *(1989),* World Poverty and Human Rights *(2002), and the collaborative volume* Global Justice *(2001).*

Pogge argues that features of our global economic system actively contribute to severe poverty and the absence of democratic processes in developing countries. As one example, he argues that the global order plays an important part in sustaining corruption and oppression in poorer countries by giving international borrowing privileges to any person or group in power and providing international resource privileges to those in power to freely dispose of their countries' resources. Pogge uses these and other descriptions of global factors to undermine the belief that the causes of severe poverty are indigenous to developing countries. He ends by suggesting policies for enhancing democratic procedures that can help eliminate the detrimental effects of the global order and improve the prospects for democracy in the developing world.

Broadly considered, our world appears to be in top condition, economically. At nearly US $30 trillion (World Bank 2001, 275), the global product is as high as never before. And even if inflation and population growth are taken into account, global economic growth has been impressive: Even while humankind has doubled during the past 40 years, from three billion people (UNDP 1997, 195) to six billion (World Bank 2001, 275), the real *global product* (i.e., the inflation-adjusted sum of all gross domestic products or GDPs) has quadrupled in the same period, so that the real *per capita* global product is now roughly twice what it was in 1960 (UNDP 1998, 142; cf. UNDP 1999, 154).[1] Looking forward one might add that, following the end of the Cold War, global military expenditures have been cut by nearly one half — from 4.7 percent of the global product in 1985 (UNDP 1998, 197) to 2.4 percent thereof in 1996 (UNDP 1999, 191) — a decline that currently releases for more productive purposes almost $700 billion annually (the so-called "peace dividend"). Is the world we are handing over to the humanity of the new millennium then an idyllic paradise in which milk and honey flow freely?

This Panglossian view is disturbed by the fact that large segments of humankind are hardly participating in our economic progress and prosperity. At the bottom, in the poorest quintile, conditions continue to be desperate: 1.2 billion persons live below the *international poverty line*, "that income or expenditure level below which a minimum, nutritionally adequate diet plus essential non-food requirements are not affordable" (UNDP 1996, 222). The World Bank currently specifies this line in terms of $392.88 PPP 1993 (Chen and Ravallion 2000, 6): People count as poor if their income per person per year has less purchasing power than $392.88 had in the US in 1993, less purchasing power than $466 have in the US today (year 2000).

As a consequence of such severe poverty, 790 million lack adequate nutrition, 1 billion lack access to safe water, 2.4 billion lack basic sanitation (UNDP 2000, 30); more than 880 million lack access to basic health services (UNDP 1999, 22); 1 billion are without adequate shelter and 2 billion without electricity (UNDP 1998, 49). 250 million children between 5 and 14 do wage work outside their household — often under harsh or cruel conditions: as soldiers, prostitutes, or domestic servants, or in agriculture, construction, textile or carpet production (World Bank 2001, 62). About 1 billion adults are illiterate (UNDP 2000, 30). Roughly one third of all human deaths, some 50,000 daily, are due to poverty-related causes,[2] easily preventable through better nutrition, safe drinking water, vaccines, cheap re-hydration packs, and antibiotics. If the European Union had its proportional share of all this suffering, we would have nearly 50 million malnourished people and well over a million poverty-related deaths each year.

Of course, severe poverty is nothing new. What is new is the extent of global inequality. Genuine affluence is no longer reserved to a tiny minority. Hundreds of millions are enjoying a high standard of living with lots of free time during and after their working years, allowing ample opportunities to enjoy travel, education, cars, household appliances, computers, and so on. The so-called "high-income countries" — 33 affluent states plus Hong Kong — contain 14.9 percent of the world's population, but have 78.4 percent of the global product (World Bank 2001, 275). Gross national product (GNP) *per capita* in these countries averages $25,725 (ibid.). By contrast, the people in the poorest quintile live, on average, 30 percent below the international poverty line[3] Thus they have, on average, $326 PPP 2000 per person per year. Since the purchasing power attributed to them by the World Bank is on average about four times their actual income,[4] the people of the poorest quintile have at current exchange rates about $82 per person per year — collectively $98 billion annually or one third of one percent of the global product.[5] In short: Half a percent of the collective GNP of the high-income countries — $115 billion

annually — would suffice to double the income of everyone in the bottom quintile.

Such extreme inequality is a recent phenomenon: "The income gap between the fifth of the world's people living in the richest countries and the fifth in the poorest was 74 to 1 in 1997, up from 60 to 1 in 1990 and 30 to 1 in 1960. [Earlier] the income gap between the top and bottom countries increased from 3 to 1 in 1820 to 7 to 1 in 1870 to 11 to 1 in 1913" (UNDP 1999, 3).[6] A detailed study of the development of income inequality among *persons* world-wide shows the same dramatic trend: "World inequality [...] has increased from a Gini of 62.5 in 1988 to 66.0 in 1993. This represents an increase of 0.7 Gini points per year. This is a very fast increase, faster than the increase experienced by the US and UK in the decade of the 1980's. [...] The bottom 5 percent of the world grew poorer, as their real incomes decreased by one quarter, while the richest quintile grew richer. It gained 12 percent in real terms, that is it grew more than twice as much as mean world income (5.7 percent)" (Milanovic 1999, 52f.).

Inequalities in wealth are significantly greater than inequalities in income. Well-off persons typically have more net worth than annual income, while the poor typically own less than one annual income. The huge fortunes of the ultra-rich have been specially highlighted in recent *Human Development Reports*: "the world's 200 richest people more than doubled their net worth in the four years to 1998, to more than $1 trillion. The assets of the top three billionaires are more than the combined GNP of all least developed countries and their 600 million people" (UNDP 1999, 3). "The additional cost of achieving and maintaining universal access to basic education for all, basic health care for all, reproductive health care for all women, adequate food for all and safe water and sanitation for all is [...] less than 4 percent of the combined wealth of the 225 richest people in the world" (UNDP 1998, 30).

One is tempted to react to such facts with moral condemnation. But it is more important, first of all, to explain these facts. How does it come about that there is so much desperate poverty in a world that, in aggregate, is rather affluent? And why is global economic inequality consistently and rapidly increasing? I am well aware that such questions do not fall within the purview of the ordinary tasks and competencies of a mere philosopher. I want to address them nonetheless, because I believe that economists and political scientists have not taken them seriously enough and have thus far given only incomplete, and even misleading accounts of the causes of current global poverty and inequality.

Let us begin with points of agreement. First, there is little controversy about the facts. Indeed, most of the data I have presented come, directly or indirectly, from the economists at the World Bank who, however, not surprisingly, prefer to dwell on the positive. Second, economists deplore the widespread persistence of severe poverty and the accumulation of enormous global inequalities in income and wealth. Third, economists agree that these facts have social causes. That so many people subsist in life-threatening poverty is not due to their own laziness, wastefulness, greater needs, or lesser natural endowments, but due to social factors over which they have no control. If these same people had been born in Italy or Norway, they would lead just as long and healthy and happy lives as those who actually did have the good fortune to be born in those places.

What then are the social causes of the persistence of poverty? Here economists divide into two main schools of thought. The libertarians on the right — also called freshwater economists because they tend to live in Chicago — argue that poverty persists because most poor countries do not follow the examples of Japan and the Asian tigers (Hong Kong, Taiwan, Singapore, and South Korea). These success stories show, so say the libertarians, that the best way to expel human misery is economic growth, and the best way to achieve economic growth is to foster free enterprise with a minimum in taxes, regulations, and red tape.

The other, left-leaning school of thought, represented by Amartya Sen, also has its favourite poster-child: Kerala, a state in India. Kerala is a poor state, but its socialist government gives priority to fulfilling basic needs. And so the people of Kerala do much better in terms of health, educa-

tion, and longevity than the people of other, more affluent Indian states.

Economists disagree then quite sharply about the causal roles of various *local* social factors in the reproduction of poverty. One side argues that poverty persists because poor countries have too much government: taxes, regulations, and red tape. The other side argues that poverty persists because poor countries have too little government: schools, hospitals, and infrastructure. As this issue is surely important, our attention is diverted from what both sides take for granted: That the social causes of poverty, and hence the key to its eradication, lie in the poor countries themselves. We find this shared belief all the more appealing because it reinforces our ever so dear conviction that we and our governments and the global economic order we impose are not substantial contributors to the horrendous conditions among the global poor. So we get drawn into believing that the crucial variable for the explanation and avoidance of severe poverty is the decision-making in the developing countries: With the right organisation and developmental policies any poor country can over time meet the basic needs of its people.[7] Yet severe poverty remains widespread, because the poor countries have bad economic institutions and bad economic policies which are generally due to the incompetence and corruption of their political leaders and public officials. This is the picture that both right-wing and left-wing economists present, and this is the view that our politicians and the general public accept and repeat.

This popular view of global poverty is quite correct in what it asserts. The eradication of severe poverty in the developing countries indeed depends strongly on their governments and political institutions. It depends on how their economies are structured and also on whether there exists a genuine competition for political office which gives politicians an incentive to be responsive to the interests of the poor majority.

But the popular explanation of global poverty is nonetheless deeply misleading, because it portrays the faulty institutions and policies and the corrupt elites prevalent in the developing world as an exogenous fact: as a fact that explains, but does not itself stand in need of explanation. "Some developing countries manage to give themselves reasonable political institutions, but many others fail or do not even try. This is just the way things are." An explanation that runs out at this point does not explain very much.

An adequate explanation of global poverty must not merely adduce the prevalence of faulty institutions and policies and of corrupt and oppressive élites in the developing world but must also provide an explanation for this prevalence. In order to understand the persistence of massive and severe poverty world-wide, we need an explanation for why incompetent, oppressive, and corrupt governments which are unresponsive to the needs and interests of "their" populations are so very frequent in the developing world.

Explanations offered in this vein generally point to the culture and/or history of particular countries. A cultural explanation might assert, for instance, that corruption or dictatorial rule are endemic to the culture of certain countries, widely accepted by the population as a familiar feature of their way of life.[8] An historical explanation may, for instance, trace Cambodia's lack of progress during the last 30 years back to the fact that this country was dragged into the Vietnam War and that its population was therefore victimised first by a pro-American military dictatorship with civil war and then, after the US withdrawal, by a crazy communist nationalism of the Khmer Rouge (who had become popular through the earlier military repression). Likewise, one might explain the frequency of corrupt elites in Africa by reference to the fact that national borders there were drawn during the colonial era without regard for tribal and linguistic boundaries. This has led to ethnically and linguistically heterogeneous states whose internal communities feel much distrust and little solidarity for one another. As a consequence, many African politicians are supported only by members of their own linguistic or ethnic community. Since such politicians must then rely on this community for their political power, they are beholden to it and obliged to favour it unfairly, which in turn reinforces mutual resentment and distrust among the various communities.

Such cultural and historical explanations are not always correct. This is especially true of cultural explanations, from which one can often learn more about the prejudices of their authors than about the countries in question. Indonesia, for instance, has long been a favourite example of a corrupt culture — but only among those who were blind to the hatred and contempt ordinary Indonesians have been feeling for their ruling elite until these feeling have finally burst forth in the late 1990s.

Historical explanations, insofar as they are correct, usefully complement and relativise the conventional analysis according to which responsibility for world poverty lies with "the poor countries themselves." But historical explanations also conveniently localise the affluent countries' contribution to world poverty in the past — when the US was still making war in South East Asia or when European states still had colonies in Africa. Such explanations therefore do not upset the popular opinion that *we now* are not involved in the reproduction of global poverty and can do only very little toward mitigating this problem.

Precisely this popular opinion is undermined when our explanation of oppression and poverty takes account of present global factors. I do not have in mind here merely (what one might call) negative factors, such as the absence of initiatives through which the rich countries *could* promote greater democratic responsiveness and economic justice. For the absence of possible causal factors can generally contribute to the explanation of actual phenomena only in a somewhat metaphysical sense. Nor am I referring to the numerous cases in which significant support from governments and secret services of powerful countries has enabled allied but domestically unpopular and corrupt groups to gain or to maintain power. Rather, I want to highlight aspects of the prevailing *global* economic and political order that contribute actively to the perpetuation of poverty.

Two such aspects are obvious, so a brief mention will suffice. The rules of our global order are shaped through negotiations among governments representing the interests of their countries and populations. It is therefore not surprising that these rules reflect the existing huge international differentials in bargaining power and expertise. This fact helps us understand the above-documented fact: That international economic inequality is steadily increasing and at an ever accelerating rate. The affluent states use their greater bargaining power to shape the rules of the global economic order in their own favour. These skewed rules in turn allow them to procure the lion's share of the benefits of global economic growth. This increases international economic inequality and thereby further strengthens the bargaining power of the affluent states, allowing them to shape the rules even more strongly in their favour. And so the cycle continues.[9]

The other obvious aspect involves the negative externalities of our affluent lifestyle: The populations of poor countries suffer from the pollution produced in the developed countries during the last 200 years — while they are, unlike us, excluded from the benefits. They suffer the effects of global warming and ozone depletion caused by our emissions of greenhouse gases. They suffer the effects of the drug trade fuelled by the huge demand for drugs in the US and Europe and of the war on drugs prosecuted by the US and European governments. They suffer from the depletion of natural resources such as crude oil and metals whose prices are much higher than they would be, if the affluent countries were prepared to moderate their consumption. They suffer from disease strains that have become resistant to ordinary drugs because of treatment practices in the developed countries. They suffer from the AIDS epidemic which affluent sex tourists are spreading around the globe with the help of patent rules that permit drug companies to suppress cheaper generic versions of medications they have patented.

Leaving these more obvious aspects aside, I will focus on showing how our global order plays an important part in sustaining oppression and corruption in the poorer countries. These phenomena are especially significant, because they cause not only poverty in the developing world, but also moral detachment among the affluent. We do not feel responsibility, but only condescending pity for peoples who somehow never get their act together and allow themselves to be ruled by incompetent kleptocrats who ruin their economies. Showing this picture's inadequacy is crucial, then, for overcoming that moral detachment.

A paradigm case of corruption is bribery. Bribes play a major role in the awarding of public contracts in the developing countries, which suffer staggering losses as a result. These losses arise in part from the fact that bribes are "priced in": Bidders on contracts must raise their price in order to get paid enough to pay the bribes. Additional losses arise as bidders can afford to be non-competitive, knowing that the success of their bid will depend on their bribes more than on the price they offer. The greatest losses probably arise from the fact that officials focused on bribes pay little attention to whether the goods and services they purchase in their country's behalf are of good quality or even needed at all. Much of what developing countries have imported over the decades has been of no use to them — or even harmful, by promoting environmental degradation or violence (bribery is especially pervasive in the arms trade). May we then conclude that poverty in developing societies is the fault of their own tolerance of corruption and of their own leaders' venality?

This comfortable conclusion is upset by the fact that, until 1999, most developed states have not merely legally authorised their firms to bribe foreign officials, but have even allowed these firms to deduct such bribes from their taxable revenues, thereby providing financial inducements and moral support to the practice of bribing politicians and officials in the developing countries.[10] Bribes encouraged by such rules divert the loyalties of officials in developing countries and also make a great difference to what persons are motivated to scramble for public office in the first place. There is hope that the recently adopted *Convention on Combating Bribery of Foreign Officials in International Business Transactions* will make blatant bribery less frequent.[11] But this Convention cannot undo the pervasive culture of corruption that is now deeply entrenched in many developing countries thanks to the extensive bribery they were subjected to during their formative years.

Moreover, huge asymmetries in other incentives remain in place. The political and economic élites of a poor country interact both with its domestic population and with foreign governments and corporations. These two constituencies differ enormously in wealth and power. The former — poorly educated and heavily preoccupied with the daily struggle for their families' survival — can do little by way of resisting or rewarding their local and national rulers. The latter, by contrast, have vastly greater rewards and penalties at their disposal. Politicians with a normal interest in their own political and economic success can therefore be expected to cater to the interests of foreign governments and corporations rather then to the interests of their much poorer compatriots. And this, of course, is what we find: There are plenty of developing-country governments that came to power or stay in power only thanks to foreign support. And there are plenty of developing-country politicians and bureaucrats who, induced or even bribed by foreigners, work against the interests of their people: *for* the development of a tourist-friendly sex industry (whose forced exploitation of children and women they tolerate and profit from), *for* the importation of unneeded, obsolete, or overpriced products at public expense, *for* the permission to import hazardous products, wastes, or productive facilities, against laws protecting employees or the environment, and so on.

To be sure, there would not be such huge asymmetries in incentives if the developing countries were more democratic, allowing their populations a genuine political role. Why then are most of the poor countries so far from being genuinely democratic? This question brings further aspects of the current global institutional order into view.

It is a very central feature of this order that any group controlling a preponderance of the means of coercion within a country is internationally recognised as the legitimate government of this country's territory and people — regardless of how this group came to power, of how it exercises power, and of the extent to which it may be supported or opposed by the population it rules. That such a group exercising effective power receives international recognition means not merely that we engage it in negotiations. It means also that we accept this group's right to act for the people it

rules, that we, most significantly, confer upon it the privileges freely to borrow in the country's name (international borrowing privilege) and freely to dispose of the country's natural resources (international resource privilege).

The international borrowing privilege includes the power[12] to impose internationally valid legal obligations upon the country at large. Any successor government that refuses to honour debts incurred by an ever so corrupt, brutal, undemocratic, unconstitutional, repressive, unpopular predecessor will be severely punished by the banks and governments of other countries; at minimum it will lose its own borrowing privilege by being excluded from the international financial markets. Such refusals are therefore quite rare, as governments, even when newly elected after a dramatic break with the past, are compelled to pay the debts of their ever so awful predecessors.

The international borrowing privilege has three important negative effects on the corruption and poverty problems in the developing world. First, this privilege facilitates borrowing by destructive governments. Such governments can borrow more money and can do so more cheaply than they could do if they alone, rather than the entire country, were obliged to repay. In this way, the borrowing privilege helps such governments to maintain themselves in power even against near-universal popular discontent and opposition. Second, the international borrowing privilege imposes upon democratic successor regimes the often huge debts of their corrupt predecessors. It thereby saps the capacity of such democratic governments to implement structural reforms and other political programs, thus rendering such governments less successful and less stable than they would otherwise be. (It is small consolation that authoritarian regimes are sometimes weakened by being held liable for the debts of their democratic predecessors.) Third, the international borrowing privilege further strengthens the incentives toward coup attempts: Whoever succeeds in bringing a preponderance of the means of coercion under his control gets the borrowing privilege as an additional reward.[13]

The resource privilege we confer upon a group in power is much more than our mere acquiescence in its effective control over the natural resources of the country in question. This privilege includes the power to effect legally valid transfers of ownership rights in such resources. Thus a corporation that has purchased resources from the Saudis or Suharto, or from Mobuto or Sani Abacha, has thereby become entitled to be — and actually is — recognised anywhere in the world as the legitimate owner of these resources. This is a remarkable feature of our global institutional order. A group that overpowers the guards and takes control of a warehouse may be able to give some of the merchandise to others, accepting money in exchange. But the fence who pays them becomes merely the possessor, not the owner, of the loot. Contrast this with a group that overpowers an elected government and takes control of a country. Such a group, too, can give away some of the country's natural resources, accepting money in exchange. In this case, however, the purchaser acquires not merely possession, but all the rights and liberties of ownership, which are supposed to be — and actually *are* — protected and enforced by all other states' courts and police forces. The international resource privilege, then, is the legal power to confer globally valid ownership rights in the country's resources.

This international resource privilege has disastrous effects in many poor countries, whose resource sector often constitutes a large segment of the national economy. Whoever can take power in such a country by whatever means can maintain his rule, even against widespread popular opposition, by buying the arms and soldiers he needs with revenues from the export of natural resources (and funds borrowed abroad in the country's name). Take Nigeria as an example. The value of Nigeria's oil exports has averaged about $20 million a day, roughly one quarter of that country's gross domestic product. Whoever controls this revenue stream can afford enough weapons and soldiers to keep himself in power regardless of what the population may think of him.[14] And so long as he succeeds in doing so, his purse will be continuously replenished with new funds with which he can cement his rule and finance a luxurious life style.

This fact in turn provides a strong incentive toward the undemocratic acquisition and unresponsive exercise of political power in these countries.[15] The international resource privilege also gives foreigners strong incentives to corrupt the officials of such countries who, no matter how badly they rule, continue to have resources to sell and money to spend. These incentives go a long way toward explaining the so-called Dutch Disease,[16] the long observed negative correlation between resource wealth (defined as the size of the natural resource sector as a percentage of GNP) and economic progress: Severe poverty is more persistent in resource-rich countries, because the special incentives arising from the international resource privilege make them more prone to corrupt government, coup attempts, and civil wars. Indeed, a recent regression analysis by two Yale economists confirms that the causal connection between resource wealth and poor economic growth is mediated through reduced chances for democracy.[17] The economists fail to note, however, that it is only because of the international resource privilege that resource wealth has so pernicious effects.

By discussing several global systemic factors in some detail, I hope to have undermined a proposition that, sustained by right-wing and left-wing economists alike, most citizens in the developed countries are all too eager to believe: The causes of severe poverty are indigenous to the countries in which it occurs, and the affluent societies and their governments do not substantially contribute to the persistence of severe poverty world-wide. This view is dramatically mistaken. The non-indigenous factors I have discussed are absolutely crucial for explaining the inability and especially the unwillingness of the poor countries' leaders to pursue more effective strategies of poverty eradication. They are absolutely crucial, therefore, for explaining why global inequality is increasing dramatically, so that income poverty and malnutrition have not declined in the last 14 years (World Bank 2001, 23), despite substantial technological progress, despite substantial global economic growth, despite a huge poverty reduction in China, despite the post-Cold-War "peace dividend," and despite a 32 percent drop in real food prices since 1985.[18]

An adequate explanation of the persistence of severe poverty requires analysis of these non-indigenous factors. And effective reduction of such poverty requires modifications in these factors, which, in turn, requires a better understanding in the developed countries of how the social causes of the persistence of severe poverty lie by no means in the poor countries alone.

To recapitulate. What I have tried to substantiate here is a point not of morality, but of causal explanation. One can put this point negatively, as a critique of the conventional wisdom, or rather ideology: Observing much political oppression and severe poverty in the developing countries, and noting that these evils are not evenly distributed among them, experts and laypersons alike are drawn to explanations invoking national factors (history, culture, climate, natural environment, leadership personalities, etc.) and international differences in such domestic factors. But these local explanations are importantly incomplete in two respects.

First, an explanation in terms of domestic factors leaves open why these domestic factors are the way they are in the first place. It is quite possible that global factors significantly affect national institutions and policies, especially in the poorer and weaker countries, and that, in a different global environment, domestic factors that tend to generate oppression, corruption, and poverty would occur much less frequently or not at all.

Second, local explanations can show at best how *in the prevailing global context* specific domestic factors are causally connected with oppression, corruption, and poverty. Such explanations leave wide open the possibility that, in a different global environment, the same domestic factors, or the same international differences, would have quite a different impact.

It may be objected that, even if our global institutional order plays an important part in the reproduction of oppression, corruption, and poverty in the developing world, there are no feasible institutional alternatives that would lead to substantial improvements. I have tried elsewhere to meet this objection by presenting such an institutional alternative in some detail (Pogge 2001). Summarising briefly, the main idea is that the international

resource and borrowing privileges are to be assigned only to governments that either came to power pursuant to democratic procedures or have legitimated themselves *ex post* through free and open elections. Governments fulfilling neither condition are not entitled to impose internationally valid repayment obligations upon their country or to effect internationally valid transfers of ownership rights in their country's natural resources.

Internationally authoritative decisions about the democratic legitimacy of a particular government are to be made by a standing Democracy Panel — composed of reputable, independent jurists and affiliated with the UN — which should have at its disposal specially trained personnel for the observation and (in special cases) implementation of elections. This commission should, as far as possible, apply the particular rules of democratic legitimisation which each country has imposed on itself in a generally democratic way.[19] By incorporating such rules into written constitutions (which should also lay down precisely how such rules may legitimately be amended), democratic governments would ensure that the Panel will make its decision pursuant to standards approved (in advance) by the country's own population and would also facilitate the work of the commission in a way that helps stabilise that country's democratic institutions. It should nevertheless be possible, in special cases, for governments that came to power by force to legitimate themselves through a newly designed democratic procedure accepted by the commission as satisfying internationally recognised general principles of democratic governance.

The modified borrowing privilege should not have a destabilising effect on existing democratic governments. Such an effect might come about as follows. If an officially illegitimate government cannot, in any case, borrow abroad in the name of the entire country, it may see no reason to service debts incurred by democratic predecessors. This fact might make borrowing abroad more difficult for democratic governments perceived to be in danger of being overthrown — which would not, of course, be in the spirit of my proposal.[20] This difficulty could be neutralized through an International Democratic Loan Guarantee Fund (IDLGF) that temporarily services the debts of countries with broadly democratic constitutions, as recognized by the Democracy Panel, in the event (and *only* in the event) that unconstitutional rulers of such countries refuse to do so. The existence of the IDLGF does not alter the fact that authoritarian rulers — no matter how illegal and illegitimate their acquisition and exercise of political power may be domestically — are obligated under international law to service their country's public debts abroad and should be sanctioned if they fail to do so. Its sole point is to neutralize precisely the risk that the institutional reform under discussion might otherwise add to the ordinary risks of lending money to countries with fledgling democratic governments.

The modified resource privilege must accommodate the fact that natural resources located within an illegitimately governed country may belong to private (domestic or foreign, individual or corporate) owners. In this case, revenues from resource sales are generally divided: One part goes to the government (as taxes and other fees) while the remainder goes to the private owners. The modified rules should, in such cases, be sensitive to three considerations. They should be sensitive to the origin of the property right in question and, in particular, to whether this right was acquired at a time when the country was governed democratically. They should be sensitive to the proportions in which the revenues are being divided and, in particular, to how much of these revenues would be diverted to the undemocratic government now in power. And these modified rules should also be sensitive to the degree of illegitimacy of this present government, which depends also on how it is affecting the fulfilment of human rights as well as the incidence of domination, corruption, and poverty. To achieve optimal incentive effects, the scheme should be both graduated (responsive to how illegitimate a government is) and rigid (not circumventable through bilateral deals with this or that powerful state).

Clearly, a reform along these lines is feasible in the sense that, with the support of the established affluent democracies, it could be effectively implemented. No less clearly, such a reform is unfeasible in the sense that it will not in fact be supported by the established affluent democracies. We would sustain some minor opportunity costs if our banks could not make safe and profitable loans to autocrats and corrupt élites in the developing world. By contrast, the opportunity costs of not recognising the power of authoritarian rulers to confer legally valid ownership rights in their country's natural resources are potentially enormous.[21] The international resource privilege brings vast benefits not only to autocratic rulers, but also to us: It guarantees us a reliable and steady supply of resources — because we can acquire ownership of them from anyone who happens to exercise effective power, without regard to whether the country's population either approves the sale or benefits from the proceeds. And it greatly reduces the price we pay for these resources — because no supplier is excluded (e.g., for lack of democratic authorisation) and also because corrupt supplier governments, made more frequent by the international resource privilege, will tend to maximise sales in the short term in order to serve their own personal interests (whereas supplier governments serving the needs of a country's present and future people are more inclined to budget its resources for maximum long-term benefit).[22] Just imagine what the price of globally traded natural resources — crude oil, for instance — would be if internationally valid ownership rights in them could not be procured from rulers who gained power unconstitutionally and exercise it undemocratically.[23]

Clearly, then, the governments and citizens of the developed countries will not agree to any meaningful restriction of the international legal powers of authoritarian and unconstitutional rulers. But this political unfeasibility does not undermine my explanatory thesis. By coercively imposing the international borrowing and resource privileges upon the rest of the world, the developed states make a major causal contribution to the persistence of oppression, corruption, and poverty in the developing world. Our refusal to allow meaningful institutional reforms does not alter the fact that we *could* allow them and are thus causally responsible for the misery such reforms would avoid.

This point has important implications for our

understanding of moral responsibilities: We tend to blame persistent oppression, corruption, and poverty in so many developing countries on their social institutions and elites. In this assessment we are correct: If those social institutions and elites were more reasonable, those problems would rapidly decline. We conclude from this that oppression, corruption, and poverty in the developing countries cannot be blamed upon external (foreign or global) factors. But this judgement, encouraged perhaps by faulty additive conceptions of causality and moral responsibility, is in error: We, too, are causally and morally responsible, because we uphold a global order in which persons and groups, if only they can seize effective power within a national territory by whatever means, may count on international recognition and support (exemplified by the international resource and borrowing privileges). This global order foreseeably contributes to the persistence of oppression, corruption, and poverty in four main ways: It crucially affects what sorts of persons shape national policy in the developing countries, what incentives these persons face, what options they have, and what impact their decisions about these options would have on the lives of their compatriots.

The flaw in the moral understanding dominant in the developed countries is closely related to a faulty interpunctuation of the situation. We see two morally significant relations: our relation to any developing country and its government's relation to its population. The former relation involves us, but it is fair — we lend money or purchase resources at going world market prices. The latter relation may be quite unjust, but we, not party to it, bear no responsibility for this injustice. The foregoing causal analysis shows how this interpunctuation, which sharply separates *us* in the developed countries from *them* in the developing countries, is deeply flawed. The morally relevant interpunctuation separates a larger *us* from the disenfranchised populations of the developing world. The morally relevant question is: What entitles us — the governments and citizens of the developed countries *and* the ruling elites of the developing ones — to enforce a global order under which we can unilaterally, on mutually agreeable terms, dispossess the majority of humankind of the world's natural

resources and burden them with the servicing of debts which they do not approve and from which they do not benefit? How can consent bought from a military strongman — someone like Sani Abacha of Nigeria — insulate Shell and its customers from the charge of having stolen the oil they took from the Nigerians? In fact, was it not worse than theft? Not only have we taken resources from them and done much environmental damage without their consent; but we have also propped up their hated dictator with funds he could spend on arms and soldiers to cement his rule. What is more, we are offering a prize to every would-be autocrat or junta anywhere: Whoever can gain effective power by whatever means will have the legal power to incur debts in the country's name and to confer internationally valid ownership rights in the country's resources. And having done all this, we lavish condescending pity on impoverished populations for their notorious "failure to govern themselves democratically"!

I hope that this essay, though it had to be brief, has lent some initial plausibility to the claims that a considerable part of the oppression, corruption, and poverty so prevalent in the developing world is foreseeably and avoidably caused by the current design of our global institutional order and that we, insofar as we co-operate in upholding this order, share moral responsibility for these foreseeable and avoidable effects. If so, further empirical exploration of the explanatory significance of central features of our global institutional order, such as the resource and borrowing privileges in particular, would seem warranted.

Author's Note

Versions of this paper have been presented at conferences in Frankfurt (December 1998), Bielefeld (February 1999), and Stanford (April 1999). I am grateful to my audiences there for valuable comments and criticisms. I am grateful also for a grant from the Research and Writing Initiative of the Program on Global Security and Sustainability of the John D. and Catherine T. MacArthur Foundation, which supported my subsequent work on updating and revising this essay.

NOTES

1. The corresponding figures in the latest report (UNDP 2000, 181) are incorrect — see <www.undp.org/hdro/errata.html>.

2. Among these causes are diarrhoea (6075) and malnutrition (1340), perinatal conditions (5760) and maternal conditions (1350), acute respiratory infections (9600, mainly pneumonia), sexually transmitted diseases (6750, mainly HIV), chronic obstructive pulmonary disease (6160), tuberculosis (4100), malaria (3040), measles (2430), tetanus (1120), and pertussis (940). See WHO 1999, Annex Table 2; cf. UNICEF 1998.

3. Chen and Ravallion 2000, Tables 2 and 4, dividing the poverty gap index by the headcount index.

4. Thus the World Bank equates China's *per capita* GNP of $780 to $3,291 PPP, India's $450 to $2,149 PPP, Indonesia's $580 to $2,439 PPP, Nigeria's $310 to $744 PPP, Ethiopia's $100 to $599 PPP, the Philippines' $1,020 to $3,815 PPP, Vietnam's $370 to $1,755, and so on (World Bank 2001, 274f.).

5. These are the poorest of the poor. The World Bank provides statistics also for a more generous poverty line that is twice as high: $786 PPP 1993 ($932 PPP or roughly $233 in the year 2000) per person per year. 2.8 billion people are said to live below this higher poverty line, falling 44.4 percent below it on average (Chen and Ravallion 2000, Tables 3 and 4, again dividing the poverty gap index by the headcount index). This much larger group of people can then, on average, buy as much per person per year as we can buy with $518 in a rich country or with $130 in a poor one. And the collective annual income of this group — nearly half of human kind — is then $367 billion or 1¼ percent of the annual global product.

6. Note that the increase in inequality is accelerating: The data just cited show that the quintile inequality ratio increased, on average, by 1.66 percent annually in the colonial period (1820 to 1960), by 2.33 percent annually from 1960 to 1990, and by 3.00 percent annually from 1990 to 1997.

7. John Rawls's latest book relies heavily on the assumption that peoples are masters of their own fate, that the causes of international inequality are purely domestic: "The causes of the wealth of a people and the forms it takes lie in their political culture and in the religious, philosophical, and moral traditions that support the basic structure of their political and social institutions, as well as in the industriousness and co-operative talents of its members, all supported by their political virtues. ... Crucial also is the country's population policy" (Rawls 1999, 108). If a society does not want to be poor, it can curb its population growth or industrialise (ibid., 117f.) and, in any case, "if it is not satisfied, it can continue to increase savings, or, if this is not feasible, borrow from other members of the Society of Peoples" (ibid., 114). With the right culture and policies, even resource-poor countries like Japan can do very well. With the wrong culture and policies, resource-rich countries like Argentina may do very poorly (ibid., 108). Everyone can succeed on their own — except only, perhaps, the Arctic Eskimos (ibid., 108n.).

8. Here is one notorious example: "It is not the sign for some collective derangement or radical incapacity for a political community to produce an authoritarian regime. Indeed, the history, culture, and religion of the community may be such that authoritarian regimes come, as it were, naturally, reflecting a widely shared world view or way of life" (Walzer 1980, 224f.). See also Landes 1998, and the essays collected in Harrison and Huntington 2001.

9. This point is well documented in the more sober reportage parts of *The Economist* (e.g., September 25 1999, 89), whose editors have outdone all others in their defence of the WTO and in their vilification of the protesters of Seattle and Washington as enemies of the poor.

10. In the United States, the post-Watergate Congress tried to prevent the bribing of foreign officials through its 1977 Foreign Corrupt Practices Act, passed after the Lockheed Corporation was found to have paid — not a modest sum to some third-world official, but rather — a US $2 million bribe to Prime Minister Kakuei Tanaka of powerful and democratic Japan.

11. The convention went into effect in February 1999 and as of April 2001 has been ratified by 31 states <http://www.oecd.org/daf/nocorruption/annex2.htm>.

This success was facilitated by public pressure generated by the innovative non-governmental organisation Transparency International <www.transparency.de> and by steady support from the US, which did not want its firms to be at a disadvantage vis-à-vis their foreign rivals.

12. As understood by Hohfeld 1919, a power involves the legally recognised authority to alter the distribution of first-order liberty rights, claim rights, and duties. Having a power or powers in this sense is distinct from having power (i.e., control over physical force and/or means of coercion).

13. The rulers of resource-rich developing countries have been especially adept at mortgaging their countries' future for their own benefit. As of 1998, Nigeria's foreign debt, run up by its succession of military dictatorships, stood at $30 billion or 79% of GNP. The 1998 ratios of foreign debt to GNP for other large resource-rich countries are as follows: Kenya 61%, Angola 297%, Mozambique 223%, Brazil 31%, Venezuela 40%, Indonesia 176%, the Philippines 70% (UNDP 2000, 219-21). The 1997 ratio for the Congo/Zaire is 232% (UNDP 1999, 195). Needless to say, little of the borrowed funds were channelled into productive investments, e.g., in education and infrastructure, which would augment economic growth and thus tax revenues that could help meet interest and repayment obligations. Much was taken for personal use or used for military and "internal security" expenditures.

14. For some background, see "Going on down," in *The Economist*, June 8 1996, 46-8. A later update says: "oil revenues [are] paid directly to the government at the highest level [...] The head of state has supreme power and control of all the cash. He depends on nobody and nothing but oil. Patronage and corruption spread downwards from the top" (*The Economist*, December 12 1998, 19).

15. To be sure, oppression, coups, and civil wars may be encouraged by the prospect of mere possession of resources. (As I have learned from Josiah Ober, this is elegantly observed already in Thucydides 1986, bk 1, ch 2.) But without the legal power to confer internationally valid ownership rights, the value of the resources, and the corresponding incentive, would obviously be much diminished.

16. This name alludes to a period in Dutch history

which began in 1959 with the discovery of huge natural gas reserves that, by the 1970's, produced revenues and import savings of about $5-$6 billion annually. Despite this windfall (enhanced by the "oil-shock" increases in energy prices), the Dutch economy suffered stagnation, high unemployment, and finally recession — doing considerably worse than its peers throughout the 1970s and early 1980s. The Dutch Disease is exemplified by many developing countries which, despite great natural wealth, have achieved little economic growth and poverty reduction over the last decades. Here are the more important resource-rich developing countries with their average annual rates of change in real GDP *per capita* from 1975 to 1998: Nigeria -0.7%, Kenya 0.5%, Angola -1.6%, Mozambique 0.7%, Brazil 1.2%, Venezuela -0.8%, Saudi Arabia -1.7%, United Arab Emirates -3.5%, Oman 2.4%, Kuwait -1.3%, Bahrain -1.4%, Brunei -0.8%, Indonesia 4.1%, the Philippines 0.5% (UNDP 2000, 182-5). For the Democratic Republic of the Congo (formerly Zaire) the average annual rate of change in GNP *per capita* for 1975-95 is -5.4% (UNDP 1999, 182). Thus, with the notable exception of Indonesia, the resource-rich developing countries fell far below the roughly 2% annual rate in real *per capita* growth of the developed countries — even while the developing countries on the whole did slightly better than the developed countries, thanks to rapid growth in China and the rest of East and South-East Asia (UNDP 1999, 83).

17. "All petrostates or resource-dependent countries in Africa fail to initiate meaningful political reforms. [...] besides South Africa, transition to democracy has been successful only in resource-poor countries" (Lam and Wantchekon 1999, 31); "Our cross-country regression confirms our theoretical insights. We find that a one percentage increase in the size of the natural resource sector [relative to GDP] generates a decrease by half a percentage point in the probability of survival of democratic regimes" (ibid., 35). See also Wantchekon 1999.

18. The World Bank Food Index fell from 124 in 1985 to 84.5 in 2000. These statistics are updated in "Global Commodity Markets" published by the World Bank's Development Prospects Group.

19. The Democracy Panel would obviously work only

in the interest of *democratic* constitutions, broadly defined. Its findings would not merely determine whether a government enjoys resource and borrowing privileges, but would also have consequences for its reputation and standing at home and abroad. A government that has been officially declared illegitimate would be encumbered in many ways (trade, diplomacy, foreign investment, etc.). In these ways, the proposed reform would tend further to reduce the incentives toward undemocratic rule, thus also further reducing the frequency of coup attempts.

20. I want to thank Ronald Dworkin for seeing this difficulty and for articulating it forcefully.

21. Still, these opportunity costs are diminished by the fact that the proposed modification of the international resource privilege would reduce the incidence of authoritarian rule in the developing world.

22. It is likely that we also benefit in terms of more lucrative business opportunities as a third dubious benefit from the international resource privilege: Corrupt supplier governments, made more frequent by the international resource privilege, tend to send much of their resource revenues right back to us, to pay for high-margin weaponry and military advisors, advanced luxury products, as well as real estate and financial investments; democratically responsive supplier governments, by contrast, tend to spend more of their resource revenues domestically (stimulating the country's economy) and tend to get better value for what they spend on imports.

23. We should remember this point whenever we hear it said that natural resources are no longer an important part of the global economy. Once we understand why this is true (relating the dollar value of resource sales to that of the global product or of aggregate international trade), we also understand why it is, in a deeper sense, false. Natural resources are of small significance only *modulo current price vectors*, which are heavily influenced by the international resource privilege and by the extreme global income inequality it helps cause. (I am grateful to Kenneth Arrow for pointing out that, with regard to some resources, consumption has a roughly linear correlation with household income so that income distribution among households has little effect on aggregate

demand for these resources.) So the small fraction of their GNP that rich countries spend on imported natural resources does not reflect the extent to which their economic prosperity depends on these resources — just as the small fraction of my income spent on water does not reflect the extent of my dependence on it. If we appraise depletable natural resources by their use value for all human beings, present and future, we must judge them grossly undervalued by current market prices. This undervaluation reflects a negative externality that the corrupt elites of resource-rich developing countries and the heavy consumers of resources together manage to impose upon the populations of those developing countries as well as on future generations, for whom such resources will be considerably less plentiful and more expensive.

REFERENCES

Chen, Shaohua, and Martin Ravallion. 2000. How Did the World's Poorest Fare in the 1990s? <http://econ.worldbank.org/docs/1164.pdf>.

Harrison, Lawrence E., and Samuel P. Huntington, eds. 2001. *Culture Matters: How Values Shape Human Progress*. New York: Basic Books.

Hohfeld, Wesley N. 1919. *Fundamental Legal Conceptions*. New Haven: Yale University Press.

Lam, Ricky, and Leonard Wantchekon. 1999. *Dictatorships as a Political Dutch Disease*. Working Paper. Yale University.

Landes, David. 1998. *The Wealth and Poverty of Nations*. New York: Norton.

Milanovic, Branko. 1999. True World Income Distribution, 1988 and 1993: First Calculation Based on Household Surveys Alone. *World Bank Policy Research Working Papers Series*, 2244.

Pogge, Thomas. 2001. Achieving Democracy. *Ethics and International Affairs* 15: 71-91.

Rawls, John. 1999. *The Law of Peoples*. Cambridge, Mass.: Harvard University Press.

Thucydides. 1986. *The History of the Peloponnesian War*. Harmondsworth: Penguin.

UNDP (United Nations Development Programme). 1996. *Human Development Report 1996*. New York: Oxford University Press.

UNDP (United Nations Development Programme).

1997. *Human Development Report 1997*. New York: Oxford University Press.

UNDP (United Nations Development Programme). 1998. *Human Development Report 1998*. New York: Oxford University Press.

UNDP (United Nations Development Programme). 1999. *Human Development Report 1999*. New York: Oxford University Press.

UNDP (United Nations Development Programme). 2000. *Human Development Report 2000*. New York: Oxford University Press. <www.undp.org/hdro/HDR2000.html>.

UNICEF (United Nations Childrens' Fund). 1998. *The State of the World's Children 1998*. New York:

Oxford University Press.

Walzer, Michael. 1980. The Moral Standing of States. *Philosophy and Public Affairs* 9: 209-29.

Wantchekon, Leonard. 1999. *Why do Resource Dependent Countries Have Authoritarian Governments?* Working Paper. Yale University. <wwTv.yale.edu/leitner/pdf/ 1999-ll.pdf>.

WHO (World Health Organisation). 1999. *The World Health Report 1999*. Geneva: WHO Publications. <www.who.int/whr/1999>.

World Bank. 2001. *World Development Report 2000/2001*. New York: Oxford University Press. <www.worldbank.org/poverty/wdrpoverty/report/index.htm>.

STUDY QUESTIONS

1 What does Amy Gutmann mean by non-ideal democracies and what are their defining features? What is "deliberative democracy" and how does it differ from non-ideal democracies?

2 How does Gutmann answer the question with which she opens the paper: "Does democracy need foundations?" Without foundations in the strong sense, are democracy and democratic values undermined? Why or why not?

3 Chenyang Li's answer to the question "what kind of democracy does China need?" is "the kind of democracy with the values of individual liberty, equality, and pluralism." According to Li, what are the points of incompatibility between these values and those in Confucianism? Does Li succeed in undermining attempts by theorists to make democracy and Confucianism compatible? Why or why not?

4 If the values of democracy and Confucianism are truly incompatible, why does Li pursue the project of introducing democratic values in China? What solution does he propose for the problem of incompatible value systems that he identifies in China? Is this a satisfactory solution? Why or why not?

5 Nadirsyah Hosen examines the perceived conflict between democratic values and Islamic law and the arguments of those who oppose the very idea of Islamic constitutional law. What are features of constitutionalism that are believed to be incompatible with Islamic law?

6 What is the basis for Hosen's rejection of fundamentalist and secularist interpretations of the Shari'ah that take it to be in conflict with democratic values? What principles does he find in the Shari'ah that would make it compatible with constitutionalism? Does he make a strong case for using the Shari'ah as a source and inspiration for democracy? Why or why not?

7 Amartya Sen examines two main arguments supporting the claim that democracy is a Western construct with little or no applicability in non-Western contexts. What are these arguments and what is the strategy Sen uses to raise objections to both?

8 What does Sen mean when he refers to some Western conceptions of democracy as too narrow? Outline features of the broader conception of democracy that Sen sketches and defends.

9 Does the use of a broader conception answer the question of whether democracy is a Western notion? Does the broader conception provide foundations for democracy in a way that gives grounds for viewing democratic values as universal? Provide reasons for your answers.

10 Thomas Pogge agrees with those who claim that many countries in the developing world lack democracy. However, he draws conclusions different from those that are normally drawn about who is responsible and what can be done. What is the story that is usually told about poverty and corruption and how does Pogge's explanation differ?

11 According to Pogge, in what ways do affluent developed countries actively contribute to the perpetuation of corruption, lack of democracy, and poverty in developing countries? What is meant by "international borrowing privileges" and "international resource privileges"?

12 What are some of the policies suggested by Pogge for eliminating the damaging effects of the global order on developing countries and for enhancing democratic processes and structures? Do you think these are good suggestions? Do you have others? Provide reasons for your answers.

13 After surveying the accounts of democracy and democratic values by the authors in this chapter, is democracy a Western notion? Can it be conceptualized as universal? Defend your answers.

SUGGESTED READINGS

Anderson, Elizabeth. "Sen, Ethics, and Democracy." *Feminist Economics*, v. 9, nos. 2-3 (2003): 239-61.

Benhabib, Seyla. "Deliberative Rationality and Models of Democratic Legitimacy." *Constellations*, v. 1, no. 1 (1994): 26-52.

Bohman, James, and William Rehg (editors). *Deliberative Democracy: Essays on Reason and Politics*. Cambridge, MA: MIT Press, 2002.

Buchanan, Allen. "Theories of Secession." *Philosophy & Public Affairs*, v. 26, no. 1 (Winter 1997): 31-61.

Couture, J., K. Nielsen, and M. Seymour (editors). *Rethinking Nationalism*. Calgary, AB: Calgary University Press, 1998.

Cunningham, Frank. *Democratic Theory and Socialism*. Cambridge: Cambridge University Press, 1987.

—. *The Real World of Democracy Revisited, and Other Essays on Democracy and Socialism*. Atlantic Highlands, NJ: Humanities Press, 1994.

Dahbour, Omar. "The Nation-State as a Political Community: A Critique of the Communitarian Argument for National Self-Determination." In *Rethinking Nationalism*, edited by J. Couture, K. Nielsen, and M. Seymour. Calgary, AB: Calgary University Press, 1998.

Dower, Nigel. *An Introduction to Global Citizenship*. Edinburgh: Edinburgh University Press, 2003.

Dower, Nigel (editor). *Global Citizenship: A Critical Reader*. Edinburgh: Edinburgh University Press, 2002.

Eschle, Catherine. "Engendering Global Democracy." *International Feminist Journal of Politics*, v. 4, no. 3 (December 2003): 315-41.

Gould, Carol C. "Diversity and Democracy: Representing Differences." In *Democracy and Difference: Contesting the Boundaries of the Political* edited by Seyla Benhabib. Princeton, NJ: Princeton University Press, 1996.

Gutmann, Amy. *Identity in Democracy*. Princeton, NJ: Princeton University Press, 2003.

Machan, Tibor R. *Liberty and Democracy*. Stanford, CA: Hoover Institution Press, 2002.

Mansbridge, Jane. "Using Power/Fighting Power." *Constellations*, v. 1, no. 1 (1994): 53-73.

Mouffe, Chantal. "Democracy, Power, and the 'Political.'" In *Democracy and Difference: Contesting the Boundaries of the Political*, edited by Seyla Benhabib. Princeton, NJ: Princeton University Press, 1996.

Nielsen, Kai. "Socialism and Nationalism." *Imprints*, v. 2, no. 3 (1998): 208-22.

Nye, Joseph S. Jr. "Globalization's Democratic Deficit: How to Make International Institutions More Accountable." *Foreign Affairs*, v. 80, no. 4 (July-August 2001): 2-13.

Ottaway, Marina. "Promoting Democracy After Conflict: The Difficult Choices." *International Studies Perspectives*. v. 4 (2003): 314-22.

Sawer, Marian. "Constructing Democracy." *International Feminist Journal of Politics*, v. 5, no. 3 (November 2003): 361-65.

Sen, Amartya. "The Importance of Democracy." In *Development as Freedom*. New York, NY: Random House, 1999.

Shapiro, Ian. *The State of Democratic Theory*. Princeton, NJ: Princeton University Press, 2003.

Sparks, Holloway. "Dissident Citizenship: Democratic Theory, Political Courage, and Activist Women." *Hypatia*, v. 12, no. 4 (Fall 1997): 74-110.

Tamir, Yael. "The Right to National Self-Determination as an Individual Right." *History of European Ideas*, v. 16, no. 4-6 (1993): 899-905.

Wellman, Christopher H. "A Defense of Secession and Political Self-Determination." *Philosophy & Public Affairs*, v. 24, no. 2 (1995): 142-71.

CHAPTER FIVE: ISSUES AND APPLICATIONS
INTRODUCTION

The readings in this chapter are designed to test the conceptions of human rights, justice, and democracy examined in Chapters Two, Three, and Four by applying them to specific contexts and issues in various parts of the world with diverse practices, conditions, and political structures. Of course, the readings represent only a narrow range of the interesting contexts in which conceptions of human rights, justice, and democracy can be explored. The ones selected raise vexing questions about the tendencies of ethnocentrism, Eurocentrism, universalism, and essentialism outlined in the Introduction to this volume. Is knowing the details of a context with a specific history, culture, and traditions relevant to the applicability and legitimacy of particular theories of human rights, justice, or democracy? Can differences in cultural beliefs be reconciled or common values found so as to engage productively in the project of articulating and justifying conceptions of human rights, justice, and democracy that avoid the pitfalls of ethnocentrism and so are truly universal? What, if anything, can we learn from challenges to traditional or Western conceptions of human rights, justice, and democracy?

The chapter opens with an examination of the issue of capital punishment and its implications for universal accounts of human rights. Stefanie Grant surveys the growing international movement to abolish the death penalty, gives some of the reasons for these changing international practices, discusses issues raised in some of the countries in which the death penalty has been abolished, and examines the role of international agencies in monitoring and condemning state practices. Grant takes this description and analysis of changing international attitudes to have implications for the U.S., one of the few countries that continue to allow capital punishment. The U.S. has faced criticism from its allies, the United Nations, and various human rights organizations such as Amnesty International for its continued defense and practice of capital punishment. The moral issue of capital punishment, therefore, allows Grant to examine a process of the revision, expansion, and reinterpretation of rights, a process that reflects the view that capital punishment is not a domestic issue but a violation of internationally protected human rights. Grant goes on to argue that global international relations and the increased permeability of borders raises questions of the rights of suspected criminals both in cases demanding their extradition to countries that have the death penalty and in cases of foreign nationals committing crimes or on death row in countries that have the death penalty.

The idea that a context of increased economic globalization is relevant to a discussion of practices within specific countries is explored in the second reading by Roland Pierik. He examines the issue of child labor in developing countries and, more specifically, the issue of what, if anything, developed countries can or should do to reduce or eliminate incidences of child labor. He argues that not every policy against child labor by rich Western countries will be in the best interest of children in developing countries. In order to know what policies will work, we need to be aware of the socioeconomic and cultural differences between developed and developing countries. Socioeconomic circumstances of the increased permeability of national, legal, and political orders enable Westerners to import commodities produced by children in developing countries where severe poverty makes this labor desirable and necessary for survival. Pierik also points to the cultural differences between developed and developing countries with respect to ideas about childhood and the role of work and education. Failure to acknowledge these differences risks having Western countries and international bodies such as the International

Labour Organization impose Western understandings of childhood on children in non-Western and developing countries. Pierik argues that we need to distinguish between child work and child labor, the former of which is the norm in most of the world where children work alongside parents on farms and in family businesses as part of their education and development into adulthood.

Support for conventions and policies, argues Pierik, must take these differences into account. He ends by providing several policy recommendations, including avoiding policies that aim at a global ban on child labor, basing policies on an inclusive conception of childhood, focusing on collaborative measures to reduce poverty, acting contextually and collectively, and having Western countries take responsibility for the maintenance of a global context in which child labor occurs and is sustained. The last point about responsibility emerges from Pierik's attention to a global economy that allows Western countries to maximize their own interests in international negotiations in ways that result in conditions of poverty that then create and increase incidences of the worse forms of child labor in developing countries.

The third reading by Kok-Chor Tan examines a history of colonialism and what it means with respect to policies for alleviating inequalities and oppression that people in the former colonies continue to suffer. Tan notes that some countries (the so-called Group of 21) have argued that there should be reparations for colonialism and that reparations should take the form of debt relief, development assistance, equal access to global markets, restitution of cultural objects, and improved cultural cooperation between countries. He claims that what is interesting about these demands is that they are also demands that have been made by some philosophers in the name of global egalitarian justice. Tan argues that reparative arguments can play a morally significant role even when egalitarian arguments are available to support the same kinds of demands that the reparative arguments aim to advance. Reparative arguments are better able to motivate action than more abstract arguments about global equality; they may be necessary for repairing the kinds of international relationships needed to achieve global

equality; and they can step in when the argument from equality is resisted.

The impact of a country's history of colonialization and oppressive practices is also explored in Jennifer Llewellyn's discussion of South Africa in the fourth reading. The specific case of South Africa provides a rare opportunity to analyze what justice demands in transitional cases, ones in which countries undergo a transition from a past of gross injustices and violations of human rights to a future committed to building a rights-respecting culture. The system of apartheid in South Africa resulted in the systematic racial oppression of the majority by a small but powerful white minority. Llewellyn argues that what we can learn from the dismantling of apartheid and the conception of justice operational in South Africa's Truth and Reconciliation Commission can be applied to conceptions of justice more generally.

The South African Truth and Reconciliation Commission was given the mandate to deal with gross injustices of apartheid, but some critics argue that the Commission is devoid of justice because it allows amnesty for disclosure of incidences of wrongdoing. Llewellyn argues that this criticism relies on an understanding of justice as retributive. On this conception, justice is a procedure of discovering and punishing individuals for wrongs done in the past. Llewellyn favors a conception of justice as restorative, a conception that is particularly suited to transitional contexts, but has broad application beyond these contexts. Restorative justice is forward-looking and relational in nature. On this conception, particular circumstances and contexts determine the set of practices that are appropriate for dealing with injustices on the road to restoring relationships in which all members of a community are treated equally and with respect. Llewellyn outlines the ways in which South Africa's Truth and Reconciliation Commission is modeled on a restorative conception of justice and highlights the challenges that a restorative model might pose for the Commission.

The final reading raises questions about the narrow conceptions of democracy and of human rights assumed in some of the readings in Chapters Two and Four. Susan Babbitt argues that Western liberal accounts of democracy assume a particular conception of human rights and of liberty, conceptions that are unquestioned and undefended in criticisms by Westerners that Cuba violates human rights and lacks democracy. Babbitt points out that these criticisms persist even in the face of evidence that Cuba guarantees rights to work, health, education, and social assistance in its Constitution and provides better medical care and education than do many developed countries. She argues that the negative assessment of Cuba is rooted in the philosophical assumptions that have shaped a world-dominant view about what constitutes democracy, human rights, freedom, and human flourishing. These assumptions have made it possible to ignore the explanations that Cuba has offered about its history and its struggle for democracy and respect for human rights.

Babbitt raises the possibility that the American notion of what it means to be human and to flourish might be wrong. For example, the notion of freedom as the capacity for unrestricted choice is a denial of freedom for many and makes it reasonable to think that some lives would be better if led from the outside by values that respect the humanity of all people. To understand Cuba is to understand that its choice is to pursue a moral vision that creates new values and new possibilities for being human. Babbitt uses this account of Cuba's story to argue that Cuba's single party system, for example, is not in itself evidence that Cuba is undemocratic because it can be seen as providing the conditions for creating a just and humane society. Babbitt holds that an account of the particular history, economic struggle, and dimensions of power in Cuba is essential to a proper understanding of the country and its aspirations for its people.

A DIALOGUE OF THE DEAF? NEW INTERNATIONAL ATTITUDES AND THE DEATH PENALTY IN AMERICA

Stefanie Grant

Stefanie Grant is Director of Program and Policy at Human Rights First. She is a lawyer specializing in and writing on issues relating to migration, nationality, and refugees. Most recently she has directed the Research and Right to Development Branch of the United Nations Office of the High Commissioner for Human Rights in Geneva.

Grant surveys the growing international movement to abolish the death penalty, gives some of the reasons for these changing international practices, and examines the increasing role of international agencies in monitoring and condemning state practices. Grant takes these features of changing international attitudes as having implications for the U.S., one of the few countries that continue to allow the death penalty. She claims that this process of the revision, expansion, and reinterpretation of rights reflects the view that capital punishment is not a domestic issue, but a violation of internationally protected human rights. Grant goes on to argue that the increased permeability of borders raises questions about the rights of suspected criminals in cases demanding their extradition to countries that have the death penalty and in cases of foreign nationals on death row in countries that have the death penalty.

The U.S. press spotlighted the recent decision by 120 governments to create an International Criminal Court (ICC) to prosecute war crimes, genocide, and crimes against humanity. That the new court would not impose the death sentence went largely unreported. But it was the high-water mark of a decade of efforts to abolish the death penalty in international law. The impact of this new abolitionism on the U.S. became clear in December 1998, when Germany agreed to extradite a suspect in the terrorist bombing of American embassies only on condition that he would not face the death penalty.

International law limits to the use of the death penalty are not new, but until recently they have been narrowly drawn. In the 1950s, when the International Covenant on Civil and Political Rights (ICCPR) was being drafted, capital punishment was not generally seen as a human rights violation,

provided the defendant was adult and sentence of death followed a trial in which due process rights had been scrupulously honored. This attitude is changing. In the last decade a growing number of states have ended capital punishment under their national laws and are using and interpreting international law as an instrument to restrict its use and, ultimately, to abolish it as a penalty.

In the same period, the U.S. has moved in a different direction, expanding the scope of federal and state death penalty laws, cutting back legal challenges by those on death row, and carrying out their execution. One effect of this divergence between the U.S. and many of its key international allies has been to isolate the U.S. on an issue which is seen increasingly by other governments not merely as a question of domestic law and policy, but as implicating internationally protected human rights. As a result, the U.S. is criticized by United

Nations (U.N.) rights bodies for breaches of international law, its extradition requests are refused by European states where the prisoner could face a death sentence in the U.S., and the Supreme Court has found itself in the uncomfortable position of refusing a stay of execution ordered by the International Court of Justice.[1]

These developments are part of an international movement to abolish the death penalty which bases itself on the human rights principles of the right to life and the right to be protected from cruel, inhuman, and degrading punishment contained in the Universal Declaration of Human Rights. Abolitionists also draw support from studies which demonstrate convincingly that a sentence of life imprisonment has as great a deterrent effect on the commission of violent crime as capital punishment.

Since 1993, this sea change in international attitudes to the death penalty has produced tangible results. The international community, led by the U.S. in the U.N. Security Council, responded to war crimes in Yugoslavia and genocide in Rwanda by creating the first international criminal tribunals. The statutes of both tribunals expressly exclude the death penalty. In 1994, abolition of the death penalty in peacetime became a treaty requirement for all new members of the forty-state Council of Europe. While this may seem no more than a logical development for stable and relatively prosperous western European democracies, it is uncharted territory for new democracies with high crime rates and weak legal systems. Nonetheless, when the Russian Federation negotiated its admission to the Council of Europe in 1996, abolition of capital punishment was one of the terms of the agreement. In 1995, the new South African Constitutional Court reviewed the range of comparative national and international legal arguments advanced for and against capital punishment and ruled it to be unconstitutional.[2] The Rome Diplomatic Conference's 1998 decision that the ICC will have no power to impose death sentences means that those convicted of the most serious international crimes will face only a life sentence.[3]

How has this dramatic change in international attitudes come about, what is the actual content of international law, and what does it mean for death penalty opponents in the U.S. and for the U.S. in its historic role as a leader of the international human rights movement?

Changing International Attitudes

On death penalty issues the positions taken by governments at the international level tend to reflect what is happening at home. As more countries have taken steps to exclude the death penalty from domestic law, their governments' support for abolition internationally has grown, as have their efforts to influence those states which retain capital punishment by developing death penalty prohibitions in international law. By 1994, the Parliamentary Assembly of the Council of Europe could express the clear view of most European governments that "the death penalty has no legitimate place in the penal system of modern civilized societies ... its application may well be compared with torture."[4]

Recently the United Kingdom translated this position of principle into foreign policy, announcing that Britain would take a clear, unequivocal stand against the death penalty. The United Kingdom had used its term as President of the European Union to make sure that Europe spoke with one voice on the subject and now planned "to use our diplomatic clout, our technical assistance and our human rights projects to persuade other countries not to use the death penalty."[5] Abolition has now become a foreign policy goal for many western European states.[6]

This approach is not restricted to European countries. When the U.N. Security Council's eighteen members drafted the Statute of the Rwanda Tribunal, the question of penalties became one of the most contentious issues. In the end, even governments like the U.S., who are retentionist at home, agreed that international judges should not be able to impose the death penalty for genocide. Sponsoring the resolution to establish the Tribunal, New Zealand articulated the prevailing abolitionist position of the Council members:

We do not believe that following the principle of "an eye for an eye" is the path to establishing a civilized society, no matter how horrendous the crimes the individuals concerned may have committed. The objective in Rwanda must be to establish a just and fair society based on respect for life and fundamental human rights.[7]

Rwanda was the only Security Council member to vote against creating the Tribunal. It argued that since Rwandan national courts could impose the death penalty, international judges should not have lesser sentencing powers than Rwandan judges hearing equivalent cases under Rwandan law. Madeleine Albright, casting the U.S. vote with the majority, noted pragmatically that although the U.S. might agree with Rwanda, "it was simply not possible to meet these [death penalty] concerns and still maintain broad support in the Council."[8]

The Roman Catholic Church has also moved closer to the abolitionist camp. Although it accepts an exception of "absolute necessity" to the abolitionist principle in those situations in which it would "not be possible otherwise to defend society," the Pope's 1995 encyclical *Evangelium Vitae* makes clear that such cases would now be very rare "if not practically non-existent."[9]

The United Nations has played an important role in facilitating this new consensus, both through its work in multilateral standard setting and by research and collection of information from individual countries. The U.N. now classifies a majority of its members, over 100 countries, as abolitionist (either for all offenses or for peacetime offenses) or as abolitionist de facto (in that capital punishment remains a lawful penalty but has fallen into disuse). Ninety countries are classified as "retentionist." In recent reports, the U.N. Secretary General described the pace of change toward abolition between 1989 and 1995 as "quite remarkable": in these five years, 24 countries had abolished the death penalty, 22 of them for all crimes, whether in peacetime or in time of war. But the trend is not uniform, and a review of the countries on the U.N.'s lists suggests some cultural and geographical denominators. The list of total abolitionists is heavily weighted towards Latin America and Europe — reflecting, at least in part, steps taken to end capital punishment as part of the transition to

democracy in the 1980s and 1990s. It also includes South Africa, Australia, New Zealand, and some south Pacific states. The United Kingdom and Israel are abolitionist, but only for ordinary crimes. The retentionist list has its own common geographical features — capital punishment is prevalent in the Middle East, the Caribbean, and a number of African countries, as well as being used in China, Japan, and the USA.[10]

Other areas of state practice are monitored by Amnesty International which, through its advocacy, campaigning, and reporting, has led and spearheaded international efforts for restriction and abolition. Amnesty reports that reintroduction of the death penalty after it has been abolished is rare. Between 1985 and 1998, thirty-five countries abolished the death penalty in law or extended the bar from ordinary to all crimes; in the same period only four abolitionist countries reintroduced capital punishment. The legal prohibition on the execution of juveniles is widely observed. Since 1990, only six countries are known to have executed prisoners who were under the age of eighteen when the crimes were committed: Iran, Nigeria, Pakistan, Saudi Arabia, Yemen, and the U.S.; the highest number of executions in these years — nine — took place in the U.S.[11] Indeed, in Amnesty International's reporting, the U.S. features prominently as one of the countries which is most dramatically out of step with the general international trend.[12]

But the trend has not gone unchallenged. Rising crime rates and criminal violence have sparked popular pressure on governments in traditionally abolitionist countries of Central America to reintroduce the death penalty. A 1998 U.N. Human Rights Commission resolution calling on retentionist states to restrict the number of capital offenses and to establish a moratorium on actual executions sparked a Statement signed by fifty U.N. members, claiming there was no international consensus that capital punishment should be abolished.[13]

The Content of International Law

It is true that general international law contains no blanket prohibition of the death penalty for adults.

Human rights treaties tend to reflect the state of national law at the time they were drafted, and it is not surprising that those international human rights and humanitarian law treaties which were written in the two decades after the Second World War recognized the death penalty as an exception to the right to life. There are nonetheless two well-established and categoric prohibitions: on imposing the death penalty for crimes committed by juveniles below the age of eighteen and on the execution of pregnant women.[14] Even though the ICCPR recognizes the death penalty as an exception, it restricts its use to "the most serious crimes" and includes specific safeguards, in addition to barring juvenile executions.[15] Thus, although governments are not obliged to abolish the death penalty totally, they are required to limit its use, and abolish it for other than "the most serious crimes." The expression "the most serious crimes" must be read restrictively to mean that the death penalty should be a quite exceptional measure.[16]

In 1977, immediately after the ICCPR came into effect, the U.N. General Assembly took an important step towards abolition when it defined "the main objective" to be pursued in the field of capital punishment as "that of progressively restricting the number of offences for which the death penalty can be imposed with a view to ... abolishing this punishment."[17] This set the scene for the next stage of international standard setting — the addition in 1989 of a Protocol to the ICCPR which bars the execution of death sentences and requires governments to take "all necessary measures" to abolish the death penalty.[18]

Similar developments have taken place at a regional level in Europe and Latin America. The European Convention on Human Rights (ECHR), like the ICCPR, contains no absolute bar on the death penalty, but a Sixth Protocol was added in 1983. It abolishes the death penalty in peacetime and states that "no-one shall be condemned to such penalty or executed." The Sixth Protocol is the first instrument in international law to make abolition of the death penalty a legal obligation for states.[19] Similarly, in 1990 a Protocol was added to the American Convention on Human Rights requiring that "states shall not apply the death penalty."[20]

The UN has also set new procedural and other standards to safeguard the rights of those facing the death penalty; these range from basic due process principles to adding "persons who have become insane" as a third category of individuals who should enjoy absolute protection from sentence of death or execution. These were further developed by the UN Economic and Social Council in 1989; it recommended inter alia that there should be a maximum age beyond which a person could not be sentenced to death or executed[21] and that persons suffering from mental retardation should be added to the list of those who should be protected from capital punishment.[22]

Abolition in Practice: Russia and South Africa

Abolition of capital punishment has been a clear consequence of political change in eastern Europe, Russia, and South Africa. In each situation, the death penalty was seen by the new political leaders as incompatible with the values of democracy and human rights, and as unconstitutional by the judges who had the task of interpreting their new constitutions.[23]

Since the fall of the Berlin wall in 1989, Romania, the Czech Republic, and Slovakia have all passed legislation to abolish capital punishment; in Hungary, the Constitutional Court has declared the death penalty unconstitutional. Although neither Poland nor Bulgaria has abolished capital punishment in law, both countries have declared a moratorium on implementation, and death sentences are not carried out. Albania is the only country in the region in which executions continue to take place.

These reforms have been accomplished in the face of substantial public opposition strengthened by rising crime rates and, in particular, an increase in violent crime. But throughout eastern and central Europe there was a popular wish to end the political isolation of the past, and the new governments realized that full compliance with internationally accepted human rights standards was a condition of their eventual integration with western Europe. The death penalty became a key issue in the unification of eastern and western Europe, and since October

1994, the Council of Europe has required all states who applied for membership to undertake that they would sign and ratify Protocol Six within a given time. Willingness to enter into a legally binding obligation to abolish the death penalty thus became a requirement for membership, and those states which were still executing prisoners under sentence of death were obliged to introduce moratoriums on execution.[24]....

South Africa

In South Africa, the decision to end the death penalty was one of the first decisions taken by the new Constitutional Court.[25] The drafters of the South African constitution, recognizing the controversial nature of the issue, had deliberately made no reference to capital punishment in the text. At the time the Constitutional Court decided *State v. Makwanyane & Others*, more than 300 people had been given death sentences and were on death row, but there had been an effective moratorium on their execution since 1989. The drafters of the 1993 constitution left to the Constitutional Court the task of determining the constitutionality of capital punishment. Accordingly, the death sentence was neither sanctioned nor excluded in the text, and it was left to the Constitutional Court to decide whether the provisions of the pre-constitutional law making the death sentence a competent sentence for murder and other crimes were consistent with the fundamental rights enshrined in the Constitution, and specifically with [sections] 11(2)'s prohibition on "cruel, inhuman or degrading treatment or punishment." "If they are, the death sentence remains a competent sentence for murder ... unless and until Parliament otherwise decides; if they are not, it is [the court's] duty to say so, and to declare such provisions to be unconstitutional." In his judgment, the court's President also noted that the absence of reference to the death sentence in the constitution distinguished the powers of his court from those of many other national and international courts which had addressed the question, including the U.S. Supreme Court. He said:

> Where challenges to death sentences in international or foreign courts and tribunals have failed,

the constitution or the international instrument concerned has either sanctioned capital punishment or has specifically provided that the right to life is subject to exceptions sanctioned by law.[26]

In holding the death penalty to be unconstitutional, the President's long and important judgment considered the South African constitution's bar on cruel, inhuman, or degrading treatment or punishment in the light of the democratic values underlying the constitution, and conducted a far-ranging review of both international and national law and practice. The judgment in *Makwanyane* is thus a compelling articulation of the position of the contemporary rights-based abolitionist movement.

The judges began by considering the dilemma which has been faced by U.S. courts since *Furman v. Georgia*; the South African judges declined to follow the U.S. jurisprudence which accepts, on the one hand, the constitutionality of the death penalty, but on the other hand must attempt to avoid arbitrariness:

> The acceptance by a majority of the Supreme Court of the proposition that capital punishment is not per se unconstitutional, but that in certain circumstances it may be arbitrary, and thus unconstitutional, has led to endless litigation. Considerable expense and interminable delays result from the exceptionally high standard of procedural fairness set by the United States courts in attempting to avoid arbitrary decisions.... The difficulties that have been experienced in following this path ... persuade me that we should not follow this route.[27]

The judges also rejected the proposition that public opinion should be a determining factor in a state's decision whether or not to use the death penalty, in part because the choice between abolition or retention is a legal decision, requiring an interpretation of the constitution, and in part because the constitution protects the rights of minorities and those very individuals who cannot protect their rights through the democratic process.[28] The court addressed the argument that capital punishment deters the commission of crime, but although it recognized the force of this in a society with a high level of violent crime, rejected its merits, saying:

> We would be deluding ourselves if we were to believe that execution of ... a comparatively few ... people each year ... will provide the solution to the unacceptably high rate of crime.... The greatest deterrent to crime is the likelihood that offenders will be apprehended, convicted and punished. It is that which is lacking in our criminal justice system.[29]

The court accepted the proposition that allowing the state to kill will cheapen the value of human life and that by not doing so the state will serve as a role model for individuals in society: "Our country needs such role models."

The judgment's final conclusion is clear:

> [T]he principal factors that have to be weighed [by the court] are on the one hand the destruction of life and dignity that is a consequence of the implementation of the death sentence, the elements of arbitrariness and the possibility of error in the enforcement of capital punishment, and the existence of a severe alternative punishment [life imprisonment] and, on the other, the claim that the death sentence is a greater deterrent to murder, and will more effectively prevent its commission, than would a sentence of life imprisonment, and that there is a public demand for retributive justice... which only a death sentence can meet.
>
> Retribution cannot be accorded the same weight under our Constitution as the rights to life and dignity.... It has not been shown that the death sentence would be materially more effective to deter or prevent murder.... Taking these factors into account, as well as the elements of arbitrariness and the possibility of error ... the clear and convincing case that is required to justify the death sentence ... has not been made out.[30]

Monitoring the United States

The U.N. has twice reviewed the use of the death penalty within America but the U.S. has resisted taking international law and U.N. norms as the frame of reference. In 1997 a U.N. expert — the Special Rapporteur on Extra-judicial, Summary and Arbitrary Executions — visited the U.S. His investigation was triggered by reports of the extension and reintroduction of the death penalty at the federal and state level, that its use was discriminatory and arbitrary, that there was inadequate defense during trial and appeal procedures, and that juvenile offenders and the mentally retarded were being executed. Two years earlier, in 1995, the U.S. had made its first report to the U.N. Human Rights Committee on how the federal government had implemented the rights contained in the ICCPR. The Committee is an international body of independent experts which supervises all states that are parties to the ICCPR Covenant.[31]

Both initiatives were met by forceful — if controversial — U.S. arguments that international law places no barrier to capital punishment under U.S. law and that the U.S. is not legally bound by the ICCPR Covenant's prohibition on juvenile executions.[32] This is clearly a threshold question for any law-based approach. The U.S. rests its position on the fact that when the Senate consented to ratification of the treaty in 1992, it did so on condition that the U.S. should insulate itself — through a set of Reservations, Understandings and Declarations [RUDs] — from obligations that would require changes to U.S. law.[33] Perhaps the most controversial of these was a reservation to Article 6(5) which prohibits capital punishment for an offense committed by anyone below the age of 18. These reservations have been harshly criticized by France, Germany, Holland, and several other western European states which formally objected to the U.S. reservation on juvenile executions.[34]

Shortly before its review of the U.S. report, the U.N. Human Rights Committee expressed its concern about the growing practice whereby governments ratified the ICCPR Covenant, but at the same time, by attaching reservations, exempted themselves from the obligation to protect specific *ius cogens* rights. In a General Comment which reviewed the scope and legality of reservations, the Committee singled out the protection of juvenile offenders from execution [Article 6(5)] as one of a number of customary international law obligations from which no government could resile.[35]

The General Comment did not mention the U.S. by name. But after reviewing the U.S. report in two days of open meetings in New York in March 1995, the Committee stated its view that the U.S. reservation on juvenile executions was "incompatible with the object and purpose of the treaty." It urged the U.S.

> to revise the federal and state legislation with a view to restricting the number of offenses carrying the death penalty strictly to the most serious crimes ... and with a view eventually to abolishing it. It exhorts the authorities to take appropriate steps to ensure that persons are not sentenced to death for crimes committed before they were 18.[36]

But any review of U.S. reservations soon became a political impossibility when the Chair of the Senate Committee on Foreign Relations, Senator Jesse Helms, inserted into the 1996-99 State Department appropriations bill a funding prohibition to bar the executive branch from undertaking any further reporting activity to the Human Rights Committee. The prohibition was accompanied by an inaccurate and damaging reference to the General Comment.[37] As drafted, the prohibition would continue until the President could certify to Congress that the Human Rights Committee had (a) revoked General Comment No. 24 and (b) "expressly recognized the validity as a matter of international law" of all the U.S. RUDs to the ICCPR. Fortunately this prohibition did not survive the legislative process, but it effectively prevented any action by the administration to follow up the committee's recommendations.

After his visit to the U.S. in October 1997, the Special Rapporteur on Extrajudicial, Summary, and Arbitrary Executions expressed his concerns in a report which he made to the U.N. Human Rights Commission.[38] They dealt with issues similar to those singled out by the Human Rights Committee: the scope of capital punishment, in particular its recent expansion and reintroduction, the reduction in procedural safeguards,[39] juvenile executions,[40]

and execution of the mentally retarded.[41] He also addressed other aspects of the justice system that raised issues of arbitrariness — namely, prosecutorial discretion, jury selection procedures, and the practice of electing judges at the state level.

The Special Rapporteur's conclusions go no further than many of the positions taken by U.S. legal and rights organizations — for example, the American Bar Association call for a moratorium — and are, if anything, more moderate than most critical assessments made by U.S. writers and critics of the death penalty.[42] Nonetheless, there was a strong negative reaction to his report from the State Department and the press, as well as from Senator Helms.[43]

Capital Punishment as a Bar to U.S. Extradition

Although extradition is not normally seen as an instrument for protecting individuals from sentence of death, it is increasingly used for this purpose. Courts in some European countries whose laws exclude capital punishment have refused to send prisoners to the U.S. if the offense is one for which the death penalty can be imposed. There is an established basis for this in the European Convention on Extradition, which allows for extradition to be refused in cases in which the offense carries a death sentence in the requesting state, but not in the state from which extradition is sought.[44] But a breakthrough with wider consequences came in 1989 when a German national named Jens Soering appealed to the European Court of Human Rights against his extradition from the United Kingdom to the United States to face murder charges in the state of Virginia. He succeeded, and the case established the wide-reaching principle that a state incurs responsibility for any reasonably foreseeable breach of a Convention right which takes place in the requesting state. In *Soering*[45] the breach was of Article Three, which prohibits degrading treatment or punishment, and related not to the death penalty but to the condition of his detention on death row in Virginia before execution. There is now a developing rule against extradition in cases in which the requesting state retains the death penalty and is unwilling to give assurances to the state in which the prisoner is held that it will not be imposed. As a result, U.S. prosecutors are increasingly faced with a choice between reducing the charges to offenses which carry no death sentence or forfeiting any realistic chance of extradition.[46] This dilemma has been highlighted recently by the case of a suspect in the 1998 terrorist bomb attacks on U.S. embassies in Kenya and Tanzania, in which 200 people died. After Mamdouh Mahmud Salim was arrested in Munich, Germany made his extradition to the U.S. conditional on guarantees that he would not face the death penalty.[47]

Obstacles to extradition arise not only from inter-state regional law — the European Extradition Convention, the European Court's reasoning under the European Convention in *Soering*, and its potential application to the Sixth Protocol, which expressly bars execution — but also from recent rulings of European national courts. The High Court of the Netherlands has held that European Convention provisions should prevail over those of the NATO Status of Forces Agreement.[48] The Italian Constitutional Court has ruled out extradition of fugitives charged with capital crimes to the U.S. because of the absolute nature of the prohibition on capital punishment in the Italian constitution.[49]

The UN Human Rights Committee has also been asked to determine the compatibility of extradition in capital cases with the rights protected in the ICCPR. Its two decisions have concerned extradition from Canada to the U.S. Both turned not on the fact of execution, but on whether the method of execution would involve a breach of the Convention's prohibition on cruel and inhuman punishment, in which case it is barred.[50]

The Rights of Foreign Nationals on Death Row

When the U.S. defends its record in the U.N. against charges that capital punishment is imposed arbitrarily, it stresses the extensive due process protections in U.S. law, which make the U.S. system of criminal justice "one of the fairest in the world."[51] This proposition has recently been challenged by two governments — Paraguay and

Mexico — in cases before the International Court of Justice and the Inter American Court of Human Rights. Paraguay and Mexico asserted, respectively, a violation of international law and a breach of due process rights when their nationals were arrested on capital charges. The legal issue raised by these cases is different in kind from those arising under general international human rights law since the violation is of a treaty right which is not only expressly protected by the Vienna Convention on Consular Relations, but which has direct effect in U.S. law.

The set of RUDs which the Senate has attached to each human rights treaty on ratification has prevented the treaty's provisions from having any direct effect through U.S. courts and from giving individuals justiciable rights.[52] This is one of the principal reasons why international human rights law is so little known, or used, by U.S. lawyers and civil rights advocates and why human rights treaties have remained essentially "off shore," and have had little visible impact on U.S. law or practice.[53]

But the Vienna Convention on Consular Relations is a clear exception to the isolationism which has long characterized the U.S. relationship to the international human rights treaty regime.[54] Although the Vienna Convention is not usually characterized as a human rights treaty, it indirectly strengthens due process rights by giving foreign nationals in U.S. prisons an immediate right to see their country's consul and thus obtain consular help in securing legal representation.[55] It also enables foreign governments to monitor the safety and fair treatment of their citizens. For those in prison in any foreign country, a consul plays a vital role in providing a "cultural bridge" by which they can navigate an unfamiliar and often hostile legal system.[56] In no situation is this more important than one in which the individual is charged with a capital offense, and in 1998 the Mexican Government told the U.N. that it regarded the right of more than thirty Mexican nationals on death row in the U.S. to consular access as

so important that it can be considered on the same level as the Miranda warning, in that it offers the detainee the possibility of having his rights explained to him in his own language through consular assistance, and to be assisted in understanding the workings of the U.S. legal system and the consequences of his possible responsibility for the commission of the crime with which he is charged.[57]

Because the treaty is self-executing, the rights in the Vienna Convention are enforceable through U.S. courts, unlike other human rights protected under international law. Law enforcement officers at both federal and state levels are required to implement its provisions by notifying a prisoner's consul that he is in custody and the prisoner that he has a right to be in contact with his consul. In addition, and of key importance, is the fact that there is a clear reciprocal interest in its domestic implementation not only on the part of other governments, but also on the part of the U.S.

The U.S. State Department Foreign Affairs Manual describes "prompt" notification as essential to protect U.S. nationals detained abroad. The logic of reciprocity is that if foreigners can contact their consuls when they are arrested in the U.S., other governments — Russia, or Iraq or Serbia — must accord Americans the same right when they travel and if they are detained....

Conclusion

Historically, the strength of national sovereignty doctrine and the weakness of international human rights law have prevented domestic rights issues from affecting bi-lateral relations, except in extreme cases. In the last two decades other states have followed the U.S. lead in making human rights a central aspect of their foreign policy. As a result violations of internationally protected human rights have become a legitimate part of international and bi-lateral discussion for democracies, as well as for dictatorships. One consequence of this development is that the U.S. is now on the receiving end of criticism about its continuing, and expanding, use of capital punishment, particularly for juvenile offenders. This is an uncomfortable experience for a country that has traditionally been an exporter of civil rights and due process guarantees.[58]....

The question that must now be answered is whether the U.S. will continue to remain separate from the emerging new international order on the death penalty, and if its resistance to this new order — combined with the very specific U.S. constitutional situation — will continue to provide effective insulation against the effects of international opinion. Alternatively, will some accommodation have to be made in due course, and, if so, what will this be?

The death penalty is, of course, only one example of a broader U.S. isolation from the evolving international human rights treaty regime. But in this wider area, U.S. attitudes may be changing. In December 1998, President Clinton signaled an important new direction, when he ordered the creation of an Inter Agency Working Group on Human Rights Treaties, to review treaty implementation.[59]

Specific accommodation was made on the death penalty in the *Soering* case, when a non-capital charge was agreed to by U.S. prosecutors as a quid pro quo for extradition. If, as seems likely, extradition of those indicted for major terrorist offenses by U.S. allies in Europe also becomes conditional on U.S. undertakings not to press capital charges, the political impact within the U.S. will be significant. It is also difficult to see how the U.S. can continue to flout the Vienna Convention without inviting reciprocal denial of consular access for U.S. nationals; enforcement of the Convention at the state level thus becomes imperative. But these situations are limited in their effect to cases in which another country forbids extradition on capital charges or in which defendants are foreign nationals. Given the depth of electoral and congressional support for the death penalty, it is unlikely that either situation will act as a catalyst for any broader reassessment by the U.S. of its own relationship to the international human rights regime.

To many outside the U.S., that relationship has too often been one in which the U.S. judged the human rights "performance" of other countries, often requiring them to bring their domestic human rights practices into conformity with the international rights regime as a condition for U.S. assistance,[60] while discouraging any review of its own domestic record. As we have seen, some skeptics within the U.S. would go further and flatly deny the relevance of international norms on the death penalty to the U.S. The radically different positions on this issue taken by the U.S. on its part, and Canada, the European Union, and other abolitionist countries on their parts, make constructive discussion difficult, if not impossible. It has become, in effect, a dialogue of the deaf.

But for the U.S., there are important consequences to rejecting even the modest prohibitions on capital punishment which at present exist in international treaty law. The rule of law is a central tenet of U.S. global policy, and one inevitable consequence of asserting U.S. moral, as well as economic and military, leadership is that other countries will increasingly judge the U.S. by its own criteria. Put in the language of public international law,

> U.S. policies abroad depend on our being able to negotiate treaties and obtain compliance with them from our foreign counterparts. Some of these treaties require other countries to make drastic changes in their domestic legal systems. A striking example is the promise to provide effective relief for violations of intellectual property rights that is contained in the new Trade-Related Aspects of Intellectual Property Agreement. A reputation for playing fast and loose with treaty commitments can only harm our capacity to be a leader in the post-Cold War world.[61]

Michael Ignatieff recently made the point in less legal terms:

> It is not just that the U.S. government disagrees with its Western partners about the death penalty. Its record of incorporating international rights documents into U.S. law is distinctly un-Western.... [T]he point of human rights language is that it maintains there are no culturally appropriate excuses for cruelty, inhuman and degrading punishment, denial of... free speech. The political culture of Texas is no less exempt from human rights scrutiny than that of Tehran or

Baghdad. To ask human rights language to be culturally sensitive is to mistake what it is. It ... makes no exceptions, and bows its knee before no power, not even those nations who proudly claim to be its inventors.[62]

NOTES

1. See 118 S.Ct. 1352 (1998), and text.
2. See note 30 infra, and text.
3. The Rome Diplomatic Conference adopted a treaty to create a permanent international court by 120 votes to 7, with 21 abstentions; the 7 no votes included the U.S., China, and Israel. See generally, *The Lawyers Committee for Human Rights, the Rome Treaty for an International Criminal Court: A Brief Summary of the Main Issues* (1998).
4. Council of Europe, *Parliamentary Assembly Recommendation 1246* (1994).
5. Statement by Foreign Secretary Robin Cook, October 16, 1998, U.N. Doc. E/CN4/1998/82 (1998).
6. "The European Union's new policy of global abolition is likely to bring it into confrontation with America, which is one of the foremost users of the death penalty.... [T]he EU has lodged a formal protest with the Americans in six separate cases," *Daily Telegraph*, Dec. 8, 1998, at 15.
7. Quoted in 1 V. Morris & M. Scharf, *The International Criminal Tribunal for Rwanda*, 583 (1998).
8. Id.
9. Pope John Paul II, *Evangelium Vitae* 100 (1995).
10. See, generally, *Capital Punishment and Implementation of the Safeguards Guaranteeing the protection of the Rights of those Facing the Death Penalty: Report of the Secretary General* E/1995/78 [hereinafter cited as *Capital Punishment and Implementation*]. The Secretary General's report of January 16, 1998, lists 61 countries as abolitionist, 14 as abolitionist for ordinary crimes, and 27 as de facto abolitionist. The U.N. has also conducted its own survey of research findings on the relationship between the death penalty and homicide rates, and in 1996 concluded that "research had failed to prove that executions have a greater deterrent effect than life imprisonment and such proof is unlikely to be forthcoming. The evi-

dence as a whole ... gives no positive support to the deterrent hypothesis." See, *Status of the International Covenants on Human Rights: Question of the Death Penalty*, U.N. Doc. E/CN.4/1998/82.

Amnesty International's April 1998 figures record slight changes, with an increase to 63 of abolitionist countries, and of abolitionists for ordinary crimes 16, with a reduction of de facto abolitionists to 25. "91 countries retain and use the death penalty, but the number of countries which actually execute prisoners in any one year is much smaller," AI International Secretariat, London.

11. Since 1990, juvenile executions have been carried out in Iran [4], Nigeria [1], Pakistan [2], Saudi Arabia [1], the U.S. [9], and Yemen [1].

The country which has carried out more documented executions of juvenile offenders than any other is the U.S.A. Sixteen U.S. states were holding 73 juvenile offenders on death row as of October 1998. Nine executions of juvenile offenders have been carried out in five states since 1990; all of those executed were 17 at the time of the offence. Of all U.S. states, Texas carried out the largest number of executions since 1990 — 127 up to 5 November 1998 — and has put to death five juvenile offenders in that time.

The background of the majority of juvenile offenders executed since 1990 was one of serious emotional or material deprivation. Many were regular users of drugs or alcohol with lower than average intelligence. Some had organic brain damage. Some had poor or inexperienced counsel. Highly relevant information was withheld at their trials due to incompetence or inexperience on the part of their lawyers. *Amnesty Int., Juveniles and the Death Penalty: Executions Worldwide Since 1990* (1998).

12. See *Amnesty Int., United States of America: Rights for All* 98, 100 (1998): "More than 350 people have been executed in the U.S.A. since 1990. The U.S.A. has the highest known death row population on earth: over 3,300.... In 1997 the U.S.A. carried out 74 executions — the highest number for four decades. Only China, Saudi Arabia and Iran were known to have executed more prisoners...."

The ramifications of the use of the death penalty in a country as influential as the U.S.A. go far beyond its borders. Officials in different countries have suggested that it is either a factor in, or justification for, their own decision to retain the punishment. In 1997 government officials from both the Philippines and Guatemala reportedly inspected execution chambers in the U.S.A. as part of their research into lethal injection as a method for killing condemned prisoners.

13. Res. 1998/8, and *Ecosoc Statement on the Question of the Death Penalty*, 29 July 1998.

14. *International Covenant on Civil and Political Rights*, Art. 6[5]: "Sentence of death shall not be imposed for crimes committed by persons below eighteen years of age and shall not be carried out on pregnant women." *Convention on the Rights of the Child*, Art. 37(a): "Neither capital punishment nor life sentence without the possibility of release shall be imposed for offences committed by persons below 18 years of age." See, too, *Fourth Geneva Convention*, Art. 68: "... the death penalty may not be pronounced against a protected person who was under the age of 18 at the time of the offence"; and Protocol I, Art. 77. Protocol II, which applies to non-international armed conflicts, goes further and Art. 6(4) bars execution of mothers of young children.

15. See Schabas "International Legal Aspects", in *Capital Punishment: Global Issues and Perspectives* (P. Hodgkinson and A. Rutherford ed. 1996) [hereinafter cited as *Capital Punishment*].

16. See *U.N. Human Rights Comm., General Comment* 14 (1994) 23, on the right to life contained in ICCPR, Art. 6.

17. G. A. Res. 32/61 (Dec. 8, 1977). See also the General Assembly in Res. 39/118 (Dec 14, 1984): *Safeguards Guaranteeing Protection of the Rights of Those Facing the Death Penalty*.

18. ICCPR, Art. 6. Second Optional Protocol to the ICCPR, aiming at the abolition of the death penalty, 1989. Thirty-three ratifications.

19. Protocol No. 6, European Convention on Human Rights, Concerning the Abolition of the Death Penalty. Thirty-three European states are parties.

20. Protocol to the American Convention on Human Rights to Abolish the Death Penalty, Art.1.

21. The American Convention on Human Rights, Art. 4(5) bars the imposition of capital punishment on

those who were over seventy when the crime was committed.

22. ECOSOC Res. 1989/64, 24 May 1989 [*Implementation of the Safeguards Guaranteeing Protection of the Rights of Those Facing the Death Penalty*] recommends "eliminating the death penalty for persons suffering from mental retardation or extremely limited competence, whether at the stage of sentence or execution" [Para.1(d)].

23. See Frankowski, "Post Communist Europe", in *Capital Punishment*, supra, note 15.

24. Council of Europe, *The Abolition of the Death Penalty in Europe*, Doc. 7589.

25. *State v. Makwanyane & Others*, CCT/3/94, June 6, 1995.

26. Id., at para.38.

27. Id., at para. 56.

28. Public opinion is no substitute for the duty vested in the courts to interpret the Constitution and to uphold its provisions without fear or favor. The very reason for establishing the new legal order, and for vesting the power of judicial review of all legislation in the courts, was to protect the rights of minorities and others who cannot protect their rights adequately through the democratic process. It is only if there is a willingness to protect the worst and the weakest of us that all of us can be secure that our own rights will be protected (id., at para. 87).

29. The need for a strong deterrent to violent crime is not open to question. The State is entitled and obliged to protect human life. Without law, individuals in society have no rights. The level of violent crime in our society has reached alarming proportions. It poses a threat to the transition to democracy.... The power of the State to impose sanctions on those who break the law cannot be doubted.... But the question is not whether violent criminals should go free.... Clearly they should not; and equally clearly those who engage in violent crime should be met with the full rigor of the law. The question is whether the death sentence for murder can legitimately be made part of that law.... We would be deluding ourselves if we were to believe that the execution of ... a comparatively few ... people each year ... will provide the solution to the unacceptably high rate of crime. There will always

be unstable, desperate and pathological people for whom the risk of arrest and imprisonment provides no deterrent, but there is nothing to show that a decision to carry out the death sentence would have any impact on the behavior of such people or that there will be more of them if imprisonment is the only sanction.... The greatest deterrent to crime is the likelihood that offenders will be apprehended, convicted and punished. It is that which is presently lacking in our criminal justice system; and it is at this level and through addressing the causes of crime that the State must seek to combat lawlessness (id., at paras. 117-22).

30. Id., at paras. 145 and 146.

31. The U.S. member is Professor Thomas Buergenthal.

32. See U.S. Response to the Report on Capital Punishment and Due Process in the United States by the Special Rapporteur on Extrajudicial, Summary and Arbitrary Executions, April 15, 1998.

33. See, generally, Stewart, "U.S. Ratification of the Covenant on Civil and Political Rights: the Significance of the Reservations, Understandings and Declarations", 14 *Human Rights L.J.*, 77-83 (1992). See also the article by Henkin, infra, note 52.

34. Multilateral Treaties Deposited with the Secretary General, Status as at Dec. 31, 1993; ST/LEG/SER. E/12, p.135 — e.g.:

> The Government of the Federal Republic of Germany objects to the United States' reservation referring to A6(5) of the Covenant, which prohibits capital punishment for crimes committed by persons below 18 years of age. This reservation ... is incompatible with the text as well as with the object and purpose of Article 6 which ... lays down the minimum standard for the right to life.

35. Although treaties that are mere exchanges of obligations between states allow them to reserve inter se application of rules of international law, it is otherwise with human rights treaties "which are for the benefit of persons within their jurisdiction. Accordingly, prohibitions in the Covenant that represent customary international law ... may not be the subject of reservations." Accordingly, a "state may not reserve the right to engage in slavery, to

torture ... to execute pregnant women or children." (General Comment # 24: "On issues relating to reservations made upon ratification or accession to the Covenant or Optional Protocol," (Nov. 1994).

36. The Committee regrets the extent of the State Party's reservations, declarations and understandings to the Covenant. It believes that, taken together, they intended to ensure that the United States has accepted what is already the law of the United States. The Committee is also particularly concerned at reservations to article 6, paragraph 5, and article 7 of the Covenant, which it believes to be incompatible with the object and purpose of the Covenant.

The Committee is concerned about the excessive number of offences punishable by the death penalty in a number of states, the number of death sentences handed down by the courts, and the long stay on death row which, in many cases, may amount to a breach of A.7 of the Covenant. It deplores the recent expansion of the death penalty in certain states. It also deplores provisions in the legislation of a number of states which allow the death penalty to be pronounced for crimes committed under the age of 18 and the actual instances where such sentences have been pronounced and executed. It also regrets that there appears to have been lack of protection from the death penalty of those mentally retarded. (*Comments of the Human Rights Committee on the United States of America*, [CCPR/C/79/Add 50; Apr. 6, 1995]).

37. The purpose and effect of General Comment No. 24 is to seek to nullify as a matter of international law the reservations, understandings, declarations, and proviso contained in the Senate resolution of ratification, thereby purporting to impose legal obligations on the United States never accepted by the United States. (Text on file with the author.)

38. E/CN.4/1998/68/Add.3.

39. It was brought to the Special Rapporteur's attention that the guarantee of due process in capital cases has been seriously jeopardized following the adoption of the ... 1996 Anti Terrorism and Effective Death Penalty Act. This law severely limits federal review of state court convictions and curtails the availability of habeas corpus at the federal level. In addition, the withdrawal of funding for post con-

viction defender organizations, which were handling capital punishment cases at the post conviction level and helping attorneys involved in death penalty cases, seriously limits the extent to which fair trial standards are fully available during the process leading to the imposition of a death sentence. (id., at para 43).

40. Out of 38 states with death penalty statutes, 14 provide that 18 is the minimum age for execution. In 4 states, 17 is the minimum age, while in 21 other states, 16 is the minimum age.... 47 offenders who committed crimes under the age of 18 are currently on death row. (id., para 51).

41. Because of the nature of mental retardation, mentally retarded persons are much more vulnerable to manipulation during arrest, interrogation and confession. Moreover, mental retardation appears not to be compatible with the principle of full criminal responsibility. (id.)

42. E.g., Bedau, The United States of America, in *Capital Punishment*, supra note 15. In many ways the U.N. report is less damning than critics such as Bedau. See, e.g., Bedau at 49:

The real scandal is the travesty of justice that unfolds all too often in the trial of a defendant charged with murder and where, if there is a conviction, the judge or the jury ... must decide the punishment. Underpaid, overworked, inexperienced, incompetent defense counsel; failure to submit any, or any adequate, evidence of mitigation during the penalty phase of the trial; indifferent judicial conduct of the trial; improper and misunderstood instructions to the jury; confusion, brow beating and impatience among the sequestered jurors — these deplorable features of actual capital trials have been cited again and again by knowledgeable observers.

43. The State Department saw the report as neglecting the "strong and effective procedural prohibitions in the US against miscarriages of justice," and (making a perhaps casuistic distinction between international treaty law and customary international law), claimed that the report "mistakes international law when it says that US use of the death penalty is a violation of international law prohibi-

tions on the death penalty. Capital punishment is not prohibited by customary international law when international standards of due process are fully protected." *The Wall Street Journal* (in a April 21, 1998, editorial entitled Murder and the UN) saw the report as raising legitimate concerns about how the UN is focusing its energies. Senator Helms described the Special Rapporteur's "strange 'investigation' as merely a platform for more outrageous accusations from US critics at the UN" (Letter to Ambassador Bill Richardson (October 6, 1997).

44. If the offence for which extradition is requested is punishable by death under the law of the requesting Party, and if in respect of such offence the death penalty is not provided for by the law of the requested Party or is not normally carried out, extradition may be refused unless the requesting Party gives such assurance as the requested Party considers sufficient that the death penalty will not be carried out. (Art. 11, *European Convention on Extradition*, 1957, E.T.S. No. 24).

45. European Court of Human Rights, *Soering v United Kingdom* A 161 (1989).

46. See, generally, Dugard and Van den Wyngaert, "Reconciling Extradition with Human Rights" 92 *AM. J. INT'L L.* 187 (1998).

47. *New York Times*, Dec. 21, 1998: "German officials said the United States had been obliged to guarantee that Mr Salim would not face the death penalty. German law prohibits extradition of suspects to countries where they could face execution."

48. See, Dugard and Van den Wyngaert, "Reconciling Extradition with Human Rights", at 193.

49. See Bianchi, Note: *Venezia v Ministero di Grazia e Giustizia*, 91 *AM. J. INT'L. L.* (1997): "Overall, practice seems to suggest the emergence of a European *ordre publique* which prohibits extradition of fugitives when this may entail ... a violation of values enshrined in either the ECHR or the forum state's constitution."

50. *Ng v. Canada*, UN Doc. CCPR/C/49/D/469/1991 [1993].

51. See supra note 37; also US Response to the Report on Capital Punishment and Due Process in the US, Geneva, April 15, 1998: Remarks by Ambassador George E. Moose.

52. See Henkin, "U.S. Ratification of Human Rights

Conventions: The Ghost of Senator Bricker" 89 *AM. J. INT'L L.* 341-50 (1995).

53. "Another problem in invoking international standards relating to the death penalty is that many are vague or aspirational, such as the increasingly fragile consensus on eventual world wide abolition. This makes international death penalty norms difficult to evoke effectively in litigation," Fitzpatrick, 25 *GA. J. INT'L and COMP. L.*, 165 (1995/96).

54. Writing as long ago as 1950, Hans Lauterpacht identified three reasons why the U.S. ("a State which has been the cradle of modern bills of rights and ... has an incomparable tradition of idealism and individualism") opposed making a new International Bill of Rights binding and enforceable:

> The first is the traditional reluctance of the U.S. to submit to obligations involving the possibility of international interference in the sphere of its domestic jurisdiction and a consequent impairment of the sovereignty of one or both branches of its supreme legislative organ. The second ... lies in the difficulty arising out of the constitutional division of powers between the Union and the component States.... [T]hirdly, the intricate problem created by the treatment of the Negro population in some of the States. (H. Lauterpacht, *International Law and Human Rights* 302-303 (1950).

55. Article 36 gives to consular officials the right to communicate with, visit, and arrange legal representation for their nationals, and to foreign nationals the right to notify their consuls of their detention.

56. See, generally, Aceves, "Litigation Under the Vienna Convention", in *ACLU INT'L CIVIL LIBERTIES REP.* 6-13 (1998).

57. See supra, note 5: UN Doc. E/CN.4/1998/82.

58. See Lester, "The Overseas Trade in the American Bill of Rights", 88 *COLUM. L. REV.*, 541 (1988):

> there is a vigorous overseas trade in the Bill of Rights in international and constitutional litigation involving norms derived from American constitutional law. Where life or liberty is at stake, the landmark judgements of the Supreme

Court of the US ... are studied with as much attention in New Delhi or Strasbourg as they are in Washington, DC, or Springfield, Illinois.

59. An Executive Order, issued on December 10, 1998, the 50th anniversary of the Universal Declaration of Human Rights, mandates the Inter Agency Working Group to provide "guidance, oversight, and coordination with respect to questions concerning the adherence to and implementation of human rights obligations and related matters," including public education.

60. The annual State Department *Country Reports on Human Rights Practices* now report and assess human rights practice in some 190 countries.

61. Vagts, "Taking Treaties Less Seriously" 92 *AM. J. INT'L. L.* 462 (1998).

62. "Keeping an Old Flame Burning Brightly", *Guardian Weekly* (London), Dec. 20, 1998.

CHILD LABOR AND GLOBAL INEQUALITY: RESPONSIBILITIES AND POLICIES

Roland Pierik

Roland Pierik is Lecturer in Political Theory in the Faculty of Law at Tilburg University in the Nether-lands. His research is in the area of contemporary political theory. He is the author of several journal articles on multiculturalism, cultural groups and identities, and issues of global justice.

Pierik asks what developed countries can or should do to reduce or eliminate incidences of child labor in developing countries. He argues that in order to know what policies will work, we need to be aware of socioeconomic and cultural differences between developed and developing countries. Socioeconomic conditions of increased permeability of national, legal, and political orders enable Westerners to import commodities produced by children in developing countries, where severe poverty makes this labor desirable and necessary. Cultural differences between developed and developing countries with respect to notions of childhood, Pierik argues, call for a distinction between child work and child labor. Support for conventions and policies must take these differences into account. Pierik ends by providing several policy recommendations to address child labor and eliminate the worse forms of it.

1. Introduction

Without doubt, most parents in Western countries want their children to experience a happy and care-free childhood and do all they can to protect their children from the responsibilities and pain of the adult world as long as possible. Childhood is viewed as a "mythic walled garden" of play and study. It is, therefore, hard to accept that children in some parts of the world have to work in sweat-shops in poor working conditions, often for ten or more hours a day. And many find it unacceptable that designer label clothes and sneakers worn by children in the West are made by children of the same age in Bangladesh and India. Child labor is a topic that evokes deep emotions and is cause for growing international concern. Most recent global estimates show that some 211 million children between the ages of five and 14 are engaged in full time economic activity, 119 million of whom are engaged in hazardous labor.

In Western liberal democracies, child labor is condemned morally, prohibited by law, and virtually non-existent. But this has not always been the case. During the Industrial Revolution, child labor was as widespread in Europe and the U.S. as it now is in India and Bangladesh.[1] Yet, one finds a near consensus in Western liberal democracies that child labor is a deplorable practice that should be abandoned. However, rejecting child labor on moral terms is one thing; devising policies for curbing it is quite another. What, if anything, should governments of liberal-democratic societies do to combat child labor?

Not every action against child labor is *ipso facto* in the best interest of the children involved, as has been shown by an already notorious example. In 1995 the U.S. Congress considered the Child Labor Deterrence Bill (*Harkin's Bill*, named after one of its sponsors, Senator Tom Harkin from Iowa), which sought to forbid the import of products made with the involvement of workers under the age of 15.

Supporters of this bill hoped (and expected) that such a boycott would result in these children returning to school. Though the bill was never passed, it sent shockwaves in the countries for which the U.S. was the largest export market. For example, the Bangladeshi Garment Manufacturers and Export Association perceived these discussions in the U.S. Congress as a threat to its exports. Nervous owners, unwilling to risk access to their most important market, quickly fired around 50,000 children, 75 per cent of the total then employed. The expectation in the U.S. that these children would return to school was not only overly optimistic, it also turned out to be dramatically naïve. As Ben White concludes:

> Not one of the dismissed children had gone back to school. Half of them had found other occupations (mainly in informal-sector and street activities, including domestic service, brick-chipping, selling flowers on the street and prostitution) but with greatly reduced earnings while the other half were actively seeking work. The children still working in the garment factories had better nutrition and better health care than those who had been dismissed.[2]

Although I do not question Senator Harkin's good intentions, the effect of his proposal was disastrous.[3] One lesson to be learned is that economic boycotts might not be the best strategy against child labor and, as the example shows, may even have the opposite effect from that intended. For one thing, boycotts only affect businesses that export goods, and these only employ 5 per cent of working children. Trade sanctions are thus unlikely to have a significant effect on the occurrence of child labor.

More generally, the lesson is that Western policies on child labor, as applied to developing countries, should not be based on impulse or good intentions but rather on careful analysis and research. Western assumptions and remedies cannot simply be applied to developing countries without reflection on the differences in socioeconomic situations and cultural convictions involved. Since such policies aim to combat practices in another society, policy-makers should be aware of

the many pitfalls risked by intervention in the complex interactions of family choices and market structures. Moreover, one needs to recognize the forces that give rise to child labor in the first place and determine which are most likely to respond to intervention and thereby curb child labor.[4]

In this paper I describe some difficulties with Western policies on child labor abroad. First I analyze liberal-democratic values concerning child labor, its socioeconomic causes, different conceptions of childhood, and the need to distinguish between child work and child labor. A brief survey of International Labour Organization (ILO) conventions on this topic serves to illustrate these issues. Moreover, I discuss the question of whether Western societies are causally responsible for the occurrence of child labor in developing countries. I then suggest some alternative approaches that may help to avoid pitfalls in Western policies seeking to curb child labor abroad and conclude with six policy recommendations.

2. Children, Child Labor, and Liberal-Democratic Values

Current debates on child labor within Western societies are closely linked to the increasing importance of globalization. Globalization is a multidimensional phenomenon that embodies a shift in the organization of human activity and the deployment of power from domestic and national orientations to interregional and transcontinental patterns.[5] One element of globalization is the increasing permeability of national, legal, and political orders, a permeability that enables Westerners to import commodities produced by children in developing countries under conditions that conflict with the norms and values that prevail in Western societies. Although supranational, international, and intergovernmental organizations such as the European Union (EU), the North American Free Trade Agreement (NAFTA), the World Trade Organization (WTO), and the United Nations (UN) may have emerged and gained influence, the basic political agency for international political affairs predominantly remains the (nation) state. I proceed from the starting point that, although political theory may be sensitive to state borders, issues of justice typically are not.[6] The aim of this paper is to reconsider the role of national governments in the international domain and to reformulate liberal-democratic values to adapt to issues of globalization and the resulting plurality. In Western states, these values are generally liberal-democratic ones, as exemplified in John Rawls's *A Theory of Justice*.[7]

Should a liberal-democratic government design policies against child labor abroad and, if so, what should these policies be? One simple answer would be to apply normative political theories that were constructed for liberal-democratic societies and developed within them. However, this implies that Western values and ideas should or can be imposed with no regard for the specific contexts of other countries. This is problematic for several reasons. The socioeconomic situation in Bangladesh or India is very different from that in the U.S. or Europe. Moreover, the fact that there is a plurality of ideas about the good life means that enacting policies based on Western values and applying them to non-Western societies is questionable. Another simple answer would be the relativist position that the issue of child labor belongs to the internal affairs of each country. This implies that every state should merely follow its own norms and that Western governments cannot criticize policies and practices within other societies or vice versa. However, most Western societies are not willing to compromise the claim to universality of some of their most deeply held values, such as a respect for the human rights summarized in the 1948 Universal Declaration of Human Rights. What might these deeply held values be and how do we get to the core of liberal-democratic values that inspire Western policies? In what ways can liberal-democratic values be reinterpreted so that they become more sensitive to socioeconomic circumstances and cultural values that differ substantially from those in Western liberal democracies?

Joseph Carens has proposed a method to distinguish core values from derivative ones. He perceives the idea of justice in terms of three concentric circles, with core values being contained within the derivative values. The idea is that "as

one moves inwards, the understanding of justice is thinner in the sense that it settles fewer questions, but more extensive in the sense that it applies to more contexts." The outermost circle contains standards of justice that are intimately linked to the history and culture of one particular society. Examples in the U.S. are the broad interpretation of free speech and the constitutionally guaranteed right to carry arms. The middle circle contains standards of justice that are not universal but applicable only to contemporary liberal-democratic societies. Such norms are more or less directly derived from liberal-democratic values and are historically and culturally specific, though they are not specific to a given society. The innermost circle contains the basic liberal-democratic ideals, non-negotiable standards of justice that should be applied to all states regardless of their particular history or political arrangements. Although this minimal standard is the product of "our" liberal-democratic values, it is applied in a universal way. For Carens, some policies, practices, and institutions can be criticized in the name of justice, "even though we recognize that the people whose policies, practices, and institutions are being criticized may not share our understanding of justice."[8]

When we apply Carens's model of justice as concentric circles to child labor, we need to find the innermost circle by distinguishing basic liberal-democratic ideals from their Western interpretations. For example, in our discussion of the conception of "childhood," we have to peel away Western interpretations to arrive at a conception that is widely acceptable. We should not start from Western policies aimed at children growing up in Western societies because their situation might differ fundamentally from children growing up in developing countries. Instead, we should seek the core values underlying these Western policies and utilize them in our policies on child labor abroad.

To formulate these basic values with respect to children, we first have to know what distinguishes children from adults. A child is a person who in some fundamental way is not developed but in the process of developing.[9] Children are therefore a vulnerable category of persons. The ultimate aim is for children to develop mentally, socially, emotionally, and physically and to become integrated persons in their society. To reach this goal, they need to be protected, nurtured, and educated. The core liberal-democratic values relating to childhood can thus be described as follows: children should be able to develop into persons who are capable of functioning in their society. Those who are responsible for children — parents, other caregivers, and government — should act on their behalf and do everything in their power to ensure that children are not hindered in their development. Although paternalism is inconsistent with liberal-democratic values, this is one of the few areas where it is permitted.[10]

The first part, being able to function in one's society, is an important element in this discussion. Different societies are organized differently, which implies that there are different situations, different ideas about what it means to be capable of functioning in a society, and different ideas about how this capability should be achieved. Western policies on child labor should be formulated in light of these considerations. There are two major differences between developed and developing countries that Western governments have to address when concrete policies are developed: socioeconomic differences and cultural ones. I will analyze each of these in turn.

3. Socioeconomic, Political, and Infrastructural Differences

In discussions on child labor, one cannot emphasize too strongly the importance of socioeconomic differences between developed and developing countries. The most important reason for the existence of child labor in developing countries is poverty.[11] Fallon and Tzannotos show that the incidence of child labor is negatively correlated with the rise in per capita GDP.[12] Even poor parents do not like to send their children to work if they can prevent it. Indeed, Kaushik Basu argues that when child labor occurs as a mass phenomenon, the alternative to child labor is usually very harsh — acute hunger or even starvation.[13] This is the main reason why boycotts like Harkin's Bill are counterproductive: boycotts focus only on the *effects* of

child labor — its products — but typically fail to investigate the *structural reasons* for the occurrence of child labor, namely, poverty. Children in the export industry usually work in comparatively good conditions. If they lose their jobs and the reason for working is not addressed, they may be forced into worse, more dangerous, less well paid jobs.[14] Legal interventions like the prohibition of child labor are a prudent policy only if we have reason to believe that it will not make the children worse off; for example, if there are alternative ways to provide for or increase the family income.

Moreover, successful policies against child labor should be founded on an awareness of the political and infrastructural situation in countries where child labor occurs. National governments usually have only a limited impact on the lives of the poorest. As William Myers concludes:

> Social welfare laws [in developing countries] have relatively little impact on the everyday life of the poor, where labor inspection services tend to be precarious and corrupt, and where national governments have extreme difficulty extending full primary education coverage to the rural and urban periphery areas where most working children live.[15]

This conclusion is important because it shows that legal interventions against child labor have only a limited effect. An important assumption used to justify Harkin's Bill was that if children did not work, they would automatically return to school. On what information was this assumption based? What if there are no schools or only ones that are a two-hour walk away? White's finding on the effects of Harkin's Bill — that none of the dismissed children had gone back to school — provides quite a sobering conclusion. A legalistic approach prohibiting child labor might not work, simply because governments in developing countries lack both the power to enforce such prohibitions and the capability to provide educational opportunities.

To conclude: awareness of the socioeconomic and infrastructural context of child labor is a prerequisite in preventing counterproductive policies against child labor. Socioeconomic circumstances dominate all the other causes that may lead to the exploitation of children. Empirical research shows that the economic recession in Ivory Coast and Cameroon in the mid-1980s led to an increase in child labor.[16] Before I discuss the policy implications of these socioeconomic circumstances further, I turn to a discussion of the second major difference between developing and developed countries: cultural differences in prevailing ideas about childhood and the role of work and education therein.

4. Different Cultural Conceptions of Childhood

Conceptions of childhood are subject to a fierce and continuing discussion. On the one hand, one finds general agreement that childhood can be described as a biologically driven natural phenomenon characterized by physical and mental growth stages.[17] On the other hand, childhood is a social construct interpreted very differently in various cultural contexts; childhood is the life space that a culture allows it to be. For a better understanding of the different conceptions of childhood, it is necessary to briefly look at Western history.

Characteristic of the Western conception of childhood is the strict separation between adulthood and childhood. The conception of childhood was established as an ideal in Britain around 1840 and can be explained as a reaction to the exploitation of children in the first decades of the Industrial Revolution. It replaced the idea of the young wage-earner by the innocent, dependent child who had to be educated and protected from the dangers of adulthood. Today, the "myth of childhood innocence" is marked by special clothing, literature, and games made to suit the interests and development of children. It is characterized as a separate stage of development with its own distinct challenges and needs: growing up is assumed to require an extended period of socialization and formalized education. Children are thus discouraged from participation in adult concerns such as economic maintenance.[18] However, this Western conceptualization of childhood is atypical, historically as well as in comparison with other societies, where a less categorical distinction between childhood and adulthood is employed and where child work is distinguished from child labor.

Distinguishing Child Work from Child Labor

The conceptual difference between *child work* and *child labor* has its origins in the industrialization of the production process during the early days of the Industrial Revolution. Child labor became an issue of concern after its detrimental effects on the health and future of children became clear. While work has different meanings in different societies and varies with social, cultural, and economic factors, child work in any form has always been part of a wider set of childhood activities. In fact, child work is the norm in most of the world.

Work in non-industrialized sectors in developing countries is usually organized in workshops or family-owned businesses, not in large-scale, impersonal factories. The fact that these children work alongside their parents protects them from the forms of exploitation common during the heyday of the Industrial Revolution.[19] A second consequence is that there is often no need for formal education to enter the labor market beyond the basic level or high school. Children learn by doing and succeed their parents in family owned businesses. In fact, in such societies work is seen as an important means of teaching and socializing children.

This reveals a less categorical distinction between childhood and adulthood than is made in Western conceptions. Children's acting in the role of adults is seen as an important element in education in some cultures and is taken as an expression of family unity and solidarity — as it was in Western societies prior to the Industrial Revolution.[20] In such situations, it is not in the best interest of children to be kept in the mythic walled garden of a separated childhood. Instead, these children need to integrate in their parents' world to be able to function in their society. Working and earning can be a positive experience in a child's growing up, or it can provide the means for additional education that would otherwise not be available. Thus, in some societies and under specific conditions, work can be beneficial for children. This depends largely on the age of the child, the conditions in which the child works, and whether work prevents the child from receiving basic education.

This implies that policy-makers must distinguish *child work* — an essential and meaningful part of education and socialization — from *child labor* — which is harmful because it prevents children from receiving education or hinders their physical, psychological, emotional, or social development. Of course, it is easier to distinguish these conceptually than to give policy recommendations on where to draw the line. We can identify the extremes, but borders can only be drawn in specific situations. However, any successful policy against child labor should bite this bullet. After all, the alternative strategy of not recognizing this distinction undermines the plausibility of the struggle against child labor. Why would one try to abolish potentially useful sources of socialization and education? Given the scarcity of energy and means, it is better to be clear about differences, set priorities, and then focus on the worst forms.

The diversity of interpretations of childhood and appropriate forms of work for children raises important questions concerning child labor, its undesirability, and the feasibility of policies to curb the practice. These debates have been dominated by Western interpretations of childhood, both with respect to theoretical conceptions of childhood and with respect to policies on child labor such as those of the ILO.

From the very start, the ILO focused on the problem of child labor, especially on the basic protection of children. The Treaty of Versailles — from which the ILO emerged — called for "an abolition of child labour and the imposition of such limitations on the labour of young persons as shall permit the continuance of their education and ensure their proper physical development." The first ILO Convention on "Hours of Work in Industry" (1919) contained a special clause for "young persons" under 15, setting a maximum working time of 48 hours a week. The second stage (1946-89) is best characterized as "the gap between aspirations and reality." In 1973, Convention No. 138 was adopted, and "with a view to achieving *the total abolition* of child labour," the *absolute* minimum age was decided to be 15 years.

This history of ILO child labor conventions illustrates Western dominance in international debates on child labor, in which a particularistic Western idea is disguised as a universal ideal.[21] In terms of Carens's model, it contains not only the innermost circle of the basic liberal-democratic ideals, but also culturally specific values of the second circle. However, one can question whether the romanticized ideal of childhood that underlies international conventions is valid, even for Western societies. Do we really think that delivering newspapers, babysitting, or mowing the lawn after school is an intolerable infringement on someone's childhood?

The third stage of child labor conventions (1989 onwards) displays signs of a new realism. In accordance with the changed world after 1989, the ILO adopted the strategy of defining only a core of forms of child labor that could not be tolerated, regardless of a country's level of economic development. Convention 182 defines and prohibits *the worst forms of child labor*. The change of terminology is evident from a rhetorical notion like the "total abolition of child labor" to a definition of the worst forms thereof. In a way, Convention 182 can be seen as an attempt to define Carens's "innermost circle" because it describes situations that every respectable nation must condemn if it wants to be part of our global trade system. It calls on governments in a very general way and focuses on the worst forms of child labor, described as "work which, by its nature or the circumstances in which it is carried out, is likely to harm the health, safety or morals of children." It includes slavery or compulsory labor, debt bondage, forced or compulsory recruitment of children for use in armed conflict, and child prostitution.

A broad support for conventions and policies against child labor is undermined if it is based on a biased conception of childhood. If Western governments and international organizations want to fight child labor, they must acknowledge the diversity in thinking about childhood. More sensitivity to culture and the way it mediates the effects of experience on children is not the same as defending cultural relativism. Instead, a more inclusive conception of childhood as the basis of policies against child labor is a way to base policies on a broader representation of human experience than only that of Euro-American values.[22] To conclude: the participation in these debates on childhood and child labor should be as broad as possible. For one thing, it can be expected that such an inclusive debate reduces the risk of parochial biases of the conception of childhood and the discussions of moral issues concerning child labor. Moreover, an inclusive character in these debates will enhance the legitimacy of their outcomes.[23]

5. Global Inequality and Responsibilities of Western Governments

Up to now I have discussed the policies of Western governments as if these governments might have some moral responsibilities to fight child labor, but have no causal responsibility for the occurrence of child labor itself.[24] Indeed, it seems obvious that we should focus our attention on the responsibilities of domestic governments for the occurrence of child labor within their jurisdiction and view them as responsible for the lot of their own citizens — including the laboring children. It is not as clear, however, that these governments have the capability and the means to fight child labor within their borders. However, taking seriously the argument that child labor in Western societies did not end at the end of the nineteenth century but was merely exported to developing countries implies that child labor today is neither an isolated phenomenon nor the sole responsibility of developing countries.[25] As we have seen in section 3, the most important cause of child labor is poverty. It could be asked, then, how we can explain the vast inequalities in wealth between developed and developing countries. More specifically, are Western societies responsible for the economic situation in developing countries that causes child labor, and do they have a responsibility to alleviate poverty in those countries?

This issue of responsibility for world poverty is one of the central debates in current political philosophy. John Rawls argues that the wealth of nations is mainly determined by domestic policies. In *The Law of Peoples* (1999) he defends principles of international law and practice that he deems consistent with, and an elaboration of, his theory of domestic justice as presented in *A Theory of Justice* (1971). He argues that inequalities between countries are mainly caused by domestic policies, and he thus focuses on domestic institutions in developing countries as the most important determinants of poverty.[26] Rawls argues that affluent societies have no causal responsibility for poverty in developing countries, because this is mainly caused by the incompetence, corruption, and tyranny entrenched in domestic governments, institutions, and cultures:

> The causes of the wealth of a people and the forms it takes lie in their political culture and in the religious, philosophical, and moral traditions that support the basic structure of their political and social institutions, as well as in the industriousness and cooperative talents of its members, all supported by their political virtues. I would further conjecture that there is no society anywhere in the world — except for marginal cases — with resources so scarce that it could not, were it reasonably and rationally organized and governed, become well-ordered.[27]

Rawls concludes that in most cases governments should be held responsible for the lot of their citizens since poverty is caused mainly by local factors. Thus, affluent societies do not have a responsibility for poverty abroad or a duty to support poor countries. Their duties are limited to assisting "burdened societies" to overcome their "unfavorable conditions that prevent their having a just or decent political and social regime."[28]

Cosmopolitans like Brian Barry, Charles Beitz, Allan Buchanan, and Thomas Pogge disagree with Rawls's emphasis on domestic institutions and focus instead on international interaction as an important causal determinant of the wealth of nations. Thomas Pogge emphasizes in *World*

Poverty and Human Rights (2002) that all states in the contemporary world are connected in one global economy as a result of the emerging globalization and global governance. Since societies are connected via the global basic structure, poverty in developing countries cannot be seen as disconnected from affluence in Western societies. States are interconnected through a global network of market trade, diplomacy, and cooperation in international and supranational institutions such as the UN, the EU, NATO, the WTO, the World Bank, and the International Monetary Fund (IMF). Pogge is critical of the foreign policies of Western societies that shaped international and supranational organizations:

> Our new global economic order is so harsh on the global poor, then, because it is shaped in negotiations where our representatives ruthlessly exploit their vastly superior bargaining power and expertise, as well as any weakness, ignorance, or corruptibility they may find in their counterpart negotiators, to shape each agreement for our greatest benefit.[29]

Pogge does not argue that this global institutional order is inherently unjust, but rather that it is designed in an unjust way because Western governments have pursued their self-interest to the extreme and thus managed to arrange these institutions in such a way that they benefit more than others societies do. He discusses the example of the current WTO treaty and argues not that it opens markets too much, but that it does not open our markets enough. Affluent societies reap the benefits of international trade, but refuse to accept the burdens thereof. The WTO treaty permits the affluent countries to protect their markets against cheap imports such as agricultural products, textiles, and steel through quotas, tariffs, and anti-dumping duties. Such protectionist measures reduce the export opportunities of developing countries by blocking their exports to the affluent countries. Moreover, subsidizing domestic producers enables the affluent countries to sell their products below the market price, pushing more efficient poor-country producers from the world markets and thereby generating severe poverty in developing countries:

> This particular aspect of the existing WTO treaty system may thus have a rather large impact on the incidence of severe poverty in the developing countries, understanding "impact" here in a counterfactually comparative way: If the WTO treaty system did not allow the protectionist measures in question, there would be a great deal less poverty in the world today.[30]

This conclusion implies that Western societies, via the global basic structure and the way international and supranational institutions are organized, do generate poverty in developing countries.

How should we assess the Rawlsian claim and its cosmopolitan alternative? Rawls's emphasis on domestic institutions in the explanations of poverty seems to be perfectly sound. No society can flourish without strong social institutions — even Pogge does not disagree with this position.[31] Less convincing, however, is Rawls's claim that domestic institutions are the *only* institutions that matter, thereby denying the normative relevance of the global basic structure. Given the enormous global interdependence that exists today — and that will only grow in the foreseeable future — we can safely conclude that Rawls's description of national states as states being "more or less self-sufficient," or "a closed system isolated from others" and "self contained" has lost its descriptive power.[32] The effects of the global basic structure on world poverty cannot be ignored because it has such profound and enduring effects on national states and individuals within them. I agree with Pogge that bad government and corruption in the developing world cannot be simply explained as "wholly native ingredients of a lesser culture" without acknowledging that they are sustained by important features of our present institutional order.[33]

However, accepting the importance of the global basic structure implies a causal link and a direct responsibility of Western societies for child labor abroad. Pogge's argument implies that affluent Western societies foster child labor indirectly by imposing an unjust global order on developing countries. They close their markets through protectionist policies, subsidize local agriculture massively, and introduce anti-dumping measures in many of the sectors where developing countries are best able to compete, such as agriculture, textiles, and clothing.

If Western liberal-democratic governments really want to fight child labor, they should not only focus on child labor itself, but also on global poverty and their role in the global basic structure. Formulated in less diplomatic words, it is gratuitous for Western governments to want to fight child labor without accepting their own responsibilities for some of the ultimate causes of child labor. If they are truly committed to curbing child labor, they would do well to open their borders to products that are now kept from their markets by protectionist policies, lift the debt burdens that disable developing countries from providing basic education for children, and support measures aimed at raising the income of parents so that children do not have to work. Moreover, they can support collaborative measures such as providing financial support for educational opportunities and helping developing countries improve governance and provide economic and political stability.

6. Policy Recommendations

In the previous sections, I emphasized some important differences between developed and developing countries: difference in socioeconomic and infrastructural situations, different conceptions of childhood, and different ideas about the role of education and work in socializing children. Moreover, I emphasized the causal role Western societies have in sustaining an unjust global basic structure. What do they reveal about the possibilities and pitfalls of Western policies against child labor abroad?

Policies against child labor should acknowledge that it is a heterogeneous phenomenon. On the one hand, different kinds of *child labor* should be distinguished. Child work that is part of education and socialization should be distinguished from child labor, which is harmful to children. Moreover, the

category of child labor should be divided into the unequivocally worst forms of child labor and other forms of child labor. The unequivocally worst forms of child labor include work that, by its nature or the circumstances in which it is carried out, hinders the physical, psychological, mental, and social development of children or is work in unhealthy and dangerous environments. These include slavery, bonded labor, and child prostitution.[34] On the other hand, different kinds of *child laborers* should be distinguished. Special attention should be given to orphans and street children as they are extra vulnerable because they have no relatives to look after them. Moreover, policies against child labor should distinguish ages and pay special attention to the fight against labor by the youngest children. Some jobs that require physical strength or mental concentration can, under certain conditions, be acceptable for older children but unacceptable for younger ones.

Policies should reflect this heterogeneity of child labor. Many past Western proposals, such as Harkin's Bill, uniformly emphasize coercive measures aimed at forbidding child labor. Coercive measures can be important but have to be used selectively; they should only be applied to the unequivocally worst forms of child labor. Such a ban might in the short run have negative effects on the poorest families if there are no alternative sources of family income. But it seems pointless to permit dangerous labor to be performed by children who cannot properly assess the long-term damage such jobs can cause (and whose parents may also be unable to make such an assessment).[35] Governments and intergovernmental organizations should take collective action to single out the unequivocally worst forms of child labor and create, implement, and monitor internationally accepted norms to abolish them.

Distinguishing the unequivocally worst forms of child labor from less harmful forms implies that the latter may have to be tolerated, at least for the near future.[36] Toleration does not imply indifference but, rather, a sense of realism. If it is impossible to ban all child labor, we should prioritize the worst forms. Rigidly fixing on a total ban on child labor excludes many policy options, such as those that focus on improving children's working conditions. Legal coercive measures are not the only policies available. Western governments could also engage in collaborative measures, designed to alter the (economic) environment of decision-makers (parents and employers), rendering them more willing to let children stay out of work and spend more time on schooling and other activities.[37] These measures do not necessarily need legislative backing. Collaborative measures enable policy-makers to consider policies that improve the conditions in which children work or that enable the combination of part-time work with part-time education. These policies are especially appropriate for situations where no alternative sources of family income may be available. Since parents typically want to keep their children out of the work place and in school, if at all possible, collaborative measures are more successful than legal bans on child labor. Empirical research on collaborative interventions shows that the most effective policies are those that enhance access to education and fight poverty.[38] Let me conclude my arguments by suggesting six recommendations for Western policy-makers that would avoid the pitfalls discussed in this paper.

1. Policies should not aim at a global ban on child labor. Some abolitionist groups argue that all child labor should be banned globally and that we will have succeeded only if all children in the world receive full-time formal education. However, such policy goals are entirely unrealistic, strategically counterproductive, and, as a result, do more harm than good. Instead of an abolitionist approach, Western governments should embrace a gradualist, step-by-step approach. There are more than 200 million child laborers today, and the practice has persisted for more than two centuries. This is a huge and complex problem that cannot be solved overnight. Child work should be distinguished from child labor, the several forms of child labor should be ranked on the basis of harmfulness, and policies should prioritize the worst forms.
2. Policies should be based on an inclusive conception of childhood. Although the Western idea of childhood is very atypical, it has been used as a universal model in many policies and conventions, such as those of the ILO. As such, this biased conception has dominated most international discussions on child labor and children's rights. The fight against child labor would be strengthened if conventions and policies were based on a more inclusive conception of childhood, including non-Western ideas on the balance between work and education in socialization. Moreover, a more inclusive conception of childhood would generate broader support for policies and conventions on child labor.

3. Western governments should act contextually. There is no single, simple policy measure that can end all child labor. Policies that have been very successful in one context did not work in another or even had contrary effects. Before proposing a specific intervention, policy-makers should be aware of the socioeconomic, political, cultural, and infrastructural characteristics of the society involved. There is an emerging body of empirical literature on the effects of different policies against child labor in developing countries, so policies should be based on a thorough analysis of the available information, not on intuitions and good faith.

4. Western governments should act collectively. Child labor is a global problem and can be fought only on a global scale. Policies against child labor can be successful only if they are the result of international cooperation. Even large countries such as the U.S. cannot achieve much on their own. Governments should work together in international and supranational organizations such as the United Nations International Children's Emergency Fund (UNICEF), United Nations Educational, Scientific, and Cultural Organization (UNESCO), the WTO, and the ILO by establishing conventions and encouraging nations to ratify them. They should encourage multinational corporations to formulate codes of conduct.[39] They should cooperate with (international) non-governmental organizations (NGOs) that have experience in the field and support promising projects, such as those addressing poverty relief and education.

5. Policies should not focus only on legal measures, but also on collaborative ones. Most policies against child labor take the form of coercive measures, intended to prohibit child labor legally. Coercive measures are important but should be applied only to the unequivocally worst forms of child

labor. Besides legal coercive measures, Western governments could also engage in collaborative initiatives designed to alter the economic environment of parents and employers, rendering them more willing to let children stay out of work and spend more time on schooling and other activities.

6. Western governments should accept their responsibilities. When Western governments formulate policies against child labor, they cannot ignore the global context in which the practice occurs. Child labor today is not an isolated phenomenon in developing countries. As a result of globalization, all states in the contemporary world are connected in one global economy. Poverty is the most important cause of child labor, and the fight against child labor should not be separated from the issue of global poverty. Western governments should forgo maximizing their own interests in international negotiations and propose reforms of the international and supranational institutions in such a way that all individuals are able to meet their basic social and economic needs.[40]

7. Conclusion

In this paper I have discussed the possibilities and pitfalls of Western policies seeking to curb child labor abroad. Since such policies aim to combat practices in another society, policy-makers should be fully aware of the different socioeconomic situations and cultural convictions in such countries. I have argued that a total ban on child labor is pointless, strategically counterproductive, and sometimes even harmful. Boycotts only focus on the effects of child labor — its products — but typically fail to acknowledge the structural reasons for the occurrence of child labor, most often poverty. Policies should not have a one-size-fits-all format, but must be tailored to suit local circumstances. Moreover, I have argued that if liberal governments are truly committed to the fate of laboring children, they should accept their own responsibilities and propose reforms towards a more just global basic structure.

Author's Note

This paper is an elaboration of my "Child Labor Abroad: Five Policy Options," *Philosophy &*

Public Policy Quarterly v. 24, no. 3 (2004). It also draws on "World Poverty, the Global Basic Structure and Individual Responsibility," which I presented at the annual meeting of the American Political Science Association, Chicago, 2-5 September 2004, and my review of Pogge's "World Poverty and Human Rights: Cosmopolitan Responsibilities and Reforms," as published in *The Leiden Journal of International Law*, v. 17 (2004): 631-35). I thank Christine Koggel and Ingrid Robeyns for their constructive comments on various versions of this paper and Mijke Houwerzijl for collaboration on a related project.

NOTES

1. For an overview of the history of child labor see Jane Humphries, "Child Labor: Lessons from the Historical Experience of Today's Industrial Economies," *The World Bank Economic Review* 17 (2003).

2. Ben White, "Globalization and the Child Labor Problem," *Journal of International Development*, v. 8, no. 6 (1996): 833-34. White's information is based on research done by the ILO and UNICEF.

3. The suspicion was widespread that the action owed more to the desire to protect American jobs in the garment industry from foreign competition than to any genuine concern with children's lives. Indeed, it is sometimes hard to determine whether such protests are primarily caused by concern for the children in developing countries or by worries about the internal market in relation to the importation of cheap commodities. However, Kaushik Basu shows that Harkin's Bill was mainly motivated by humanitarian concerns. Kaushik Basu, "Child Labor: Cause, Consequence, and Cure, with Remarks on International Labor Standards," *Journal of Economic Literature*, v. 37 (1999): 1092.

4. Kausik Basu and Zafris Tzannatos, "The Global Child Labor Problem: What Do We Know and What Can We Do?" *The World Bank Economic Review*, v. 17, no. 2 (2003): 164.

5. David Held, "Regulating Globalization? The Reinvention of Politics," *International Sociology*, v. 15, no. 2 (2000): 398; Malcolm Waters, *Globalization* (London and New York: Routledge, 1995) 3.

6. Jeremy Waldron, "Special Ties and Natural Duties," *Philosophy & Public Affairs*, v. 2 (1993): 776.

7. John Rawls, *A Theory of Justice* (Oxford: Oxford University Press, 1971).

8. Joseph Carens, *Culture, Citizenship and Community: A Contextual Exploration of Justice as Even-handedness* (Oxford: Oxford University Press, 2000) 33-34. For reasons of clarity, the presentation of his model has been changed slightly.

9. Tamar Schapiro, "What is a Child?," *Ethics* v. 109, no. 4 (1999): 716.

10. For a treatise on the status of children in political theory, see David Archard and Colin Macleod (editors), *The Moral and Political Status of Children* (Oxford: Oxford University Press, 2002).

11. Basu and Tzannatos, "The Global Child Labor Problem," 157-60; Ulrike Grote, Arnab Basu, and Diana Weinhold, *Child Labour and the International Policy Debate* (Bonn: ZEF, 1998; ZEF-Discussion Papers on Development Policy, no. 1) 10.

12. Peter Fallon and Zafiris Tzannotos, *Child Labor: Issues and Directions for the World Bank* (Washington, DC: World Bank, 1998) 3.

13. Basu, "Cause, Consequence, and Cure..." 1015.

14. Grote, Basu, and Weinhold, *International Policy Debate* 10.

15. William E. Myers, "The Right Rights? Child Labor in a Globalizing World," *Annals* 575, May (2001): 46; Christiaan Grootaert and Ravi Kanbur, "Child Labor: An Economic Perspective," *International Labour Review*, v.134, no. 2 (1995).

16. On Ivory Coast, see Grootaert and Kanbur, "Child Labor: An Economic Perspective." For Cameroon, see Aloysius Ajab Amin, "The Socio-economic Impact of Child Labour in Cameroon," *LABOUR, Capital and Society*, v. 27 (1994).

17. Myers, "The Right Rights?" 40; Alec Fyfe, *Child Labor* (Oxford: Polity Press, 1989) 13-14.

18. Myers, "The Right Rights?," p. 40; Fyfe, *Child Labor*, p. 13.

19. Basu, "Cause, Consequence, and Cure..." 1089.

20. Myers, "The Right Rights?" 40; Fyfe, *Child Labor* 2.

21. Cf. Jo Boyden, "Childhood and the Policy Makers: A Comparative Perspective on the Globalization of Childhood," in *Constructing and Reconstructing Childhood: Contemporary Issues in the Sociological Study of Childhood*, edited by Allison James and Alan Prout (London: Falmer Press, 1997).

22. Myers, "The Right Rights?" 43.

23. Cf. Allen Buchanan *Justice, Legitimacy, and Self-Determination: Moral Foundations for International Law.* (Oxford: Oxford University Press: 2004) 120-21.

24. For the distinction between moral and causal responsibility, see David Miller, "Distributing Responsibilities," *The Journal of Political Philosophy* (2001).

25. Basu, "Cause, Consequence, and Cure..." 1089; Basu and Tzannatos, "The Global Child Labor Problem" 148.

26. John Rawls, *The Law of Peoples*, (Cambridge, MA: Harvard University Press, 1999).

27. Rawls, *The Law of Peoples* 108.

28. Rawls, *The Law of Peoples* 37.

29. Thomas Pogge, *World Poverty and Human Rights*, (Oxford: Polity Press, 2002) 20.

30. Thomas Pogge "What is Global Justice?," in *Real World Justice*, edited by Andreas Føllesdal and Thomas Pogge, forthcoming.

31. Cf. Pogge, *World Poverty and Human Rights* 21-22.

32. Rawls, *A Theory of Justice* 4, 8, 457.

33. Pogge, *World Poverty and Human Rights* 22.

34. Cf. ILO Convention 182 (3).

35. Basu and Tzannatos, "The Global Child Labor Problem" 166-67.

36. Debra Satz, "Child Labor: A Normative Perspective," *The World Bank Economic Review*, v. 17 (2003): 298.

37. Basu and Tzannatos, "The Global Child Labor Problem" 164.

38. For surveys of empirical research on collaborative measures, see Basu and Tzannatos, "The Global Child Labor Problem" 166-67; Grootaert and Kanbur, "Child Labor: An Economic Perspective"; Basu, "Cause, Consequence, and Cure..." 1093, 1114-16.

39. Ans Kolk and Rob van Tulder, "Child Labor and Multinational Conduct: A Comparison of International Business and Stakeholder Codes," *Journal of Business Ethics*, v. 36 (2002).

40. Pogge, *World Poverty and Human Rights* 67, 145, 172.

REPARATIONS AND JUSTICE: THE CASE OF COLONIALISM

Kok-Chor Tan

Kok-Chor Tan teaches philosophy at the University of Pennsylvania. His area of specialization is political philosophy and, more specifically, global justice, nationalism, and human rights. He is the author of Justice Without Borders *(2004) and* Toleration, Diversity and Global Justice *(2000).*

Tan examines inequalities and injustices that people in former colonies continue to suffer. He notes that some countries (the so-called Group of 21) have argued that there should be reparations for colonialism, reparations in the form of debt relief, development assistance, equal access to global markets, restitution of cultural objects, and improved cultural cooperation between countries. Tan claims that these demands for reparations are also demands that have been made by some philosophers in the name of global egalitarian justice. He argues that reparative arguments can play a morally significant role because they are better able to motivate action than more abstract arguments about global equality; they may be necessary for repairing the kinds of international relationships needed to achieve global equality; and they can step in when the argument from equality is resisted.

Some countries have argued that there should be reparations for colonialism and that reparations should take the form of debt relief, development assistance, equal access to global markets, restitution of cultural objects, and improved cultural cooperation between countries. For example, paragraph 116 of the draft declaration prepared by the Group of 21 for the 2001 World Conference Against Racism proposed that

> reparations to victims of slavery, the slave trade, and colonialism and their descendants should be in the form of enhanced policies, programmes and measures at the national and international levels to be contributed to by States, companies and individuals who benefited materially from these practices, in order to compensate, and repair, the economic, cultural and political damage which has been inflicted on the affected communities and peoples, through inter alia, the creation of a special development fund, the improvement of access to international markets

of products from developing countries affected by these practices, the cancellation or substantial reduction of their foreign debt and a programme to return art objects, historical goods and documents to the countries of origin.[1]

Predictably, this proposal for reparations for the injustices of slavery and colonialism did not make the final version of the Resolution that was adopted at the Durban Conference.[2] In this paper, I want to examine the demand for reparations with regard to colonialism. Specifically, I am interested in the kinds of claims that independent sovereign nations have on account of their past colonial subjection. The claims of formerly colonized nations are quite distinct from the claims for reparations by Indigenous peoples who have been colonized. The reparations demanded by Indigenous peoples often involve repatriation of territory or compensation of some form for the loss of territory, as well as demands for greater political self-determination. The reparative claims that are made by formerly colonized countries normally do not involve territory and formal political autonomy (which were largely restored when these countries were granted independence) but involve claims of the sorts identified in paragraph 116 noted above. They include financial compensation for the economic exploitation of colonialism in the form of debt relief, improved access to global markets, and development assistance. They also include claims for cultural restoration in the form of restitution of cultural objects removed during colonial rule, as suggested by the draft declaration. Other claims commonly made in the name of cultural restoration include the granting of special cultural rights to formerly colonized peoples in the form of exempting cultural products from free trade agreements in order to enable the revitalization of local cultural industries and the special protection of local cultural (tangible and intangible) goods through international organizations such as the United Nations Educational, Scientific, and Cultural Organization (UNESCO) and so on. For this reason, it is worth examining the demands for reparations for colonialism as it applies to independent countries separately from that of reparations for Indigenous peoples even though the latter are victims of colonization as well.[3]

The question of reparations raises several difficult and challenging philosophical questions, such as the scope of past injustices, the basis of the claim of persons in the present for reparations of injustices committed in the past, and the nature of the responsibility of those in the present to repair these past wrongs. In this paper, I am interested in a different issue, that of the normative force and purpose of making arguments from reparations. Given that the demands made in the name of reparations presented in paragraph 116 of the Draft Resolution are also demands that arguably could be made in the name of global distributive equality, it might be thought that arguments from reparations are superfluous and that arguments from equality can do all the justificatory work. I will suggest, however, that reparative arguments can supplement arguments from equality, that they may even be necessary if egalitarian justice is to be realized, and that they can substitute for egalitarian arguments when the latter are resisted (see sections 2 and 3 below). To

begin, however, let me make some remarks about the injustice of colonialism (section 1).

1. Colonialism as an Injustice

It is generally taken for granted that colonialism was an injustice because, among other things, it violated the self-determination rights of nations, exploited the natural resources and natural environment of colonized territories, economically exploited the colonized peoples, and undermined their cultural identity. The history of colonialism is, of course, a highly complex one. There is no denying that colonized peoples have also benefited in different ways from their encounter with the colonizing power. Some commentators consider the global dominance of the English language as a positive legacy of British colonialism. As Salman Rushdie writes, "peoples who were once colonized by the [English] language are now rapidly remaking it, domesticating it, becoming more and more relaxed about the way they use it. ... The children of independent India seem not to think of English as being irredeemably tainted by its colonial provenance. They use it as an Indian language, as one of the tools they have to hand."[4] It has also been suggested in some quarters that Britain's gift to its colonies include the introduction of parliamentary democracy and the idea of common law, as well as more tangible contributions to the economic infrastructure of colonized countries (such as the railway system in India).

But there is also no denying that the loss to the colonized nations is significant. Colonial intervention disrupted the economic development and thwarted the industrialization of colonized nations. It also undermined — even destroying in the cases of many Indigenous groups — the local cultures of colonized societies, thus eroding one of the bases of self-respect of persons. As Frantz Fanon argues, the economic exploitation of the colonial powers was assisted by a policy of "cultural estrangement." The cultures of colonized peoples were degraded and devalued, and it was "consciously" driven into "the natives' heads ... that if the settlers were to leave, they would at once fall back into barbarism, degradation and bestiality." The result is a sense of cultural inferiority among colonized subjects, says Fanon, especially among the local elites who have been schooled in the ways of their colonial rulers. The sense in which the effects of cultural estrangement of colonialism is "conscious" can be further debated, but Fanon does not exaggerate when he says that one of the central struggles of post-colonialism is the rehabilitation and revitalization of local national cultures that have been eroded by colonialism.[5] And while colonialism often introduced new forms of government to the colonized peoples, some commentators rebut that this was at the price of disrupting and transplanting local political organizations and practices. If there is some gain to colonized nations from the imposed contact with the culture of the colonizing power, it is still reasonable to conclude that colonialism violated the right of peoples to political, economic, and cultural self-determination and was on the whole an injustice. At any rate, I will take this point as a given for the purpose of this paper. If colonialism was indeed an injustice, a challenging question that follows is whether reparations are owed by former colonial powers to their former colonies.

2. Why Make Reparative Arguments?

Some philosophers have argued that debt relief, development assistance, and greater or at least equal access for developing countries to global markets can be advanced on principles of global distributive justice.[6] Even special cultural rights for some nations, such as allowing developing countries to exempt cultural products from free trade agreements, the return of cultural artifacts to their countries of origin, and the establishment of international organizations to sustain and support cultural activities and practices of formerly colonized nations can be defended by appeals to what global justice here and now requires. A theory of minority rights along the lines of the one developed by Will Kymlicka can, potentially, be modified and extended to the global domain, by showing that certain nations, even though politically independent, face unfair disadvantages with regard to their cultural development and protection

due to the inequalities of the global cultural marketplace.[7] So, like minorities within a single state, some independent nations are entitled to certain cultural rights so as to rectify the unfair cultural disadvantages they are facing.

In short, the specific demands for economic and cultural rights as forwarded in paragraph 116 and elsewhere can possibly be made on the basis of what it means to treat contemporary individuals with equal respect and concern. On this approach, a global arrangement that does not support the right to development, that treats the foreign debt of developing countries as acceptable market outcomes, that allows governments of developed countries to subsidize certain industries and agricultural products (thereby blocking off these markets from producers in developing countries), and that does not recognize the cultural rights of peoples fails to live up to the ideal of treating individuals with equal respect and concern. The call for development assistance, improved or equal market access, debt relief, and cultural rights can be grounded on the duty of global justice to treat all persons equally. For simplicity, I will call this the argument from global equality or the egalitarian argument.

If these claims — for debt relief, development assistance, access to markets, and so on — are claims that could be made in the name of global equality, why, one might ask, obscure and complicate the matter by introducing arguments from reparation? If the disadvantages that some people are now facing are *unjust* disadvantages that cannot be condoned under some defensible criteria of global equality, then these disadvantages should be criticized under these criteria, whether or not they are due to past injustices. Justice *here and now*, rather than injustice *then*, demands the rectification of these disadvantages. It is not the fact that individuals have been wronged in the past that is calling for greater global redistribution, but the fact that they are being wronged now. They are being wronged now because of the imposition of unjust global arrangements on them, that is, arrangements that fail to treat them with equal respect and concern, independently of whether or not they were also wronged in the past.

To be sure, a present unjust distributive arrangement can be the result of unjust events of the past. As Janna Thompson has put it, injustice can "cast a very long shadow."[8] Past injustices can spill over into the present and can have effects that can *unjustly* harm people now. That is, unjust events of the past can be responsible for bringing about a present arrangement that violates the requirements of egalitarian justice. This is not the case of a past injustice persisting into the present, as when my stolen car is never returned to me (to use Jeremy Waldron's example), but that of a past injustice creating *new and present* social, economic, and political relations that are in turn unjust.[9] For example, it might be thought that the present unjust disadvantages faced by many African Americans, disadvantages that offend against the ideal of equality, are the result of the great evil of slavery and other forms of racial injustice continuing beyond the abolition of slavery in the U.S.

But in this situation, reference to past injustices, while useful as a *diagnosis* of a present injustice, is not necessary as a *remedy* for the injustice. Or, to put it more exactly, the fact of past injustices is not a necessary condition for our having a reason to remedy a present injustice. If a current distributive arrangement offends against the prevailing standards of egalitarian justice, there is a reason of justice to take action and to rectify the situation, independently of how the arrangement came about. Talk of the past may help us understand how the present unjust arrangement came about, but it plays no necessary justificatory role with respect to why we should do something about the current situation. There can be reasons independently of any past injustice to mitigate the disadvantages faced by persons if these disadvantages are unjust on other grounds.

Many of the economic and social disadvantages that many African Americans face are objectionable on most defensible criteria of egalitarian justice, regardless of the origin of these disadvantages. This is not to deny that reparative claims with regard to slavery can be made in addition to that of egalitarian justice here and now. My point is that many of the social and economic disadvantages that African Americans currently face can also be criticized on forward-looking terms by reference to what egalitarian justice now requires. There is no need to invoke the past wrong of slavery to show why these current disadvantages are unacceptable. None of this is incompatible with the possibility that there can be reparative claims for slavery over and above what distributive equality for African Americans requires.

Suppose it is true that the current economic disadvantages faced by individuals in the developing world can be traced to the injustice of colonialism. If these disadvantages are also unjust according to principles of global equality, then the fact that these economic disadvantages have their roots in the history of colonialism is *normatively irrelevant* in a sense. References to a country's colonial past can contribute to a causal explanation as to why it had to borrow a massive amount of money to (re)build its economic infrastructure or why its economic development is lagging behind that of more developed economies. But invoking its colonial past is not necessary for the purpose of *justifying* why we now have a duty of justice to forgive its debt or to assist in its development. If there is a duty based on egalitarian justice on the part of the better off to assist the less well off in developing their respective economies, then the foreign loans that poor countries have received should be seen not as a debt to be serviced and repaid, but as an entitlement based on distributive justice.

So it might be thought that reparative arguments are superfluous in the context of global injustice. The demands being made in the name of colonial reparations — the demands for development assistance, for debt relief, and so on — can be defended by appealing to egalitarian principles. Drawing attention to the injustice of colonialism seems to do no extra normative work as far as forwarding these specific demands. Indeed, it might be thought that introducing the notion of reparations to the debate on global justice will only distract and confuse the discussion unnecessarily.

3. The Normative and Practical Force of Reparative Arguments

I find the argument from equality very persuasive and would support the view that egalitarian considerations can ground many of the global proposals made in paragraph 116 (for debt relief, development assistance, and so on).[10] However, I want to suggest some reasons why reparative arguments can be useful even if the demands for greater global redistribution of resources from rich to poor countries can be justified on global egalitarian grounds. Reparative arguments can complement and motivate egalitarian arguments in different ways and so merit serious consideration in their own right.

First, arguments about reparation can supplement arguments about global equality by providing additional motivation for compliance with the demands of egalitarian justice. While reparation claims have to confront some difficult philosophical questions, as mentioned at the start of this paper, it is nonetheless the case that the core moral principle behind the idea of reparation speaks more immediately to the moral sensibility of most individuals and, hence, is better able to move them to action than the claim that one has positive duties of justice to assist strangers. This is because reparations appeal to a moral intuition that most persons hold, namely, that if we wrong another, we can be rightly asked to make amends. The positive action that is required in the making of amends is an action to make up for our (past) failure to avoid harming others and so is strictly speaking a belated fulfillment of a negative duty. There is no need to invoke claims about positive duties, but only the non-contentious claim that we have a negative duty not to inflict harm, and the duty to make up for the harm that we do inflict. The positive duty (to make repairs) is ultimately "a debt of honor" (to borrow Kant's phrase). It is a (positive) duty we have because we have not previously complied with our negative duty not to harm others.

So supplementing arguments from equality with arguments from reparation for colonialism can help motivate compliance with the demands of egalitarian justice. It appeals more directly to people's moral intuitions that individuals must take responsibility for their wrongdoing. The sentiment associated with the principle that one ought to return what has been wrongly taken from another is stronger than that associated with the

principle that one ought to assist a stranger in need. Most ordinary and well-meaning people are more likely to take action to correct their past transgressions than to act as required by egalitarian justice (even if they are convinced of the demands of equality).[11] In this respect, reparative arguments have a practical advantage over egalitarian arguments.[12]

A second reason for introducing reparative arguments is this: while a current arrangement may be unjust on terms defined independently of the past, the fact that the present injustice has roots in a past injustice may mean that the present injustice cannot be corrected without acknowledging and making some amends (even if only symbolically) for the past injustice. Relations based on justice require mutual respect, trust, and reasonableness on the part of the parties concerned. A relationship based on justice would require that both sides be willing to make only reasonable demands on each other and to respect each other's reasonable demands. Accordingly, parties in a just relationship must also be willing to make concessions on their own demands (for example, to adjust one's claim against the legitimate entitlements of others) and to meet each other part way where necessary.

Historical injustices can have spill-over unjust effects in an indirect way, then, by tainting present relations that make justice between the affected parties difficult to achieve.[13] Failure to acknowledge a grave historical wrong on the part of the unjust and to show remorse can be interpreted as a lack of respect for their (former) victims. As Rahul Kumar and David Silver put it well, one legacy of past injustice is that it can have the effect of taking present individuals (belonging to the group that was wronged) "to be *deserving* of an inferior social, political and legal status."[14] Indeed, in this sense, past injustice can have ongoing harmful effects on present persons who were not themselves personally wronged by inculcating social attitudes that continue to accord them less than equal respect. In turn, the victims of the past injustice will not be in a position to trust their former aggressors. Those who have suffered grave but unacknowledged wrong may also find it hard to be reasonable and to make concessions to those who have wronged them, even if the demands that their former violators are now making are reasonable on other criteria. Unacknowledged past wrongs not only distort parties' perceptions of each other, but can also infect their self-perception. Victims may internalize the morally inferior status they have in the eyes of their aggressors, while violators may come to have a distorted sense of their own moral superiority, furthering the asymmetry that makes a just relationship impossible.

So, even if the present global arrangement is objectionable by reference to justice here and now, it is arguable that international justice is impossible until a certain level of mutual trust and respect between different nations is attained, and the realization of this must require, among other things, an acknowledgement, by the perpetrators, of the great injustices in recent human history, including that of colonialism, and the making of reparations for these injustices in some form. So long as the relationship between formerly colonized peoples and their former rulers remains on unequal terms characterized by distrust and suspicion because of the failure on the part of the latter to acknowledge and make reparations for their past deed, justice here and now may not be realizable.[15] Past injustices can cast a very long shadow, then, because of their corrosive effects on human relationships that can make justice now and into the future difficult to achieve.

Arguments from reparation, on this reasoning, have more than a supplementary role in the quest for global justice. They will have the important function of helping to repair the kind of human relationship on which global justice depends. Justice is a relationship between equals, and the aim of reparations is to restore the moral equilibrium between the wrongdoer and the wronged.[16] In this regard, reparative arguments are not just supplementary to arguments for global equality, they are necessary if we want to achieve real justice. They help to realize the goal of egalitarian global justice.

A third reason for invoking claims of reparation to support demands for debt relief, development assistance, improved access to global markets, and so on, is already suggested above. While specific claims of reparations are sometimes shrouded by controversy concerning the question of *who* is to compensate *whom*, it seems to me that the fundamental principle informing the idea of reparation is less controversial in the minds of most people than the idea of global egalitarianism. As mentioned, the underlying idea behind reparative claims — that one should make amends for the wrongs that one has committed — is intuitively more obvious than the idea that one has a positive duty to assist strangers in need. Arguments from reparations for colonialism (as suggested in paragraph 116) can therefore be invoked to justify greater global redistribution of resources when arguments from global equality are met with skepticism (as they often are in the real world). In this regard, reparative arguments can serve as an alternative to global egalitarian arguments where necessary.

Not all present disadvantages are unjust. There can be disadvantages that a person faces that are not necessarily unjust by reference to egalitarian principles. For example, these disadvantages might be due to the person's free choice taken within an institutional scheme that satisfied egalitarian principles. Critics of global egalitarianism might think, then, that if the foreign debt incurred by debtor nations has been freely and fairly assumed in a global marketplace that is fair, there is no reason of justice why this debt should be forgiven. On this reasoning, that some countries are severely hobbled by their heavy foreign debt is not itself an injustice. Or critics might think that there is no right to development, and so there is no duty of assistance to provide aid to developing countries. The fact that some countries are economically underdeveloped, regrettable as it is, is itself not a matter of injustice because countries have to take responsibility for their own development and the choices that they have collectively made in this regard as self-determining nations.[17]

Arguments from reparations offer alternative reasons for global redistribution that do not appeal to global egalitarianism and so can avoid these anti-egalitarian objections. Even if it is conceded that the present disadvantages that some nations are currently facing are not unjust disadvantages by reference to egalitarian criteria, the fact that the disadvantages that they are facing are due to unmitigated past injustice presents a reason of justice for ameliorating these existing disadvantages. The argument from reparation will explain why a current arrangement that is not objectionable on egalitarian terms is nonetheless morally unacceptable because the disadvantages that some are facing under this arrangement are due to uncorrected historical injustices.

In the case of the demands made in paragraph 116, an argument from reparation can say that *even if* the debt burden of developing countries cannot be objected to in terms of global egalitarian justice, this debt should nonetheless be forgiven as a form of compensation for colonial exploitation, particularly in cases where the debtor and creditor have a past colonial relationship. Or, to take another example, the duty of some developed countries to provide assistance to some developing countries for economic development can be explained not as a duty of egalitarian justice but as a duty to make amends for their past colonial exploitation.

Reparative arguments for special cultural rights can also work in lieu of arguments based on minority rights when the latter are contested. Indeed, in contemporary philosophy, minority cultural rights arguments face even more resistance than arguments for economic justice. Cultural rights and the rights of peoples are commonly associated with the so-called "third generation" of human rights, which is presumably a more advanced and less accepted phase in the development of the concept and practice of human rights than the so-called "second generation" rights that include social and economic rights. Basing the call for special cultural provisions in the form of reparations for the culturally destructive consequences of colonialism — for example, the loss of cultural self-respect, the undermining of local languages, and the loss of tangible cultural objects — can be a useful argumentative strategy when arguments about global inequality and its impact on the cultural identities of some peoples fail to persuade. Indeed, Fanon's point about the culturally destructive and degrading aspects of colonialism can provide forceful reasons why former colonized peoples are entitled to special support and provisions to help with the rehabilitation and revival of their respective cultures, either directly in the form of special assistance from their former colonial rulers or indirectly through international organizations such as UNESCO that former colonial powers are especially obligated to support.

Thus, reparative arguments, if successful, can provide a "morally minimalist" approach to global justice similar to the argumentative strategy adopted by Thomas Pogge.[18] Instead of invoking claims about positive duties of justice, Pogge's minimalist approach to global justice begins with relatively uncontroversial moral premises that are limited to the negative duty not to harm others and the corollary duty to make good on the harm one inflicts or helps to inflict on others. For Pogge, the current global institutional order that contributes in pervasive ways to the plight of the global poor is not a natural fact, but an arrangement that individuals in well off countries help to sustain through their choices and institutional participation. On this approach, the expectation that rich countries offer developing countries development assistance and forgive their foreign debt are to be seen as responses to their own failure not to impose harmful arrangements on others. These demands for global redistribution can be understood, in a sense, as demands of "compensations" for the injustices that the world's rich are inflicting on the world's poor. They are "debts of honor" rather than positive duties of beneficence as such. While Pogge focuses on prevailing institutional injustices and does not dwell on past injustices (of colonialism, for example), it is clear that arguments for redistribution and special cultural rights that appeal to the past wrong of colonialism are consistent with the spirit of Pogge's minimalist approach. The past injustice of colonialism, that is, the failure of some people not to unjustly interfere with the lives of others and not to impose harmful arrangements on them, is what morally grounds the positive obligations of global redistribution that are now being demanded by the formerly colonized developing world. Reparative arguments for global redistribution and cultural rights, unlike arguments based on global equality, can begin from minimalist and widely shared moral commitments.

To preempt a potential misunderstanding of the moral minimalist approach to global justice, it is worth stressing that what is minimalist in this approach are not the actions that will be expected of the global well off. On Pogge's account, the well off will be called on to make significant amends, including transferring wealth and resources to the less well off, in order to make good their failure to avoid imposing harmful arrangements on others. What is minimalist are the moral premises of the argument, not its conclusion. That is, beginning from a modest claim about the nature of moral obligations — that our primary moral duties are limited to the duty of forbearance — the minimalist approach nonetheless results in rather robust normative conclusions about the responsibilities of the well off. The aim of the minimalist approach is not to convince the "weak-willed" who know what the right thing to do is but who are reluctant to do the right thing. The intended audience of the minimalist approach are those who do not see that they have a reason grounded on justice to assist the global poor due to their (mis)understanding that the duties of justice are fundamentally limited to the duty to avoid harming others. The strategy of the argument is to show that even if it were true that our duties of justice are ultimately confined to the negative duty to avoid harming, the well off still have the obligation grounded on justice to take positive steps to improve the lot of the worst off (because their being worst off is due to the failure of the well off to avoid harming them). The minimalist approach, which takes redistribution to be grounded on the obligation to correct one's own wrongdoing, allows for a morally less contentious route for supporting substantive global responsibilities on the part of the rich.

Moreover, in saying that reparative arguments can serve as a morally minimalist substitute for egalitarian arguments, I mean only that it can step in when egalitarian arguments fail to persuade, not that its invocation guarantees success. A minimalist argument based on reparations avoids making contentious moral claims, but its acceptance is highly dependent on the persuasiveness of the empirical claims about factors of injustice and causal responsibility on which the argument relies. My point is that reparative arguments are not redundant, not that they are decisive.

4. Conclusion

Arguments from reparation can be useful in three ways even though arguments from global equality can also ground many of the demands that have been made in the name of reparations. One, they are better able to motivate action than more abstract arguments about global equality. Two, they may be necessary for repairing the kinds of international relationships that are necessary for global equality to be realized. And, three, they can step in when the argument from equality is resisted.

But it is important that reparative arguments be understood in the context of global egalitarian justice. Some former colonies may be doing better than countries that have not been colonized (compare, say, Singapore and Thailand), and it would be perverse to argue that the former should be the beneficiary of global redistribution but not the latter. Therefore, reparative arguments for debt relief, economic assistance, and so on are to be understood within the paradigm of what global justice requires. The demands of global justice will set limits on the kinds of reparations that may be demanded and who may demand them. Nonetheless, I have tried to argue that reparative arguments are not necessarily superfluous. Where applicable, reparative arguments for colonial injustices supplement, motivate, and even help realize the goals of global egalitarian arguments.

Author's Note

Thanks to Karen Detlefsen, Christine Koggel, Jon Miller, David Reidy, and David Silver for their helpful comments and discussion on earlier drafts. This paper draws on the first part of a paper presented at the "Conference on Reparations," Queen's University, February 2004, and at the "Symposium on Truth and Power," Bryn Mawr College, March 2004. I am grateful to Colin Macleod for his written comments at the Queen's University conference, and to Jay Drydyk, Rahul Kumar, Michael Krausz, Will Kymlicka, Erin LaFarge, Alistair Macleod, Debra Satz, and other participants and members of the audience at these two events for their helpful questions and suggestions.

NOTES

1. See http://www.racism.gov.za/substance/conf doc/decldraft89b.html for the declaration.
2. See paragraph 99 of the final Declaration in http://www.unhchr.ch/html/racism/02-documents-cnt.html.
3. I thus take European colonialism in Asia and Africa as my model example of colonialism. But in so restricting my discussion, I do not mean to endorse the so-called "salt water" doctrine that confines colonialism to European colonialism, thereby limiting the right to colonial independence and self-determination to just these cases.
4. Salman Rushdie, "'Commonwealth Literature' Does not Exist," in *Imaginary Homelands* (New York, NY: Penguin, 1992) 64. See also Chinua Achebe, *Morning Yet on Creation Day* (New York, NY: Doubleday, 1975) 91-103.
5. Frantz Fanon, *The Wretched of the Earth* (New York, NY: Penguin, 1967) 166-68.
6. See for example, Thomas Pogge, *World Poverty and Human Rights* (Oxford: Polity, 2002).
7. Will Kymlicka, *Multicultural Citizenship* (Oxford: Oxford University Press, 1995).
8. Jana Thompson, "Historical Injustice and Reparation: Justifying Claims of Descendants," *Ethics*, v. 112 (2001): 116.
9. Jeremy Waldron, "Superseding Historic Injustice," *Ethics*, v. 103 (1992): 14.
10. I try to defend the egalitarian view in *Justice Without Borders* (Cambridge: Cambridge University Press, 2004).
11. For the seemingly common disconnect between the commitment to egalitarianism and the motivation to be egalitarian, see G.A. Cohen, *If You're an Egalitarian, How Come You're so Rich?* (Cambridge, MA: Harvard University Press, 2000).
12. Perhaps another way of making the same point is to say that duties of assistance are thought to be imperfect duties and so open to agent's discretion, whereas duties of reparations are perfect duties and so are binding without exception.
13. Janna Thompson, *Taking Responsibility for the Past* (Oxford: Polity, 2002) 34-35.
14. Rahul Kumar and David Silver, "The Legacy of Injustice," in *Justice in Time*, edited by Lukas Meyer (Baden-Baden: Nomos Verlagsgesellschaft, 2004) 152.
15. Not surprisingly, many individuals in former colonies continue to regard the foreign policies, even when well-meaning, of former colonial powers with deep suspicion, often interpreting them from the paradigm of neo-colonial domination. For example, attempts (some of which are sincere) by Western countries to support the development of human rights institutions in some of their former colonies are sometimes dismissed as neo-colonial interventions.
16. Aristotle says that corrective justice aims to "redress the inequality between persons" (*Nicomachean Ethics*, Book 5, Chap. 4).
17. For one rejection of global egalitarianism on grounds of national responsibility, see David Miller, *Citizenship and National Identity* (Oxford: Blackwell, 2000) Chap. 10.
18. Pogge, *World Poverty and Human Rights*.

JUSTICE FOR SOUTH AFRICA:
RESTORATIVE JUSTICE AND THE SOUTH AFRICAN TRUTH AND RECONCILIATION COMMISSION

Jennifer Llewellyn

Jennifer Llewellyn is in the Faculty of Law at Dalhousie University in Halifax. She has worked on restorative justice issues for the Law Commission of Canada, has been involved in the recently established International Criminal Court, and in the late 1990s worked for the South African Truth and Reconciliation Commission. She is the author of articles on restorative justice, justice in South Africa, and human rights.

Llewellyn uses the South African Truth and Reconciliation Commission as a point of departure for discussing conceptions of justice. She defends the Commission against critics who charge that it is devoid of justice by highlighting aspects of the restorative conception of justice that it upholds. Restorative justice relies on an understanding of human beings as relational, an understanding in sharp contrast with the individualism in traditional conceptions of justice as retribution. Restorative justice is about restoring relationships to the ideal of social equality — to relationships of dignity and equal concern and respect. Llewellyn argues that this conception serves South Africa well in its transition from a past marred by the abuse of human rights to a peaceful and rights-respecting society.

Issues of justice are particularly poignant in the South African context. The system of Apartheid introduced by the National Party government in 1948 was maintained and perpetuated by acts of manipulation, coercion and violence. The result was a country premised on lies, secrecy, and the abuse of basic human rights. South Africa endured decades of war, waged for liberation from this racial oppression. Apartheid was an all-pervasive system seemingly secure and unstoppable. Thus, it surprised even those closest to the inner workings of this system when at the opening of Parliament in 1990 F.W. De Klerk, President of the National Party government, announced the systematic dismantling of Apartheid. The living symbol of its imminent demise was the release of South Africa's most famous political prisoner — Nelson Mandela. What followed his release was transformation swifter than anyone dared to imagine. The world

watched in awe as South Africa negotiated the transfer of power resulting in their first ever truly democratic elections. The magnitude of the transition will be represented forever by the results of these elections — Nelson Mandela once prisoner would now be president. He would lead a transitional government, the Government of National Unity, until the next elections in 1999.

The election of a government of national *unity* was not enough, however, to make such unity a reality. The transition from a past marred by mass human rights abuses to one based on the principles of democracy and respect for human rights could not be had simply by a transition in government. In the words of the Interim Constitution, South Africa faces the challenge of building a bridge "between the past of a deeply divided society characterized by strife, conflict, untold suffering and injustice, and a future founded on the recognition of human rights, democracy and peaceful co-existence."[1] The constitution called this the bridge of unity and reconciliation indicating the hope that a rights respecting culture would be waiting on the other side. If it is to begin construction of this bridge, South Africa, as other countries undergoing transition, must face the task of dealing with a past marked by gross human rights violations committed under Apartheid, a task placed before the first democratic government of South Africa.

Arguments for the necessity of dealing with the past arise from a common moral intuition that justice demands "something be done" to address the wrongs of the past. Traditionally the debate over how to "deal" with the past has been a debate over the two options of prosecution or impunity. It is questionable, however, whether the latter of these two qualifies as "dealing with the past" at all. Many have successfully argued that impunity, as it is generally accomplished through blanket amnesties, is tantamount to official amnesia. Impunity seems more akin to forgetting rather than dealing with the past. Thus, advocates of criminal trials argue that the only viable option for "dealing" with the past is prosecution and punishment of the guilty. Were the original terms of the debate exhaustive of all the options for dealing with the past, advocates of criminal trials might be justified in this assertion. However, a new approach has entered the picture to dissolve the all or nothing dichotomy between prosecution and impunity — namely truth commissions. While truth commissions have generally been accompanied by amnesties, their fundamental purpose has been to *prevent* the amnesia brought by traditional impunity. Contrary to the impunity resulting from blanket amnesties, truth commissions "deal" with the past by discovering and telling the truth about it.[2]

This new model for dealing with the past has been utilized in many contexts in the last decade. Current examples include South Africa, Guatemala, and Ireland and plans are underway for a Rwandan truth commission. In *Truth and Reconciliation: Obstacles and Opportunities for Human Rights,* Daan Bronkhorst notes two distinct periods since the mid-1980s marking substantially differ-

ent approaches to the truth commission model. For the most part, commissions in the early period (before 1991) lacked independence and were thus little more than government puppets or propaganda agents. Bronkhorst takes the report of the Chilean Truth and Reconciliation Commission in 1991 as the line of demarcation between these two periods. According to Bronkhorst's research, "[s]ince 1991 'truth commissions' to investigate past human rights abuses have appeared in around thirty countries" and in contrast to their predecessors they have been empowered to undertake serious independent investigation.[3]

The truth commission model, as embodied in this later period, offers a conception of justice, of the "something that must be done", that is different from that offered by advocates of criminal prosecution. Current models of truth commissions are rooted in a restorative conception of justice, a conception that deals with human rights violations of the past by working *toward* restoring a particular society to one that respects human rights. As such, this approach stands in stark contrast to the traditional alternative of criminal prosecution rooted in retributive justice, a conception centered on punishing individual wrongdoing.

In this paper, I will use the example of the South African Truth and Reconciliation Commission (TRC)[4] as a point of departure for examining the nature of justice and the mechanisms appropriate for achieving it in a transition to democracy. Through this examination, I will argue that the truth commission approach exemplified by the South African TRC is grounded in a restorative conception of justice that stands juxtaposed to the retributive approach of criminal trials; that central to restorative justice is a relational approach to dealing with the past; and that this relational approach stands in stark contrast to the individualist approach underlying a retributive conception of justice. The relational approach underlying restorative justice is better not only for addressing issues of justice in transitional contexts than approaches that are retributive in nature, but also for satisfying the demands of justice more generally. To defend the case for restorative justice, I will outline the history and structure of the South African Truth and Reconciliation Commission; introduce the justice problem in that context; outline and evaluate responses to this problem; pursue restorative justice as the conception behind the Truth and Reconciliation Commission as distinct from retributive approaches; show that the TRC is a model of restorative justice at work in South Africa; and, finally, examine some of the problems with its implementation.

South Africa and its Truth and Reconciliation Commission

South Africa, if not the clearest, is certainly one of the most familiar contemporary examples of a transitional context. After much national and international consultation and consideration,[5] the South African government chose to establish The Truth and Reconciliation Commission to fulfill the transitional imperative of dealing with the past. The Commission was charged with the difficult task of establishing "as complete a picture as possible of the causes, nature and extent of gross violations of human rights[6] which occurred between 1 March 1960 and 10 May 1994."[7] The Commission is made up of three committees with different responsibilities pertaining to this mandate:

1) The Human Rights Violation Committee (HRV) — is responsible for conferring victim status on those individuals who qualify under the Act[8] and come forward to the Commission to make a statement.[9] Victim status will be used to determine eligibility for government reparations. The HRV committee also holds hearings to receive public testimony on a representative number of cases. In addition, they hold special hearings concerning particular events or incidents.

2) The Amnesty Committee — is responsible for fulfilling the imperative contained in the Interim Constitution that "amnesty shall be granted in respect of acts, omissions and offences associated with political objectives and committed in the course of the conflicts of the past." While the Interim Constitution mandated the provision of amnesty, it left open the mechanisms, criteria and

procedures by which it might be granted. By embedding the amnesty provision in the process of the TRC, the government provided accountability in amnesty rather than a blanket amnesty.[10] Thus, *individuals* must apply for amnesty in respect of *specific acts*. Such acts must have been committed in pursuit of a political objective and must have occurred before the cut-off date[11] provided for in the Act. In addition, in order to qualify for amnesty, application must be made before the deadline and individuals must offer full disclosure to the Commission. Amnesty is located in the context of the mandate of the Commission — amnesty is provided in exchange for truth.

3) The Reparation and Rehabilitation Committee (R and R) — is responsible for making recommendations to the government regarding the provision of reparations to and rehabilitation of victims. It is also to make recommendations concerning the prevention of future abuses and the steps necessary to create a culture of respect for human rights in South Africa. Such recommendations might include institutional, administrative, or legislative initiatives aimed at these objectives.

In addition to the work of the specific committees, the Commission itself has undertaken certain investigations and held hearings on matters related to the overall objective of establishing a picture of the past. These have included soliciting submissions from the political parties, holding hearings on the role of various institutions in upholding Apartheid (i.e.: the health sector, business community, legal profession)[12] and compiling chronologies and histories of particular phenomena under Apartheid (i.e.: massacres, commissions of inquiry, Apartheid legislation). Such work will provide the context and background for the Commission's final report which must be submitted to the President three months after its work is finished.[13]

The South Africa commission is a part of the larger phenomenon of truth commissions as a model for dealing with the past. South Africa's experiment, however, stands apart from its predecessors in a number of ways. The South African TRC is the first of its kind to be established by an act of parliament. Other truth commissions have been either informal, unofficial or established through a decree of the head of state. The TRC is also unique in its commitment to transparency. All hearings, testimony and proceedings are open to the public and many are broadcast on public television and radio.[14] This commitment to transparency and public participation was also reflected in the Commission's selection process for its 17 Commissioners. The government undertook an open and public process, accepting public nominations for each of the positions. Members of the public could also submit questions to be put to specific candidates during the nationally televised interview process. The Commission also sets itself apart through its emphasis on victims. The TRC understands itself to be a "victim centered process" in contrast to previous commissions which have focused almost exclusively on perpetrators. These developments in the truth commission model offer guidance to other countries considering this model. Just as Chile's TRC in 1991 stands as a line of demarcation in the development of truth commission models from "spin doctors" to serious investigative mechanisms, South Africa's commission stands poised to mark the beginning of another wave of development — toward the truth commission model as a viable option for nations reckoning with their own past.[15] These distinctive elements of South Africa's TRC fit the model of restorative justice that I shall outline and defend later.

Critics of the TRC — the "Justice Problem"

Given the preceding description, one might ask why the Commission is not simply called the "truth" Commission. In fact, this common reference for the South African Commission may reflect a public perception that the Commission is focused on truth but has little or nothing to do with reconciliation. The Commission's slogan "Truth the road to reconciliation" might offer some explanation. The attainment of truth is seen as a *prerequisite* for reconciliation. The questions posed by one of the first witnesses to testify in front of the HRV committee are a poignant reminder of this fact. She asked: how can we forgive when we do not know whom we are to forgive and for what? The Commission attempts to provide answers to these questions. It seeks the truth about the past and *then*, truth in hand, works toward reconciliation. The Commission must be understood as *one part* of the road to reconciliation.[16]

While this answer may satisfy some who express concern that the Commission fails to offer reconciliation, it does not meet the concerns of others. A deeper concern is that the Commission itself is *harmful* to the aim of reconciliation. For example, Fred Rundle, a political analyst and member of the AWB (the militant right wing Afrikaner movement), commenting on the South African television program "Two Way," suggested that the TRC should stand for "Total Revenge Commission." Mr. Rundle, while perhaps slightly more extreme than most, is certainly not alone in this criticism. Some suggest that the Commission will simply rip open old wounds that ought to be left to heal. Others are concerned less with unleashing skeletons than with the haunting impact of the revelations on victims. At the root of all of these concerns and complaints is the perception that the Commission fails to do justice. Such concerns have led many to suggest that justice is not only conspicuously absent from the title of the commission but from its achievements as well. Bronkhorst suggests that the consistent absence of the term "justice" from the titles of the various truth commissions may result from the fact that justice "attracts far more controversy than the other two concepts — truth and reconciliation."[17]

The South African Truth and Reconciliation Commission has certainly not managed to avoid controversy by omitting justice from its name. The perceived lack of justice in the TRC presents itself in the media, the courts, and on the street in pointed calls for "No Amnesty, No Amnesia, Just Justice." It is clear that "just justice" is a call for retributive justice. It means catch, prosecute and punish (by imprisonment or worse) the perpetrators. This position is typically an uneasy hybrid of the view that justice, in the sense of retribution, must be done regardless of the impact on the transition and of the instrumentalist view that, in fact, retributive justice is necessary to achieve the very goal of reconciliation. The Commission, it is argued, fails on both these terms to offer justice. Further, it actually *denies* justice, since by granting amnesty it robs victims of their right to seek their own justice through either the criminal or civil courts.[18] This is cutting condemnation of the TRC (and the truth commission model more generally). If the Commission is to fulfill its assigned role in the transition it seems it must find some way to respond to critics who charge that it is devoid of justice.

Possible Responses to the Justice Problem

Three responses to this justice problem seem possible. The first is to concede that justice does mean retributive justice. This option openly acknowledges that the granting of amnesty (and therefore the TRC) is unjust. The second alternative is to argue that the Commission offers "transitional justice." Transitional justice can mean one of two things: either the retributive *standard* of justice is different for transitional contexts or there is a different *kind* of justice applicable in transitional contexts. The third and final option is to re-examine our assumptions about the nature of justice. On this account, the Commission may in fact offer justice — justice understood as restorative and not retributive in nature.[19]

It is important to look at the first two options in order to understand the nature of the debate. However, it is the explanation and exploration of the third option which is the particular interest of this paper. The third option, restorative justice, not only appears to hold the most promise for offering a full response to opponents of the Commission, it may, in fact, prove a more appropriate means of conceptualizing both the ambitions of the TRC and justice more generally.

1) Retributive Justice

Advocates of "just justice" in the sense of retribution believe that criminal trials are necessary to satisfy the demands of justice. They are not alone in their belief; criminal prosecution of perpetrators has historically seemed the most obvious avenue, especially to Western human rights activists or international lawyers, for dispensing justice and dealing with the past. Currently this belief is the driving force behind the push for a World Criminal Court.

Criminal trials respond to the powerful, if not overwhelming, moral intuition that the something that must be done in the wake of gross violations of human rights is that the "monsters" responsible for the acts in question must be punished. Indeed, there is a tendency among public international lawyers to cast arguments in terms of a *duty* to prosecute and punish crimes against humanity.[20] As a result, there has been very little analysis of whether such trials actually serve the needs of a transitional society or meet the objectives behind attempts to deal with the past let alone whether they meet the demands of justice in general. This very argument — regarding a "duty" to prosecute — was invoked in the constitutional proceedings aimed at blocking South Africa's alternative approach to dealing with the conflicts of the past.

Advocates of criminal prosecutions claim that trials serve a range of purposes related to the overall goal of dealing with the past and the successful transition to democracy. First, they argue that trials promote the value of legality or the rule of law, which is crucial for a stable and lasting transition to democracy. Second, they maintain that trials allow for discovery and disclosure of what happened in the past and that this disclosure will bring with it an understanding of how such abuses could have happened — how human beings became "monsters." Third, by attributing responsibility for the worst human rights abuses committed during conflicts of the past to individuals rather than groups, it is believed that such trials can produce "closure." Fourth, it is claimed that trials allow victims an opportunity to tell their stories, to confront those who harmed them, and to begin the process of healing. Trials it is argued, present an alternative to private vendetta or vengeance. Finally, supporters of criminal prosecutions make the familiar claim that trials promote deterrence. They stand as a warning to those who might be inclined to commit such human rights violations in the future.

These are all fundamentally laudable goals. The problem is not with the content of these claims made in support of criminal trials. Rather, the problem is that criminal trials do not actually achieve what advocates claim they do. But before I examine some of the deficiencies of a retributive approach more generally, there is the pragmatic point that in the context of South Africa, the transition itself (at least in the manner and time it took place) *required* amnesty and thus precluded the possibility of criminal trials. Had criminal trials been an open possibility there is little doubt that the Apartheid government would have refused to turn over power and the country would have been plunged into civil war. The fact that even those closest to the regime were shocked by the transition and had not foreseen an end to Apartheid in the near future, makes it questionable whether the transition would have occurred (at least any time soon) through any other means than peaceful negotiation. Thus, a retributive stance would have inhibited if not prohibited transformation. It seems clear, then, given the South African realities, the raging debate over amnesty is misplaced.

However, there are general problems with a retributive conception of justice as exemplified by criminal trials, problems rooted in the inherent individualism underlying this approach to dealing with injustices of the past. Criminal trials focus on the individual as the source of the wrong and therefore as the proper subject of punishment. They "deal" with crime by "dealing" with the criminal, an objective that is achieved by extracting individual wrongdoing from the social context in which the actions occurred. There is a delinking of gross human rights violations from what Judith Shklar calls "complex social events" because, as Shklar suggests, "[a] criminal trial demands *mens rea,* and there is often no *mens rea* to be found in the development of socially complex events such as war."[21] The result is a distorted understanding of the past and, perhaps even more dangerous for transitional contexts, a complete lack of information about what political, social, and economic choices could help to avoid repeating the past.

In addition, the criminal process does not lend itself to the discovery of morally and socially relevant "truth" that can only be disclosed through the narratives of victims, perpetrators, and others. The pretence of legal objectivity actually makes it a priority of war crimes tribunals and their prosecutors to exclude or minimize such statements as highly subjective and influenced by an individual's perceptions, affiliations, and so forth. The process, Alvarez confirms, attempts to curtail precisely just such expressions, to avoid the appearance that victims are partial or are testifying in order to further the cause of one side or the other in the conflict.[22] Instead, victims are encouraged to present calm and "dead-pan" recitation of "facts." It is hard to imagine that a process, which by its own nature and aspirations makes these demands, can permit victims to feel they have been able to express their suffering and receive understanding and sympathy for their experiences. As Nino argues, what is crucial for achieving the necessary goal of enabling "the victims of human rights abuses to recover their self-respect as holders of human rights" is not the retributivist outcome of punishment but rather "the fact that their suffering is listened to in the trials with respect and sympathy."[23] Thus, there appears to be an inherent tension between the adversarial criminal process, which is ultimately aimed at the determination of guilt of particular individuals, and the goal of a complete understanding concerning the past, an understanding that is achieved when we examine the individuals and actions in the social and political context in which they occurred.

Furthermore, criminal trials are not well-suited to exploring the margins of individual choice or to obtaining any nuanced account of moral responsibility in cases of such difficult choices as obedience to orders, passive vs. active resistance, and the perception of oneself as under threat. Even less do war crimes trials provide, generally speaking, a means of identifying and telling the stories of those who made admirable moral choices in these situations, stories that are crucial to affirming free will and demonstrating that such choices are more than hypothetical.[24] Criminal trials focus on the cases where there is no moral ambiguity. Prosecutors go after the "monsters" and leave unconsidered any sense of the range of moral choices available or operating at the time they acted. By attempting to prosecute not the "ordinary" individuals but the heroes or leaders of the various groups in conflict, criminal trials undermine their claim to affirm individual responsibility.

This brief critique makes it clear that criminal trials, owing to their individualist approach, fail to deliver on their promises for transitional contexts. The puzzle remains then, why, given these failings, theorists continue to advocate trials as the best or necessary means to dealing with the past. In other words, what is it that continues to propel people toward a solution that doesn't really work? Quite simply criminal trials, even in the face of their inadequacies, match the strong moral intuition that justice demands retribution in the sense of meting out punishment to individuals for wrongdoing. If justice is understood in this retributive sense, the TRC would indeed appear to be devoid of justice. The TRC trades amnesty for disclosure about events and acts of the past. In doing so, the Commission precludes the possibility of punishment (beyond the public censure and humiliation of coming forward and admitting one's actions). Amnesty is then, by definition, unjust on a retributivist account. The TRC further fails if judged against a retributivist account as its mechanisms represent a rejection of the isolationist and individualist approach of retribution. Thus, if advocates of criminal trials are correct and justice does actually demand retribution, there is little hope of the Commission providing justice.

The first option available in response to the justice problem accepts this retributivist conception of justice and thus concedes that the TRC is unjust. Or rather, and perhaps more accurately, that *amnesty* is unjust and as a result the Commission cannot achieve justice. Such an admission, while it does render it impossible to mount a *positive* defense against the critics' charge that the commission fails to do justice, does not leave the commission altogether defenseless.[25] One might argue, in support of the TRC, that justice does not encompass the whole of the moral universe. There may be other values against which justice might be weighed in deciding what is the right thing to do. Thus, the Commission might respond to accusa-

tions that it fails to do justice by conceding this point and then claiming that its work is not about justice. The Commission might still claim that its work is *justified* because in the context of the transition, justice may need to be sacrificed to ensure instrumental goals such as peace, stability and avoidance of civil war.

2) Transitional Justice

The second option open to supporters of the TRC in their efforts to respond to the justice problem is to accept that justice ought to have some pull on the Commission. It is not acceptable, on this account, to simply claim that the TRC is not concerned with doing justice. At the same time, however, advocates of this option question the very possibility of realizing justice (i.e.: "just justice" or retributive justice) in a transitional context like South Africa. This alternative is often referred to as transitional justice. "Transitional justice" as a distinct approach to justice holds that there is a different content of justice specific to transitional situations. This position varies in degree. Some advocates claim transitional justice is the same in kind as justice for other situations (that is, they claim it is retributive justice), but differs in the extent to which it is to be applied or achieved. Advocates have in mind here a compromising or tempering of justice (read: retributive justice) for transitional contexts. Other advocates of transitional justice argue, however, that such contexts demand a special and decidedly different *kind* of justice. It follows that this kind of justice would not be appropriate for other stable and established contexts.

The Chilean Truth and Reconciliation Commission employed the different standards approach (the former of the two positions).[26] It accepted that justice required retribution. It recognized, however, the need to protect the fragile process of transition. Chile's TRC attempted to strike a balance between these two goals with the claim that under the circumstances of transition one must be content with "justice to the extent possible." Recognizing that the political nature of the crimes at issue and the transitional context itself made the likelihood of "just justice" minimal at best, the Chilean Commission set itself the task of achieving justice as far as possible without threatening the transition. This version of transitional justice holds transitional contexts to a different *standard* of justice. On this account, justice is satisfied in transitional situations by the *attempt* to achieve it to the extent possible given the context.

Advocates of the other version of transitional justice make a slightly different claim. They do not suggest that one must accept a compromise of justice in transitional contexts — finding consolation in the fact that some justice is better than none. Transitional contexts, on this version, do not simply demand a variation of the standard of justice but call for a different *kind* of justice. Transitional justice conceived of in this way requires inquiry into the specific demands of justice in a transitional context. One can not simply apply a slightly compromised version of retributive justice to a transitional context. This does not preclude the possibility that there may be retributive aspects in this second form of transitional justice. But while it may include punishment, it is not a necessity as it is under a purely retributive conception of justice.

Thus, there is a theoretical distinction between these two understandings of transitional justice. The former accepts that justice is retributive in nature while the latter maintains that a distinct kind of justice is required for transitional contexts. Despite this difference, both versions allow that justice requires or means something different in transitional contexts. Thus, each offers the same defense of the TRC; namely, that the TRC is doing justice in a special way — it is doing transitional justice.

3) Restorative Justice

While the second option restricts its inquiry to transitional contexts, it opens the door for a third approach to the justice question. Restorative justice takes the exploration of the nature of justice a step further. By examining what we mean by justice generally rather than positing a theory of justice singularly appropriate to transitional con-

texts, advocates of this option provide a defense of the TRC that need not rely on the particulars of a transitional context while recognizing that the dilemmas posed by transitional contexts offer insight into the true nature of justice. The differences between the respective approaches of restorative and transitional justice in the case of transitional contexts can be highlighted in the mechanisms each would favour for achieving justice. A transitional justice perspective would maintain that if criminal trials are feasible without jeopardizing the transition or helpful in dealing with the past, they ought to occur. In contrast, a restorative justice theorist maintains that even if it were possible to have criminal trials they would not be appropriate. Restoration on this account is a first best option not simply an alternative in the face of the impossibility of retributive methods.

What is Restorative Justice?

Tony Marshall offers a workable *description* of restorative justice in practice: "Restorative justice is a process whereby all the parties with a stake in a particular offence come together to resolve collectively how to deal with the aftermath of the offence and its implications for the future."[27] This description is very general. Its lack of specificity leaves several questions open. Who is to be restored? To what are they to be restored? While Marshall is offering us a "one size fits all" or general description and not a theory of restorative justice, the open nature of his description holds important clues for the nature of a restorative justice theory. Restorative justice does not force situations to fit theory. Rather, as a theory, it is open and flexible enough to apply on a variety of levels and to different contextual imperatives. Braithwaite argues that "restorative justice is about restoring victims, restoring offenders and restoring communities" and suggests that it is aimed at "whatever dimensions of restoration matter to the victims, offenders and communities affected by the crime."[28] In this way, restorative justice is sensitive to context and thus appropriate to a variety of situations. A restorative justice approach, on his account, is not limited to the individual level, but can be applied to the institutional level as it has been in recent programs aimed at corporations and as it is applied in the case of the TRC.

Restoring Equality — Restoring Relationships

The suggestion that justice is or ought to be restorative means it is best conceived of in relational terms. This has implications for the way in which justice is to be achieved. The mechanisms of justice must, according to this conception, be judged by their ability to restore the kind of relationships in a community that are respectful of each person's right to dignity and to equal concern and respect. Evaluated against this restorative conception of justice, the TRC, far from lacking justice or representing some compromise or special kind of justice, serves as a model of justice.

Once we understand that the concept of restoration is not that of re-establishing the *status quo ante*, that it is not aimed at restoring things to the way they were immediately before the wrong occurred, it is possible to appreciate how restoration will ultimately depend on a broad social transformation to create full equality in society among victims and perpetrators. At the same time, however, it addresses discrete offences such as gross human rights violations. Such offences may require special measures that address the *particular* way in which they disrupted the ideal possibility of victims and perpetrators living as equal members of society. In sum, restoration of social equality entails neither the *isolation* of each individual wrong as a source of disequilibrium, nor the *submergence* of each wrong to social equality more generally.[29]

Once we understand the challenge that crime poses for justice as that of restoration of *social* equality, of equality in relationship, we can begin to grasp the way in which restorative justice theory and retributive theory begin to diverge from their common goal of addressing injustice. They differ in that retributive theory imposes on the goal or purpose of restoration of social equality a particular set of historical practices (typical of a wide range of societies) often known as "punishment." It identifies the very idea of restoration with these

particular practices, practices which are premised on isolating individuals from social relationships. Restorative theory, in contrast, problematizes the issue of what set of practices can or should, in a given context, achieve the goal of restoration of equality in society. Identifying these practices requires dialogue among victims, perpetrators and community and involves concrete consideration of the needs of each for restoration.[30] These practices may vary widely, from place to place and time to time — including therapy for victims, apology or acceptance of responsibility, what Braithwaite calls "reintegrative shaming,"[31] or financial compensation for victims.

Restorative justice theory preserves the intrinsically social dimension in the moral intuition that "something must be done" in response to the offence. It claims that equality or equilibrium must be restored, only it is an equality or equilibrium *in relationships within* society. Establishing equality in relationship means ensuring equal concern and respect between the parties in the relationship. This helps us then to better understand the contrast between restorative and retributive theory in terms of the social practices they justify and generate. It is not a crude contrast between punishment vs. everything else, but rather between paradigmatically isolating measures and paradigmatically reintegrative ones; between a focus on the individual isolated and abstracted from social relationship and a focus on the individual inherently embedded in relationship. What restorative justice theory asserts is not the preferability of the latter from some external point of view, such as social welfare or social self-protection. Rather, it asserts reintegrative measures as a *logical necessity* flowing from the facts of selves as inherently relational. By this claim, I do not intend to deny the individuality of selves. Rather I mean to highlight what is perhaps an obvious truth — that human selves live and develop (constitute themselves) in and through relationships with other selves. Thus, while we are each individual selves we are not wholly independent of one another, but are rather interdependent.[32] It is not enough, however, to simply assert the fact of our relationality. Not any and all relationships will serve to fulfill our needs. For human beings to flourish, there must be relationships that respect each person's right to dignity and to equal concern and respect.

The case of the South African transition is particularly stark as it is moving from a history of severe power imbalances, resulting in the systematic racial oppression of the majority of the population at the hands of the small (yet powerful) white minority. This same minority had the power to define and enforce rights. In so doing, they had the power to structure relationships to ensure inequality and disrespect for the majority. In its efforts to create a rights respecting culture, South Africa is working toward establishing relationships of equality. Restoration after such gross violations of basic human rights is the restoration of equality in all relationships; between the perpetrator of the offence and other members of society, including the victim. It is the restoration to the ideal of relationships of mutual concern and respect with which restorative justice is concerned.

Theory in Practice — Restorative Justice for South Africa?

Given the discussion of restorative justice, we are now in a position to explore how this model of justice is at work in South Africa. After decades of violent abuse of human rights, oppression and essentially civil war, South Africa needs transformation, reconciliation. Reconciliation in this context is not some idyllic notion of forgive and forget. Rather, what is sought in terms of reconciliation (as described in the South African Interim Constitution) is peaceful co-existence. This may be more difficult than it sounds. Reconciliation requires the very opposite from forgetting; it demands remembering so that each citizen can know the history of the abuses of the past and commit to live together in a different way. This notion of reconciliation seems to offer content to the idea of restoration in South Africa. In contrast to the alternative retributive model, restorative justice does not seek to avenge the wrongs of the past. Restorative justice looks backwards in order to look forward and build a different future; it is thus inherently oriented toward transformation.[33]

The establishment of the TRC reflects the commitment to create a new society mindful of the lessons of the past. Such a commitment is best served by a theory of justice which is not purely retrospective or concerned with the re-establishment of the *status quo ante*.

For restorative justice, community is both subject and object; restorative justice is realized in community and is at the same time transformative of that very community. Under this model, justice can only be achieved when all those with a stake in the situation come together to collectively resolve the problem. This dimension of restorative justice has many advantages for a transitional situation like South Africa. First, much of the abuse in South Africa was perpetrated, supported and maintained in a systematic manner implicating most if not all of the population in some way. Thus, in order for any real transformation to occur, the process must include not just the individuals who were perpetrators and victims in the conventional sense, but those in their communities who were supporters, silent witnesses, and those painfully affected by particular incidences of injustice. Second, transformation by definition involves the creation or rebuilding of community, that is, the restoration of an inherently social equilibrium. Restorative justice involves different communities in coming to a resolution and requires them to assist in building the bridge to the future. Having been a part of the process, these communities have a stake in its successful outcome.[34] Lastly, through community involvement, members can learn and reconstitute themselves in a commitment to the justice process itself. Community involvement is key because in order to establish this new rights respecting society, the people must be part of the process through which it is created.[35] Restorative justice facilitates this involvement by bringing communities into the process.

Conclusion — TRC as a Restorative Process

Archbishop Desmond Tutu, chairperson of the TRC, has explicitly stated that he understands the Commission to be an exercise in restorative justice.[36] However, as the theory developed throughout this paper has suggested, there is no single institutional model for restorative justice. Thus, it is not possible to test the TRC process against some abstract procedural ideal of restorative justice. Each restorative justice process may be fundamentally different and still be entirely restorative in nature. Thus, there might exist two restorative approaches to political transformation that are considerably different but still informed and guided by the same restorative commitments. The reason for this, as discussed in an earlier section of this paper, is that restorative justice pays attention to and is informed by context. This results in room for and indeed a necessity to develop different processes depending on context.

Underlying these various forms, however, must be common commitments; to restoration over retribution, to relational over isolating mechanisms, and to understanding communities as an integral part in the creation and solution of the social phenomenon of crime. Thus, whether it is focusing on restoring the victim, perpetrator, or the community, the focus is always broader than the individual. The focus now is on relationships. Further, these processes have a commitment to be forward looking — to look at the implications of offences for the future and to bringing together all those who have a stake in the development of that future.

It is clear, then, how the Truth and Reconciliation Commission attempts a restorative approach in dealing with South Africa's past. The Commission embeds the granting of amnesty in a process which seeks the truth of the past in order to build a different future. A comprehensive analysis of the ways in which the TRC lives out these restorative commitments is beyond the scope of this paper. However, if we return to our previous description of the TRC, we can get a picture of it as a restorative process.

First, the TRC's process implicates a wide spectrum of the society. The selection of Commissioners was a public process and driven by public nominations resulting in the appointment of individuals from several different communities and segments of society. Further, the work of the Commission is public. Sessions are open to the public and broadcast on television and radio drawing in a wider

population than would be possible in person. This commitment to transparency takes the work of the Commission into the public arena for debate and discussion. It enables the community to participate in the process as a party with a great stake in the issues of transition.

Second, the Commission is clearly committed to the restoration of victims. It is by its own identification a victim centered process. The Commission attempts to listen to victims and address their needs. Such a focus enables them to ask the important question about what is required for restoration, namely, to bring the victim, perpetrator and the community together to understand the dynamics of relationships that permitted such abuse and to look for ways to restore these relationships to ones of social equality.

The Commission is also operating within a restorative model with respect to its treatment of perpetrators. Through the amnesty process, perpetrators are called to account for their actions. However, they are not removed from society, but rather left free to re-enter the community and rebuild relationships. Thus, the Commission leaves open the possibility of restoring relationships as it keeps the perpetrator in relationship with others to work toward a better future. While the amnesty provision is clearly important to the restorative approach of the TRC, it raises an interesting challenge to the TRC and restorative justice practices more generally. The challenge is that created by the need for an "axe" (or whip) to motivate people to participate in the process. There is a question about whether using punishment as this "axe" implies a retributive approach and whether it can be accommodated within restorative justice theory. It is entirely consistent with a restorative conception of justice to admit the necessity of some "axe" in order to motivate participation. Conceived of in another way, this problem asks the question: what if a person refuses to participate or for some reason cannot participate in the process of restorative justice? In short, what reason do people have to participate in the process given that the alternative is freedom?

The response must be that an "axe" is required not for justice itself but for social protection. In order to protect relationships from further disruption and to protect the restorative process itself, it is necessary to remove those who, owing to their unwillingness to participate in the restorative process, pose a threat to the achievement and stability of social equality. However, claiming this is outside the scope of justice does not mean that anything goes, that justice (restorative justice) holds no sway, for the overarching *goal* in all of these activities is still justice. Thus, whatever measures are utilized as an "axe", we cannot lose sight of this goal. In other words, such measures cannot preclude justice. Even measures taken in the name of social protection must work toward bringing the perpetrator into the restorative process, a central goal evidenced in the forward-looking nature and commitment of the Commission. The Commission is focused, on a macro scale, at the restoration of communities. At its core, it is motivated by the goal of nation-building and reconciliation. Its work is done in this spirit and mindful of this goal.

Further, the focus of the Commission is not centered solely on individual responsibility, as it is in the criminal system. Rather, the TRC views individual responsibility through the context of community responsibility. It places individual acts in the context of organizational, institutional and state actions. This is clear as amnesty is granted with respect to politically motivated acts. Determinations of whether or not an act was politically motivated rest on the individual's membership or association with a political group or operation. Thus, the connection between individual and collective responsibility is clearly recognized.

Viewing the Commission through the lens of restorative justice is indeed helpful in fending off those who would condemn its lack of justice. However, this perspective also raises challenges for the way in which the Commission attempts to provide restorative justice. If the TRC is about restorative justice, then this model of justice must also serve as an evaluative tool. Thus, I want to end by highlighting one of the challenges a restorative justice model, taken seriously, might pose to the TRC.

Specific to the South African TRC (and perhaps truth commissions in general) is the problem of the lack of connection between the perpetrators and the victim. This separation causes problems for addressing the restorative needs of both. Structurally the victim and the perpetrator are dealt with separately by the TRC. The HRV committee deals with the victims and the Amnesty committee with the perpetrators. While there is some provision made for victims to face the perpetrators in an amnesty hearing, there is no room for dialogue between the two and their respective communities.[37] In fact, the question of reparations is taken out of this process altogether and has no relationship to amnesty. The rationale behind this move is that it is the state who is granting amnesty (thereby removing the victim's right to choose to seek redress through the courts as amnesty includes immunity from both criminal prosecutions and civil actions) and thus it is the state's responsibility to repay the victim. What this precludes in the process, however, is any possibility of the offender making reparation to the victim. This has implications on all levels — for the victim, perpetrator and the community. Removing reparation from the amnesty process seriously limits the connection between amnesty and restoring the victim. It restricts this connection solely to that restoration achieved through hearing and knowing the truth of the past. Practically, the victim sees the offender go free and still receives no direct reparations until the government considers proposals for reparation at some later date. As far as the perpetrator is concerned, amnesty without any way to make amends for one's actions could result in what Braithwaite refers to as a "shaming machine" serving to stigmatize rather than reintegrate perpetrators. Without at least the possibility of reparations, perpetrators are left with no way to re-enter the community and try to "make things right."[38] Further, this separation ignores the large role that reparations can play in rehabilitation. By focusing on reparations and rehabilitation only with regard to victims, the Commission forgets the importance of reintegrating perpetrators in order to heal or reconcile damaged relationships in society. The difficulty here is how far one can go and still be granting amnesty. Would a conditional amnesty have served the political purposes of facilitating the transition? It seems, however, that even if a conditional amnesty was not possible, at the very least provision for involvement in reparations or access to rehabilitation programs could have been made *available* to perpetrators. This problem might yet be addressed by the Commission through its recommendations to the President on reparations and rehabilitation.[39]

In both its strengths and weaknesses, the South African TRC stands as a compelling example of restorative justice, as a model for transitional contexts. Supporters of the TRC are able to respond to its critics who charge that it is devoid of justice. Viewed through this lens, the Truth and Reconciliation Commission does not lack justice; quite the contrary, the TRC serves as a powerful example of justice in a transitional context and offers lessons on how justice might be better achieved.

Author's Note

Jennifer Llewellyn served as an intern with the Research Department of the Truth and Reconciliation Commission. This internship was supported through CIDA's Technical Assistance Fund and a research grant from the Wright Foundation. The views expressed here are those of the author alone and do not reflect those of the Commission. The author is grateful to her colleagues at the Commission, in particular Charles Villa Vicencio, Wilhelm Verwoerd, Michelle Parleveliet, and Ronald Slye for their assistance and guidance. Special thanks is owed to Robert Howse for many discussions which provided invaluable challenge and support for the development of these ideas. The author is indebted to Christine Koggel, Jennifer Nedelsky, and Hallett Llewellyn for their insightful comments.

NOTES

1. Interim Constitution, section 232 (4).
2. For further reference, see David Crocker, "Transitional Justice and International Civil Society," National Commission on Civic Renewal, Working Paper #13; Luc Huyse "Justice after Transition: On the Choices Successor Elites Make in Dealing with the Past" (1995) *Law and Social Inquiry: Journal of the American Bar Association*; Juan E. Mendez "Accountability for Past Abuses" (1997) 19 *Human Rights Quarterly* 255; Carlos S. Nino "The Duty to Punish Past Abuses of Human Rights Put into Context: The Case of Argentina" (1991) 100 *Yale L.J.* 2619; Diane F. Orentlicher, "Settling Accounts: The Duty to Prosecute Human Rights Violations of a Prior Regime" (1991) 100 *Yale L.J.* 2537; Sam Seibert et. Al., "War Crimes: To Punish or Pardon? — Justice from Bosnia to Rwanda to Chile, a Searing Moral Debate over Amnesty" (November 21, 1994) *Newsweek* 32; M.R. Rwelamira and G. Werle (eds) *Confronting Past Injustices: Approaches to Amnesty, Punishment, Reparation and Restitution in South Africa and Germany* (Butterworths, 1996); and, Naomi Roht-Arriaza (ed) *Impunity and Human Rights in International Law and Practice* (Oxford: Oxford University Press, 1995).
3. Daan Bronkhorst, *Truth and Reconciliation: Obstacles and Opportunities for Human Rights* (Amsterdam: Amnesty International Dutch Section, 1995) at 10.
4. The Truth and Reconciliation Commission has come to be known by many names throughout its life. I tend to use several of them interchangeably for the sake of literary convenience. Most common among these is "the TRC," "the Commission," and "the Truth Commission."
5. The parliamentary bill regarding the creation of the Truth and Reconciliation Commission was the longest debated bill in the history of South Africa.
6. The Commission is not charged with the task of investigating all of the abuses, or even all of the human rights abuses committed under the Apartheid regime. The mandate of the TRC quite clearly draws the parameters of the Commissions investigations. The Commission is only concerned with "gross violations of human rights." Section 1(1) (ix) of The Promotion of National Unity and Reconciliation Act which governs the TRC defines gross violations of human rights as:

   ... the violation of human rights through B
   (a) the killing , abduction, torture or severe ill-treatment of any person; or

(b) any attempt, conspiracy, incitement, instigation, command or procurement to commit an act referred to in paragraph (a), which emanated from the conflicts of the past and which was committed during the period 1 March 1960 to the cut-off date within or outside the Republic, and the commission of which was advised, planned, directed, commanded or ordered, by any person acting with a political motive.

7. Promotion of National Unity and Reconciliation Act, The Republic of South Africa, Act No. 34 of 1995, as amended by The Promotion of National Unity and Reconciliation Amendment Act No. 84 of 1995 (hereafter "the Act"). This act was amended to extend the latter of these two dates. The date was initially 10 December 1993, but was changed in an effort to include the events leading up to the elections in 1994.

8. Under the Act, section 1(xix), victim includes B

(a) persons who, individually or together with one or more persons, suffered harm in the form of physical or mental injury, emotional suffering, pecuniary loss or a substantial impairment of human rights B

(i) as a result of a gross violation of human rights; or

(ii) as a result of an act associated with a political objective for which amnesty has been granted,

(b) persons who, individually or together with one or more persons, suffered harm in the form of physical or mental injury, emotional suffering, pecuniary loss or a substantial impairment of human rights, as a result of such person intervening to assist persons contemplated in paragraph (a) who were in distress or to prevent victimization as may be prescribed.

(c) Such relatives or dependents of victims as may be prescribed.

9. Given the size of the country and the conditions under which many of the victims of gross human rights live, it would have been impossible for most of them to go to the Commission to make their statement. While the Commission does have regional offices in four locations throughout the country they were still inaccessible to many

victims living in small communities, townships and homelands throughout South Africa. Thus, the HRV Committee undertook a statement taking process which involved sending statement takers throughout the country to meet with, listen to and record victim's testimony.

10. It is important to note that this is one of the unique features of the South African TRC. We will return to a discussion of the other ways in which the South African TRC stands apart from its predecessors.

11. There are two important dates with respect to the Amnesty provision. The "cut-off" date is the date that marks the period during which acts must have been *committed* to be eligible for amnesty. This date was extended by Parliament to include acts leading up to the election in 1994. The second important date is the "deadline." This is the date by which one must make *application* for amnesty in order to qualify. This date was also extended from May 10, 1997 until September 30, 1997 in order to account for the change in the cut-off date.

12. See David Dyzenhaus, *Judging the Judges, Judging Ourselves: Truth, Reconciliation and the Apartheid Legal Order* (Oxford: Hart Publishing, 1998).

13. The original legislation gave the Commission a mandate of eighteen months with a possible extension of six months at the President's discretion. An additional extension, beyond the six months contemplated in the act, was granted by an act of parliament in September 1997. The extension was granted so that the work of the Amnesty Committee could be completed during the life of the Commission and before the Commission submitted its final report to the President. The amendment calls for the extension of the Commission's mandate from its intended completion in December 1997 (final report in March 1998) to April 30 1998 (final report to be submitted by July 1998). The amendment prohibits the Commission from undertaking any new work after December 14, 1997. See Statement by Archbishop Desmond Tutu, Chairperson, Truth and Reconciliation Commission, September 18, 1997.

14. The only exception to this rule is under section 33 of the Act. Section 33 provides:

Hearings of Commission to be open to public —
1 (a) Subject to the provisions of this section, the

hearings of the Commission shall be open to the public.

(b) If the Commission, in any proceedings before it, is satisfied that —

i) it would be in the interest of justice; or

ii) there is a likelihood that harm may ensue to any person as a result of the proceedings being open, it may direct that such proceedings be held behind closed doors and that the public or any category thereof should not be present at such proceedings or any part thereof: Provided that the Commission shall permit any victim who has an interest in the proceedings concerned, to be present.

Such an exception is most commonly made with respect to hearings held under section 29 of the Act where individuals have been subpoenaed to appear before the Commission.

15. For further comparisons of Truth Commissions see Daan Bronkhorst, *Truth and Reconciliation: Obstacles and Opportunities for Human Rights* (*Supra* note 3); Priscilla B. Hayner "Fifteen Truth Commissions — 1974 to 1994: A Comparative Study" (1994) 16 *Human Rights Quarterly* 597; and, Michelle Parleviet "Considering Truth: Dealing with a Legacy of Gross Human Rights Violations" (1998) 16:2 *Netherlands Quarterly of Human Rights* at 141.

16. The other obvious components of the journey toward reconciliation are the Land Claims Commission, The Reconstruction and Development Plan (RDP), and the pending reparation program for victims.

17. Bronkhorst at 11.

18. This very argument was, in fact, the subject of a court challenge to the Amnesty provision in the new South African Constitutional Court. See *Azanian People's Organization (AZAPO) and Others v. President of the Republic of South Africa and Others*, 1996 (8) BCLR 1015 (CC). The challenge, brought by a few prominent victims' families, failed on the grounds that the Constitution provided for the violation of their rights in the interest of national unity and reconciliation. It is interesting to note that these families are not typical of victims in South Africa. They were very prominent cases and as such might have had access

to enough information to contemplate legal action. Most victims, however, do not have any information concerning their cases and come to the commission in search of it.

19. See Charles Villa-Vicencio, "A Different Kind of Justice: The South African Truth and Reconciliation Commission" (Unpublished); and, Wilhelm Verwoerd, "Reflections from within the TRC" *Current Writing: Text and Reception in South Africa*, Vol. 8(2), October 1996, 66-85.

20. See Payam Akhavan, "Justice in the Hague, Peace in the former Yugoslavia?: A Commentary on the United Nations War Crimes Tribunal." Unpublished manuscript, The Hague; and, Carlos S. Nino, "The Duty to Punish Abuses of Human Rights Put in Context: The Case of Argentina" *Yale L.J.* Vol. 100, 1991 at 2619.

21. Judith Shklar, *Legalism: Law, Morals and Political Trials* (Cambridge Mass.: Harvard University Press, 1964) at 172.

22. José Alvarez, "The Tadic Judgement and the Nuremberg Model of Closure" unpublished manuscript, University of Michigan Law School, 1997.

23. Carlos Santiago Nino, *Radical Evil on Trial* (New Haven: Yale University Press, 1996), 147.

24. See the important work of Tzetvan Todorov, *Facing the Extreme*: *Moral Life in the Concentration Camps*, tr. Denner and Pollack, (New York: Henry Holt, 1996).

25. See generally Wilhelm Verwoerd *supra* note 19.

26. See Neil Kritz (ed), *Transitional Justice — Volume II: Country Studies* (Washington DC: United States Institute of Peace Press, 1995) at 487.

27. John Braithwaite, *Restorative Justice: Assessing an Immodest and a Pessimistic Theory*, 1997 (this paper is available on the World Wide Web, Australian Institute of Criminology Home Page B Http://www.aic.gov.au), 5 (Hereafter Braithwaite 1). See also Jim Consedine, *Restorative Justice: Healing the Effects of Crime* (New Zealand: Ploughshares Publications 1995).

28. Braithwaite ch 1, 5.

29. See Jennifer Llewellyn and Robert Howse "Dealing with the Past and the Building of a Pluralistic Society," Conference Proceedings for UNESCO International Conference on Multiculturalism and Post-Communism Tradition and Democ-

ratic Processes, Dubrovnik, Croatia, November 1997.

30. For an example of the role of dialogue in the realization of social equality, see J. Nedelsky and C. Scott "Constitutional Dialogue" in J. Bakan and D. Schneiderman, (eds) *Social Justice and the Constitution: Perspectives on a Social Union for Canada* (Ottawa: Carleton University Press, 1992) at 59.

31. John Braithwaite, *Crime, Shame, and Reintegration* (New York: Cambridge University Press, 1989) (Hereafter Braithwaite 2).

32. See generally Jennifer Nedelsky "Reconceiving Rights as Relationship" *Review of Constitutional Studies* 1, 1993 and Christine Koggel *Perspectives on Equality: Constructing a Relational Theory* (Lanham, MD: Rowman & Littlefield Publishers, Inc., 1998).

33. In fact there has been some suggestion that restorative justice might be better called by the name of transformative justice. Ruth Morris, *A Practical Path to Transformative Justice* (Toronto: Rittenhouse, 1994).

34. See the evidence that there is a much higher rate of performance of reparations decided upon through restorative justice programs than those ordered by courts in Braithwaite 1.

35. See generally J. Habermas, *Between Facts and Norms*, tr. W. Rehg (Cambridge, Mass.: MIT Press 1995).

36. In conversations with the author.

37. It is important to note that the failure to make room for dialogue in the Amnesty setting is contrasted in other areas of the Commission, in particular some of the special event hearings held by the HRV committee, where dialogue and the meeting of different communities is central.

38. Consult, for example, the case of Brian Victor Mitchell who was granted amnesty with respect to the Trust Feeds Massacre — *Amnesty Application No. 2586/96*. Brian Mitchell was convicted and sentenced to death in 1992 for the murder of eleven people in the Trust Feeds area. The killings were a part of a police operation headed by Mitchell. A mistake was made and the wrong house was fired upon. The eleven people killed were not the intended victims. Mitchell was granted amnesty in 1996 and upon his release wanted to make reparation for his actions, but when he turned to the commission for assistance, there were no such programs in place. Mitchell then went back into the community where the murders took place. For over a year he would try to find ways to give back to the community from which he took so much.

39. Although the outline for these recommendations was released October 23, 1997, and further implementation details released March 11, 1998, it gave no indication that the commission was considering a move in this direction. See "Introductory Notes to the Presentation of the Truth and Reconciliation Commission's Proposed Reparations and Rehabilitation Policies" — Truth and Reconciliation Press Release October 23, 1997; and, "Statement By Archbishop Desmond Tutu on Allocation for Reparations in the Minister of Finance's Budget" Truth and Reconciliation Commission Press Release March 11, 1998. Available at the TRC website: www.truth.org.za.

FREEDOM AND DEMOCRACY IN CUBA:
A PROBLEM OF UNDERSTANDING

Susan E. Babbitt

Susan E. Babbitt teaches philosophy at Queen's University in Kingston, Ontario. Since 1993 she has been spending large amounts of time in Cuba. More recently, she has been involved in a large interdisciplinary project (York University) entitled "Diaspora, Islam, and Gender." She is the author of Impossible Dreams: Rationality, Integrity and Moral Imagination *(1996) and* Artless Integrity: Moral Imagination, Agency, and Stories *(2001) and the editor of* Racism and Philosophy *(with Sue Campbell, 1999).*

Babbitt considers the difficulty of interpreting and understanding the Cuban situation. It is widely recognized, for instance, that children in Cuba are better taken care of in terms of health and education than children in any developing country and in many developed countries. Yet, to many, these accomplishments do not matter as much as the belief that Cuba is not democratic and Cubans are not free. Babbitt argues that whether there is democracy in Cuba can only be investigated in the context of understanding globally dominant expectations about democracy and freedom. These assumptions have made it possible to ignore the explanations that Cuba has offered about its history and its struggle for democracy and respect for human rights.

After a two-hour discussion about Cuba in a graduate seminar, a student says, without explaining what she means or to what it is relevant, "But there's no freedom," and leaves the room. At an APA conference, when I mention my interest in and passion for Cuba, someone I have not seen for a long time suggests that we must have serious disagreements. In explanation, she describes evidence of lack of freedom of expression in Cuba.

I am often impressed that freedom, in a quite undefined sense, is taken to trump any other consideration of a positive sort about Cuba. Moreover, it has this trumping role without argument. The issue about Cuba is often whether or not a certain kind of freedom or openness exists, not whether it matters and to what. In the following, I try to make some suggestions about what matters to a useful discussion of freedom and what this implies for understanding democracy in Cuba.

Expectations and Power

A Cuban newspaper tells the story of a Martian visitor who wants to understand how Earth people conceive of human rights.[1] He is taken first to the United States to know a society that respects human rights, and learns that the Constitution makes no mention of rights to work, health, education, and the rights of women and children. He sees that 59 per cent of those condemned to death are members of minority racial groups; that 5 million people are in prisons; that funding for prisons has increased 30 per cent in the past 10 years while funding for education decreased by 18 per cent during the same period; that police in New York torture and even kill those they arrest; that 78 people have been killed trying to cross the Mexican/US border; that illegal immigrants are denied medical treatment; that, according to the US President himself, 60 per cent of the children at

290

age eight do not know how to read; that 54 per cent of the suicides of young people in developed countries take place in the US; and that social assistance has been reduced by 60 per cent. The Martian is then taken to Cuba to see what it is like in a country where human rights are not respected, to see an example of failure to respect human rights and sees that the Constitution guarantees all human rights — individual, political, and social. He sees that the Constitution guarantees rights to work, health, education, and social assistance, and he notices that it makes reference to the rights of families, children, and women. He sees that education is free at all levels, including books and materials, and that health care is free as well. And he sees that there are 54 doctors for each 10,000 citizens, an average higher than that of the much more wealthy United States. Then he learns that the United States proposes every year to the United Nations that Cuba be condemned for violation of human rights. He takes his ship and returns to Mars convinced that Earth people are both stupid and frightening.

The point of this story, I take it, is not that Cuba expresses greater respect for human rights than does the United States. Such a point does not need to be made in a Cuban newspaper. Instead, the point of the story is that it would take something like a Martian to be able to draw such conclusions. The facts mentioned in the story are common knowledge. They are widely repeated in the United States and are often in the news. It is not news, for instance, to point out that illegal immigrants are denied medical care or that those condemned to death are mostly non-white. What is not so common is to put these facts together in such a way that one draws the conclusion that many people are confused about the meaning of human rights, that there exists a general sort of erroneous thinking about human rights and their importance. What is surprising is not the information, but the conclusions that are drawn about the importance of the information, that, for instance, such thinking about human rights is frightening, as the Martian concludes. The point, I take it, is that one would have to be a Martian to see that what these facts mean is significant in a certain way. The Martian listened to the facts and fled. Many would listen to all the

same facts, and even believe them, and think that nothing follows of interest for how we understand respect for human rights in general.

In the case of Cuba, it is not enough to consider empirical evidence; it is also necessary to consider the conceptual and practical background which explains the importance given to evidence. Moreover, one has to consider the fact that relevant philosophical assumptions are now very powerful, that they constitute the basis for a world view, informing the way people see themselves and interpret stories and experiences. We always interpret the world on the basis of background beliefs and traditions, and in the particular case of Cuba we have to become aware of certain beliefs and traditions, if we are to be fair.

When people talk sympathetically about Cuba, for instance, it is common to say that although Cuba is not democratic, although the Cuban government does not respect the autonomy of its people,[2] the Cuban revolution has succeeded in bringing about a social system which provides better medical care and education than many developed countries. Indeed, the statistics that generally follow the "but" which follows the claim that Cuba is not democratic indicate that in fact Cuba takes better care of its smallest and weakest citizens than probably any country in the world. One could think that this is a story about democracy, and many do. One might think that if "democracy" has to do with the people ruling themselves, and if "autonomy" has to do with individuals controlling their own destinies, it is hard to see how it can be irrelevant to democracy or autonomy what happens to people when they are in the most helpless states. But we often listen to the facts about Cuba and think somehow that recognized successes in caring generally for the weak and the sick do not *matter* to democracy, that these issues are just not the same sort of thing.

Consider the following example regarding the situation of women in Cuba. In *Sex and Revolution: Women in Socialist Cuba*, we find the following claim explaining the life of women in Cuba: "Fidel Castro marched through the public arena dressed in the uniform of the perpetual warrior," and, for three decades "life in Cuba was a succession of military emergencies, sudden campaigns and heroic efforts which disrupted the civilian economy upon which women depended."[3] Now it is true, of course, that Fidel Castro wears military uniforms most of the time and that most women in Cuba have spent a lot of time training militarily. What is interesting about this account of women in Cuba, though, is that it does not provide any explanation of why this is the case. No explanation is offered for Fidel Castro's being the "perpetual warrior" and the women's engaging in military activity. And if no information is provided in a book published by Oxford University Press, it must be because none is needed, because, perhaps, there is no surprise. This may be so either because it is assumed that everyone knows who the enemy is or because there is no enemy. But since the authors say that women "were taught to perceive [Cuba] as an embattled revolution in [a] hostile world" (185), the missing explanation cannot be accounted for by the expectation that the enemy, or that there is an enemy, is well-known. If the women had to be taught to perceive hostility, the suggestion is that the hostility wasn't obvious to them. And since we the readers are not being taught, the expectation taken for granted must be that there is no enemy.

The authors of *Sex and Revolution* indicate that women and men in Cuba have been offered a particular explanation for the hostility directed toward Cuba in the world. Indeed, this is true. Many important documents and speeches include lengthy explanations for the hostility directed toward Cuba and what it implies. These explanations are stories, or rather, one single story, about a struggle for certain goals and values, and of the central cause of the humiliation, degradation and death endured throughout the struggle, i.e., the dominant classes of the United States. It is the story of how Cuba, the last Spanish colony, fought over a period of 30 years against the Spanish without outside help and just when the Spanish were ready to give up, the United States intervened and occupied the country, insultingly buying back the guns of the Cuban Mambises for 75 pesos each, and imposing a constitution according to which the United States had the right to intervene whenever it saw fit. It is a story of increased American investment in Cuba after 1902 until American companies owned most of the best agricultural land in Cuba and most Cubans lived a kind of slave existence, receiving coupons for their labour which they were able to exchange for goods provided by the plantation owner. It is a story of humiliating sabotage and defeat of brief revolutionary outbursts in 1933 and 1944, interludes in the succession of American supported governments some of which proclaimed openly that Cuba would be better off being a dependent colony of the United States. And it is a story of constant attempts after the 1959 revolution to liquidate the revolution and its leadership, of the most massive disinformation campaign ever, of biological warfare and of the longest and most cruel economic blockade in the history of the world.[4]

It is, in short, a history of US interest in and desire for Cuba's dependence and of Cuba's interest in and desire for independence. Now, there are those who deny that there exists a history of aggression toward Cuba by the United States. In his response to Ricardo Alarcón on Nov. 5, 1997, the representative of the United States to the United Nations said, as had the US representative in 1996, that the United States was not blockading Cuba economically, that it was only protecting its interests, and that it was justified in doing so because Cuba does not respect human rights. But since 143 countries, including the US's most powerful allies, voted on that day to condemn the US blockade of Cuba, the sixth such vote in as many years, each year with increased numbers, the claim that the United States does not have a history of aggression toward Cuba is at least not obvious.[5]

My interest here is not in discussing US policies toward Cuba. Instead, I am interested in the fact that the authors of *Sex and Revolution,* for instance, leave this story out. They point out that Cuba has been preparing itself militarily for forty years and that people are given a story about why this is so. But they do not provide the story explaining this activity. Why, when the story is offered so often by Cuba's defenders as an explanation of Cuba's position and policies, do the authors just ignore the story? It is true that Cubans are offered explanations for what is and has been happening to them as a nation. And maybe the explanation is not correct. But the authors of *Sex and Revolution* do not *refute* the explanation. They ignore it.

Now, one might think, in reading *Sex and Revolution*, that there is a kind of refutation of the story in the authors' allusions to the various reforms that were brought about by Cuban governments before 1959. For instance, they make reference to an "unprecedented era of democratic politics" from 1940-1952 (19) and to the Constitution of 1940 which included rights for women.

But this is not a refutation of the Cuban story. The Cuban *response* to this position is that what existed between 1940 and 1952 was *pluripartidismo*, or a system of several political parties, and *not* democracy. The story explains how these parties all represented similar expressions of the interests of the rich, that there was a lot of corruption and only a small percentage of the people showed up to vote. The Cuban story explains how *pluripartidismo* is not the same as democracy because having several parties does not amount to rule by the people, or at least it did not in Cuba in the 1940s. Moreover, the Cuban story also explains that the 1940 Constitution, while progressive in promise, did not turn out to be progressive in fact, and that this was because the constitutional reforms were not supported by progressive laws according to which such reforms could be actualized.

Smith and Padula do not refute or respond to a story that has been told repeatedly for almost half a century in Cuba explaining Cuba's aspirations for democracy and respect for human rights. Whereas almost every response by Cuban officials and spokespeople makes reference to the history of Cuba's struggle for democracy and respect for human rights, to what it means and why, as well as to the US government's commitment to undermining Cuban sovereignty, this story is often just left out of the stories told about Cuba by many who try to evaluate the Cuban Revolution from outside.

Now, one might think that there is nothing particularly interesting about this. It is simply a manifestation of ideological power. The more powerful entity does not need to tell its own story and is of course not interested in promoting the point of view of those it wants to dominate. But I am interested in this problem as it applies to those who are sympathetic to Cuba. I am not interested in why members of the US government ignore the Cuban story; I am interested in why people who are sympathetic to Cuba — like the authors of *Sex and Revolution* — ignore the story, and what is required in order to not ignore it. I will suggest that it is an issue about the consequences of ideological power, but that it is also an issue about the nature of understanding and of the role of a particular sort of commitment and engagement in the investigation of beliefs about ideological influence: The authors of *Sex and Revolution* can leave the explanatory story out because the dominant expectations are that Cuba engages militarily *unnecessarily*. And in order to think that the explanation is important, that it must be taken seriously in order to properly appreciate empirical evidence, one must not only question relevant expectations but also think that it matters that we do so.

Philosophers of science have pointed out that when we look for explanations we look for causes that play a particular explanatory role within an investigative program generating certain cognitive needs. According to Philip Kitcher, rational decisions are those that issue from a process that has high expectations of cognitive progress, for we have to have expectations of success to generate certain directions of evaluation.[6] Causes become explanatory ones when they explain what needs to be understood. So, for instance, we wouldn't say that Smith's going to buy cigarettes explains his death on the highway, even though he would not have died if he had not gone out to buy cigarettes. Jones' drunk driving better explains Smith's death because it is the sort of action that is relevant to understanding highway deaths.[7] Drunk driving in this case is explanatory and smoking is not because of what each contributes to a direction of understanding. The rationale is that we can pursue our concern about car crashes if we know more about drunkenness and inattention, whereas knowledge about the errands that lead people to be in the wrong place at the wrong time does not help.

Suppose we did not care about vehicular accidents. Suppose this were something that we did not see a need to try to understand or avoid. In that case, the search for an explanatory cause lacks a certain motivation, and we might well think that Smith died because he happened to like smoking late at night. Thus, certain sorts of understanding cannot be acquired or evaluated unless there is first the commitment which can generate relevant cognitive needs. This is most interestingly the case in situations in which the understanding being pursued conflicts with expectations, in which expectations need to be pursued and developed.

Speaking to the United Nations in 1960, Fidel Castro invited the audience to suppose "that a person from outer space were to come to this assembly, someone who had read neither the Communist Manifesto of Karl Marx nor UPI or AP dispatches or any other monopoly-controlled publication. If he were to ask how the world was divided up and he saw on a map that the wealth was divided among the monopolies of four or five countries, he would say, 'The world has been badly divided up, the world has been exploited'."[8] The suggestion is that without the aid of ideology or propaganda, or at least without the aid of certain ideologies and propaganda, someone from outer space might have good reason to think something is *wrong* with the way the world is divided up.

Now, it would seem that Fidel Castro's point here is not interesting primarily because it refers to a different perspective, or the suggestion of one, but rather because it refers to the difficulty of properly understanding something that is obviously true. The truth of the claim "The world is divided up badly" is hard to dispute; its truth is somewhat obvious. But its *understanding* is difficult. It might be possible for someone from outer space to think it *matters* that the world is wrongly divided up because someone looking from outer space would not have expectations generated by how the world is currently divided up. Such a person would be reasoning without a certain set of expectations. The suggestion seems to be that someone from outer space might see differences in a different way and might indeed find certain differences irrelevant. The point in this case, however, is not that they *could* be irrelevant from another perspec-

tive but that they *are* in fact irrelevant and that the only way this might be properly understood would be from something like outer space.

The question of properly understanding certain truths may be more important in some cases than questions about their possession. Fully understanding the true statement "The world is divided up badly" requires not only a desire to understand how the world *ought* to be divided up but also, more fundamentally, a commitment according to which it *matters* that the world is divided up wrongly. The problem is not just that one has to see that there is an issue before one can appreciate the usefulness of the information. The more important problem is what is *involved* in seeing that there is an issue. Thus, it would appear that what is significant for the acquiring of understanding is not so much the discovery or identification of truth, but rather the commitment to the kinds of directions of development — particularly human development — that can make the right sorts of truths relevant. The difficulty of understanding that the world is divided up wrongly, even if one believes correctly that it is, is that such understanding requires an interest in the kind of possibilities for human existence its pursuit would make possible.

To get back to the story of the Martian visitor: What sends the Martian fleeing is the last bit of information, which is that Cuba has been condemned in the United Nations for abuse of human rights. That is, what sends the Martian fleeing in terror is not the bits of empirical evidence and what they indicate, but the information he receives about how the bits of information are assessed. What is terrifying is awareness of the context within which the results of investigation are interpreted. The Martian *flees*, presumably, not just because human rights are not respected. What sends the Martian fleeing is that it does not seem to matter that human rights are not understood.

Redefining Options

Consider the story of Sethe in Toni Morrison's *Beloved*, which I have discussed elsewhere.[9] When Sethe, an escaped slave, sees her ex slave-master coming down the road to take her and her children back to slavery, from which she had fled 28 days before, she decides, with certainty, that she should kill her children rather than let them go back to slavery. There are lots of ways in which we might think the choice a strange one. But the novel is powerful in particular because we understand Sethe's choice in terms of what becomes important to Sethe, even though that importance is not entirely articulable. We understand Sethe's choice in terms of the awareness that Sethe acquires as she proceeds in action according to certain specific interests and needs.

Sethe tries to kill her children, succeeds in killing one, and is considered crazy by both the slave master and her own community. But Sethe has no regrets about her choice. She knew that she had to do it. Now, as Christine Korsgaard points out, the kind of normativity that most requires philosophical explanation is not that which explains why people feel compelled to choose as they do, but rather that which explains why *I* feel compelled, in other words, that which explains the first-person compulsion.[10] We might say for instance that people act morally for the sake of the continuation of the species. But this doesn't explain why *I* might feel compelled in a particular situation to do or not do something at the possible cost of my life, or the lives of others. And it seems right to say, as Korsgaard does, that an account of moral compulsion must make reference to a person's practical identity. For when someone feels compelled to act in a certain way even if the cost is death, there is an important sense in which what she feels is that to not act in a certain way is to not be the person she thinks she is.

Thus, we might say about Sethe that she decides to kill her children because if she does not act to protect their capacity for moral responsibility, she will not be able to live with herself. During her 28 days of freedom Sethe has learned that she can love her children. She has taken the risk, being a slave, of loving her children. Paul D, for instance, tells her that used-to-be-slaves should pick the smallest stars in the sky to own because dreams can be taken away and one has to be able to go on living.[11] But Sethe commits herself to sewing on a button for her daughter as if it were right that she

be able to sew a garment for her daughter. So, when Sethe faces her slave master and *knows* that she cannot let her children go back to slavery, we might think that the compulsion that she tries to explain later to Paul D is that according to which she would rather be dead than go back to slavery and she would rather that her children be dead than that she allow them to go back to slavery. The moral compulsion according to which Sethe feels that she *has* to try to protect her children from slavery by killing them is that according to which to not do so would be to not be able to continue on as a sort of person.

But this is too simple. For Sethe's experience in the 28 days of freedom is not that of becoming a *sort* of person; it is that of becoming a person. It is not that of gaining a sort of awareness of herself and her possibilities; it is that of gaining awareness, of becoming aware of the possibility and importance of self-awareness. We might say about Sethe's compulsion that, given the person she has become and what is now important to her, the life that is offered to her under slavery is *worse* than death, as if there were a kind of comparison, a choice between discrete entities. But given that what she has become in her view *is* a person, it would seem more appropriate to say that what compels her is that what is offered to her under slavery is not offered to *her*, since she is not, under slavery, a person at all, but rather an animal.

What matters more than continuing on as a sort of person, for Sethe, is the possibility that *persons* be a sort that applies to her, and to her children. So Sethe's statement to Paul D that she absolutely could not "let all that go back to where it was"[12] is reference not just to a way of life, but more importantly, it would seem, to an orientation toward that life. What she would not let her children go back to was not just the life of slaves, but a world in which it was expected that she *ought* to be a slave because she is not a person. If Sethe were a slave and it were *wrong* that she be a slave, the situation might have been a little different. But if she is just an animal and if it is appropriate, even to those who share her experience as a slave, that she pick only the smallest stars in the sky to own, then the issue is not just about being a slave but also about how it can even be wrong that she be a slave, about the expectations according to which it is okay that she be a slave. It is important to Sethe that she be able to flee from slavery and to love her children. But what is more important, according to her, is her realization that she *ought* to be able to love her children.

To the extent that Sethe's compulsion is explained in terms of identity, it is explained in terms of expectations about and interest in a certain possibility for identity, and for the conditions that would allow such expectations and interests to be maintained, and pursued. To choose *not* to recognize expectations that she is an animal, and not human, is to choose at least the possibility, even if not fully articulatable, of an understanding of *human*, or *person*, that applies to her.

If Sethe kills her children, of course, they will not have the possibility of realizing themselves as human beings. But if she doesn't kill them, they also do not have the possibility of realizing themselves, for they are slaves. If Sethe kills them or not, her children do not have the possibility of realizing themselves, but if she doesn't try to kill them to protect the possibility, she also risks losing the expectation of the possibility. So what Sethe chooses is not an option, or an action by itself, as much as it is a unifying perspective, a way of thinking of herself and her children in ways that generate certain expectations. What is maintained and preserved by her choice to try to protect her children from slavery is the control of the possibility of a certain (human) identity, not the identity itself, which must still be pursued in thought and action.

What seems crucial to understanding the situation of Cuba is the possibility, not the truth, of the claim that the options offered by US dominated capitalism might be wrong, that the available options for humanity rest upon mistaken liberal conceptions of what it means to be human. Understanding Cuba is not a problem in the first instance of beliefs. For one can possess all the relevant propositional beliefs about Cuba and interpret the information according to a perspective which is inadequate for attributing appropriate importance to such beliefs. This is what *Sex and Revolution*

does so effectively. It presents all the relevant information but does not adequately present the story that explains, or could explain the significance of that information.

When we read the story of Sethe, we make a mistake if we ask whether or not she did the right thing when she tried to kill her children. We make a mistake because the story that she has told is one according to which she does what she does in order to be able to ask such a question. We ask the wrong question because the reason Sethe tries to kill her children is that as slaves, she and her children are not able to do right or wrong; concepts of right and wrong do not apply to them because as non-human animals, they do not possess moral responsibility. Thus, the question about the moral status of her act demonstrates failure to understand her story and what it is about, or to respect it, because the story that Sethe tells raises questions about morality itself. If it can even make sense for someone to go against morality to claim its very possibility, then to the extent that we have understood the story, we have at least to acknowledge that there is a question to be asked first about morality itself and what it involves.

The point is not that we have to believe Sethe's story. The point is that if we understand Sethe's story with a certain respect for Sethe and her situation, we have to acknowledge that there are certain difficulties in deliberating about what it is reasonable to believe. The problem here is *not* that there are different perspectives, that for instance Sethe sees slavery in a way that is different from how her neighbours see slavery, the uninteresting "now it's a duck, now it's a rabbit" insight. Instead, the problem is that there is a difficulty understanding Sethe's view because one way of thinking of slavery is not only more powerful than the other, but that it generates expectations according to which Sethe's perspective becomes implausible, and thereby difficult to articulate. Sethe's explanation of what she chooses is that she just couldn't let her children go back to "all that," by which she means a system in which they could not choose from amongst options appropriate for human beings, as a human being. So, the issue is not in the first instance one about believing or not; it is first a question about the conditions under which it becomes possible to effectively evaluate certain beliefs, or even to be able to identify what they are beliefs about.

Similarly, if there is any possibility at all that the Cuban story makes sense, then one cannot just choose between two systems. For one system and not the other defines the terms according to which the evaluation takes place. Indeed, in the theory and expression of the Cuban Revolution, it is often made explicit that there is a commitment to redefinition of options. In May, 1982, Fidel Castro said ideas do not come together easily in revolutionary situations; they cannot be expected like a ray of light, in a clear, precise and linear fashion. But what must be linear is the commitment to action in a certain direction.[13] Action must be linear because theory cannot be, and action must be linear in order that theory *be* theory, in order that there be expectations of the sort that can make it possible to consider evidence as evidence. In May, 1982, Fidel said that commitment to direction has to have priority because ideas take their form as a result of that commitment, through development and action. Then, in October, 1997, at the Fifth Party Congress, Fidel said that what is necessary for survival in an unjust and threatening world is, in the first instance, unity and direction:

> Luego una enseñanza histórica para nosotras es que hay que garantizar la dirección y que la dirección no puede fallar, el Partido no puede darse el lujo de que un día falle su dirección, porque el precio es inpagable. Esa es una idea clave: tenemos que arreglárnoslas para garantizar eso durante un largo período histórico. En los tiempos en que estamos viviendo y con el largo enfrentamiento que tenemos ante el imperialismo y el capitalismo, no es posible renunciar a la idea de la necesidad de una dirección unida y eficiente.[14]

This is a commitment to action of a certain sort, in a certain direction, as a result of which it becomes possible to maintain certain expectations. The *direction*, it is suggested, is important for unity; it is not, as is often assumed, the unity that

determines the direction. Thus, there is something epistemologically, as well as politically, significant about the constant reference in the Cuban literature to the fact that there is an option to make the option that of winning or dying, that there is a choice about the choices. This was what Fidel Castro said in 1956 before a small group of people set sail from Mexico in an old yacht, in preparation for the Revolution, and it is what many in Cuba say today as the United States approves yet another amendment (the Graham Amendment declaring Cuba a security risk) and makes further suggestions about justifying military aggression.[15]

When Fidel Castro spoke at the Fifth Party Congress in October, 1997, he did not just say that the choice was between socialism or death, as he usually does. He also said that there was a choice that the choice be between socialism and death. After describing the desperate situation of the first half of 1992, when during a period of five months almost nothing arrived in the country, Fidel Castro suggested that there was an alternative that had been there for a long time. He did not propose another option, besides capitalism and death by starvation, or invasion. He proposed a reformulation of the options:

> Pero también siempre hay una alternativa que ha estado presente desde el primer día...:Si no es posible vivir con honor y con justicia, si no es posible ser hombre y ser hombre libre,)para que queremos la vida?; es preferible la muerte.... cuando los hombres escogen el deber y el honor, cuando escogen lo que es justo, es precisamente cuando más viven, porque viven mientras viva una idea, y las ideas no mueren, las causas justas se perpetúan a lo largo de los tiempos, como se perpetuarán nuestras ideas y se perpetuará nuestra causa justa.... Y nosotros escogimos hace rato, en este dilema...[16]

In other words, the question is not about choosing between life and death, but about choosing to choose the pursuit of a certain kind of meaningful life, with a certain purpose; it is to choose to reject the meaningfulness of life as otherwise defined, to not engage with options made available by such meaningfulness.

This is not to say that there is no question about freedom. There is a burdensome question of freedom that arises within this choice, just as there is a question for Sethe about morality. But the suggestion is that there is sometimes a question about how social values and norms are defined, and how, as a result, options are made meaningful as options for life. There is a deep-seated and popular view in North American and European philosophical traditions that someone acts or chooses autonomously when she weighs her options in light of relevant information, and does or chooses that which is most likely to advance more of her aims than other options. Freedom, according to this picture, has to do, ultimately, with realization of a person's actual desires and interests. Certainly, no one would say that someone acts freely when they act upon *any* desires, since desires can be compulsive or based upon ignorance. But the popular assumption is that respecting people's autonomy involves respecting people's freedom to act on their settled values and aims, without interference other than the providing of appropriate resources.

However, when we consider the extent to which social norms and values prescribe and limit people's choices, when we consider the extent to which such norms and values constitute, as Frantz Fanon says, "a definitive structuring of the self and the world,"[17] this picture is naive. Will Kymlicka's defence of minority rights in *Liberalism, Community and Culture* involves a lengthy argument attempting to show that concern for group rights does not involve overriding individuals' essential interests in, as he puts it, living their lives "from the inside," with true beliefs.[18] Kymlicka thinks that it is uncontroversial that "no life goes better by being led from the outside according to values the person does not endorse."[19] But one might wonder why some lives might not go better if they were led by more humane values, even if these are not easy to endorse, or even to identify, as they will not be if they are expected. To the extent that societies, or global world views can be systemically unjust, to the extent that available options are defined by norms and values that deny the humanity of some people, it *is* reasonable to think that at least some lives would indeed go better if led from the outside

according to values the person involved might well not endorse, or even recognize.

Freedom has to do, among other things with identifying, understanding and being able to control forces — including one's own impulses — that would compel one to act in ways that are the result of arbitrary, unchosen aspects of one's situations. The idea that freedom is the capacity for unrestricted choice amongst available options is for some people a denial of freedom, since those available choices, and the values that explain them, are the result of arbitrary, unjust aspects of one's unchosen situation. It may be then that freedom requires above all, resistance to such choices, and the system that explains them, before one can identify what would be required to act — freely— in one's human interests.

When people approach Cuba concerned above all with the existence of a certain understanding of freedom, they are like readers who insist on concerning themselves with the morality of Sethe's choice. The question is inappropriate in the case of Sethe because Sethe does what she does in order to claim the possibility of real moral agency in a situation in which available understandings of morality are inadequate. When we insist on trying to understand her choice in terms of existing understandings of morality, we apply to Sethe's situation concepts the power and control of which Sethe struggles above all to resist, in order to be human. It may turn out to be true that human freedom depends primarily upon being able to choose from amongst many options, whatever they happen to be. And it may turn out to be true that as human beings we are incapable of transforming ourselves morally, and realizing ourselves through participation in the transformation of the social and political conditions that transform us. That is, it may be that what matters most to the realization of human worth is choice, and not the conditions under which we choose and imagine. But it's not clear that we know this yet, and if we don't we should avoid dismissing the meaningfulness of struggles the full understanding of which depends in part upon our own struggles to develop relevant expectations (for freedom and democracy) and to pursue them.

Democracy in Cuba

The single party system should be understood as the direction that is necessary for the unity (of vision), not as the unity that determines the direction and vision. This is how it is defended in the literature. What is referred to in reference to the Party is unity of direction, and it is the direction that explains the unity, not the reverse. Because Leninist parties and regimes have tended historically to become highly centralized and oligarchic, it is assumed that they were defined that way in the beginning. But the notion of the vanguard party in Antonio Gramsci's writing needs to be considered in conjunction with Lenin's and Che Guevara's ideas that socialist revolution is impossible without the bringing about of new values, new morals and new possibilities for being human. It is true that there is in Marxist-Leninist thought the idea that the moral person is a product of the superstructure. But what is important in Lenin's thought for Cuban revolutionary theory is Lenin's suggestion that the biggest mistake that could be made by the Communist Party in the Soviet Union would be to forget that the past still had to be overcome, to think that knowledge was secure and that there wasn't still a constant battle to be fought against the heritage of past traditions.[20]

The pursuit of Cuban identity — cubanidad — has its roots in important arguments for solidarity, for unity, in resisting the devastating consequences — psychological, ideological, political and economic — of the collapse of the Soviet Union. But liberal philosophy, especially ideas of what solidarity and unity consist of, seem to lead to a conflation in some literature and in popular conversation of the significance of moral vision with a preservation of traditional cultural values contradicting and sometimes actively undermining that vision. For instance, in an attempt to explain how it was that Cuba, despite universal predictions about its imminent collapse, not only has continued in its commitment to socialism but has begun slowly to rebuild its economy and strengthen its political system, Dario Machado lists among other factors Cuban patriotism.[21] "La Patria," however, is, in the theory, a moral concept.[22] That is, it is not

a notion referring to what actually or who actually exists within the Cuban nation, but rather to what *ought* to characterize the Cuban people if indeed they are to be able to go forward as an independent entity. And if "la Patria" is a normative concept, then not only is it possible to change cultural values without undermining solidarity, but in certain cases it is crucial. The unity, the solidarity, that has explained the going forward in question is unity beneath a cause.[23] Offered in explanation of how to go ahead, it is not a sharing of social and cultural characteristics; it is a shared vision. And hence the defence of that unity, the unity needed to resist, is defence not of shared qualities between people who happen to share a geographical space, but defence of a moral vision, a vision the pursuit of which may in important and painful ways, transform those shared qualities, or at least bestow a different importance to them.

The Cuban Revolution, the theory of which can be found in the writings of Che Guevara and Fidel Castro, does not express the idea that culture and moral values are a mere reflection of the superstructure and that individuals are an appendix of the economic motor, the stereotypical notion of marxist development.[24] Instead, it reflects the less orthodox, "humanist" understanding of revolution and revolutionaries that can be found in Marx's earlier writings, for instance, in the *1844 Manuscripts*,[25] and in Gramsci's *The Prison Notebooks*.[26] Che Guevara followed Gramsci in arguing for a conception of the person, and for a notion of self-realization and human growth. In the work of Gramsci, for instance, the development of awareness, of creativity, of intelligence, is both dependent upon and determining of the development of material conditions. And the unity upon which so much depends, according to this philosophy, is not imposed upon people or decreed; it cannot be. Instead, it is the result of a process characterized by the development of individuals' awareness and capacities, what Gramsci referred to as "the lifting up of simple souls."

In other words, it is not a certain sort of (structural or theoretical) unity that defines and/or determines who and what people can do and be, but rather a process of transformation of values and ways of being that makes it possible for people to be and do more than they could before, as human beings. According to Che Guevara, Marx was as interested in the spiritual repercussions of the economy as he was in the economy itself, what he called "hechos de conciencia,"[27] and Guevara thought that if communism is not interested in *los hechos de conciencia*, it can provide a method of distribution of goods but it can never be a moral revolution.[28]

The single Party system, then, has an epistemological and metaphysical justification having to do with the need for direction and organization in both the increase of understanding and the bringing about of the conditions that make such understanding desirable and possible. The argument for the Party is the following: In order to be able to control their lives people have to have the resources; they have to have the understanding and the capacity to apply it. Cuban society has a history of oppression and injustice as a result of which the values that define the society and that define the people who live in it are questionable at best and in many ways inhuman. If it is to be possible to find ways of living better, it has to be possible to examine and analyze such values, and this is a long and difficult process. A just and humane society is not a matter of decree: It must be the result of a process in which people acquire moral understanding and responsibility. What is essential to such a process is participation, and individual and social growth, moral growth. But people learn by acting and they understand through participation. So the priority is to find ways to bring about the sort of social change that makes such participation possible. The role of the Party is to find ways to do this in which people can be fully and meaningfully involved in the conditions of their own social formation. But the authority of the Party does not consist in the fact that it is a single party; instead, the Party *is* a Party in the first place to the extent that it acquires authority as a result of its capacity to respond to the interests and desires of the people.[29]

The difference between Gramsci and Guevara, and those Marxists called "historical materialists,"[30] is that Gramsci and Guevara thought that capitalism had to be overthrown, that it would not fall as a result of "objective forces." And the process according to which it would be overthrown was one of raising consciousness, of increasing awareness, of faith in human beings and what they could do and be. Yet if individuals are to take an active role in the overthrowing of capitalism, they have to be prepared to struggle also against its heritage. And Gramsci and Guevara recognized that this was a daily struggle, a struggle against values, attitudes, presuppositions, against the subjective elements. Indeed, it is primarily such a struggle. Military struggle is sometimes necessary, but it is not as important or as difficult as the struggle for ideas, and for direction.[31] For this struggle is daily and requires patience. The struggle against the *heritage* of capitalism is a constant, daily struggle in which people must be able to be involved, to participate, to bring about results and to recognize them as results. For people only learn when they can act, and people must always be *persuaded* to believe, not coerced.

The single party has an epistemological explanation in the very important suggestion that without theoretical vision, without working constantly to revise and enlarge such a vision, the freedom of individuals is limited by unexamined and unacknowledged traditions and values. And in order for people to acquire greater awareness and understanding, they must be able to participate in the bringing about of the conditions that make possible such vision. They must be able to act according to their understanding, and to recognize the results. Marx's early vision of human nature, the one that inspired Che Guevara, was that human beings realize themselves as they relentlessly strive to create the conditions that create us as certain sorts of persons. And such striving, according to Lenin, Gramsci and Guevara must be informed by the practical and theoretical education that makes it possible for people to resist certain traditional values and to assess for themselves the results.

Those who think that any argument about what happens in Cuba is trumped by tired, unimaginative remarks about freedom, are both metaphysically and epistemologically naive. For Cuba's pursuit of communism depends upon certain beliefs about human capacities for moral and personal development, beliefs which may turn out to be mistaken. The point here has been that if they are mistaken, it cannot be easy to know this, and there is no reason to think that we know it yet. To the extent that such beliefs about human development presume a different conception of human freedom, they cannot fairly be shown to be wrong on grounds that they conflict with a current conception of freedom, however powerful.

Che Guevara made the point at the beginning of the Revolution, in response to critics who worried about the freedom of the individual, that they failed to understand the *narrow* dialectical relationship between theory and practice in a revolutionary setting.[32] By this, it seems, he was referring to the fact that the justification for the party and its direction depends upon what becomes possible for people as they participate, and as they acquire for themselves awareness of the direction in which they are painstakingly advancing. The *narrow* dialectical unity is required in situations of redefining options because understanding requires not just truth, but the development of the conditions for ascribing importance to truths, for seeing how such truths matter, or could matter.

The liberal view according to which one acts autonomously when one considers one's options on the basis of full understanding and instrumental reasoning makes sense in certain situations, as does *pluripartidismo*. It makes sense, for instance, when there is no reason to think not only that the options are inadequate but, worse, that one may easily fail to see *that* and how the options are inadequate. It makes sense, that is, where justice already exists. The problem for liberal philosophy is not just that the options offered to people by unjust societies are inadequate. The more difficult problem is that in situations in which the *explanations* for options are wrong, it is sometimes necessary to first reject the options in order to pursue conditions in which it is possible to see *how* they are wrong, or even *that* they are wrong.

Pluripartidismo might make sense if there were no struggle against and for subjective attitudes. But if there is such a struggle, developing theoretical vision requires, not just theories and analysis, but

the organization and effective social change necessary for control of such a vision. It may still not be clear how best to define Cuban democracy, its merits and defects, but the fact that there is one political party involved cannot mean that there is no possibility of examining the democratic experience, without begging crucial questions about what democracy and freedom mean.

Conclusion

The theory of the Cuban Revolution is full of references to the epistemological role of the Party and to the explanation for it, but these are often ignored in discussions of democracy. Gramsci claimed that "political science, as far as both its concrete content and its logical formulation are concerned, must be seen as a developing organism."[33] It cannot be merely or mostly empirical, at least not if the object is effective criticism. The active politician, the creative intellectual, according to Gramsci, is not one who moves "in the turbid void of his own desires and dreams" but one who "applies one's will to the creation of a new equilibrium among the forces which really exist and are operative — basing oneself on the particular force that one believes to be progressive and strengthening it to help it to victory."[34] In Gramsci's view, the active theorist is one who works to change the balance, the equilibrium, and he does so relative to a vision that is being actually pursued but which may not be easily realized, even conceptually. If one does not grapple with the general vision, including the metaphysics and epistemology, one cannot rely with confidence upon what one sees and hears.

The point about the Martian story in *La Gramna* seems to be that there is a particular kind of difficulty involved in appreciating certain facts about the Cuban situation, even though it is generally recognized that these facts are true. Cubans often comment on the fact that US papers keep talking about the need for elections in Cuba, and then they ignore completely the elections in Cuba. Presumably, the reason the elections in Cuba are ignored is that they are not *like* the American elections in certain respects. This should not be a reason to think they are not elections unless one argues first for that unifying perspective according to which the participation of more than one party is an essential characteristic of an election's being what it is. Cubans point out that what happens in the US would fail to count as elections if it were stipulated that elections should involve at least an 80 percent turn-out.[35] Again, the point here is not the issue about elections in Cuba, but the argumentative strategy that is employed, and that is able to be employed, against Cuba, specifically because of the existence of dominant expectations. It is not clear that it matters much how we think about elections, but understanding freedom and democracy certainly do matter. Thus, it is important to take seriously the possibility that there is still something to learn about what these mean and what might be implied for how we move ahead as human beings pursuing human flourishing.

Author's Note

I would not have been able to write this paper without the friendship of, discussions with, and bibliographic help from Sonia Enjamio, Juscarid Morales, Inés Rodríguez, Amelia Suárez, and Ernesto Tornín. Some sections of the paper have been presented at St. Mary's University, Queen's University, and the University of Oregon, at Eugene. I am grateful to Christine Koggel for her interest in the paper and to the Social Sciences and Humanities Research Council of Canada for support during two fall semesters in Havana.

NOTES

1. Santiago Cuba Fernandez, "Derechos humanos: Ficción y realidad," *La Gramna* (La Habana, Dec. 6, 1997), p. 4.

2. E.g., Jennifer Stiff, "The Question of National Autonomy: The Case of Cuba," paper presented at North American Society for Social Philosophy conference at Queen's University, July 20, 1997.

3. Lois M. Smith and Alfred Padula, *Sex and Revolution: Women in Socialist Cuba* (New York: Oxford University Press, 1996), p. 185. References in the text are to this edition.

4. E.g., *Proyecto: El partido de la unidad, la democracia y los derechos humanos que defendemos,* V Congreso del partido comuista de Cuba, October, 1997 (Havana: Editora Política, May, 1997).

5. "¡Sexta Victoria!," *La Gramna*, Havana, Nov. 6, 1997, pp. 1, 4, 5.

6. Philip Kitcher, *The Advancement of Science* (New York: Oxford University Press, 1993). e.g. p. 193.

7. This example is from R. Miller, *Fact and Method* (Princeton: Princeton University Press, 1987), p. 93-4.

8. "The Case of Cuba is the Case of Every Underdeveloped Country," Address to the General Assembly, Sept. 26, 1960, reprinted in Fidel Castro, Che Guevara *To Speak the Truth* (New York: Pathfinder, 1992), p. 76.

9. Toni Morrison, *Beloved* (New York: Penguin Books, 1987). Discussed in *Impossible Dreams: Rationality, Integrity and Moral Imagination* (Boulder: Westview Press, 1996), esp. ch. 1.

10. Christine M. Korsgaard, *The Sources of Normativity* (Cambridge: Cambridge University Press, 1996), p. 7-18.

11. Toni Morrison, *Beloved* (New York: Penguin Books, 1987), p. 44-45.

12. *Ibid*, p. 163.

13. Discurso en la Clausura del VI Congreso del ANAP, Havana, May 17, 1982 rpt. In *Discurso en Tres Congresos* (La Habana: Editora Política, 1982), p. 153.

14. Claurura del V Congreso, *La Gramna*, Havana, Nov. 1, 1998, p. 7: "Later we learned a historical lesson, that we had to guarantee the direction, that the direction could not fail, the Party could not allow itself the luxury of failing in direction, for the price is unpayable. This is the key idea: we have to organize ourselves to guarantee direction for a long time. In the times in which we are living, and with the confrontation with imperialism and capitalism, it is not possible to renounce the idea of an efficient and united direction" (my translation).

15. Nicanor Leon Cotayo, "Enmienda Graham: Una amenaza militar contra Cuba," *La Gramna*, La Habana, # 225 (Nov. 12, 1997), p. 5.

16. *Informe Central, V Congreso, La Gramna* (Havana, Oct. 29, 1997), p. 4: "There has always been an alternative, that has been there from the beginning,

that if we cannot live with honour, why do we want to live. It is better to die... when people choose duty and honour, when they choose what is just, it is when they most live, because they live with an idea, and ideas don't die, just causes continue through time, as our ideas will continue, and our just cause... and we chose a long time ago, in this dilemma...." (my translation).

17. Frantz Fanon, "The Fact of Blackness," reprinted in D.T. Goldberg, *The Anatomy of Racism* (Minneapolis: University of Minnesota Press, 1990), p. 109.

18. Will Kymlicka, *Liberalism, Community and Culture* (New York: Oxford University Press), p. 12.

19. *Ibid*.

20. V.I. Lenin, March, 1923, cited in Isabel Monal, "Tiene la palabra el camarada Lenin," *Juventud Rebelde Dominical* (La Habana, Nov. 2, 1997), p. 9.

21. See e.g., Dario L. Machado, "La coyuntura sociopolítica actual de la sociedad cubana," in *Contracorriente: Una revista cubana de pensamiento*, Ene-Feb-Mar 1996, Año 2, Número 3, p. 42-58.

22. Fidel Castro, "La Patria es inseparable del concepto de la justicia, de la dignidad, de la libertad, de la Revolución," *La Gramna*, Havana, December 17, 1996, p. 1.

23. Fidel Castro, "*Unidos en una sola causa, bajo una sola bandera*" April 19, 1991 (Havana: Editora Politica, 1991).

24. See e.g., Néstor Kohan, "El Che Guevara y la filosofía de la praxis," *Debates Americanos*, No. 3 (enero-junio) 1997 La Habana, p. 55-70.

25. Karl Marx, *Economic and Philosophic Manuscripts of 1844* in Karl Marx and Frederick Engels, *Collected Works, Vol. 3* (London: Lawrence and Wishart, 1975), p. 249-346.

26. Antonio Gramsci, *Selections from the Prison Notebooks of Antonio Gramsci*, ed. and tr. Quinton Hoare and Geoffrey Nowell-Smith (New York; International Publishers, 1971), esp. "The Intellectuals," p. 3-23.

27. "deeds of conscience" (my translation).

28. Che, "El Plan y el Hombre" en *El Socialismo y el hombre nuevo*, p. 69 rpt. in Kohan, 66.

29. *Fidel Castro: Ideología, conciencia y trabajo político, 1959-1986* (Havana; Editorial Pueblo y Educación, 1991).

30. E.g., Kohan, *op.cit.*

31. E.g., *Informe Central* of the Fifth Congress of the Cuban Communist Party, Oct. 8, 1997, rpt. In *La Gramna*, Oct. 29, 1997, p. 5.

32. Che Guevara, "El socialismo y el hombre en Cuba" in *Ernesto Che Guevara: Obras 1957-1967* (Havana: Casa de las Américas, 1970), p. 370.

33. Antonio Gramsci, "The Modern Prince," *Selections from the Prison Notebooks of Antonio Gramsci*, ed. and tr. Quinton Hoare and Geoffrey Nowell-Smith (New York; International Publishers, 1971), p. 133-4.

34. *Ibid*, p. 172.

35. E.g., Edda Diz Garcés, "Podemos medir el tamaño de nuestro pueblo por el tamaño de los obstáculos que ha tenido," *Trabajadores*, Oct. 20, 1997, p. 16.

STUDY QUESTIONS

1 Stefanie Grant takes the U.S. to be out of sync with a growing international movement to abolish capital punishment. What are features of this growing international movement and are they significant with respect to American policy and practice? What is Grant's view? What is yours? Defend your answers.

2 What are some of the arguments underlying the growing movement to abolish capital punishment and can these be the basis for a universal account of the wrongness of capital punishment?

3 Is capital punishment a domestic issue or a violation of internationally protected human rights? Should there be international bodies that monitor and condemn state practices? Provide reasons for your answers.

4 Are the rights of suspected criminals being violated when they are extradited to or commit their crimes in countries with capital punishment? What does Grant argue? What would you argue?

5 What are the socioeconomic and cultural differences between developed and developing countries that Roland Pierik takes to be relevant to an account of child labor? Do you think these differences matter for a proper assessment of what should be done about child labor?

6 Outline and evaluate the policies that Pierik recommends for addressing child labor in developing countries.

7 Did learning about child labor and a global order that sustains child labor influence your thinking about who is responsible and what can be done? Provide reasons for your answer.

8 According to Kok-Chor Tan, why are former colonies demanding reparations and what kinds of reparations are being demanded?

9 Tan claims that injustices and inequalities that continue to be part of the lives of people in colonized countries can also be addressed by arguments for global egalitarian justice. How do these arguments work and how do reparative arguments differ?

10 What are some of the moral arguments in favor of reparations? Do you think reparative arguments can play the morally significant role that Tan sketches for them? Why or why not?

11 What reasons does Jennifer Llewellyn give for rejecting a retributivist conception of justice as inappropriate not only for dealing with the past in transitional contexts like South Africa but also for addressing injustices more generally?

12 What is restorative justice and how does it differ from what has come to be known as transitional justice? According to Llewellyn, what are some of the features of the mandate and mechanisms of the South African Truth and Reconciliation Commission that fit a conception of justice as restorative?

13 In your view, is restorative justice a better way of addressing human rights violations than a conception of justice based on retribution? Is this conception of justice limited in its application to transitional contexts or even more specifically to South Africa? Provide reasons for your answers.

14 According to Susan Babbitt, how do globally dominant expectations about democracy and freedom interfere with a fair investigation of and constructive debate about Cuba? What are these globally dominant expectations?

15 What moral truths about human flourishing might we learn if we take seriously the stories told by Cubans about their aspirations for and ways of achieving human dignity and equality?

16 Does Babbitt's analysis of the situation in Cuba undermine the accounts of democracy given by Gutmann and Li in the previous chapter? Does what we learn about Cuba cast doubt on the validity of claims about the lack of freedom and democracy in Cuba? Defend your answers.

SUGGESTED READINGS

Amsterdam, Anthony G. "Race and the Death Penalty." *Criminal Justice Ethics*, v. 7, no. 1 (Winter/Spring 1988): 2, 84-86.

Bacic, Roberta. "Dealing with the Past: Chile — Human Rights and Human Wrongs." *Race & Class: A Journal for Black and Third World Liberation*, v. 44, no. 1 (July 2002): 17-31.

Berns, Walter. *For Capital Punishment: Crime and the Morality of the Death Penalty*. New York: Basic Books, 1979.

Byron, Michael. "Why My Opinion Shouldn't Count: Revenge, Retribution, and the Death Penalty." *Journal of Social Philosophy*, v. 31, no. 3 (Fall 2000): 307-15.

Chayes, Antonia, and Martha Minow (editors). *Imagine Coexistence: Restoring Humanity After Ethnic Conflict*. San Francisco, CA: Jossey-Bass, 2003.

Crocker, David. *Transitional Justice and International Civil Society*. Working Paper no. 13. Institute for Philosophy and Public Policy, University of Maryland: The National Commission on Civic Renewal, 1998.

Hamber, Brandon. "'Ere their Story Die': Truth, Justice and Reconciliation in South Africa." *Race & Class: A Journal for Black and Third World Liberation*, v. 44, no. 1 (July 2002): 61-79.

Logan, Wayne A. "Declaring Life at the Crossroads of Death: Victims' Anti-Death Penalty Views and Prosecutors' Charging Decisions." *Criminal Justice Ethics*, (Summer/Fall 1999): 41-57.

McCloskey, James. "The Death Penalty: A Personal View." *Criminal Justice Ethics* (Summer/Fall 1996): 2-8.

McLaughlin, Cahal. "Reparations in South Africa — a Visit to Khulumani." *Race & Class: A Journal for Black and Third World Liberation*, v. 44, no. 1 (July 2002): 81-86.

Minow, Martha. *Between Vengeance and Forgiveness: Facing History After Genocide and Mass Violence*. Boston, MA: Beacon Press, 1998.

—. *Breaking the Cycles of Hatred: Memory, Law, and Repair*. Princeton, NJ: Princeton University Press, 2002.

Rolston, William. "Assembling the Jigsaw: Truth, Justice and Transition in the North of Ireland." *Race & Class: A Journal for Black and Third World Liberation*, v. 44, no. 1 (July 2002): 87-105.

Rosenfeld, Michel. "Restitution, Retribution, Political Justice and the Rule of Law." *Constellations*, v. 2, no. 3 (1996): 309-32.

Seils, Paul F. "Reconciliation in Guatemala: The Role of Intelligent Justice." *Race & Class: A Journal for Black and Third World Liberation*, v. 44, no. 1 (July 2002): 33-59.

Simson, Rosalind S. "Does Capital Punishment Deter Homicide? A Case Study in Epistemological Objectivity." *Metaphilosophy*, v. 32, no. 3 (April 2001): 293-307.

Stanley, Elizabeth. "What Next? The Aftermath of Organised Truth Telling." *Race & Class: A Journal for Black and Third World Liberation*, v. 44, no. 1 (July 2002): 1-15.

Strang, Heather and John Braithwaite (editors). *Restorative Justice: Philosophy to Practice*. Burlington, VT: Dartmouth, 2000.

Thompson, Janna. *Taking Responsibility for the Past: Reparation and Historical Injustice*. Cambridge: Polity Press, 2002.

Torpey, John. *Politics and the Past: On Repairing Historical Injustices*. Lanham, MD: Rowman & Littlefield, 2003.

Von Hirsch, Andrew *et al.* (editors). *Restorative Justice and Criminal Justice: Competing or Reconcilable Paradigms?* Oxford: Hart, 2003.

Wheeler, Samuel C. "Gun Violence and Fundamental Rights." *Criminal Justice Ethics* (Winter/Spring 2001): 19-27.

Whiteley, Diane. "The Victim and the Justification of Punishment." *Criminal Justice Ethics* (Summer/Fall 1998): 42-60.

CHAPTER SIX: WAR AND TERRORISM

INTRODUCTION

In the previous chapter we applied concepts central to moral and political theory to specific issues and contexts. Conceptions of human rights, justice, and democracy are tested when they are placed in particular contexts, practices, histories, and conditions. We examined the ways in which discussions of issues such as capital punishment increasingly involve awareness of a global context and of pressure by the international community to extend understandings of human rights. We explored the possibility that the debate on capital punishment in the global context has implications for countries that continue to justify and use it. We also examined the ways in which child labor is impacted by factors of globalization and the unequal relationships between countries that are rich and poor, developed and developing. Child labor does not exist in isolation from a global economic system in which children in developing countries produce products for consumers in developed countries, and these factors may be relevant to an account of responsibilities and policies. We also examined the ways in which histories of colonialism may call for extended understandings of justice as reparations for harm done to peoples of former colonized countries. Traditional conceptions of justice are also challenged by cases in which countries are in transition from a history of human rights violations to a future that restores relationships of dignity and respect. And Cuba's history and conditions raise questions about globally dominant expectations of the meaning of democracy and human rights.

In this chapter, we explore the applications of human rights, justice, and democracy to the specific and timely issue of political violence in the context of war and terrorism. How should states and the international community respond to violence against states and the people in them? Can responding to violence with violence be justified? Can war be justified and, if so, under what circum-

stances? Can terrorism be justified? Are dimensions of power in relationships between countries that are rich and poor relevant to an analysis of war and terrorism? How do these dimensions work in a global context in which violence by particular groups and countries impacts on individuals, other countries, and the world as a whole?

The collapse of the Soviet Union in the late 1980s spelled the end of Cold War; the beginning of regional, national, and civil conflicts in different parts of the world; and responses by other countries, international bodies, and agencies to these conflicts. Some claim that the attacks on the World Trade Center of September 11, 2001 (commonly known as 9/11) have permanently changed theories about war and terrorism and justifications for them. The attack on a country that for much of its history was protected from the direct impact of war was a serious shock to the global community and to the American people. The responses to the attack in the form of the declaration of a war on terrorism, the invasion of Afghanistan, and the war in Iraq have changed international relations and reshaped American policy and relations with many countries and peoples.

These features of the contemporary context of war and terrorism have led some to claim that new life has been given to the tendencies of ethnocentrism and Eurocentrism and to moves to defend universalism as described in the Introduction to Chapter Two of this volume. It has also led theorists and politicians to reexamine arguments from just war theory, a tradition that goes back millennia, in order to defend or criticize responses to terrorism that have already been taken or to identify the conditions under which a country is justified in going to war. This literature has enriched political theory in the area of dealing with violence to groups and countries. It is this literature and the fact of a global context of increased political violence that called for the addition of this chapter on war and terrorism to this Second Edition of *Moral Issues in Global Perspective*.

The chapter opens with a reading by Michael Walzer. Walzer surveys the theory of just war beginning with Augustine's argument that war could only be fought for the sake of peace, to Christian Europe using military force against unbelievers, to theorists incorporating just war theory into international law, to states claiming a right to fight based on arguments for the supreme sovereignty of the state and of decisions by rulers of states. The latter has been referred to as "realism," a theory justifying force when it is calculated to serve the "national interests" of power and wealth. Walzer argues that Vietnam changed this turn to realism by injecting morality back into the debate: moral arguments were made about the wrongness of American imperialism and of the exposure of Vietnamese civilians to the violence of war. This spelled, according to Walzer, the return to the language of just war and the moral arguments identifying the conditions under which wars could be fought and justifying the methods and conduct of soldiers during and after war.

Walzer applies these insights about the "triumph of just war theory" to contemporary wars, arguing that politicians, political theorists, clerics, generals, lawyers, and the media merely use the language of just war theory to justify their positions and actions. He worries that this use of just war theory risks having it lose the critical role it has always claimed by deflecting attention from the actual business of war and what soldiers do. He argues that justice still needs to be defended in a world where militarization, methods, and contexts for war have changed. Decisions about when and how to fight, as well as what happens when wars end, require constant scrutiny and critical analysis.

In the second reading, Neta Crawford picks up on the idea that warfare has changed to examine arguments by the Bush administration that war is justified to preempt further attacks. She grants that the contemporary context of unconventional adversaries using unconventional methods increases fear and the perception of vulnerability. She notes that joining these with the idea that the U.S. faces rogue enemies who hate everything about the U.S. and what it stands for has allowed the U.S. to take the offensive — to act in self-defense and thereby preempt further attacks. In the process, Crawford argues, important distinctions have been blurred (such as that between preemption and prevention and between terrorists and those states in which terrorists reside), and conditions for legitimate preemption have been violated. Crawford identifies and defends four conditions necessary for legitimate preemption: the "self" in self-defense against aggression should be defined narrowly and not in terms of what will protect imperial interests or increase economic well-being; there should be strong evidence that war is inevitable and will happen in the immediate future; preemption should be likely to succeed in reducing the threat and be restricted to finding the source of the threat and eliminating the damage it was about to do; and military force must be necessary and other options exhausted.

The third reading by Asma Barlas discusses preemptive measures from within the U.S. Barlas moves the discussion from state and global responses to the 9/11 attacks to those responses as they affect American citizens, specifically Muslims. She argues that new laws such as the Patriot Act bring to the surface patterns of racism that mirror and reproduce colonialist thinking and relationships. Barlas claims that the Patriot Act has legalized racial profiling, surveillance, preemptive arrests and detentions, secret courts, and the denial of legal rights both to those accused of terrorism and to those suspected of harboring hostile intent toward the U.S. These laws, she argues, represent a frontal attack on civil liberties, a set of measures that some worry will be made permanent. They have also made it easy to typecast Muslims and Arabs as terrorists, so that entire peoples are held culpable for the acts of a tiny minority of extremists that many Muslims and Arabs themselves condemn. Barlas takes the depersonalization and dehumanization of Muslims to be reflective of the deeply racist nature of fear and paranoia, a racism that categorizes Muslims as "other" and casts them as unpredictable and unknowable. It is a stance all too easy, she argues, for a powerful nation in which citizens of that nation become convinced they do not need to know others because the U.S. can and will take care of itself and its "citizens." These attitudes and beliefs parallel those of colonizers. Barlas notes the difficulty of voicing dissent and being heard in a context in which criticism can be silenced through legal sanctions and by the media. She also notes the tension of voicing dissent in her own case as someone who fled military rule in Pakistan and has benefited from the American legal and educational system.

The specific idea that the phenomena of racism and oppression are connected with terrorism and responses to terrorism is explored by Frank Cunningham in the fourth reading. Cunningham examines those arguments that suggest that terrorism is a response to oppression and as such can be justified as a necessary means of countering or combating oppression. He argues that once we are clear about the meaning of some of the central concepts of terrorism, oppression, and the phenomenology of terrorism, doubt is cast on the argument that terrorism is necessary or effective for combating oppression. Cunningham grants that moral arguments for the wrongness of terrorism cannot just be assumed but must be defended. It is best, therefore, to employ a value-neutral conception of terrorism that enables interrogation of the characteristics and contexts unique to terrorist activities. He then defines oppression as the harm suffered by those who are members of a category of people just by virtue of the fact that they are members of a group. An example of oppression is that of people in formerly colonized countries who are structurally and systemically barred from improving their lives. The utilitarian defense of counter-oppressive terrorism rests on the idea that oppression is morally wrong and calls for a response. Cunningham agrees but asks whether terrorism is an effective and necessary response.

Cunningham argues that the phenomenology of terrorism demands that group hatred be nurtured and sustained, a hatred that molds one's character in psychologically debilitating ways. Moreover, because terrorist acts often target and kill innocent civilians, hatred must not discriminate but be directed at everyone in the group. Counter-oppressive terrorism, therefore, closes off possibilities for finding the underlying causes of oppression, makes cross-group alliances difficult, and sparks downward spirals of revenge-motivated violence. But while counter-oppressive terrorism cannot be justified on the utilitarian grounds of eliminating oppression and improving relations, Cunningham also argues that the "war on terrorism" needs to pay attention to combating policies that sustain oppression in other countries and across cultures.

The final reading by Antonio Tujan, Audrey Gaughran, and Howard Mollett provides further discussion of the "war on terrorism" in the context of examining its effects on development policy and practice and, more specifically, on policies of aid allocation to developing countries. They argue that the war on terror has generated policies that undermine the achievement of development goals and run counter to international commitments on human rights. They cite examples of donor countries changing their aid policies from alleviating poverty in developing countries to providing military aid and resources to countries to fight terrorism. They reject the idea that terrorist groups can be isolated from the overall social and political matrix of poverty and underdevelopment. Terrorism, they argue, can only be effectively combated within a framework of peace and development that upholds social justice and human rights, promotes inclusion and empowerment, and enhances international understanding. The current move from foreign aid to military aid will result in increasing levels of poverty for people in many parts of the world and only succeed in jeopardizing human security by escalating local conflict.

THE TRIUMPH OF JUST WAR THEORY
(AND THE DANGERS OF SUCCESS)

Michael Walzer

Michael Walzer is a Professor at the School of Social Science, Institute for Advanced Study. He is the author of a number of books including Arguing about War *(2004),* Politics and Passion: Toward a More Egalitarian Liberalism *(2004),* On Toleration *(2000), and* Spheres of Justice: A Defense of Pluralism and Equality *(1983).*

Walzer surveys the history of just war theory to claim that arguments for the realist position that force is justified if it serves the interests of the sovereign state lost sway when moral arguments were injected back into the debate during the Vietnam War. Walzer then applies these insights about the "triumph of just war theory" to the contemporary context of war, arguing that politicians, political theorists, clerics, generals, and lawyers use the language of just war theory merely to justify their positions. Walzer worries that this use of just war theory risks having it lose the critical role it has always claimed by deflecting attention away from the actual business of war and of what soldiers do. He argues that justice still needs to be defended in a world where militarization, methods, and contexts change. Decisions about when and how to fight, as well as what happens when wars end, require constant scrutiny and critical analysis.

I

Some political theories die and go to heaven; some, I hope, die and go to hell. But some have a long life in this world, a history most often of service to the powers-that-be, but also, sometimes, an oppositionist history. The theory of just war began in the service of the powers. At least that is how I interpret Augustine's achievement: he replaced the radical refusal of Christian pacifists with the active ministry of the Christian soldier. Now pious Christians could fight on behalf of the worldly city, for the sake of imperial peace (in this case, literally, *pax Romana*); but they had to fight justly, only for the sake of peace, and always, Augustine insisted, with a downcast demeanor, without anger or lust.[1] Seen from the perspective of primitive Christianity, this account of just war was simply an excuse, a way of making war morally and religiously possible. And that was

indeed the function of the theory. But its defenders would have said, and I am inclined to agree, that it made war possible in a world where war was, sometimes, necessary.

From the beginning, the theory had a critical edge: soldiers (or, at least, their officers) were supposed to refuse to fight in wars of conquest and to oppose or abstain from the standard military practices of rape and pillage after the battle was won. But just war was a worldly theory, in every sense of that term, and it continued to serve worldly interests against Christian radicalism. It is important to note, though, that Christian radicalism had more than one version: it could be expressed in a pacifist rejection of war, but it could also be expressed in war itself, in the religiously driven crusade. Augustine opposed the first of these; the medieval scholastics, following in Aquinas's footsteps, set themselves against the second. The classic statement is Vitoria's: "Difference of religion cannot be a cause of just war." For centuries, from the time of the Crusades to the religious wars of the Reformation years, many of the priests and preachers of Christian Europe, many lords and barons (and even a few kings), had been committed to the legitimacy of using military force against unbelievers: they had their own version of *jihad*. Vitoria claimed, by contrast, that "the sole and only just cause for waging war is when harm has been inflicted."[2] Just war was an argument of the religious center against pacifists, on the one side, and holy warriors, on the other, and because of its enemies (and even though its proponents were theologians), it took shape as a secular theory — which is simply another way of describing its worldliness.

So the rulers of this world embraced the theory, and did not fight a single war without describing it, or hiring intellectuals to describe it, as a war for peace and justice. Most often, of course, this description was hypocritical: the tribute that vice pays to virtue. But the need to pay the tribute opens those who pay it to the criticism of the virtuous — that is, of the brave and virtuous, of whom there have been only a few (but one could also say: at least a few). I will cite one heroic moment, from the history of the academic world: sometime around 1520, the faculty of the University of Salamanca met in solemn assembly and voted that the Spanish conquest of Central America was a violation of natural law and an unjust war.[3] I have not been able to learn anything about the subsequent fate of the good professors. Certainly, there were not many moments like that one, but what happened at Salamanca suggests that just war never lost its critical edge. The theory provided worldly reasons for going to war, but the reasons were limited — and they had to be worldly. Converting the Aztecs to Christianity was not a just cause; nor was seizing the gold of the Americas or enslaving its inhabitants.

Writers like Grotius and Pufendorf incorporated just war theory into international law, but the rise of the modern state and the legal (and philosophical) acceptance of state sovereignty pushed the theory into the background. Now the political foreground was occupied by people we can think of as Machiavellian princes, hard men (and sometimes women), driven by "reason of state," who did what (they said) they had to do. Worldly prudence triumphed over worldly justice; realism over what was increasingly disparaged as naive idealism. The princes of the world continued to defend their wars, using the language of international law, which was also, at least in part, the language of just war. But the defenses were marginal to the enterprise, and I suspect that it was the least important of the state's intellectuals who put them forward. States claimed a right to fight whenever their rulers deemed it necessary, and the rulers took sovereignty to mean that no one could judge their decisions. They not only fought when they wanted; they fought how they wanted, returning to the old Roman maxim that held war to be a lawless activity: *inter arma silent lege* — which, again, was taken to mean that there was no law above or beyond the decrees of the state; conventional restraints on the conduct of war could always be overridden for the sake of victory.[4] Arguments about justice were treated as a kind of moralizing, inappropriate to the anarchic conditions of international society. For this world, just war was not worldly enough.

In the 1950s and early 1960s, when I was in graduate school, realism was the reigning doctrine in the field of "international relations." The standard reference was not to justice but to interest. Moral argument was against the rules of the discipline as it was commonly practiced, although a few writers defended interest as the new morality.[5] There were many political scientists in those years who preened themselves as modern Machiavellis and dreamed of whispering in the ear of the prince; and a certain number of them, enough to stimulate the ambition of the others, actually got to whisper. They practiced being cool and tough-minded; they taught the princes, who did not always need to be taught, how to get results through the calculated application of force. Results were understood in terms of "the national interest," which was the objectively determined sum of power and wealth here and now plus the probability of future power and wealth. More of both was almost always taken to be better; only a few writers argued for the acceptance of prudential limits; moral limits were, as I remember those years, never discussed. Just war theory was relegated to religion departments, theological seminaries, and a few Catholic universities. And even in those places, isolated as they were from the political world, the theory was pressed toward realist positions; perhaps for the sake of self-preservation, its advocates surrendered something of its critical edge.

Vietnam changed all this, although it took a while for the change to register at the theoretical level. What happened first occurred in the realm of practice. The war became a subject of political debate; it was widely opposed, mostly by people on the left. These were people heavily influenced by Marxism; they also spoke a language of interest; they shared with the princes and professors of American politics a disdain for moralizing. And yet the experience of the war pressed them toward moral argument. Of course, the war in their eyes was radically imprudent; it could not be won; its costs, even if Americans thought only of themselves, were much too high; it was an imperialist adventure unwise even for the imperialists; it set the United States against the cause of national liberation, which would alienate it from the Third World (and significant parts of the First). But these claims failed utterly to express the feelings of most of the war's opponents, feelings that had to do with the systematic exposure of Vietnamese civilians to the violence of American war-making. Almost against its will, the left fell into morality. All of us in the antiwar camp suddenly began talking the language of just war — though we did not know that that was what we were doing.

It may seem odd to recall the '60s in this way, since today the left seems all too quick to make moral arguments, even absolutist moral arguments. But this description of the contemporary left seems to me mistaken. A certain kind of politicized, instrumental, and highly selective moralizing is indeed increasingly common among leftist writers, but this is not serious moral argument. It is not what we learned, or ought to have learned, from the Vietnam years. What happened then was that people on the left, and many others too, looked for a common moral language. And what was most

available was the language of just war. We were, all of us, a bit rusty, unaccustomed to speaking in public about morality. The realist ascendancy had robbed us of the very words that we needed, which we slowly reclaimed: aggression, intervention, just cause, self-defense, noncombatant immunity, proportionality, prisoners of war, civilians, double effect, terrorism, war crimes. And we came to understand that these words had meanings. Of course, they could be used instrumentally; that is always true of political and moral terms. But if we attended to their meanings, we found ourselves involved in a discussion that had its own structure. Like characters in a novel, concepts in a theory shape the narrative or the argument in which they figure.

Once the war was over, just war became an academic subject; now political scientists and philosophers discovered the theory; it was written about in the journals and taught in the universities — and also in the (American) military academies and war colleges. A small group of Vietnam veterans played a major role in making the discipline of morality central to the military curriculum?[6] They had bad memories. They welcomed just war theory precisely because it was in their eyes a critical theory. It is, in fact, doubly critical — of war's occasions and its conduct. I suspect that the veterans were most concerned with the second of these. It is not only that they wanted to avoid anything like the My Lai massacre in future wars; they wanted, like professional soldiers everywhere, to distinguish their profession from mere butchery. And because of their Vietnam experience, they believed that this had to be done systematically; it required not only a code but also a theory. Once upon a time, I suppose, aristocratic honor had grounded the military code; in a more democratic and egalitarian age, the code had to be defended with arguments.

And so we argued. The discussions and debates were wide-ranging even if, once the war was over, they were mostly academic. It is easy to forget how large the academic world is in the United States: there are millions of students and tens of thousands of professors. So a lot of people were involved, future citizens and army officers, and the theory was mostly presented, though this presentation was also disputed, as a manual for wartime criticism. Our cases and examples were drawn from Vietnam and were framed to invite criticism (the debate over nuclear deterrence also used, in part, the language of just war, but this was a highly technical debate and engaged far fewer people than did Vietnam). Here was a war that we should never have fought, and that we fought badly, brutally, as if there were no moral limits. So it became, retrospectively, an occasion for drawing a line — and for committing ourselves to the moral casuistry necessary to determine the precise location of the line. Ever since Pascal's brilliant denunciation, casuistry has had a bad name among moral philosophers; it is commonly taken to be excessively permissive, not so much an application as a relaxation of the moral rules. When we looked back at the Vietnamese cases, however, we were more likely to deny permission than to grant it, insisting again and again that what had been done should not have been done.

But there was another feature of Vietnam that gave the moral critique of the war special force: it was a war that we lost, and the brutality with which we fought the war almost certainly contributed to our defeat. In a war for "hearts and minds," rather than for land and resources, justice turns out to be a key to victory. So just war theory looked once again like the worldly doctrine that it is. And here, I think, is the deepest cause of the theory's contemporary triumph: there are now reasons of state for fighting justly. One might almost say that justice has become a military necessity.

There were probably earlier wars in which the deliberate killing of civilians, and also the common military carelessness about killing civilians, proved to be counterproductive. The Boer war is a likely example. But for us, Vietnam was the first war in which the practical value of *jus in bello* became apparent. To be sure, the "Vietnam syndrome" is generally taken to reflect a different lesson: that we should not fight wars that are unpopular at home and to which we are unwilling to commit the resources necessary for victory. But there was in fact another lesson, connected to but not the same as the "syndrome": that we should not

fight wars about whose justice we are doubtful, and that once we are engaged we have to fight justly so as not to antagonize the civilian population, whose political support is necessary to a military victory. In Vietnam, the relevant civilians were the Vietnamese themselves; we lost the war when we lost their "hearts and minds." But this idea about the need for civilian support has turned out to be both variable and expansive: modern warfare requires the support of different civilian populations, extending beyond the population immediately at risk. Still, a moral regard for civilians at risk is critically important in winning wider support for the war ... for any modern war. I will call this the usefulness of morality. Its wide acknowledgement is something radically new in military history.

Hence the odd spectacle of George Bush (the elder), during the Persian Gulf war, talking like a just war theorist.[7] Well, not quite: for Bush's speeches and press conferences displayed an old American tendency, which his son has inherited, to confuse just wars and crusades, as if a war can be just only when the forces of good are arrayed against the forces of evil. But Bush also seemed to understand — and this was a constant theme of American military spokesmen — that war is properly a war of armies, a combat between combatants, from which the civilian population should be shielded. I do not believe that the bombing of Iraq in 1991 met just war standards; shielding civilians would certainly have excluded the destruction of electricity networks and water purification plants. Urban infrastructure, even if it is necessary to modern war-making, is also necessary to civilian existence in a modern city, and it is morally defined by this second feature.[8] Still, American strategy in the Gulf war was the result of a compromise between what justice would have required and the unrestrained bombing of previous wars; taken overall, targeting was far more limited and selective than it had been, for example, in Korea or Vietnam. The reasons for the limits were complicated: in part, they reflected a commitment to the Iraqi people (which turned out not to be very strong), in the hope that the Iraqis would repudiate the war and overthrow the regime that began it; in part, they reflected the political necessities of the coalition that made the war possible. Those necessities were shaped in turn by the media coverage of the war — that is, by the immediate access of the media to the battle and of people the world over to the media. Bush and his generals believed that these people would not tolerate a slaughter of civilians, and they were probably right (but what it might mean for them not to tolerate something was and is fairly unclear). Hence, although many of the countries whose support was crucial to the war's success were not democracies, bombing policy was dictated in important ways by the demos.

This will continue to be true: the media are omnipresent, and the whole world is watching. War has to be different in these circumstances. But does this mean that it has to be more just or only that it has to look more just, that it has to be described, a little more persuasively than in the past, in the language of justice? The triumph of just war theory is clear enough; it is amazing how readily military spokesmen during the Kosovo and Afghanistan wars used its categories, telling a causal story that justified the war and providing accounts of the battles that emphasized the restraint with which they were being fought. The arguments (and rationalizations) of the past were very different; they commonly came from outside the armed forces — from clerics, lawyers, and professors, not from generals — and they commonly lacked specificity and detail. But what does the use of these categories, these just and moral words, signify?

Perhaps naively, I am inclined to say that justice has become, in all Western countries, one of the tests that any proposed military strategy or tactic has to meet — only one of the tests and not the most important one, but this still gives just war theory a place and standing that it never had before. It is easier now than it ever was to imagine a general saying, "No, we can't do that; it would cause too many civilian deaths; we have to find another way." I am not sure that there are many generals who talk like that, but imagine for a moment that there are; imagine that strategies are evaluated morally as well as militarily; that civilian deaths are minimized; that new technologies

are designed to avoid or limit collateral damage, and that these technologies are actually effective in achieving their intended purpose. Moral theory has been incorporated into war-making as a real constraint on when and how wars are fought. This picture is, remember, imaginary, but it is also partly true; and it makes for a far more interesting argument than the more standard claim that the triumph of just war is pure hypocrisy. The triumph is real: what then is left for theorists and philosophers to do?

This question is sufficiently present in our consciousness that one can watch people trying to respond. There are two responses that I want to describe and criticize. The first comes from what might be called the postmodern left, which does not claim that affirmations of justice are hypocritical, since hypocrisy implies standards, but rather that there are no standards, no possible objective use of the categories of just war theory.[9] Politicians and generals who adopt the categories are deluding themselves — though no more so than the theorists who developed the categories in the first place. Maybe new technologies kill fewer people, but there is no point in arguing about who those people are and whether or not killing them is justified. No agreement about justice, or about guilt or innocence, is possible. This view is summed up in a line that speaks to our immediate situation: "One man's terrorist is another man's freedom fighter." On this view, there is nothing for theorists and philosophers to do but choose sides, and there is no theory or principle that can guide their choice. But this is an impossible position, for it holds that we cannot recognize, condemn, and actively oppose the murder of innocent people.

A second response is to take the moral need to recognize, condemn and oppose very seriously and then to raise the theoretical ante — that is, to strengthen the constraints that justice imposes on warfare. For theorists who pride themselves on living, so to speak, at the critical edge, this is an obvious and understandable response. For many years, we have used the theory of just war to criticize American military actions, and now it has been taken over by the generals and is being used to explain and justify those actions. Obviously, we must resist. The easiest way to resist is to make noncombatant immunity into a stronger and stronger rule, until it is something like an absolute rule: all killing of civilians is (something close to) murder; therefore any war that leads to the killing of civilians is unjust; therefore every war is unjust. So pacifism reemerges from the very heart of the theory that was originally meant to replace it. This is the strategy adopted, most recently, by many opponents of the Afghanistan war. The protest marches on American campuses featured banners proclaiming, "Stop the Bombing!" and the argument for stopping was very simple (and obviously true): bombing endangers and kills civilians. The marchers did not seem to feel that anything more had to be said.

Since I believe that war is still, sometimes, necessary, this seems to me a bad argument and, more generally, a bad response to the triumph of just war theory. It sustains the critical role of the theory vis-à-vis war generally, but it denies the theory the critical role it has always claimed, which is internal to the business of war and requires critics to attend closely to what soldiers try to do and what they try not to do. The refusal to make distinctions of this kind, to pay attention to strategic and tactical choices, suggests a doctrine of radical suspicion. This is the radicalism of people who do not expect to exercise power or use force, ever, and who are not prepared to make the judgments that this exercise and use require. By contrast, just war theory, even when it demands a strong critique of particular acts of war, is the doctrine of people who do expect to exercise power and use force. We might think of it as a doctrine of radical responsibility, because it holds political and military leaders responsible, first of all, for the well-being of their own people, but also for the well-being of innocent men and women on the other side. Its proponents set themselves against those who will not think realistically about the defense of the country they live in and also against those who refuse to recognize the humanity of their opponents. They insist that there are things that it is morally impermissible to do even to the enemy. They also insist, however, that fighting itself cannot be morally impermissible. A just war is

meant to be, and has to be, a war that it is possible to fight.

But there is another danger posed by the triumph of just war theory — not the radical relativism and the near absolutism that I have just described, but rather a certain softening of the critical mind, a truce between theorists and soldiers. If intellectuals are often awed and silenced by political leaders who invite them to dinner, how much more so by generals who talk their language? And if the generals are actually fighting just wars, if *inter arma* the laws speak, what point is there in anything we can say? In fact, however, our role has not changed all that much. We still have to insist that war is a morally dubious and difficult activity. Even if we (in the West) have fought just wars in the Gulf, in Kosovo, and in Afghanistan, that is no guarantee, not even a useful indication, that our next war will be just. And even if the recognition of noncombatant immunity has become militarily necessary, it still conflicts with other, more pressing, necessities. Justice still needs to be defended; decisions about when and how to fight require constant scrutiny, exactly as they always have.

At the same time, we have to extend our account of "when and how" to cover the new strategies, the new technologies, and the new politics of a global age. Old ideas may not fit the emerging reality: the "war against terrorism," to take the most current example, requires a kind of international cooperation that is as radically undeveloped in theory as it is in practice. We should welcome military officers into the theoretical argument; they will make it a better argument than it would be if no one but professors took an interest. But we cannot leave the argument to them. As the old saying goes, war is too important to be left to the generals; just war even more so. The ongoing critique of war-making is a centrally important democratic activity.

II

Let me, then, suggest two issues, raised by our most recent wars, that require the critical edge of justice.

First, risk-free war-making. I have heard it said that this is a necessary feature of humanitarian interventions like the Kosovo war: soldiers defend-ing humanity, in contrast to soldiers defending their own country and their fellow-citizens, will not risk their lives; or, their political leaders will not dare to ask them to risk their lives. Hence the rescue of people in desperate trouble, the objects of massacre or ethnic cleansing, is only possible if risk-free war is possible.[10] But, obviously, it is possible: wars can be fought from a great distance with bombs and missiles aimed very precisely (compared with the radical imprecision of such weapons only a few decades ago) at the forces car-rying out the killings and deportations. And the technicians/soldiers aiming these weapons are, in all the recent cases, largely invulnerable to coun-terattack. There is no principle of just war theory that bars this kind of warfare. So long as they can aim accurately at military targets, soldiers have every right to fight from a safe distance. And what commander, committed to his or her own soldiers, would not choose to fight in this way whenever he or she could? In his reflections on rebellion, Albert Camus argues that one cannot kill unless one is prepared to die.[11] But that argument does not seem to apply to soldiers in battle, where the whole point is to kill while avoiding getting killed. And yet there is a wider sense in which Camus is right.

Just war theorists have not, to my knowledge, discussed this question, but we obviously need to do so. Massacre and ethnic cleansing commonly take place on the ground. The awful work might be done with bombs and poison gas delivered from the air, but in Bosnia, Kosovo, Rwanda, East Timor, and Sierra Leone, the weapons were rifles, machetes, and clubs; the killing and terrorizing of the population was carried out from close up. And a risk-free intervention undertaken from far away — especially if it promises to be effective in the long run — is likely to cause an immediate speed-up on the ground. This can be stopped only if the intervention itself shifts to the ground, and this shift seems to me morally necessary. The aim of the intervention, after all, is to rescue people in trouble, and fighting on the ground, in the case as I have described it, is what rescue requires. But then it is no longer risk-free. Why would anyone undertake it?

In fact, risks of this sort are a common feature of *jus in bello*, and while there are many examples of soldiers unwilling to accept them, there are also many examples of their acceptance. The principle is this: when it is our action that puts innocent people at risk, even if the action is justified, we are bound to do what we can to reduce those risks, even if this involves risks to our own soldiers. If we are bombing military targets in a just war, and there are civilians living near these targets, we have to adjust our bombing policy — by flying at lower altitudes, say — so as to minimize the risks we impose on civilians. Of course, it is legitimate to balance the risks; we cannot require our pilots to fly suicidal missions. They have to be, as Camus suggests, prepared to die, but that is consistent with taking measures to safeguard their lives. How the balance gets worked out is something that has to be debated in each case. But what is not permis-sible, it seems to me, is what NATO did in the Kosovo war, where its leaders declared in advance that they would not send ground forces into battle, whatever happened inside Kosovo once the air war began. Responsibility for the intensified Serbian campaign against Kosovar civilians, which was the immediate consequence of the air war, belongs no doubt to the Serbian government and army. They were to blame. But this was at the same time a foreseeable result of our action, and insofar as we did nothing to prepare for this result, or to deal with it, we were blameworthy too. We imposed risks on others and refused to accept them for our-selves, even when that acceptance was necessary to help the others.[12]

The second issue concerns war's endings. On the standard view, a just war (precisely because it is not a crusade) should end with the restoration of the status quo ante. The paradigm case is a war of aggression, which ends justly when the aggressor has been defeated, his attack repulsed, the old boundaries restored. Perhaps this is not quite enough for a just conclusion: the victim state might deserve reparations from the aggressor state, so that the damage the aggressor's forces inflicted can be repaired — a more extensive understanding of restoration, but restoration still. And perhaps the peace treaty should include new security arrangements, of a sort that did not exist before the war, so that the status quo will be more stable in the future. But that is as far as the rights of victims go; the theory as it was commonly understood did not extend to any radical reconstitution of the enemy state, and international law, with its assumptions about sovereignty, would have regarded any imposed change of regime as a new act of aggression. What happened after World War II in both Germany and Japan was something quite new in the history of war, and the legitimacy of occupation and political reconstitution is still debated, even by theorists and lawyers who regard the treatment of the Nazi regime, at least, as justified. Thus, as the Gulf war drew to a close in 1991, there was little readiness to march on Baghdad and replace the government of Saddam Hussein, despite the denunciation of that government in the lead-up to the war as Nazi-like in character. There were, of course, both military and geopolitical arguments against continuing the war once the attack on Kuwait had been repulsed, but there was also an argument from justice: that even if Iraq "needed" a new government, that need could only be met by the Iraqi people themselves. A government imposed by foreign armies would never be accepted as the product of, or the future agent of, self-determination.[13]

The World War II examples, however, argue against this last claim. If the imposed government is democratic and moves quickly to open up the political arena and to organize elections, it may erase the memory of its own imposition (hence the difference between the western and eastern regimes in post-war Germany). In any case, humanitarian intervention radically shifts the argument about endings, because now the war is from the beginning an effort to change the regime that is responsible for the inhumanity. This can be done by supporting secession, as the Indians did in what is now Bangladesh; or by expelling a dictator, as the Tanzanians did to Uganda's Idi Amin; or by creating a new government, as the Vietnamese did in Cambodia. In East Timor, more recently, the UN organized a referendum on secession and then worked to set up a new government. Had there been, as there should have been, an intervention in Rwanda, it would certainly have aimed at replacing the Hutu Power regime. Justice would have required the replacement. But what kind of justice is this? Who are its agents, and what rules govern their actions?

As the Rwandan example suggests, most states do not want to take on this kind of responsibility, and when they do take it on, for whatever political reasons, they do not want to submit themselves to a set of moral rules. In Cambodia, the Vietnamese shut down the killing fields, which was certainly a good thing to do, but they then went on to set up a satellite government, keyed to their own interests, which never won legitimacy either within or outside of Cambodia and brought no closure to the country's internal conflicts. Legitimacy and closure are the two criteria against which we can test war's endings. Both of them are likely to require, in almost all the humanitarian intervention cases, something more than the restoration of the status quo ante — which gave rise, after all, to the crisis that prompted the intervention. Legitimacy and closure, however, are hard tests to meet. The problems have to do in part with strategic interests, as in the Vietnamese-Cambodian case. But material interests also figure in a major way: remaking a government is an expensive business; it requires a significant commitment of resources — and the benefits are largely speculative and nonmaterial. Yet we can still point to the usefulness of morality in cases like these. A successful and extended intervention brings benefits of an important kind: not only gratitude and friendship, but an increment of peace and stability in a world where the insufficiency of both is costly — and not only to its immediate victims. Still, any particular country will always have good reasons to refuse to bear the costs of these benefits; or it will take on the burden, and then find reasons to perform badly. So we still need justice's critical edge.

The argument about endings is similar to the argument about risk: once we have acted in ways that have significant negative consequences for other people (even if there are also positive consequences), we cannot just walk away. Imagine a humanitarian intervention that ends with the massacres stopped and the murderous regime overthrown; but the country is devastated, the economy in ruins, the people hungry and afraid; there is neither law nor order nor any effective authority. The forces that intervened did well, but they are not finished. How can this be? Is it the price of doing well that you acquire responsibilities to do well again ... and again? The work of the virtuous is never finished. It does not seem fair. But in the real world, not only of international politics, but also of ordinary morality, this is the ways things work (though virtue, of course, is never so uncomplicated). Consider the Afghan-Russian war: the American government intervened in a major way, fighting by proxy, and eventually won a big victory: the Russians were forced to withdraw. This was the last battle of the cold war. The American intervention was undoubtedly driven by geopolitical and strategic motives; the conviction that the Afghan struggle was a war of national liberation against a repressive regime may have played a part in motivating the people who carried it out, but the allies they found in Afghanistan had a very restricted idea of liberation.[14] When the war was over, Afghanistan was left in a state of anarchy and ruin. At that point, the Americans walked away and were certainly wrong, politically and morally wrong, to do so; the Russians withdrew and were right to do so. We had acted (relatively) well, that is, in support of what was probably the vast majority of the Afghan people, and yet we were bound to continue acting well; the Russians had acted badly and were off the hook; even if they owed the Afghan people material aid (reparations), no one wanted them engaged again in Afghan affairs. This sounds anomalous, and yet I think it is an accurate account of the distribution of responsibility. But we need a better understanding of how this works and why it works the way it does, a theory of justice-in-endings that engages the actual experience of humanitarian (and other) interventions, so that countries fighting in wars like these know what their responsibilities will be if they win. It would also help if there was, what there is not yet, an international agency that could stipulate and even enforce these responsibilities.

This theory of justice-in-endings will have to include a description of legitimate occupations,

regime changes, and protectorates — and also, obviously, a description of illegitimate and immoral activity in all these areas. This combination is what just war has always been about: it makes actions and operations that are morally problematic *possible* by constraining their occasions and regulating their conduct. When the constraints are accepted, the actions and operations are justified, and the theorist of just war has to say that, even if he sounds like an apologist for the powers-that-be. When they are not accepted, when the brutalities of war or its aftermath are unconstrained, he has to say that, even if he is called a traitor and an enemy of the people.

It is important not to get stuck in either mode — defense or critique. Indeed, just war theory requires that we maintain our commitment to both modes at the same time. In this sense, just war is like good government: there is a deep and permanent tension between the adjective and the noun, but no necessary contradiction between them. When reformers come to power and make government better (less corrupt, say), we have to be able to acknowledge the improvement. And when they hold on to power for too long, and imitate their predecessors, we have to be ready to criticize their behavior. Just war theory is not an apology for any particular war, and it is not a renunciation of war itself. It is designed to sustain a constant scrutiny and an immanent critique. We still need that, even when generals sound like theorists, and I am sure that we always will.

NOTES

1. Augustine's argument on just war can be found in *The Political Writings of St. Augustine* (1962: 162-183); modern readers will need a commentary: see Dean (1963: 134-171).

2. See Vitoria (1991: 302-304), and for commentary, Johnson (1975: 150-171).

3. See Boswell (1952:129), quoting Dr. Johnson: "'I love the University of Salamanca, for when the Spaniards were in doubt as to the lawfulness of conquering America, the University of Salamanca gave it as their opinion that it was not lawful.' He spoke this with great emotion...."

4. With some hesitation, I cite my own discussion of military necessity (and the references there to more sympathetic treatments): Walzer (1977: 144-151, 239-242, 251-255).

5. The best discussion of the realists is Smith (1986); chapter 6, on Hans Morgenthau, is especially relevant to my argument here.

6. Anthony Hartle is one of those veterans, who eventually wrote his own book on the ethics of war: *Moral Issues in Military Decision Making* (1989).

7. See the documents collected in Sifry and Cerf (1991: 197-352), which include Bush's speeches and a wide range of other opinions.

8. I made the case against attacks on infrastructural targets immediately after the war (but others made it earlier) in DeCosse (1992: 12-13).

9. Stanley Fish's op-ed piece in *The New York Times* (October 15, 2001) provides an example of the postmodernist argument in its most intelligent version.

10. This argument was made by several participants at a conference on humanitarian intervention held at the Zentrum fur interdisziplinare Forschung, Bielefeld University, Germany, in January 2002.

11. "A life is paid for by another life, and from these two sacrifices springs the promise of a value." Camus (1956: 169). See also the argument in act I of *The Just Assassins*. Camus (1958, esp. pp. 246-247).

12. For arguments in favor of using ground forces in Kosovo, see Buckley (2000: 293-94, 333-335, 342).

13. Bush's statement on stopping the American advance, and his declaration of victory, can be found in Sifry and Cerf (1991: 449-451); arguments for and against stopping can be found in DeCosse (1992: 13-14, 29-32).

14. Artyom Borovik (1990) provides a useful, though highly personal, account of the Russian war in Afghanistan; for an academic history, see Goodson (2001).

REFERENCES

Augustine. *The Political Writings of St. Augustine.* Ed. Henry Paolucci. Chicago: Henry Regnery Company, 1962.

Borovik, Artyom. *The Hidden War: A Russian Journalist's Account of the Soviet War in Afghanistan.* London: Faber and Faber, 1990.

Boswell, James. *Life of Samuel Johnson LL.D. Great Books of the Western World.* Vol. 44. Ed. Robert Maynard Hutchins. Chicago: Encyclopedia Britannica, 1952.

Buckley, William Joseph. *Kosovo: Contending Voices on Balkan Interventions.* Grand Rapids: William B. Eerdmans Publishing Company, 2000.

Camus, Albert. *The Rebel.* Trans. Anthony Bower. New York: Vintage, 1956.

—. *Caligula and Three Other Plays.* Trans. Stuart Gilbert. New York: Vintage, 1958.

Dean, Herbert A. *The Political and Social Ideas of St. Augustine.* New York: Columbia University Press, 1963.

DeCosse, David E., ed. *But Was It Just? Reflections on the Morality of the Persian Gulf War.* New York: Doubleday, 1992.

Goodson, Larry P. *Afghanistan's Endless War: State Failure, Regional Politics, and the Rise of the Taliban.* Seattle: University of Washington Press, 2001.

Hartle, Anthony E. *Moral Issues in Military Decision Making.* Lawrence: University Press of Kansas, 1989.

Johnson, James Turner. *Ideology, Reason, and the Limitation of War: Religious and Secular Concepts, 1200-1740.* Princeton: Princeton University Press, 1975.

Sifry, Micah L., and Cerf, Christopher, eds. *The Gulf War: History, Documents, Opinions.* New York: Times Books, 1991.

Smith, Michael Joseph. *Realist Thought from Weber to Kissinger.* Baton Rouge: Louisiana State University Press, 1986.

Vitoria, Francisco de. *Political Writings.* Ed. Anthony Pagden and Jeremy Lawrance. Cambridge: Cambridge University Press, 1991.

Walzer, Michael. *Just and Unjust Wars.* New York: Basic Books, 1977.

THE SLIPPERY SLOPE TO PREVENTIVE WAR

Neta C. Crawford

Neta Crawford teaches political science at the University of Massachusetts, Amherst. She is the author of Argument and Change in World Politics: Ethics, Decolonization and Humanitarian Intervention *(2002) and* How Sanctions Work: Lessons from South Africa *(1999).*

   Crawford examines arguments for the preemptive doctrine used by the Bush administration to justify war. She argues that the contemporary context of increased fear and the perception of vulnerability coupled with the idea that the U.S. faces rogue enemies who hate everything about the U.S. and what it stands for has made it possible for the U.S. to justify taking the offensive to preempt further attacks. She outlines four conditions for legitimate preemption: the "self" in self-defense against aggression should be defined narrowly and not in terms of what will protect imperial interests or increase economic well-being; there should be strong evidence that war is inevitable and will happen in the immediate future; preemption should be likely to succeed in reducing the threat by finding the source of the threat and eliminating the damage it was about to do; and military force must be necessary and other options exhausted.

The Bush administration's arguments in favor of a preemptive doctrine rest on the view that warfare has been transformed. As Colin Powell argues, "It's a different world ... it's a new kind of threat."[1] And in several important respects, war has changed along the lines the administration suggests, although that transformation has been under way for at least the last ten to fifteen years. Unconventional adversaries prepared to wage unconventional war can conceal their movements, weapons, and immediate intentions and conduct devastating surprise attacks.[2] Nuclear, chemical, and biological weapons, though not widely dispersed, are more readily available than they were in the recent past. And the everyday infrastructure of the United States can be turned against it as were the planes the terrorists hijacked on September 11, 2001. Further, the administration argues that we face enemies who "reject basic human values and hate the United States and everything for which it stands."[3] Although vulnerability could certainly be reduced in many ways, it is impossible to achieve complete invulnerability.

Such vulnerability and fear, the argument goes, means the United States must take the offensive. Indeed, soon after the September 11, 2001, attacks, members of the Bush administration began equating self-defense with preemption:

> There is no question but that the United States of America has every right, as every country does, of self-defense, and the problem with terrorism is that there is no way to defend against the terrorists at every place and every time against every conceivable technique. Therefore, the only way to deal with the terrorist network is to take the battle to them. That is in fact what we're doing. That is in effect self-defense of a preemptive nature.[4]

The character of potential threats becomes extremely important in evaluating the legitimacy of the new preemption doctrine, and thus the assertion that the United States faces rogue enemies who oppose everything about the United States must be carefully evaluated. There is certainly robust evidence to believe that al-Qaeda members desire to harm the United States and American citizens. The National Security Strategy makes a questionable leap, however, when it assumes that "rogue states" also desire to harm the United States and pose an imminent military threat. Further, the administration blurs the distinction between "rogue states" and terrorists, essentially erasing the difference between terrorists and those states in which they reside: "We make no distinction between terrorists and those who knowingly harbor or provide aid to them."[5] But these distinctions do indeed make a difference.

Legitimate preemption could occur if four necessary conditions were met. First, the party contemplating preemption would have a narrow conception of the "self" to be defended in circumstances of self-defense. Preemption is not justified to protect imperial interests or assets taken in a war of aggression. Second, there would have to be strong evidence that war was inevitable and likely in the immediate future. Immediate threats are those which can be made manifest within days or weeks unless action is taken to thwart them. This requires clear intelligence showing that a potential aggressor has both the capability and the intention to do harm in the near future. Capability alone is not a justification. Third, preemption should be likely to succeed in reducing the threat. Specifically, there should be a high likelihood that the source of the military threat can be found and the damage that it was about to do can be greatly reduced or eliminated by a preemptive attack. If preemption is likely to fail, it should not be undertaken. Fourth, military force must be necessary; no other measures can have time to work or be likely to work.

A Defensible Self

On the face of it, the self-defense criteria seem clear. When our lives are threatened, we must be able to defend ourselves using force if necessary.

But self-defense may have another meaning, that in which our "self" is expressed not only by mere existence, but also by a free and prosperous life. For example, even if a tyrant would allow us to live, but not under institutions of our own choosing, we may justly fight to free ourselves from political oppression. But how far do the rights of the self extend? If someone threatens our access to food, or fuel, or shelter, can we legitimately use force? Or if they allow us access to the material goods necessary for our existence, but charge such a high price that we must make a terrible choice between food and health care, or between mere existence and growth, are we justified in using force to secure access to a good that would enhance the self? When economic interests and vulnerabilities are understood to be global, and when the moral and political community of democracy and human rights are defined more broadly than ever before, the self-conception of great powers tends to enlarge. But a broad conception of self is not necessarily legitimate and neither are the values to be defended completely obvious.

For example, the U.S. definition of the self to be defended has become very broad. The administration, in its most recent Quadrennial Defense Review, defines "enduring national interests" as including "contributing to economic wellbeing," which entails maintaining "vitality and productivity of the global economy" and "access to key markets and strategic resources." Further, the goal of U.S. strategy, according to this document, is to maintain "preeminence."[6] The National Security Strategy also fuses ambitious political and economic goals with security: "The U.S. national security strategy will be based on a distinctly American internationalism that reflects the fusion of our values and our national interests. The aim of this strategy is to help make the world not just safer but better." And "today the distinction between domestic and foreign affairs is diminishing."[7]

If the self is defined so broadly and threats to this greater "self" are met with military force, at what point does self-defense begin to look like aggression? As Richard Betts has argued, "When security is defined in terms broader than protecting the near-term integrity of national sovereignty and borders, the distinction between offense and defense blurs hopelessly.... Security can be as insatiable an appetite as acquisitiveness — there may never be enough buffers."[8] The large self-conception of the United States could lead to a tendency to intervene everywhere that this greater self might conceivably be at risk of, for example, losing access to markets. Thus, a conception of the self that justifies legitimate preemption in self-defense must be narrowly confined to immediate risks to life and health within borders or to the life and health of citizens abroad.

Threshold and Conduct of Justified Preemption

The Bush administration is correct to emphasize the United States' vulnerability to terrorist attack. The administration also argues that the United States cannot wait for a smoking gun if it comes in the form of a mushroom cloud. There may be little or no evidence in advance of a terrorist attack using nuclear, chemical, or biological weapons. Yet, under this view, the requirement for evidence is reduced to a fear that the other has, or might someday acquire, the means for an assault. But the bar for preemption seems to be set too low in the Bush administration's National Security Strategy. How much and what kind of evidence is necessary to justify preemption? What is a credible fear that justifies preemption?

As Michael Walzer has argued persuasively in *Just and Unjust Wars*, simple fear cannot be the only criterion. Fear is omnipresent in the context of a terrorist campaign. And if fear was once clearly justified, when and how will we know that a threat has been significantly reduced or eliminated? The nature of fear may be that once a group has suffered a terrible surprise attack, a government and people will, justifiably, be vigilant. Indeed they may, out of fear, be aware of threats to the point of hypervigilance — seeing small threats as large, and squashing all potential threats with enormous brutality.

The threshold for credible fear is necessarily lower in the context of contemporary counterterrorism war, but the consequences of lowering the threshold may be increased instability and the pre-

mature use of force. If this is the case, if fear justifies assault, then the occasions for attack will potentially be limitless since, according to the Bush administration's own arguments, we cannot always know with certainty what the other side has, where it might be located, or when it might be used. If one attacks on the basis of fear, or suspicion that a potential adversary may someday have the intention and capacity to harm you, then the line between preemptive and preventive war has been crossed. Again, the problem is knowing the capabilities and intentions of potential adversaries.

There is thus a fine balance to be struck. The threshold of evidence and warning cannot be too low, where simple apprehension that a potential adversary might be out there somewhere and may be acquiring the means to do the United States harm triggers the offensive use of force. This is not preemption, but paranoid aggression. We must, as stressful as this is psychologically, accept some vulnerability and uncertainty. We must also avoid the tendency to exaggerate the threat and inadvertently to heighten our own fear. For example, although nuclear weapons are more widely available than in the past, as are delivery vehicles of medium and long range, these forces are not yet in the hands of dozens of terrorists. A policy that assumes such a dangerous world is, at this historical juncture, paranoid. We must, rather than assume this is the present case or will be in the future, work to make this outcome less likely.

On the other hand, the threshold of evidence and warning for justified fear cannot be so high that those who might be about to do harm get so advanced in their preparations that they cannot be stopped or the damage limited. What is required, assuming a substantial investment in intelligence gathering, assessment, and understanding of potential advisories, is a policy that both maximizes our understanding of the capabilities and intentions of potential adversaries and minimizes our physical vulnerability. While uncertainty about intentions, capabilities, and risk can never be eliminated, it can be reduced.

Fear of possible future attack is not enough to justify preemption. Rather, aggressive intent, coupled with a capacity and plans to do immediate harm, is the threshold that may trigger justified preemptive attacks. We may judge aggressive intent if the answer to these two questions is yes: First, have potential aggressors said they want to harm us in the near future or have they harmed us in the recent past? Second, are potential adversaries moving their forces into a position to do significant harm?

While it might be tempting to assume that secrecy on the part of a potential adversary is a sure sign of aggressive intentions, secrecy may simply be a desire to prepare a deterrent force. After all, potential adversaries may feel the need to look after their own defense against their neighbors or even the United States. We cannot assume that all forces in the world are aimed offensively at the United States and that all want to broadcast their defensive preparations — especially if that means they might become the target of a preventive offensive strike by the United States.

The conduct of preemptive actions must be limited in purpose to reducing or eliminating the immediate threat. Preemptive strikes that go beyond this purpose will, reasonably, be considered aggression by the targets of such strikes. Those conducting preemptive strikes should also obey the *jus in bello* limits of just war theory, specifically avoiding injury to noncombatants and avoiding disproportionate damage. For example, in the case of the plans for the September 11, 2001, attacks, on these criteria — and assuming intelligence warning of preparations and clear evidence of aggressive intent — a justifiable preemptive action would have been the arrest of the hijackers of the four aircraft that were to be used as weapons. But, prior to the attacks, taking the war to Afghanistan to attack al-Qaeda camps or the Taliban could not have been justified preemption.

The Risks of Preventive War

Foreign policies must not only be judged on grounds of legality and morality, but also on grounds of prudence. Preemption is only prudent if it is limited to clear and immediate dangers and if there are limits to its conduct — proportionality, discrimination, and limited aims. If preemption

becomes a regular practice or if it becomes the cover for a preventive offensive war doctrine, the strategy then may become self-defeating as it increases instability and insecurity.

Specifically, a legitimate preemptive war requires that states identify that potential aggressors have both the capability and the intention of doing great harm to you in the immediate future. However, while capability may not be in dispute, the motives and intentions of a potential adversary may be misinterpreted. Specifically, states may mobilize in what appear to be aggressive ways because they are fearful or because they are aggressive. A preemptive doctrine which has, because of great fear and a desire to control the international environment, become a preventive war doctrine of eliminating potential threats that may materialize at some point in the future is likely to create more of both fearful and aggressive states. Some states may defensively arm because they are afraid of the preemptive-preventive state; others may arm offensively because they resent the preventive war aggressor who may have killed many innocents in its quest for total security.

In either case, whether states and groups armed because they were afraid or because they have aggressive intentions, instability is likely to grow as a preventive war doctrine creates the mutual fear of surprise attack. In the case of the U.S. preemptive-preventive war doctrine, instability is likely to increase because the doctrine is coupled with the U.S. goal of maintaining global preeminence and a military force "beyond challenge."[9]

Further, a preventive offensive war doctrine undermines international law and diplomacy, both of which can be useful, even to hegemonic powers. Preventive war short-circuits nonmilitary means of solving problems. If all states reacted to potential adversaries as if they faced a clear and present danger of imminent attack, security would be destabilized as tensions escalated along already tense borders and regions. Article 51 of the UN Charter would lose much of its force. In sum, a preemptive-preventive doctrine moves us closer to a state of nature than a state of international law. Moreover, while preventive war doctrines assume that today's potential rival will become tomorrow's adversary, diplomacy or some other factor could work to change the relationship from antagonism to accommodation. As Otto von Bismarck said to Wilhelm I in 1875, "I would ... never advise Your Majesty to declare war forthwith, simply because it appeared that our opponent would begin hostilities in the near future. One can never anticipate the ways of divine providence securely enough for that."[10]

One can understand why any administration would favor preemption and why some would be attracted to preventive wars if they think a preventive war could guarantee security from future attack. But the psychological reassurance promised by a preventive offensive war doctrine is at best illusory, and at worst, preventive war is a recipe for conflict. Preventive wars are imprudent because they bring wars that might not happen and increase resentment. They are also unjust because they assume perfect knowledge of an adversary's ill intentions when such a presumption of guilt may be premature or unwarranted. Preemption can be justified, on the other hand, if it is undertaken due to an immediate threat, where there is no time for diplomacy to be attempted, and where the action is limited to reducing that threat. There is a great temptation, however, to step over the line from preemptive to preventive war, because that line is vague and because the stress of living under the threat of war is great. But that temptation should be avoided, and the stress of living in fear should be assuaged by true prevention — arms control, disarmament, negotiations, confidence-building measures, and the development of international law.

NOTES

1. Colin Powell, "Perspectives: Powell Defends a First Strike as Iraq Option" interview, *New York Times*, September 8, 2002, sec. 1, p. 18.
2. For more on the nature of this transformation, see Neta C. Crawford, "Just War Theory and the U.S. Counterterror War," *Perspectives on Politics* (March 2003).
3. "The National Security Strategy of the United States of America September 2002," p. 14; available at www.whitehouse.gov/nsc/nss.pdf.
4. Donald H. Rumsfeld, "Remarks at Stakeout Outside ABC TV Studio," October 28, 2001; available at www.defenselink.mil/news/Oct2001/t10292001_t1 028sd3.html.
5. "National Security Strategy," p. 5.
6. Department of Defense, "Quadrennial Defense Review" (Washington, D.C.: U.S. Government Printing Office, September 30, 2001), pp. 2, 30, 62.
7. "National Security Strategy," pp. 1, 31.
8. Richard K. Betts, *Surprise Attack: Lessons for Defense Planning* (Washington, D.C.: Brookings Institution, 1982), pp. 14-43.
9. Department of Defense, "Quadrennial Defense Review," pp. 30, 62; and "Remarks by President George W. Bush at 2002 Graduation Exercise of the United States Military Academy, West Point, New York," June 1, 2002; available at www.whitehouse.gov/news/releases/2002/06/20020601-3.html.
10. Quoted in Gordon A. Craig, *The Politics of the Prussian Army, 1640-1945* (Oxford: Oxford University Press, 1955), p. 255.

A REQUIEM FOR VOICELESSNESS:
PAKISTANIS AND MUSLIMS IN THE US

Asma Barlas

Asma Barlas is in the Politics Department at Ithaca College in New York. She is the author of Islam, Muslims, and the U.S.: Essays on Religion and Politics *(2004),* "Believing Women" in Islam: Unreading Patriarchal Interpretations of the Qur'an *(2002), and* Democracy, Nationalism, and Communalism: The Colonial Legacy in South Asia *(1995).*

   Barlas examines what state and global responses to the attacks on 9/11 have meant for citizens within the U.S., specifically Muslims. She argues that new laws such as the Patriot Act bring to the surface patterns of racism that mirror and reproduce colonialist thinking and relationships. These laws, she argues, have made it easy to typecast all Muslims and Arabs as terrorists. Barlas takes the depersonalization and dehumanization of Muslims to be reflective of the racist nature of fear and paranoia, a racism that categorizes Muslims as "other" and casts them as unpredictable and unknowable. She notes the difficulty of voicing dissent and being heard in a context in which criticism can be silenced through legal sanctions and by the media. She also notes the tension of voicing dissent in her own case as someone who fled military rule in Pakistan and has benefited from the American legal and educational system.

I have been asked to address the situation of Pakistanis in the US at this historical conjuncture. However, it is difficult to do that without also speaking about Muslims in the US. But, a great deal of what is happening to Muslims reflects the attitudes and actions of those who are not Muslims. As such, a commentary on Pakistanis cannot help being a commentary on nonPakistanis as well.

At the outset, I should note that I view racism as part of a larger system of historically existing oppression whose quintessential expression was colonialism. In fact, I believe that contemporary racism mirrors and reproduces colonialist discourses and relationships. Accordingly, I draw upon some of the concepts and terminology of colonialism to speak about racism. My intent in doing this isn't to erase historical particularities, but to stress the universality of those modes of misrecognition in which racism is embedded.

Also, what I offer here is not a systematic analysis, but some reflections on civil liberties, the challenges I face as a Muslim-Pakistani-American in the present political milieu, and the psychology of racism, in particular, the mindset of the colonizer, which I address by way of a selective reading of Albert Memmi's work.[1]

"The Mark of the Plural"[2]

The assault on civil liberties in the wake of 9/11 has been stunning as much for its speed as for its content and its ever-widening scope. New laws — notably the hideously mis-named Patriot Act — have legalized racial profiling, surveillance, pre-emptive arrests and detentions, secret courts, and the denial of legal rights not only to those accused of terrorism, but also those suspected of harboring hostile intent toward the US.

Most of these measures target Muslim and Arab men. For instance, all men over 16 from several Muslim countries, including Pakistan, are now required to "be fingerprinted, photographed and interviewed" by the INS. Since the start of the program, "3,000 Pakistanis have fled to Canada and 1,100 have been deported"; as many as 50,000 are expected to return to Pakistan on their own "before it's all over."[3]

A measure currently under debate would change citizenship laws so that not everyone born in the US will be entitled to citizenship any more while those who are citizens can have their citizenship revoked if they engage in activity considered hostile to the US (this provision isn't new, but it has rarely been used thus far). Meanwhile, at least one state is considering declaring antiwar protestors terrorists and incarcerating them for 25 years.

Disturbingly, there is talk of making these measures — which have been represented as provisional safeguards at a time of war — permanently into the law of the land, and given how quickly some of these laws have been adopted, this doesn't seem impossible.

I will leave it to the legal experts to discuss the impact of such laws on various groups, as well as on the constitutional framework within which citizens in electoral democracies exercise their rights. Instead, I want to focus on three other aspects.

First, as I noted, these measures basically are targeting Muslims and Arabs and while racial profiling is nothing new, it still begs the question of why it has been so easy to typecast Muslims and Arabs as terrorists, *notwithstanding* 9/11. I say "notwithstanding" because a tragedy, of whatever proportions, does not determine how one responds to it; nor are entire people always held culpable for the crimes of a few. Certainly, white people can claim uniquely individualized identities as a way of freeing themselves from the burdens of collective responsibility; thus Hitler remains Hitler and Timothy McVeigh Timothy McVeigh; neither becomes the essentialized essence of white folks.

But Muslims and Arabs and people of color cannot claim such individuality because they are always branded with the "mark of the plural," as Memmi calls it. As he says,

The colonized is never characterized in an individual manner [but] ... entitled only to drown in an anonymous collectivity ('They are this.' 'They are all the same.'). If a colonized servant does not come in one morning, the colonizer will not say that she is ill, or that she is cheating, or that she is tempted not to abide by an oppressive contract. ... He will say, 'You can't count on them.' ... He refuses to consider personal, private occurrences in his maid's life; that life in a specific sense does not interest him, and his maid does not exist as an individual.[4]

This could be an elegy for Muslims and Arabs in the US today, who are being held hostage for the acts of a tiny minority of extremists that they themselves decry. I don't want to underestimate the role of fear and paranoia in generating a suspicion of Muslims but, again, this does not explain why the fear and paranoia take the form they do, namely, the depersonalization and dehumanization of Muslims. To understand that, we need to understand the deeply racist nature of the fear and paranoia.

And this brings me to the second point. It isn't accidental that such a massive assault on civil liberties has taken the form of an attack on the familiar, but still unrecognizable, "Muslim Other," to use a clichéd phrase that is still evocative of certain realities. The most obvious of these realities is that after more than 1,400 years, a majority of non-Muslim Westerners still don't know Muslims. Their humanity remains opaque like that of the colonized who "remains so mysterious after years of living with the colonizer." As the colonizer insists "('They are unpredictable!' 'With them, you never know!')"[5] And so it is with Muslims today, who are seen as unpredictable and unknowable.

That is why I believe that it is not just knowledge of 9/11, but also the *lack* of knowledge of Muslims and Arabs that has shaped the dominant US-American response to them. In fact, I believe it is the fear generated by an absence of recognition that explains most people's willingness to yield up rights that heretofore they had considered inalienable.

Such people view the problem of civil liberties

as a trade-off in which they agree to give up some of their rights — or, at least, don't protest overmuch when those rights are taken away — in order to ensure that the dreaded (Muslim) Other has none.

The fact that such a situation can appear as a trade-off reveals the extent to which most US-Americans can't see any commonalities between themselves and Muslims or Arabs, and, of course, this also keeps them from seeing the connections between what is being done to Muslims today and what might happen to them tomorrow. After all, once a law is on the books, it can target everyone equally.

Lastly, I cannot help seeing the parallels between the assault on civil liberties at home and preemptive wars and killing of civilians, including women and children, abroad. In fact, the doctrine of hostile intent first seems to have been tried out abroad.

Last year, a soldier from Ithaca said in an interview that US troops in Afghanistan "were told there were no friendly forces … If there was anybody there, they were the enemy. We were told specifically that if there were women and children to kill them." Later on, seemingly in an attempt to take the edge off his bald statement, he wrote a letter to the paper clarifying that "we were made aware that the hostile forces of the Whaleback might include women and children. In that event, if those women and children showed hostile intent, we were ordered to kill them as hostile forces …We were further informed that some of these children are trained starting at a very young age to be soldiers. Knowing this, we could not afford to just dismiss them as noncombatants."[6] Yet, there was no public outcry against the doctrine of hostile intent or killing children because US soldiers can't "afford" to see them as noncombatants, whatever *that* means!

It is no secret that most US-Americans aren't interested in what their governments do abroad even though methods of repression and control that governments use abroad are eventually imported for the purpose of domesticating critics and "minorities" at home.

My own view is that it is largely a belief in their own particularism that keeps most US-Americans from realizing "what it means to be part of a larger world; in the US, as the song goes, 'we are the world.' And, when the world does intrude upon people's consciousnesses, it generally is in the form of wars, natural disasters, and tales of horrific destitution. Between the violence and the charity that such representations inspire, there is little room for cultivating relationships with others based in mutual recognition or understanding. In fact, the very scale of US power has convinced its citizens that they don't need to know others since they can go it alone in everything. But one cannot live knowledgeably, ethically, or safely with people if one does not understand them or know in what ways one may be connected to or beholden to them. Ironically, then, US power renders Americans vulnerable to the world by estranging them from it."

This alienation results also from "a Manichean view of the universe in which a morally unique and uniquely moral US is juxtaposed to an evil and dangerous world mired in fanaticism, hatreds, and jealousies. To embrace such a view, however, is to do away with any notion of humility, and even with a sound view of morality since it is not given to a person, let alone to an entire people, to be only good."[7]

It is this view of themselves and others — this peculiar mode of self and Other recognition — that I believe explains the US-American response to 9/11 and Muslims and, therefore also the precarious situation of Muslims and Arabs in the US today.

On Voicelessness

A few hours before the US invasion of Iraq, I wrote a short essay in which I say that trying not to despair and bracing myself emotionally for what is to come, I can't help wondering what it means to live in the world's largest democracy today. As someone who grew up in a country (Pakistan) that has been under the shadow of military rule for most of its life, I was made aware of the powerlessness of people's voices early on. After all, that is essentially what life in a dictatorship is about:

the lack of a voice. And, yet, Pakistan's first military ruler, General Ayub Khan, was driven from office because several thousand people came out in the streets to protest his policies. Suddenly, people were willing to give voice to their anger, and their voices *mattered*.

Today, hundreds of millions of people all around the world, not just the US, have come out in the streets to denounce the Bush administration's policies on Iraq, as well as their own leaders who are backing him. But these voices of protest have produced not a single ripple of recognition from those hunkered down in their ideological bunkers in the White House. The genocidal massacre that is masquerading as a war is to go ahead anyway. Policies, Mr. Bush said, are not made by masses of people in the street. And, yet, it is in the name of giving voice to the Iraqi people that he is going to "liberate" Iraq!

Of course, the US invasion of Iraq has done much more than merely underscore people's voicelessness, but I keep struggling with this issue in part because I haven't had the right to speak freely, in a legal sense, for most of my life and I take it very seriously. However, now that I *do* have this right, I find that the right to speak does not ensure the right to be heard, that not all voices are equal and that voices of dissent and criticism can be silenced even in a democracy through legal sanctions or through the practice of shaming people by impugning their integrity in the media.

For criticizing US foreign policies that are unjust and are breeding anger and resistance on the part of many people and not just Muslims, I have been denounced as a bin Laden sympathizer and a voice that speaks "against us" in both the local and national press. Significantly, my critics have focused not on my arguments, but on the fact that I am a Muslim. Thus, a local critic advised his readers to start asking me why I hate America, a nice sleight of hand that allowed him to displace onto me all the rhetoric about evil Muslims generated by Mr. Bush's "why do they hate us?" demagoguery. I call it demagoguery because "love and hate, good and evil, are never mutually exclusive and ... each of us is equally capable of both." Similarly, US policies "may be good and bad and

evoke both disapproval and approbation." In fact, this duality defines my own experiences of the US.

I came to the US after General Zia ul Haq sacked me from the foreign service for having criticized him. Brought to power with US help, Zia had deposed the first democratically elected prime minister of Pakistan, Z.A. Bhutto, and had him executed.

I was among the first women to have been inducted into the foreign service, and would have been an ambassador today, but, dismissed without a trial and fearing for my safety and that of my son's, I fled Pakistan, leaving behind family, home, and friends.

But for the United States' supporting Zia, my life would have been very different.

In the US I returned to graduate school, receiving political asylum during the course of my studies. My life initially was one of newfound poverty, loneliness, single motherhood, and racial hatred directed against my son and myself. Eventually, however, both he and I completed our education and began new careers and new relationships.

But for the United States' giving me asylum, my life would have been very different.

Over the years, I have struggled to make sense of my two lives, lived and unlived, and of my relationship with the US. Clearly, on the one hand, I am a victim of its foreign policy that has brought military rulers like Zia to power in Pakistan. On the other hand, I am also a beneficiary of the US legal and educational systems.

This dual relationship I have with the US mirrors the duality of the US itself. This duality exists in the US's reverence for freedom, democracy and human rights, and its denial and violation of such values when it comes to Muslims, the poor, women and peasants in the 'Third World.' It exists in my neighbor's warning that people who criticize the United States should get out and in a friend's offer of a haven in her home. It exists in the attitude of those who embrace my differentness — as a way to validate their own liberalism — even as they retreat into hurt at any sign of differences between us. It exists in ... my being told that, unlike Pakistan, the US is a 'free' country, and in my being labeled 'anti-American' when I use that freedom to decry war and oppression."[8]

I contend that encountering this duality means eventually mirroring it, and this sense of a split self has only been enhanced by the circumstances in which Muslims in the US live today: living in a democracy, we don't enjoy all the rights that come with it.

Memmi on Colonialism

I have so far spoken about Muslims and as a Muslim and I want now to talk about some parallels between colonizers and those US-Americans who are enabling or countenancing the assault on civil liberties of Muslims and Arabs and also those who are perched on the sidelines, paralyzed by fear and uncertainty.

These parallels are suggested by Memmi's critique of French colonialism in Africa; for those who may not know, Memmi was a Tunisian Jew who wrote from the vantage point of both the colonizer and the colonized. As a Jew, he says he identified with the colonizer and yet, the reality of being an African in a colony ensured that he was part of the colonized.

I generally am not an advocate of quoting random passages from texts, but I thought it might not be inappropriate to do that today. I have purposely maintained Memmi's language, but as you are listening to these passages, you are free to substitute "racism" or "white privilege" or "US domination" every time you hear the word "colonialism."

It is true that discouraged citizens of free countries tell themselves that they have no voice in the nation's affairs, that their actions are useless, that their voice is not heard, and that the elections are fixed. Such people claim that the press and radio are in the hands of a few, that they cannot prevent war, or demand peace, or even obtain from their elected representatives that for which they were sent to parliament. However, they at least immediately recognize that they possess the right to do so; the potential if not the effective power; that they are deceived or weary, but not enslaved. They try to believe they are

free men, momentarily vanquished by hoaxes or stunned by demagogy. Driven beyond the boiling point, they are seized by sudden anger, break their paper chains and upset the politicians' little calculations. ....Thinking it over, they may feel guilty for not revolting more often; after all, they are responsible for their own freedom and if, because of fatigue or weakness or skepticism, they do not use it, they deserve their punishment.[9]

Who can completely rid himself of bigotry in a country where everyone is tainted by it, including its victims?

Not to be the only one guilty can be reassuring, but it cannot absolve.

It is not without detriment that one is willing to live permanently with one's guilt. The eulogizing of oneself and one's fellows, the repeated, even earnest, affirmation of the excellence of one's ways and institutions, one's cultural and technical superiority do not erase the fundamental condemnation which every colonialist carries in his heart.

For me, oppression is the greatest calamity of humanity. It diverts and pollutes the best energies ... of oppressed and oppressor alike. For if colonization destroys the colonized, it also rots the colonizer."[10]

Author's Note

This is a slightly amended version of a talk I gave at the forum on "Homeland Insecurity: Attack on Civil Liberties and Domestic Racism," held at Cornell University on April 12, 2003. Parts if it have been published before. I am thankful to Mecke Nagel for wanting to publish it in a journal on feminist studies.

NOTES

1. Albert Memmi, *The Colonizer and the Colonized*, Boston: Beacon Press, 1991.
2. Memmi, 85.
3. Traci Hukill, "A Safe Haven Turns Hostile," *AlterNet*, March 26, 2003.
4. Memmi, 85.

5. Memmi, 85.
6. Asma Barlas, "Hostile Intent: the elisions of war," *Daily Times*, June 18, 2002.
7. "9/11, the Academy and Renewal," talk given at Ithaca College, September 13, 2002.
8. Asma Barlas, "Reclaiming 'the duality within ourselves,'" *Ithaca Journal*, February 22, 2002.
9. Memmi, 91-92.
10. Ibid., 23; 9; 56; xvii.

COUNTER-OPPRESSIVE TERRORISM

Frank Cunningham

Frank Cunningham is Principal of Innis College and Professor of Philosophy and of Political Science at the University of Toronto. He is the author of Theories of Democracy: A Critical Introduction *(2002),* The Real World of Democracy Revisited and Other Essays on Socialism and Democracy *(1994), and* Democratic Theory and Socialism *(1987).*

Cunningham examines the utilitarian defense of counter-oppressive terrorism that rests on the idea that oppression is morally wrong and calls for a response. He argues that once we get clear about the meaning of the central concepts of terrorism, oppression, and the phenomenology of terrorism, doubt is cast on the argument that terrorism is necessary or effective for combating oppression. The phenomenology of terrorism demands that hatred be sustained and directed at everyone in a group, and this cannot but mold one's character in psychologically debilitating ways. Counter-oppressive terrorism, Cunningham argues, closes off possibilities for finding the underlying causes of oppression, makes cross-group alliances difficult, and sparks downward spirals of revenge-motivated violence. But while counter-oppressive terrorism cannot be justified on the grounds of eliminating oppression and improving relations, Cunningham argues that the "war on terrorism" needs to pay attention to combating policies that sustain oppression in other countries and across cultures.

Can a case be made for terrorism on counter-oppressive grounds? In many public forums, a simple response is that since terrorism can never be justified, the question is answered without examining this ground or any other. However, some not obviously demented or immoral people see terrorism as a sometimes unavoidable defense against oppressive relationships. Moreover, it is inimical to the discipline of philosophy to rule positions out of bounds without argumentation. In this contribution a case in favor of terrorism on counter-oppressive grounds is constructed and critically examined.

The core of the contribution was first prepared for a meeting of the Radical Philosophy Association on the topic of terrorism[1] where it treated the interface between terrorism and systematic oppression. No effort is made in the paper to defend the claim that such oppression is still alive and well in the world — being *radicals*, its original audience needed no proof of this. On the other hand, because they were also *philosophers*, the paper does proffer analyses of key terms and of the structure of some arguments regarding terrorism. It also, and mainly, aims to explicate and to refute the only defense of terrorism with any claim to plausibility: a utilitarian justification that terrorism is an unavoidably necessary means for combating oppression. Though seldom systematically advanced by political philosophers,[2] the defense is informally expressed by many who champion anti-oppressive struggles. Central to its refutation are some hypotheses about the phenomenological world-view of terrorism.

"Terrorism"

"Terrorism," as the term will be employed in this contribution, refers to violence or the threat of violence deliberately inflicted upon non-combatant civilians. This is a necessary condition for terrorism, to which two features of the attitudes of its perpetrators must be added: indifference to the victims and political intent. Each condition is complex.

To say that terrorists are indifferent to their victims means that they do not typically take into consideration whether, as individuals, the victims have engaged in activities that call for self-defense by the terrorists or that merit punishment for crimes committed against them or against those the terrorists see themselves as representing. However, this condition is not clear-cut, since though terrorists may not think of victims as *individually* guilty, they might consider them as somehow *collectively* guilty. (We shall return to this point.) As to the political motivation condition, while this is aptly included in most definitions of "terrorism,"[3] a broad conception of what counts as "political" must be held. For example, the deliberate bombing of civilians in a war counts as political since it aims to change the policies of a political regime or to unseat the regime altogether. By contrast, such things as violence by criminal extortionists cannot be construed as having political intent.

This characterization of terrorism departs from much journalistic or propagandistic use of the term to brand something as morally unacceptable, since, as it stands, the characterization does not entail that terroristic acts are always morally reprehensible. Rather, arguments need to be given for or against this view. Terrorists not infrequently describe their activities as forms of warfare, which, certainly in modern times, involve inflicting violence on civilians, sometimes deliberately. Perhaps this form of terrorism is morally unjustified, but arguments need to be marshalled to demonstrate this just as they are required in the case of other forms of terrorism. Or, if it is granted that violence against civilians in conventional wars may be justified, but it is denied that terrorist activities are comparable to such warfare, this denial itself needs justification.[4]

The aim of employing a value-neutral conception is to avoid blanket charges and counter charges — where one person's terrorism is another's war of liberation — in favor of interrogating the characteristics and contexts unique to terrorist activities, both to understand and to evaluate them. While terrorism may be classified into several types,[5] this paper will examine the situations where it is employed with broadly political intent in what its perpetrators see as an unavoidable tactic in countering their oppression. In these situations — subway bombing by the IRA, suicide attacks on Israeli civilians by Hamas, and the like — a central aim is political, and the terrorists are as passionately convinced of the moral justification of their deeds as critics are of their immorality.

"Oppression"

The notion of oppression pertains to protracted harm suffered by those who are members of a category of people just in virtue of being in this category. Sometimes such harm is deliberately inflicted, but this is not essential for oppression, which, at its core is structural or systemic. A well-known example is the way such things as workplace hours impede job advancement for women. Closer to the sort of oppression that sparks terrorism are the occupational ghettos and downward spirals in which people in formerly colonized countries find themselves in lacking the language, schooling, and respected cultural traits that have been inherited from protracted colonial occupation as requirements for upward mobility. While the line between structural oppression and non-structural, deliberately inflicted harm is often blurred, there is still a difference between them.

The Holocaust was a morally ghastly and quite deliberately planned campaign of annihilation. By contrast, if one accepts the explanation that the situation of Palestinian peoples in exile or enduring subordinated positions within Israel results from the geopolitical circumstance of a Jewish state superimposed on a relatively small land of preexisting Arab populations, this is an example of systemic oppression. To be sure, among the background conditions that made the Holocaust possible were centuries-old social, economic, and cultural structures of isolation and marginalization of Jewish peoples, and anti-Arab sentiment on the part of some Israelis and their supporters not infrequently prompts or sanctions violence, including state violence, directed against Palestinians. The difference is that perpetrators of the Holocaust were primarily motivated by malevolent intent specifically directed against Jews. No analogue of an Oslo Accord aimed at finding a way for Nazis and Jewish people in Europe to coexist is imaginable, and it would have been hard, if not impossible, to find Nazi supporters of the Holocaust who sincerely wished there could be "some other way" of realizing their goals.

An additional connotation of the term "oppression" is that harm inflicted on the oppressed is morally unjustified. It would be peculiar, for example, to describe thieves as oppressed, though they confront ongoing structural as well as deliberate impediments to their chosen way of making a living. That is, it would be odd to describe thieves as oppressed *qua* thieves, though some may have been led to thieving partly in virtue of membership in some other groups, which can properly described as oppressed.

Terrorists with political, religious, or national motives normally claim that morality is on their side, but, as in the case of the blurred line between oppressive and non-oppressive harm, the merits of such claims are not always clear. Despite U.S. President Bush's astoundingly inept description shortly after the 9/11 attacks on New York's World Trade Center of his country's war on terrorism as a "crusade," there is little evidence for a claim by Islamic extremists that the U.S. is spearheading a Christian and Jewish attack on the Islamic religion. On the other hand, to the extent that American actions are partly motivated by the political economy of oil and by the residual habits of Cold War geopolitics, a case can be made that such things as persisting inequalities, subjection to autocratic rule, denigration of people's religious or national identifications, and denial of national self-determination are unjustifiably oppressive.

These two features of oppression — its non-deliberate and its morally unjustified dimensions — complicate the scenarios this contribution addresses, where terrorism is used as a counter-oppressive instrument. To the extent that oppression is purely structural, it is inaccurate to describe oppression, no matter how terrible for the oppressed, as terrorism simply in virtue of being oppressive, since, as defined above, the latter must be deliberate. Insisting that terrorism is a matter of actions deliberately undertaken by specifiable individuals against people in some category means that the mere fact that some or all of those in an oppressor group profit from systemic harm suffered by others does not by itself warrant charging them with terrorism.

Rather, it is apt to speak of oppression as itself terroristic when part of being structural or systemic is that, in addition to breeding prejudicial attitudes on the part of those who profit from oppression, a disposition to threaten or carry out violence with political intent is engendered as well. One example is the employment of rape as a strategy for demoralization in ethnic warfare. Another is indiscriminant death squad violence directed against inhabitants of class or racial ghettos thought to be inhabited by political opponents of dictatorial rule. Not infrequently, oppression also prompts behavior by the oppressed that, in turn, is met with deliberate violence. Organized resistance on the part of some is often met with police, military, or vigilante violence directed against civilian communities as a whole.

A complication implicated by the "morally unjustified" condition of oppression is that members of a group may be subject to systemic constraints that they believe to be morally unjustified, though in fact they are not. I suppose, for instance, that Whites in the American South who fought a losing battle against racial desegregation of schools and other public places in the 1960s and 1970s sincerely thought themselves unjustifiably treated by the federal government. Some of the arguments against terrorism, shortly to be outlined, apply equally to terrorists who correctly believe themselves oppressed and to those, such as the Ku Klux Klan in the desegregation example, who falsely believe this. However, the force of cases *for* terrorism that appeal to oppression are affected by whether one is confronting what might be called "objective" oppression or not. That terrorists and their defenders sincerely believe themselves to be reacting to oppression allows one to comprehend and perhaps even empathize with them, but a case for justifying terrorism is substantially weaker when these beliefs are false.

An Anti-Oppressive Case for Terrorism

What about those situations where terrorists or the people on whose behalf they act are in fact oppressed? I take it that the most plausible argument for terroristic activity in these cases is the essentially consequentialist or, more specifically, utilitarian one that this is an unavoidably necessary means for overcoming oppression such that the harm suffered by victims of terrorism is outweighed by the benefits of those relieved from the burdens of oppression. One alternative claim is that terrorism on behalf of oppressed people is justified because those who profit from the oppression, even unwittingly, *deserve* to be punished. Another, sometimes related, conviction is that inflicting harm on members of an oppressor group is required to achieve justice conceived of as a matter of moral balance — "they must suffer as we do." And there are justifications, often standing behind these, from the direction of religious fundamentalism, which sees punishment of those from oppressor groups as a divine mandate. There can be no doubt that many defenders of terrorism passionately endorse one of these non-consequentialist justifications. Indeed, I am inclined to think that these, and not utilitarian reasoning, are foremost in the minds of many who actually engage in acts of terrorism. It is probably also the case that some terrorists are acting out of pure rage, with no clearly defined purpose.[6]

Without pursuing the point, it will suffice here to announce my view that these stances are too tenuous to merit detailed philosophical examination for the purpose of ascertaining their soundness (though they no doubt do merit historical, social-psychological, or theological interrogation). In addition to requiring some problematic philosophical theses about the nature and will of the deity, religiously based justifications are challenged by the mainstreams of every one of the world's religions on behalf of which they are advanced, and the notions of deserving punishment or achieving a balance of suffering are such that it would be diffi-

cult to construct a plausible, non-theistic explication and defense of them.

Many philosophers maintain that utilitarian arguments are also flawed. The term "utilitarian" is being used here in the technical sense associated with the ethical theories of philosophers such as John Stuart Mill. It is thus a broad enough term to cover all of the three general moral perspectives in which the political theorist, Jonathan Barker, sees defenses of the morality of terrorism (as well as of extraordinary state measures to combat it).[7] These are the protection of an ethnic, national, religious or other sort of "moral community"; combating violations of basic human rights; and "consequentualist" justifications of short-term harmful measures by reference to long-term goals.

On the utilitarian defense of counter-oppressive terrorism, systematic threats to or denigration of a religious, ethnic, or national community and denial of human rights count as forms of oppression that are supposed to necessitate terrorist acts to be overcome. Barker is sceptical about justifying the morality of group or state actions on the basis of consequentialism (which, depending on one's understanding of ethical theory, either includes utilitarianism or the terms are synonymous). This stance is shared by many anti-utilitarian ethical theorists. If their rejection of utilitarianism is sound, then defenders of terrorism are either thrown back onto ultimately theistic justifications or they must seek support in some other non-utilitarian ethical theory.

Perhaps defenses of terrorism can be constructed by reference to an ethics focused on basic rights, appeal to fundamental duties in the manner of Kantian ethics, or contractarianism, but these options will not be addressed in this paper. One reason is that, like what I see as theistically based views, attempts to turn these ethical theories to the defense of terrorism are extraordinarily weak.[8] Another reason pertains to the strategy of the next part of this paper. Critiques of political-philosophical positions (or any other kind for that matter) are traditionally sorted into "external" and "internal" categories, where the former try to defeat a position by giving reasons to reject basic principles employed or presupposed by its adherents, while the latter accept the principles and show that they do not support the intended conclusions. The advantages of internal critiques are that they do not require defending fundamental philosophical principles and they have a better chance than external critiques of making contact with and persuading adherents of a position to abandon it. The strategy of this paper is "quasi-internalist."

It is internalist because, while it does not accept all or even the main principles by which actual terrorists likely defend terrorism, it still aims to maintain a certain level of contact with supporters of terrorism, since even someone whose stance toward terrorism is coherently constructed in theistic, rights, Kantian, or contractarian terms could (and I think likely would) also welcome subsidiary support from a utilitarian direction. It is not a full-blown internalist critique, since a defender of anti-oppressive terrorism may as well, or instead, appeal to non-utilitarian grounds. It is only being assumed in this paper that other grounds cannot, themselves, withstand criticism, so a fully internal criticism would have to address them as well.

One kind of utilitarian argument can be constructed making reference to sentiments of terrorists and their defenders. The argument might run that success in terroristic retribution brings with it great psychological relief and satisfaction, while inability to achieve retribution is a source of overwhelming frustration. A similar argument could be advanced taking desire for revenge as the motive for terrorism. I intend to set aside this sort of justification as well.

In addition to requiring the crudest and most unrealistic sort of utilitarian calculations (adding up the sum of pleasures gained, for example, by a sated thirst for revenge and subtracting this sum from that of the pains suffered by the victims of terrorism), this argument more likely figures in a *reductio ad adsurdum* critique of utilitarianism itself than as a plausible argument to justify some instances of terrorism. Suppose that enough Ku Klux Klan members and their sympathizers were so intensely fearful of equality for African Americans that the psychological discomfort they would endure should desegregation succeed would outweigh, if only slightly, the relief this would afford southern African Americans. There would be something intuitively wrong with a moral theory that therefore condoned continuing segregation. The anti-oppressive case for terrorism taken seriously here, however, is more of the "rule" than of the "act" version of utilitarianism, where this means that certain principles or rules are endorsed for having generally beneficial consequences.

The advantage of this approach is that it avoids having to add up anticipated costs and benefits of specific acts each time they are being entertained, and it allows the utilitarian to recognize the legitimacy of general rules of moral behavior (for instance, against killing or theft). To be consistent, the utilitarian still must allow that the consequences of following a rule might sometimes be so detrimental that breaking it is justified, but in these instances the burden of proof rests on those who advocate deviating from the rule to show that this really is justified. Whatever else terrorism is or does, it inflicts widespread pain and suffering — indeed, it is essential for it to do so if the terrorists' aims are to be realized. Defenders of terrorism on anti-oppressive grounds who employ a "rule" version utilitarianism need not callously ignore or discount such pain, but, on the contrary, they can endorse a principle against such infliction and recognize that they have an obligation to justify violating this rule.

In the case of counter-oppressive terrorism, two explicit claims and one implicit one seem central for marshalling this justification. The explicit claims are, first, that sometimes terrorism is the only means available to the oppressed to combat their oppression. Second, whereas terrorism is a temporary measure, oppression is ongoing so that, unless successfully combated, if necessary by terrorism, it will continue to afflict large bodies of people into indefinite futures. So the pain and suffering caused by terrorism, terrible as it might be for some in the short run, pales by comparison to the ongoing misery of oppressive conditions of life for generations of entire peoples. The implicit claim is, of course, that terrorism at least has a chance of effectively combating oppression.

Counter-Arguments to Counter-Oppressive Terrorism

Counter-oppressive terrorism, then, is directed against non-combatant members of a society seen as implicated in the ongoing oppression of a body of people, which oppression the terrorist aims to combat. Some grounds for challenging terrorism simply require identifying it as a species of the infliction of pain and suffering on innocents and hence worthy of condemnation in virtue of this fact. A variation is Ted Honderich's view that while it is certain that pain will be inflicted on innocents by terrorist acts, there is "no certainty or significant probability" that anti-oppressive goals will be achieved.[9]

The first challenge has the virtue of directness but confronts the problem of civilian casualties in wartime. Those waging a modern war will know that a certain number of innocent civilians will perish or be harmed by military actions they initiate. An inviolate principle against harming others would lead to thoroughgoing pacifism, and perhaps this position can be defended, though few who wish their moral theories to have real-life application try. To argue that an exception to a pacifistic rule is sanctioned when a war is conducted in self-defense or otherwise in pursuit of some worthy cause invites the same defense regarding terrorism. A well-known justification of wartime violence is to maintain that harm of non-combatants is not intended in a (just) war, even though it is a regrettable and foreseeable consequence of military actions. This defense is obviously not available to the terrorist (whose deliberate targets are non-combatants), but, despite the ingenious arguments given in favor of this perspective, it is very difficult not to see in it an element of hypocrisy.[10] Terrorists can react by saying that at least they are honest about knowingly inflicting pain on civilians.

Honderich's challenge holds more promise, but as it stands it requires substantiating argumentation. By demanding of the defender of terrorism a demonstration of "significant" probability (if not certainty) of success in countering oppression, he flags a general problem, well known to philosophers of induction. Without some absolute standard against which degrees of significance can be measured, subjective estimates of the practical importance of being wrong or right will unavoidably come into play. (For instance, medical scientists will have to weigh the importance of making a new drug publicly available against the dangers of its possible side effects in deciding how extensively to test it.) Here there will be a standoff between the critic and the defender of counter-oppressive terrorism: the critic will consider it of paramount importance to preserve innocent lives, while the defender will maintain that the extent of suffering engendered by continuing oppression merits sanctioning a high degree of risk that terrorist tactics will fail.

Perhaps this problem for inductive reasoning can never be entirely overcome, but it can be mitigated by offering grounds, in the present case, for or against confidence in the success of counter-oppressive terrorism. A question now arises about how general such grounds must be. One problem with adducing such general grounds as pacifism or setting standards of probable success close to certainty is that the resulting arguments are unlikely to engage those who see terrorism as at least analogous to warfare and are therefore neither receptive to pacifistic values nor averse to the sorts of risk-taking endemic to military strategies. At an opposite extreme are grounds for criticizing terrorism, not *per se*, but as the issue comes up case-by-case. Such arguments have the disadvantages of getting mired down in contested details and, more seriously, of being more appropriate to after-the-fact critiques than to motivating a general rejection of the case for counter-oppressive terrorism. In the remainder of this paper, I shall advance some grounds for such rejection in a way that is intended both to have general application and to engage those sympathetic to the position in question on terrain they must take seriously.

The argument initially focuses on the third of the utilitarian argument's three premises. Recall that these are that terrorism is necessary for combating oppression; that the misery of ongoing oppression is worse than the effects of terrorism; and that terrorism can, in fact, make headway in overcoming oppression. The first and second of these will be set aside until the conclusion of the paper. Suffice it here to note that they can be challenged only in specific cases. To address the first claim, alternative means must be adduced and their potential effectiveness persuasively argued, which is not the sort of thing that can be shown in general. In comparing miseries, again, specific cases must be addressed. Though the third claim might also be argued with respect to specific instances, I wish to suggest that it is open as well to a more general critique.

Moreover, of the three claims, if it can be shown that in general terrorism has virtually no chance of overcoming structural oppression, then the entire counter-oppressive justification fails, and the other two parts of the justification turn on themselves. When the first claim is accurate, but terrorism cannot succeed in overcoming oppression, engaging in it ceases to be anything but an act of futile violence or vengeance. If terrorism cannot undo oppression, it will only compound an already bad situation.

As long as the arguments of this paper are assuming utilitarian principles, it must be granted that it might always be possible to imagine exceptions to any prescription. However, by sticking close to the perspective of at least supporters of terrorism (one that regards terrorism as an unfortunate but unavoidable necessity in the face of ongoing oppression) and advancing some hypotheses about features of a world-view engendered by terrorism, I submit that a burden that is in fact insurmountable can be placed before anyone who claims that the exceptional circumstances of oppression justify terrorism. The case being examined in this paper for terrorism-justifying circumstances is a general one — appeal to the pervasive and intractable nature of oppression; hence, a counter case must be likewise general. The attempt at such a case explicated below depends on some admittedly speculative views about the phenomenology of terrorism (or, for those who are wary of the philosophical connotations of this word, its social psychology).[11]

The Phenomenology of Terrorism

A political assumption is that counter-oppressive terrorism requires at least the passive support of large numbers of the people in whose name the terrorism is undertaken. This terrorism is protracted, often spanning generations, so pools of recruits are needed. Because police or military surveillance is typically extensive, support on the part of non-terrorists is required similar to the way that combatants in guerilla warfare depend upon support within civilian populations. At the very least the terrorists must depend upon passive acquiescence, so they are not turned in for engaging in activities which, were they conducted out of criminal motives, would not be tolerated by their neighbors or co-workers.

As to the phenomenological mind set or social world-view of the terrorist, it is hard to understand how willingness to engage in terrorism could be sustained without an element of group enmity, or, even if terrorism begins in a dispassionately calculating way, how it could avoid becoming infused with hatred toward members of what are seen as an oppressor group. If so (and again I speculate), then some features common to situations of group hatred are germane to the current discussion.

One of these is that while it is individuals who hate, the object of their hatred in places where group animosity is severe and protracted is not other individuals, but entire groups — the Jews, the Arabs, the English, the Serbs, the Americans. The other feature is that close to the center of a world-view in the grip of group hatred is the ascription of blame to the group as a whole. The hated group is seen, as a group, as responsible for the ills of one's own group — its economic circumstances; threats to its religion, national identity, or language; its ability to exercise political sovereignty; and so on. Taken together these features of the phenomenology of group hatred help to make it understandable how individuals could engage in terroristic activities: the victims of terrorism are not innocent at all but are responsible for the oppression of the terrorist's people just by being members of an oppressor group.

Examination of some moral implications of the phenomenology of group hatreds also suggests reasons why, in general, terrorism is incapable of combating oppression. A simple argument is that hatred is a morally undesirable character trait, and therefore any practice that foments it is to be avoided. While this argument is on the right track, without adumbration it does not suffice. Defenders of counter-oppressive terrorism on the utilitarian grounds being considered here can retort that attitudes of group enmity are necessary for terrorists to carry out actions, which, being self-sacrificing servants of their peoples' liberation as opposed to sadistic killers or the like, they would normally recoil from.

One rejoinder appeals to the psychological dynamics of hatred. It can be granted that group hatred begins as a facilitator of activities carried on or sanctioned in a cause viewed as noble (and which in the case of counter-oppressive terrorism as defined here does, indeed, have unobjectionable ultimate aims), but it can also be observed that attitudes like hatred are not the sorts of things that can be turned off like tap water once having served their purposes. Rather, hatred can easily become all-consuming and mold one's character in a psychologically debilitating, vengeful direction. Bad enough in itself, this stance and the terroristic acts it facilitates create or exacerbate attitudes of counter-hatred in people from what the terrorists and their supporters regard as their oppressor groups.[12] To the extent that oppression is sustained by prejudicial attitudes held by the latter, there is already a basis for the nurturing of such hatred.

Implicated in the defense of terrorism on counter-oppressive grounds is that part of what makes oppression systemic or structural is that it comes to be seen as a way of life, both by those from the oppressed and the oppressor groups, and terrorism is necessary for its value in calling attention to an intolerable situation. If the suggestions about terrorism and group hatred are more or less on target, however, a downward spiral is created which has the exact opposite effect by entrenching oppression even more deeply, and this in three, mutually reinforcing ways.

1. The moral blame dimension of group hatred impedes seeking the underlying causes of oppression. Arguably, a major breakthrough in feminist theory occurred when feminists began to direct attention to structures of women's oppression which victimize men as well as women (albeit in less obvious or violent ways), thus putting on the agenda such things as reforms in education, the law, labor policies, and so on. Moral blame of men as a group for the subordination of women distracts from such attention and the resulting structural campaigns. The same point applies to oppressive relations that prompt terrorism.

2. Attitudes of mutual group hatred make cross-group alliances extraordinarily difficult if not impossible. The point is often and aptly made that the "shock value" of terrorists' activities may realize one of their aims, namely, to put their causes into local and world news, but this is more likely than not to backfire in creating hostility toward them. The situation is worsened when mutual group hatred is added to the mix. This severely jeopardizes alliances between anti-oppressive members of the "oppressor" group (since they are all the more isolated when their peers are in the grip of reactive hatred) and those of the oppressed group (because the holistic object of group hatred sees only enemies on "the other side").

3. Mutual hatreds spark downward spirals of revenge-motivated violence, the destructiveness and tenacity of which we have seen in all-too-many parts of the world in recent times. This effect of group hatreds is, perhaps, the most pernicious, since it also prompts or sustains terroristic oppression. That economic, national, religious, or political oppression is (by the definition of the term) structural and therefore not at its core deliberate does not mean that it cannot also become deliberate and even terroristic. Sometimes this is undertaken in covert ways by states or state-sanctioned agents such as paramilitary death squads as a calculated way of dampening resistance, but it is easier to carry out overtly, which, in turn, is greatly facilitated when a state's own population harbors vengeful sentiments.

Concluding Remarks

The last conjecture has implications for the two premises of a counter-oppressive justification of terrorism earlier set aside. If terrorism breeds revenge-motivated violence, then an attempt to picture it as a temporary measure is called into question. Cycles of such violence are themselves entrenched sources of ongoing pain and destruction, sharing at least the systemic character of oppression. Also, even if, as some defenders of terrorism anticipate, terrorism prompts a negotiated truce and some concessions (once it is realized that it cannot be completely eradicated by police measures), the resulting peace cannot be secure among populations who have come to hate each other.

In response to the other premise set aside — that terrorism is sometimes the only means available to those in oppressively subordinated positions — it was suggested that whether there are alternatives to terrorism is a contextual matter. Standing by this judgment, I hope that the arguments of the paper have shown that terrorism is a non-starter for champions of the oppressed, so there is no alternative except to look for alternatives even though no generally applicable formulas are likely available. Moreover, it is not the place of North American philosophers to give concrete advice on this matter to those living where actual terrorism is an unfortunately live option. But this does not mean that there is nothing for those in the relatively oppression-free pockets of life in affluent societies to do.

After 9/11, some in the U.S. expressed the view that their country bore some of the ultimate blame for pursuing economic and political policies in the Middle East that created widespread, deeply felt, and largely justified hostility among its Muslim populations. Such outspokenness was met with harsh, sometimes hysteric denunciations from the government and the mainstream press, as if those who dared to say such things condoned the attacks and were giving aid and comfort to the terrorists. If the arguments of this paper have any merit, then those denunciations could not be more misguided. Rather, the critics should be seen as exposing the one source of terrorism that can render it justified in the eyes of otherwise moral and non-psychopathic people. Nor need or should those who recognize this consequence of oppression be satisfied simply with announcing it. The best way for them to join a "war on terrorism" is politically to combat oppression-sustaining policies originating within their own societies.

Author's Note

This paper was originally presented at a session of the Canadian Philosophical Association meetings, Congress of the Humanities and Social Sciences, Halifax, May 31, 2003. Thanks are due to participants in this session and to Jonathan Barker and Y. Michael Bodemann, who commented on an earlier draft of this paper.

NOTES

1. At a session of the Canadian Philosophical Association meetings, Congress of the Humanities and Social Sciences, Halifax, May 31, 2003.
2. Ted Honderich is an exception in his defense of terrorism on the part of Palestinians in Israel on broadly consequentialist ethical grounds, *Journal of Ethics*, v. 7, no. 2 (2003): 178-79.
3. For example, Jonathan Barker in *The No-Nonsense Guide to Terrorism* (Toronto, ON: Between the Lines, 2003) 23, and Honderich, *op. cit.* and in his *After the Terror* (Edinburgh: Edinburgh University Press, 2002) 97-9, where terrorism is a species of political violence.
4. Paul Dumouchel notes that in declaring a "war on terrorism," the Bush Administration in the U.S. sanctioned classifying terrorism as a species of warfare, and he draws out the consequences of this conception in a way that bears on some of the speculations of this paper, "Le terrorisme entre guerre et crime, ou de l'empire," *Esprit*, août-septembre (2002): 134-46.
5. A useful classification of species of terrorism is provided by Barker, *The No-Nonsense Guide to Terrorism* 25.
6. Loren Lomansky claims that all acts of terrorism are of this sort and are motivated by "unregulated opposition to the preconditions of successful civility" or to civil society *per se*, in "The Political Significance of Terrorism," in *Violence, Terrorism, and Justice*, edited by Raymond G. Frey and Christopher W. Morris (Cambridge: Cambridge University Press, 1991) 105. While some such unreasoned, brute hostility to civil order may be a component of the mind set of some or even all terrorists, I doubt that it is the only component. In any case no empir-

ical basis for Lomansky's claim is provided.

7. Barker, *The No-Nonsense Guide to Terrorism* 87-100.

8. In the collection edited by Frey and Morris, arguments to justify terrorism by reference to basic rights, Kantian, and contractarian ethical theories are, in my view, adequately criticized in the contributions by, respectively, Virginia Held, Thomas Hill, and Jan Narveson.

9. Honderich advances this view in *After the Terror* (118) in a criticism of terrorism as a generally acceptable practice. This is compatible with his subsequent endorsement of terrorism in the Palestinian cause, if (as seems obvious) he is arguing from a broadly rule utilitarian perspective, which allows for exceptions to usually inviolate rules.

10. A concise summary and criticism of the "double effect" argument to justify what is today called "collateral civilian damage" in warfare is in Robert L. Holmes, *On War and Morality* (Princeton, NJ: Princeton University Press, 1989) 193-200. A more extended and nuanced discussion with reference to current literature on double effect and related topics is by Richard Norman, *Ethics, Killing, and War* (Cambridge: Cambridge University Press, 1995) 83-93.

11. I explicate these speculations in "Group Hatreds and Democracy," in *Liberalism and its Practice*, edited by Daniel Avnon and Avner de Shallit (New York, NY: Routledge, 1999) 125-45; and in "Group Hatreds and Antioppressive Politics," in, *Race, Class and Community Identity*, edited by Andrew Light and Mechthild Nagel (Amherst, NY: Humanity Press, 2000) 182-98.

12. Trudy Govier focuses on this tendency in her discussion of terrorism, *A Delicate Balance: What Philosophy Can Tell Us about Terrorism* (Boulder, CO: Westview Press, 2002) Ch. 4.

DEVELOPMENT AND THE "GLOBAL WAR ON TERROR"

Antonio Tujan, Audrey Gaughran, and Howard Mollett

Antonio Tujan works with IBON, an education and development non-governmental organization (NGO) committed to studying and exploring solutions to the socioeconomic issues confronting Philippine society. Audrey Gaughran and Howard Mollett work with BOND, a network of British based NGOs working in international development and education.

Tujan, Gaughran, and Mollett discuss the "war on terror" in the context of examining the effects of it on policies of aid allocation to developing countries. They cite examples of donor countries changing their aid policies from ones designed to alleviate poverty in developing countries to ones that provide military aid and resources to countries to fight terrorism. They reject the idea that terrorist groups can be isolated from the overall social and political matrix of poverty and underdevelopment. Terrorism, they argue, can be effectively combated only within a framework of peace and development that upholds social justice and human rights, promotes inclusion and empowerment, and enhances international understanding. The current move from foreign aid to military aid, they argue, will result in increasing levels of poverty for people in many parts of the world and an escalation of local, national, and international conflict.

The global "war on terror," launched after the September 11, 2001 attack on the World Trade Center, has become an important defining influence on global affairs. It covers more than the wars against Iraq and Afghanistan and other military actions, as initiated by the US and supported by countries such as the UK and the Philippines. For fighting terrorism is not just a matter of identifying and neutralising terrorist groups in a war effort. Since terrorism does not represent the humanist, democratic aspirations of the people, but, in its narrow extremist logic, is more akin to fascism, the implication is that terrorist groups can be isolated from the overall social and political matrix of poverty and underdevelopment by a combination of social, economic and political measures coupled with police action. Isolating terrorist groups is not that simple, however.

It is frequently assumed that there is a development dimension to fighting terrorism and that a causal relationship exists between terrorism and the conditions of poverty and underdevelopment commonly associated with the countries where terrorism thrives. While a causal relationship has not been established, what is clear is that terrorism is able to utilise the conditions of dehumanisation that result from poverty, the militarisation of society, violent occupation and war as a justification for gathering some sympathy for indiscriminate, inhuman acts of violence against perceived oppressors and their supporters. In this sense only is the dehumanisation arising from poverty and injustice turned into a social base for terrorism.

In *apprehending* terrorism, the issues of social justice and development become of paramount concern. Terrorism can only be effectively combated within a framework of peace and development that upholds social justice and human rights, promotes inclusion and empowerment and enhances international understanding. In this sense, a war on terrorism in which ending terrorism itself is the paramount objective or the singular focus cannot be successful. But, too, development cannot be made an appendage to a war on terrorism.

The post-September 11 war on terror, by its very definition, takes a primarily militarist approach. But unless the social, economic, cultural and political contexts of terrorism are addressed, military action cannot solve the problem of terrorism. Rather, such action exacerbates it, as terrorism tends to thrive and further escalate in the face of military suppression alone.

The war on terror has made the world hostage to a definition of "global security" understood as the security of the global powers. For example, the identification of Iraq, Iran and North Korea as the "axis of evil" addresses the security interests of some global powers, but not necessarily the security of the Middle East or, indeed, much of the rest of the world. The designation of the National Democratic Front of the Philippines as a foreign terrorist organisation and the particular identification of its leader, José María Sison, as a terrorist may be valid for the United States and the Philippine government under the Arroyo administration, but is not widely supported by the Filipino population.

In a matter of two years, then, the war on terror has significantly reshaped the world according to its objective of so-called global security. In the US, human rights have been recast, with the "right to freedom from fear" paramount, according to Harold Hongju Koh, professor of international law at Yale Law School.[1] (It has to be presumed that the right to freedom from fear is not, however, viewed as a universal right.)

The war on terror has resulted in the militarisation of globalisation, according to which the integration of markets remains the main economic imperative, but is pursued within the framework of the global security agenda. The militarisation of globalisation effectively allows the global powers to bring military force to bear in securing their economic interests, removing opposition and threats and, with them, people's economic, social, cultural and political rights. Such political repression and

military suppression mainly affect the poorest and most marginalised sectors and communities. As a result, political and social conditions that foster exclusion, poverty and underdevelopment are exacerbated. Weaker sectors of the domestic economy, often the means of livelihood of the poorest groups in society, are the most vulnerable to the negative impacts of military operations.

Security considerations provide justification and opportunity for strengthening the boundaries between the global North and the global South. While globalisation espouses economic integration and the free movement of capital, this has never included the free movement of people. The war on terror has, in fact, provided an excuse for pursuing vigorously the pre-September 11 agenda of increasing constraints on the movement — and the human rights — of refugees and economic migrants.

As the war on terror becomes the number one global political priority, development co-operation is increasingly being influenced or captured by the global security agenda. Security considerations are being promoted as key in the granting of development aid, either in the selection of programmes or partners or in the actual promotion of military or quasi-military assistance as development aid. Governance and the rule of law, promoted in development co-operation, are also being reinterpreted to encompass more effective anti-terror legislation and enforcement.

Even without the complications arising from the war on terror, however, the problem of terrorism has become increasingly unmanageable and internationalised — also as a result of globalisation. This situation makes the objective of global security increasingly urgent, requiring effective international co-ordination, based on a commonality of objective and action among all peace-loving nations.

Peace and security are essential conditions for the development and well being of people and communities. But at what cost and through what means are these to be achieved? The more important question, however, is what kind of peace and security would achieve the goals of development and well being for all people? Pacification through a military solution or genuine peace and security through social justice, inclusion and international understanding?

The War on Terror and Trends in Foreign Aid

Since September 11, leading foreign aid donors have been reorienting their aid programmes to address the war on terror. The "securitisation" of aid is increasingly obvious; several donors, including the US and the EU, have strengthened formal links between their foreign, security and development policies, with long-term consequences for development co-operation and developing countries. Such trends have serious implications for the development of many poor countries that depend on foreign assistance.

Below, we examine how the war on terror has influenced the development policies and practices of four major donors: the US, Japan, Australia and the EU. Southeast Asia is considered the "second front" in the US-led war on terror and the US claims that the region, home to 200 million Muslims, hosts groups belonging to the al Qaida network.

US bilateral aid is increasingly allocated according to concerns related to the war on terror. Countries with large Muslim populations and insurgency movements are automatic priorities for US assistance. After September 11, Washington substantially increased its foreign aid to Pakistan, India, the Philippines and Indonesia — these countries are now the foci of the Bush administration's anti-terrorism efforts in South and East Asia.

Statistics on US bilateral assistance in South and East Asia show an increasing emphasis on military aid:

- US official development assistance (ODA) to East Asia grew by 47 per cent between 2000 and 2003. In addition, the US economic support fund (ESF) grew by 104 per cent during the same period. However, these rises are dwarfed by huge increases in military-related aid. Expenditure through the US foreign military fund (FMF) in East Asia, for example, grew by 1,614 per cent between 2000 and 2003; during the same period,

expenditure on US international military education and training (IMET) grew by 4,575 per cent. IMET is currently the largest US aid programme in East Asia, displacing ODA, which now accounts for only 30 per cent of total US bilateral aid to the region.

- A similar trend can be observed in South Asia. US ODA to the region grew by 85 per cent from 2000–03. But this increase pales in comparison with the large expansion in US IMET in South Asia, which grew by 593 per cent in the same period. The largest increase in US bilateral aid in South Asia, however, is in ESF. From zero allocation in 2000, US ESF in the region is pegged at $242 million. Consequently, the share of ESF to total US bilateral assistance in South Asia jumped to 40 per cent in 2003. It is now the largest US aid programme in South Asia, followed by ODA with 36 per cent.[2]

Increased military funding to Indonesia is a case in point. The world's largest Muslim country, Indonesia, even before September 11, played a strategic role in world geopolitics. It borders the Malacca Strait, the world's busiest shipping lane and Japan's "lifeline." The Malacca Strait also borders the deployment route that US forces use when travelling from Asia to the Middle East.[3] US military intelligence claims that the Java-based Jemaah Islamiyah is an active member of the Al Qaida network.

Shortly after September 11, the US began manoeuvring to loosen the restrictions on military aid to Jakarta that had been imposed by the Clinton administration following the human rights abuses committed by Indonesia in East Timor in 1999. At present, Indonesia stands accused of human rights violations in the context of suppressing independence movements in the Aceh province and West Papua.[4] But in spite of Indonesia's poor human rights record, the US wants to reestablish military-to-military relations. From zero allocation in 2000, the State Department requested $800,000 in IMET assistance to Indonesia for 2002 and 2003. Other US military aid, such as FMF and excess defence articles (EDA), may also be provided to Indonesia.[5]

US military and security-related aid to Africa

has also increased post-September 11, for example:

- During his July 2003 trip to Africa, George Bush committed $100 million to security in East Africa, mainly intended to increase security at air- and seaports.
- Countries that have hitherto been of little importance to the US have garnered new funding via the war on terror. Djibouti, for example, received $31 million from the US in return for allowing it to set up a permanent military base in the country.
- Under the Pan-Sahelian Initiative, established in October 2002, US military advisers provide weapons, vehicles and military training to special anti-terrorism squads in Mali, Niger, Chad and Mauritania.[6]

Trends in Japanese Aid

Since September 11, Japan has supposedly embraced an aid policy that is based on "peace diplomacy"[7] and which involves the active use of ODA for conflict resolution. Japanese foreign minister Yoriko Kawaguchi identified Afghanistan, Aceh in Indonesia, Mindanao in the Philippines and Sri Lanka as some of the conflict zones on which Japan's aid would focus. In July 2003, the Japanese government released a new draft ODA charter, which refers to promoting Japan's own security and to combating terrorism.

The shift in Japan's aid policy can be seen in the type of programmes it supports. For example, Japan has sent experts to Cambodia to draw up a civil code and a civil procedure code for the country. This is aimed at providing support for projects such as election monitoring and the development of human rights legislation. Japan also funds a programme to collect small weapons as a condition for providing reconstruction assistance. Such programmes are quite different to the big infrastructure projects that Japan has traditionally supported.

Trends in Australian Aid

The Australian government has strongly taken up the counter-terrorism theme in its aid policy and

budgeting since September 11. In a statement on Australia's overseas aid programme 2003-04, the minister for foreign affairs, Alexander Downer, stated that:

> terrorism is a trans-national phenomenon that threatens peace, security and prosperity. The tragic events of 11 September 2001 and Bali in October 2002 emphasised the importance of a concerted response to terrorism. The Australian aid program is helping to build the capacity of developing countries in the region to respond effectively to potential terrorist threats.

A key initiative announced in the budget was a new A$7.5 million peace and security fund for post-conflict assistance and "initiatives to counter trans-national crime and terrorism" in Pacific island countries. Another was a counter-terrorism initiative in Indonesia, focused on policing, tracking terrorist financing and a "travel security program," to cost A$10 million (over four years).[8] The initiative includes A$3.5 million to strengthen the Indonesian National Police's capability to combat terrorism and related crimes. Another A$3.5 million is to be used to reinforce Indonesia's anti-money laundering regime. The support includes Australian participation in drafting legislation and training in the investigation of suspicious financial transactions. The final part of the package established a A$3 million fund to foster Australian-Indonesian capacity-building links related to travel security.[9]

Trends in European Union Aid

The war on terror has affected EU member state and European Community ODA policy and aid budgets in a number of ways. According to Joseph Nye, in contrast to the "hard power" global presence of the United States, the EU is endowed with "soft power" a hybrid of economic, social and political influence. Several recent analyses have concluded that democratic governance and human rights in developing countries come far below trade, regional stability and security on the list of foreign policy priorities.[10] EU external policy projects its "civil power" role by prioritising regional stability and democracy promotion in countries and regions of strategic importance — themes that also help articulate a distinctly "European identity" at home and abroad. Conflict resolution and crisis management (the so-called "Petersberg tasks" as defined in the treaty of the EU) are now the favoured trajectory for the promotion of Europe as a global player. Sub-Saharan Africa has been identified as an important region precisely because "it could contribute to the global affirmation of the European Security and Defence identity."[11] Some analysts fear that, in this context, EU assistance will increasingly emphasise foreign policy-led initiatives focused on high-profile conflicts rather than long-term development co-operation.[12] Other foreign policy advocates welcome this move as an expression of the EU's assumption of a more coherent, liberal internationalist role in international affairs.

Development aid budgets have been eroded to address reconstruction in countries directly affected by the war on terror. After the war in Afghanistan, the EU pledged a total of US$3.6 billion for reconstruction in that country. While the aid came partly from humanitarian aid budget lines, a significant share came from 2002 EC development funds for Asia and Latin America (US$67 million or 15 per cent of the Asia and Latin America budget).[13] The issue is not the amount of aid to Afghanistan, which is clearly important in itself, but rather the politics around siphoning off aid from other budgets, instead of making additional allocations, and that such aid is then subject to the short-termist objectives of foreign policy.

The type of project funded is also under review. The EC is now providing targeted technical assistance for anti-terror projects in Indonesia, Pakistan and the Philippines.[14] There are also calls to redefine aid eligibility criteria under the European Development Fund for African, Caribbean and Pacific countries to include the financing of peacekeeping missions. While nobody disputes that additional resources for peacekeeping and peace enforcement intervention are essential, there are concerns about EC aid resources being directed within a foreign and security policy framework.

In the draft EU constitutional treaty, published in July 2003, development co-operation and humanitarian assistance were accorded separate chapters. However, the chapters on the Common Foreign and Security Policy and the Common Security and Defence Policy propose that "Union instruments," including aid resources, are placed at the disposal of a new EU foreign affairs minister. One Article in the Common Security and Defence Policy proposes that humanitarian aid contribute to "the fight against terrorism." This would compromise the fundamental principles of humanitarian aid: those of independence, impartiality and neutrality.

Escalating Local Conflicts and Increasing Poverty

The events of September 11 provided political justification for the military agenda of some of the world's most powerful countries. The US, for example, is using them to justify its heightened military presence in so-called "critical areas." Japan also took advantage of September 11 to justify the expansion of the global role and significance of its "Self Defence Forces." The presence of groups designated terrorist, such as Jemaah Islamiyah and Abu Sayyaf, is used to justify external intervention through military aid.

An increased military presence has been viewed in some quarters as linked to the importance of protecting the economic interests of some donor countries. The US, for instance, has significant investment interests in both mining and oil exploration in West Papua, Indonesia. Japanese interests in Indonesia are underscored by the fact that 80 per cent of the oil and 90 per cent of the liquid petroleum gas that the Japanese consume has to pass through the Malacca Strait.[15] The US also has significant investments in Mindanao in the Philippines. There are at least twenty-six American-owned or affiliated corporations exploiting the war-torn region's rich natural resources; there are also twenty-nine Japanese-owned or affiliated corporations operating in Mindanao.[16] ...

The war on terror appears to have altered the primary objective of aid giving, which is development co-operation. Donors have been quick to reframe the war on poverty in the context of the war on terror. In October 2003, President Bush proposed a six-year education programme for Indonesia, apparently aimed at reducing the flow of students to Islamic boarding schools. This is the first education intervention by the US in Indonesia for a decade. Many concerns have been expressed at US involvement in education, including fears that the US will seek to influence curricula.[17] Some donors have already begun to use their official development aid budgets to fund global security programmes. The Danish government, for example, has made security and the fight against terrorism the second of its five main development objectives for the period 2004-08. Much of the aid allocated under this priority will be spent in countries that do not fall into the least developed countries category, hitherto the focus for Danish aid.

Not only can development aid be used to address security; it can also be used as a tool for pacification. "Peace and stability" are achieved not for people's development, but rather to serve the donor's security agenda.

Countries like the Philippines and Indonesia need development assistance that is focused on poverty reduction and development rather than militarised aid that results in ever more militarised societies, increased conflict and displacement and, of course, profits for western arms manufacturers. Out of 168 countries, the Philippines ranks 75th and Indonesia 107th in the UN Human Development Index. Meanwhile, these countries maintain some of the largest armed forces in Southeast Asia.

The Militarisation of Globalisation

The September 11 attacks on the World Trade Center were initially seen as a direct strike on a symbol of globalisation. But if anyone thought that the attacks would dent pro-globalisation zeal, they were wrong. The dust had not settled on ground zero before proponents were recasting globalisation as a key weapon in the war on terror. US Federal Reserve Board chairman Alan Greenspan, in a speech made shortly after the attacks, claimed that: "globalisation is an endeavour that can spread worldwide the values of freedom and civil contact — the antithesis of terrorism."[18] Writing in the Washington Post nine days after the attacks, US trade representative Robert Zoellick argued that global trade liberalisation was vital to counter terrorism: "The terrorists deliberately chose the World Trade towers as their target," he wrote. "While their blow toppled the towers, it cannot and will not shake the foundation of world trade and freedom."[19] The UK secretary of state for trade went further and said that the world "should fight terror with trade."

Efforts to integrate countries into the globalisation process are now driven in part by security concerns. As globalisation, counter-terrorism and (western) security agendas converge, the nature of relations between developed and developing countries is affected....

Financial Flows

If developing countries have been dealt a sideways blow by the new dimension in global trade negotiations, they have been hit head-on in terms of direct financial inflows. The major inflows from official aid, foreign direct investment (FDI), tourism revenues and migrant remittances have all been affected negatively by the counter-terrorism and security agenda. Official development assistance has been skewed by geopolitical considerations, with a number of donors redefining the conditions under which they select developing country partners — shifting the emphasis from "well-run countries" to countries perceived as "security threats."

Globally, FDI has declined almost everywhere since 2000. The events of September 11 and the war on terror are not the sole — or even the main — causes of this downswing, but they are a factor, particularly for developing countries. The designation of many countries in Africa and Asia as terrorist havens or areas of potential danger is influencing investment. A recent study on investment trends by Deloitte Research noted that global US manufacturing investment slid in 2002 to an estimated $23 billion, down from $36 billion in 2001.[20] The same report noted that "the political and economic stability of nations [has] become a much more important factor in the decision process of U.S. manufacturing firms" and that the "majority of funding actually goes to developed nations in North America, Europe and Asia."

And it is not just FDI that is staying in developed countries; European and American tourists are spending their tourist cash in western tourist locations. Post-September 11 fears have been exacerbated by the attacks on tourist resorts in Kenya and Bali. But the travel advice that influences tourist decisions does not always appear to be even-handed.

The UK organisation Tourism Concern has published research which looks at, among other things, how UK Foreign and Commonwealth (FCO) travel advice is affecting developing countries.[21] The report highlights the sometimes different treatment of countries affected by terrorism. For example, the impact of advice on travel to Bali on the local economy and livelihoods has been severe and tour operators in Asia and the UK have called for a change in the FCO's advice. In contrast, the FCO travel advice for Spain before the Madrid bombing — at a time when the Basque separatist group ETA was still warning that it would target tourists during the season — seemed "to be so protective of the Spanish tourism industry, it is hardly surprising that developing countries should suspect political motivation."

African livelihoods have been among those hardest hit by terrorism warnings. Kenya's President Kibaki made repeated appeals to the US to lift a travel ban which has affected the Kenyan economy and thousands of livelihoods. Kenya estimated that it lost US$14 million in revenue in just a few weeks immediately following terror warnings in May 2003.[22] ...

The pursuit of the war on terror has also had an impact on the policing of global financial systems, with an unintended negative consequence hitting poor families in several developing countries. New controls aimed at closing off the financing of terrorism are creating increasing difficulties for immigrants trying to send much-needed cash back to families at home. Remittances are an important source of development

financing and Somalia is one country particularly dependent upon them. However, in 2002, the US government maintained that companies involved in transferring remittances to Somalia from Somalis living abroad might have links to "terror networks" and has sought to shut them down. Such moves failed to take into account their impact on the thousands of Somali families that rely on remittances in a country where few, if any, international money transfer operations exist.

The Movement of People

According to the *Economist's* 2003 review of migration issues, it is impossible to separate the globalisation of trade and capital from the global movement of people. But it is on the global movement of people that the effects of September 11 have been most tangible. While western governments continue to promote the movement of money and goods, they have been swift to curtail the movement of people. The EU, for example, is pursuing a "conservative alliance containment model," according to Statewatch.[23] "In practice this means the construction of a Fortress Europe and attempts to control migration 'at source' by the use of aid and trade as 'leverage' to secure the co-operation of developing countries."

While such policies often pre-date the September 11 attacks, the war on terror has strengthened the call for controls in many quarters. Anti-terror legislation and measures have been used as a pretext by some countries to limit their responsibilities over accepting refugees and asylum seekers. For example, the number of refugees resettled in America declined from 90,000 a year before September 11 to 27,000 in 2003.

The impacts on developing countries of the new restrictions on the movement of people are many. Remittances, an important source of development revenue for many countries, are down. Education opportunities, particularly for young Muslim males, have been restricted.[24] In its impact on the movement of people, the irony of the war on terror is at its most marked: combating terrorism by increasing injustice and resentment.

Development or Destruction? Impact of the War on Terror on Communities

....

Shattered Hope for Development

The forgotten — or ignored — victims of the war on terror are ordinary people with no links to terrorism. The experiences of wartorn Afghanistan and Iraq, as well as the experiences of communities such as those in the Philippines, Somalia, Kenya and Bali, have highlighted the damage that the war on terror can do to innocent people, diminishing their prospects for economic and social development.

As the war on terror moves swiftly forwards, even its own direct casualties are often forgotten. The reconstruction of Afghanistan took a backseat to the invasion of Iraq. During the International Conference on Reconstruction Assistance to Afghanistan in Tokyo (January 2002), donors pledged US$5.1 billion for the period January 2002 to June 2004. However, not all the pledges have been honoured. Most worrying was the decline in American attention to reconstruction since, in 2002, President Bush had likened the American commitment to a "Marshall Plan" for Afghanistan.

Rhetoric has been belied by reality. This plan has never materialised and nor have the finances to support reconstruction on anything like a Marshall Plan scale. In a spectacular example of forgetfulness, the Bush administration failed to request any money for reconstruction in Afghanistan in the budget announced in February 2003. The US Congress had to step in to find nearly $300 million in humanitarian and reconstruction funds for the country.[25]

Undermining Human Rights

World leaders have repeatedly stated that efforts to tackle terrorism should be seen as complementary to initiatives to strengthen human rights, the rule of law and judicial reform. In reality, the war on terror is being used to justify actions — in both developed and developing countries — that undermine all of these aims. Organisations across the globe have highlighted the threat to human rights posed by the war on terror: "The 'war on terror', far from making the world a safer place, has made it more dangerous by curtailing human rights, undermining the rule of international law and shielding governments from scrutiny," according to Irene Khan, secretary general of Amnesty International.[26]

There are three main contexts in which human rights are undermined in relation to the war on terror: the introduction of repressive anti-terrorism legislation; the condoning of human rights abuses in combating terrorism; and the growth in arms sales and military aid, particularly to regimes with poor human rights records.

Anti-terror Legislation

Anti-terrorism legislation threatens human rights in many countries and legalises practices, such as arbitrary arrest and prolonged detention without trial, that are contrary to international human rights laws and standards. Apart from entrenching human rights abuses, this type of legislation has allowed discrimination to be practised, based on nationality and ethnicity, in the way it is applied. Following the declaration of the war on terror, a number of countries with poor human rights records introduced new anti-terrorism legislation or extended powers under existing legislation — moves that human rights monitors have seen as opportunistic attempts to justify human rights abuses and political repression.

The main rights compromised by much of the anti-terrorism legislation introduced across the world have been the rights of detained persons and the rights to freedom of expression and assembly. While legislation that undermines fundamental freedoms is by no means confined to developing countries, an added dimension from a human rights perspective is that oversight mechanisms in many developing countries are weak or non-existent, and legal advice — particularly legal aid — can be difficult to obtain. Consequently, poor people are often at greater risk when repressive legislation is introduced.

The fundamental rights of detained persons include the right to be informed of the reason for detention, the right to independent legal advice and the right to be brought before a legal authority at the earliest opportunity. Anti-terrorism legislation often removes these basic rights under the guise that increased detention times are needed in order to carry out investigations or by only allowing contact with approved lawyers. Amongst the examples of such legalised abuses are the following:[27]

- Pakistan's Anti Terrorism (Amendment) Ordinance, which came into force in November 2002, allows for the detention of a suspected person for up to twelve months. The Human Rights Commission of Pakistan has constantly lobbied for an end to illegal detentions. It has also lobbied on the issue of suspects extradited to the US without due process.
- India's Prevention of Terrorism Act (POTA, 26 March 2002) has been criticised for targeting minorities and political opponents. Under the Act, suspects can be detained for up to three months without charge; this can be extended for a further three months with permission from an appointed judge.
- Mauritius has enacted the Prevention of Terrorism Act, the Financial Intelligence and Anti-Money Laundering Act and the Prevention of Corruption Act. The Prevention of Terrorism (Special Measures) Regulations were introduced on 25 January 2003. A person who is suspected of engaging in terrorist acts can be detained for up to thirty-six hours without access to any person other than a police officer or, on request, a government medical officer. The bill was only enacted after two presidents stepped down rather than give their assent to it.

Freedom of expression is a fundamental right, enshrined in a number of international agreements, including the International Covenant on Civil and Political Rights. The freedom to criticise and voice opposition to government activities has borne the brunt of anti-terrorist rhetoric as media groups and peaceful protesters are labelled "terrorists."

- Under India's POTA, journalists are obliged to inform the police about any information that is terrorist related. The government has accused the media of giving too much publicity to terrorists.
- In Zimbabwe, the Broadcasting Services Act 2001 gives the minister of state for information the authority to issue licences for independent radio broadcasters. While registration itself is not an unusual phenomenon, the minister also retains the authority to ban any broadcaster deemed to be a threat to national security. The Access to Information and Protection of Privacy Act 2002 (AIPPA) has been used to suppress news media and to restrict the information that is available on public bodies. AIPPA also demands the registration of journalists by a government-appointed board.

Acceptance of Human Rights Abuses

Legalised human rights abuses, while posing a significant and long-term threat to human rights, are at least highly visible. However, far less visible are those abuses quietly condoned — or even encouraged — as expedient in the prosecution of the war on terror.

The use of torture is one such abuse. In international law, the prohibition of torture is universal and total. However, human rights groups have reported on human rights abuses, including torture, being carried out in the name of combating terrorism in developing (and developed) countries. Indeed, torture is facilitated by prolonged and incommunicado detention — both practices that have been legalised in several countries. The publication in the Economist of a lead article on torture ("Is torture ever justified?"), in the specific context of the war on terror, gives some indication of the manner in which the war on terror is undermining human rights.[28] Although the article came out against the use of torture in the fight against terrorism, it concluded that "given the gravity of the terrorist threat, vigorous questioning short of torture — prolonged interrogations, mild sleep deprivation, perhaps the use of truth serum — might be justified in some cases."

A recent paper published by the Development Assistance Committee of the OECD, "A development co-operation lens on terrorism prevention:

key entry points for action," notes as a concern that "OECD governments might overlook *severe* abuses taking place because they need co-operation from [a] particular country's government" (emphasis added). The qualification of "severe" has been criticised as not compatible with the obligation, rooted in international human rights law, not to ignore any derogation of international human rights standards.[29]

Many countries have been quick to use the war on terror to justify human rights abuses, pre-and post-September 11. Shortly before leaving office, Malaysian prime minister Mahathir Mohamad defended the detention of terrorist suspects without trial under Malaysia's controversial Internal Security Act. The prime minister pointed out that some suspects had been detained before 11 September 2001 and that, at that time, Malaysia had been condemned for not applying appropriate standards, but now "other people realise you cannot wait until bombs are exploded before you take action."[30]

President Mubarak of Egypt, expressing similar sentiments, has claimed that the US decision to authorise military tribunals "proves that we were right from the beginning in using all means, including military tribunals."[31] Egypt has received substantial US aid in what many see as a tacit acceptance of its human rights violations.

Djibouti, too, has received substantial US aid in the context of the war on terror, and its benefactor appears to have turned a blind eye to the expulsion, in early October 2003, of 100,000 residents (about 15 per cent of its population). Djibouti authorities described the foreign-born residents as possible terrorists and a "threat to the peace and security of the country."

Military Aid, Human Rights, and Development

Relaxing arms export controls compromises the long-term goals of development, conflict prevention and human rights. Global security and the war on terror have already altered the military aid spending of the US in ways that have raised concerns amongst development and human rights advocates.

In 2002, the US-based organisation Human Rights Watch released a report, "Dangerous dealings: changes in US military assistance after September 11," in which it outlined concerns that the US government was extending new military assistance to governments responsible for serious human rights abuses. Among Human Rights Watch's concerns were the lifting of an eight-year-old ban on arms sales to Tajikistan and military aid to Uzbekistan, a country guilty of serious human rights violations. According to Human Rights Watch:

> Uzbekistan's proximity to Afghanistan, and its willingness to host US airbases, has made it a valued partner in the international campaign against terrorism. In order to allow for increased aid to its new ally the US sometimes exaggerated Uzbekistan's progress in meeting its human rights commitments ... In August 2002, the State Department prematurely certified that Uzbekistan was making the progress demanded by supplemental aid legislation, allowing for the release of $16 million in military and security assistance.[32]

UK foreign affairs think-tank Saferworld has raised concerns that UK arms export controls have been relaxed in the war on terror.[33] Although potential impacts on human rights and development are among the criteria used by the UK government to assess UK arms exports, Tajikistan, Turkmenistan and Uzbekistan — all countries that had received highly critical human rights assessments in the UK's 2002 *Human Rights Report* — were granted open individual export licences in that year. These licences allow for unlimited exports of a wide range of military equipment, from small arms to rocket systems and battle tanks.

The war on terror has dealt a severe blow to human rights worldwide. Short-sighted measures have far-reaching consequences. Repressive legislation, illegal counter-terrorism measures and the arming of countries based solely on their status as "allies" put power into the hands — most often — of those who abuse it. In pursuing their security, the US and Europe have been willing to sacrifice security and justice elsewhere in the world. And, while this will doubtless come back to haunt them, in the meantime it is the innocent — as always — who will suffer.

NOTES

1. *Economist* (30 October 2003). For general background to the issues covered in this article, see Mark Curtis, *Web of Deceit: Britain's real role in the world* (London, Verso, 2003); Hans Kochler, "The war on terror, its impact on the sovereignty of nations, and its implications for human rights and civil liberties," paper delivered at the International Ecumenical Conference on Terrorism in a Globalized World, Manila (25 September 2002); and Alexandra Poolos, "US opens new phase in war on terror," *Radio Free Europe/Radio Liberty* (23 January 2002), <http://www.rferl.org/>.

2. Thomas Lum, "US foreign aid to East and South Asia: selected recipients," *Congressional Research Service Report for Congress* (10 April 2002).

3. Yumiko Nakagawa, "A vital triangle: Indonesia and the US-Japan alliance," *Issues & Insights*, Pacific Forum CSIS, Honolulu, Hawaii (Vol. 3, no. 4, July 2003).

4. Conn Hallinan, "Supporting Indonesia's military bad idea — again," *Foreign Policy in Focus*, <http://www.atimes.com/se-asia/DF14Ae01.html> (homepage of *Asia Times Online*, 14 June 2002).

5. Lum, op. cit.

6. BOND, "Global security and development updates" (September 2003 and October 2003), <http://www.bond.org.uk/advocacy/globalsecurity.htm>.

7. Suvedrini Kakuchi, "Japan's new embrace of peace diplomacy," <http://www.atimes.com/atimes/Japan/EB06Dh01.html>.

8. BOND, "Global security and development project, September 23 update," <http://www.bond.org.uk/advocacy/gsdsept.htm#aus>.

9. "Counter-terrorism and Australian aid," Commonwealth of Australia (August 2003).

10. Gorm Rye Olsen, "Promotion of democracy as a foreign policy instrument of 'Europe': limits to international idealism," *Democratization* (Vol. 7, no. 2, 2000), pp. 142-67.

11. G. Lenzi, "WEU's role in sub-Saharan Africa," pp. 46-65 in W. Khune, G. Lenzi and A. Vasconcelos, *WEU's Role in Crisis Management and Conflict Resolution in Sub-Saharan Africa* (Paris, Institute for Security Studies of WEU, 1995), p. 48.

12. See Gorm Rye Olsen, op. cit.; and Chris Alden and Karen E. Smith, LSE, "Strengthening democratic structures and processes in Africa: a commentary on the role of the EU," presentation at IISS seminar in Lisbon (November 2003).

13. BOND, "Tackling poverty in Asia" (2002), <http://www.bond.org.uk/eu/ eupolicy.html#tackling poverty>.

14. For further in-depth analysis of the relationship between EU foreign, security and development policies, see BOND, *Europe in the World: Essays on EU foreign, security and development policies* (May 2003), <http://www.bond.org.uk/eu/euinworld.htm>.

15. Nakagawa, op. cit.

16. Arnold Padilla, "Mini-Marshall plan for Mindanao: will foreign aid end the Moro war?" *IBON 'Facts & Figures'* (November 2003).

17. *Financial Times* (23 October and 7 November 2003).

18. Alan Greenspan, "Globalization: the Institute for International Economics" first annual Stavros Niarchos lecture" (Washington, Institute for International Economics, 24 October 2001).

19. *Washington Post* (20 September 2001).

20. "Globalization on hold? Global investment trends of US manufacturers" (New York, Deloitte Research, June 2003).

21. Report is available at <http://www.tourismconcern.org.uk>.

22. *Africa Online*, <http://www.africaonline.com/site/Articles/1,3,53156.jsp> (accessed 7 November 2003).

23. BOND, *Europe in the World*, op. cit., ch. 8.

24. "America slams the door (on its foot): Washington's destructive new visa policies," *Foreign Affairs* (Vol. 82, no. 3, May 2003).

25. "Afghanistan omitted from US aid budget," *BBC News World Edition* (13 February 2003).

26. *Amnesty International, Annual Report 2003: human rights threatened by "war on terror,"* <http://www.amnesty.org.uk/deliver?document'14553>.

27. This section draws heavily on work done by the Commonwealth Human Rights Initiative by

Dominic Bascombe in "Anti-terrorism legislation in the Commonwealth: a briefing paper for the Commonwealth Human Rights Initiative" (May 2003). Any errors in the reproduction are the responsibility of BOND.

28. *Economist* (11 January 2003).

29. To view the international civil society position paper on the DAC statement, see: <http://www.bond.org.uk/advocacy/gsddac.htm>.

30. *Financial Times* (25 September 2003).

31. Human Rights Watch, "In the name of counter-ter-rorism: human rights abuses worldwide: a Human Rights Watch briefing paper for the 59th session of the United Nations Commission on Human Rights, March 25, 2003," <http://www. hrw.org/un/chr59/counter-terrorism-bck4.htm#P202_39289>.

32. Ibid.

33. The UK-based think-tank Saferworld made this statement in 2002 in a memo to the House of Commons Quadripartite Select Committee (made up of the Foreign Affairs, Defence, International Development and Trade and Industry Committees).

STUDY QUESTIONS

1　Summarize some of the main theories in the just war tradition that Michael Walzer surveys on the road to providing an account of contemporary responses to war. Specifically, what is "realism" and what replaced it and why?

2　What does Walzer mean by the "triumph of just war theory" and why is he worried about the use of just war theory by contemporary politicians, political and legal theorists, the media, and the military?

3　According to Walzer, why does just war theory have an important role to play in a world where war and methods of war have changed? Do you think that this critical role could change attitudes and the discourse of war in our time? Why or why not?

4　Neta Crawford examines preemption as a justification for war. What is the argument for preemption? In her view, what contributes to the popularity of this argument in the contemporary context of war? Do you agree with Crawford that fear and vulnerability play a role with respect to theory and policy on war? Provide reasons for your answer.

5　Crawford outlines four conditions necessary for legitimate preemptive attacks. What are they? Are they being violated by current American policy? What is Crawford's view? What is your view? Defend your answers.

6　What are some of the measures allowed by the Patriot Act as described by Asma Barlas? Do you agree with Barlas that these are "frontal attacks on civil liberties"? Do you think these measures should be made permanent? Defend your answers.

7　What does Barlas mean by her claim that responses to the attacks on 9/11 reflect and bring to the surface deeply entrenched racist and colonist thinking?

8　Do you think that dissenting voices on war and responses to war are being silenced? Should they be? Defend your answers.

9　What is the utilitarian argument for counter-oppressive terrorism examined by Frank Cunningham?

10　How does Cunningham define terrorism? How does he define oppression? Are these definitions important to the analysis of counter-oppressive terrorism? Why or why not?

11　What does Cunningham mean by the phenomenology of terrorism? According to Cunningham, how does what terrorists do and think undermine the argument that terrorist acts are needed to fight oppression?

12　Cunningham concludes that counter-oppressive terrorism cannot be justified on the utilitarian grounds of eliminating oppression and improving relations. What does he recommend by way of policy? Do you agree? Provide reasons for your answers.

13　Antonio Tujan, Audrey Gaughran, and Howard Mollett call attention to the ways in which the "war on terror" has had effects on development policy and practice and has changed policies on foreign aid. What are these changes and why are they critical of them?

14　How does providing military aid and resources to countries to fight terrorism undermine the achievement of development goals? Do you agree with Tujan, Gaughran, and Mollett that these policies violate human rights? Defend your answer.

SUGGESTED READINGS

Barber, Benjamin R. *Fear's Empire: War, Terrorism, and Democracy*. New York, NY: W.W. Norton & Co., 2003.

Barker, Jonathan. *The No-Nonsense Guide to Terrorism*. Toronto, ON: Between the Lines, 2002.

Betts, Richard K. "Striking First: A History of Thankfully Lost Opportunities." *Ethics & International Affairs*, v. 17, no. 1 (2003): 17-24.

Byers, Michael. "Letting the Exception Prove the Rule." *Ethics & International Affairs*, v. 17, no. 1 (2003): 9-16.

Dershowitz, Alan M. *Why (understanding the threat) Terrorism (responding to the challenge) Works*. New Haven, CT: Yale University Press, 2002.

Frey, Raymond G., and Christopher W. Morris (editors). *Violence, Terrorism, and Justice*. Cambridge: Cambridge University Press, 1991.

Govier, Trudy. *A Delicate Balance: What Philosophy Can Tell Us about Terrorism*. Boulder, CO: Westview Press, 2002.

Haynes, Jeff. "Religion and Politics: What is the Impact of September 11?" *Contemporary Politics*, v. 9, no. 1 (2003): 7-15.

Holgzrefe, J.L., and Robert Keohane (editors). *Humanitarian Intervention: Ethical, Legal and Political Dilemmas*. Cambridge: Cambridge University Press, 2003.

Holmes, Robert L. *On War and Morality*. Princeton, NJ: Princeton University Press, 1989.

Honderich, Ted. *After the Terror*. Edinburgh: Edinburgh University Press, 2002.

—. *Terrorism for Humanity: Inquiries in Political Philosophy*. Sterling, VA: Pluto Press, 2003.

Ignatieff, Michael. *The Lesser Evil: Political Ethics in an Age of Terror*. Toronto, ON: Penguin Canada, 2004.

—. *Virtual War: Kosovo and Beyond*. New York, NY: Henry Holt, 2000.

Petchesky, Rosalind P. "Phantom Towers: Feminist Reflections on the Battle Between Global Capitalism and Fundamentalist Terrorism." *The Women's Review of Books*, v. XIX, no. 2 (November 2001): 2-6.

Sterba, James (editor). *Terrorism and International Justice*. New York, NY: Oxford University Press, 2003.

Tosteson, Daniel C. "Unhealthy Beliefs: Religion & the Plague of War." *Daedalus*, v. 132, no. 3 (Summer 2003): 80-82.

Von Clausewitz, Karl. *On War*. Princeton, NJ: Princeton University Press, 1976.

Walzer, Michael. *Just and Unjust Wars*. New York, NY: Basic Books, 1977.

ACKNOWLEDGEMENTS

"The Categorical Imperative" by Emmanuel Kant. *Groundwork for the Metaphysics of Morals*. Ed. Lara Denis. Peterborough, ON: Broadview Press, 2005. Reprinted by permission of Broadview Press.

"Utilitarianism" by John Stuart Mill. *Utilitarianism*. London: Longmans, 1907.

"Ethics: The We and the I" by V.F. Cordova from *American Indian Thought: Philosophical Essays*. Ed. Anne Waters. Oxford: Blackwell Publishing, 2004. Reprinted with the permission of the publisher.

"What does the Different Voice Say? Gilligan's Women and Moral Philosophy" by Margaret Urban Walker in *The Journal of Value Inquiry*, v. 23, 1989: 123-134. Reprinted with permission of Kluwer Academic Publishers and the author.

"Changing Moral Values in Africa: An Essay in Ethical Relativism" by Egbeke Aja in *The Journal of Value Inquiry*, v. 31, 1997: 531-543. Reprinted with permission of Kluwer Academic Publishers and the author.

"Human Rights: A Western Construct with Limited Applicability" by Adamantia Pollis & Peter Schwab. *Human Rights: Cultural and Ideological Perspectives*. Eds. Adamantia Pollis & Peter Schwab. Copyright © 1979 by Praeger Publishers. Reproduced with permission of Greenwood Publishing Group, Inc., Westport, CT.

"Globalization and Human Rights" by Jay Drydyk. *Global Justice, Global Democracy*. Eds. Jay Drydyk and Peter Penz. Winnipeg: Fernwood Publishing, 1997. Reprinted with permission of the Society for Socialist Studies.

"A Buddhist Response to the Nature of Human Rights" by Kenneth Inada. *Asian Perspectives on Human Rights*. Eds. Claude E. Walsh and Virginia Leary. Boulder, CO: Westview Press, 1990. Reprinted with permission of the author.

"Reconceiving Rights as Relational" by Jennifer Nedelsky in *Review of Constitutional Studies/Revue d'etudes constitutionnelles*, v. 1, no. 1, 1993: 1-26. Reprinted with permission of Centre for Constitutional Studies and the author.

A Theory of Justice by John Rawls. Cambridge, MA: Harvard University Press, © 1971 by the President and Fellows of Harvard College. Reprinted with permission of the publisher.

"Libertarianism, Insurance Arguments, and General State Welfare" by Richard A. Garner in *Philosophical Notes*, no. 67, 2004. Reproduced with permission of the Libertarian Alliance. < http://www.libertarian.co.uk>

"Care and Justice in the Global Context" by Virginia Held in *Ratio Juris*, v. 17, no. 2, June 2004: 141-155. Reprinted with permission of the publisher.

"Confucianism, Globalisation and the Idea of Universalism" by A.T. Nuyen in *Asian Philosophy*, v. 13, nos. 2/3, 2003: 75-86. Reprinted with permission of the publisher.

"Women, Citizenship and Difference" by Nira Yuval-Davis in *Feminist Review*, no. 57, Autumn 1997: 4-27. Reprinted with permission of the publisher.

"Democracy, Philosophy, and Justification" by Amy Gutmann from *Democracy and Difference: Contesting the Boundaries of the Political*. Ed. Selya Benhabib. Princeton: © 1996, Princeton University Press. Reprinted with permission of the publisher.

"Confucian Value and Democratic Value" by Chenyang Li in *The Journal of Value Inquiry*, v. 31, 1997: 183-193. Reprinted with permission of Kluwer Academic Publishers and the author.

"In Search of Islamic Constitutionalism" by Nadirsyah Hosen in *American Journal of Islamic Social Sciences*, v. 21, no. 2, Spring 2004: 1-24. Reprinted with permission of the publisher.

"Democracy and its Global Roots: Why Democratization is Not the Same as Westernization" by Amartya Sen in *New Republic*, vol. 229, October 6, 2003. Reprinted with permission of The New Republic, Inc. and the author.

"The Influence of the Global Order on the Prospects for Genuine Democracy in the Developing Countries" by Thomas W. Pogge from *Ratio Juris*, v. 14, no. 3, September 2001: 326-343. Reprinted with permission of the publisher.

"Dialogue of the Deaf?: New International Attitudes and the Death Penalty in America" by Stefanie Grant in *Criminal Justice Ethics*, v. 17, no. 2, Summer/Fall 1998: 19-32. Reprinted by permission of The Institute for Criminal Justice Ethics, 555 West 57th Street, Suite 607, New York, NY 10019-1029.

"Child Labor Abroad: Just and Effective Policies" by Roland Pierik. Published with permission of the author.

"Colonialism, Reparations and Global Justice" by Kok-Chor Tan. Published with permission of the author.

"Justice for South Africa: Restorative Justice and the South African Truth and Reconciliation Commission" by Jennifer Llewellyn. Published with permission of the author.

"Freedom and Democracy in Cuba: A Problem of Understanding" by Susan E. Babbitt. Republished with permission of the author.

"The Triumph of Just War Theory (and the Dangers of Success)" by Michael Walzer from *Social Research: An International Quarterly of the Social Sciences*, v. 69, no. 4, Winter 2002: 925-944. Reprinted with permission of the publisher.

"The Slippery Slope to Preventive War" by Neta C. Crawford in *Ethics & International Affairs*, v. 17, no. 1, 2003: 30-36. Reprinted with permission from Carnegie Council on Ethics and International Affairs and the author.

"A Requiem for Voicelessness: Pakistanis and Muslims in the US" by Asma Barlas in *Wagadu: Journal of International Women's and Gender Studies*, v. 1, no. 1, Spring 2004. Reprinted with permission of the author. <http://web.cortland.edu/wagadu/issue1/Requiem.html>

"Counter-Oppressive Terrorism" by Frank Cunningham. Published with permission of the author.

"Development and the 'Global War on Terror'" by Antonio Tujan et al. in *Race and Class*, v. 46, no.1, 2004: 53-74. Reprinted by permission from SAGE Publications, Inc. and the authors.

The editor of the book and the publisher have made every attempt to locate the authors of copyrighted material or their heirs and assigns, and would be grateful for information that would allow them to correct any errors or omissions in a subsequent edition of the work.